Anatomy of Wonder: Science Fiction

Neil Barron

R. R. Bowker Company
A Xerox Education Company
New York & London, 1976

Published by R. R. Bowker Company (A Xerox Education Company)
1180 Avenue of the Americas, New York, N.Y. 10036
Copyright © 1976 by Xerox Corporation
All rights reserved
Printed and bound in the United States of America

Second printing, July 1977

Library of Congress Cataloging in Publication Data
Main entry under title:
Anatomy of wonder, science fiction.
(Bibliographic guides for contemporary collections)
Includes indexes.
1. Science fiction—Bibliography. 2. Science
fiction—History and criticism. I. Barron, Neil,
1934—
Z5917.S36A52 [PN3448.S45]   016.8083'876   76-10260
ISBN 0-8352-0884-2 (hardbound)
ISBN 0-8352-0949-0 (paperbound)

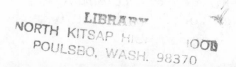

Contents

Foreword

The concept of the Bibliographic Guides for Contemporary Collections Series was derived from a realization that many librarians, students, teachers, and lay persons lack in-depth guidance to subjects of current interest. Too often, librarians are faced with inadequate, or even a total lack of, selection assistance when developing specific areas for their libraries or individual studies. "Contemporary Collections" seeks to help fill this need. The word "contemporary" refers to a subject, old or new, that is now experiencing a high level of interest throughout America and across the educational spectrum. A sudden upsurge of interest in a specific area emphasizes the lack of guidance, in many instances, to the best and most necessary materials for reading and research. The "Contemporary Collections" series will attempt to meet such information crises by presenting the reader with a selective basic guide to the literature. Each book will be written by an expert or group of experts who will develop each subject through selection, annotation, and commentary. The emphasis is on in-print materials but, obviously, some subjects cannot be adequately explored without citing titles of landmark quality and some of these may be out of print. Where appropriate, media other than books will be included for most titles in the series. These bibliographic guides will give librarians, students, scholars, and the general public a frame in which to approach certain immediate topics with solid organization.

Peter Doiron
Series Editor

Preface

Anatomy of Wonder, a critical guide to science fiction, is intended to serve a variety of overlapping audiences:

1. Public, school, college, and university libraries desiring to develop well-rounded collections of science fiction books, whether for recreational reading or for support of instructional programs.

2. Interested readers, including librarians and SF fans, who wish to become more familiar with the best or representative works in the field.

3. High school, college, and university faculty who use SF books in their courses, whether general in nature, devoted to SF only, or to the emerging specialty of futurology, and who wish to select titles for possible course use or background reading.

4. Students enrolled in such courses wishing to broaden their backgrounds or select titles for more intensive study, or merely for recreational reading.

The scope of this book has been deliberately limited to books, although frequent mention is made of the original pulp magazine sources. The major emphasis is on twentieth century American works, although careful attention has been paid to British, European, Russian, and other foreign works in translation. Because our audiences are likely to be large-

ix

ly English-speaking, we usually limited ourselves to works available in English.

Basic ordering information is given for all annotated titles, based on the following sources: *Books In Print*, 1975; *Paperback Books in Print*, January 1976; *Forthcoming Books*, January 1976; *British Books in Print*, 1975; and current dealer and publisher catalogs. British editions are listed only when no American edition was in print. When no price appears, the book was believed to be out of print in the United States and Britain in winter 1975/76, although some dealers may still carry selected recent titles in their inventory. Libraries and individuals should realize that the large number of mass market paperback reprints and originals means that current availability of such works will fluctuate rapidly. The introduction to the Directory of Publishers has ordering suggestions for individuals and libraries.

The annotations include these elements:

Name of author or editor. Books are listed under the name most commonly used by the author, even if this is a pseudonym. The true name is shown in parentheses and cross-references from the name to pseudonym are provided in the Author Index.

Nationality of author or editor, if known and if other than American.

Title, including known variant titles. Unquestionably some variant titles were missed, since title changes are extremely common in SF.

Publisher and year of first American or British publication in English. Because most users of this guide are likely to be American, the American publisher was shown even if a British edition appeared a year or two earlier or simultaneously. Variations in contents between British and American editions is common for short story collections. A few foreign language titles are included in Chapter 6, and somewhat fuller bibliographic information is given for some of the early-period titles.

Price and publisher for all titles determined to be in print. Wherever possible, prices are up-to-date as of January, 1976. Specialty dealers can often supply copies of o.p. books. Paperback reprints are sometimes abridged and are so indicated when known.

Succinct plot summary, noting principal themes, critical strengths or weaknesses, comparable works, and any awards or nominations received (see Chapter 10). Notable stories in collections and anthologies are usually mentioned. Clareson's selections in Chapter 2 are often based on the fact that they are representative of the period, and his introduction frequently provides the critical evaluation rather than the annotations themselves. This synoptic approach permits the reader to grasp evolving themes more effectively.

Each annotated entry is preceded by a key number which is used for cross-reference whenever the title is mentioned elsewhere in the text.

First purchase (core collection) titles are starred, and a large majority are in print, although many of the works from the modern period are available only in paperback. Starred titles were selected on the basis of one or more of these characteristics: awards or nominations received (see Chapter 10); influence of the work; outstanding or unique treatment of a theme; critical and/or popular acceptance; importance of the work in the author's total output; or historical importance, especially for early works.

Nonstarred titles are those which are *relatively* less important but which should be found in a more comprehensive collection. This category includes many of the less distinguished but still respectable efforts in the field. It necessarily reflects substantial personal judgment by individual contributors, and no attempt was made to secure unanimity of judgment. Certain titles were selected as representative of their type, e.g., space opera. Equally good alternates could have been selected.

As should be clear, this is a critical guide, not a comprehensive handbook. But a conscientious attempt has been made to direct the reader to more specialized works which provide much of the information which would be part of such a handbook; Chapters 6-10 list many such works along with background information which should be useful to the several audiences of this book.

I hope that this guide will encourage the reprinting of selected works, especially first-purchase titles which are out of print. Several efforts along this line are already evident, such as the series from Hyperion, Arno and Gregg.

Although each of the contributors had primary responsibility for the selection of books in his respective period, preliminary lists were reviewed by all and by a number of outside readers listed below. The intent was to be reasonably comprehensive without becoming exhaustive. We hope knowledgeable readers will find almost every work they would judge of major significance annotated, even if their individual judgments may differ from that of the contributors. Because we cast our net widely, we have occasionally included titles which fall at the fantasy end of the spectrum but which for various reasons stated elsewhere, are important in the history of science fiction.

In addition to the contributors who have given generously of their knowledge and time, thanks are due the individuals shown below who have critically reviewed various portions of this guide. While they are not responsible for the individual selections and judgments, the guide has been greatly improved because of their enthusiasm and knowledge.

James Gribben, a very knowledgeable SF reader who suggested titles and drafted a number of annotations; Frank Varela, a research librarian who copy edited portions of Chapter 4, as well as suggesting titles in Spanish; Stephen Dark, Cy Chauvin, Tom Barber, Peter Nicholls, Clinton Price, Darko Suvin, Robert J. Wilson, Marshall Tymn, and Nicole

Ballard, for suggestions as to inclusions and exclusions; Howard De-Vore, a dealer who generously made available the resources of his store; Cecily Little, Doris Miller, and the supporting staff of the Central Michigan University library; and Tom Jones and Donna Wilson for their help in researching Chapter 4. Denise De Bolt and Linda Sutliff were invaluable in the preparation of the final manuscript.

Neil Barron

Contributors

(Richard) Neil Barron, 1934– . A graduate of two Univ. of California campuses, he was an active SF fan in the late 1940s and 1950s in the Los Angeles area. A librarian for 12 years, he left library work in 1973 for a sales management position with the publisher of *World Book Encyclopedia*. This guide is an outgrowth of his two bibliographic essays in *Choice*, January 1970 and September 1973. Address: 2319 Fern Place, Tampa, Fla. 33604.

Thomas D. Clareson, 1926– . A professor of English at the College of Wooster, he specializes in American literature and nineteenth- and twentieth-century fiction. As the founding editor of *Extrapolation*, he has long been active in the SFRA. He edited *SF: The Other Side of Realism* [6-23], *Science Fiction Criticism* [7-5], and *A Spectrum of Worlds* [4-663], among other works. He is now readying for publication a study of Charles Reade and is writing a history of American SF to 1926. Address: Box 3186, College of Wooster, Wooster, Ohio 44691.

Joseph W. De Bolt, 1939– . An associate professor of sociology at Central Michigan University, he has authored articles in scholarly journals and is the editor of *The Happening Worlds of John Brunner* [6-27]. His major academic interests are social change, small groups, and the community, and his long-standing SF interests are used to illustrate topics in his courses. Address: Dept. of Sociology, Central Michigan University, Mount Pleasant, Mich. 48859.

H(al) W(eldon) Hall, 1941– . Born in Waco, he holds degrees from the Univ. of Texas, Austin (biology) and North Texas State Univ. (library science). A former high school biology teacher, he is now the serials librarian at Texas A&M. He is a member of the SFRA's board of directors, editor of their publication series, and book and production editor for the *SFRA Newsletter*. He edited the *Science Fiction Book Review Index, 1923–1973* [8-8]. Address: 3608 Meadow Oaks Lane, Bryan, Texas 77801.

Francis J. Molson, 1932– . An associate professor of English at Central Michigan University, specializes in nineteenth-century American literature and children's literature, especially fantasy. He is currently engaged in a full-length study of Frances Burnett, best known for her *Little Lord Fauntleroy* (1886), and hopes to write a history of fantasy in the United States. Address: English Dept., Central Michigan Univ., Mount Pleasant, Mich. 48859.

John R. Pfeiffer, 1938– . With degrees from the University of Detroit and Kentucky, he is now associate professor in the English department of Central Michigan University. The author of scholarly articles and bibliographies dealing with G. B. Shaw, Durrenmatt and Gunter Grass, he also wrote *Fantasy and Science Fiction: A Critical Guide* [7-16]. Forthcoming is an annotated bibliography of writings about Shaw. Address: English Dept., Central Michigan Univ., Mount Pleasant, Mich. 48859.

Robert M. Philmus, 1943– . A professor of English at Montreal's Loyola College, Concordia University, he is the author of *Into the Unknown* [6-74] and a number of essays on writers like Borges, C. S. Lewis, Swift, and Wells. With David Hughes, he coedited a critical anthology, *H. G. Wells: Early Writings in Science and Science Fiction* (Univ. of Calif. Press, 1975). He is currently working on a study entitled *Jonathan Swift and the Poetics of Indirection*. Address: English Dept., Loyola College, Concordia University, 7141 Sherbrooke St. West, Montreal, Quebec H4B 1R6, Canada.

Ivor A. Rogers, 1930– . His Time Machine bookstore specializes in fantasy and SF, juveniles and other twentieth-century popular literature. While on the faculties at Drake University and the University of Wisconsin, Green Bay, he taught film, theater arts and SF courses, and was active in theater arts. He contributed a critical forward to Silverberg's *The Mirror of Infinity* [4-693], is the art editor of *Orcrist: A Journal for Fantasy in the Arts*, and has several works in progress. Address: Box 1068, Des Moines, Iowa 50311.

Introduction

Neil Barron

All this world is heavy with the promise of greater things, and a day will come, one day in the unending succession of days, when beings who are now latent in our thoughts and hidden in our loins, shall stand upon this earth as one stands upon a footstool and shall laugh and reach out their hands amidst the stars.

—*"The Discovery of the Future"* (1902), H. G. WELLS

But one thing is certain. Man himself, at the very least, is music, a brave theme that makes music also of its vast accompaniment, its matrix of storms and stars. Man himself in his degree is eternally a beauty in the eternal form of things. It is very good to have been man. And so we may go forward together with laughter in our hearts, and peace, thankful for the past, and for our own courage. For we shall make after all a fair conclusion to this brief music that is man.

—*Last and First Men* (1930), W. OLAF STAPLEDON

That Man is the product of causes which had no prevision of the end they were achieving; that his origin, his growth, his hopes and fears, his loves and his beliefs, are but the outcome of accidental collocations of atoms; that

no fire, no heroism, no intensity of thought and feeling, can preserve an
individual life beyond the grave; that all the labours of the ages, all the
devotion, all the inspiration, all the noonday brightness of human genius,
are destined to extinction in the vast death of the solar system, and that the
whole temple of Man's achievement must inevitably be buried beneath the
debris of a universe in ruins—all those things, if not quite beyond dispute,
are yet so nearly certain, that no philosophy which rejects them can hope to
stand.

—*"A Free Man's Worship"* (1903), BERTRAND RUSSELL

In 1962 Mark Hillegas taught the first science fiction course at Colgate University. A measure of the change in the critical acceptance science fiction as a legitimate field of scholarly study is that many hundreds of courses were devoted to the genre in American colleges and universities in 1975, with additional hundreds offered in high schools. A relatively new organization, Instructors of Science Fiction in Higher Education, now presents the Jupiter Award (see Chapter 10). Popular acceptance has grown as well. The subscription and newsstand sales of the five leading SF magazines total close to 300,000, and multiple readership would inflate this figure several times over. Many American and foreign publishers regularly include SF titles in their trade publishing programs, and the number of texts on the market has grown rapidly.

Most modern American science fiction appeared originally in the pulp magazines beginning in the 1920s. The 1950s and 1960s saw extensive reprinting of this material, much of it by specialty houses, few of which now survive. In 1972 a major change occurred: the paperback and hardcover book market became the most important single market for original SF. The steady decline in the number of magazines publishing original SF was also responsible for this important shift.

According to *Publishers Weekly*, about 2,400 new works of fiction were published in 1974. *PW*'s tabulations, however, slight mass market paperbacks, a key format for SF books. Although *PW* showed only 137 new SF titles in 1974, contributors to *Locus*, a news magazine in the SF field, tabulated 172 new hardbacks and 201 original SF paperbacks, with 59 and 288 reprints and reissues in these respective categories. This total of 373 original works of SF—even allowing for differences in definition—is a respectable 16 percent of all new fiction published. Few works of fiction, SF or otherwise, achieve distinction, and one major purpose of this guide is to identify the more significant works worthy of the reader's time.

The demand in libraries for science fiction, like mysteries, is predictable if modest. A few new titles are added each month, usually from the better known authors. But there is rarely any attempt to develop an SF book collection systematically. There is also the buckram syndrome still too prevalent in libraries, which regards the paperback as a second class book. Although original SF paperbacks and reprints may be purchased, it is rare for these to be cataloged because of the relatively high processing costs. Yet many important works in SF have been published only in paperback. Card catalog users are therefore unaware of their existence unless they browse the paperback racks. And because SF is still suspect as serious literature in many libraries, older titles tend to be discarded, and the collection accordingly lacks historical depth.

There are still other problems facing the library user in search of SF. Science fiction as a subject heading used by libraries in their card catalogs and in various standard bibliographies and indexes came into use around 1950. The term's usage in libraries varies widely, depending on the cataloging (indexing) policies followed. Some public libraries use the term for any work labeled SF, whether novel, short story collection or anthology. Others are more restrictive, limiting the term only to anthologies, although the library may provide users with copies of a typed list of SF titles not otherwise so identified in the card catalog. Others may use a special symbol to denote SF, sometimes shelving them separately, like biographies. The Library of Congress, whose subject heading lists are usually accepted by most college and university libraries and some large metropolitan libraries, uses the heading science fiction only for anthologies (SCIENCE FICTION—COLLECTIONS), not for single author works which are listed in LC's subject book catalogs as FICTION IN ENGLISH, hardly a helpful heading. However, the *Cumulative Book Index* of books in English published worldwide has for some years used the heading for single author works as well as for anthologies. The specialist bibliographies listed in Chapter 7 are the essential tools for the interested reader. A recommended survey is Hal Hall's "The Bibliographic Control of Science Fiction," *Extrapolation*, 15 (December 1973), 42–50.

Hal Hall, who compiles an annual index of SF book reviews [8-8] remarks that the reviewing of science fiction is still heavily concentrated in the SF magazines and fanzines, although coverage in general reviewing sources is improving. Library publications such as *Library Journal* and *Choice* are paying more attention and use reviewers who are conversant with the field. The quality of reviewing varies widely and is not easily characterized by source of the review. Fanzine reviews, for example, include both poorly written plot summaries and some of the best critical reviews. The most informative reviews are usually found in the professional SF magazines, followed closely by library journals such as the two mentioned. Users of book reviews should be cautioned to consider the source and purpose of the review. For example, *Publishers Weekly* has a different goal in reviewing than does *Analog*, and the reviews often reflect this difference. Major writers in the field, such as Clarke, Vonnegut, Heinlein and Asimov, are receiving somewhat more attention than in the past, but reviewing in the general media is still sketchy at best, probably reflecting the lingering suspicions of SF by book review editors.

In a 1955 talk to the Cambridge University English Club, C. S. Lewis remarked of SF: "There seems, in fact, to be a double paradox in its history: it began to be popular when it least deserved popularity, and to excite critical contempt as soon as it ceased to be wholly contemptible." (From his essay, "On Science Fiction," in his posthumous collection, *Of Other Worlds* [6-57]).

There has long been controversy over by whom and how SF should be judged. The more devoted fans have always been suspicious of "outsiders"—either nonfans or non-SF writers. This defensive attitude was reinforced by the usually uninformed criticism and reviewing in the general media until at least the 1960s. As noted above, there has been considerable improvement. There is still some uneasiness, even among professional SF authors, as to whether the growing academic study of SF, with its ponderous analyses, bloodless schema, critical in-fighting, and other features, is likely to benefit the field.

Linked to this suspicion is the attitude that the conventional methods of literary criticism are largely inapplicable to SF, which for years was regarded as *sui generis* and thus required separate standards. This attitude is—or seems to be—much less common than it once was. But SF usually has certain characteristics which require comment.

In the essay quoted from earlier, C. S. Lewis noted that most SF criticism prior to his 1955 talk was not informed, and that the people who wrote it clearly hated SF, and too often wrote drivel, because hatred obscures all distinctions. Amis [6-6] begins his lectures with two quotes from SF novels and suggests that those for whom the quotes held little or no interest would do better to ignore SF altogether.

Lewis admits his own critical limitations in his likes and dislikes. He dislikes the stories "which leap a thousand years to find plots and passions which they could have found at home." The emphasis on scientific gadgetry held little appeal for him. As to the lack of deep or sensitive characterization in SF, Lewis felt such characterization would be a fault, noting that if Gulliver or Alice had been other than commonplace, they would have wrecked their stories. "To tell how odd things struck odd people is to have an oddity too much: he who is to see strange sights must himself not be strange" (p. 65). For Lewis, one must have at least a minimal sense of wonder, a feeling for the mythopoetic, to appreciate fantasy and SF. Those who lack these characteristics are, he feels, poorly qualified to judge SF.

Martin Green, in his *Science and the Shabby Curate of Poetry* [6-42], provides an excellent discussion of C. P. Snow's famous two cultures, with their emphases on literary versus scientific sensibilities. In Chapter 6, "Two Surveys of the Literature of Science," Green remarks: "It is universally agreed that the people one meets in these SF stories, even the good ones, are unconvincing and uninteresting by comparison with quite a low grade of conventional fiction; they are neither freshly observed, deeply explored, nor carefully selected . . . . For most readers with literary training, this disposes of science-fiction altogether, because, unconsciously or not, they identify literature with the moral-psychological exploration of personal relations" (p. 129). Green rejects the view of many defenders of SF that SF "*cannot* offer interesting characterization, because that would over-involve the reader in the individual character, and distract the attention from the species or the society or the experiment which is the main subject" (p. 129). He adds: "Though the best of these novels excite the imagination in dozens of ways, they never really satisfy it" (p. 132). He argues that there lie in SF inherent contradictions which limit it to "a kind of writing which cannot develop into forms which engage major talents and deliver major meanings, though it can reinvigorate the forms of conventional literature by merging into them" (p. 133), adding ". . . its writers have undertaken major imaginative enterprises without attempting minor literary standards of style and characterization. That is why its commentators identify it with its limitations (with the literary things it does *not* do) and why they are so uneasy in their tone about it" (p. 135). But he concludes: ". . . this fiction brings with it an atmosphere of literary possibility which a writer can find hardly anywhere else today. When he puts down one of these short stories or novels, he finds his imagination reverberating with a dozen possibilities of rewriting it, and of related subjects" (p. 133). The concerns of Lewis and Green are also explored very effectively in Robert Conquest's "Science Fiction and Literature," *Critical Quarterly*, 5 (Winter 1963), 355–367. And Robert Scholes' recent work, *Structural Fabulation* [6-83] argues that traditional fiction is moribund and that SF holds great promise as an invigorating force.

I quote these contrasting views to suggest that a different type of literary experience awaits the reader wholly or largely unfamiliar with SF. Most SF does not correspond to the dominant expectations of the academy, which still uses the nineteenth-century novel of psychological exploration as its norm, as Green suggests. I hope *Anatomy of Wonder* will enlarge the more knowledgeable reader's awareness of SF's variety and scope. And for all readers, I hope many of the annotated and mentioned books provide both pleasure and stimulus to thought.

Readers of SF vary widely in their interest in the field and do not run to type. Fans, while sometimes unfairly depicted as pimply adolescents, are far more varied. The growing popularity and seriousness of the field has been paralleled by the increasing number attending the world SF conventions held around Labor Day. The thirty-second such convention held in Washington, D.C. in September 1974 attracted over 4,000

people. The number of casual and "hardcore" (fan) readers of SF probably numbers several million. David Hartwell, writing in *Locus* (24 December 1974), comments, "There are regular SF readers, numbering
about 50,000, who buy more than one SF book a month for years, continuously. And then there are about two million people who buy SF infre-
quently, do not really know anything about it, and make all the difference in the long run."

Several readership surveys have been made. A twenty-one-year-old article ("A Profile of Science Fiction," by S. E. Finer, *Sociological Review*, December 1954) cites several studies which suggest a predominantly youthful readership (under thirty-five), heavily male. The news fanzine, *Locus*,
polled its 2,000 or so readers each year from 1971 through 1974. The
respectable 20 to 25 percent return summarized in issue 158, 20 April
1974, showed a number of constants. The median age was about twenty-
five, with 80 percent of the readers male. Many students were among the
varied occupational categories, and of 247 nonstudents who responded,
71 percent were college graduates, and 29 percent held advanced degrees. Liberal arts majors appear to make up a growing percentage of
readers, which is reflected in the rapid growth of college courses cited
earlier. The *Locus* editor noted that publishers tend to regard the average SF reader as a teenager who reads SF for three to four years and
"matures" to something else, a portrait quite at variance with the *Locus*
reader. But the *Locus* reader is probably a fan, and a profile of the much
larger number of less-devoted readers would probably reveal a quite different picture.

One of the most entertaining studies of pseudoscience is *Fads and Fal-
lacies in the Name of Science* (Dover, 1957), by Martin Gardner, a freelance
writer and the author of the mathematical games department in *Scientific
American*. He takes a decidedly sour view of the SF fan, based on his reading of *Astounding* (now *Analog*) in the 1950s, when its late editor, John W.
Campbell, was pushing dianetics, "psionics," and similar favorites. Gardner remarks: "It suggests once more how far from accurate is the stereotype of the science fiction fan as a bright, well-informed, scientifically literate fellow. Judging by the number of Campbell's readers who are impressed by this nonsense, the average fan may very well be a chap in his
teens, with a smattering of scientific knowledge culled mostly from science fiction, enormously gullible, with a strong bent toward occultism,
no understanding of scientific method, and a basic insecurity for which
he compensates by fantasies of scientific power" (p. 348).

While I have personally seen some evidence for the "we precious few"
syndrome among SF fans, it seems to me no more common than in any
other group of readers. If they are not scientifically knowledgeable, SF is
not to be blamed, since a major intent of most SF is to entertain, not instruct. Many of the common fictional conventions in SF are scientifically

indefensible, e.g., time travel, interstellar travel, controlled telepathy, etc., but these are accepted by SF readers as making many of the memorable stories possible.

The credulity sometimes attributed to SF readers is more of a general human characteristic. The will to believe is a strong one. Of likely interest to readers of this guide is the study, *When Prophecy Fails* (1956), a social and psychological study of a modern group that predicted the destruction of the world (to quote the subtitle), by Leon Festinger, H. W. Riecken, and Stanley Schachter. The belief in UFO's as something beyond objects which are simply unidentified is one common to many SF readers for obvious reasons. The role which evidence plays in beliefs is explored in detail in this fascinating and disturbing case study. A more recent work, akin to Gardner's, is Charles Fair's *The New Nonsense: The End of Rational Consensus* (Simon & Schuster, 1974).

As Chapter 1 indicates, the limits of SF as a literary genre are impossible to specify with any exactitude. But even a narrow definition would include several thousand titles. It is both this sheer bulk and the increasingly widespread popular and critical acceptance which has made this guide necessary.

Part 1.
The Literature

1.
Science Fiction: From Its Beginning to 1870

Robert M. Philmus

Let me think: was I the same when I got up this morning? . . . But if I'm not the same, the next question is, "Who in the world am I?" . . .

I'm sure I'm not Ada . . . . for her hair goes in such long ringlets, and mine doesn't go in ringlets at all; and I'm sure I can't be Mabel, for I know all sorts of things, and she, oh, she knows such a very little! Besides, she's she, and I'm I, and—oh dear, how puzzling it all is!

—*Alice in Wonderland*, LEWIS CARROLL

Down the Rabbit-Hole

Attempts to define science fiction suffer from perplexities that out-perplex Alice's. It is generally agreed that it is not quite what it was when it, so to speak, "got up in the morning." Heinlein or Le Guin or Lem are not the same as Lucian or Plato or Swift. Yet the question "What in the world is science fiction?" cannot be answered without at least tacitly assuming something about the genre's earliest influences—and vice versa.

3

Definitions of science fiction and accounts of its literary history, accordingly, tend to chase one another around in logical circles. A given definition and the specific "prototypic" examples selected to validate it—or those proposed as its culminating apotheoses—determine one another. To perplex matters further, *science fiction* often serves as a catchall term for Alices and Mabels (and sometimes Adas also). From this unhappy mélange arises a dilemma: to introduce distinctions, especially if they are exclusive, risks being arbitrary, and not to do so is to be left in Alice's confused despair ("I must be Mabel after all, and I shall have to go and live in that poky little house, and have next to no toys to play with, and oh, ever so many lessons to learn!").

One possible way out of this dilemma is to speak of science fiction as a class of literature whose works collectively share certain generic characteristics (as Alice and Mabel presumably do) while also belonging to a variety of subclasses, and other literary classes, which diverge with regard to their backgrounds, upbringings, and personalities. Many of the perplexities about what science fiction is originate in its affiliations with groupings that include non-science fiction. Consequently, a survey that recognizes both the pluralism and the unity obtaining among works of science fiction may not resolve all the perplexities, but it might at least provide the schematic means and the terminology for clarifying them.

A Matter of Definition—or, What's in a Name?

A class of literature as heterogenous as science fiction does not readily accommodate definitions that aim at homogenous universality. As a result, efforts to define science fiction as an undifferentiated whole are rarely, if ever, satisfactory. Usually the formulation is either so general that it says little about what science fiction is and lets in what it isn't, or so specific that it applies to some science fiction but not to all. The following examples illustrate the point, claiming variously that science fiction is:

(1) "fiction based on rational speculation regarding the human experience of science and its resultant technologies" (Reginald Bretnor)[1];

(2) "narrative[s] of an imaginary invention or d:scovery in the natural sciences and consequent adventures and experiences" (J. O. Bailey)[2];

(3) "that class of prose narrative treating of a situation that could not arise in the world we know, but which is hypothesized on the basis of some innovation in science or technology, or pseudo-science or pseudo-technology, whether human or extra-terrestrial in origin" (Kingsley Amis)[3];

(4) "a branch of fantasy identifiable by the fact that it eases the 'willing suspension of disbelief' . . . by utilizing an atmosphere of scientific credibility for its imaginative speculation in physical science, space, time, social science, and philosophy" (Sam Moskowitz)[4];

(5) "the search for a definition of man and his status in the universe

which will stand in our advanced but confused state of knowledge (science), and is characteristically cast in the Gothic or post-Gothic mould." (Brian Aldiss)[5].

Some of these statements are obviously too encompassing; others, perhaps less obviously, are too restrictive. Bretnor and Aldiss in effect take into the category of science fiction much of Western literature since the Industrial (if not the Copernican) Revolution, including (as more or less randomly chosen examples) Dickens' *Hard Times* and Elizabeth Gaskell's *Mary Barton*. On the other hand, Bailey and Amis would seem to leave out those fictions whose basis is "real" or "non-innovative" science—e.g., Darwinian biology (which Moskowitz also omits from his list of subjects for imaginative speculation)—or the social sciences (Bailey). Amis would also exclude science-fictional poetry, which does exist, albeit marginally, along with the by now numerous instances—notably anti-utopian science fiction—depicting situations that could arise "in the world we know" (regardless of where the emphasis falls in that ambiguous phrase).

Critical consideration of the five propositions above reveals that the criteria each puts forward so confidently can be reformulated in problematic terms. While all seem to agree that science fiction has something to do with science, there is some disagreement as to what counts as science (see Judy Merril's essay in *SF: The Other Side of Realism*)[6]. Nor is there much of a consensus about how the science figures in the fiction. Is science the basis of the hypothesis on which the fictional situation is predicated (Amis) or the starting point out of which the plot comes as a consequence (Bailey)? Or is it simply an "atmosphere" that dispels disbelief (Moskowitz)? Does the fiction deal with science itself or with its human and social impact (Bretnor)? Is science in the foreground of the fiction, in the background, or, as Aldiss seems to suggest, merely an external ground of reference? As for science fiction as a genre, is it a species of "rational speculation" (Bretnor), "fantasy" (Moskowitz), or Gothic romance (Aldiss)?

Virtually all the possibilities these questions imply can be affirmed by citing particular examples. But this only postpones, without resolving, the problem of what science fiction is, a problem which can be restated in terms of whether a particular example is eccentric or paradigmatic. It would therefore appear more useful to investigate instead the areas of complementarity and contradiction among the competing claims about science fiction. For this purpose, it will be necessary to discard the simplistic notion of a homogenous class and to talk rather of science fiction as a genre with identifiable, if not absolutely definite, boundaries, and consequently with a center and a periphery relative to those boundaries.

At the perimeter of science fiction and theoretically outside its domain are "realistic" or "re-presentational" fiction and the literature of the supernatural. The more or less ordinary incidents in pure "re-presentational" fiction do not require any special scientific explanation. The more or less extraordinary incidents in pure supernatural fantasy do not allow any. Science fiction, by contrast, both allows and requires some kind of scientific, or seemingly scientific, rationale for its contraventions of "mundane actuality."

Whether stated or implicit, the rationale behind the science-fictional "invention" (in the largest, Wellsian, sense) may derive from the natural or the social sciences, the former being generally the more central, or "hard core." It usually entails an imaginative extension or application of scientific theory to account for the invention—the hitherto unknown machine or species or what-not—which impinges upon or altogether displaces mundane reality. Both the invention and its rationale may be more or less essential to the fiction. The more incidental the invention, the closer the story comes to being "re-presentational"; the more dispensable its rationale, the closer the story approaches to supernatural fantasy. Verne's *Mysterious Island*, for example, verges on "re-presentational" fiction, to which its prototype, *Robinson Crusoe*, surely belongs (since Crusoe's technological creations are really re-creations, unless Defoe's work is read as if it were hermetically self-contained). As an instance of the opposite extreme, H. P. Lovecraft's tales involving discoveries of grotesque forms of life (underground, under the sea, in old New England ports, or wherever) would count as supernatural fantasies were it not for their last-minute invocations of biological theory or pseudo-theory.

To say that scientific theory supplies the necessary premise, expressed or implied, of the fictional hypothesis, or invention, does not exhaust the relations between science and science fiction or delimit the range of themes in the fiction itself. The scientific rationale may serve the purpose of literal credibility as part of an "argument" for the realizability of an imagined technological breakthrough, with or without its social consequences. But the fiction need not concern itself with real scientific possibilities, in the narrow sense, at all. Whatever scientific rationalizing goes on may belong to, and signal, a nonliteral, interpretative connection between the fiction and sociohistorical reality. The fiction might thus share the "cognitive" intent of science in its broadest (and also its etymological) sense by presenting heuristic models of the empirical world. But in science fiction these "models" usually come in the guise of apparent unlikeness, offering "a world radically discontinuous from the one we know" and only "indirectly" confronting "that known world in some cognitive way" in the "estranged" terms of what it seemingly or actually is not (the quotations are from Robert Scholes,[7] borrowing in large part from Darko Suvin[8]). Nor does the cognitive element rule out the critique of cognition itself—scientific or otherwise—a perennial theme in science fiction, from Lucian's *True History* to Lem's *Solaris*.

"Scientific" content, then, provides the lens of the fiction or its focal point or both, and the explanatory function it thereby serves may accordingly be "immediate" or "derivative." Science fiction that focuses, seriously or not, on future technological possibilities—the kind of science fiction exemplified, prototypically, in many of the works of Jules Verne—invokes scientific theory as "immediate" justification for speculation that is to be taken more or less literally. But in the kind of science fiction that might be called Wellsian (though its antecedents go back to Plato), meaning resides in the fiction as a cognitive parable rather than in the scientific content per se. The explanatory role of that scientific content would therefore derive from its participation in the metaphoric substance of the fiction and from its use as rhetorical means for establishing the fiction's cognitive character.

To propose that science fiction is the sort of literature that implicates scientific theory as an immediate or derivative explanation for its departures from—and fictional surrogates for—mundane reality does not dispose of all the disagreements about it. What deserves to be called "scientific" is, after all, to some extent a relative matter, partly dependent both on historical considerations (as in the case of mesmerism in the nineteenth century) and on the opinion of reader and writer (as in the case of extrasensory perception). This relativity of science confers a degree of indeterminacy on the criterion of "explanatory scientific content," which is unquantifiable anyway, and that in turn affords the genre a latitude that accentuates the continuities (in respects other than scientific content) between science fiction and other classes of literature. For example, if Hawthorne's anti-utopian *Blithedale Romance* is accounted science fiction because of the role that mesmerism assumes in it, its inclusion within the perimeters of the genre establishes a connection with the Hawthornian romance generally. But while there does exist a similarity between the two in the freedom each allows for imagination in the treatment of the fictional scene, the Hawthornian romance aims at "the truth of the human heart" in a moral and psychological sense which science fiction, centrally concerned with the human species collectively rather than individually, does not share.

Further (and more readily admissible) examples indicate areas of intersection with other literary classes, and subclasses, that resemble some science fiction in some ways but not in all. Mary Shelley's *Frankenstein*, for instance, points to a kinship between science fiction and the Gothic novel in the evocation of a feeling of strangeness and horror through the manipulation of scenic convention. But though the typical Gothic conventions—haunted castles or abbeys, mysterious apparitions and disappearances, and so forth—may have a parallel in the alien islands and planets of science fiction, the typical Gothic novel differs from most science fiction in vigorously subordinating cognitive elements for the sake of atmosphere and its attendant affects. Moreover, *Frankenstein* is not cognitively typical of the Gothic novel, which, apart from its "rationalizing" of the supernatural, manifests affinities with the so-called psychological novel, its Richardsonian predecessor, and the Hawthornian romance, its "post-Gothic" descendant.

By contrast, cognitive as well as formal considerations are the basis for enlisting works like *The Time Machine* and *The Sirens of Titan* in the category of "apocalyptic" fiction (a term David Ketterer[9] adopts from Northrop Frye to designate literary visions that reveal the human condition *ad terminem*). Apocalyptic fiction does not, of course, entirely coincide with science fiction. But where the two classes do intersect, it is arguable that the notion of apocalypse may subtly transmute the intention of science-fictional cognition. For a category whose prototype and paradigm is the Book of Revelation, though it admits more or less secular versions of apocalypse under the jurisdiction of the "type" of Apocalypse, it nonetheless tends to ally the cognitive aspects of the fiction with eschatology rather than science and with other-worldly rather than this-worldly preoccupations.

Subsuming science fiction under the rubric of fantasy, on the other hand, directs attention away from cognitive content altogether. This can permit recognition of elements in science fiction that, while meaningful, might be called "subliminative" (Scholes) as distinguished from "cognitive," since they are *relatively* private and subjective (for a case in point, see Alexei Panshin on A. E. van Vogt[10]). The problem with "fantasy," however, is that it is ambiguous enough as a term and amorphous enough as a concept to be a source of considerable confusion. In the sense that is primarily pejorative, it denotes whatever has no discernible meaningful connection with reality—a sense barely applicable to some of the space operas on the fringes of science fiction. As a Freudian concept that carries with it a theory of how the imagination transforms reality through the pleasure principle into the stuff of fiction (or dream or neurosis), fantasy applies in kind to all literature, though perhaps in greater degree to literary genres like science fiction whose formal conventions allow for less restraint, on a literal level, at least, by a reality principle. Finally, in literary parlance, fantasy has the vaguest meaning of all, signifying only an undifferentiated mass of writings that do not belong with mimetic or "re-presentational" fiction. It is consequently useless for distinguishing the Adas of non-science-fictional fantasy (e.g., most of the works of George MacDonald) from the fundamentally "cognitive" Alices and the fundamentally "subliminative" Mables of science fiction.

Thus, the various proposals for defining science fiction in terms other than "explanatory scientific content" are all open to objection as being too inclusive, or not inclusive enough, or both. At the same time, while these alternative definitions can be criticized for their selectivity, notions like "apocalypse," "rational speculation," "cognitive estrangement," "sublimation," and so forth largely complement one another in offering an access to understanding, in whole or in part, the works of science fiction they select—thereby testifying to a generic diversity to which no homogenous definition of science fiction can do justice. It would accordingly seem appropriate to acknowledge that diversity by indicating the ways in which the genre can be divided into subgroupings, most of them inclusive of examples that would not qualify strictly as science fiction. Such a procedure is especially necessary in dealing with the history of science fiction before Wells, a history which takes in many examples that are at best borderline science fiction and are otherwise "precursors" solely in their influence upon the subsequent history of the genre.

On the Plurality of Science-Fictional Worlds: Ideas of Generic Order

Explanatory scientific content, though it is the one common factor among works of science fiction in the strict sense, does not afford an adequate basis for a system to bring conceptual order to the genre's multiplicity. Apart from the difficulty—often the impossibility—of abstracting and isolating scientific content from fiction without distorting both, any such conceptual scheme would depend upon science for a framework of historical analogies and logical categories. But for the purposes of that kind of systematization, the historical correlation between science and science fiction is not simple and exact enough, nor do the categories provided by the usual disciplinary division of the sciences prove commensurable with the variety of explanatory scientific content. While the fiction attests and responds to a social concern with scientific thought—which is the precondition of its existence—the particular theory it selects to work upon, though more often than not current, is not necessarily a predominant one. Ludwig Holberg, for instance, refers in passing to Newtonian physics in *Nils Klim* (written perhaps a decade or more prior to its publication in 1741), but the operative idea behind Holberg's satiric invention is a belief he himself rather facetiously entertains, that there is another world at the center of a hollow Earth. More significantly, and regardless of what status a scientific theory may have in itself, the fiction may assimilate the theory in a manner that makes it less accessible to the historian of science than to the historian of ideas. In Swift's hands, Newton's celestial mechanics turn into another absurdly reductive explanation of mind in terms of the behavior of matter; and from Edward Bulwer-Lytton's *The Coming Race* (1871) through Wells' *Men Like Gods* (1923), science-fictional visions of "alternative evolution" transform Darwinian theory into a hypothesis about the nature of human society and the grounds of social ethics.

Earlier, and more recondite, parallels can be found as far back as Plato. *The Republic* (c. 387 B.C.), particularly in its ideal curriculum, evidences the influence on Plato of a Pythagorean absorption with mathematics and astronomy, and the cosmology the Pythagoreans derived from their theory of number enters into Timaeus' exposition in the dialogue bearing his name. But Plato transfigures Pythagorean thought to such an extent that considerable guesswork is required to reconstruct it. Again, the myth of an Atlantis destroyed by earthquake and flood, as outlined in the *Timaeus* (23A.–26D.) and developed more fully in the fragmentary *Critias* (both composed sometime after 360 B.C.), employs a theory of geological change—or, precisely, geological degeneration. But this geological theory can be accounted for more satisfactorily as manifesting a *zeitgeist* obsession with the notion of the world's decline (which also governs Hesiod's *Theogony* and is consistent with another datum of Plato's myth—namely, that in the time of Atlantis, 9,000 years before— Athens was the realization of his ideal Republic) than it can by recourse to Greek science per se. Where the explanatory scientific content does not come from science at all, or at least not directly, the heuristic applicability of the history of science in structuring the history of science fiction is more dubious still. Yet eclectic borrowing from one's predecessors is an ancient and widespread practice among writers of science fiction: Poe's ransacking of literary sources for his "science"—from Francis Godwin's *The Man in the Moone* (1638) to *Symzonia* (1827)—is unusual only in degree. Nor is it exceptional to find that scientific content, whatever its source, does not fit neatly into any one of the ready-made categories of the sciences. For example, Francis Godwin's explanatory apparatus in the first "scientific" extraplanetary voyage in fiction relies on principles of Galilean physics and of the "new astronomy" of Galileo, Copernicus, and Kepler, as well as on the biological pseudodox that a certain species of wild geese migrates to the moon. To consign *The Man in the Moone* arbitrarily to the category of, say, physics, astronomy, or biology would therefore be misinformative; whereas the compounding of categories (by substituting "and" for "or") multiplies them ad hoc and thereby nullifies their value as a system of clear and distinct classifications. Even an ill-sorted conglomeration of makeshift rubrics cannot convey an accurate idea of explanatory scientific content, which tends to be complex and indivisible in itself and inseparable from the fictional invention as a whole.

The difficulty of imposing on science fiction a logical or historical order based on science and oriented towards explanatory scientific content demonstrates the necessity of looking elsewhere for the means and object of classification—specifically, to the fictional invention and the ways of regarding it. Among the numerous possibilities, virtually all of which are implicit in the foregoing discussion, perhaps the most essential might be termed "topical," "structural," "modal," and "mythic" approaches. Each offers a system of logical categories for analyzing various aspects of science-fictional content; and if none can claim to apply exclusively to science fiction as such, this logical defect also enables them to assimilate works which, while they are not strictly science fictional themselves, nevertheless have a historical bearing on the genre's development.

Of the four systems mentioned, the first is probably the most familiar. Its "topics" include utopia and anti-utopia, the tale of the future or of the prehistoric past, the imaginary technological discovery or experiment or the voyage connected therewith, the lost or alien race, and the catastrophic event. These topics are logically distinct entities; they do not in themselves necessarily denominate generic subdivisions, since any combination or permutation of them may be present in a given fiction. Even so, one can trace the history of each topic and map its intersections with others. Utopia, for example—excepting myths of a Golden Age or a Land of Cockaigne—can be said to begin with Plato, both in his *Republic* and in a late dialogue, *The Laws*, especially Book III, which contains an ontogenetic account of an ideal but practicable commonwealth. This topic merges almost immediately, in Plato's myth of Atlantis, with the catastrophic event and the lost or alien race. The latter figures again in Euhemerus' (fl. 311–298 B.C.) tale of the island of Panchaea and in Iambulus' Island(s) of the Sun (second century B.C.—this narrative, like that of Euhemerus, is preserved only in abstract, in Diodorus Siculus' *Bibliotheke*). As early as the second century A.D., Lucian of Samosata, in his *True History* (or *True Story*), parodies the utopia of Iambulus and his ilk. His nameless hero, after being carried, ship, crew, and all, by whirlwind or waterspout, and then by the winds, to the moon, and having witnessed an epic battle between its inhabitants and those of the sun, notices that the moon is a utopia of plenty, peopled by beings whose noses drip honey and who sweat milk. Book II of Thomas More's *Utopia* (1516) revives the topic and gives it its name; it can also be argued that Book I adumbrates the first anti-utopia. Utopia continues to be a principal topic in Bacon, Campanella, Cyrano, Gabriel de Foigny, and Swift, through the socialist utopians (Rousseauesque, Fourierist, et al.) of the late eighteenth and the nineteenth centuries. Anti-utopia does not begin to come into its own as a topic much earlier than Lytton's *The Coming Race*, by which time technological progress had made anti-utopian technological oppression foreseeable, if not available.

The Idea of Progress, gaining ascendancy as a result of the Industrial and French Revolutions, with its dreams of the ameliorability of the material conditions of man's existence and the perfectibility of the human spirit, gave rise to the tale of the future, which had a precocious exponent in the anonymous author of *The Reign of George VI, 1900–1925* (1763), a book not especially noteworthy beyond its possibly being the first "future history." The tale of the future, or future history, joins with the castastrophic event in Mary Shelley's *The Last Man* (1826) and with the imaginary technological experiment in Mrs. Webb's *The Mummy!* (1827), but on the whole it does not command an overwhelming interest in its pre-Darwinian phase. Its post-Darwinian history—including one of the first tales of evolutionary prehistory, "A Story of the Stone Age" (1897, though again the topic in general refers back to Plato's Atlantis)—is almost synonymous with that of modern science fiction, commencing in Wells. His *Time Machine* (1895) is a virtual compendium of topics; together with the rest of Wells' early science fiction it can be thought of as a focal point for "topical" traditions that elsewhere are somewhat diffuse.

A historical outline of utopia or the tale of the future suggests the paradigm for treating other topics. It also indicates how topical categories can organize the generic connections inherent in the tradition of science fiction and coordinate them with the history of ideas, especially scientific ideas. In addition, the generic connections identified by a system of topics conform more easily—and more sensibly—to chronological arrangement than do those categorically stipulated by the other approaches being considered. But this does not mean that any other scheme of classification is useless or even ancillary. There are essential aspects of the science-fictional invention which topical categories in themselves are incapable of dealing with and which consequently require for their analysis wholly different sets of distinctions—"structural," "modal," and "mythic."

Structural distinctions, reduced to a minimum, can be characterized as "extrapolative," "analogical," and "alternative." These terms identify, in their logically pure form, structural principles, or models, which heuristically stipulate how the fictional "invention" is arrived at and, accordingly, what cognitive relationship it bears (in itself or in conjunction with the totality of the fiction) to the outside world (compare Suvin[11]). Regardless of the structural principle involved, the cognitive invention in theory supposes as its basis of departure a given state of affairs, technological, sociological, or otherwise. The extrapolative principle generates the invention by projecting the ("prophetic") consequences of that state of affairs, specified or assumed. Analogical models depend upon the state of affairs to establish the grounds of likeness, overt or implicit, on which the analogical invention is predicated. In this context, alternative structures can be thought of as negated or inverted analogies, originating in, and founded on, unlikeness.

The alternative invention as negated analogy antedates Iambulus— the inhabitants of whose Island(s) of the Sun live in a land of peace and plenty virtually free from all natural or moral causes of suffering—by several centuries. It can be traced at least as far back as Aristophanes' *Lysistrata* (411 B.C.), in which the women of the Greek city-states collectively sequester themselves until their men agree to put a stop to the Peloponnesian War, and its basis in unlikeness is clear from his *Ecclesiazusai* (c. 391 B.C.), in which the women of Athens again turn the world upside down, this time by directly taking over political power. Nor has the alternative model advanced much in sophistication since Plato (and not at all since More and Swift), especially compared to its analogical and extrapolative counterparts, with which it is often juxtaposed (particularly in "voyages to the moon," from Francis Godwin through the anonymous *History of a Voyage to the Moon* [1864]). This relative lack of development is not to be attributed to some notion that the alternative structure is inherently more—or less—primitive than any other, but rather to the fact that it is more patently recognizable for what it is. By contrast, extrapolative and analogical models, from Plato onwards, exhibit a compulsion, which still marginally persists, to call attention to, and explain, their structural nature. Though the compulsion may be justified (some readers manage to mistake Lilliput for pure fantasy, despite Swift's broad analogical hints), it tends to abate as writers assume a conversance with such models on the part of their audience. Sometimes that assumption originates in the author's own habits of mind: this is the case with Hawthorne, who, because of his addiction to reading, and thinking in terms of allegories, felt no need to explain his analogical fictions (including "The Birthmark" [1843] and other short stories) further than by interjecting a few brief moralistic asides. Sometimes the author supposes an awareness in his readers of the nature of structural models because he himself has deliberately inculcated that awareness: this is the case with Wells, who, having drawn extensively from the tradition of science fiction to construct a highly complex "analogical-extrapolative" (and to some degree also "alternative") model in *The Time Machine*, whose workings he explains at some length, thereafter takes a familiarity with such models for granted and in consequence abbreviates considerably the explanatory rationale of his subsequent extrapolative and analogical inventions. Whatever the motive, the overall historical direction of cognitive science fiction is towards structural complexity and sophistication.

A system of structural classifications is not sufficient without modal ones as well. Viewed solely in terms of structure, the inventions of a means for getting to the moon in Godwin's *Man in the Moone* and in the pseudonymous Murtagh McDermot's *A Trip to the Moon* (1728) are similarly extrapolative (the former relies on Galileo's principles of the pulley, the latter on Newton's laws of motion). However, their modalities of extrapolation are quite antithetical. Where Godwin is serious, McDermot is satirical; where Godwin is naive, McDermot is ironic. If they are not self-explanatory, these modal categories—serious vs. satiric, naive vs. ironic—define themselves relationally as antinomies, and differentiate among authorial attitudes towards matters of topical and structural content. By and large, modal categories comprise the system least susceptible to historical orientation: determinations of chronological order and precedence are seldom relevant to them since they exist practically irrespective of history and literary tradition. But the satiric mode can be excepted from this generalization by virtue of its connection with formal satire, which can be treated historically (see, for example, Robert C. Elliott's *The Power of Satire*), and which—beginning with its most informal variant, Menippean satire, as in Lucian's *Icaromenippus*—does pertain to the development of science fiction.

The "formal" fluidity of science fiction is manifest in its history. At one time or another it or its prototypes merge not only with formal satire but with the detective story (as in Poe—and also in Asimov), the psychological tale of horror (as in E.T.A. Hoffman), the ghost story (as in Melville and Fitz-James O'Brien), and others. The same sort of diversity characterizes the specific "mythic" content of the genre. For this reason—and also because the historicity of that content precludes any simple equation with a handful of timeless archetypes—any mythic categories, if they are to be manageable in number, must apply not directly to the multitudinous particularity of mythic content in itself but to its nature generally (and thus might be more properly called "meta-mythic"). The logical categories answerable to this requirement can be designated as "mythopoetic," "mythomorphic," and "demythologistic." According to these distinctions, the invention—or the fiction as a whole—may in theory either conform to the pattern of an already existing myth (mythopoesis, as T. S. Eliot employs the word in regard to James Joyce's *Ulysses*), or embody a myth-like paradigm original with it (mythomorphosis), or negate the one process or the other (demythology). The possibilities, though they are distinct in theory, are not so clearly differentiated in practice. *Frankenstein* (1818), for instance, as its subtitle, *A Modern Prometheus*, suggests, intends to be mythopoetic, but in effect also succeeds in being mythomorphic—as does, say, *The War of the Worlds* (1898), which sets out principally to be demythologistic by debunking the "Battle of Dorking" myth.

The demythologistic tendency, as it pertains to science fiction, appears in Aristophanes' *The Birds* (414 B.C.), in which two citizens fleeing from the corruption of Athens organize a Cloudcuckooland as intermediary between men and the gods. It continues in Euhemerus' account of Panchaea, where the gods once lived as men, and, more pronouncedly, in Lucian (also in Rabelais, Cyrano, Swift, and so on). Its early and persistent presence is instructive in that it demonstrates—and infuses into the generic tradition—an awareness of the historical relativity of myths. It consequently points to the crucial difference between myth per se and the mythic content of science fiction. Mythic content may aspire to the "primitive" status of myth as timeless explanation of cosmic processes and principles, but it cannot reach that status. Indeed, it is arguable that such status, sustained in oral tradition, is incompatible with literary self-consciousness, that as myth enters a literature aware of itself, it becomes time-bound, and its explanatory power (at least relative to what it was) becomes contingent and provisional instead of absolute. Whether this be admitted or not, the fact remains that the connotations of myth most useful in regarding science fiction are Sophoclean (with reference to his subjecting myth to history by transforming the vengeful Erinys into the merciful Eumenides in the course of the *Oresteia*). Historical coordinates deriving from the "scientific" or "extra-scientific" material incorporated in the invention do apply to the specific mythic content of the fiction. Hence, the mythic, and meta-mythic, systematizing of mythic content (in the stipulated sense of "mythic") agrees in substance with the approach to the cognitive content of science-fictional models and complements it in emphasis. Where the one primarily concentrates on the particulars of structural content as they cognitively relate to reality, the other focuses above all on the connections obtaining among various models as viewed in terms of their mythic content. Where the one might point to, say, *The Invisible Man* (1897) as an "extrapolative-analogical" model of the moral perplexities entailed by modern science, the other would consider Wells' fiction in its relation to *Frankenstein* and *The Strange Case of Dr. Jekyll and Mr. Hyde* (1886) as one more analogue of the myth of Faust (see *Into the Unknown* [6-74]).

This outline of various approaches to a genre definable on the basis of explanatory scientific content and otherwise highly diverse does not pretend to circumscribe all systems of logical and historical categories relevant to science fiction. Those that have been discussed may be able to subsume, through syncretic combination, some that have not, such as thematic classifications. But the main intent has been to suggest the plurality of possible systems, not to propound, with Panglossian assurance, the best of all possible systems.

Notes

1. "Science Fiction in the Age of Space," in Bretnor, *Science Fiction, Today and Tomorrow* [6-17].

2. *Pilgrims through Space and Time* [6-9], p. 10.

3. *New Maps of Hell* [6-6], p. 14.

4. *Explorers of the Infinite* [6-65], p. 11.

5. *Billion Year Spree* [6-2], p. 8.

6. "What Do You Mean: Science? Fiction?," reprinted in Clareson, *SF: The Other Side of Realism* [6-23], p. 53–95.

7. *Structural Fabulation* [6-83].

8. Suvin, Darko, "On the Poetics of the Science Fiction Genre," *College English*, 34 (December 1972), 372–82.

9. *New Worlds for Old* [6-53].

10. Panshin, Alexei, "Metaphor, Analogy, Symbol and Myth," *Fantastic*, February 1972.

11. Suvin, *op. cit.*, and "Science Fiction and the Geneological Jungle," *Genre*, 6 (September 1973), 251–73.

The brackets refer to the entry numbers in Chapter 6, where fuller bibliographic information is provided for the cited books.

Bibliography: Science Fiction From Its Beginning to 1870

The earliest of the following annotations is More's *Utopia* (1516). Classical works, notably the Greek, are discussed in the introductory section of this chapter. The annotations continue through 1870, a significant year in European history and also one of some importance in the history of science fiction. After 1870 comes a deluge of science fiction—including most of Verne's, along with works by Butler, Greg, Morris, G. C. Griffith, and a host of others—that reaches its high water mark, as it were, in H. G. Wells and modern science fiction.

Within its chronological boundaries, this bibliography is deliberately selective. It lists some works that are marginally science fictional, or relevant to the generic tradition, if they are little known or not often thought of in that connection (e.g., Diderot's *Supplement*), but it omits mention of, or subsumes under other entries, those marginal cases (e.g., Defoe's *Consolidator*) recorded and discussed in Bailey's *Pilgrims through Space and Time* [6-9], Nicholson's *Voyages to the Moon* [6-67], my *Into the Unknown* [6-74], or elsewhere.

The entries attempt to give the reader accurate information about first publication in book form, or in periodicals in the case of short stories. An effort has been made to track down first translations from foreign languages. Works that have never been translated are generally excluded. Where a particular edition or translation is recommended, the reason for preference is usually stated or implied; where none is singled out, the reader can assume that any edition will do (e.g., the stories by Hawthorne and Poe that Franklin does not include in *Future Perfect* [6-35] can be found in a number of other sources).

The place of publication is shown because it has a socio-historical significance for foreign-language works initially published abroad (e.g., Voltaire's *Micromégas*).

1-1. Anonymous. **The History of a Voyage to the Moon . . . An Exhumed Narrative, Supposed to Have Been Ejected from a Lunar Volcano.** London: Lockwood, 1864.
Thanks to a monk's legend, a German student of science discovers an antigravitational substance and, accompanied by a friend, propels a kind of flying greenhouse to the Moon. The story has a certain science fictional interest up to this point, especially as a precursor of Wells' *First Men in the Moon*. But a haze of metaphysical and theological speculation beclouds the rest of a remarkably boring narrative about a lunar utopia.

1-2. Anonymous. **The Reign of George VI, 1900–1925.** London: W. Nicoll, 1763.
This work, possibly the first "future history," projects into the early twentieth century a jingoistic resolution of England's political problems of the eighteenth. After repelling a Russian invasion and finally subduing the combined power of Russia and France, England begins to enjoy a moral and cultural renaissance. There are no technological innovations in this world, but otherwise it anticipates the science fiction emergent from the "Battle of Dorking controversy" at the close of the nineteenth century.

1-3. Anonymous. **A Voyage to the World in the Centre of the Earth. Giving an Account of the Manners, Customs, Laws, Government and Religion of the Inhabitants . . . in which Is Introduced the History of an Inhabitant of the Air. . . .** London: S. Crowder and H. Woodgate, 1755.
The hero falls through Mt. Vesuvius into " a World like ours" at the center of the Earth. There he finds a human species that is vegetarian because everyone recognizes man's proper place in the natural order. Counterpointing the utopian state of affairs in this world is a history of a transmigrating soul victimized by tyranny and injustice on three other worlds (Jupiter, Saturn, and Earth). A subterranean bird flies the hero back to the Earth's surface. This curious book borrows from a variety of earlier *voyages imaginaires*, notably those of Voltaire and Holberg.

*1-4. Atterly, Joseph (pseud. of George Tucker). **A Voyage to the Moon: With Some Account of the Manners and Customs, Science and**

Philosophy, of the People of Morosophia, and Other Lunarians. New York: E. Bliss, 1827. Gregg, $13.00.

Atterly obtains from a Brahmin an antigravitational metal and applies it to the outside of the space vehicle in which he and the Brahmin fly to the Moon. On the way they discuss various theories of astronomy and physics suggested by what they observe. They protect themselves from the cold of space with thermal energy from certain chemical reactions, and experience (like Domingo Gonsales before them) a gravitational shift as they approach the Moon. They land in Morosophia, whose Laputanesque inhabitants have a warped sense of utility (e.g., they attempt to invent a kind of internal combustion engine!) or none at all. After visiting the political utopia of Okalbia, they return to Earth.

*1-5. Bacon, Francis (U.K.). **The New Atlantis**, in *Sylva Sylvarum*. London: William Lee, 1627. Odyssey, $3.50; Oxford Univ. Press, $11.25 (includes *Advancement of Learning*).

In this incomplete work, a ship lost in the South Seas happens upon the island of Bensalem, a monarchical and patriarchal utopian community. The most outstanding innovation in this work is Salomon's House, a kind of research center founded 1,900 years previously by King Salomona. Here studies are carried out in meteorology, astronomy, botany, and other fields. Researchers also attempt such things as imitating the flight of birds and constructing ships that can sail underwater.

1-6. Balzac, Honoré de (France). **La recherche de l'absolu.** Paris: C. Bechet, 1834. Tr. as *Balthazar; or, Science & Love*, by William Robson. London: Routledge, 1859. Modern translations follow the original title. French & European Pubs., $1.75 (in French).

Balthazar Claes sacrifices all his earthly happiness—and that of his wife and children—to his quest for the Absolute, the "single element" to which "all natural productions might be reduced." He becomes fatally ill when the awareness is brought home to him of "the contrast between the ideal world in which he lived and the real world about him." This is an early "mad scientist" story, later grouped with the Études Philosophiques of Balzac's *Comedie Humaine*.

1-7. Bray, John Francis (U.K.). **A Voyage from Utopia.** London: Lawrence & Wishart, 1957. Kelley, $10.00; Melvin McCosh, $9.50.

Instead of having a visitor to utopia report directly on the state of affairs there, Bray has a visitor *from* utopia go on a tour of England and America, offering a satirical critique of their socioeconomic systems and leaving the outlines of his socialist utopia largely to inference. This novel treatment of the topic of utopia, completed in 1842, remained unpublished for more than a century.

1-8. Brunt, Samuel (pseud.) (U.K.). **A Voyage to Cacklogallinia. With a Description of the Religion, Policy, Customs and Manners of That Country.** London: J. Watson, 1727. Columbia Univ. Press, 1940. Garland, $25.00 (as vol. 49 of Foundations of the Novel series).

Captain Samuel Brunt, the eponymous author and hero of this imitation of *Gulliver's Travels*, finds himself shipwrecked in Cacklogallinia, an island populated by a society of fowls. He describes their customs and social and political institutions, and especially their preoccupation with projects for paying off their huge national debt. One of these projects is to extract gold from the Moon, and the Cacklogallinians eventually fly Brunt there for that purpose. But the inhabitants of that sphere, the vegetarian souls of the virtuous dead who live there until the soul dies and the understanding returns to its Creator, are inhospitable to this project, and show Brunt from their lunar vantage point the diverse vices, follies and evils of the Earth below. Brunt's satire throughout is directed primarily at John Law and the South Sea Bubble.

*1-9. Butler, Samuel (U.K.). **The Elephant in the Moon**, in **The Genuine Remains in Verse & Prose of Mr. Samuel Butler.** 2 vols. London: J. & R. Tonson, 1759. Reprinted as Augustan Reprint Society Pub. No. 88, Kraus, $16.00.

Butler's satiric verse describes how a group of "virtuosi" (i.e., scientists) gather to view what they imagine to be a Lucianic lunar battle between Kepler's Privolvans and Subvolvani. This epic battle is soon interrupted by the entrance on the scene of an elephant. A footboy standing by deflates the territorial pretensions to empire and knowledge on the part of the virtuosos by opening the far end of their telescope and discovering a swarm of flies and gnats—and a mouse. This posthumously published satire, probably written in the last quarter of the seventeenth century, belongs to the history of SF not merely because of its allusions to Lucian and Kepler but also because of its technical sophistication in making the virtuosos' "lunar vision" a projection of their *magnified* sense of their own worth.

1-10. Campanella, Tommaso (Italy). **City of the Sun.** Tr. of *Civitas Solis*, in *Realis philosophie epilogisticae partes quatuor*. Frankfurt: G. Tampach, 1623. Reprinted in *Ideal Commonwealths*, Kennikat, $12.50.

In dialogue form, Campanella describes the City of the Sun, a communistic utopian community governed by Metaphysic with the help of the triumvirate of Power, Wisdom, and Love. The city itself consists of seven concentric circular walls, in accordance with the number of planets then known. At its center is a planetarium-like temple. The inhabitants practice eugenics, and the city itself provides a kind of euthenic environment, each of its walls being inscribed with a pictorial compendium of one of the sciences.

1-11. Carroll, Lewis (pseud. of Charles Lutwidge Dodgson) (U.K.). **Through the Looking Glass.** London: Macmillan, 1872. Recommended editions: *The Annotated Alice*, intro. and notes by Martin Gardner, Potter, $10.00; New American Library, $3.95; *Alice in Wonderland*, ed. by Donald J. Gray, Norton, $2.45, $10.00.

Alice's "cognitively estranged" adventures down the rabbit hole lack the scientific rationale of science fiction (but see William Empson's Freudian interpretation in *Some Versions of Pastoral*, 1960). Its sequel, however, is at least a borderline case. The chess model used to differentiate the world-on-the-other-side-of-the-mirror from that of "common sense" is akin to the mathematical analogy at the basis of Abbott's *Flatland* [2-1], for instance, and more generally, to the mathematical structuring of much SF since Wells (given X, what logically follows?).

*1-12. Cyrano de Bergerac, Savinien (France). **The Comical History of the States and Empires of the Worlds of the Moon and Sun.** Tr. of *Histoire comique des états et empires de la lune*, 1651. Authoritative title: *L'autre monde, ou les états et empires de la lune et du soleil.* Larousse, $1.50 (in French). Recommended tr. by Geoffrey Strachan, *Other Worlds*, Oxford Univ. Press, 1965.

Depreciated for centuries as a "comical history" (of which an unexpurgated French text became available only as late as 1921), Cyrano's work is really a metaphysical fable about the nature of man and the universe. The various adventures of the hero take him to the Moon and the Sun. In a lunar Eden he interviews Enoch and Elijah; rationalistic Selenarians encage him with Domingo Gonsales, in the hope that the two will mate; in the Kingdom of the Birds he is condemned to be eaten by flies as punishment for man's inexcusable anthropocentricity; and finally he finds himself near the Sun among infinitesimal "animals" capable of the most marvelous transformations. Along with the satire on man's pride and superstition, *Other Worlds* seeks to give a metaphysical understanding of, and ultimately a sense of imaginative participation in, the fundamental being—and freedom of being—of the cosmos. On this level Cyrano remains unsurpassed—indeed, has few imitators. But compare Calvino's *Cosmiccomics* [4-136].

1-13. Diderot, Denis (France). **Supplement to Bougainville's "Voyage"** (tr. of *Supplement au voyage de Bougainville* . . . in *Opuscules philosophiques et literaires*, 1796), in *Rameau's Nephew and Other Works*, ed. by Barzun and Bowen, Bobbs, $3.00, $6.00.

Under the guise of an addendum to Louis-Antoine de Bougainville's *Voyage autour du monde* (*Voyage around the World*, 1771), Diderot presents an imaginary diatribe by a Tahitian elder against the probable evil effects of civilized imperialism, followed by an imaginary debate on morality and religion between a Tahitian named Orou and Bougainville's chaplain.

Framing these set pieces is a dialogue between A and B, in which the advantages of man in a state of nature are balanced against those of civilization. The *Supplement* is many ways the prototype of anthropological SF (as exemplified by LeGuin). It circulated in manuscript as early as 1773 but was published only posthumously.

1-14. Erskine, Thomas (U.K.). **Armata: A Fragment.** London: John Murray, 1817.
The hero of this "alternate history" reaches a planet that articulates with Earth through a channel at the South Pole. Here he finds an island whose history, institutions, and customs parallel and counterpoint England's. The satire is for the most part didactic and dull, though not nearly as dull as its continuation in Erskine's sequel.

*1-15. Godwin, Francis (U.K.). **The Man in the Moone; or A Discourse of a Voyage Thither.** London: Joshua Kirton and Thomas Warren, 1638. British Book Center, $6.95; Scolar Press, £1.50.
Wild geese ("gansas") migrate to the Moon, carrying Domingo Gonsales in a flying machine. On his way, Gonsales makes scientific observations confirming the truth of the "new astronony" of Kepler and especially Galileo. (Poe's criticism in his afterword to "Hans Pfaall" [1-43] conceals his debt to Godwin on this score). He spends enough time in the lunar utopia to learn that its inhabitants live in "another Paradise" and have perfected their scientific researches to the point of discovering the Philosopher's Stone. Returning from the Moon, he lands in China and makes his way back to Europe to record his adventures. Though its science is far from sophisticated by modern standards, this little book by an Anglican bishop is nevertheless the first to give a Moon voyage any kind of scientific credibility.

*1-16. Hawthorne, Nathaniel. **"The Artist of the Beautiful"** (1844).
Hawthorne is widely available, and his *Complete Short Stories*, Doubleday, $5.95, is a convenient source for all the annotated stories.
Owen Warland, a watchmaker, devotes years of his life to making a mechanical butterfly. He offers his butterfly as a belated wedding present to the woman with whom he has been secretly in love and who has since married someone of greater use to society than the artist. On one of its flights around the room the butterfly is seized by their child, in whose grasp it disintegrates. Unlike Melville's "The Bell-Tower," which it probably influenced, Hawthorne's story is less a metaphysical tale than a fable about the nature of art and the artist.

*1-17. Hawthorne, Nathaniel. **"The Birth-Mark"** (1843).
Obsessed by his wife's birth-mark, Aylmer attempts to remove it surgically. He succeeds, but the patient dies. While the idea can be considered

science fictional, its main significance, as in Hawthorne's other tales, pertains to the moral—and in this case also theological—allegory it suggests.

1-18. Hawthorne, Nathaniel. **"The Celestial Railroad"** (1843).
This is a satiric revamping of *Pilgrim's Progress* into an allegory of modern salvation-made-easy. The up-to-date pilgrim, thinking to take advantage of the technological progress of his materialistic way of life, travels by rail to the Celestial City, but the railroad lands him at a ferry going to Hell. While not itself SF, the parable foreshadows the utopia that turns out to be anti-utopian. In this regard it resembles another of Hawthorne's critiques of the utopian enterprise, *The Blithedale Romance* (1852).

*1-19. Hawthorne, Nathaniel. **"Rappaccini's Daughter"** (1844).
Giovanni Guasconti, a student newly arrived in Padua, develops an infatuation for Beatrice Rappaccini, who inhabits the "Eden" of poisonous plants adjoining his lodgings. He at first fancies her an alien and terrifying being whose very breath is poison, but his fears recede through his conversations with her. One day he receives a visit from Professor Baglioni, who reawakens his doubts about Beatrice's alien and evil nature and leads him to discover that he has caught the contagion of poisonous breath. Guasconti goes to Beatrice and scornfully offers her an antidote Baglioni has given him. As she drinks the antidote and dies protesting the innocence of her heart, Baglioni exults in having foiled Dr. Rappaccini's experiment in adaptation. As in most of Hawthorne's stories, the theme here is the betrayal of human sympathy by cold experimental objectivity.

1-20. Hoffmann, Ernst Theodore Wilhelm (Germany). **"The Sandman."** Tr. of "Der Sandmann" in *Die Elixiere des Teufels* (under pseud. Bruder Medarus), Berlin, 1815. Recommended tr. by Michael Bullock, *The Tales of Hoffmann*, Ungar, $2.95, $7.00.
A psychological horror story about a young man's obsession with the diabolic Sandman (Coppelius, alias Coppola), who he imagines covets his eyes. Nathanael falls in love with Olympia, only to find that she is an automaton. Under the delusion that his former love is also an automaton, he tries to kill her and, foiled in the attempt, commits suicide. Alchemy and superstition figure in the background, and Hoffmann leaves ambiguous the question of whether Nathanael's is a case of diabolic possession or psychosis.

*1-21. Holberg, Ludwig (Denmark). **A Journey to the World Underground. By Nicolas Klimius**, tr. anonymously. London: T. Astley, 1742. Tr. of *Nicolai Klimii iter subterraneum*, n.p: Hafniae and Lipsiae, 1741. Greenwood, $11.50; Garland, $25.00.
In this Danish classic (in Latin) of science-fictional satiric fantasy, Nils

Klim, a science student at the University of Copenhagen, goes off on a spelunking expedition and falls through a cave to the center of the Earth. He has occasion to verify the theories about the motion of bodies in space as he orbits around the planet Nazar, though his status as a satellite is only a three days' wonder. He lands on Nazar and proceeds to acquaint himself with the institutions and habits of thought in its various nations, many of them populated by rational trees. All of this gives Holberg scope for his satire, comparable in its encyclopedic breadth to *Gulliver's Travels*. By introducing such "improvements" as weapons of destruction, Klim eventually subdues the other nations of Nazar to the authority of Quama, and becomes its king. But a palace revolt against his tyrannous pretensions forces him to flee, and in so doing he falls back up to Earth.

*1-22. Kepler, Johannes (Germany). **Somnium, seu opus posthumum de astronomia lunari.** Frankfurt: Sagani Silesiorum, 1634. Tr. as *Kepler's Dream* by Patricia Kirkwood, Univ. of California Press, $10.00; tr. by Edward Rosen, Univ. of Wisconsin Press, $17.50.

Kepler recounts a dream in which a daemon of Levania (the Moon) tells Duracotus, a student of Tyco Brahe, and his mother, Fiolxhilde, about the nature of the Moon. He states that this satellite consists of two hemispheres, one of which, the Subvolva, always faces the Earth and one of which, the Privolva, never does; that it has an atmosphere and water; and that life forms, animal and vegetable, all of them prodigious in size and speed of growth, though short-lived, exist there. When it was first circulated in manuscript in 1609, the *Somnium*'s true meaning was disguised by its use of allegory and supernatural machinery, most of which Kepler deciphered in footnotes before his death—revealing the work to be basically a treatise, albeit a highly imaginative one, on the astronomy of the Moon.

1-23. Locke, Richard Adams. **"Great Astronomical Discoveries Lately Made by Sir John Herschel . . . at the Cape of Good Hope."** New York *Sun*, August–September 1835. The Gregg edition of *The Moon Hoax*, ed. by Ormand Seavey, $7.50, reproduces the longer 1854 edition, several contemporary reviews, and Poe's "Hans Pfaall" as well.

As the original title indicates, Locke purports to give an account of the discoveries Sir John Herschel made through a kind of reflecting telescope, twice as large as the one the English astronomer actually had transported to the Cape of Good Hope. In the hoax, Locke claims that Sir John and a colleague observed all manner of life on the Moon: various kinds of vegetation, including trees, animals like sheep and cows, and no less than three distinct humanoid species, at least two of which were winged (compare Paltock's *Peter Wilkins* [1-36]), and the third apparently worshippers of some geometrical deity (in their architecture and tribal gatherings they conform to geometrical patterns). Poe discusses Locke's hoax in his postscript to "Hans Pfaall" [1-43].

1-24. Loudon, Jane (U.K.). **The Mummy! A Tale of the Twenty-Second Century.** 3 vols. London: Henry Colburn, 1827.
A historical romance of the future which focuses primarily on the byzantine political intrigues in an England under a female monarchical succession. In this advanced world of the future, where weather control is possible and people travel in high-speed balloons, a man named Edric journeys to Egypt—now totally industrialized—with a Frankensteinian plan for reanimating the mummy of Cheops. The attempt appears successful, but afterwards Edric passes out and the mummy escapes, taking Edric's balloon to England and entering into the plotting and counter-plotting there. Thereafter, the romance reads more like something out of Sir Walter Scott. In the final scene the Cheops' tomb, the mummy, who has for the most part been presented as a diabolic figure, reveals to Edric that supernatural rather than natural forces caused him to come to life again temporarily to "assist the good and punish the malevolent" as penitence for his misdeeds as pharoah.

*1-25. Lytton, Edward Bulwer (U.K.). **The Coming Race.** Blackwood, 1871. Philosophical, $6.95.
In a subterranean world an American finds the Vril-ya, a race far in advance, both personally and socially, of the nineteenth century. They do not know sorrow, sin, or passion; there is no war, crime, poverty. All of this is made possible through the use of vril, "which Faraday would perhaps call 'atmospheric magnetism' "; it is the universal essence behind "the various forms under which the forces of matter are made manifest. . . . " The many mechanical contrivances, including wings, which the Vril-ya use make this utopia individual among the British utopias of the period. American life is satirized.

1-26. Lytton, Edward Bulwer (U.K.). **A Strange Story.** Leipzig: Tauchnitz, 1861, Shambala, £1.75.
Margrave, a philosophical materialist, seeks to cheat death by discovering the elixir of life. Through a woman named Lillian, who is his spiritual antithesis, he enlists the help of Dr. Allen Fenwick in his desperate and nefarious quest. From that point on the plot concerns Fenwick's ultimately successful efforts to disentangle himself and Lillian from Margrave's evil clutches. Like Balzac in *La recherche de l'absolu* [1-6], Lytton portrays the scientist as alchemist.

*1-27. McDermot, Murtagh (pseud.) (U.K.). **A Trip to the Moon.** Dublin: J. Roberts, 1728. Scholar's Facsimiles, $20.00 (as *Gulliveriana No. 1*, including Humphrey Lunatic's *Trip to the Moon*, 1764).
In this Swiftian satire—primarily on science (in the manner of the Third

Voyage of Gulliver, to whom the book is dedicated)—the hero is swept upward from Mt. Tenerife (also Domingo Gonsales' starting point) and becomes a satellite of Earth. Resolving not to remain permanently in this situation, McDermot grabs hold of a cloud and by a timely application of Newton's laws of motion accidentally propels himself to the Moon. There he finds a society of natural philosophers—many of them part beast—who engage in such absurdities as a project for building a house out of light, and who also have a contraption like a primitive submarine-bathyscope. Eventually McDermot blasts himself back to earth by igniting a large accumulation of gunpowder.

*1-28. Melville, Herman. **"The Bell-Tower"** (1855). Included in *Piazza Tales*, Hendricks House, $5.00 and in Franklin [6-35].
In the Italian Renaissance, the "mechanician" Bannadonna undertakes to build a Babel-like bell-tower, atop which is to be a giant bell rung by an automaton. He succeeds, except that the bell is flawed where the remains of a workman Bannadonna murdered for his incompetence have settled into the cast metal. As the hour arrives for the bell to strike, the mechanician is too absorbed in the study of the presumably unintentional individuality of one of the female figures graven on the bell to notice the silent advance of the automaton along its track, and he is fatally impaled on its spike. The terrified townspeople cast the automaton into the sea, and the bell and tower are destroyed. While Melville's automaton is an imaginary invention only within the internal time scheme of the story, it foreshadows the robots of SF from Capek to Asimov. As his epigraphs indicate, Melville's primary concern in his fable is with the metaphysics of the machine (on which see Leo Marx on *Moby Dick* in *The Machine in the Garden*, Oxford, 1964). But the story also deals in various points of view: what is first presented as a tale of the supernatural is glossed over again with a scientific explanation and then again with a moralistic one.

1-29. Mercier, Louis Sebastian (France). **Memoirs of the Year Two Thousand Five Hundred.** London: G. Robinson, 1772; rev. ed., 1802. Tr. by William Hooper from *L'an deux mille quatre cent quarante*. London: pub. anonymously, 1771. Clearwater Pub., 3 vols., $80.75 (in French).
A Parisian falls asleep to wake up 760 years old in 2500 (2440 in the original) in a society with a rational system of government and without the abuses and corruptions of eighteenth-century Paris. Generally considered the first utopian work of fiction published in America (Philadelphia, 1795), it provided a pattern followed by many similar works in the nineteenth century.

1-30. Mitchell, Silas Weir. **"Was He Dead?"** *Atlantic Monthly*, 32 (July 1873), 211–218. Reprinted in Franklin's *Future Perfect* [6-35].
A science-fictional detective story of sorts. Over a period of time the con-

versations of Purpel, Gresham, and Vance tend towards the possibility of reviving a human being after death. Purpel finally tries the experiment on a recently hanged criminal, who is resuscitated long enough to confess that he was the one who committed a murder for which a mutual friend of the threesome had been executed.

*1-31. More, Thomas (U.K.). **A Fruteful and Pleasaunt Worke of the Beste State of a Publyque Weale, and of the Newe Yle Called Vtopia**, tr. by Ralphe Robynson London: Abraham Vele, 1551. Originally *Libellus vere aureus nec minus salutaris quam festivus de optimo reip[ublicae] statu deq[ue] noua insula Vtopia*. Louvain: T. Martens, 1516. Of the many translations of *Utopia*, those by H. V. S. Ogden, Appleton, $1.25, and Edward Surtz and J. H. Hexter, Yale Univ. Press, *Collected Works*, vol. 4, $35.00, or *Selected Works*, vol. 2, $1.95, $7.00, are recommended.

Implicity contrasts the state of England, described in Book One, where men are hanged for theft while the state engorges acres of land in enclosures, with the communistic society on the island of Utopia (More's coinage of a term meaning "no place," with a pun on "the good place"), which Ralph Hythloday describes in Book Two. Divided into 54 city-states, Utopia is a planned society governed by principles of justice. In addition to the rational planning of cities, there is also socialized medicine, religious toleration, and other features. *Utopia* was a seminal work in defining utopia as a *literary* genre.

1-32. Morris, Ralph (U.K.). **The Life and Astonishing Adventures of John Daniel. . . .** London: M. Cooper, 1751. Arno, $16.00.

John Daniel's son Jacob builds a sort of flatcar-cum-trampoline by means of which he and his father get to the Moon. There they find—among other creatures that are grotesque variations on their terrestrial counterparts—a somewhat monstrous humanoid species, at least some of whom are the result of miscegenation with sea monsters (compare Lovecraft's 1936 story, "The Shadow over Innsmouth").

*1-33. O'Brien, Fitz-James. **"The Diamond Lens"** (1858). This and "What Was It?" are included in the author's *Collected Stories*, Books for Libraries, $11.25.

A man named Linley resorts to a medium to consult Leeuwenhoek on how to make a universal lens of unheard-of penetrating power. He procures the large diamond necessary for such a lens by murdering a fellow lodger. He makes the lens, through which he sees in a drop of water a microscopic nymph, Animula, with whom he falls in love. As Animula dies in the evaporating water droplet, Linley goes mad.

1-34. O'Brien, Fitz-James. **"How I Overcame My Gravity."** *Harper's New Monthly Magazine*, March 1864. Never reprinted in book form.

A would-be physicist who dreams of mastering the problems of flight is inspired by a toy machine something like a gyroscope. He catapults himself into the air in a large copper globe designed to overcome gravity by centrifugal force, but his globe cannot take the stress of that force and begins to disintegrate. At that point, he awakes.

*1-35. O'Brien, Fitz-James. **"What Was It?"** (1859).
A ghost story with a vaguely science fictional twist. A scientific rationale is proposed for the invisibility of a monster which attacks the narrator in the night. The latter overcomes this creature, and with the help of plaster of Paris discovers that it is "shaped like a man,—distorted, uncouth, and horrible, but still a man." Compare Bierce's "The Damned Thing" [2-17] and de Maupassant's "The Horla."

1-36. Paltock, Robert (U.K.). **The Life and Adventures of Peter Wilkins. A Cornish Man.** London: J. Robinson and R. Dodsley, 1751. Hyperion, $4.50, $12.95.
Shipwrecked near the South Pole, Peter Wilkins passes along a subterranean river and emerges into a dimly lighted world inhabited by "glums" and "glawries." With one of the female members of this species—who are essentially human except that they are born with a detachable set of wings which enables them to fly—Wilkins lives for many years, producing no less than seven children, and in time he makes up for the biological deficiency of not having wings by inventing a machine in which he can be borne aloft by eight glums. Eventually he returns to this world to tell his tale.

1-37. Poe, Edgar Allen. **"The Balloon Hoax"** (1844). Any standard edition of the tales includes this and the following six stories.
Poe describes a dirigible that carries four men across the Atlantic in 75 hours. Balloons were popular in many early works; Verne used them in several of his. Poe's story is the first transatlantic balloon voyage in fiction.

1-38. Poe, Edgar Allan. **"The Facts in the Case of M. Valdemar"** (1845).
A dying man is mesmerized and remains in a state of suspended animation for several months until the mesmerist is forced to wake him, whereupon he instantly decomposes.

*1-39. Poe, Edgar Allan. **"Mellonta Tauta"** (1849).
An ambivalent sketch of life in the twenty-ninth century. Men fly in high-speed balloons or move across the sea in propeller-driven boats and communicate via a floating transatlantic telegraph cable. Imaginative intuition has replaced reasoning by induction or deduction. Democracy is scorned: only humanity in the aggregate counts; individuals are expendable. This is one of the earliest stories to open directly in the future.

*1-40. Poe, Edgar Allan. **"The Murders in the Rue Morgue"** (1841).
M. Dupin, a precursor of Sherlock Holmes, scientifically deduces the
nurderer of Mme. L'Espanaye and her daughter to be an orangutan.
H. G. Wells, in his 1894 essay, "Popularising Science," singles out this story and those of Doyle as the prototypes for "the fundamental principles
of construction" of SF.

1-41. Poe, Edgar Allan. **The Narrative of Arthur Gordon Pym.** Harper,
1838.
Poe's only novel-length tale at first appears to be realistic fiction, describing Pym's first shipwreck, his stowing away in the hold of the *Grampus*,
the mutiny aboard that ship, and its consequences. The turning point
from realism towards symbolism occurs after the two survivors of the
Grampus, Pym and Dirk Peters, are rescued off Cape St. Roque by the
Jane Guy and proceed with Captain Guy towards the South Pole. The
ship stops at an island well inside the Antarctic Circle, inhabited by an
alien dark-skinned race who are hostile to anything white (their very
teeth are black). Captain Guy and his crew are buried alive by the savages, but Pym and Peters escape in a canoe and head south. As they approach the pole, the temperature of the sea gets warmer. The novel concludes abruptly, giving rise to arguments about whether it is complete, as
Pym and Peters, nearing a cataract that descends towards a chasm "open
to receive us," behold a dream-like vision of an enshrouded human figure much larger than life. The cataract and chasm—imaging the vertigi-
nous dream-experience of the absolute—recall the whirlpools of Poe's
"Manuscript Found in a Bottle" (1833) and "Descent into the Mael-
strom" (1841).

*1-42. Poe, Edgar Allan. **"A Tale of the Ragged Mountains"** (1844).
This tale speculates on dislocated and parallel space and time. Augustus
Bedlow, wandering in the Ragged Mountains, experiences a dream or
hallucination whose details correspond to those attending the demise of
a British officer named Oldeb in Benares sixty-five years before. About a
week later, Bedlow, who bears a physical resemblance to Oldeb, dies
from the bite of a poisonous leech applied accidentally by his doctor
friend, who was also a friend of Oldeb. Poe's concluding paragraph
draws attention to the anagrammatic similarity in the names of the two
dead men.

*1-43. Poe, Edgar Allan. **"The Unparalleled Adventures of Hans
Pfaall"** (1835) (commonly known as "Hans Pfaall").
A manuscript dropped from a balloon gives an account of how a Dutch
bellows maker constructs a balloon to escape his creditors. Filling it with
a gas, he begins his ascent to the Moon, first blowing up three particularly obnoxious bill collectors. The bulk of the narrative describes his sensa-
tions and observations during the voyage, and ends with a promise to

publish an account of his stay among the ugly and dwarfish lunarians if there is sufficient interest to warrant it. Poe's story concludes with reasons (also fictional) for supposing Pfaall's manuscript a hoax. In a postscript, Poe criticizes Locke's *The Moon Hoax* [1-23] and Godwin's *The Man in the Moone* [1-15] for their scientific inaccuracies and goes on to insist that this sort of fiction should preserve a kind of scientific verisimilitude within the imaginative premises of the tale.

1-44. Restif de la Bretonne, Nicolas Edmé (France). **La découverte australe par un homme volant, ou Le dedale français.** Leipsig: pub. anonymously, 1781. No English translation known.
Victorin invents a method of flying by means of wings and a small parachute-like contraption. He then swoops down and abducts his girl friend, Christine, and the two of them form the nucleus of the utopian community he founds on the slopes of Mount Inaccessible in the Alpine region of Daupine. He later flies with his son to the Southern Hemisphere, where they go from island to island meeting various sorts of man-beast—dog men, goat men, elephant men—representing an "allegory" of the physiological varieties of aboriginal man. Father and son finally arrive among the Metapatagonians, a utopian society based on natural/rational principles and advanced scientific knowledge. These Metapatagonians "follow Nature step by step," pointing to the moral of this literary farrago.

1-45. Sadeur, Jacques (pseud. of Gabriel de Foigny) (France). **A New Discovery of Terra Incognita Australis, or the Southern World.** London: J. Dunton, 1693. This is based on the drastically expurgated 1692 revision de Foigny made as a result of his persecution and conversion. Tr. of *La terre australe connu. . . .* Vannes [Geneva]: J. Verneuil, 1676. Clearwater Pub., $74.00 (in French).
Sadeur, after a shipwreck, happens upon a southern world inhabited by an androgynous human species that follows Nature and Reason. An aged "australian" philosopher engages him in many conversations in which the conventional thinking of Europe, as expounded by Sadeur, is compared unfavorably with the rationalistic ideas and practices of the australians, much in the manner of the later dialogues between Gulliver and his Houyhnhnm master. Since Sadeur did not arrive on a ship, the australians are not sure that he is a "demiman," their arch-enemies; but after he spends 30 years among them, their suspicions grow, and he finds it politic to take flight on a large bird.

*1-46. Seaborn, Adam (pseud. of John Cleves Symmes). **Symzonia: A Voyage of Discovery.** New York: J. Seymour, 1820. Arno, $14.00.
Captain Seaborn takes his ship through an opening in the earth at the South Pole and discovers Symzonia, a utilitarian utopia with a strong moral bias. It is governed by a Best Man under the advice of a Council of

the Good, the Wise and the Useful. The work reveals probable Swiftian influence, especially in the last interview between Seaborn and the Best Man, where the latter, observing that Seaborn and his crew belong to a race of "pestiferous beings, spreading moral disease and contamination by their intercourse," determines to expel them as a source of corruption in utopia. One of the earliest works suggesting a hollow Earth.

*1-47. Shelley, Mary Wollstonecraft (U.K.). **Frankenstein; or, A Modern Prometheus.** London: Lackington, Hughes, 1818. London: Henry Colburn, rev. ed., 1831. Recommended ed. edited by James Rieger, Bobbs, $3.25, $7.50.

In this classic tale of monster-making, Frankenstein assembles an inanimate human form and by some mysterious process (undisclosed in the novel proper) brings it to life. Frankenstein attempts to repudiate his creation, and his neglect sets the monster on a murderous course in which he and Frankenstein alternately pursue and are pursued by each other. The opening of the novel implies an analogy between Frankenstein's Promethean quest for the secret of life and Captain Walton's desire to reach the North Pole, which Frankenstein dissuades him from attempting. Apart from Shelley's probable revision of his wife's manuscript before its first publication (see Rieger's introduction), Mary's conception of the novel was undoubtedly influenced by her father, William Godwin's, novels, *Things as They Are* (*Caleb Williams*, 1794) and *St. Leon* (1799), the second of which deals with the psychological consequences of the hero's obsession with the two absolutes of the alchemist, the philosopher's stone and the elixir of life. Brian Aldiss [4-4] exalts *Frankenstein* as the prototype of SF; but, as H.G. Wells points out, the means by which Frankenstein animates his monster is more magical than scientific.

1-48. Shelley, Mary Wollstonecraft (U.K.). **The Last Man.** 3 vols. London: Henry Colburn, 1826. Univ. of Nebraska Press., $1.95, $10.95.

This romance focuses on the closing years of the twenty-first century as recorded by Lionel Verney, "the last man." The first part of the narrative deals with England after the abolition of the monarchy and with the political ambitions and career of Raymond, who is modeled on Lord Byron. The apocalyptic motif centers on the death of Raymond in plague-devastated Constantinople. The plague finally comes to England, from which Adrian (based on Shelley), the former king's son, leads an ever-diminishing number of survivors to France. In the end, two of the three humans remaining drown off the Italian coast, and the third, Verney, making his way to Rome, waits in the hope that he is not the last member of the human species. This novel inspired Thomas Campbell and Thomas Hood to write poems with the same title.

*1-49. Swift, Jonathan (U.K.). **Travels into Several Remote Nations of the World . . . by Lemuel Gulliver** [*Gulliver's Travels*]. 2 vols. London:

Benjamin Motte, 1726; rev. ed., Dublin: George Faulkner, 1735. Recommended ed. edited by Herbert Davis, Blackwell, 1941. Many acceptable editions are available.

Drawing upon the tradition of travel literature and *voyages imaginaires*, Swift has his (anti-) hero, Lemuel Gulliver, visit the "remote nations" of Lilliput, Brobdingnag, Laputa, and Houyhnhnmland. The first two books—whose presentation of the Lilliputians and Brobdingnagians as models of human life undoubtedly owes something to the telescope and the microscope—hold up a satiric mirror to man's moral and political pettiness and his physical grossness. Book Three, the most science-fictional in the strictest sense of term, makes use of Newton's *Principia* and the *Transactions* of the Royal Societies of London and Dublin in ridiculing the absurdities of science and its materialistic premises. The Fourth Book offers a contrast between anthropomorphic life reduced to its most brutal and irrational—the Yahoos—and the perfect rationality of hippomorphic beings, the Houyhnhnms, whose utopian community admits no deviation from the dictates of Reason. With its sources and influence, *Gulliver's Travels* is the crucial nexus between its predecessors and modern SF from Wells onward. Swift's other book-length masterpiece, *A Tale of a Tub* (1704), also introduces science-fictional elements in its satiric assault on metaphysical materialism—principally in its "physico-logical" account of "the mechanical operation of the spirit" (vulgarized by Defoe in *The Consolidator*, 1705).

*1-50. Voltaire, Françoise-Marie Arouet (France). **Micromégas: A Comic Romance, Being a Severe Satire upon the Philosophy, Ignorance, and Self-Conceit of Mankind.** London: D. Wilson and T. Durham, 1753. Originally *Le Micromégas de M. Voltaire.* London: pub. anonymously, 1752. Modern Library, $1.95 (in *Candide and Other Writings*).

Micromegas, banished from the court of Sirius for 800 years and on a grand tour of the universe, picks up a Saturnian as a traveling companion. These two giants, landing on Earth, assume it to be uninhabited on account of its irregular topography. But an ersatz microscope enables them to see a group of scientists on an expedition in the North Sea. The ensuing dialogue between these men and the visitors from outerspace gives Voltaire ample scope for satirizing the pretensions and limitations of human understanding, much as he did in *Candide*.

2.
The Emergence of the Scientific Romance, 1870-1926

Thomas D. Clareson

However much and for whatever reasons contemporary literary critics may wish to impose restrictive definitions upon science fiction, they cannot dismiss the widespread impact of the so-called "new science," both at the levels of theoretical speculation and technological achievement, from the last third of the nineteenth century onward. As suggested in "SF: The Other Side of Realism,"[1] on the one hand this impact laid the foundations for literary realism and naturalism, especially in France and America; on the other, it produced that wide spectrum of stories which gained the name "scientific romance." Such a generalization, however, does not illuminate vividly the manner in which writers not traditionally associated with science fiction made use of the new theories and speculations in each field of science.

The indebtedness of the embryonic science fiction to such individual works as Shelley's *Frankenstein* and O'Brien's "The Diamond Lens," as well as to the fiction of Poe, is obvious. What may be less apparent is the manner in which the Gothic and post-Gothic concern for abnormal (or heightened) states of psychology, as in Poe's *The Narrative of A. Gordon*

33

Pym, provides a means by which one may observe the transition from fantasy to science fiction. For example, the best fiction of Ambrose Bierce is united by his dramatization of fear, as in "The Man and the Snake," a hallucination whose technique and symbolism anticipate Eugene O'Neill's *The Emperor Jones*. Throughout his stories, Bierce refers to racial memory, particularly in terms of man's inheritance from prehistoric ancestors of a terror of death and the unknown. In some ways he most effectively completed the evolution from fantasy to science fiction and gave a new dimension to horror by drawing upon biology in "The Damned Thing" (*Can Such Things Be?*, 1893). He assigned to the traditional, invisible creatures of such stories as O'Brien's "What Was It?" (1858) and Maupassant's "Le Horla" (1887) a scientific explanation: just as there are sounds which man cannot hear, so, too, "at each end of the spectrum the chemist can detect the presence of what are known as 'actinic rays,' representing colors man cannot see. And, God help me [writes the diarist] The Damned Thing is of such a color."

Although giving little or no explicit attention in his texts to scientific data, Henry James, like Bierce, showed an awareness of the new psychology in his ghost stories in which he studied obsession and hallucination, such as "Maud Evelyn" (1900): what Ford Madox Ford referred to as James's "analysis of an anxious state" of mind.[2] Much of the explanation of his development may be reflected in one of his early discussions of the supernatural in fiction: "A good ghost story, to be half as terrible as a good murder story, must be connected at a hundred different points with the common objects of life."[3] Again, he praised Wilkie Collins' *The Woman in White* (1861) for "its introduction into fiction of the mysteries at our own door."[4] Between them, James and Bierce did as much as, if not more than, any of their British and American contemporaries to transform the traditional ghost story into a psychological case study.

Meanwhile, as early as 1861, Oliver Wendell Holmes' *Elsie Venner* had anticipated the interest in multiple personality, while Thomas Bailey Aldrich's "The Queen of Sheba" (1877) centered upon the amnesia of its heroine. Edward Bellamy's first novel, *Dr. Heidenhoff's Process* (1880) focused upon a scientific experiment which made possible the erasure of the memory of evil at the same time that an individual's heart was being purified (the novel obviously gave expression to Bellamy's Christian mysticism). This moral transformation was made possible by "the discoveries of modern psychologists and physiologists as to the physical basis of intellect. . . ." Such authors anticipated the finest of the studies of multiple personality, Stevenson's *Strange Case of Dr. Jekyll and Mr. Hyde* (1888), in which a scientist carries out a deliberate experiment attempting to purify his moral nature and thereby "frees a monster of evil who finally dominates him."[5] James explored the problem of an alter ego, as did Conrad. The first American novel to imitate Stevenson appears to have been Albert Bigelow Paine's *The Mystery of Evelin Delorme: A Hypnotic Story* (1894). Although the main interest of the narrative is a love story, as was so often the case during the period, Paine did attach a special introduction in which he explained his heroine's duality in terms of "Mesmeric Sciences." The case study of multiple personality dominated Vincent Harper's *The Mortgage on the Brain* (1905), the self-styled confession of a medical student who was the subject of an experiment giving him a new personality by a process closely resembling that in Bellamy's earlier novel; in contrast, however, the novel remains most significant because of its attack upon orthodox religion and orthodox philosophical concepts of personality.

In a sense, the most obvious evolution of these stories from fantasy to science fiction was completed by William Dean Howells in those tales collected under the titles *Questionable Shapes* (1903) and *Between the Darkness and the Daylight* (1907). Although he could not bring himself to dispense entirely with the "occult [sciences]," Howells did introduce the psychologist Wanhope, who gave scientific explanations in terms of the theories of the day to the ghost stories told him by the various members of his dinner club.

Important as was the interest in psychology at the time and important as it is to the student who would trace the evolution of modern science fiction, it remained peripheral to the central interests of the scientific romances of the late nineteenth and early twentieth centuries. Quantitatively, the first dominant motif is the portrayal of future wars. In May 1871, *Blackwood's Magazine* published the anonymous "The Battle of Dorking: Reminiscences of a Volunteer." It was not the first British narrative of a future conflict, but coming fresh upon the outcome of the Franco-Prussian war, amid the growing hysteria of nationalism and imperialism which swept Europe, "The Battle of Dorking" caught the British populace in "a mood of foreboding and anxiety for the future." Published throughout the English-speaking world and widely translated, it triggered a reaction throughout Europe, particularly in Britain, France, and Germany, serving as the prototype of a legion of books that predicted an inevitable holocaust. Its author, Sir George Tomkyns Chesney, who had been recalled from India to establish a Royal Indian Engineering College at Staines, warned his countrymen of a German invasion and the defeat of Britain, because as a nation she had been unwilling to accept the cost of defense and so had remained militarily unprepared. Most importantly, perhaps, he predicted that the use of new weapons would decide the outcome of such a struggle. This attention to the "hardware" of the period proved to be the distinctive innovation of the story.

These novels are important to intellectual history in that they give insight into the military strategy and armaments race of the turn of the century, although, ironically, many of the authors felt that any future conflict would be decided by a great naval battle. One exception was H. G. Wells' *The War in the Air* (1908), in which he saw the imminent world war and the social collapse after it resulting from both man's inability to solve his social and political problems and his inability to control such new inventions as the airplane. In contrast, although his *The World Set Free* (1914) envisions atomic holocaust, there is ultimately a rational settlement of world affairs and, thus, a utopia. In retrospect, perhaps the most grimly realistic prediction occurred in Arthur Conan Doyle's short story, "Danger." Scoffed at by naval experts, it portrayed unrestricted submarine warfare. Written in 1912–1913, it was published in *Strand Magazine* in July 1914.

I. F. Clarke has analyzed the wildfire spread of this literary phenomenon in his *Voices Prophesying War* [6-25], which must stand, to date, as the model for any intensive, scholarly study of a specific phase of science fiction. Of the motif Clarke wrote: "In their own strange way these writers were trying to create a Beowulf myth for an industrial civilization of ironclads and high-speed turbines, a new and violent *chanson de geste* for an age of imperialism, told in the inflammatory language of the mass press. They were popular epics for a period of universal literacy, the counterpart of the many tales about the deeds that won the Empire, all written to the glory of the nation-state; for in the closing years of the 19th century the agressive nation-states of Europe had everything on their side except common sense."[6]

With the persistence of the concept of Manifest Destiny, as well as the flirtation with imperialism at the turn of the century, America did not escape the wildfire. With the advent of World War I, writers envisioned German hordes occupying the territorial United States, as in Thomas Dixon's *The Fall of a Nation* (1915) and Clevelands Moffett's *The Conquest of America* (1916), but from the first, American treatment of the future war motif had a distinctive quality of its own. Pierpont W. Dooner's *Last Days of the Republic* (1880) warned of an "impending catastrophe" owing to the importation into California of cheap Coolie labor; because its citizens remain loyal and support its plot to rule the world, China conquers the United States, destroying it as a nation. The theme of the "yellow peril"—this time Japanese—recurred in such fiction as J. U. Giesy's *All for His Country* (1915), in which an invasion of Mexico and the western U.S. is finally beaten back by the invention of an "aero destroyer," and in the essay-like *The Great Pacific War: A History of the American-Japanese Campaign of 1931–33* (1925), by Hector C. Bywater, the author of *Sea Power in the Pacific* (1925). It persisted in Gawain Edwards' more fanciful *The Earth Tube* (1929), in which nameless "mongol" legions stalk across both American continents. During the 1930s these nameless Asiatic hordes ravaged the United States in the monthly exploits of such pulp heroes as *Dusty Ayres and his Battle Birds*, *Operator 5*, and, finally, even *The Spider*, whose Richard Wentworth had been created originally to compete with that master crime fighter, Lamont Cranston, *The Shadow*.

One should not forget that this obsession was deeply ingrained in the American imagination, appearing as early as the three-part, "factual" prediction in *Cosmopolitan* (1908), "If War Should Come," by Captain Pearson Hobson, identified as "one of the greatest living experts in the sciences of war,"[7] who predicted a sneak attack upon Hawaii not unlike that at Pearl Harbor. One is tempted to infer that this body of popular literature made conflict with the Japanese inevitable, and one wonders how a continued portrayal of rampaging Asiatic hordes would have influenced the public reaction to the Vietnam affair.

The second main trend of the future war motif in American hands found expression in *The Battle of Siwash and the Conquest of Canada* (1888); Samuel Barton addressed his "historical forecast" to those responsible for America's unpreparedness and celebrated the enthusiasm with which Canada throws off the yoke of Great Britain to become part of the United States. Yet the British fleet sacks such eastern cities as New York, and victory does not come until an American inventor develops a self-destroying torpedo boat that annihilates Her Majesty's fleet. Canada and the West Indies are ceded to the United States, and Great Britain becomes an impotent island kingdom. The following year, Frank Stockton serialized *The Great War Syndicate* in *Collier's Weekly*. In *The Unpardonable War* (1904), James Barnes combined an attack upon a third party composed of labor, socialists, and populists with a secret plot to incite America to war with Britain, a war which would annex Canada and promise that "Ireland would be free."

As the crises leading to the 1914–1918 conflict continued, an increasing number of authors portrayed the attempts of scientists—not statesmen—to bring all war to an end: there were Simon Newcomb's *His Wisdom: The Defender* (1900); Hollis Godfrey's *The Man Who Ended War* (1908); Roy Norton's *The Vanishing Fleets* (1908); J. Stewart Barney's *L.P.M.: The End of the Great War* (1915); and the "mad" scientist of Arthur Train and Williams Wood's *The Man Who Rocked the Earth* (1915), first serialized in *The Saturday Evening Post* in the autumn of 1914. Newcomb and Barney foresaw a world state dominated by science; however, earlier books such as Stanley Waterloo's *Armageddon* (1898) and Benjamin Rush Davenport's *Anglo-Saxons Onward: A Romance of the Future* (1898) envisioned a future dominated by America and Great Britain. Frequently over a conference table their representatives told the lesser peoples of the world—even those of Eastern Europe and the Mediterranean—that the two countries proposed to direct the affairs of the world, perhaps for centuries. In *The Vanishing Fleets*, Roy Norton permitted a recalcitrant Kaiser to become part of an Anglo-Saxon triumvirate after he had repented his ways as a result of an enforced encampment in a lumbercamp in the Pacific Northwest. Significantly, only in Train and Wood's *The Man Who Rocked the World*, after the death of the mad scientist, does a conference of nations assemble in Washington to abolish all war and form a federated, utopian world state. This emphasis upon an international conference of rulers leads one to speculate what influence, if any, such idealism had upon Henry Ford's peace mission and upon President Wilson.

If speculation about future wars provided the motif which first catches the eye of the student of the period, then Jules Verne is the single author who first attracts attention. Immediately his interest in and indebtedness to Edgar Allan Poe (although he lamented Poe's lack of scientific accuracy) and his emphasis on the differences between his own fiction and that of H. G. Wells come to mind. For some individuals, like Hugo Gernsback, who have emphasized both the prophetic nature of science fiction and its role in accurately extrapolating future technological achievement, Verne has often held a place even higher than that of Wells in the development of the new genre. Even after Gernsback had lost control of *Amazing Stories*, a sketch of "Jules Verne's Tombstone at Amiens Portraying His Immortality" formed a part of its masthead.

By 1862, Verne had written a number of comedies and comic operettas for various theatres in Paris, as well as a few short stories. In that year he sought to complete a factual article dealing with African exploration, incorporating into it the idea that the use of a balloon would make such a venture easier. The publisher, Pierre Hetzel, asked that he change the article into fiction; apparently it was he who spoke of an adventure story based upon scientific fact. *Five Weeks in a Balloon* (1863) resulted, the first of *Les voyages extraordinaires*. Its protagonist, Dr. Samuel Ferguson, an English explorer, not only develops a special furnace that will control the temperature of the hydrogen gas inside the balloon bag (supposedly making the balloon more navigable, but ignoring the possibility of the explosion of the hydrogen), but he is also the source for vast amounts of factual information as the three explorers drift in the balloon from Zanzibar across the interior of Africa, sighting Lake Victoria, which is declared to be the source of the Nile (in the same year John Speke confirmed that observation). Here, then, are the basic ingredients of Verne's stories: a man of reason (a scientist) who will both invent the necessary gadgetry and provide factual information; a journey to some exotic destination, generally somewhere on earth; and a series of largely disconnected adventures, most often involving the threat of pursuit and capture.

By 1864, Hetzel had launched a new magazine for young readers— the *Magasin d'education et de Récréation*—and in the initial March issue appeared the first installment of Verne's second *voyage, The Adventures of Captain Hatteras*, whose explorers attained the elusive North Pole at the expense of Captain Hatteras's sanity. It was not published in book form until after the success of *A Journey to the Center of the Earth* (1864) and *From the Earth to the Moon* (1865). In the former, Verne relied upon the theory that volcanoes are joined by subterranean passages permitting them to be fed by some fiery source within the earth. His "gadget" was the so-called Ruhmkorff coil, for which the German physicist, Heinrich Ruhmkorff, received a cash award in the same year that Verne wrote the story. One can certainly call it a rudimentary form of the flashlight, but at the time of the novel such an application of electricity was unknown to the general public. (Verne's attitude toward electricity throughout his works seems to be almost one of awe. In *Propeller Island* [1895], a four-mile-long, mechanical island that is initially a utopia, everything, including the preparation of food and the growing of plants, is accomplished by electricity. Again, the *Twenty Thousand Leagues under the Sea* [1870], the motive power of the submarine *Nautilus* is electricity.) Verne also displayed the nineteenth-century fascination with geology, for as his explorers venture deeper into the earth they find relics of the prehistoric past, ranging from the bones of extinct animals and men to the sight of a gigantic manlike creature acting as shepherd of a herd of mastodons. In this way he dramatized, to some extent at least, the highly controversial theory of evolution.

For *From the Earth to the Moon*, in order to rely only upon knowledge and materials available to the mid-nineteenth century, he spent much of the novel developing a cannon capable of firing a projectile at a velocity of seven miles per second—that is, escape velocity. He later defended this practice while condemning Wells for making use of a metal which negated the law of gravity (a convention introduced by Percy Greg in *Across the Zodiac* [1880] when he made use of Apergy, a "*repulsive* energy" counteracting gravity). In the second part of this story, *All around the Moon* (1870), the projectile fails to land upon the Moon because it is deflected by a comet; it returns to earth and splashes down in the Pacific, and its voyagers, not unlike the modern astronauts, are picked up by a U.S. naval vessel. *Twenty Thousand Leagues under the Sea* provides the romantic figure of Captain Nemo, that self-willed outcast of society who loves freedom and hates despotism, but it is primarily a veritable encyclopedia of oceanography, an underwater travelog ranging from sunken Atlantis to shipwrecks and Spanish bullion. Significantly, Verne named the *Nautilus* for the submarine which Robert Fulton built in France under the sponsorship of Napoleon I and demonstrated in the river Seine and in the harbor at Brest.

Perhaps these examples will suffice to capture the essence of Jules Verne. Although humor and occasional insight color his work, he did not have the profound insight of H. G. Wells. His hatred of the Germans after the Franco-Prussian War led him to write *The Begum's Fortune*

(1879), in which he compared the two cities of the future: Frankville, "a model city, based on strictly scientific principles," a utopia; and Stahl-stadt, a totalitarian society built by German science solely to operate a giant munitions factory. But this is the exception, for like so many of his contemporaries, Verne was fascinated by the changes that science and technology were bringing to society, and he remained essentially optimistic. He gained acceptance in Britain because he presented "to the public, in a series of fantastic romances and marvelous travels, the results of the wonderful discoveries and theories of modern men of science."[8] In America his works were serialized in *The Contemporary Review*. The prefatory "In Memoriam" to William H. Rhodes' posthumous collection of short stories, *Caxton's Book* (1876), suggests that had Rhodes been able to devote himself more to his fiction than the practice of law, "the great master of scientific fiction, Jules Verne, would have found the field of his efforts already sown and reaped. . . ." For many of his contemporaries, then, the name of Jules Verne had become synonymous with the new fiction.

But any examination of the developing field indicates that its diversity makes this at best an oversimplification. For example, in two of the dominant motifs in the scientific romance of the period, other authors used imaginary voyages, which are as old as narrative literature, much differently than did Verne. In that motif dealing with journeys to the moon and especially Mars among the planets, the voyage became the framework for an intellectual battle between traditional religious beliefs and the implications of the new science; in the so-called "lost race" motif, the journey allowed the authors to retreat to some haven where they could escape the industrial–urban civilization that had engulfed the West by the time of World War I.

In writing of "The Grammar of Science," Henry Adams asserted, ". . . according to Helmholz, Ernst Mach, and Arthur Balfour, he [Adams] was henceforth to be a conscious ball of vibrating motions, traversed in every direction by infinite lines of rotation or vibration, rolling at the feet of the Virgin of Chartres . . . a centre of supersensual chaos. The discovery did not distress him. A solitary man of sixty-five years or more . . . need fret himself little about a few illusions more or less. . . . Nevertheless he could not pretend that his mind felt flattered by this scientific outlook." He later remarked, "If Karl Pearson's notions of the universe were sound, men like Galileo, Descartes, Leibnitz, and Newton should have stopped the progress of science before 1700, supposing them to have been honest in the religious convictions they expressed. In 1900 they were plainly forced back on faith in a unity unproved and an order they themselves disproved. They had reduced their universe to a series of relations to themselves. They had reduced themselves to a motion in a universe of motions. . . ."[9] It takes little imagination to see here an expression of that nightmare vision which has swept the Western intellectual world; here, too, is a traumatic landmark in the evolution of C. P. Snow's concept of the two cultures.

On the other hand, there was the popular celebration of the new technology—an enthusiasm seemingly unaware, at least for some decades, of the underlying implications of science. One must recall that the half century ending in the 1920s saw the greatest flourishing of the literary utopia. What mattered the loss of a traditional heaven so long as the man in the street, the working man, could gain an "earthly paradise" brought about by the new technology? This is the stuff that many dreams were made of. Unlike many of his British contemporaries, who by midcentury viewed their iron-and-coal technology as a mixed blessing, Verne remained optimistic; unlike Wells, Samuel Butler (*Erewhon*, 1872), or W. H. Hudson (*A Crystal Age*, 1877), for example, he essentially celebrated the machine. In doing this, he captured the popular imagination, perhaps especially in America, where so many of the inventions which were to produce modern civilization occurred between the Civil War and the early years of the twentieth century. He stood at the heart of an optimism leading to such enthusiasts as Hugo Gernsback and the pulp magazines of the 1930s with their vision of what Robert Silverberg has called "galactic man"—"man . . . and his technology triumphant throughout the universe."[10] That vision flourished briefly and died amid the ashes of dystopia.

From 1870 onward, an increasing number of scientists, inventors, engineers, medical men, archeologists, and even students of such exotic topics as Egyptology and the occult became the protagonists of popular fiction. Quantitatively, perhaps because so many of the new developments were taking place in the United States—one has only to turn to nonfiction to find Thomas A. Edison a folk hero—one at least gains the impression that the majority of them were American, heroes of fiction intended for a juvenile or adult audience, or both. To put it another way, one is aware of scientists in British popular fiction of the period, but they most often seem incidental, as in F. Hernaman-Johnson's *The Polyphemes* (1906)—supposedly the official history of the warfare between England and giant, intelligent ants capable of technology because of their control of "X-magnetism." That so many American stories turned upon some invention may measure the American infatuation with the machine. Boy inventors proliferated, either in series or in individual issues of such weeklies as *Pluck and Luck*, as in the instance of Richard R. Montgomery's *A Sheet of Blotting Paper*, or *The Adventures of a Young Inventor* (August 2, 1916).

At one end of the spectrum intended for an adult audience, in Charles E. Bolton's *The Harris-Ingram Experiment* (1905), the protagonists develop the finest steel mill in the world by powering it completely with electricity; they also created a utopian community for their workers. At the other, the brilliant chemist of Harriet Stark's *The Bacillus of Beauty* (1900) transforms a plain, midwestern country girl into the most beautiful woman in the world, while the Russian scientist in Martin Swayne's *The Blue Germ* (1918) discovers a germ which destroys all others and thereby brings immortality to mankind. Both plots, however, provided their authors with vehicles to remind their readers that beauty (which begets pride) and immortality may not be best for mankind.

Such achievements could not go unopposed. Edgar Franklin's *Mr. Hawkins' Humorous Adventures* (1904) described the misadventures of an eccentric genius whose gadgets, such as the pumpless pump and the auto-aero-mobile, fail. One of Street and Smith's writers, William Wallace Cook, who parodied all of the major motifs of the period, produced *The Eighth Wonder* (1906–1907), whose protagonist, an inventor who has been cheated out of his patents by the oil trusts, seeks revenge by attempting to "corner the electrical supply of the country"; since there is only so much electricity—so that it must be used over and over again—he hopes to attract every particle of it into the giant magnets which he has set up in the Black Hills of South Dakota. His experiments deflect the North Pole and threaten to tilt the Earth; although troops are sent after him, the government rights previous wrongs by retiring him with a pension. His companion, the youthful narrator, goes to work for the government and is permitted to marry the "girl of his choice." Love and marriage also dominate Robert W. Chambers' *The Green Mouse* (1910), which involves a machine capable of intercepting psychic waves and thereby discovering the person one should marry; an advertisement for the machine reads in part: ". . . Wedlock by Wireless. Marriage by Machinery. A Wonderful Wooer without Words." Chambers thus amusingly anticipates the computer dating system, although his protagonists decide in favor of their irrational hearts.

Satire seldom occurred in those stories purporting to deal with the activities of the inventor in the familiar social world of the here and now or the immediate future. It was used—and was most bitter—either in picturing imaginary societies such as those which grew out of the *Looking Backward* controversy, those societies in which women dominated—whether in some far corner of the earth or the future, as in Frank Cowan's undated *Revi-Lona* or Owen M. Johnson's *The Coming of the Amazons* (1931) [3-28]—or those novels which attacked some specific phase of scientific thought, usually evolution, as in John Uri Lloyd's *Etidorpha* (1895). Similarly, although the evil scientist appeared occasionally and the Frankenstein theme may be found in such major works as Wells' *The Island of Dr. Moreau* (1896) and *The Invisible Man* (1897), in the years at the turn of the century the scientist was as often portrayed as the savior of a society facing natural catastrophe, especially in American fiction.

This was the period when the scientist–inventor was a hero, a man devoted to truth. Perhaps some insight may be gained into the differences between the American and British handling of the new science fiction by contrasting their most famous fictional scientists. Craig Kennedy, created by Arthur B. Reeve, was the best known of the so-called scientific detectives. From 1910 until late in 1915 (with the single exception of November 1912), his monthly adventures graced the pages of *Cosmopolitan*. Beginning with *The Silent Bullet* (1912), they were issued in book form, the last titles being *Pandora* and *The Radio Detective* (1926). Once called the "American Sherlock Holmes,"[11] Kennedy exploited current developments in all fields of science—"mechanical wonders," medical discoveries, physical and chemical data, and—increasingly—psychology, especially the theories of Freud. Often he retired to his laboratory to invent the device needed to solve the crime at hand. He dealt with assassination and adultery, witchcraft and white slavery. Always the pattern was the same: either someone "in desperate plight" came to him, or he visited the scene of a baffling crime; he interviewed the persons involved and often found a seemingly meaningless item which became an essential clue; after briefly retiring to his lab, he assembled everyone, either explained a theory or proposed some test (he was the first to make use of wiretapping and once developed "a love meter [which] registers the grand passion [because] even love can be attributed to electrical forces. . ."). In short, he was never more than a puppet who at best voiced and popularized the knowledge of the moment or extrapolated from it.

In sharp contrast—not only in regard to his interests—stands Arthur Conan Doyle's George Challenger. One may argue that he is no more than a skillfully drawn stereotype of the brilliant, eccentric scientist far in advance of his contemporaries; one recalls his confrontation with members of the Zoological Institute early in *The Lost World* (1912). Yet he is memorable as a colorful individual—something one certainly cannot say of Craig Kennedy or a multitude of Challenger's fellow-protagonists. In *The Lost World* he leads an expedition to a plateau rising sheer from the South American jungle, on which survives a remnant of prehistory. In *The Poison Belt* (1913), after reminding the readers of *The Times* that the Earth floats "towards some unknown end, some squalid catastrophe which will overwhelm us at the ultimate confines of space" and suggesting that we may be entering some strange belt of ether, he is denounced, but the world does undergo a "death" for twenty-eight hours, and then awakens from a cataleptic trance caused by the changed atmosphere. As in Wells' short story "The Star" (1897), mankind has been given a second chance. Challenger's role changes somewhat in *The Land of Mist*, first published in *The Strand* in 1925. It is one of Doyle's explorations of psychic experience, brought about by his traumatic reaction to his son's death. In it Challenger plays a peripheral role, remaining the scientific skeptic until he is converted to the belief that through at least some mediums one can communicate with the dead and that, therefore, there is eternal life. The novel ends with a denunciation of modern materialism, concluding that man must not let his "intellectual side [become] more developed than his spiritual." In contrast to Craig Kennedy, George Challenger triggers a larger action capable of sustaining some theme other than a mere belief in inevitable progress.

Yet an emphasis upon the scientist–inventor and the "wonderful machine" does point to the heart of the scientific romance as it evolved during the period, particularly in America, for increasingly the utopian societies sketched by the authors—whether placed upon some other planet or projected into the future—had achieved their perfection through the blending of advanced technology and some form of socialism. Only a few, like H. G. Wells in *A Modern Utopia* (1905), realized that perfection was not static but only "a hopeful stage leading to a long ascent of stages." So far as an evaluation of the whole field of science fiction is concerned, however, there are many who argue that the concern for technology comprises the heart—the "hard core"—of modern SF as a fiction of ideas, of prophecy. They would insist that its other chief element was to become space travel.

As Marjorie Nicolson [6-67] has demonstrated so ably, from Kepler and Godwin onward, voyages to the Moon occurred frequently in Western literature, usually for purposes of satire. As suggested elsewhere, two events in the 1870s changed this destination. In 1877, not only did Asaph Hall discover the twin moons of Mars, but Giovanni Schiaparelli announced that he had discovered "canals" on Mars. The issue was simple and battle lines were drawn: if the canals did exist, were they the work of intelligent creatures? One has only to turn to the journals like *Popular Science* to see how bitterly the controversy raged for a generation. Percival Lowell championed the theory of intelligent life, and perhaps only the recent Mariner photographs have laid the dream to rest. If Schiaparelli gave the writers a new destination, then three years earlier John Fiske's *Cosmic Philosophy* had provided the cornerstone for the speculations of many writers of scientific romance, proposing that a parallel evolution existed throughout the universe. Culminating in the creation of man, its ultimate goal was the perfection of the human soul. Although there were to be exceptions, practice insisted that Mars, an older world than Earth, was inhabited by an advanced civilization; Venus, being younger than Earth, was at a primitive stage of development, sometimes being likened to some period of prehistory. Percy Greg, in *Across the Zodiac* (1880), established a number of the conventions, including that of the advanced civilization. Hugh Maccoll's *Mr. Stranger's Sealed Packet* (1889) describes a similar civilization, which a second race seeks to destroy.

While space flight and utopian civilizations seemed to satisfy the British authors, as noted elsewhere,[12] in American hands Mars became heaven, where, in some stories, one could actually encounter departed friends and relatives. Theosophy, incorporating some of Fiske's ideas, permitted American writers to use the journey to Mars or other planets in an attempt to reconcile traditional religious beliefs with the new sciences. This pattern dominated the motif until, on the one hand, H. G. Wells and his American imitator, Garrett P. Serviss, portrayed wars between the worlds, while on the other hand, in *A Columbus of Space* (1911), Serviss allowed the plot to be dominated by the love story of a scientist far ahead of his time and a beautiful Venusian princess. He undoubtedly adapted that story line from the so-called "lost race" novel as it had been created by Sir H. Rider Haggard.

Just as the voyage to the Moon had become a convention from the seventeenth century onward, so the picturing of a hitherto unknown, often exotic civilization located somewhere beyond man's known frontiers had become a widespread convention at least as early as the medieval travel books. It produced More's *Utopia* (1516) and the imaginary kingdoms visited by Gulliver, as well as the Robinsonades. Some of those countries had reflected man's fear of the unknown, but a greater number of them—the Hesperides, the Kingdom of Prester John, *terra australis incognita*, the "American dream" of an Edenic Western continent, El Dorado, Atlantis, Lemuria—represented the dream of a sought-after land in which life attained a perfection it had never known in Europe, or, later, America. However fabulous might be the courts of Kubla Khan, the cities of Montezuma, the simple life of the Tahitians, more intimate acquaintance with newly discovered lands proved that they, too, fell short of the dream. And so the idealized kingdom once more was pushed beyond known frontiers. So long as great portions of the world remained unexplored, it could be placed on an island, in a valley beyond the next range of mountains, in one of the polar regions, or inside the Earth itself. But as the Earth was ever more fully mapped, the writers who sought such lands were forced, increasingly, to rely upon the scientific romance.

They could either place the new-found civilization on another planet or discover that it had flourished at some period in prehistory, as in Olof W. Anderson's *The Treasure Vault of Atlantis* (1925). Because orthodox Christianity, with its literalism—witness the American geologist Louis Agassiz's long debate against the mutability of the species—came under such heavy attack as the century progressed, a third alternative setting arose. As soon as the cosmic drama ending in a fixed Day of Judgment for all of mankind was no longer a certainty, writers could project their dreams into a future which might well contain an "earthly paradise." This, in part at least, may explain why the millenial year 2000 became so important. Increasingly, then, in the early twentieth century both flight to other planets and the future as a setting became essential in the evolution of modern science fiction.

Robert Silverberg, among others, has condemned much of twentieth-century science fiction, particularly that part which found its place in the specialist pulp magazines, for becoming a kind of story "that was all action and no content."[13] One might say the same for those works appearing in such general magazines as *All-Story* and *Argosy*. The view is essentially correct; what it may well overlook, however, is that the issues that made the scientific romance an intellectual battleground late in the nineteenth century became dated. What remained were narrative frames and conventions in search of new themes, often settling for a yearning toward mysticism and a plethora of adventure.

Perhaps the best illustration of this problem may be seen in the creation and flourishing of the "lost race" novel, quantitatively—in Britain especially—the most popular form of the scientific romance from the 1880s until after World War I at least, although it persists to the present day.[14] It reflected the impact upon the literary and popular imaginations of at least three interrelated areas: first, the last great wave of exploration, which mapped the interiors of Asia, Africa, South and Central America, as well as both polar regions (it is intriguing to follow the progress of that exploration by the changes in setting in novels; whereas the polar areas were perhaps most popular in the nineteenth century, by the 1920s China and Southeast Asia dominate); second, the cumulative effect of the discoveries in paleontology, which filled the vast geologic past with saurian monsters and strange half-men (the missing link was a burning issue which at the turn of the century produced innumerable novels, like those of Gouverneur Morris (*The Pagan's Progress*, 1904 [2-115]), the Danish writer Carl Eward (*Two-Legs*, 1906 [2-76]), and F. Britten Austin (*When Mankind Was Young*, 1927 [3-2], dramatizing the moment when mankind became human); and third, the equally powerful impact of those archeological discoveries and theories which raised mysterious empires from pre-Columbian America to the valley of the Indus (significantly, it was only after actual exploration that man's imagination again needed Atlantis and Lemuria).

The imaginary voyages of many of the novels sought and found the Edenic homeland of mankind. But it was one writer, Sir H. Rider Haggard, who gave the lost race novel its lasting, most popular form. After producing *King Solomon's Mines* (1885)—a panorama of Africa drawing upon his personal knowledge of the land—he created *She* (1887) and *Allan Quatermain* (1887). In *She*, his explorers reached the Valley of Kor in the unknown heart of Africa. Ruling the descendants of Egyptians living near the ruins of a once-great city, was Ayesha: "She-Who-Must-Be-Obeyed." Given immortality by the Flame of Life, she languished impatiently, awaiting the reincarnation of her beloved Kallikrates, who lived again in Haggard's protagonist, Leo Vincent. Death, however, cut short their love. *Allan Quatermain* changed that, for the narrator took as his wife the lovely queen of the sun-worshipping Zu-Vendis, Nyleptha, who bore him an heir—"a regular curley-haired, blue-eyed young Englishman in looks . . . destined to inherit the throne of the Zu-Vendis." In short, Haggard created a form which told the love story of a modern man for a primitive beauty, a pagan princess so beautiful that "language fails me when I try to give some idea of the blaze of loveliness" (of Nyleptha and her sister). He was immediately parodied and endlessly imitated. Undoubtedly one must interpret the motif as an expression of neo-primitivism, a kind of revolt against the complex, urbanized society—so conscious of its manners—which had come into existence by the turn of the century.

In this regard, what Rider Haggard was to one generation, Edgar Rice Burroughs was to the next. He remains best known, of course, for Tarzan, Lord Greystoke. Raised by the great apes, beloved of Jane Porter of Baltimore, Tarzan rejected an effete Britain in favor of the vastness of Africa; nor should one forget how often he found some lost race, as in the city of Opar, that last remnant of Atlantis, whose bewitching princess was dazzled by his masculinity. Burroughs' first work was *Under the Moon of Mars*, serialized in *All-Story* (1912) and published in book form as *A Princess of Mars* (1917), in which John Carter literally wishes himself to the planet Mars, where Dejah Thoris awaits his love. Similarly, the narrator–protagonist of the Pellucidar series finds Dian the Beautiful in that strange, prehistoric world within the earth, while Carson of Venus is the beloved of Duare, princess of Vepaja. Outside of these four series Burroughs duplicated the pattern from *The Land that Time Forgot* (1924), set on an island in the Pacific, and *Jungle Girl* (1931), with its lost cities in Cambodia.

Thus, the scientific romance ranged from Verne to Haggard and Burroughs: from the adulation of the scientist–inventor and his gadgetry to the love story in exotic, primitive settings. That may explain in part why, although Wells' contemporaries were attracted to his fiction and often were to speak of him as the individual who had most influenced the thought of a generation, they also tended to dismiss him as a strident voice crying the need of utopia, the need of well-intentioned men. By and large, perhaps until after World War II, they acknowledged that his early romances were entertaining stories, but they remembered the Wells of *A Modern Utopia* (1905) and *Men Like Gods* (1923).

A student of Thomas Huxley, Wells did not succumb to the popular concept of inevitable progress. Repeatedly he dramatized the precariousness of man's very existence amid universal flux and change, of which man has only partial knowledge. Mark Hillegas quite properly identifies him as the source of the dystopian mood which has seized increasingly both the literary and popular imaginations in the twentieth century.[15] On the one hand, his story "The Star" (1897) permits the Earth to survive a natural catastrophe and gives man a second chance by calling attention to the new spirit of brotherhood that follows the ordeal; on the other hand, in "The Sea Raiders" (1896), he reports the appearance of *Haploteuthis ferox* in the English Channel in order symbolize "the violence of a changeable nature and the complacency with which man views his immutable world."[16] *The Time Machine* (1895) climaxes with the vision of a dying Earth where only dark shapes scuttle across the beach of a tideless ocean. So much attention has been given the conflict between the Eloi and the Morlocks during that intermittent moment—the year 802,701—that too many critics have read the novel solely as Well's statement of the inevitable outcome of Western industrial society, the evolution of man into two distinct species. The Marxian projection, however, is but one of the dichotomies of the period which the conflict of the Eloi and Morlocks may suggest. *The Island of Dr. Moreau* (1897), in which Moreau transforms various animals into the Beast People, may be read at the level of the Frankenstein myth, but Robert Philmus makes two provocative assertions: first, that it is a symbolic reinstatement of God into "the tortuous process of evolution"—that is, that "God becomes Moreau, a vivisectionist insensitive beyond all humanity to the pain of his creatures"; and secondly, "what Wells has substantiated in *Moreau* [is] the prophetic myth of man's partial animality as an irrational creature motivated by fear and desire. . . ."[17] *The War of the Worlds* (1898) suggests to Wells' narrator that "our views of the human future must be greatly modified by these events. We have learned now that we cannot regard this planet as being fenced in and a secure abiding-place for Man. . . ."

Repeatedly Wells sounded the same basic warning, but his contemporaries did not hear it, for many of them who wrote the scientific romance were enchanted with the prospects held forth by science and technology. The alternative was to embrace the escapism of Haggard and Burroughs. In his *Billion Year Spree* [6-2], Aldiss metaphorically speaks of the thinking pole, symbolized by Wells, and the dreaming pole, symbolized by Burroughs and his many imitators.

The dystopian note which has increasingly dominated much of contemporary science fiction was first sounded most clearly by several Continental writers. In Karel Čapek's *R.U.R.* (1921) [2-37], which opened in Prague and immediately became a classic of modern theatre, Rossum's Universal Robots revolt and destroy mankind, explaining that they did so because to be human is to dominate and destroy anything which opposes one. His neglected novel, *Krakatit: An Atomic Phantasy* (1925) [2-36], noteworthy as a study of the protagonist—the young Czech engineer, Prokop—explores the dangers inherent in the release of atomic energy. In 1922, Eugene Zamiatin praised Wells highly in a brief study,

Herbert Wells; in 1924 the English-language edition of his novel, *We* [2-177], was released. Its portrayal of the United State in the twenty-sixth century, a glass-enwalled city-state inhabited by those who have survived a great war and kept separate from the irrational, "ugly" natural world, is obviously an attack upon the Soviet Union. Its citizens are building a spaceship to carry word of the state's mathematical, antiseptic perfection to other worlds. Inside the city, man has imposed a rational order upon society, carefully regulating all emotions and activities so that no one is different, except in terms of intelligence and specific service to the United State. Zamiatin portrays a revolt that fails; the protagonist, who has momentarily learned what it means to be human after falling in love, surrenders himself and permits brain surgery which removes the last possibility of his being an individual. He is an automaton, a servant of society. With *We*, utopia dies. Thereafter the motifs which dominated the scientific romance for almost half a century lose their content, to recall Silverberg, and become no more than plot action as a new generation of writers searches for its own themes in order to give voice to its own concerns. Significantly, the English-language version of Zamiatin's *We* was published two years before American science fiction, by and large, was relegated to the specialist pulp magazines, a publishing phenomenon which did not occur in Europe.

Reference Notes

1. Thomas D. Clareson, "SF: The Other Side of Realism," in *SF: The Other Side of Realism* [6-23], pp. 1–28.

2. Ford Madox Ford, *Henry James: A Critical Study* (London: 1913), p. 225.

3. Henry James, *Notes and Reviews*, Pierre de Chaignon la Rose, ed. (Cambridge: 1921), p. 110.

4. James, p. 110.

5. Robert Philmus, *Into the Unknown: The Evolution of Science Fiction from Francis Godwin to H. G. Wells* [6-74], p. 90.

6. I. F. Clarke, *Voices Prophesying War* [6-25], p. 127.

7. Hobson Pearson, "If War Should Come," *Cosmopolitan*, 45 (June 1908), 38.

8. "Jules Verne," *Men of Mark* (London: 1877), no. 24.

9. Henry Adams, *The Education of Henry Adams* (Boston: Houghton Mifflin Sentry Edition, 1961), pp. 460, 495.

10. Robert Silverberg, *The Mirror of Infinity* [4-693], p. xxi; Thomas D. Clareson, *A Spectrum of Worlds* [4-663], p. 25.

11. Howard Haycraft, *Murder for Pleasure* (New York: Biblio and Tannen, 1968), pp. 98–99.

12. Clareson, *SF: The Other Side of Realism* [6-23], p. 14.

13. Silverberg, *The Mirror of Infinity* [4-693], p. ix.

14. For a detailed discussion of the "lost race" novel as the "respectable erotica" of the period, see Thomas D. Clareson, "Lost Lands, Lost Races: A Pagan Princess of his Very Own," *Journal of Popular Culture*, 8 (Spring 1975), 714–723. The persistence of the motif may be seen by the fact that Ian Cameron's *The Lost Ones* (1961) served as the basis for the Walt Disney film *Island at the Top of the World*, and has been reissued under that title by Avon.

15. Mark Hillegas, *The Future as Nightmare: H. G. Wells and the Antiutopians* [6-47].

16. Clareson, *A Spectrum of Worlds* [4-663], p. 60.

17. Philmus, p. 118.

The brackets refer to entry numbers in chapters 4 and 6, where fuller bibliographic information is provided for the cited books.

Bibliography:
The Emergence of
the Scientific Romance

2-1. Abbott, Edwin A. (as A. Square) (U.K.). **Flatland: A Romance of Many Dimensions.** Roberts Brothers, 1885. Dover, $1.25; Barnes & Noble, $6.00.

The narrator, citizen of a two-dimensional country, uses the land as a basis for some satire, especially of education and women. He briefly envisions a one-dimensional world where motion is impossible ("Lineland"), and a sphere intrudes into the plane, giving him knowledge of "Spaceland." He tries unsuccessfully to teach the concept of three dimensions. The book becomes a mathematician's delight, an exercise in the limitation of perception.

2-2. Aldrich, Thomas Bailey. **The Queen of Sheba and My Cousin the Colonel.** J. R. Osgood, 1877. AMS Pr., $10.00 (*Works*, vol. 5).

The Queen of Sheba provides an early example of the psychological "case study." In the terms of the day, a medical doctor discusses the affliction of the heroine, which appears to be primarily amnesia.

2-3. Anderson, Olof W. **The Treasure Vault of Atlantis.** Midland, 1925.

Explorers find in South America a vault in which Atlantean leaders have placed themselves in suspended animation so that they may transmit

51

their vast knowledge to the future. Science is taken care of by a "radio machine." The young modern protagonist has visions, including those of having ruled Atlantis and loved a beautiful princess. He had, and she is one revived. The thematic core of the book centers, however, on such issues as reincarnation and successful communication with the dead.

2-4. Anet, Claude (pseud. of Jean Schopfer) (France). **The End of a World.** Knopf, 1927. Tr. by Jeffrey E. Jeffrey (pseud.). of *La fin d'un monde*.
The prehistoric "Bear People," living in a river valley at the end of the Ice Age, are identified as the artists of the grottoes near Dordogne. Merchants of a supposedly advanced culture visit them; a roundheaded people absorbs them and thereby destroys their culture. Modern sensibilities are assigned to the cavemen.

*2-5. Astor, John Jacob. **A Journey in Other Worlds.** Appleton, 1894.
The book opens with utopian descriptions of the Earth in 2000 A.D., but quickly shifts to a series of voyages to the planets. Mysticism dominates all the voyages, particularly the one to Saturn.

*2-6. Balmer, Edwin, and MacHarg, William. **The Achievements of Luther Trant.** Small, Maynard, 1910.
Trant is a psychologist turned detective. In a preface the authors insist that the theories, methods, and tests employed have a factual basis. This is apparently the first use in fiction of the lie detector.

*2-7. Barney, John Stewart. **L.P.M.: The End of the Great War.** Putnam, 1915.
An American scientist, Edestone, defeats all warring nations with his advanced weapons. Victorious, he calls for an authoritarian world government to be ruled by "the Aristocracy of Intelligence."

2-8. Barr, Robert. **The Face and the Mask.** Stokes, 1895.
"The Doom of London" portrays a catastrophe in which a mixture of coal smoke and fog threatens to suffocate everyone. "A New Explosive" involves a liquid set off by evaporation in sunlight.

2-9. Barton, Samuel. **The Battle of Siwash and the Capture of Canada.** Charles T. Dillingham, 1888.
A future war between America and Britain is decided by the use of self-destroying torpedo boats which annihilate the English navy.

2-10. Beale, Charles Willing. **The Secret of the Earth.** F. T. Neely, 1899. Arno, $14.00.
The lost race is a tribe of ancients in a Symmesian world inside the earth.

2-11. Bellamy, Edward. **The Blindman's World and Other Stories.** Houghton Mifflin, 1898. MSS Information Corp., $20.75; Somerset Pubs., $9.50.

"To Whom This May Come" describes an unknown race on a Pacific island; they have mastered telepathy and brought about a utopia. William Dean Howells wrote the introduction to the book.

*2-12. Bellamy, Edward. **Dr. Heidenhoff's Process.** Appleton, 1880. AMS Press, $6.50.
A medical doctor perfects a machine which erases the memory of evil; the process is described in terms of the psychological and physiological theories of the period. Much emphasis is given to repentance and Christian forgiveness.

2-13. Bellamy, Edward. **Equality.** Appleton, 1897. AMS Press, $10.00; Greenwood, $15.25.
This sequel to *Looking Backward* [2-14] served as a rebuttal to Bellamy's critics. It argues that economic equality is the cornerstone upon which the complete life—political, intellectual, ethical—of an industrial democracy rests. He emphasizes the important place of religion in the world of 2000, but there is no need of an established church or ordained ministers. Despite the thread of a love story, this is more an essay than a novel.

*2-14. Bellamy, Edward. **Looking Backward: A.D. 2000–1887.** Ticknor, 1888. Harvard Univ. Press, $10.00.
Without doubt the most famous of the American utopias, this was the progenitor of several hundred utopias, both in America and Europe. Science is incidental in the text, although technology and socialism have made utopia possible.

2-15. Beresford, John Davys (U.K.). **The Hampdenshire Wonder.** Sidgwick and Jackson, 1911. Arno, $17.00; Garland, $11.00.
Long celebrated as one of the first "superman" novels, the narrative tells the story of a boy wonder who confounds adult society. He has a mind thousands of years in advance of contemporary man's, but society regards him as little better than a macrocephalic idiot because of his silence. His major enemy is the local vicar, and when he is found drowned, the question remains open as to whether he was murdered. Perhaps most interesting for its suggestions regarding the future development of the human mind and for the mood of awe and wonder with which the narrator regards a superior and rational mind. Compare Stapledon's *Odd John* [3-58], Wylie's *Gladiator* [3-73], and van Vogt's *Slan* [4-591].

2-16. Bierbower, Austin. **From Monkey to Man, or Society in the Tertiary Age.** Dibble, 1894.
A pseudo-historical treatment of the earliest cavemen gives supposedly scientific bases for various Christian beliefs. Oncoming glaciers force the apemen from their fruitful valley, which their descendants remember as a kind of paradise, an Eden.

*2-17. Bierce, Ambrose. Although many of Bierce's stories involve supernatural themes or the humor of horror, there is the attempt to explain such events rationally. In "The Secret of Macarger's Gulch" and "A Tough Tussle" Bierce speaks of fear of the supernatural, especially the dead, as a racially inherited trait. "A Watcher by the Dead" and "The Suitable Surroundings" establish a much imitated plot which supposedly proves the existence of this fear. "The Man and the Snake" uses hallucination to suggest racial memory. "Moxon's Master" employs a robot chess player much like Poe's "Maelzel's chess player" (1836), while "The Damned Thing" is explained in terms of the wavelength of light. Many editions of Bierce's works are available. *The Collected Writings of Ambrose Bierce*, Citadel, $4.95, contains all cited stories as well as Bierce's major work.

2-19. Blot, Thomas. **The Man from Mars.** Bacon, 1891.
By metempsychosis (teleportation) a Martian appears on Earth. He describes a superior, utopian civilization to a hermit.

2-20. Bolton, Charles E. **The Harris-Ingram Experiment.** Burrows Brothers, 1905.
The love story of a hard-working young genius and the daughter of the man who becomes his sponsor–partner is combined with a description of practical accomplishments. The two men develop the finest steel mill in the world and establish a utopian community for labor and management.

2-21. Boussenard, Louis (France). **10,000 Years in a Block of Ice.** Tr. by John Paret. F. Tennyson Neely, 1898.
Frozen into suspended animation by exposure in the Arctic, the protagonist awakens to find a utopian state in which a race descending from a blend of the Chinese and Africans is the dominant people. Much emphasis is given to psychic powers; the technology is advanced.

2-22. Bouve, Edward T. **Centuries Apart.** Little, Brown, 1894.
An American naval expedition finds lost sixteenth-century colonies, British (South England) and French (La Nouvelle France), in Antarctica. The majority of the narrative reads like an historical romance: political intrigue, chivalry, knightly warfare. A love story assumes greatest importance, but the American officer returns to the United States and is killed in the Civil War. A now-lost diary provides the narrative frame.

*2-23. Bradshaw, William Richard. **The Goddess of Atvatabar.** J. F. Douthitt, 1892. Arno, $19.00.
The lost race inhabits a Symmesian world in the Arctic. Highly extravagant magic combines with mysticism to distinguish this novel from its contemporaries. It is perhaps most important for the introduction, in which Julian Hawthorne condemns such writers as Zola.

2-24. Burgess, Frank Gelett. **The White Cat.** Bobbs, 1907.

By hypnosis a villainous doctor summons up the alter ego of the heroine. Much attention is given to the process of hypnotism, but there is less psychological theory than in a number of contemporary works.

*2-25. Burroughs, Edgar Rice. **At the Earth's Core.** McClurg, 1922. Ace, $1.25; Peter Smith, $5.00.

*2-26. Burroughs, Edgar Rice. **Carson of Venus.** Burroughs, 1939. Ace, $1.50; Canaveral, $6.95.

*2-27. Burroughs, Edgar Rice. **The Gods of Mars.** McClurg, 1924. Ballantine, $1.25; Canaveral, $6.95.

*2-28. Burroughs, Edgar Rice. **The Land that Time Forgot.** McClurg, 1924. Ace, $1.95; Canaveral, $6.95.

*2-29. Burroughs, Edgar Rice. **Lost on Venus.** Burroughs, 1935. Ace, $1.25; Canaveral, $6.95.

*2-30. Burroughs, Edgar Rice. **Pellucidar.** McClurg, 1923. Ace, $1.50; Canaveral, $6.95.

*2-31. Burroughs, Edgar Rice. **A Princess of Mars.** McClurg, 1917. Ballantine, $1.25; Dover, $3.00.

*2-32. Burroughs, Edgar Rice. **Tarzan of the Apes.** McClurg, 1914. Ballantine, $1.25.

The above titles provide a cross-section of the more than fifty novels making up the canon of Burroughs' work. It consists primarily of four series: John Carter of Mars (Barsoom), which includes his first story, *Under the Moons of Mars*, published in book form as *A Princess of Mars*; Tarzan of the Apes; Pellucidar, the world within the Earth; and Carson of Venus. Many of the stories were first issued in popular magazines of the period. Implicit in all of them—perhaps most obviously in the Tarzan stories—is a neoprimitivism, but Burroughs wrote at a time when the burning issues of the earlier period—including its mysticism—had become dated, although they never disappeared completely. Thus, writing in the tradition of Rider Haggard, he could concentrate upon producing an adventure story seemingly divorced from serious thematic materials. He skillfully manipulated the conventions which he had inherited from the nineteenth century, and his basic theme, the rejection of modern civilization, stands always behind his apparent escapism.

*2-33. Butler, Samuel (U.K.). **Erewhon; or Over the Range.** Truebner, 1872. Signet, $.95; Dutton, $3.95 (includes *Erewhon Revisited*).

In the interior of an unnamed British colony [New Zealand], the narrator discovers a utopian culture which has rejected the use of the machine because the machine will supersede man, and which lives in an agrarian culture in which both illness and poverty are considered immoral. Through the device of irony the narrator satirizes many of the beliefs of England, particularly those regarding religion and personality. He escapes and intends to return to convert the Erewhonians—the high point of the irony.

2-34. Butler, Samuel (U.K.). **Erewhon Revisited Twenty Years Later.** G. Richards, 1901. Dutton, $3.95 (includes *Erewhon*).
The account of Higgs' second journey to Erewhon is told by his son, whose own visit forms the epilogue. Higgs finds that he is remembered as the Sunchild and is worshipped as a supernatural being. This provides the basis for satire not only of the clerical establishment but also of the beliefs of some of its leaders.

2-35. Bywater, Hector Charles (U.K.). **The Great Pacific War: A History of the American–Japanese Campaign of 1931–33.** Houghton Mifflin, 1925.
Without individualized characters or fully dramatized scenes, this story is presented as history rather than fiction. To avert the rise of a leftist government, Japan begins aggression against China and propaganda against the United States. The war ends after the Chinese overrun Manchuria, Sakhalin is surrendered to Russia to prevent her entry into the war, and the United States achieves victory at sea (fifty airplanes appear over Tokyo). The war-weary Japanese sign a truce.

2-36. Čapek, Karel (Czechoslovakia). **Krakitit: An Atomic Phantasy.** Macmillan, 1925. Arno, $23.00. Tr. by Lawrence Hyde.
An early novel treating a proto-atomic bomb and man's inability to control his weapons. A Czech scientist discovers a very powerful new explosive, Krakatit, which disables its discoverers when accidentally detonated. Imprisoned by munitions makers, he is later captured by anarchists who destroy themselves and a town they were terrorizing. This second explosion causes the scientist to forget his discovery, and he devotes his remaining years to peaceful research. The romantic subplot is dated, but the novel still retains topical interest.

*2-37. Čapek, Karel (Czechoslovakia). **R.U.R.: A Fantastic Melodrama.** Doubleday, 1923. Washington Square Press, $.75; Oxford Univ. Press, $3.75 (includes *The Insect Play*).
Originally produced by the National Theatre of Czechoslovakia (January 1921), this drama introduced the modern concept of robots (Rossum's Universal Robots). The elder Rossum wished "to become a sort of scientific substitute for God"; his son simply wished to make money. Helena Glory persuades the technicians who build the robots to change the process slightly so that the robots will have feeling, "soul." Europe teach-

es them to fight and serve in the military forces. The robots destroy humanity. Terror and pain have given them souls; they are aggressive and destructive in order to be like men.

2-38. Chambers, Robert William. **The Gay Rebellion.** Appleton, 1913. Arno, $17.00.
This light-hearted spoof of the suffragette movement and the science of eugenics is perhaps most important for the dated attitude it expresses toward women and love. Each young woman foregoes her principles when she falls in love. The novel is episodic and is not sustained.

*2-39. Chambers, Robert William. **The Green Mouse.** Appleton, 1910.
A "wireless apparatus" guarantees happy marriage by intercepting and matching psychic waves, but scientific invention cannot overcome the impulses of the irrational heart.

2-40. Chambers, Robert William. **Some Ladies in Haste.** Appleton, 1908.
The hero, a student of mental suggestion, causes people to fall in love by post-hypnotic suggestion.

2-41. Chapman, Samuel. **Doctor Jones' Picnic.** Whitaker & Ray, 1908.
Dr. Jones invents an aluminum balloon two hundred feet in diameter, with which to journey to the North Pole. More important, perhaps, are the cures—including one for cancer—which he effects along the way.

2-42. Chester, George Randolph. **The Jingo.** Bobbs, 1912.
This satire of modern materialism uses the lost race motif as a framework. The protagonist, a salesman, brings "improvements" to a civilization in the Antarctic.

*2-43. Cook, William Wallace. **Adrift in the Unknown.** Street & Smith, 1904. Arno, $17.00.
Four Capitalists are kidnapped and taken on a journey to Mercury; this provides a frame for social criticism. This is one of the few novels in which the aliens are nonhuman.

2-44. Cook, William Wallace. **Cast Away at the Pole.** Street & Smith, 1904.
This is a satire both of lost race novels and of Arctic exploration.

2-45. Cook, William Wallace. **The Eighth Wonder.** Street & Smith, 1906–1907.
Satirizes the scientist–inventor by concentrating upon the plot of an eccentric to corner the nation's supply of electricity in revenge against the trusts which have stolen his patents.

2-46. Cook, William Wallace. **Marooned in 1492.** Street & Smith, 1905.
Time travel is achieved by means of a drug.

*2-47. Cook, William Wallace. **A Round Trip to the Year 2000.** Street & Smith, 1903. Hyperion, $3.85, $10.95.
The first and probably most successful of Cook's satires deals with a group of nineteenth-century writers who travel in various manners to the year 2000 and become marooned there.

2-48. Copley, Frank Barkley. **The Impeachment of President Israels.** Phillips Pub., 1912.
Impeachment occurs because the President will not let public clamor force him to declare war on Germany. A Jew, he is an heroic but isolated leader. Much emphasis is given to a natural and scientific basis for moral law; the next step in evolution will be to perfect the human soul.

2-49. Cowan, Frank. **Revi-Lona.** Tribune Press, 188-.
The lost race has a communistic state in Antarctica. The novel becomes satirical when the arrival of an American man disrupts this society dominated by women.

*2-50. Cowan, James. **Daybreak: A Romance of an Old World.** G. H. Richmond, 1896. Arno, $15.00.
When the Moon falls toward the Earth, the protagonists fly to it successfully in a balloon; some magnetic phenomenon repels the Moon from Earth so that it flies to Mars. The book is most significant for its use of the concept of parallel evolution and its defense of Christianity, including the idea that Christ must be incarnated on every planet.

2-51. Craig, Alexander. **Ionia: Land of Wise Men and Fair Women.** G. Hill, 1898. Arno, $12.00.
The lost race is a Greek settlement in the Himalayas. A young English reformer visits the society and brings back such ideas as prohibition, sterilization of the unfit, and communal ownership of land.

2-52. Cromie, Robert. **The Next Crusade.** Hutchinson, 1896.
In a future war the combination of Britain, Austria, and their allies defeats Russia and Turkey; the result is that "with Constantinople on the east and Gibraltar on the west, the Mediterranean was at last a British lake."

2-53. Cromie, Robert. **A Plunge into Space.** Frederick Warne, 1890. Hyperion, $12.50.
By means of a steel globe the protagonist and his party fly to Mars, where they find an advanced, utopian civilization, including The City of Delight with its boulevards lined with flowering shrubs. The book is dedicated to Jules Verne.

*2-54. Cummings, Ray. **The Girl in the Golden Atom.** Harper, 1923. Hyperion, $3.95, $10.95.

This volume is made up of Cummings' fusion of two novelettes, "The Girl in the Golden Atom" (*All-Story Weekly*, 1919) and "The People of the Golden Atom" (*All-Story Weekly*, 1920). In an atom of his mother's wedding ring, "The chemist" discovers a beautiful woman on a subatomic world. He develops chemicals permitting him to decrease and increase his size and goes alone to find and woo Lylda, the "fragile beauty." He returns to tell his story but then goes back to his beloved. After five years his friends follow him. The second portion of the story focuses upon the love of "The very young man" and Aura. The adventures portrayed typify the Munsey stories, are essentially those of the lost race novel, and anticipate the contemporary sword and sorcery romance.

2-55. Cummins, Harle Owen. **Welsh Rarebit Tales.** Mutual Book, 1902.
"The Man Who Made a Man" deals with the Frankenstein theme. "In the Lower Passage" reveals the survival of a beast-man apparently from prehistory. "The Fool and His Joke" imitates Bierce's "A Watcher by the Dead." "The Space Annihilator" introduces a machine capable of instantaneously transporting objects over long distances.

*2-56. Dake, Charles Romyn. **A Strange Discovery.** H. J. Kimball, 1899. Gregg, $14.00.
The lost race is Romans in the Antarctic. The book combines the further adventures of Poe's Gordon Pym with a love story in the manner of Rider Haggard.

2-57. Davenport, Benjamin Rush. **Anglo-Saxons, Onward! A Romance of the Future.** Hubbell Pub., 1898.
In a future war the Americans and British defeat Russia, Turkey, and their allies. The hero is the American President, whose wise decisions save Canada from invasion and bring about a British-American alliance. The book not only celebrates Anglo-Saxon supremacy but hails the American victory over Spain as an event which opened "a new vista of . . . grandeur and glory" to America.

*2-58. DeMille, James. **A Strange Manuscript Found in a Copper Cylinder.** Harper, 1888. Arno, $16.00.
A lost race survives in the Antarctic. This narrative is important in several ways: the echoes of Poe and Symmes, the survival of prehistoric creatures, and the use of a series of intrusive scenes in which the discoverers of the manuscript cite scientific data and theory to substantiate the events reported in the manuscript.

2-59. DeMorgan, John. **He: A Companion to She.** Norman L. Munro, 1887. **It.** Norman L. Munro, 1887.
These are the two most famous parodies of Rider Haggard's *She*, although *He* shifts its scene from Africa to Easter Island.

2-60. Dixon, Thomas. **The Fall of a Nation.** Appleton, 1916. Arno, $20.00.
Germany reduces America to a conquered province. This savage tirade against Germany has no scientist as hero.

*2-61. Donnelly, Ignatius. **Caesar's Column.** F. J. Schulte, 1890.
A socialist revolution overthrows a government controlled by the trusts. Incidental although important use is made of dirigible balloons.

2-62. Donnelly, Ignatius. **Doctor Huguet.** F. J. Schulte, 1891. Arno, $11.00.
By transmigration the protagonist awakens in the body of a Negro, thus providing a framework for social criticism.

2-63. Donnelly, Ignatius. **The Golden Bottle.** D. D. Merrill, 1892. Gregg, $9.50; Johnson Reprint, $17.50.
Obtaining a bottle which turns iron into gold, the protagonist first overthrows the capitalists, then wins a war against all of Europe, and finally establishes a utopian world state. Much emphasis is placed upon Christian values. The protagonist awakens to find that it all has been a dream.

2-64. Dooner, Pierton W. **Last Days of the Republic.** Alta California Pub. House, 1880.
Written as a protest against importing Chinese coolie laborers and suggesting that they remain agents of the Chinese government, this is the first warning of "the yellow peril." The federal government will not pass legislation to aid California; the Chinese "fifth column" becomes more active. America is finally destroyed as a nation. The narrative is presented as history, without individualized characterization or fully developed scenes of fiction.

2-65. Dostoyevsky, Feodor (Russia). **"The Dream of a Ridiculous Man"** (1877). In *Best Short Stories*, tr. by David Magarshack, Modern Library, $1.95.
A man apathetic to the suffering of his fellow humans and periodically under the delusion that the existence of the world depends upon his perceiving it dreams that he has been carried through space to a planet that is identical to Earth except that its inhabitants are exempt from suffering, whether natural or moral. He dreams that he corrupts these people, introducing all the evils of earth among them. Awaking convinced of the truth of his dream, he attempts to evangelize about a world of love without suffering, but feels he is regarded as a fool or a madman.

2-66. Doyle, Arthur Conan. **The Land of Mist.** Doran, 1926. Transatlantic, $9.75 (*The Complete Professor Challenger Stories*).
In this last novel dealing with Professor George Challenger, the protagonists learn that it is possible to communicate with the dead. Man is thus seen to be part of a universal order.

*2-67. Doyle, Arthur Conan. **The Lost World.** Hodder & Stoughton, 1912. Transatlantic, $9.75; Berkley, $.95.
The novel introduces Professor George Challenger, who leads a party of explorers to the remnant of a prehistoric world on a plateau in South America. It remains the most famous of its type and has served as a model since its publication.

*2-68. Doyle, Arthur Conan. **The Maracot Deep.** Doubleday, 1929.
Believing (correctly) that the concept of the extreme pressure at ocean depths is erroneous, Professor Maracot leads his companions to explore the extreme depths of the Atlantic basin, some 26,000 feet. A crab-like creature breaks their hawser line, and they plunge to the sea floor where they discover survivors amid the ruins of Atlantis. A love story figures in the narrative, but Doyle writes more in the tradition of Verne, giving a panorama of undersea wonders. The explorers save themselves by means of a "vitrine ball" (plastic?) and a gas lighter than hydrogen which permits them to reach the surface. Doyle pronounces nature to be cruel, but his increasing mysticism shows itself in a long, final confrontation between the explorers and "the lord of the dark face," obviously Satan.

*2-69. Doyle, Arthur Conan. **The Poison Belt.** Hodder & Stoughton, 1913. Transatlantic, $9.75.
Professor Challenger's party isolates itself and survives a seeming worldwide catastrophe. They explore the vacant world before all life reawakens, not realizing that everything has been in a cataleptic state for twenty-four hours. Although not so explicit as in Wells, for example, the idea of mankind being given a second chance—so typical of the British treatment of the catastrophe motif—is present.

2-70. Drayton, Henry Sinclair. **In Oudemon.** Grafton Press, 1901.
The book portrays a lost race of English colonists in South America. The colony originated as a conscious effort to achieve an ideal Christian socialist state and has long been marooned by earthquake and landslide. Its technology is far in advance of that of the outside world.

*2-71. Emerson, Willis George. **The Smoky God.** Forbes, 1908. Amherst Press, $3.00.
The lost race is a conventional utopia in a Symmesian world. The smoky god is a small sun within the Earth. Much attention is given to arguments supporting the view that either the Arctic or the inner world was the Edenic homeland of man.

2-72. England, George Allan. **The Air Trust.** P. Wagner, 1915. Hyperion, $12.95.
A scientist in the hire of the trusts perfects a device to remove oxygen from the air so that the trusts can control and sell even the air people breathe. A socialist revolution overthrows the existent tyranny.

*2-73.   England, George Allan. **Darkness and Dawn.** Small, Maynard, 1914. Hyperion, $5.95, $15.00.
"The Vacant World," "Beyond the Great Oblivion," and "The Afterglow" form the trilogy which recounts how, after more than a thousand years of suspended animation, the engineer–hero and his beloved awaken to rebuild a finer, better civilization than that which was destroyed by natural catastrophe in the twentieth century.

2-74.   England, George Allan. **The Flying Legion.** McClurg, 1920.
A scientist far in advance of his contemporaries forms his wartime flying companions into a group, with himself as absolute head. They intend to reform Islam, which he believes to be the true religion. After stealing sacred religious objects from Mecca, they go to a hidden, golden city in Africa, where the legion is destroyed except for the hero and his beloved.

2-75.   England, George Allan. **The Golden Blight.** H. K. Fly, 1916. Arno, $19.00.
A scientist invents a machine which disintegrates gold, and thus helps to effect a revolution which overthrows the trusts.

2-76.   Ewald, Carl (Denmark). **Two-Legs.** Tr. by Alexander Teixera de Mattos. Scribner's Sons, 1906.
Animals tell of the rise of man, who has dominated the whole earth.

2-77.   Franklin, Edgar (pseud. of Edgar Franklin Stearns). **Mr. Hawkins' Humorous Adventures.** Dodge, 1904.
A series of stories recounts the misadventures of an inventor whose gadgets invariably fail. The style is gentle, not satirical.

*2-78.   Fuller, Alvarado M. **A. D. 2000.** Laird and Lee, 1890. Arno, $16.00.
By means of an experiment inducing suspended animation, a scientist projects himself into a future utopia dominated by science. Much attention is given to descriptions of inventions. A natural catastrophe has changed the American continent and turned scientific attention to electricity, the chief source of energy for the utopia.

2-79.   Futrelle, Jacques. **The Diamond Master.** Bobbs, 1909.
This mystery story involves the successful production of synthetic diamonds. Much attention is given to scientific data and experiments.

*2-80.   Gernsback, Hugo. **Ralph 124C41+: A Romance of the Year 2660.** Stratford, 1925; Fell, 1950.
First published as a serial in *Modern Electrics* in 1911, this story sketches a science-dominated utopia and contains a virtual catalog of brief descriptions of advanced machinery. It is one of the early narratives to which individuals turn when they stress the "prophetic" element of science fic-

tion, for to them such prophecy is limited to technological advancement. The creaky plot concentrates upon a love story involving the world's foremost scientist and is unique in the period in having a Martian as the "other man."

2-81. Godfrey, Hollis. **The Man Who Ended War.** Little, Brown, 1908.
A scientist perfects the ultimate weapon—an electrical/radioactive wave which disintegrates warships. The novel ends with a world peace conference.

*2-82. Gratacap, Louis Pope. **The Certainty of a Future Life on Mars.** Irving Press, 1903.
The protagonist successfully communicates with Mars by "wireless telegraphy," establishing contact with his deceased father. Early chapters are dominated by science and the concept of parallel evolution, but the narrative turns to mysticism as well as a description of the utopian Martian civilization.

*2-83. Greg, Percy. **Across the Zodiac: The Story of a Wrecked Record.** Truebner, 1880. Hyperion, $5.50, $15.00.
In many ways this became the prototype of interplanetary voyages to Mars, lending its "apergy"—an electric force counteracting gravity—to a number of narratives. The Martian civilization has advanced technology and is a monarchy, for communism had been tried but failed.

2-84. Griffith, George (U.K.). **The Angel of the Revolution, a Tale of the Coming Terror.** Tower, 1894. Hyperion, $4.75, $12.95.
Originally serialized in *Pearson's Magazine* in 1893, this novel combines several plot lines popular in the future war motif. The protagonist invents an airplane and is persuaded to join a group of "Terrorists" (socialists) who wish to bring about political reform; they organize the trade unions in America, overthrow the government, and propose an Anglo-American Federation. At first Britain rejects the idea, although war has broken out with Russia. Not until London has been devastated do the British agree to the Federation. The Russians are routed, and a world state is organized.

2-85. Griffith, George (U.K.). **Olga Romanoff; or, The Syren of the Skies.** Tower, 1894. Hyperion, $4.25, $12.00.
By 2030, a century of socialism has brought about a utopia. But Olga Romanoff, descendant of the Russian royal house, combines with the Sultan of Turkey to begin a terrible war. The Aerians (as the Terrorists are now called) learn that a comet will soon strike the earth, and build a subterranean refuge. The comet devastates the surface of the earth, but the Aerians emerge to build a new, even better society.

*2-86. Haggard, Henry Rider. **Allan Quatermain.** Longman's, 1887.

Dover, $3.95. (includes *King Solomon's Mines* and *She*).
Published in the same year as *She*, this novel provides the basic pattern for the lost race novel which Haggard's imitators most often followed. It allowed the protagonist to marry NylepFtha, the beautiful queen of the Zu-Vendis, and remain in the primitive kingdom.

*2-87. Haggard, Henry Rider. **King Solomon's Mines.** Cassell, 1885.
The protagonist and his party search for and find the mythical source of King Solomon's wealth. The romance of this novel draws upon Haggard's own experience and the panorama of Africa instead of imagined peoples and societies.

*2-88. Haggard, Henry Rider. **She: A History of Adventure.** Longman's, 1887.
This is the most famous of Haggard's novels; it has all of the ingredients of the lost race novel except the happy ending.

2-89. Harben, William Nathaniel. **The Land of the Changing Sun.** Merriam, 1904. Gregg, $11.50.
A great subterranean cavern near the Arctic has been colonized by men who wish to escape such unpleasantnesses as taxation. They build an electrical sun to heat the cavern, but their main interest is the field of eugenics. In advocating a world-wide eugenics program, the novel bitterly attacks the medical profession.

2-90. Harper, Vincent. **The Mortgage on the Brain.** Doubleday, 1905.
A scientific experiment involving electrical force—seemingly a kind of shock treatment—successfully changes personality and cures amnesia. The book contains a strong attack upon both traditional religious views and traditional concepts of personality.

*2-91. Hastings, Milo. **City of Endless Night.** Dodd, Mead, 1920. Hyperion, $3.95, $11.50.
Faced with defeat after starting a third war, Germany has built a subterranean city under its last stronghold, Berlin, from which it still wages war against the world community. Millions now live in a totalitarian state, in which a careful eugenics program breeds the different classes. The portrait of the society undoubtedly influenced later dystopian fiction. Here, however, the protagonist infiltrates the city, organizes a fifth column, and eventually leads the army which defeats the Germans.

2-92. Hatfield, Richard. **Geyserland: 9262 B.C.: Empiricism in Social Reform.** Richard Hatfield, 1908.
The lost race inhabits an Edenic continent in the Arctic. The major emphasis of the book is an attempt to reconcile Marxism both historically and philosophically to Christianity, but the early chapters contain much geological theory and speculation.

*2-93. Hertzka, Theodor (Austria). **Freeland: A Social Anticipation.** Appleton, 1891. Gordon Press, $39.95. Tr. of *Freiland; Ein Sociales Zukunftsbild*, 1890.

The book describes the successful effort of men "from all parts of the civilized world" to found a socialist society, Eden Vale, in East Africa. Technology plays an important part in the society. Sharing the assumptions regarding man and society expressed in other utopias of the period, *Freeland* has particular significance because Hertzka was a distinguished Viennese economist and because he gave a careful blueprint showing how the society would be brought into existence and operate. It had wide popularity and influence, upon the Continent especially, but soon became dated because of its very specificity of detail.

*2-94. Howells, William Dean. **Between the Dark and the Daylight.** Harper, 1907.

These short stories feature the psychologist Wanhope, who explains scientifically the ghost stories told by members of his dinner club.

*2-95. Howells, William Dean. **Questionable Shapes.** Harper, 1903. Books for Libraries, $10.25; Folcroft, $15.00.

These stories first introduce Wanhope.

*2-96. Howells, William Dean. **Through the Eye of the Needle, a Romance.** Harper, 1907. AMS Press, $15.00.

A sequel to *A Traveler from Altruria*, it is not so effective. The early chapters retain the strength of the earlier book as Aristides Homo comments upon the quality of life which he sees in New York City, but once he returns to Altruria and his American friends join him there, the narrative becomes no more than the portrait of another utopia, which is indebted to Howells' contemporaries.

2-97. Howells, William Dean. **A Traveler from Altruria, a Romance.** Harper, 1894. Hill & Wang, $2.65.

Originally serialized in *Cosmopolitan*, this utopian romance records the visit of Aristides Homo to the United States. He describes his homeland as "the first Christian commune after Christ" and is critical of all things American, especially slavery, class inequality, and the belief in competition. Howells gains some strength by reversing the usual technique of the utopian romance: that is, by the use of a dialogue about the United States rather than a direct description of utopia.

2-98. Hudson, William Henry (U.K.). **A Crystal Age.** Duckworth, 1913. AMS Press, $15.00; Folcroft, $14.50.

The narrator, a botanist, suffers a fall and awakens in an unspecified future which has no knowledge of his world. It is a pastoral scene, with no industralization apparent; the unit of society is the family, living in isolated manorial homes (its members are known as the "children of the house"). There is a strong sense of right and wrong, and other character-istics include matriarchy and longevity, but there is no marriage and no recognition of sexual love. In a preface in his collected works, Hudson asserted that such "romances of the future" grew out of "a sense of dis-satisfaction with the existing order of things" and the hope of a better order to come.

2-99.   Jane, Frederick T. (U.K.). **To Venus in Five Seconds.** A. D. In-nes, 1897.
A woman who reveals that she is a descendant of ancient Egyptians kid-naps the narrator and takes him to Venus, where he and other earthmen are to be subjected to various experiments. His efforts to escape provoke a final battle between the "Thothens" (Egyptians) and the Venusians (nonhuman creatures).

2-100.   Janvier, Thomas Allibone. **The Aztec Treasure House.** Harper, 1890. Gregg, $14.50.
The lost race is a surviving remnant of the Aztecs in Mexico. The protag-onist, a professor of linguistics, undertakes an expedition as part of his research for a book on pre-Columbian America. Much reference is made to scholarly sources, including Stephens.

2-101.   Jensen, Johannes Vilhelm (Denmark). **The Long Journey: Fire and Ice.** Tr. by A. G. Chater of *Den lange rejse.* Knopf, 1923.
Based on the premise that mankind originated in the northern latitudes of Scandinavia, this is one of several volumes attempting to put the his-torical cycle into story form, thereby "tracing the long journey from pri-meval chaos to modern civilization."

2-102.   Kipling, Rudyard (U.K.). **"With the Night Mail,"** in *Actions and Reactions.* Doubleday, 1909. (Consult the *Short Story Index* for collections in which this appeared. One recent source is Damon Knight, ed., *One Hundred Years of Science Fiction,* Simon & Schuster, $7.95).
"A story of 2000 A.D." recounts the flight of Postal Packet 162 from Lon-don to Quebec. Dirigible balloons fly the air currents; the world is gov-erned by the Aerial Board of Control (A.B.C.), whose laws are deter-mined by "traffic and all it implies." The narrative ends with "extracts from the magazine in which the story appeared"; these include letters to the editor, advertisements, and notices regarding lights, missing ships, and weather.

*2-103.   Lasswitz, Kurd (Germany). **Two Planets.** Tr. of *Auf zwei Plan-eten.* 1897. Ed. by Mark Hillegas, Southern Illinois Univ. Press, 1971, $10.00.
Widely popular and influential on the Continent, this novel was not is-sued in English until recently. This account of how Martians establish a

protectorate over Earth, thereby bringing reason and utopia to the planet, has been widely praised for its influence upon the scientific imagination. For example, it mentions artificial satellites manned by the Martians. It contains a war of the worlds finally settled by peace treaty, a glimpse of Martian culture, and satire of contemporary society.

2-104. LeQueux, William (U.K.). **The Great War in England in 1897.** Tower, 1894.
France and Russia invade Britain. The calamity occurs because Britain has permitted herself to become unprepared and to lose control of the seas.

*2-105. Lloyd, John Uri. **Etidorpha.** Author, 1895. Amherst Press, $3.50; Sun Pub., $7.50, $12.00.
A journey in the great caverns within the Earth is made by the man who betrayed the guarded secrets of alchemy and was condemned to eternal life. The book contains one of the periods most violent attacks upon science, especially biology.

*2-106. London, Jack. **Before Adam.** Macmillan, 1906. New English Library, £0.30.
A pseudo-historical romance of the life of a caveman, in which the protagonist makes inventions and becomes aware of emotions which permit him to begin the long ascent to the level of humanity. Through racial memory the narrator dreams of this previous existence. Stanley Waterloo accused London of plagiarizing his *The Story of Ab* [2-160].

*2-107. London, Jack. **The Iron Heel.** Macmillan, 1907. Journeyman Press, £0.75.
The Everhard Manuscript records the early stages of the struggle between socialists and a fascist-type state ruled by the trusts. After seven centuries, the socialists have triumphed and established a utopia.

*2-108. London, Jack. **The Red One.** Macmillan, 1918. Gregg, $15.00 (in *The Science Fiction of Jack London*).
In the title story, the protagonist, dying on Guadalcanal among headhunters, agrees to an immediate death if he is permitted to see the god of the savages—called "The red one" or "The star-born"—whose metallic echo lured him into the jungle. He finds it to be a spaceship vastly superior to man's technology that has long rested in the jungle. The story is most notable for the manner in which London attempts to fuse literary naturalism and scientific romance.

*2-109. London, Jack. **The Scarlet Plague.** Macmillan, 1915. Gregg, $15.00 (in *The Science Fiction of Jack London*); Arno, $10.00.
A fascist-type society has been destroyed by an unknown disease for which there is no antitoxin. The remnant of mankind reverts to savage-

ry; the narrative closes with the deterministic prediction that the cycle of civilization's rise and fall will be repeated "without end." This is the most credible of the early novels dealing with world catastrophe.

*2-110.   London, Jack. **The Star Rover.** Macmillan, 1915. $4.95.
By means of self-induced cataleptic trance, a prisoner in solitary confinement frees his mind to wander in other times, other worlds. No explanation is given, although the process is described. This is the most extravagant of London's scientific romances.

2-111.   Mitchell, John Ames. **Drowsy.** Stokes, 1917. Arno, $17.00.
A young scientist discovers antigravity and an ultimate energy permitting space flight to the moon. He is recalled from a second voyage to Mars by the "psychic" call of his beloved, who has finally decided that she loves him.

2-112.   Mitchell, John Ames. **The Last American.** Stokes, 1889. Gregg, $9.00.
Parallels Poe's "Mellonta Tauta" [1-39]; a Persian expedition of the thirtieth century visits America. One of the earliest suggestions of the catastrophe motif occurs in references to climatic changes which brought about America's downfall. It serves primarily as the vehicle for a bitter attack upon American materialism.

*2-113.   Moffett, Cleveland Langston. **The Conquest of America.** Doran, 1916.
In a future war with Germany, victory is not attained until after Thomas Edison develops a radio-controlled torpedo permitting an "insignificant airforce" to annihilate the German navy. The book is dedicated to the Aero Clubs of America.

2-114.   Morris, Gouverneur. **It and Other Stories.** Scribner, 1912.
"Back There in the Grass" turns upon the discovery of a foot-high man–serpent; the suggestion is made that the creature is the product of another line of evolution.

2-115.   Morris, Gouverneur. **The Pagan's Progress.** Barnes, 1904.
A pseudo-historical romance of the caveman, this narrative has as its focus the spiritual awareness of man; specifically, after the death of his mate, the caveman "sees" her in the forest and realizes the fact of eternal life rather than "dissolution—decay—dust—nothing."

2-116.   Moskowitz, Samuel, comp. **Science Fiction by Gaslight: A History and Anthology of Science Fiction in the Popular Magazines 1891–1911.** World, 1968. Hyperion, $4.25, $12.00.
This collection shows the context from which Wells emerged as well as the pervasiveness of science fiction as a form of popular literature during the early period. The stories are preceded by a useful survey of Brit-

ish and American magazine publishing of the period. The selection of twenty-six stories covers topics from "Catastrophes" and "Marvelous Inventions" to "Scientific Crime and Detection" and "Medical Miracles."

2-117. Moskowitz, Samuel, ed. **Under the Moons of Mars: A History and Anthology of "The Scientific Romance" in the Munsey Magazines, 1912–1920.** Holt, 1970. Hyperion, $7.95.

This volume provides a significant sampling of nine Munsey romances, ranging from Edgar Rice Burroughs' "Under the Moons of Mars" (1912) to A. Merritt's "The Moon Pool" (1918) and Austin Hall and Homer Eon Flint's "The Blind Spot" (1921). It is most important in that it provides the original texts of stories that later (often revised and extended) became "classics" of the field. The stories are followed by a history of the Munsey pulps, focusing on the featured writer but discussing dozens of others. No index or bibliography.

*2-118. Newcomb, Simon. **His Wisdom, the Defender.** Harper, 1900. Arno, $19.00.

A professor of molecular physics discovers ultimate energy and produces advanced weapons. After defeating European nations, he establishes a government with himself at its head, abolishes war, and outlines a method by which "dependent peoples" may rule themselves. The story is told by future historians of the state he set up.

2-119. Norton, Roy. **The Toll of the Sea.** Appleton, 1909.

A series of terrible earthquakes changes the contour of the Pacific, making re-exploration necessary. Several ships disappear. An American naval vessel discovers a new land; a love story dominates the remainder of the plot.

2-120. Norton, Roy. **The Vanishing Fleets.** Appleton, 1908.

On the eve of a threatened American-Japanese war, the Japanese and British fleets disappear. A flashback reveals that an American scientist has developed an ultimate metal and antigravity. A council of world rulers outlaws war.

2-121. Odle, E. V. (U.K.). **The Clockwork Man.** Heinemann, 1923.

During a cricket game a man-robot that has a clock built into him appears. He apparently comes from the future, a time after man had surrendered his free will and allowed the rulers who had survived the last wars to install the clocks. One senses an attempt at an allegory in which man hopes that God does take him seriously.

2-122. Paine, Albert Bigelow. **The Great White Way.** J. F. Taylor, 1901. Arno, $18.00.

The lost race is a utopian civilization in the Antarctic. The young scientist of an American expedition remains behind to marry the queen of an agrarian culture, whose people have developed telepathy. The novel serves as a vehicle for an attack upon modern materialism.

2-123.   Paine, Albert Bigelow. **The Mystery of Evelin Delorme.** Arena, 1894.
The book imitates Stevenson's *Dr. Jekyll and Mr. Hyde* [2-141], using alter egos as symbols of good and evil. The story is presented as the case study of an experiment in hypnosis which went wrong.

2-124.   Pallen, Condé B. **Crucible Island: A Romance, an Adventure and an Experiment.** The Manhattanville Press, 1919. Gordon Press, $35.00.
The importance of this volume lies in its denunciation of socialism. A young revolutionary is transported for life to the Spielgarten on the island of Schlectland, where by secret agreement among themselves the governments of Europe have allowed exiles to pursue the socialist ideal for the past fifty years. The state is the supreme good; individualism is completely destroyed. The inclusion of a diary permits a change in narrative voice while restating essentially the same arguments. A love story provides the thin narrative line, and eventually the lovers and their companions escape to America.

2-125.   Parry, David MacLean. **The Scarlet Empire.** Bobbs, 1906. Arno, $16.00.
In this lost-race story, Atlantis exists at the bottom of the Atlantic as a glass-domed city. Although attention is given the past glories of Atlantean science, the novel is primarily a vehicle for a bitter attack against socialism.

*2-126.   Pope, Gustavus W. **Journey to Mars.** G. W. Dillingham, 1894. Hyperion, $5.25, $14.50.
This was to be the first in a series of novels involving visits to every planet. Although the conventions of parallel evolution and advanced Martian civilization are introduced, the plot is dominated by the love story of an American naval officer and a Martian princess, so that it must be associated with the tradition of Haggard and Burroughs rather than the older interplanetary voyages. It is perhaps most significant for its introduction, a defense of the scientific romance as a literary genre.

2-127.   Pope, Gustavus W. **Wonderful Adventures on Venus.** Arena, 1895.
In this sequel to *Journey to Mars*, the naval officer and his princess find Venus a younger world, comparable to some stage of Earth's pre-history. The parallel is kept, even to the sinking of an "Atlantean" continent.

*2-128.   Reeve, Arthur Benjamin. **The Poisoned Pen.** Harper, 1911. Books for Libraries, $13.75.
This was the first book publication of the Craig Kennedy stories and nov-

els. The stories first appeared in *Cosmopolitan* beginning in 1910, while the last novels were issued in 1926. Kennedy was the best known of the scientific detectives, and most of his cases turn upon the use of some new gadget, often of his invention. In *The Dream Doctor* (1917), he made use of and explained in detail Freudian theory.

*2-129. Rhodes, William Henry. **Caxton's Book.** A. L. Bancroft, 1876. Hyperion, $3.75, $10.50.
Daniel O'Connell edited this posthumous work, calling Rhodes the potential equal of Verne and acknowledging "scientific fiction" as a distinct genre. The stories themselves emphasize interests held by Poe and Verne, but Rhodes was no mere imitator. The longest and best of the works, "The Case of Summerfield," presents an evil scientist who threatens to destroy the world's oceans if he is not paid a ransom. It was published separately in 1918, after its original newspaper appearance in 1871.

2-130. Robinson, Charles Henry. **Longhead: The Story of the First Fire.** L. C. Page, 1913.
This is the episodic story of a caveman and his mate, moving from the use of fire to the first attempts at social organization, art, and religion. The realization of the importance of marriage is also an essential part of the story.

2-131. Rousseau, Victor (pseud. of Victor Rousseau Emanuel). **The Messiah of the Cylinder.** McClurg, 1917. Hyperion, $3.85, $10.95.
By an experiment inducing suspended animation, the protagonist awakens in a future world dominated by socialism and science. The rulers believe that science has already made a complete revelation to man so that new inquiry is impossible; they worship such men as Darwin, Marx, Mendel, Nietzsche, and Wells. During the protagonist's sleep, legend has made him a kind of messiah who will deliver the world from this domination. He leads a successful revolt.

2-132. Sedberry, James Hamilton. **Under the Flag of the Cross.** C. M. Clark, 1908.
The Caucasian and Asiatic races fight a future war, the battleground being primarily Asiatic Turkey. Against this background two love stories are told. In the more important, a young Virginian saves the life of the daughter of the British commanding general. They fall in love, but the father rejects the suit; he relents only after the protagonist has risen through the ranks to become the commander of the allied armies.

*2-133. Serviss, Garrett Putnam. **A Columbus of Space.** Appleton, 1911. Hyperion, $3.95, $10.95.
A scientist develops atomic power and voyages to Venus. There, against the background of an advanced civilization, he falls in love with the beau-

tiful Queen of Venus. As they are about to be married, they die in a catastrophic fire.

*2-134. Serviss, Garrett Putnam. **Edison's Conquest of Mars.** Carcosa House, 1947.
First serialized in the New York *Evening Journal* in 1898, this was intended as a sequel to Wells' *The War of the Worlds*, which had been published in *Cosmopolitan* in 1897. Although technical detail and explanation are dismissed, the novel becomes a eulogy to the inventiveness of Edison. Except for giantism, evolution on Mars parallels that of Earth.

*2-135. Serviss, Garrett Putnam. **The Moon Metal.** Harper, 1900.
A scientist assumes almost dictatorial powers because he has a monopoly on the metal which replaces gold as a basis for the world's monetary system. Investigation discloses that he has invented a method of drawing the metal from the Moon.

*2-136. Serviss, Garrett Putnam. **The Second Deluge.** McBride, West, 1912. Hyperion, $4.50, $12.50.
When a watery nebula threatens the Earth, a scientist builds an ark and chooses the people who will help to found a new civilization after the catastrophe. A geological phenomenon causes a portion of the Rockies to rise so that others are also saved. The new society is dominated by science. This novel provides perhaps the most fully developed statement of the scientist as actual savior of society.

*2-137. Shaw, George Bernard. (U.K.). **Back to Methuselah: a Metabiological Pentateuch.** Constable, 1921. *The Bodley Head Bernard Shaw* edition of Shaw's plays (London 1970–1974, 7 v.) is the definitive edition. V. 5 (£4.20) contains this play and others, and it is found in *Complete Plays with Prefaces*, v. 2, Dodd, $7.50, and alone, Oxford U.P., $2.95.
Shaw's reputation crested about 1905, yet he lived to write his greatest plays in the three decades after, dying in 1950. This is his longest play, requiring several sessions for a complete performance of its five parts. Part 1 reconstructs the events of Genesis, emphasizing the hopefulness of man for improvement. Part 2 presents a post-World War I speculation on the possibility of longevity by "Creative Evolution." Part 3, in the 22nd century, reveals Bill Haslam at age 283. He and Ms. Lutestring, 274, contemplate marriage. In them and a few others the longevity gene has emerged. Part 4, in 3000 A.D., recounts the death of the "Elderly Gentleman," symbolically the end of the short-lived man. Part 5, set in 31,920 A.D., is titled "As Far as Thought Can Reach," and presents the human species ready to become beings of pure thought. A vehicle for Shaw's theory of Creative Evolution, this bears the brilliant stamp of Shavian satire upon virtually every major human problem. His last play, *Far-fetched Fables* (1950), presents six scenarios of post-World War II civ-

ilization and may be a partial reworking of the themes in *Back to Methuselah*. Compare Stapledon's *Last and First Men*, Lewis's space trilogy, Heinlein's *The Past Through Tomorrow* and Asimov's Foundation trilogy. Contrast Wells' *Time Machine*.

2-138. Shiel, Matthew Phipps. **The Purple Cloud.** Gollancz, 1901. Warner, $.95.
Because he is on an expedition to the pole, the narrator escapes the world-wide catastrophe which wipes out mankind. For seventeen years he wanders alone but finally finds the daughter of a sultan in Constantinople. They will be the new Adam and Eve. For whatever symbolic purposes, the narrator kills most of his companions during the quest for the pole and is extremely brutal to the girl.

2-139. Slee, Richard, and Cornelia Atwood Pratt. **Dr. Berkeley's Discovery.** Putnam, 1899.
A scientist discovers "cerebral localisation" and develops a method of photographing the content of specific memory cells of the brain. When his beautiful wife is found murdered in a hotel (registered as the wife of the accused), he uses the process to prove her innocent of any infidelity. But the experience proves too much for him; he flees to his old tutor and dies without making known the secrets of his discovery.

2-140. Stark, Harriet. **The Bacillus of Beauty.** Stokes, 1900.
A brilliant chemist infects his prize pupil with a bacillus, causing her to become the most beautiful woman in the world. The remainder of the novel becomes an account of her ever-increasing pride, selfishness, and greed. She finally dies, and those who love her lament the effect of her beauty upon her.

*2-141. Stevenson, Robert Louis (U.K.). **Strange Case of Dr. Jekyll and Mr. Hyde.** 1886. (Any complete edition will suffice).
This classic nineteenth-century presentation of a dual personality dramatizes the good and evil within each man. Aware from his youth of a certain wickedness within his nature, Dr. Jekyll experiments and develops a potion which brings that other self into ascendancy, thereby transforming him physically into Hyde. One learns of the mystery through the eyes of the lawyer Utterson, but only a final manuscript, the full statement of Henry Jekyll, explains the relationship between him and his alter ego.

*2-142. Stockton, Frank. **The Great Stone of Sardis.** Harper, 1908.
Against the background of the utopian world of 1947, a scientist invents a kind of X-ray machine permitting him to see the strata of the earth. He burrows through the shell of the earth to find its core, a diamond, while friends make a successful submarine voyage to discover the North Pole. There is an incidental love story.

*2-143. Stockton, Frank. **The Great War Syndicate.** Scribner, 1889. Gregg, $9.00.
Twenty-three American businessmen assume responsibility for the war effort during a future struggle with Britain. They develop an armored vessel and an electric-powered "instantaneous motor," which seems to be a cross between a jet-propelled shell and an atomic bomb. After victory, an Anglo-American alliance is formed to outlaw all war.

2-144. Swayne, Martin (U.K.). **The Blue Germ.** Doran, 1918.
A Russian scientist develops a strain of bacillus that seems to make anything infected with it immortal. He and his English friend release it into the Manchester reservoir; an epidemic—called the "blue disease" because of the accompanying coloration—spreads throughout Britain, causing unforeseen results, including warfare between the young and the old. The protagonists decide that immortality brings with it "the end of disease and the end of desire." The populace falls asleep, and the infection comes to an end.

2-145. Tarde, Gabriel de. **Underground Man.** Duckworth, 1905. Hyperion, $2.95, $9.50.
Published in the same year as Wells' *A Modern Utopia*, this book opens with a portrait of a utopian society. But world catastrophe—the extinction of the sun—forces mankind to burrow deep into the earth to survive. There a society powered by wonderful machines has a chance to develop aesthetically and spiritually. Wells wrote the book's introduction.

2-146. Thomas, Chauncey. **The Crystal Button.** Houghton Mifflin, 1891. Gregg, $15.00.
The protagonist, an engineer, is transported to the utopian forty-seventh century, where science dominates society. There is much praise of the engineering profession as a public service; a technocratic state is preferable because of the efficiency it brings to government.

*2-147. Train, Arthur Cheyney, and Robert Williams Wood. **The Man Who Rocked the Earth.** Doubleday, 1915. Arno, $13.00.
Serialized in *The Saturday Evening Post* in the autumn of 1914, this gives an account of the efforts of a mad scientist to end the stalemated European war. He increases the length of the sidereal day, disintegrates a part of the Atlas Mountains, and threatens to change the poles of the Earth. His weapons and airship use atomic power; the novel seems to contain the first detailed discussion in fiction of atomic power, including radiation sickness. Although an explosion kills him and destroys his base, an American scientist saves his inventions. A conference of nations convenes in Washington to end all war and form a federated, utopian world state.

*2-148. Verne, Jules (France). **Five Weeks in a Balloon (Cinq semaines en balloon).** 1863.

*2-149. Verne, Jules. **A Journey to the Center of the Earth (Voyage au centre de la terre).** 1864.

*2-150. Verne, Jules. **From the Earth to the Moon (De la terre à la lune).** 1865.

*2-151. Verne, Jules. **The Adventures of Captain Hatteras (Les adventures du Capitaine Hatteras).** 1866.

*2-152. Verne, Jules. **All around the Moon (Autour de la lune).** 1870.

*2-153. Verne, Jules. **Twenty Thousand Leagues under the Sea (Vingt milles lieues sous les mers).** 1870.

*2-154. Verne, Jules. **Around the World in Eighty Days (Le tour du monde en quatre-vingts jours).** 1870.

*2-155. Verne, Jules. **The Begum's Fortune (Le cinq cent millions de la Bégum).** 1879.

*2-156. Verne, Jules. **Propeller Island (L'Ile à hélice).** 1895.
Verne adapted the traditional imaginary voyage to his own ends. No longer was the portrait of an unknown society of primary importance, as it had been from Mandeville and More; rather, the voyage itself was the *raison d'etre* of the narrative. Verne's contribution to the emerging science fiction lay in his emphasis upon the new technology—particularly the "hardware" of transportation—and his encyclopedic inclusion of factual information about the settings through which his travellers journeyed. His voyagers usually included a man of reason who both invented the gadgets and supplied the factual information, a man of action, and—often for comic relief—a loyal servant. Unlike Wells, he did not question the concept of progress. His celebration of the new technology for its own sake explains his importance to such later devotees of science fiction as Hugo Gernsback, for it is this affirmation which characterizes much of the so-called "hard core" science fiction.

Les Voyages Extraordinaires were first published by Pierre Hetzel in Paris. The most authoritative modern edition is that issued by Hachette during the 1860s. Unfortunately at present there is no standard edition in English, although one can recommend such individual translations as that of *Twenty Thousand Leagues under the Sea* by Walter James Miller (New York: Washington Square Press, 1966). Frequently the translations into English have not faithfully reflected the original French text. Various reasons may explain this: for example, the very popularity of Verne, which has led to hasty work and reliance upon available translations, and the conversion of the *voyages* into works aimed at a juvenile audience. Hachette is still Verne's official publisher. The Le Livre de Poche French paperbacks are reliable and inexpensive but are going out of print. The English titles vary somewhat from edition to edition. Check *Books in Print* for various editions.

2-157. Wallace, King. **The Next War.** Martyn, 1892.
This is an early novel portraying a future war between blacks and whites in America. It is little more than an hysterical diatribe against the blacks. Under torture and because of the pleading of his beloved, the protagonist–scientist gives the black secret societies the formula for a poison he has developed to kill English sparrows, but he gives them a dilute form so that when they try to use it in conjunction with a revolt, they fail. Like lemmings, the blacks vanish into southern swamps to be seen no more. Compare Corley [4-179] and Greenlee [4-275] for modern and quite different treatments of this theme.

*2-158. Waterloo, Stanley. **Armageddon.** Rand McNally, 1898.
In a future war, America uses a dirigible-type craft to destroy the attacking European navies. Aluminum and electricity are enshrined as the ultimate metal and the ultimate energy. An Anglo-American alliance is established to rule the world until the "lesser breeds" are capable of ruling themselves. This provides one of the most pronounced statements of Anglo-Saxon supremacy of the period.

2-159. Waterloo, Stanley. **A Son of the Ages.** Doubleday, 1914.
By combining ideas on reincarnation and racial memory, the stories trace the protagonist through his various lives—from that of Scar, "The Link" to the Phoenicians, Germanic tribes, and Vikings. One episode dramatizes the sinking of Atlantis.

*2-160. Waterloo, Stanley. **The Story of Ab: A Tale of the Time of the Caveman.** Way and Williams, 1897. Arno, $12.00.
This is apparently the first American pseudo-historical novel of prehistory from which previously dominant religious matters are completely absent. It dramatizes within the lifespan of a single protagonist those inventions and developments which helped man begin his ascent from savagery; the plot became the prototype for later novels.

*2-161. Wells, Herbert George (U.K.). **The Time Machine.** Heinemann. 1895.†

*2-162. Wells, Herbert George. **The Island of Dr. Moreau.** Heinemann. 1896.†

*2-163. Wells, Herbert George. **The Invisible Man.** Pearson, 1897.†

*2-164. Wells, Herbert George. **The War of the Worlds.** Heinemann, 1898.†

*2-165. Wells, Herbert George. **When the Sleeper Wakes.** Harper, 1899.

*2-166. Wells, Herbert, George. **The First Men in the Moon.** George Newnes, 1901.†

*2-167. Wells, Herbert George. **The Food of the Gods.** Macmillan, 1904.†

*2-168. Wells, Herbert George. **A Modern Utopia.** Chapman and Hall, 1905.

*2-169. Wells, Herbert George. **In the Days of the Comet.** Macmillan, 1906.†

*2-170. Wells, Herbert George. **The War in the Air.** G. Bell, 1908.

*2-171. Wells, Herbert George. **The World Set Free.** Macmillan, 1914.

*2-172. Wells, Herbert George. **Men Like Gods.** Cassell, 1923.
Any complete edition is acceptable. *Seven Science Fiction Novels of H. G. Wells* (Dover, $5.00) includes unabridged reprints of the titles followed by a (†), and is a bargain. Dover also reprints *Three Prophetic Novels by H. G. Wells* (*The Time Machine, When the Sleeper Wakes, A Story of the Days to Come*) in a $2.00 paperback, and *Men Like Gods, Star Begotten* and 26 shorter stories in *Twenty-eight Science Fiction Stories of H. G. Wells*, $5.00, hardbound. St. Martin's distributes *The Complete Short Stories*, $12.50, which includes *The Time Machine* and 62 shorter pieces.

The above novels represent the parameters of the canon of H. G. Wells' fiction. They can be divided, by and large, into two groups: early romances written before the turn of the century, and from *A Modern Utopia* (1905) onward, those essentially utopian writings in which he insisted ever more desperately upon the need for social and political reform. By general consensus, at least at the present time, the earlier romances have proved more crucial to the evolution of modern science fiction. Some individuals, like Robert Silverberg, assert that in them Wells laid out the themes explored by contemporary writers. In them Wells dramatized (mythologized) the never-ending flux and change of which modern man is so aware. The constant theme is the precariousness of man's position in a universe of which he knows little and, perhaps, understands less. In terms of his contemporary England, he ceaselessly attacks both the concept of inevitable progress and of man as a final expression of evolution. Yet even in the early works the pessimism is blunted by the hope that man will gain a second chance or that he will live as though this precariousness were not true.

2-173. Wharton, Edith. **Tales of Men and Ghosts.** Scribner, 1910. (The cited stories may be found in other collections as well, such as

Wharton's *Collected Short Stories* [Scribner, 1968].)
Several of the ghost stories, like "The Bolted Door," deal with obsession
or hallucination, but "The Debt" stands unique in the period. It turns
upon the conflict which arises when a young scientist produces a Darwin-
ian-type study which completely replaces the work of his teacher, one of
the great scientists of the period.

*2-174. White, Stewart Edward, and Samuel Hopkins Adams. **The Mystery.** McClure, Phillips, 1907. Arno, $16.00.
The majority of the manuscript is presented as a mystery echoing the
Marie Celeste affair. In the last portion, the narrator reports the scientist–
hero's successful search for the ultimate energy. The book gives one of
the finest portraits of the idealized scientists at the turn of the century.

*2-175. White, Stewart Edward, and Samuel Hopkins Adams. **The Sign
at Six.** Bobbs, 1912.
A "mad" scientist develops a method of cutting off light, sound, and heat
waves. He threatens to use it against the whole of New York—instead of
test spots—but is thwarted by the protagonist, who destroys the machine
and notes because, though brilliant, they represent an area into which
man should not venture.

2-176. Wicks, Mark. **To Mars via the Moon.** Lippincott, 1911. Arno,
$19.00.
The first chapters of the novel read like a textbook in astronomy, but
once Mars has been reached, the work is dominated by mysticism and
portrays a conventional utopia. It is dedicated to Percival Lowell.

*2-177. Zamiatin, Eugene. **We.** Dutton, 1924. $1.95; Viking, $6.95; Bantam, $1.75; Gregg, $13.00.
This is a satirical portrait of the United States of the twenty-sixth century; the nation is fully regimented and works with machine-like precision. There is no room for individuality. The narrative frame is provided by the journals of a protagonist who is helping to build a rocket
ship to carry news of the state's perfection to other worlds; by this device
one sees the conflict arise within the protagonist as he falls in love and
begins to realize his humanity. But a revolt fails, and he permits the state
to operate on his brain so that he can never again deviate from the ap-
proved norm. An attack upon Soviet Russia, it has never been published
there.

3.
The Gernsback Era, 1926·1937

Ivor A. Rogers

The period from 1926, when Hugo Gernsback founded *Amazing Stories*, to 1937, when John Campbell became editor of *Astounding*, saw the growth of science fiction from the traditions of the scientific romance, especially in the earliest pulps, to more modern themes and techniques. This was also the heyday of the general fiction magazines and the specialist pulp magazines as well as a period of popular fiction published in book form. The movies and radio still appealed mostly to nonreaders. Modes of transportation and life styles encouraged the consumption of light reading: detective novels, scientific, sentimental, and historical romances, and almost every other form of escape literature.

Only by reading widely in this period can one realize the extent of this literature. Because of its very bulk, few critical writers on the period are wholly reliable. Sam Moskowitz [6-65] and Donald Wollheim [6-98] have the advantage of having lived through the era and give the picture as they saw it. But neither is trained in literary analysis, and much that occurred in the wider world of literature escaped their view.

Writers trained in literary techniques are seldom better. J. O. Bailey's *Pilgrims through Space and Time* [6-9] does not emphasize the pulps and popular fiction of this period, and Brian Aldiss's *Billion Year Spree* [6-2], weakest in this particular era, is filled with aberrant interpretations and misstatements of fact. Sam Lundwall's *SF: What It's All About* [6-60] is weak on European science fiction, just where one would expect the best information, and his judgments for this period are sometimes questionable. Some shorter and specialized studies are excellent, but they have a tendency to see with tunnel vision and leave large holes. The annotations for books in this period are intended to reflect the best that was printed as well as to give representative samples of the wide variety of work available, but much has necessarily been omitted.

No matter who writes about SF, he is compelled to come to grips with what it is. The average SF reader knows what he is reading when he reads it, but what was science for H. G. Wells or Mary Shelley is fantasy today. I prefer an eclectic approach, sticking closely to a definition that came out of a class taught by Dr. Barton Hacker at Iowa State University: "Science fiction is the fantasy of an era of technological change." This might eliminate Aristophanes' *The Birds* (one of the earliest utopias), Lucian's, *Le Pélerinage de Charlemagne*, and other works before Kepler's *Somnium* [1-22], but a historian might also observe that the widespread social stresses in Athens during the Peloponnesian War and in Europe during the high middle ages were at least partly due to technological change.

Imaginary voyages, future wars, prehistoric or alternate world tales have all been published in the SF specialty magazines, and many readers consider them science fiction. Lost race, hollow Earth, astral mind projection, and "dream" stories have all been considered SF by some writers, although their relationship to science is very tenuous. Most stories that appeared under the editorship of such "hard science" proponents such as Hugo Gernsback and John W. Campbell, Jr., are actually technological fiction rather than science fiction. Tom Godwin's much-anthologized "The Cold Equations" (1954) shows not really science but technology impinging on human concerns. The science in the story is engineer's mathematics, not pure science. The pure mathematics of J. W. Dunne's *An Experiment with Time* (1936) is the basis for several plays and novels by J. B. Priestley that involve prescient dreams, alternate futures, clairvoyance, and much that is considered fantasy. (See my article, "The Time Plays of J. B. Priestley," *Extrapolation*, 10 [December 1968], 9–16.)

Science fiction is more of a process or an attitude than a genre. I can think of no definition better than this: science fiction is a state of mind in the reader and a rationally explained or coherent fantasy in an age of technological change. In addition, the categories of Bailey in his cited study are useful and are used in this section.

It is traditional to call the period from 1926 to 1937 the Gernsback era, because Hugo Gernsback founded *Amazing Stories* in 1926, and John Campbell started to come into his own as editor of *Astounding* in 1938, thus signaling the beginning of a new era. Some commentators speak of the pulp science fiction "ghetto" as stemming from these years or speak of the specialty SF pulps as the sole or major force in SF during this era. This view is erroneous in several respects.

First, if there ever was a pulp ghetto, the publication of *Amazing Stories* was the final brick in the ghetto wall, not the foundation stone. Science fiction and the scientific romance had been published in pulp magazines for decades before *Amazing Stories*, and even long before Gernsback started editing. Among Sam Moskowitz's other virtues, we must credit him for tracing the development of the scientific romance in the Munsey magazines from 1912 to 1920 (see *Under the Moons of Mars* [2-117]). Thomas Clareson takes the roots of popular SF back to before the turn of the century (*A Spectrum of Worlds* [4-663]), and readers of Robert D. Mayo's *The English Novel in the Magazines, 1740–1815* (1962) will discover that 238 periodicals printed long prose fiction in England alone. This list of 1,375 novels and novelettes includes utopias, gothic romances, fantasies, and other predecessors of modern science fiction. It should also be noted that novels like *Rasselas* and *Robinson Crusoe* were reprinted, in abridged or excerpted form, almost as soon as the original book appeared. Fiction written specifically for these magazines soon appeared. It was as badly written as pulp fiction, and while writers from Smollett to Dickens were to write for the popular magazines, most of their writing, like that of their pulp descendents, was of very poor quality. Given this pedigree, it is surprising to see so much made of the first appearance of *Amazing Stories*. The pulp tradition was a long if not an honorable one.

Amazing was the first of many pulps devoted primarily to SF, but the earlier issues included many reprints of Verne and Wells. Many of the stories printed were SF by courtesy only, and many stories appearing in other, nonspecialized magazines were similar to the stories printed by Gernsback or were out-and-out SF. Paging through Tony Goodstone's *The Pulps* (1970), one can see the extent of science fiction from the cover art alone.

Air war pulps often featured a future war story, notably *Terence X. O'Learny's War Birds; Dusty Ayres and his Battle Birds; Bill Barnes, Air Adventurer*, and *Dare-Devil Aces*. Even the pulps devoted to recapping the air battles of World War I had occasional fantasies and, later, future air war stories. *G-8 and His Battle Aces* regularly featured advanced technology when "The Hun" invented bacteriological or psychological warfare, or even a monstrous armored fort that chewed its way through Allied lines, leaving neat cartons of ersatz "tinned beef" behind.

Scientific and occult crime fighters like *The Shadow, The Spider, Operator 5*, and especially *Doc Savage* [3-48] often contained extensive fictional elements. Unhappily, there is no way to obtain much of this material today, and practically no scholarly work has been done on the pulps

(Goodstone's book is a sketchy outline at best, omitting more than it includes).

Even the historical pulps had technical features and data that were as strange as SF to the average reader in the 1920s and 1930s. In the urban and rural enclaves of the pre-World War II United States, the only "real" exposure to the outside world, especially for pre-teen and teenage youth, was through fiction, movies, and radio. These media were the sugar-coated pills of experience. Through them you learned how to cope with the future shock of technological change, how to adapt to your social environment—fiction was the key to living.

If science fiction existed long before the advent of *Amazing*, and if more SF existed outside the specialty magazines than in them, what was so special about the SF pulps? Part of the answer lies in the fact that SF fans felt that they had magazines which were peculiarly their own. Fans—short for fanatics—took to the SF pulps more than to any other type of pulp. Partly this was a deliberate strategy encouraged by Gernsback and other editors to increase sales, but the letters to the editor column, a feature in many pulps, took on a special tone in SF magazines.

Well before the first "world" SF convention took place in 1939, SF fans were more organized and serious about their specialty than other pulp readers. Air war pulp fans might write that "You can't *do* an Immelman like that," or "Despite your story, the Fokker triplane was not introduced on the Western front until. . . ." Railroad pulp fans would write about niggling errors in terminology or practice. Science fiction fan letters were different. There were many of the "I am ten years old and have been reading your mag for two years, and I think that the September ish was the greatest thing ever published . . ." sort of letter, but some serious correspondence was also printed, amateur publications were started, and intense fan activity led to the phrase, "fandom is a way of life." This was atypical behavior for most pulp readers but the norm for SF readers.

Fandom and fanzines and the later SF conventions were so important that practically every critic who read the early SF pulps has commented on it. Wertham, in his book on fanzines [9-92], not only gives incorrect definitions of the jargon but omits the most typical fan activities and, in his concern with violence, does not even see the endemic paranoia that was the dominant theme of SF fandom. Sam Moskowitz's *The Immortal Storm* (1954) is a far better picture of fandom if one already knows that this is a personal and limited version, disputed by almost everyone else as to interpretation, and that the "press battles" of which he writes so well were carried out in fanzines limited to a few dozen to a few hundred copies. Even though the cast of characters was small, the influence was great. One can see the genesis of much that has influenced modern SF by reading the fan letters and publications of the era. It is interesting to see the immature James Blish sharpening his critical insights in the early 1930s' *Astounding*, or the furor that greeted Don Wollheim's first editorship (he was formerly editor of the Ace SF paperback line and is now editor of his own DAW books). Warner's *All Our Yesterdays* [6-94] usefully supplements the Moskowitz account for the 1940s.

Most fan writers stress the importance of fandom in the development of SF, while most critical and scholarly writers are unqualified to judge. It is hard to overstress this influence on the editors and writers who came up through fandom, but fandom constitutes a miniscule percentage of SF readers (see figures cited in the guide's general introduction). Some writers have picked up a reverence for Gernsback as the "Father of Science Fiction" from the fans and fan-oriented writers without checking to see whether the title was deserved. The influence was there, but it was hardly enough to explain all the results.

Not all the influence was benign. Other writers have commented upon the devastating effect fandom had on certain authors, and its effects can still be felt. Gernsback and later editors wanted fast-action, pseudo-scientific stories that read easily, could be broken into suitable chunks for serialization, and could be shortened or stretched to fit into their magazine format. There are numerous tales of writers being called to editorial offices, given a title, shown the cover art, and asked for 10,000 words by next Tuesday. Charles Dickens could write well under such circumstances, but few others have been able to match his accomplishment. One need look no further than early assembly-line Ellison and Silverberg or the later *Star Trek* Blish to see this particular influence at work today.

Writing in the pulps was often puerile, prolix, awkward, hurried, and hackneyed, but some of it had a raw vigor and power that was exciting if somewhat routine and repetitious. Lester Dent [3-48] in the *Doc Savage* magazine was very good, as were a few of the SF writers, especially Jack Williamson and Campbell himself. There were also some fine second-class writers, such as Abraham Merritt and Stanley Weinbaum who wrote for the SF magazines, but the writing there was usually worse than in the other types of popular fiction.

During the first quarter of the twentieth century, romantic sentimentality lingered on in mainstream literature. Novels, stories, and plays for general consumption reflected an anemic romanticism, to which realism and naturalism acted as refreshing antidotes. But the latter modes of writing are often dull for many readers, and many readers were alienated by the newer realism. The form-over-content avant-garde crowd held temporary sway and fragmented into dozens of "isms." It was a period not so much of art for art's sake as obscurity for obscurity's sake.

Much of the product of the avant-garde was exciting, vital, and imaginative, but it was too often obscure, thus alienating readers. Much that had been written before had been obscure and difficult to understand, but it was so because of the difficulty of the material presented, not because the author was deliberately obscure or was writing for a coterie. Few people other than the literary "in" crowd read what was being written, and like similar movements in art and music, they tended to repel more readers than they attracted.

If realistic techniques put the reader to sleep and the avant-garde put him in a daze, what did appeal to the reader? Not much except light fiction and genre fiction. Master writers such as Dashiell Hammett and Dorothy Sayers were writing distinguished work in the detective field, although it might be fair to characterize Hammett as a pulp writer making realism work as a myth, and Sayers as a detective writer remaking the genre into a novel of manners. They, and others like them, were the best writers of quality popular literature that the period could produce.

Despite the death of the more popular writers or the failure to continue their mythmaking, more fiction that could be classified as scientific romance was written during the second quarter of the century than was written in earlier periods. This was an era of change from earlier scientific romance to the modern SF of the 1940s and 1950s. With the best writers working in other genres, alienating their audiences with formalistic experimentation, or working the mainstream of the realistic novel, few competent writers were producing anything resembling science fiction.

The impact of realistic and naturalistic writing was particularly severe in the United States. In the nineteenth century, almost every major writer had included utopias, imaginary voyages, and scientific romances as part of his stock in trade. Realism, except in one special instance, is particularly antagonistic to the nonrealistic framework of the proto-science fiction story. Also, fantasies and the scientific romance were anathema to the newer breed of naturalistic writers. In Sinclair's *The Jungle*, there was no time for speculation about the future, and Lenny in *Of Mice and Men* was incapable of imagining anything except rabbits in his utopia.

Ironically, the special instance where realism did influence the fiction of the 1920s and 1930s was in the genre we no longer consider science fiction. Peter Penzoldt, in his *The Supernatural in Fiction* [6-73], devotes an entire chapter to the metempsychosis of the supernatural story into SF. His thesis is that in modern fiction (post-realism), any supernatural theme is changed into a scientific or pseudo-scientific story. The traditional magician is the modern chemist or biologist, the vampire is scientifically explained, and apparitions are explained by psychology. His book is strongly oriented toward classic Freudian and Jungian analysis, and his most startling observation is that the traditional ghost story has been most affected by the science of psychiatry. He points out that there are stories which can only be explained by recourse to the supernatural, but they are minor and appear mostly in the more traditional forms by English authors. Thus, any story with a basis in anthropology, neurotic imaginations, or "scientific" explanations of traditional supernatural subject matter, is science fiction. He is almost alone in the extreme position he has taken, listing as SF stories that most critics would dismiss as fantasy, but his training and arguments are persuasive.

Writers found themselves in a curious situation because of the growth of the specialist SF pulps: there was an outlet for the older scientific romance in the pulp magazines, the masters of the older styles were no longer writing, and mainstream literature was concerned with either the realistic novel or experimentation. The new writers either had to conform to the restrictions and limitations of the pulps or try to sell their work in a market that was vitiated by a loss of readers. Major critics slighted their works. They were reviewed, when they were able to get published, but reviewed as genre fiction, as a second-class type of writing. Much was written but little was noted or long remembered.

It is not surprising that so little really memorable SF was written during this period. Stapledon, Huxley, and Tolkien are almost the only major authors whom we immediately think of, and Tolkien had written only a juvenile. There were other writers of power and technical skill who wrote single novels or a limited number of pieces, but it has been a major job to rehabilitate them. One immediately wonders why Charles G. Finney had such a limited output, or why such a brilliant novel as E. C. Large's *Sugar in the Air* [3-33] did not receive more attention when it was published or why it is not on every college reading list. Even more surprising is the failure of modern critics to recognize Vincent McHugh's two excellent novels, *Caleb Catlum's America* [3-38] and *I Am Thinking of My Darling* [4-400]. Even Robert Heinlein's act of homage in writing *Time Enough for Love* [4-303] as an outer-space version of *Caleb Catlum* stirred little critical notice of the earlier and better work.

One of the most abused phrases in fan jargon is "sense of wonder." It is used to lament the good old days when everything was better, finer, and more exciting. It is also used to cover up the fact that no one has ever come up with a good explanation of why much SF, written so badly that it can scarcely claim to be literate, is still entertaining, if no more than that. It applies with special meaning to the SF published in the early 1930s. What appeared in pulp magazines and hard cover alike was often incredibly bad by modern standards. John Campbell wrote one of the most acid comments ever penned about Skylark of Space and the Hawk Carse stories in his "Editorial Number Three" (quoted in *A Requiem for Astounding* [6-77]). He thought that the science was poor and the writing equally bad. (His own space operas were a little better, but not as well liked by the readers.) Quality and sense of wonder had nothing in common.

Sense of wonder is composed of several elements, all acting in different ways at different times on different people. There are aspects of archetypal themes and characters, and there is an unconscious use of other psychological mechanisms, especially in escape from reality and wish fulfillment. SF is a subgenre of fantasy however you define it, and one would expect to find a large area of equivalence between normal wish fulfillment fantasy and the plot outlines of SF novels and stories. Robert Plank is the only critic to address himself to this problem to any extent (see his *The Emotional Significance of Imaginary Beings*, 1968). Most critics and scholars have not yet explored these areas of apparent equivalence.

It is impossible to do more than suggest a few themes and plot elements that evoke common fantasies. Repressed sexual drives contribute to a great many plot twists and devices for two reasons: first, because *no* sex of any kind was allowed in the pages of the SF pulps, and second, because the readership was predominantly teen-age males, most of them sufficiently introverted to have problems expressing their sexual drives. This partly explains the frequent device of buried cities, caves in the earth, and secret caverns. In classic Freudian analysis these symbols usually represent repressed sexuality, but because there is a leakage of the repression, these symbols become charged with emotional overtones for most readers. The reader remembers these images with special pleasure and searches for further examples of them in books. Perhaps the most inspired use of the cave image was in Herbert Read's *The Green Child* [3-46]. Films, such as the early Tarzan films, also incorporated muted sexual feelings.

Usually the women (girls in name but not in age) involved in the action of a space opera are sufficiently androgynous to pass for men in the close confines of a space ship, but female enough to arouse the male instinct of protection. The woman clad in diaphanous scarves and a brass bra, in the clutches of a bug-eyed monster (BEM) or other hideous extraterrestrial, was a cliché of the cover art of the period. Everyone knew what the monster had on his mind, the main question being not what but how.

One of the few examples of fiction where one felt that the male might break down and express his suppressed drives is E. E. Smith's *Spacehounds of IPC* [3-53]. Protected from all eyes by the fragment of a destroyed spaceship, the "boy" and the "girl" live out a sylvan interlude in a small cave in a hidden valley. Their clothes are beginning to disintegrate under the demands of rural life, and the two have been living together secluded but celibate. One day after the noon meal Steve, the hero, lies on the grass, apparently under some strain—the author uses the word "rigid." The heroine, Nadia, proposes that if they are unable to get off the world on which they are marooned, they have a marriage "before God" and continue the race. *She* must do the proposing; he still calls her his "little fellow." They embrace, he disengages himself, and he pulls out his last cigarette! There is a temptation to call the scene a parody of the entire genre, but too many readers have taken Smith's books as gospel for us to deny the unconscious sexual material in this scene *for the reader*, no matter what Smith's intention was.

Oedipal fantasies play a major role in SF. A continual theme of many stories might be expressed as "showing daddy how strong I am." There is often an older man whose daughter is attracted to a younger man who lacks the father's knowledge, position, or experience. Nevertheless, he is the one who stops the strange ball of force or the long-tentacled horror that is about to devour Cleveland. He shows up the older man and gets the woman/girl/mother. This is a common element in most popular fiction, but there is a heavy emphasis on this type of plot in the Gernsback era.

Campbell sums up the whole problem of sense of wonder by caustically remarking that everyone was younger then and taste buds worked better and everything was new and fresh, but the element of repressed sexuality in the SF stories also left strong impressions on the juvenile mind. Burroughs and E. E. Smith still sell today, and the Robert E. Howard books have been reprinted in many editions, from comics to books. Conan, the major character created by Howard (see annotation 3-25), is a stock symbol of immature sexual fantasies.

There is another element to the sense of wonder, one to which we should perhaps pay most attention. SF is, after all, a literature of ideas, particularly since Wells. This is the hardest thing to explain to the scholarly critic, because literature, particularly Good Literature, has always been a medium of ideas. The "ideas" expressed in pulp fiction were usually puerile at best and were often mere action plotting and sentimentality disguised as ideas. SF had a few statements to make: mankind will leave this planet by physical means; the creation of life is not the sole prerogative of God; there is other intelligence in the universe.

Although these were not the only ideas SF had to present, they were the major ones, and they were not new. SF did not make up all those "crazy ideas" out of whole cloth; they were the product of a whole tradition in science. SF took the ideas of a Rutherford, a Mendel, a Freud, a Darwin, or an Einstein and made them into popular literature. Other writers had done something similar before: Tennyson owed much to Lyell's *Principles of Geology*, Chambers' *Vestiges of Creation*, and Darwin's *Origin of Species*, but he did not espouse their theories in his poetry, create new forms to more appropriately call attention to their existence, or envisage a life in which these beliefs could make a new social order. Tennyson, like most writers of the later nineteenth century, wrote in opposition to these ideas or at best found no solace in them. There were writers who did write in the joy of new scientific theories, but they either lacked skill to write anything other than arid polemics, or their work was ignored. Nikolai Chernyshevsky wrote an immensely popular novel, *What Is to Be Done*, in 1862, but it was not published for almost forty-five years and created little impact outside Russia. What he did in the middle of the nineteenth century (see Darko Suvin's preface to *Other Worlds, Other Seas* [4-698]) was what the SF writers of the 1920s were to do: use scientific ideas, favorably presented, as the focus for an entire body of literature.

Wells had done it, as had other writers, but they tended to be isolated islands in a sea of romantic pessimism and naturalistic despair. Starting in the second quarter of the twentieth century, an entire body of fiction was to develop that denied the earlier theses of romanticism and naturalism.

One must also realize that the ideas which created a sense of wonder in the SF reader during the Gernsback era were at second or third removed from the original. By the time they reached the corner newsstand, they had a markedly shopworn air. In 1974, Samuel Delany was able to take classic SF concepts, a red sun and a blue sun, and transmute them with and by the philosophy of Ludwig Wittgenstein to create *Dhalgren* [4-199]. In 1926, the concept of a blue sun, in and of itself, would have been sufficient to create a sense of wonder; the simplest ideas did so, but complex ideas generated rejection slips.

The exceptions to these generalities were great writers who had an immense influence on their generation and who eventually had great popular success. Three of them in particular—Stapledon, Huxley, and Tolkien—will be discussed later. Still, the main thrust of this period was the popularization of scientific ideas and a technological ambience in the mass audience. Young and unsophisticated readers, whose prior reading experience was (at best) some ill-taught Tennyson, Shakespeare, Longfellow, and Sir Walter Scott, felt as if the Sun had gone nova in their brains. For many individuals SF was a whole brave new world of ideas, more a state of ecstasy than a sense of wonder.

The Gernsback era was primarily a transitional period between the older scientific romance and a newer style of SF culminating in the 1940s and 1950s. What happened in the pulps shaped the new SF, but this may be attributed partly to the dying of the older forms. Again we must return to realism, which led to forms of writing which clashed with the old subject matter and plots. Realism and naturalism may exist without a realistic or naturalistic style of writing, although there is a tendency for style to follow form. Perhaps the greatest triumph in the Campbell era was the development of fairly realistic writing styles for nonrealistic plots and subject matter. Asimov's grainy, grey style of prose is simply inelegant. It is very efficient for the type of pseudo-scientific story that he was writing, as it gave one the solid feel of reporting or lucid technical writing. When one attempts to read aloud Asimov, Heinlein, Clarke, and the other giants of the Campbell era, the flat, bald narrative style becomes immediately apparent.

The mannerisms and circumlocutions of Haggard or Burroughs were stylistically no better than the style of Asimov or Clarke, but they suited the complex plotting and more fantastic subjects of *She* or *Chessmen of Mars* very well. This older style was unsuited to the newer fiction appearing in the pulps. Even Campbell at his space opera worst had a better sense of dialogue than most of the practitioners of pulp fiction, and by the time he wrote "Who Goes There?" he had mastered the more straightforward forms that others were to develop later. It does no good to attack Campbell or Asimov on the grounds that their style was poor or that the characters were two-dimensional. Their style was efficient, which was more important, and they were writing about characters who would function in their plots as nicely shaped cardboard cutouts. The characters of *Vanity Fair* are hardly three-dimensional, but they are memorable and serve the purpose of the author.

While the change to more realistic dialogue and writing styles was occurring, the subject matter was also changing. Following the categories in Bailey's *Pilgrims through Space and Time* [6-9], we notice a greater emphasis on the story of the wonderful machine or the wonderful invention and the wondrous journey. Lost race novels still appeared frequently, but far less often as scientific romance than as a minor type of light fiction. I. F. Clarke noted the change in future war stories brought about by World War I in *Voices Prophesying War* [6-25]. This period was to continue the tendency toward pacificism in Earth settings but was to become incredibly bloody off this planet. The gothic romance continued its decline despite several pulps devoted almost exclusively to the field and the presence of one of the greatest gothic horror writers of modern times, H. P. Lovecraft. With the advent of the Oxford Christian group of writers (Williams, Tolkien, Lewis, et al.), new excursions were made into the realms of Fäerie in a way that would create a new genre in the 1950s.

When reading the pulps of the Gernsback era, one is struck by the large number of great invention or discovery stories. This is partially due to Gernsback's championing of "practical" science or technology. Long before C. P. Snow discovered the "two cultures" of science and literature, Gernsback was trying to effect a detente, but his science was more technology than science. This led to plots based on ingenious devices assembled in basements and attics. There was a surprising twist:

Gernsback was a self-taught radio expert and enthusiast, but a large body of fiction owed more to the biological sciences than to the physical sciences.

There are several reasons for this. Warfare and the preparation for warfare had been the stimulus for a great many of the wonderful invention stories, not only in the future war stories, but even as far back as Verne's *20,000 Leagues under the Sea*. The *Nautilus* was an engine of war as much as a wonderful invention—motivated as much by the crushing defeat of the Franco-Prussian War as by an interest in technology. Clarke points out that after the holocaust of the Western front during World War I, future war stories laid less emphasis on the glories of defeating the enemy than on the absolute horrors of the next war. Audiences would not accept gratuitous slaughter simply to show the cleverness of some inventor, but a wonderful machine isn't very wonderful if it simply sits and blinks lights.

There must be conflict, and the wondrous invention must therefore either leave the Earth to destroy ugly extraterrestrials, or the writer must find a different menace. If the product of the laboratory is a biological creation rather than a metallic device, as in Shelley's *Frankenstein*, it can provide a suitably horrifying thrill for the reader and meet a suitably horrible end. Blobs, masses, and fungoidal monstrosities as tall as skyscrapers may be bombed, rayed, electrocuted, or shot off into the Sun because they don't look human, but are human creations, and thus lack an immortal soul.

If one classes spaceships as machines, the second change was the amalgamation of the machine theme with the wondrous voyage theme. This was necessitated by the shrinking of the globe, especially the portions marked "unknown." After the flight of Admiral Byrd over the South Pole, practically the only *terra incognita* left was extraterrestrial. Stories of astral projection and other nonphysical means of leaving the Earth were becoming fantasy rather than SF as the researches of Goddard and Tsiolkovsky promised an eventual physical means for escaping Earth. Once the audience was conditioned to accept a flight to the Moon, Venus, or Mars by spaceship, the entire range of the solar system, from Mercury to the newly discovered Pluto, was available to the writer. Extrapolating further, the writer could suppose the existence of worlds in other solar systems, and who knows what might be found there.

Einstein's theories were percolating down to the level of the pulp reader, opening up other dimensions, time sequences, microcosmic and macrocosmic universes, and other galaxies for the pulp writer. The imaginary voyage could lead to other times and other universes as well as to other places, and the voyage itself was often a sidelight to the fast action encountered by the scientists and technicians en route. There was so much involved in a typical plot of this era that it is difficult to determine whether a story was primarily one of a machine, a voyage, or a meeting with strange beings whose heads grew under their arms.

Typical is E. E. Smith's space opera. The Skylark series [3-52] covered whole galactic clusters in a single bound, while fleets of spaceships destroyed entire solar systems (galactic clusters in later imitations). A more restrained story is Smith's *Spacehounds of IPC* [3-53], which begins with a simple trip to one of the inner planets. Attacked by a strange spaceship and towed to the orbit of Jupiter, the hero and heroine land on Ganymede, a Jovian moon, meet no less than three new sentient races on Jupiter and one of Saturn's moons, catch a ride on a comet, fall in love, rescue survivors of the attacked spaceship, fight three interplanetary wars, and help invent at least a dozen new machines. We also get a glimpse of two other sentient races on Mars and Venus. It is no wonder that this might instill a sense of wonder in the reader, despite some of the worst pulp prose ever to see print. Campbell's *The Mightiest Machine* [3-7] starts with an invention, but it progresses through the same complex intertwining of extra-solar travel, future war, extraterrestrial races, and a multitude of new inventions.

It cannot be overstressed that these are tales of pseudo-science. Despite Einstein and well-known laws about mass and velocity, it is not unusual to see space vehicles flit about from planet to planet on fifty gallons of mass or a small ribbon of "atomic tape." Campbell, Smith, and the better writers either followed known limitations or used a convincing pseudo-scientific doubletalk to evade them, but the poorer writers simply accepted them as conventions of the genre and ignored every known law of physical science. By the 1940s, writers with a little better scientific education or better imaginations were able to have fun with the clichés of the Gernsback era, but the majority of the writing was comic-book level or worse. (It must be remembered that the creators of the comic *Superman* had a rational scientific explanation for the powers of their hero, and that the worst offender, *Buck Rogers*, was based on a solid piece of scientific romance [3-44]).

The other major change in the future war stories was the increasing use of strife between sexes or economic classes as thematic material. The writers who wrote to bring about change in the army regulations or order of battle in the navy began to write less fiction and more nonfiction. The writers who wrote for a living wrote about outer space. Writers oriented toward the social sciences took the place of the military man turned writer. To bring about the millenium of pie in the sky, social critics used the future war as part of their cautionary tales. In this category we find books like Nathan Fialke's *The New City* [3-18], *Intrigue on the Upper Level* by Hoyne [3-26], and Johnson's *The Coming of The Amazons* [3-28]. Jingoists, racists, and other less savory types write occasional future wars for profit or propaganda. The "yellow peril" or some other form of racist fears was usually at the bottom of these novels. The best-written was Gibbons' *The Red Napolean* [3-21]. Gibbons played on every neurotic fear that he could and even used a first-person narrator in the persona of Floyd Gibbons to enhance verisimilitude.

As the depression deepened in the 1930s, this type of story became rarer and more subdued. There was little left to warn the general reading population about: there were coups in Germany, China, and Spain and civil strife in America and Europe. These amply demonstrated what discontented or power-mad classes or groups could do given proper leadership and weapons. Again the thrust was toward the galacticalization of the future war story or the cautionary tale of doomsday. There was even a fair number of atomic armageddons and atomic future war stories printed in the pulps during the later 1930s, but at the time, nuclear and thermonuclear reactions seemed much less likely than the conquest of space. Even in the pulps, air bombardment and gas were usually the ultimate horrors.

No future war stories during the Gernsback era were as well written and as popular as Ernest Childers' *The Riddle of the Sands* (1903). Part of the reason why audiences were turning away from the genre to interstellar conflicts may be seen in the history of the author. Childers was to renounce the use of the future war story as a means of preparedness—if one prepares for war, war will come. Childers wrote his book after serving in the Boer War and before his service in World War I. But he died in a conflict that was representative of the new social and class-oriented struggles. Executed during the Irish Revolution, he ended a life spent in preparing for and fighting wars of imperialist aggression in a conflict that was sectarian and nationalistic.

The changing attitude toward the supernatural has already been mentioned, but as it became more and more difficult to get an easy suspension of disbelief for supernatural and ghost stories, there was no way left for readers to exercise their need for an occasional shiver. On the Continent, German writers such as Hans Ewers [3-16] continued to write *Schauerromane* in the old tradition of magic as well as in the new tradition of the scientist's laboratory. Thea von Harbou [3-23] also was to work between these two poles in her writing career. The strong mystical quality of her work was best brought out by the Fritz Lang production of *Metropolis*. The workshop of Rotwang is straight out of a medieval alchemist's dungeon, while the factory workers are no more than *Maschinenmenshen*, and even Rotwang has an artificial hand. The false Maria and the soulless Alraune of *Metropolis* are conceived and created equally of the laboratory and the magician's spell.

In England there was always a large body of readers content to read about fairies at the bottom of the garden and things that go bump in the night. As Penzoldt [6-73] suggests in his book, the new rationalism was eroding the base for straight tales of the supernatural while increasing the number of stories with rational or pseudoscientific elements. The English reader has never felt as uncomfortable with fantasy as the American, so it was possible for major writers such as Huxley, and Orwell a few years later, to write fantasy in a realistic style.

There is another solution to the dilemma faced by a writer of non-realistic subject matter in an era of realism. J. R. R. Tolkien suggested the way in two critical articles, one of which, "Beowulf: The Monster and the Critics," was to turn medieval scholarship on its head. He suggested that the monsters of *Beowulf* were the central theme of the work and not peripheral nonsense to be scanted with an embarrassed apology for our superstitious ancestors. In his later critical study, "On Fairy Stories," he was to suggest the importance of a complete and unified secondary world for tales of Fäerie. (Note the distinction he makes between fairy tales and tales of Fäerie.)

The secondary world, or secondary universe as I have used the term, partakes of all the elements of a created mythology in which the natural laws of the universe, *as we know it*, are changed. This secondary universe may be based on mathematics, as in Abbott's *Flatland* [2-1], or on the mathematical constructs of J. W. Dunne (see above).

This mythos may also be based on a universe in which the images and objects of Christianity exist literally. Charles Williams writes of a universe—our own as it happens—in which the Holy Grail was brought to England by Joseph of Arimathea and is still to be found in a small country church. C. S. Lewis can write of a universe in which Earth is the home of "the Bent One" and Venus and Mars are capable of supporting human life. Tolkien can write of Middle Earth (an Old English phrase meaning *this* earth), in which elves, dragons, dwarfs, orcs, and magic exist, although in an age of post-Atlantean prehistory. To many this seems to be the merest fantasy, but the element of mythic creation (Tolkien would insist on the phrase "sub-creation," as only God can create) is, I believe, sufficiently strong to place Middle Earth, Thulcandra, and Narnia in the same category as Opar, Barsoom, and the lost city of *She*.

Within this framework of speculative fabulation we can find many works that are difficult to explain otherwise. Outside the group of Oxford Christians, there are only isolated instances of novels so well written that they create a myth in terms of their own secondary universe. *Lost Horizon* [3-24] is a good example of this mythic creation. Ostensibly just another lost race or lost city novel, it generated its own believability and scientific plausibility. *The Green Child* [3-46], James Branch Cabell's multi-volume history of Dom Manuel, White's *The Once and Future King* (1967), and Richard Adams' *Watership Down* (1974) and *Shardik* (1975) are other examples.

The gothic romance and weird or horror story did not prosper as much as other genres during the Gernsback era, but the greatest modern practitioner did his best writing during this period. Although H. P. Lovecraft wrote short stories and verse as a teen-ager, he was not published until 1916, and did not publish in a regular paying market until 1923, when his work began to appear in *Weird Tales*, a gothic/horror pulp. His writing is repetitious and redundant, and he has a passion for unnamed and unmentionable horrors, usually signs of bad writing. However, there is a strangely compelling fascination to his writing that has lasted over several generations. His enthusiasts have an intense devotion that is almost cultish, and there are numerous biographies and appreciations written about him, as well as numerous paperback reprints of his works.

The two titles annotated [3-35, 3-36] are indisputably science fiction with overtones of the horror or weird tale, but much else that he wrote is clearly over the line into fantasy. Much of his writing is part of what has come to be called the Cthulhu Mythos, a rather diffuse secondary universe that grew more by accretion than by design. Robert E. Howard, Robert Bloch, August Derleth, Clark Ashton Smith, Frank Belknap Long, and others were to contribute ideas to the mythos.

Despite the cultish aspects of Lovecraft's followers, the man was a neurotic genius who produced several viable works of fiction and influenced many writers and readers. If one can get beyond the repetition and purple writing, the stories themselves are fascinating. James Branch Cabell was a far better writer, but his use of ironic realism in the Dom Manuel volumes does not have the enrapturing quality of Lovecraft's turgid nineteenth-century prose. As in the case of Robert E. Howard, Burroughs, or Haggard, the myth transcends the writing. In Cabell, one is continually being pulled back into our real world by the ironic commentary and deliberate anachronisms. In Lovecraft and Howard, one is lost in the secondary universe.

The works of these writers have created devoted followers. We see it today in the huge Star Trek fan groups, the Tolkien enthusiasts, and even in a writer such as Philip José Farmer, who has written entire volumes on the "real" Tarzan and Doc Savage. It starts with the pretend game of: if the secondary creation of the *Enterprise* or Middle Earth were real, what is the genetic explanation for Mr. Spock or the Elvish/human intermarriage? Books "explaining" the linguistic structure of Elvish and blueprints for the *Enterprise* exist, and the readers argue the finer points as if they were real. Such imaginings may have a neurotic basis (see the fascinating account in "The Jet Propelled Couch" in Robert Lindner's *The Fifty Minute Hour*, 1955), but hundreds of Baker Street Irregulars have spent parts of their waking hours in the secondary creation of Conan Doyle, and thousands continue to play similar games today. This is evidence of the strong archetypal myths which these writers tap in their works.

The real test is what happens when the secondary universe no longer casts its spell. Conan, Doc Savage, and Tarzan are no deeper than the immediate spell they cast. It may take twenty years or more for these creations to wear thin, but under the froth of mythic enchantment there is often much solid material. Cabell is like an onion: the more you peel him, the more layers you find. I am continually impressed by the scholarship and ambience of the early middle ages which Tolkien brings to his work. Cabell really was the last of the great writers of the romance, and Tolkien really did write the last literary masterpiece of the middle ages. H. P. Lovecraft, who also has this quality of greatness, is the latest descendent of M. G. "Monk" Lewis.

Closely allied to the gothic romance is the story based on psychoanalytic discoveries of infant sexuality, repression, and psychosomatic manifestations. In the first quarter of the twentieth century, it was possible to write a story using the discoveries of Charcot, Freud, and others as a basis for a scientific romance or even an SF story, but by the 1920s realism had so taken over mainstream writing that a psychological interpretation of character was almost obligatory and not really SF anymore. E. Arbuthnot Robertson's *Three Came Unarmed* [3-47] is one of the finer examples of this type of literature that may still be read as science fiction. In a treatment of semiferal children exposed to modern technical civilization, the author is writing about culture shock, a very new concept at that time. She uses three white children raised as primitives as her leading characters rather than three children of "colour" to emphasize the difference between cultures, avoiding any implication that racial differences might be at the root of the cultural estrangement. Much attention is focused upon their psychological difficulties in adapting to a new way of life, but the anthropological aspects of her work have had the most impact on later writers. Literally hundreds of stories were printed in the 1940s through the 1960s, especially in *Astounding/Analog* and *Galaxy*, which used culture shock as a theme or as the dominant message. The dangers of giving metal tools to stone-age extraterrestrials were stressed over and over. Part of this can be traced to the guilt many individuals felt over the destruction of "native" cultures by white explorers and missionaries in the nineteenth and twentieth centuries, and part was a natural outgrowth of the introduction of the social sciences to the writing of SF. Robertson's novel, while not the first to point out these problems, is one of the earlier treatments of this theme and pointed the way for many later writers.

Darwin's impact on thinkers was somewhat attenuated by the twentieth century, but a large body of books that can best be classed as prehistory were still being written. Like all scientific hypotheses, Darwin's ideas had an almost immediate impact, usually negative, on the major creative writers. Less skilled writers then took the theories and fictionalized them slightly. As the public came to accept the ideas, they were used as the basis for popular literature for both adults and children. Darwin's theories suggested to many writers that man had evolved (although not from monkeys as many anti-evolutionists misquote) into his present state. Therefore, novels which attempt to show mankind as subhumans living in caves or discovering fire are SF novels based on the "science" of evolutionary theory. Bogoraz' *Sons of the Mammoth* [3-4] and even Austin's charming little stories of prehistory [3-2] became part of the genre, continued today by William Golding's *The Inheritors* (1962).

Much of what I've written so far concerns popular fiction of little or no lasting significance except perhaps to other writers. In addition to writers such as Lovecraft and Tolkien, who captured archetypal images and the imaginations of several generations, there are two giants who stand out in the writing of the Gernsback era. Aldous Huxley achieved recognition and fame as a writer in his own time and left a body of science fiction and mainstream novels that are bound to become classics. Olaf Stapledon is a genius of a different sort. More philosopher than writer, his works were mined for ideas by many pulp writers. His writing style is bald and emotionless and reminds one of a really bad translation of Aristophanes. But he had ideas!

Others have written about both Huxley and Stapledon, but few have explored the intellectual basis for their writing—especially Stapledon's. As Huxley was the grandson of the greatest champion Darwin had, one would expect to see some evidence in his works of the clash between science and religion that so occupied the nineteenth century. It is there, but it is third-generation stuff and so thoroughly integrated into the attitudes of the writer that it is difficult to spot its influences. Stapledon is still fighting the old battles of science vs. God.

What Stapledon did is not really apparent at first, for as one becomes enmeshed in his millenial time spans, one often forgets to ask why. Stapledon's religious heresy is the same as that of Darwin's most atheistic supporters. For Stapledon, God is not dead; he never was. It would never have occurred to him to stand on a lecture platform, stopwatch in hand, waiting for God to strike him dead in two minutes. Stapledon was not looking at what man had created to warm his soul in the cold reaches of the universe, but he was looking forward to the day when man, perfected of his limitations and failings, would achieve godhood. His denial of the necessity for Christ's redemption was to lead to C. S. Lewis's angry rebuttal in *That Hideous Strength* [4-394]. To Stapledon, man could become a god himself.

Most rationalistic and atheistic thinkers should supposedly lead a gloomy and depressing spiritual life. For them there is no promise of Nirvana, Heaven, or even the gloomier prospects of an afterlife. To some individuals, even Hell is a more enticing prospect than the end of consciousness. Wells could see nothing happier than a universe motionless and cold. Stapledon was not anti-God so much as anti-entropy. For him the power of the life force could create ever higher levels of consciousness and awareness until it could transcend the limitations of the physical universe itself. Others—J. P. Priestley, P. D. Ouspensky, and more mystical writers—played at this game, but no one made it into a fictive world as all-encompassing as Stapledon's.

Even in the Gernsback era SF never sold much better than the other types of pulp magazines. The SF magazines have lasted longer than most other genres of popular literature, but today their sales and print runs are modest in spite of the much greater acceptance of SF. They did lead to the SF paperback; many of the best-selling SF authors today learned their trade in the old magazines. Influence evaluation is difficult. I have read an article by Charles G. Waugh in manuscript, and it would appear that the influence of SF on scientists was probably quite limited. My own opinion is that the influence of SF was minimal on scientists and writers outside the pulps. Within the field, however, countless writers have written about the impact Gernsback's *Amazing* or *Argosy* had on them, and many younger writers derived much of their knowledge of SF from Campbell's *Astounding/Analog*.

This is probably the greatest influence of the SF pulps: they provided a ghetto where one was removed from the mainstream story of sex in the street and seduction in the suburb. Realism was antithetical to the development of science fiction, particularly in the United States. A ghetto was needed, not to keep others out—which it did until the mid-1960s—but to protect the inhabitants. The scientific romance was moribund by 1926 and probably would have died without issue but for the SF ghetto. The walls had been going up for decades, but the founding of *Amazing* in 1926 closed the last gap in the wall.

A few English writers like Huxley, Stapledon, and Tolkien could publish and win fame and fortune outside the ghetto, but other writers, far better than the ones who wrote for the pulps, found their seed sown on the barren ground of realism and did not survive.

Inside the ghetto there were changes. From the crude beginnings of the earliest pulp magazines, writers developed who were to build the traditions on which the writers of today rely. SF pulps were the lowest of the low: there was no Picasso with his passion for comics or Kittridge and his detective story to give prestige to the genre. Some writers were able to make a living from their work, a very few becoming affluent. But above all, they were able to write, and from their writing came Campbell, Asimov, Heinlein, Silverberg, Ellison, and Delaney.

Bibliography: The Gernsback Era

3-1. Abdullah, Achmed. **Steel and Jade.** Doran, 1927.
Twelve short stories, several of which are fine fantastic romances, representative of author's career. Best known for his *Thief of Bagdad* (1924), Abdullah specialized in romantic settings in the Near and Far East. Most works are slight but competently written and retain some interest today.

3-2. Austin, Frederick Britten. **When Mankind Was Young.** Doubleday, 1927. Books for Libraries, $11.00.
Plausible and well plotted, these ten stories are good if minor examples of the rewritten prehistory popular in the early twentieth century. Their slight SF flavor derives from the attempt to blend history, archaeology, and Darwinian philosophy.

3-3. Balmer, Edwin, and Philip Wylie. **When Worlds Collide.** Stokes, 1933. Lippincott, $8.95 (includes sequel); Warner, $1.25.
The 1951 George Pal film dramatized the threatened collision of the Earth with an invading planet. A handful of Americans build and launch a spaceship and land on the companion of the invader planet, which goes into an orbit around the Sun and proves capable of sustaining life. There is fast plotting with much suspense and action, but the writing

strikes a false note today with its obligatory love interest and WASPish hero. The sequel, *After Worlds Collide* (Stokes, 1934, Warner, $1.25), is poorer in writing and plotting. The Americans discover that a British group and Asiatic communists have also landed on the new world. In a fight for planetary control, the communists are defeated.

3-4. Bogoraz, Vladimir Germanovich (U.S.S.R.). **The Sons of the Mammoth.** Cosmopolitan, 1929, Tr. by Stephen Graham.
Anthropology and evolutionary theory are the scientific base for this novel of prehistory, which purports to show the change in the human race seen from the viewpoint of tribal hunters. Often grim, it is essentially a story of sympathetic magic, taboos, ritual observances, and one individual's attempt to break out of this pattern.

3-5. Brunngraber, Rudolf (Germany). **Radium; A Novel.** Random, 1937. Tr. by Eden and Oedar Paul.
It's hard to know whether the author or the translators are to blame for the awkward, stilted writing, especially the dialogue. Students of Marie Curie are attempting to use radium to cure cancer in an English hospital but are hampered by the difficulty in obtaining radium. A Belgian tycoon is cornering the radium supply and raises the price until the hospital cannot buy any more. This interesting, semidocumentary novel is not as badly written as much pulp fictions, and it has parallels with contemporary drug pricing practices.

3-6. Campbell, John Wood, Jr. **The Black Star Passes.** Fantasy Press, 1953. Ace $.75. **Islands of Space.** Fantasy Press, 1956. **Invaders from the Infinite.** Fantasy Press, 1961.
These stories chronicle the space adventures of Arcot, Wade, and Morley. Wade, a twenty-second-century super pirate, pilots an invisible space ship. When he is tracked down by Arcot and Morley, they form an invincible trio and take off for extravagant adventures on many worlds. Revised from their appearance in the pulps of the early 1930s, the stories are typical of Campbell's space opera period. Published as *John W. Campbell Anthology*, Doubleday, 1973.

3-7. Campbell, John Wood, Jr. **The Mightiest Machine.** Hadley, 1947. Ace, $.95.
Originally published in *Astounding* in 1934, this book combines interstellar war and great invention themes. It is typical Campbell space opera with fast action, incredibly inept dialogue and characterization, and a cluttered plot. Aarn Munro and his friends invent and build a spaceship capable of utilizing energy directly from suns and go exploring in the galaxy. Their return after being lost in space is chronicled in three novelettes written in the 1930s and printed in 1949 as *The Incredible Planet* (Fantasy Press).

*3-8.   Campbell, John Wood, Jr. **Who Goes There?** Shasta, 1951. Hyperion, $12.50.
This is a collection of short stories from *Astounding*, 1934–1938, most written under the pseudonym Don A. Stuart. The title story is best known, an ingenious detective-horror story with an SF basis. (The inept 1951 film, *The Thing*, substitutes stock horror elements.) Other stories include "Blindness," "Dead Knowledge," "Elimination," "Twilight," "Night," and "Frictional Losses." Characterization is shallow, but the stories are free of the gross stylistic and period eccentricities and far above the usual low level of the 1930s pulps.

*3-9.   Čapek, Karel (Czechoslovakia). **The Absolute at Large.** Macmillan, 1927. Hyperion, $3.50, $10.00; Garland, $11.00. Tr. of *Tovarna na absolutno*, 1922.
This is one of the rarities in SF: an ironic treatment of science. Marek invents an atomic source, the Karburator, but as each atom is smashed, a bit of "God" is released. Karburator operators are able to perform miracles, and as mass production spreads the devices, religious fanaticism develops and leads to international conflict. With civilization in peril, the Karburators are destroyed and peace prevails. Thematically typical of the younger Čapek's work, it shows less of his older brother's influence than his other works. Well received critically, it still holds interest in spite of a dated translation.

3-10.   Čapek, Karel. **War with the Newts.** Putnam, 1937. Gregg, $15.00. Tr. by Marie and Robert Weatherall of *Valka S Mloky*.
Like most Čapek novels, this ends in *Sturm und Drang*, with the enslaved newts, docile, small sea creatures of modest intelligence raised by man for economic gain, undermining the continents and bringing human civilization down in a worldwide catastrophe. Not up to his usual standard, this is still one of the better examples of the type of novel arguing man's inhumanity to man. Čapek's newts are perfectly suited to make his point and are better suited to express the slave mentality (read: oppressed working classes) than creations by other writers. Like his other novels, this one expresses Čapek's ambivalence toward industrial progress at the expense of humanity.

3-11.   Chester, William L. **Hawk of the Wilderness.** Harper, 1936.
Kioga, or the Snow Hawk, is an arctic Tarzan. Raised by Shoni Indians after his parents are killed in a Siberian land warmed by volcanic action, he becomes a friend to the great bears of the region. He becomes the leader of the Shoni, saves some explorers, falls in love with a girl they bring with them, and goes to New York, but returns to his home with the girl. Three other novels about Kioga appeared in *Blue Book* between 1935 and 1938. Not as preposterous as the Tarzan novels, they never quite captured the public as the apeman did.

3-12. Coblentz, Stanton Arthur. **The Sunken World.** Fantasy Pub. Co. Inc., 1948.
First published in *Amazing Stories Quarterly* in 1928, five years after his first volume of verse, this is his first published novel. Curiously stiff and wooden for even a second rate poet, it lacks sensitivity to the use of language. A submarine is caught in a whirlpool and hits a large domed city on the ocean bottom housing a pacifist, utopian, Atlantean civilization and a beautiful girl, Aelios. The sub-commander and Aelios are married, the dome is crushed, everyone dies except the hero and the heroine, and they escape to America. Compare Doyle's *The Maracot Deep* [2-68].

3-13. Collier, John (U.K.). **Tom's A-Cold.** Macmillan, 1933. (U.S. title: *Full Circle.* Appleton, 1933.)
Collier is a superlative craftsman of short supernatural and weird tales. His *Fancies and Goodnights* (1951) won an International Fantasy Award. His short stories have sometimes overshadowed his longer works, which are less preciously written and grimmer in tone. *Tom's A-Cold* is a mordant story of civilization in a society struggling to rebuild after a catastrophic war. Set in England, this book set the tone for countless post-atomic holocaust stories. Considering the gloom of the time, this book is optimistic in its hope that civilization *could* be rebuilt, but not as optimistic as most pulp stories. Well written and literate, it still retains great interest.

3-14. Cox, Erle (Australia). **Out of the Silence.** Henkle, 1928. Hyperion, $13.95 (complete ed.).
The complex plot features an ancient civilization of high scientific achievement that foresaw the destruction of all life and placed two men and a woman in suspended animation. An Australian discovers their chamber, revives the woman, and falls in love with her. She has plans for remaking our world in her own version of perfection but is killed and her discoverer commits suicide as he destroys all evidence of the earlier civilization. Shallowly written, overplotted, and racially prejudiced, it is typical of the period's pulp fiction, although originally published in Australia in 1925, outside the pulp ghetto.

3-15. Cummings, Ray. **Brigands of the Moon.** McClurg, 1931.
Cummings was a prominent pulp writer in the 1920s and 1930s after the appearance of *The Girl in the Golden Atom* [2-54]. This work and its sequel, *Wandl the Invader* (1932; book, 1961), are good examples of his better and worse pulp writing habits: heavy plotting, shallow writing, and pseudo-science are the dominant elements. This novel involves a space mutiny, valuable radium deposits, space battles, and space pirates, and inevitably a happy ending with a victorious hero.

3-16. Ewers, Hans Heinz (Germany). **Alraune.** Day, 1929. Tr. by S. Guy Endore from *Alraune,* 1919.
The most SF-oriented of the Frank Braun series, this is basically a competent retelling of the Frankenstein myth. Braun and his uncle conduct experiments on animal mutations and intelligence and finally create an android. She is Alraune, who proceeds to cast a baleful influence on all men who come under her spell, including Braun. He wastes away to the point of death, but she destroys herself to save him.

3-17. Farley, Ralph Milne (pseud. of Roger Sherman Hoar). **The Radio Man.** Fantasy Pub. Co., Inc., 1948.
A 1924 serial in *Argosy, The Radio Man* has two novelized sequels, *The Radio Beasts,* Ace 1964, $1.50, and *The Radio Planet,* Ace 1964, $1.50, and four other uncollected radio stories. Myles Cabot, an electrical engineer, "awakes" on Venus, where he fights a race of giant ant-like creatures and wins the love of Lilla, princess of a subhumanoid race held captive by the ant-like Formians. The Formians are destroyed by gunpower, and Cabot lives happily ever after. This reads like second-rate Burroughs.

3-18 Fialke, Nathan. **The New City.** Margent, 1937.
The author is responsible for the uneven translation, which often reads like a schoolboy's translation of the Gallic Wars. It sometimes comes alive, as in the chapter on the winged man, where it approaches greatness. It is partly a future utopia in what was the U.S.S.R., where people live lives of unbelievable regimentation. It was influenced by Chernyshevsky and probably by Zamiatin. The final portion depicts the perversion of the new social system in the United States by class exploiters and the resultant class wars. The novel is so uneven that one recommends it with strong reservations, but the ideas and concepts used are seldom met in other SF translated into English.

3-19 Forester, Cecil Scott. **The Peacemaker.** Little, Brown, 1934. New English Library, £.30.
The author of the Hornblower series also wrote several SF stories. This, his only SF novel, concerns a mathematician who builds a machine which disrupts magnetic forces and stops all engines. A pacifist, he plans to force disarmament in England by stopping all transportation and machinery. He is betrayed and killed by a mob. Forester never writes badly, but seldom rises above mere competence, a level well above most SF of the period. There is a realistic love story involving such elements as divorce and adultery, taboo topics in the family- or youth-oriented pulps. See also his "If Hitler Had Invaded England," *Saturday Evening Post,* April 16, 1960.

3-20. Ganpat (pseud. of Martin Louis Alan Gompertz). **Mirror of Dreams.** Doubleday, 1928.

This is typical of the lost race novels set in India and, like most of the author's novels, reeks of the British Raj and the white man's burden. It was originally well received, but the modern reader notes racist elements and the ever-present British concern with Russian encroachment. There is also a bitter attack on Blavatsky-type mysticism, but the plot advances the author's own style of mind-power pseudo-science. A white girl is brought up by mystic adepts. There is a native revolutionary, and several other villains meet satisfactory ends, with hints of a lost civilization and supernormal powers.

3-21. Gibbons, Floyd Phillip. **The Red Napoleon.** Cape & Smith, 1929.
Gibbons, a famed war correspondent, used the framework of this future war novel to display his prejudices and to plug for his favorites, mostly the navy and air power. A descendent of Ghenghis Khan becomes a force in the Soviet Union and emerges as a dictator, conquering all Europe and Asia. He sets out on a deliberate policy of miscegenation to reduce racial tension and inequality. Invading the United States, he is defeated. Today one has more sympathy for the red Napoleon than for the WASP heroes. The dialogue is very inept and the book is filled with romantic, sentimental stereotypes, but the action scenes have some holding power.

3-22. Hamilton, Edmond. **Crashing Suns.** Ace, 1965. **Outside the Universe.** Ace, 1964.
Space opera from the 1929–1930 *Weird Tales* is typical of Hamilton's early work. These two books comprise most of the Interstellar Patrol series of stories. Hamilton authored many of the Captain Future stories as well. They are similar to but not the equal of E. E. Smith's Skylark series.

3-23. Harbou, Thea von (Germany). **Metropolis.** Hutchinson, 1927. Gregg, $12.50; Ace, $1.25.
The movie by Fritz Lang has become something of a camp masterpiece, which is a shame. The expressionist acting style of the major actors seems peculiar to modern audiences because they've seen so little of it, but this and the lush futuristic settings and direction of Fritz Lang make it a priceless treasure. The plot of the film is its weakest point, and this is not helped in the novel by a barely adequate translation. The mixture of the super-scientific elements of a future city with the simplistic symbolism of occultism is more apparent in the film than in the novel, but there is nothing in the novel to take the place of the film's stunning visuals except a thin sense of wonder. Read the book only if the film is unavailable.

*3-24. Hilton, James. **Lost Horizon.** Morrow, 1933, $8.95. Pocket Books, $1.50; Washington Square Pr., $1.50.
With a movie, play, and musical based on this book it still retains its own

popularity. Surprisingly, many of the original reviewers complained that it was too "heavy," philosophical, and serious. Later dismissed as a romantic lost race fantasy, it is still a fine (and perhaps the most rational) lost race tale, and the High Llama's prediction that the lost valley in Tibet would be a refuge for civilization during the coming dark ages held great appeal during World War II and its aftermath. The writing is a bit thin, the characters a trifle wooden, but they effectively show the author's antitechnological philosophy, and the ending is agreeably ambiguous.

*3-25. Howard, Robert Ervin. **Conan the Conqueror.** Gnome, 1950. Sphere, £.30.
The SF reader should know the Conan books, which have inspired dozens of others in the so-called sword and sorcery vein. Conan is a barbarian who wanders around prehistoric Europe getting into fights, wooing women, and escaping from supernatural and monstrous enemies. The SF element is minimal, but the sword and sorcery books are often called SF because they are written by SF writers. The Conan books are racist, sexist trash which combine a simpering sexuality with thud-and-blunder adventure. They appeal mostly to readers as simple-minded as Conan himself, but I confess to a liking for them in small doses. At least one is required reading; any will do.

*3-26. Hoyne, Thomas Temple. **Intrigue on the Upper Level.** Reilly & Lee, 1934.
The basic society is a capitalistic oligarchy based on gold and stock ownership and manipulation. Life on the upper level is hedonistic but violent, destructive, and wasteful of human life. The lower level is cowed, desperate, and ready for revolution. After one of the most promising beginnings of any anti-utopian novel of its period, sentimental romance and weakly plotted adventure follow. There are interesting ideas, poorly realized.

*3-27. Huxley, Aldous Leonard (U.K.). **Brave New World.** Doubleday, 1932. Harper, $1.25, $7.95, $3.25 (last includes *Brave New World Revisited*).
One of the few SF novels of the 1930s that was considered a major work by the critics, this is a bitterly dystopian novel of 632 A.F. (After Ford). Funnier than the totally grim *1984*, it stresses cloning, test tube babies, and genetic, hypnopedic, and drug control of the population, by a benevolent ruling class. One takes an ambivalent attitude toward the society because of its built-in paradoxes. The Savage, a sexually repressed mass of neuroses who has escaped the training and regimentation of the larger society, is faced with instant sensory gratification: drugs, sex, "feelies," and proper use of his abilities. He is destroyed by this world and commits suicide. In the other subplot, the love story of Marx and Le-

nina, we see the treatment afforded dissidents. They are not tortured or executed, simply removed from positions where they might disturb the even tenor of society, to live their lives in isolated frustration. Huxley seems to be commenting on the unsuitability of modern man to live in any sort of utopia. The characters who most nearly resemble contemporary man in attitudes and sensitivity are the most unhappy. But for the majority this is a genuine utopia: coupling in obligatory orgies, senses dulled by drugs, a bland life followed by a painless death; such is the individual's fate. But by comparison with the Savage and Bernard Marx, or perhaps even with our own lives, this is indeed Eden. Deeply thought-provoking and exceptionally well written, this is a seminal novel for modern SF. For later editions Huxley wrote an interesting preface, whose ideas were expanded still further in a nonfiction work, *Brave New World Revisited* (Harper, 1958, $.95, $7.95).

*3-28. Johnson, Owen McMahon. **The Coming of the Amazons.** Longmans, 1931.
An intelligent, attractive, complacent young man is frozen until 2181 and awakens in a future in which females dominate. The sleeper attempts to restore men from their position as sexual objects to a position of equality. Written with humor, its tone is polemic, attacking by inversion sexual stereotypes (men are emotional and belong to clubs; women are efficient, logical, and businesslike). It is especially germane today.

3-29. Jones, Neil Ronald. **Planet of the Double Sun.** Ace, 1967. Garland, $11.00. **The Sunless World.** Ace, 1967. **Space War.** Ace, 1967. **Twin Worlds.** Ace, 1967. **Doomsday on Ajiat.** Ace, 1968.
These five volumes feature Professor Jameson in sixteen stories from the 1931–1950 period, in the lengthiest and longest running of any SF series. Rescued from suspended animation by robots in the far future, Jameson visits a variety of worlds with them. This is enjoyable if undistinguished space opera in the Edmond Hamilton tradition.

3-30. Kline, Otis Adelbert. **Maza of the Moon.** McClurg, 1930.
Misinterpreting a projectile from Earth as the start of an interplanetary war, the yellow P'an-ku launch a devastating attack on the Earth. The hero travels to the Moon where he meets a white race led by Princess Maza, and together they destroy the nasty P'an-ku. Poorly written and filled with romantic and racist nonsense, this book was very highly regarded by SF readers of the time.

3-31. Kline, Otis Adelbert. **The Planet of Peril.** McClurg, 1929.
This is the first of three novels that originally appeared in *Argosy* and *Weird Tales*. The recent reprints are often abridged, especially the ones by Avalon. The planet is Venus, where Robert Grandon is involved with monsters, sword fights, beautiful maidens, and all other hackneyed ele-

ments of the pulps' romantic fantasies. The stories' locale gives them a claim to be SF, and they are frankly imitative of the interplanetary novels of Burroughs. But Kline does not tap into the collective unconscious' archetypal symbols as well as Burroughs.

3-32. Knight, Damon F., ed. **Science Fiction of the Thirties.** Bobbs, 1975, $12.50.
Of these eighteen stories from the 1931–1939 period, none duplicates those in the larger Asimov collection covering the same period. Brief introductions precede the three sections, and eighteen period illustrations complement the stories. The editor suggests that this period has been unfairly neglected by anthologists, who tend to select from the Campbell period. It is a well-chosen and representative collection of pulp fiction, but Asimov [4-652] is preferable. A critical and historical introduction and survey of the period would have added a great deal to this collection.

*3-33. Large, Ernest Charles. **Sugar in the Air.** Scribner, 1937.
Although there is a detailed and fairly plausible description of the invention and marketing of a nutritious food syrup from waste gases, the novel's focus is on international finance, corporate structure, and stock manipulation. A product which would have prevented starvation and malnutrition becomes a cattle-feed additive. Grimly pessimistic about society and industrial/corporate greed, the novel manages to make both science and high finance interesting. The love interest is used to develop character and give depth, and a good picture of the working scientist/engineer adds interest. While not a literary success, it is one of the better SF novels of the period, and deserves reprinting.

3-34. Lewis, Sinclair. **It Can't Happen Here.** Doubleday, 1935.
This is one of the first novels to suggest the serious possibility of an American fascist regime. The plot closely follows events in Germany, little adapted to the United States, and the characters are cardboard figures. Dated today, it is of more historical than literary interest.

*3-35. Lovecraft, Howard Phillips. **At the Mountains of Madness.** Arkham, 1964, $7.50; Ballantine, $1.50.
Originally published in *Astounding* in 1936, this story is the closest to SF Lovecraft could come. An exploration team from Miskatonic University goes to the Antarctic, where it discovers the deaths of an advance party and a huge city abandoned for 500,000 years. This was the last surviving outpost of an extragalactic race, the Old Ones, who settled on Earth and created life on this planet, finally dying during an ice age. After a multitude of events, the narrator and a colleague narrowly escape and return to civilization, one man mad and the narrator writing this tale to warn other expeditions against going to the evil city. The complete 42,000

word story is in Lovecraft's *The Outsider and Others* (Arkham, 1939). This 1964 edition, which includes seven other stories, contains an abridged version, which has been reprinted elsewhere as well.

3-36. Lovecraft, Howard Phillips. **"The Shadow Out of Time"** in *The Dunwich Horror and Others*. Arkham, 1963, $7.50.
This story also appeared in *Astounding* in 1936 and has more SF elements than most of Lovecraft's stories, which emphasize dread and terror. The shadow is a mind force that periodically infects humans, permitting them to absorb what is current in the scientific world but forcing them to do ghastly deeds. The mind of a professor at Miskatonic University is taken over and used for over five years. After building a machine which returns the mind of the professor to his body, the professor, Peaslee, and his son begin to solve the mystery of the amnesia and go to a desert site in Australia. Peaslee descends into huge caves where he finds evidence to confirm his dimly remembered, nightmarish visions. The story, which abounds in Lovecraft's named and nameless horrors, was his last major work.

3-37. McClary, Thomas Calvert. **Rebirth, When Everyone Forgot.** Bartholomew House, 1944. Hyperion, $10.50.
Rewritten from its original 1934 appearance in *Astounding*, this is a post-catastrophe novel which assumes an intact world where the survivors lack even basic skills such as eating and drinking. Within a decade, basic skills are regained, fire is discovered, and the United States is reunited. A bit creaky and implausible, it still retains some value as an interesting variant of a common theme. Compare Stewart's much better *Earth Abides* [4-558].

*3-38. McHugh, Vincent. **Caleb Catlum's America.** Stackpole, 1936. Gale, $14.00.
This ludicrous novel demonstrates the author's versatility and literary talents (as did his other SF novel, *I Am Thinking of My Darling* [4-400]). Heinlein called this work the best romantic fantasy written in America and used many of the techniques, attitudes, content, and stylistic devices in his own *Time Enough for Love* [4-303]. Well received, the story chronicles the immortal Catlum family, which includes many American folk heroes, such as Eric the Red, Abe Lincoln, Davy Crockett, and John Henry (a major character). Routed by Ben Franklin and a following of merchants and opportunists, the family discovers a new world entered by a cave. The book is occasionally repetitious but still very funny.

3-39. Margulies, Leo, and Oscar J. Friend, eds. **From off This World.** Merlin Press, 1949.
These eighteen short stories, all from the 1929–1937 pulps, include Weinbaum's "A Martian Odyssey," C. A. Smith's "The City of the Sing-

ing Flame" and its sequel, and Edmond Hamilton's "The Man Who Evolved." They are typical of the period, which has more recently been mined by Asimov [4-652] and Knight [3-32] with minimal duplication.

3-40. Maurois, André (France). **A Private Universe.** Appleton, 1932. Books for Libraries, $14.25. Tr. by Hamish Hiles.
Combines advice to a young French man of letters on how to behave in England, pungent commentaries on the French and English political and governmental structures, and bits of a utopian vision. Although listed here for its utopian, future history sections, the book is an urbane, witty, and well-written book of ideas.

3-41 Merritt, Abraham. **The Face in the Abyss.** Liveright, 1931. Collier, $.95.
One of the most popular writers of scientific romances was A. Merritt, whose lush prose does not wear well today. A mining engineer finds a lost city in the Andes. His greedy companions are turned into blobs of gold, but Nicholas Graydon is saved by the Snake-Mother of Yu-Atlanchi and her beautiful handmaiden, Surra. Together they fight the evil Nimir, the nasty thing in the abyss.

*3-42. Merritt, Abraham. **The Ship of Ishtar.** Putnam, 1926.
Perhaps the best of Merritt's romances, this fuses the romantic and symbolic elements for which the author was well known. John Keuton receives a block of stone from Babylonian ruins, inside of which he finds a miniature ship which puts him into a trance. He awakens in the universe of the ship, split between the followers of Ishtar and her priestess Sharane, and the evil Nergal. The book features lots of pulpy adventure and a downbeat ending. The Virgil Finlay illustrated reprint (Borden, $4.50) is preferred. Other popular Merritt titles include *Burn, Witch, Burn* (1933) and *Dwellers in the Mirage* (1932).

*3-43. Mundy, Talbot. **Jimgrim.** Century, 1931.
One of several books on India by Mundy, and a continuation of the scientific detective/explorer romances of the late nineteenth and early twentieth centuries, this novel uses many of their plot elements but is much better than most. The Gobi Desert, a lost Atlantean civilization, a WASP hero and a Eurasian antagonist, mind-enhancing drugs, an antigravity airship—all the familiar elements are here. The lost valley and lost race are conveniently destroyed in the final battle, along with the hero and villain, in a variant of the usual formula. This is an early example of the collective superhero as featured in Doc Savage, G-8, and the Mission Impossible crew. Doyle's Sherlock Holmes and Professor Challenger and their imitators were accompanied by a fumbling amanuensis or a pair of young lovers, but in the twentieth century this is not enough.

3-44. Nowlan, Philip Francis. **Armageddon 2419** A.D. Bouregy, 1962. Ace, $1.25.

First printed in the August 1928 *Amazing* (along with the first installment of Smith's *Skylark of Space*), this story has had great general influence. A "yellow peril" novelette combined with future war and marvelous invention themes, it is a trifle creaky but is surprisingly modern in places (women fight in armies with the men). Anthony Rogers awakens in a strange America where Asiatic conquerors, who live in huge cities protected by domes of force, have almost exterminated the Americans. There are death rays, missiles, and most of the other stock gadgetry of future "science." In addition to sequels, Nowland wrote the Buck Rogers comic strips, adapted as movie serials and as TV series. Better than E. E. Smith's space epics, the book was far from the lowest common denominator of popular taste and does not deserve the scorn usually accorded it.

3-45 Pseudoman, Akkad (pseud. of Edwin Fitch Northrup). **Zero to Eighty.** Scientific Pub. Co., 1937.

This is what Gernsback meant when he suggested fiction should stimulate scientific interest. While not as badly written as most Gernsback-inspired pulp fodder, it's not much better. Forty pages of scientific proof are included with the text to demonstrate the factual basis of the book. This involves launching a spaceship by an electric gun, a trip around the Moon, and return to Earth: there are no rockets, just pure ballistics. It is also the life history of a man born in 1920 who dies in 2000. The high point of his life is the lunar flight. Tame today, the book should be remembered as a monument to those who said it couldn't be done.

*3-46. Read, Herbert Edward (U.K.). **The Green Child.** Heinemann, 1935. New Directions, $1.75, $6.00.

Two green children appear on the moors. One wastes away, but the other, Siloen, leads the narrator, Olivero/Oliver, into a pool and an underground world of grottoes. Once a revolutionary and the president of a fictitious South American country, Olivero sheds the conflict and pain of the outside world through contemplation and an ordered, regimented existence. Freed from the demands of the body, he achieves a Nirvana state, dies, and is petrified in a statue with Siloen at his side. Oliver, the man seeking freedom by revolutionary acts, eventually finds freedom by turning inward. Oriental rather than occidental in ambience, this work has a deep stratum of repressed sexuality running through it, despite the asexual relations between Olivero and Siloen.

*3-47. Robertson, Eileen Arbuthnot. **Three Came Unarmed.** Garden City, 1929.

Three semiferal children raised by primitives are taken from their island utopia to England, where they are destroyed by sex, power, and the struggle between capital and labor. A fiercely satiric attack on contemporary values and a rebuttal of all the Rousseau-like myths on which works like *Tarzan of the Apes* [2-32] are based, this novel received high critical acclaim. Somewhat neglected today, the author has a readable style, and her ideas are sound and interesting. She should be better known.

3-48. Robeson, Kenneth (pseudonymous house name). **The Man of Bronze.** Street & Smith, 1933. Bantam, $1.25.
Doc Savage is one of the longer lived of the pulp super-heroes. Most of the series was written by Lester Dent. Resurrected from the pulps of the 1930s and 1940s into a current paperback series, Savage has appeared in comic books and a film. Doc Savage was a scientifically reared superman who used science and his superhuman abilities (unlike Superman or Captain Marvel, he was just a *little* stronger and smarter) to defeat crime. Doc works with a group of associates, making him a corporate hero (see introduction to this chapter). In the tradition of the scientific gadget detective, these novels, of which this one is typical, include lost race and supernatural elements.

*3-49. Schuyler, George Samuels. **Black No More.** McCauley, 1931. Collier, $1.50; Negro Univ. Press, $10.25.
Written by a black author about the effects of bleaching blacks white, this is a well-written and ironic commentary on racial relations from an era when black citizens were first starting to mount a campaign to retain the rights they had lost during the previous fifty to sixty years. Unfairly forgotten today, it is a superior work in spite of partially stereotyped characters, both black and white.

3-50. Simak, Clifford D. **Cosmic Engineers.** Gnome, 1950.
The cosmic engineers are a race of super-robots who are trying to save our galaxy from the bad guys. Suspended animation, interstellar travel, a trip to the future, and humanoid robots that have become "human" over the centuries are all plot elements. Many elements remind one of his far better, more intimate writing, such as *City* [4-535]. Popular in its day, it is dated, like most 1930s space opera. It is important as a good example of its kind and because it shows the direction of Simak's writing.

3-51. Siodmak, Curt (Germany). **F.P. 1 Does Not Reply.** Little, Brown, 1933. Tr. by H. W. Farrel of *F.P. 1 antwortet nicht*, 1931.
Floating Airport No. 1 is part of a transatlantic line run by Atlantic Airways. Competitors try to sabotage the airfield's anchoring. This is good technological fiction, but curiously unprophetic, as clipper ships were only a few years away and routine, nonstop transatlantic flights only a few more. Lindbergh's flight was in everyone's mind, and a transatlantic tunnel or floating midocean airport were popular fictional subjects. This is an example of technological advance almost outstripping a writer's fantasies.

3-52. Smith, Edward Elmer. **Skylark Three.** Fantasy Press, 1948. Garland, $11.00; Pyramid, $1.25.

One of the favorite space operas by "Doc" Smith, this 1928 serial exhibits most of the subgenre's features, including its many faults. "Blackie" DuQuesne, in conflict with Seaton and Crane, discovers a group of supernasty, semihumanoid extraterrestrials who are ready and more than willing to destroy the Earth. Seaton and Crane discover friendly aliens on the planet of Noralimin, acquire an indestructible spaceship, and the battle is on. It is preceded by *The Skylark of Space* (Hadley, 1947; Garland, $11.00; Pyramid, $1.25) and followed by *Skylark of Valeron* (Fantasy Press, 1949; Garland, $11.00; Pyramid, $1.25) and *Skylark DuQuesne* (Pyramid, 1966, $.95), this last title was a HN, 1966. The later Lensman series by Smith [4-548] is much the same. Compare Campbell and Williamson during this era.

3-53. Smith, Edward Elmer. **Spacehounds of IPC.** Fantasy Press, 1947.

This 1931 story has a fascination despite execrable writing; e.g., the hero calls his beloved "Ace" and "you square little brick." But the Robinson Crusoe aspect of a boy and a girl marooned on Ganymede makes their stay, complete with man-eating plants, air, water, and food, memorable. The plot goes stale after they repair the spaceship, hop on a convenient comet, and get involved with assorted Jovian aliens. Badly dated slang, rays, and things that go zap impede today's reader, but the book retains a period charm.

3-54. Snell, Edmund. **Kontrol.** Lippincott, 1928.

This early brain transplant novel is more scientific than Heinlein's *I Will Fear No Evil* (1970). It is still an interesting story, although marred by a cliché ending. A slightly mad doctor transplants the minds of a potential power elite into young, healthy bodies. The story is told by Wildash, who is kidnapped and taken to the island where the doctor works, sees the operations there, and survives the explosion and destruction of the island.

3-55. Stapledon, William Olaf (U.K.). **Darkness and the Light.** Methuen, 1942. Hyperion, $2.95, $9.50.

The narrator tells of his twofold vision of the future. In one, a series of wars and struggles results in mankind's extinction by mutated rats; in the other, mankind almost meditates itself into extinction before it finds its purpose in the production of a new mutant race, superior to us. The old race passes. There is much more in the book, and one can see the influence of World War II in the author's concern with ethics and government. A sort of Book of Revelations, it is filled with vague apocalyptic forebodings and a personal symbolism that is difficult to decipher. More than his other works, it has a strange mystic quality, reflecting the author's inner struggle.

*3-56.   Stapledon, William Olaf (U.K.). **Last and First Men; A Story of the Near and Far Future.** Methuen, 1930. Dover, $3.00 (with *Star Maker*); Peter Smith, $5.00 (ditto); Penguin, $2.45 (with *Last Men in London*); Gregg, $35.00 (in the omnibus *To the End of Time*, including *Star Maker*, *Odd John*, *Sirius*, and *The Flames*).

Most of the early reviews of the book were favorable, with most critics impressed by its scope and sweep, few by its style and writing. More a philosopher than a writer, Stapledon wrote outside the tradition of the pulp magazines but within the tradition of the scientific romance. This, his first published work, spans millenia as mankind spirals upward to become an immensely wise, telepathic race covering the solar system, its progress interrupted by periodic descents into savagery and barbarism. In opposition to a Wellsian dystopian vision of the future, this book is based firmly on Darwinian evolutionary theory as a positive force. Anathema to Christian writers like C. S. Lewis, it suggests that man himself can achieve godhood. Though one of the most imaginative pieces of fiction of this century, much of it seems clichéd because so many later writers have borrowed its elements and themes, and the introductory chapters describing the past forty-five years are badly dated. The philosophy is not original, but the work is a brilliantly imagined piece of fiction.

3-57.   Stapledon, William Olaf (U.K.). **Last Men in London.** Methuen, 1932. Penguin, $2.45 (with *Last and First Men*).

A partial sequel to *Last and First Men*, this fills in some of the gaps and explains how the first book came to be written through the development of the racial mind. The narrator, a member of the last race of mankind, is experiencing the twentieth century through a member of today's race. He attempts to influence and guide our society through this contemporary individual. This is close to a didactic novel, for the author puts more of his personal philosophy into it than in his other works. Not as preachy as one might expect, it is still less impressive than his first novel, and many of its ideas may be traced to Jung, Shaw, and others.

*3-58.   Stapledon, William Olaf (U.K.). **Odd John; A Story between Jest and Earnest.** Dutton, 1936. Garland, $11.00; Dover, $2.50 (with *Sirius*); Peter Smith, $5.00 (ditto).

John Wainwright is so advanced mentally that he may properly be considered *homo superior*, a new species. He finds other members of his species and founds a utopian, scientific community on a Pacific island. Threatened by the "civilized" nations, John and his fellows destroy themselves rather than destroy the rest of humanity or allow themselves to be mastered and used by them. Fairly well written, it is very different from Stapledon's other work, for it focuses upon a relatively small time span and group of people. It is also essentially pessimistic, suggesting that a superior race would find itself unable to survive in the contemporary world. Compare Beresford's *The Hampdenshire Wonder* [2-15] and van Vogt's *Slan* [4-591].

*3-59. Stapledon, William Olaf (U.K.). **Sirius; A Fantasy of Love and Discord.** Secker & Warburg, 1944. Penguin, $.95; Dover, $2.50 (with *Odd John*); Peter Smith, $5.00 (ditto).
Perhaps better than *Odd John*, this also deals with the uses of super intelligence but has an ending of greater emotional impact. The writing is better, and the characters often seem well developed. The mutated dog, Sirius, becomes believably human and is far more interesting than the usual stereotypes used by authors attempting to allegorize the human condition. Probably this comes from Stapledon's concern with the evolution of mankind to ethical and mental supermen or perhaps from his focus upon an extremely short span of time. Always a writer of ideas, which are often central to his works, he is at his best when he deals with one-to-one relationships. Sirius and his human companions offer ideas but also the realization of human ideals of love and friendship.

*3-60. Stapledon, William Olaf (U.K.). **Star Maker.** Methuen, 1937. Penguin, $1.25; Dover, $3.00 (with *Last and First Men*); Peter Smith, $5.00 (ditto).
The two billion year span of *Last and First Men* is but the dust on the end of a meter stick compared to the time span of this novel. A contemporary Englishman uses his mind to project his consciousness through all of time and space. He finds other inhabited planets and encounters other sentient mentalities, some physical, some disembodied. He discovers that all life stystems are the work of a Star Maker, who creates a succession of universes, each more perfect than the earlier, in an eternal series. The Star Maker is not so much God as the ultimate perfection of life force or consciousness. Even more mind-boggling than his earlier books, this is a tremendously exciting exposition of Stapledon's philosophy, which extends his thought to its logical conclusion.

3-61. Stout, Rex. **The President Vanishes.** Farrar, 1934. Pyramid, $.95.
Originally published anonymously, this near-future political prognostication is an early form of *Seven Days in May* [1962] and similar novels. The American President vanishes during critical national and international discussions and must be found to save the nation. Unlike Heinlein's *Double Star* [4-296], the President is found safe and more or less sound after a series of closely packed action sequences. Stout deals with the problems of the 1930s, such as labor unrest, communism, and fascism, which are naturally a bit dated today, but the writing remains acceptable. One interesting feature is the use of retouched photographs of street violence of the era as illustrations.

3-62. Taine, John (pseud. of Eric Temple Bell). **Green Fire.** Dutton, 1928.
The mathematician–author of this book was a fairly prolific writer from the 1920s to the 1950s, and this work is typical. Popular and well reviewed in the SF pulps, his works have an overblown and prolix style, and the science is often little short of fantasy. Based on the search for atomic power, this work features a mad scientist who is willing to destroy entire galaxies for personal profit. There is a theme of public responsibility vs. private power, which Asimov handled better in *The Gods Themselves* [4-39]. Among Taine's other works are *Before the Dawn* (1934) and *The Iron Star* (1930).

3-63. Thompson, Vance. **The Green Ray.** Bobbs, 1924.
A series of colored lights makes the young old and bleaches blacks white, also removing dialects. It is ultimately revealed as a hoax, but the bleaching process is never fully explained. A racist piece of trash, this is interesting as a sample of popular quasi-scientific poppycock current in the period, and as a possible prefiguration of a theme used later by Schuyler [3-49].

3-64. Viereck, George Sylvester, and Paul Eldridge. **My First Two Thousand Years.** Macaulay, 1928. Sheridan, $10.00; Scholarly, $19.50.
The "lost" MS of this story, found in a monastery, tells the tale of three immortals: the Wandering Jew, Lilith, and the Missing Link. Although this could have served as the basis for a serious look at some of our shibboleths, it is little more than an antireligious, pro-fornication romp through history. Underneath the sexual byplay (somewhat revolutionary in its day), there are some interesting ideas on civilization. There are also two sequels, but after the first 10,000 years, two replays as seen by the Missing Link and Lilith are too much.

3-65. Weinbaum, Stanley Graham. **The Black Flame.** Fantasy Press, 1948.
Originally two short novels in the 1930s' *Astounding*, these were considered among the best SF of their period. Unhappily, they don't hold up well. The plot is fast, action-packed, and furious, with a deep romantic sentimentality fused to a sense of wonder. A group of immortals rule a postwar semi-savage society. Joaquim Sith and his sister, Margot (the Black Flame), conquer the little city-states and warring tribes. The major interest today lies in the intense sexuality and repressed maternal drive of the Black Flame. Sterile because of her immortality treatments, she is a well-conceived character. Falling in love with a twentieth-century man, she renounces immortality for love and children.

*3-66. Weinbaum, Stanley Graham. **A Martian Odyssey and Other Science Fiction Tales.** Hyperion, 1975, $5.75, $15.00.

Includes *A Martian Odyssey and Others* (Fantasy Press, 1949) and *The Red Peril* (Fantasy Press, 1952), plus "Graph," a previously uncollected short story, and an autobiographical sketch. The 1934 title story is easily the author's best-known work, whose Martian creatures are sharp departures from the tentacled monsters of the 1930s pulps. Other stories include "The Lotus Eaters," a fascinating look at a Venus creature, "The Adaptive Ultimate," and "The Mad Moon."

*3-67. Wells, Herbert George (U.K.). **Things to Come.** Macmillan, 1935. Gregg, $10.50.
Written from his novel, *The Shape of Things to Come* (Macmillan, 1933), this scenario includes seventeen stills from the 1935 production. An influential film in the SF field, comparable in some respects to *Metropolis*, the 1927 film directed by Fritz Lang (see 3-22). The film retains some of Wells' ideas and suggests that futuristic hardware and technical gadgets may not be enough. Compare Clarke's *2001: A Space Odyssey* [4-158].

3-68. Williams, Charles (U.K.). **War in Heaven.** Gollancz, 1930. Eerdmans, $3.25.
A good example of the quasi-mystical novels of Williams, a peripheral figure for SF but one whose works may appeal to some SF readers. This is ostensibly a Grail quest set in modern England and also something of a detective story. Williams transcends his genre by good writing, much as Dorothy Sayers did. The least appreciated of the three main members of the Oxford Christian group (Tolkien, C. S. Lewis, and Williams), his work is more readable than Lewis at his most didactic. This title and *The Greater Trumps* (1950) are strongly recommended.

3-69. Williamson, Jack. **The Legion of Space.** Fantasy Press, 1947. Garland, $11.00.
From the heights (or depths) of the space opera era, this features Williamson's usual tricks of characterization and mixture of SF and fantasy. Incredible characterization and motivation are not helped by choppy plotting and writing, but the uncritical will enjoy the story. Greatly misunderstood, maligned and cheated, John Star and beautiful Aladorea Anthor team up to destroy horrible extraterrestrials, the Medusae, rescue Earth, and save the galaxy. In this stickily romantic tale, we learn the "secret" of Aladorea and her weapon, but the hero and heroine never consummate their love (in print).

*3-70. Williamson, Jack. **The Legion of Time.** Fantasy Press, 1953.
A 1938 serial in *Astounding*, this is one of Williamson's better efforts. Superior to *Legion of Space*, it has action, romance, and adventure. The plot involves a time nexus where a young boy can either, by his early interest in science, create the benevolent future society of Lethonis or, through a failure to develop such an interest, create the malevolent society of So-

rayina. After many adventures, Lanning's Legion of Time succeeds in structuring events to create the proper outcome.

3-71. Wright, Sydney Fowler. **Deluge.** Cosmopolitan, 1928. Arno, $42.00 (includes *Dawn*).
A catastrophic shifting of the Earth's surface brings floods and near-obliteration. Martin Webster, a lawyer, is one of the survivors. He leads a group through the dangers of the new society to form a utopia. Style and writing are tolerable, and the plot moves well but slowly. The plot is mostly adventure but contains some material on social structure and power. The sequel, *Dawn* (1929), is much more interesting as it deals with the problems of this post-catastrophe society.

*3-72. Wright, Sydney Fowler. **The World Below.** Longmans, 1930. Hyperion, $12.95.
Consisting of two novels, *The Amphibians* (1924) and its sequel, *The World Below* (1929), this chronicles the adventures of a man projected 300,000 years into a future of telepathic, furry amphibians, mutant men, unusual forms of intelligent animal life, and imprisonment by the Dwellers, who control the planet. With touches of Dante's *Inferno*, which Wright translated, this story retains considerable power and satiric bite.

3-73. Wylie, Philip. **The Gladiator.** Knopf, 1930. Hyperion, $3.95, $11.50.
A scientist discovers a drug which gives immense strength. He injects his pregnant wife, and their son is extremely strong, with quick reflexes and a superior mind. He quits sports after killing a student, but becomes a super-soldier in World War I. There is no place for him in postwar society, so he goes to the Yucatan and is about to start a super race when he is killed by lightning. This is poor writing even for hack Wylie, with little characterization or motivation except for the gladiator, who is at least interesting as a semi-messiah. The Hyperion reprint is the preferred edition.

4.
The Modern Period, 1938·1975

Joe de Bolt and John Pfeiffer

In the first section of this chapter, we attempt to present a brief history of science fiction from 1938 to the present, agonizingly aware of its oversimplification and inevitable arbitrariness, but convinced of its necessity to an apprentice historian of the field and of the challenge it may offer to those who have formed a mature view of the period. In the second section, we highlight the principles and circumstances that governed the making of the list.

We have divided the period into five parts, each roughly representing a decade or part of a decade. For each part we have blended salient details from contemporary history representing the aspects of popular consciousness that might have been expected to supply inspiration for science fiction. Second, we have mentioned events in the history of the media (print, radio, films, television) that can suggest the modes in which SF was transmitted. Finally, we have represented SF itself, in its topics, titles, and authors, both from the literary mainstream and traditional genre sources.

Three additional matters must be briefly mentioned, because they remain important in a definitive history of SF. The first is an earnest caution against ignoring the quintessential importance of short fiction both in the history and modern progress of SF, especially in view of the fact that most general readers have discovered SF in the form of the novel, film, or TV show. A fundamental history of SF must be recounted largely in terms of the short story. To a considerable extent, anthologies and single-author collections supply the representative titles. The second is SF fandom with its conventions that began in the late thirties. Its influence upon the genre is enormous and incalculable. The third is the parent genre of SF—fantasy. With a few exceptions in cases of award nominees, this guide is restricted to SF, but fantasy can hardly be ignored in a full account of the field. By our definition, fantasy is the genus under which SF is collected as a historically local species. In other ages it appears as Aesop's fables, saints' legends, or Arthurian romance. The issues tend to remain the same while the scenes, furniture, government, technology, and culture change with the times. Modern fantasy is distinct because it is not time- and culture-locked. This is true of the work of three of the most popular writers of fantasy in the last forty years, J. R. R. Tolkien, Mervyn Peake, and Ursula LeGuin, as well as an impressive roster that includes Richard Adams' *Watership Down* (1972), Poul Anderson's *Three Hearts and Three Lions* (1961), John Brunner's *Traveler in Black* (1971), Fritz Leiber's *Conjure Wife* (1953) and the Gray Mouser and Fafhrd series (1939–1968), James Blish's *Black Easter* (1968), Jorge Luis Borges' *Labyrinths* (1962), George Orwell's *Animal Farm* (1946), Miguel Angel Asturias' *Mulata* (1967), Avram Davidson's *The Phoenix and the Mirror* (1969), L. Ron Hubbard's "Fear" (1940), Fletcher Pratt's "The Blue Star" (1952), and the collaborative and editorial efforts of L. Sprague de Camp and Lin Carter on Robert E. Howard's unfinished fantasy works. Such works evoke the mood of our time and must be regarded as a definitive element of the context in which we view SF.

Compilation of the critical list required a rigorously explicit yet flexible index of elements to define SF. Shown below are the titles of many of the best or better works of the period to illustrate and perhaps authenticate the nine elements of our working definition. Titles are presented in one category only, though overlapping of several categories is usually warranted. This list not only supplies a definition of SF but also displays almost graphically the historical weave of the best works with the topology of the genre. Entry numbers are not shown; see under author, or check the index.

A. Demonstration polemics (includes utopias and dystopias)— **Thirties/Forties:** Graves, *Watch the North Wind Rise*; Orwell, *1984*. **Fifties:** Bradbury, *Fahrenheit 451; The Martian Chronicles*; Heinlein, *Double Star*; Kelley, *A Different Drummer*; Pohl and Kornbluth, *The Space Merchants*; Tucker, *The Long Loud Silence*; Vonnegut, *Player Piano*; Wylie, *The Dis-*

appearance. **Sixties:** Barth, *Giles Goat-Boy*; Brunner, *Stand on Zanzibar*; Burgess, *Clockwork Orange*; Disch, *Camp Concentration*; Durrell, *Tunc; Nunquam*; George, *Dr. Strangelove*; Heinlein, *The Moon is a Harsh Mistress*; Vonnegut, *Slaughterhouse Five.* **Seventies:** Aldiss, *Barefoot in the Head*; Carter, *The War of Dreams*; Compton, *The Unsleeping Eye*; Le Guin, *The Dispossessed*; Malzberg, *Beyond Apollo*; Percy, *Love in the Ruins.*

B. Human destiny stories (includes future histories)—**Thirties/Forties:** Asimov, *Foundation Triology*; Heinlein, *The Past Through Tomorrow* (continues through 1950's); Stewart, *Earth Abides.* **Fifties:** Blish, "Cities in Flight" series; Miller, *Canticle for Leibowitz*; Simak, *City*; Pangborn, *Mirror for Observers*; Yefremov, *Andromeda.* **Seventies:** Merle, *Malevil.*

C. Alternate and lost worlds—**Sixties:** Dick, *The Man in the High Castle*; Roberts, *Pavane.*

D. Descriptions of alien and noncontemporary Earth life—**Fifties:** Clement, *Mission of Gravity*; Norton, *Star Man's Son*; Wyndham, *The Midwich Cuckoos.* **Sixties:** Delany, *Einstein Intersection*; Farmer, *The Lovers*; Herbert, *Dune*; Le Guin, *The Left Hand of Darkness*; Leiber, *The Wanderers*; Lem, *Solaris*; Tevis, *The Man Who Fell to Earth*; White, *The Watch Below.* **Seventies:** Asimov, *The Gods Themselves*; Gunn, *The Listeners*; Wolfe, *The Fifth Head of Cerberus.*

E. Objective trips to inaccessible places or with new means of transportation (includes time travel, teleportation, faster-than-light travel, matter transmission)—**Thirties/Forties:** de Camp, *Lest Darkness Fall.* **Sixties:** Anthony, *Macroscope*; Leiber, *The Big Time.* **Seventies:** Anderson, *Tau Zero*; Finney, *Time and Again*; Moorcock, *Behold the Man.*

F. Latent effects of technology—**Thirties/Forties:** Williamson, *The Humanoids.* **Fifties:** Shute, *On the Beach.* **Sixties:** Aldiss, *Greybeard.* **Seventies:** Brunner, *The Sheep Look Up.*

G. New Technology—**Fifties:** Brown, *The Lights in the Sky Are Stars*; del Rey, *Nerves*; Heinlein, *Starship Troopers.* **Sixties:** Spinrad, *Bug Jack Barron.* **Seventies:** Clarke, *Rendezvous with Rama*; Niven, *Ringworld*; Shaw, *Other Days, Other Eyes.*

H. New belief systems (includes new sciences, ideologies, and religions)—**Thirties/Forties:** Hesse, *The Glass Bead Game*; Lewis, "Space Trilogy." **Fifties:** Blish, *A Case of Conscience.* **Sixties:** Budrys, *Rogue Moon*; Delany, *Babel-17*; Heinlein, *Stranger in a Strange Land*; Panshin, *Rite of Passage*; Simak, *Way Station*; Zelazny, *Lord of Light.* **Seventies:** Farmer, *To Your Scattered Bodies Go*; Silverberg, *A Time of Changes.*

I. New physical and/or mental capacities for living or nonliving things (includes stories of supermen, mutations, and transcendence)—**Thirties/ Forties:** Smith, "Lensmen" series; van Vogt, *Slan.* **Fifties:** Anderson, *Brain Wave*; Bester, *The Demolished Man; The Stars My Destination*; Clarke, *Childhood's End*; Clifton and Riley, *They'd Rather Be Right*; Sturgeon, *More Than Human.* **Sixties:** Ballard, *The Crystal World*; Dick, *The Three Stigmata* *of Palmer Eldritch*; Keyes, *Flowers for Algernon*; Lem, *The Cyberiad*; Zelazny, *This Immortal*. **Seventies:** Bass, *Half Past Human*; Silverberg, *Dying Inside*; Wilson, *The Philosopher's Stone*.

Within the perennial themes, historical events have shaped SF as well.

Pre-1940s. With the rise of fascism, the advent of World War II, and the experience of the Depression, a coming to terms with hard reality began to characterize SF. Stanton A. Coblentz's "Lord of Tranerica" (1939) cautioned against the victory of the Axis powers, a theme to be resurrected in such works as Dick's *Man in the High Castle* (1962) and Spinrad's *The Iron Dream* (1972). P. Schuyler Miller erected an architecture of the Depression in *The Titan* (1935; 1952). Movies and pulp literature proliferated for the huge audience otherwise idled by the Depression. American comic books emerged with Superman in the June 1938 *Action Comics*, the beginning of the "golden age" of comics that would be the vulgar assimilation of the more disciplined fantasy of SF. The reaction to Orson Welles' "War of the Worlds" radio production in 1938 illustrated the incredible influence the electronic media would have upon the public consciousness. And John W. Campbell became editor of *Astounding* late in 1937 to shepherd in the first "new wave" in SF. In the literary mainstream, Balmer and Wylie's *When Worlds Collide* was out. C. S. Lewis's famous "Space trilogy" was in progress, while Aldous Huxley's *Brave New World* had been available since 1932. Campbell, within the field, would turn from the adolescently conceived superman, space opera, gadget-fascinated stories marking the apprenticeship of the Binder brothers, Nelson Bond, E. E. Smith, and Jack Williamson to more probable and plausible scenarios represented by Stanley Weinbaum's *Martian Odyssey* (published in 1949 as a book), Campbells' own pieces, and the work of such fledglings as Isaac Asimov and Robert A. Heinlein. Nearly single handed, Campbell focused the visions of important SF writers for decades to come.

1940s. From the outset of the forties, few significant historical developments failed to find treatment in SF. Heinlein in "Sixth Column" (1941) expressed the general anxieties of World War II. Lester del Rey's "Nerves" (1942) depicted the terrible danger of atomic experiments, while Cleve Cartmill predicted the actual development of the atom bomb with now-legendary accuracy in "Deadline" (1944). It was tragically fitting that by his death in 1946, H. G. Wells had lived to see his prediction of nuclear warfare come to pass. The bomb ended the war, but raised new fears over the possibility of genetic alteration in victim populations, fears mirrored in Poul Anderson's "Tomorrow's Children" (1947). Moreover, the real possibility of global catastrophe found metaphor throughout the decade, from Best's *Twenty-fifth Hour* (1940) to Farjeon's *Death of a World* (1948). Meanwhile, the new threat of the U.S.S.R.–United States cold war was expressed in Engel and Piller's *The World*

Aflame (1947), Koestler's *Age of Longing* (1951), and Bradbury's *Fahrenheit 451* (1953). The war had also forced the rapid development of automation, for which robots became the obvious symbol—displayed in the Binders' *Adam Link* (1965), Asimov's *I, Robot* (1950), and Williamson's *Humanoids* (1949). The first of the modern series of UFO flaps occurred to characterize the postwar mood—caught in Ray Jones' *This Island Earth* (1952) and Heinlein's *Puppet Masters* (1951) as the decade ended. Meanwhile, the comic book flourished; Hollywood produced *The Thing*, a bastardization of Campbell's "Who goes there?," and pulp SF serials multiplied. In the mainstream, Orwell's *1984* (1949), Rand's *Anthem* (1946), and Stewart's *Earth Abides* (1949) represented, respectively, the political left, the political right, and a socio-anthropological view of the decadence of human civilization. In the SF field, Campbell's disciplining influence pervaded. Fascination with the gifts and dangers of science waxed, along with concentration upon the refinements of superman in the stories of Asimov, Heinlein, Kuttner, George O. Smith, Williamson, de Camp, and Bradbury—the early greats. Their overall message was earnestly, if tentatively, optimistic.

1950s. Our critical list will show that the bulge in production of memorable SF novels begins in this period and continues unabated to the present. They are so numerous, in fact, that it is a maverick task indeed to select just a few from the nearly 200 annotated entries to represent the signs of the times. Vonnegut's *Player Piano* (1952) challenged the illusion of progress and increasing affluence, while Collins' *Tomorrow's World* (1956) highlighted the struggle between the hedonism and vicariousness of the "beat" generation and traditional puritanism. In Korea the cold war flared and the specter of the H-bomb loomed; so readers were ready for Kornbluth's *Not This August* (1955) and Frank's *Alas, Babylon* (1959). Heinlein's *Starship Troopers* (1959) triangulated a future implied in the success of Sputnik and the rise of the U.S. space program. Leiber's "The Silver Eggheads" (1959) seems more and more prescient of the fruits of war-born computer science, given the breakthrough invention of the transistor. Cities sprawled and made metropolitan life nightmarish; Pohl and Kornbluth's *Gladiator-at-Law* (1955) told the story. And no one could forget Bradbury's "The Pedestrian," predicting the mind-numbing, ubiquitious effects of television. Radio languished. Many SF pulps floundered, while the paperback book began to prosper. Remarkably, a number of mainstream writers produced SF—including Frank, Golding, Shute, "Vercors," Wylie, Wouk, Vidal, and Drury. Good writers in the field increased: Pohl, Clement, Norton, Leinster, Kornbluth, Leiber, Sturgeon, Blish, Bester, del Rey, Wyndham, Clarke, Simak, and Miller. Their works made a golden age for SF.

1960s. In such a tumultous decade, we can only suggest influences. There was the Vietnam war—Ballard's *Love and Napalm: Export USA*

(1972); the continuing H-bomb hysteria—George's *Dr. Strangelove* (1964); the U.S. moon landing—Malzberg's *Universe Day* (1971); McLuhan's media theory—Brunner's *Stand on Zanzibar* (1968) and Spinrad's *Bug Jack Barron* (1969); the wide use and abuse of consciousness-altering drugs—Chester Anderson's *The Butterfly Kid* (1967); the explosive civil rights revolution in progress—Seymour's *The Coming Self-Destruction of the U.S.* (1969); the rise of welfarism—Pohl's *Age of the Pussyfoot* (1968) and Jensen's *Epp* (1967); recognition of the population explosion—Burgess' *The Wanting Seed* (1963), del Rey's *The Eleventh Commandment* (1962), Blish and Knight's *Torrent of Faces* (1967), and Harrison's *Make Room! Make Room!* (1966); the sexual revolution—Heinlein's *Stranger in a Strange Land* (1961), Burrough's *Nova Express* (1964), and Rimmer's *The Harrad Experiment* (1966); the recognition of the threat to ecology by modern industry—Ballard's *The Burning World* (1964) and Merle's *The Day of the Dolphin* (1969). Moreover, the perennial question of man's ability to survive in the chaotic world he makes was asked anew in Brunner's *The Whole Man* (1964), Delany's *Babel-17* (1966), Disch's *Camp Concentration* (1969), and Keyes' *Flowers for Algernon* (1966). Alvin Toffler preceptively caught the syndrome of these years with the label "future shock." Meanwhile, all but a few of the SF pulps had died; SF paperbacks flourished, while SF films peaked with Kubrick's *2001*, and television's *Star Trek* furnished a phenomenon that is still strong in the seventies. Wider and more appreciative audiences than ever developed for SF, and writers both from the mainstream and the field met their appetite:

Mainstream Writers: John Barth, Eugene Burdick, Anthony Burgess, William Burroughs, Lawrence Durell, Sam Greenlee, John Hersey, Fletcher Knebel, Robert Merle, Alan Seymour, B. F. Skinner, Kurt Vonnegut, Irving Wallace.

Writers in SF Field: Poul Anderson, Philip Jose Farmer, Frank Herbert, Ursula Le Guin, Robert Silverberg, Cordwainer Smith, Roger Zelazny.

Furthermore, the mood of the sixties was so stark and wrenching that a special group of writers became identified who seemed to express it most appropriately. For lack of better a term they might be referred to as the "Second New Wave," including Aldiss, Ballard, Brunner, Delany, Disch, Ellison, Malzberg, Moorcock, Spinrad, Reed, and Russ (to name a core). These authors were distinguished from the general field for their emphasis on formerly constrained subject matter and literary experiment. They explored with often painfully ruthless objectivity topics once taboo in most SF, such as sex, radical politics, and religion. Simultaneously, they attacked SF's sacred cows: the conquest of space, man's progress through technology, the success of the male-dominated capitalistic state. Much of the sixties' moods, themes, and developments in writing are summed up in story collections such as Spinrad's *No Direction Home* (1975), Ellison's *Alone Against Tomorrow* (1971), Malzberg's *Final War and Other Fantasies* (1969), and Disch's *Fun With Your New Head* (1971).

In literary art and craft, the new wave authors introduced to SF techniques long common in the mainstream. Their characters were unique and analyzed, not stereotypes. Narratives featured stream of consciousness, word play, prose/poetry counterpoint, and scenario structuring techniques borrowed from such nonprint media as radio, film, and television. In addition, they were often appallingly erudite, employing eclectic vocabulary and displaying consummate control of the esoteric detail of virtually all the sciences. Having appeared upon the scene first in Britain's *New Worlds*, they reached maturity in Ellison's anthology, *Dangerous Visions* (1967). They would meet the malaise of the seventies head on.

1970s. Cynicism and civil anarchy combined with the onset of the food and energy crises and the spreading awareness of a shrinking planet to provide the mood of the past five years. Malzberg's *Beyond Apollo* (1972) drips with cynicism, and Delany's *Dhalgren* (1975) turns page upon page in a world from which government has fled. Famine and filth ravage Earth in Brunner's *The Sheep Look Up* (1972), while Asimov's *The Gods Themselves* (1972) may be an ironic depiction of just how preposterously desperate man's search for energy sources will become. Instead of the prophesied greening of the West, reaction, division, and isolation bridge the decades, as in Brunner's *The Jagged Orbit* (1969) and Priest's *Darkening Island* (1972). The pathology of institutionalized paranoia and oppression wars with the tentatively wholesome search for brotherhood and sisterhood in a world state, as in Hjortsberg's *Gray Matters* (1971) and Russ's *The Female Man* (1975). China has risen, the Vietnam war has ended, and both Russian communism and Western capitalism are on the defensive, as in Harrison's *The Daleth Effect* (1970), and Shaw's *Ground Zero Man* (1971). For the longing eye in this storm of despair is Ursula Le Guin's *The Dispossessed* (1974), a novel whose violent referents in present reality merge into an organization that permits hope and newly innocent joy. Likewise, there is Reynold's utopia, *Looking Backward from the Year 2000* (1973). Watergate broke, radically depreciating the charisma of the American presidency and adding to a nearly universal decline of public confidence in traditional institutions; Knebel's *Night of Camp David* (1965) and Sapir and Murphy's *Destroyer* (1971) series hardly seem fiction. One form of surcease is sought in religious revivals and new cults, epitomized in Silverberg's *Tower of Glass* (1970), Simak's *A Choice of Gods* (1972). Gary's *The Gasp* (1973), MacLean's *Missing Man* (1975), and Goulart's *After Things Fell Apart* (1970). Another form is nostalgia, presented in recent SF anachronistically set in a culture that no longer exists, such as Clarke's *Rendezvous with Rama* (1973) and Niven and Pournelle's *Mote in God's Eye* (1974). Finally, many look to alien gods to lift them from their troubles, as in Cowper's *The Twilight of Briareus* (1974), even to the point of scouring the Earth of its unfit, as the Hoyles do in *The Inferno* (1973).

SF itself has become a matter for serious study in the literature and humanities departments of American universities. All the moods, traditions, and resources of SF have coalesced. The golden age writers are still publishing, and more new authors emerge who are immediately polished and professional. There is a convergence of the mainstream with the SF writers' ghetto that strongly implies that once unthinkable proposition—science fiction or "speculative fiction"—may indeed become the mainstream's heart. Certainly, it is for the first time authentically international, as represented in the dissemination of works by European, Asian, and South American writers. Even so, mainstream and "field" continue to be distinguishable. Associated with the field are Niven, Russ, Lem, Malzberg, Bishop, and James Tiptree. Beyond are Drury, Crichton, Kosinski, Lange, Percy, Gardner, and Boulle. Thus ends an overview of nearly forty years of SF, of thousands of works by hundreds of writers. To represent them in the list that follows, we have had to be satisfied with naming only a few hundred authors and their works.

The preparation of this list has been an occasion for elation in the systematic exploration of a wonderful and important cultural phenomenon, nearly four decades of science fiction. We are challenged by the frustration that a definitive history of this literature does not exist, that the identification of many thousands of works which constitute its body is not completely accomplished, and that a commonly negotiable definition of it is not available. We have presented a critically selected, annotated list of science fiction, moved principally by the pleasant anticipation that it might stimulate the exciting reading and study necessary to identify it, establish its history, grasp its meaning, and enjoy it.

In compiling this list, we found that the works we chose would fall within the following three categories:

1. With the exception of four titles from two of the first-ballot Nebula nominations, we include all novels that were winners and nominees in the awards listing. We note other honors, such as the National Book Award, when appropriate and known to us.

2. We have extracted two content indexes that generally describe the basis for inclusion or exclusion of a given work:

Include:
Demonstration polemics (includes utopias and dystopias)
Human destiny stories (includes future histories)
Alternate and lost worlds
Descriptions of alien and noncontemporary Earth life

Objective trips to inaccessible places or with new means of trans-
portation (includes time travel, teleportation, faster-than-light
travel, matter transmission)
Latent effects of technology
New technology
New belief systems (includes new sciences, ideologies, and religions)
New physical and/or mental capacities for living and nonliving things
(includes stories of supermen, mutations, and transcendence)
Exclude:
Hard fantasy
Pure gothic
Detective stories
Sword and sorcery and/or occult
Cold war/spy stories
Drug trips and/or internal visions
Absurd fiction
Divine intervention or miracles
3. Possessing acceptable elements of content, a work's reputation met
one or more standards.
It was exceptional as literary art.
It presented unusually interesting ideas.
It was important to the history and/or the definition of science fiction.
It was popular either in the field, the literary mainstream, or both.
Though not meeting other criteria, it was the best, or representative
of the best of an important author not otherwise included in the list—
usually a collection of short stories.

Core collection recommendations for libraries were selected on the
basis of one or both of two criteria. They had won a first place in the International Fantasy, Hugo, Nebula, or Campbell awards, or they were
exceptional works in a list already selected according to carefully considered critical standards, as outlined above.

With a few exceptions, we have handled and read a copy of every annotated work. However, for identification and selection of works, we employed numerous published and printed sources. Our individual debts
to them have blurred beyond our ability to specify them. Those who
know them will appreciate their service to us. In addition to many of the
sources listed in chapter 6 and 7, we have relied on many of the "best"
lists appearing in SF magazines, fanzines, and books as a basis for selection
and a source of bibliographic information. The book review columns in
professional and selected amateur magazines were scanned. And as noted
in the introduction, many individuals contributed suggestions.

The following abbreviations are used in this chapter to denote award
winning titles: A (Apollo), H (Hugo, J (Jupiter), IFA (International Fantasy Award), N (Nebula). W after the first initial means winner; N means
nominee; SFHF means Science Fiction Hall of Fame.

Bibliography: The Modern Period

4-1. Abé, Kobo (Japan). **Inter Ice Age 4**. Knopf, 1970, $5.95. Tr. by E. Dale Saunders of *Dai yon kampyo-ki*.

Foreseeing worldwide flooding due to melting ice caps, an underground group of Japanese scientists forces aquatic adaptive changes on human fetuses in the name of survival. Katsumi, information scientist whose work helps develop a machine to forecast the future, faces the moral dilemma of whether or not to support this effort after his own child has been turned into a water-dwelling "aquan." Creative story with doses of philosophy; includes a philosophic postscript by Abé. Writing awkward, perhaps due to translation.

*4-2. Aldiss, Brian Wilson (U.K.). **Barefoot in the Head: A European Fantasia**. Doubleday, 1970.

One of SF's most ambitious, complex books. Aldiss re-Joyces in Yugoslavian Colin Charteris' odyssey across a Europe made mad by psychedelic bombs. Under the influence of the anti-novel, Aldiss strews the work with a full repertoire of writing techniques, including numerous pop songs and poems. Originally appeared, sans verse, as the Acid Head War series in *New Worlds* in 1967. An under-appreciated book even in the genre. Compare Brunner's *Stand on Zanzibar* [4-118] and Dick's *The Three Stigmata of Palmer Eldritch* [4-213].

4-3. Aldiss, Brian Wilson (U.K.). **Cryptozoic!** Doubleday, 1968. Sphere, £.30. (British title: *An Age*, 1967).
A complex science-fantasy novel of mind/time travel. Artist Ed Bush, who sketches the untouchable landscapes of the distant past (reminiscent of the ocean in Lem's *Solaris* [4-390]), runs afoul of his decaying, authoritarian society of 2093 and is labeled mentally ill. But he has seen the truth, that time runs in reverse of our mind-betrayed perception, so that past is future, death is birth. Our common end/beginning is the dead "Cryptozoic Age," the final union of ourselves, descendents of the "Cosmic God," with His creation. Contrast Dick's very different treatment of time reversal theme in *Counter-Clock World* (1967).

4-4. Aldiss, Brian Wilson (U.K.). **Frankenstein Unbound**. Random, 1974, $5.95. Fawcett, $1.50.
A clever tour de force that merges the original *Frankenstein* story and the real characters of Mary Shelley and her circle, along with macabre affectation of a monster-mate with the head of Justine (monster's victim in original story). Adventure story, irony, and social criticism. Compare Farmer's *The Other Log of Phileas Fogg* (1973).

4-5. Aldiss, Brian Wilson (U.K.). **Galaxies like Grains of Sand**. Signet, 1960. (British title: *The Canopy of Time*, 1959, Faber, £1.50).
Eight stories from 1957 to 1958 plus poetic interstitial sequences make up a "chronological novel," sketches of a future history that depicts the universe's end and rebirth. *Starswarm*, another "chronological novel," is similarly organized, except divisions, "surveys," are of different galactic sectors named for various colors; eight stories (from 1958 to 1963) and connective sections. Both collections slightly overlap *Who Can Replace a Man?* [4-12] ("A Kind of Artistry," "Old Hundredth," and the title story), but are illustrative of Aldiss's major concerns with time, change, and the unfolding of uncontrollable, irresistible forces. Stories comparable with those of James Ballard.

*4-6. Aldiss, Brian Wilson (U.K.). **Greybeard**. Harcourt, 1964. Panther, £.40.
After World War III, the human race is confronted with infertility and sterility. There is fear the species will die out. Many people despair, but Greybeard and Martha search and are rewarded with the discovery that children are still being born, guaranteeing mankind's survival. The scenario is the basis for a thoroughgoing critique of what is wrong with mid-twentieth century civilization. Compare Stewart's *Earth Abides* [4-558] and Bass's *Half Past Human* [4-59].

4-7. Aldiss, Brian Wilson (U.K.). **The Long Afternoon of Earth**. Signet, 1962. (British Title: *Hothouse*, 1962). Gregg, 1976 (as *Hothouse*), price not set.
Novelization of the five Hugo-winning (1962) Hothouse stories. In the far future, Earth's rotation has stopped and one hemisphere continually faces the bloated Sun. Vegetation has evolved to fill every ecological niche, and giant plant-spiders spin webs that entwine Earth and Moon. Of animal life, the only survivors are a few social insects and treetop dwelling man, and he, like his star and world, is devolving and close to extinction. An intelligent morel explains the approaching end to a group of humans it befriends and offers to take them with it to seed younger worlds, but they refuse. Perhaps man has finally attained wisdom. Contrast Herbert's *The Green Brain* (1966) and Clarke's *The City and the Stars* [4-150].

4-8. Aldiss, Brian Wilson (U.K.). **Moment of Eclipse**. Faber, 1970, £1.50. Fourteen stories including title story about organism that incubates for four years and, then, membrane-like, occludes eyeball, and "Super-Toys Last All Summer Long," about people who must substitute androids for children. Sophisticated and experimental narrative and points of view; a basic collection of more recent Aldiss.

4-9. Aldiss, Brian Wilson (U.K.). **Report on Probability A**. Doubleday, 1969.
Mary watches on TV men who are watching men who are watching men who . . . are watching through the windows of her house—her. In a circular schema of voyeurs, which is really real? Answer: all realities are subjective. Skillfully constructed mirror maze; compare Dick's *The Three Stigmata of Palmer Eldritch* [4-213].

4-10. Aldiss, Brian Wilson (U.K.). **The Saliva Tree and Other Strange Growths**. Faber, 1966, £1.25. Sphere, £.30.
Excellent collection of ten stories, including the title story, a pastiche of H. G. Wells about the "invasion" of an English farm by aliens from Auriga, which won a Nebula (1965). Also outstanding are "Day of the Doomed King," "Parental Care," and "The Source."

4-11. Aldiss, Brian Wilson (U.K.). **Starship**. Criterion, 1959. Avon, $1.25. (British title: *Non-stop*, 1958).
Man's cosmos shrinks to the vast but limited interior of an uncontrolled derelict interstellar ship. A jungle grows from its hydroponic tanks, wherein savage tribes live, testifying to Aldiss's version of social devolution. But the stalwart, creative few fight and eventually find the control room, pull the brake, and liberate man once again. Good writing and plot. Contrast with its prototype, Heinlein's *Orphans of the Sky* (1964).

4-12. Aldiss, Brian Wilson (U.K.). **Who Can Replace a Man?** Harcourt, 1966. (British title: *Best Science Fiction Stories of Brian W. Aldiss*, Faber, 1965, £1.75, £.80.)

Fourteen early and middle Aldiss stories from 1954 to 1966. Title story, a classic, tells of the attempted self-emancipation of the robotic machines on an automated farm following the collapse of human society; the machines are trapped again by their programmed subservience to man. Also noteworthy are the time-twisting "Man in His Time" (NN, 1966; HN, 1967); "Not for an Age," winner of a 1957 *Observer* contest; "Man on Bridge," "Poor Little Warrior," and the haunting "Old Hundredth." Some of the stories are collected in *Galaxies like Grains of Sand* [4-5] and other Aldiss collections.

4-13. Allighan, Garry (South Africa). **Verwoerd—The End; A Lookback from the Future**. Cape Town: Purnell & Sons, 1961.

In 1987, a historian recounts how apartheid in South Africa, brutally established by Prime Minister Hendrik Frensch Verwoerd, was made to work acceptably and prestigiously under later benevolent rule. Apartheid properly administered can work. Energetically argued polemic. Would not persuade anti-racist reader. Contrast Brunner's *The Jagged Orbit* [4-111].

4-14. Amosov, Nikolai Mikhailovich (as N. Amosoff) (U.S.S.R.). **Notes from the Future**. Simon & Schuster, 1970, $6.95. Tr. by George St. George of *Zapiski iz budushchego*.

A leading Russian scientist (as is the author), dying of leukemia, is frozen until 1991 when he is awakened and cured. Beginning life anew, he acquires a mistress and child, tours the world, and ponders questions of materialism, immortality, and the meaning of life. Much technical and medical information included, but author's aim seems more philosophic than predictive. Contrast with Lem's satirical *Futurological Congress* [4-386] and Reynold's serious and slow-paced *Looking Backward from the Year 2000* [4-476].

4-15. Anderson, Chester. **The Butterfly Kid**. Pyramid, 1967.

Hippies in Greenwich Village obtain a blue pill that makes people's fantasies real. Sean hallucinates real butterflies. The pill-givers are blue lobsters from space who hope through this means to effect a nonviolent conquest of Earth. Hippies stop lobsters with weapons "dreamed up" by the pills. Battle is memorable, including assault by army of blond five-year old boys (illusion created by lobsters) which hippies (sympathetic heroes) repel with machine guns. Enormously energetic and literate narrative texture: "Home was several billion butterflies distant, on St. Mark's Place in the mysterious east." Recalls style and themes of Joseph Heller and Jack Kerouac. HN, 1968.

*4-16. Anderson, Poul. **Brain Wave**. Ballantine, 1954, $1.50.

Anderson's first adult novel and one of his best. Earth moves out of a shower of galactic radiation that has retarded the development of intelligence during the evolution of life; intellect, both human and animal, makes a quantum leap. The genius becomes the super genius, the retarded and higher animals become the old-style normal; neither Earth, now inherited by the former meek, nor the galaxy, watched over by the new super intellects, can ever be the same again. Like Charlie in Keyes' *Flowers for Algernon* [4-336], humanity suffers the trauma of mental growth, and while it is truly a *Childhood's End* [4-149] for man, it is one he makes for himself. Poetic and insightful.

4-17. Anderson, Poul. **The Byworlder**. Signet, 1971, $.75.

Skip Wayburn, artist, minstrel, and free spirit "sigaroon," beats the experts to the reason for Earth's first interstellar visitor; it is looking for art. Story suffers from contrived tension before reader is "let in" on Skip's brainstorm and from worn-out cold war intrigue with Chinese villains. But alien is interesting, as is slang and picture of twenty-first century United States composed of unique subcultures made possible by advanced technology. Contrast Brunner's *The Shockwave Rider* [4-116]. NN, 1971.

4-18. Anderson, Poul. **The Enemy Stars**. Lippincott, 1959.

Four men strive to survive when their matter transmitter is destroyed while they are exploring a dead star. Lots of physics, but in-depth characterization as well: wealthy liberal aristocrat Maclaren, the sole survivor; Buddhist Nakamura, who overcomes his fear of space; young Ryerson, god-haunted descendant of ancient Norsemen, who finds his manhood; revolutionary Sverdlov, who learns to see beyond mere politics. An affirmation of man's dangerous quest into the unknown; original title, from Kipling, was "We Have Fed Our Seas." HN, 1959.

4-19. Anderson, Poul. **Fire Time**. Doubleday, 1974, $5.95. Ballantine, $1.50.

A giant red star scorches the northern hemisphere of the planet Ishtar every 1,000 years, driving the barbarian Centauroid natives to destroy the budding civilization of their counterparts to the south. However, human scientists, on Ishtar to study its unique natives and triple sun system, intervene this time. They persuade the garrisoned Earth navy, there because of a senseless preoccupying war involving Earth, to destroy the nearly victorious barbarian horde. Although against the home government's orders, these acts are pardoned by Earth's leaders. Surrounding the lectures are good action, the well worked-out environment of Ishtar, and interesting aliens. Compare Clement's *Cycle of Fire* [4-161]. HN, 1975.

4-20. Anderson, Poul. **The High Crusade**. Doubleday, 1960. Manor Books, $.95.
Humorous tale of English knights in 1345 A.D. who capture a Wersgorix Empire spaceship. Carried back to the empire through treachery, the knights resist surrender and eventually destroy the empire, replacing it with an interplanetary feudal system "united in Christiandom, the English tongue, and the English crown." Entertaining action, historical color, and consistency of internal logic that makes it all seem possible. Compare Leinster's *The Pirates of Zan* [4-384]. HN, 1961.

4-21. Anderson, Poul. **The Many Worlds of Poul Anderson**, ed. by Roger Elwood. Chilton, 1974, $6.95. (Alternate title: *The Book of Poul Anderson*. DAW, 1975, $1.50).
Seven stories from Anderson's first, "Tomorrow's Children" (1947), one of the earliest post-nuclear war mutation stories, to a new work, "A World Named Cleopatra" (1974), more an encyclopedia entry about a planet than a story. Also contains the excellent "The Queen of Air and Darkness" (NW, 1971; HW, 1972), a poetic tale of telepathic aliens whose defense against colonizing earthmen is the creation of a realm of man's myths, and "The Longest Voyage" (HW, 1961), where a viking-like leader destroys a galactic castaway's ship in order to prevent the benign destruction of his own people's future through cultural contact.

4-22. Anderson, Poul. **People of the Wind**. Signet, 1973, $.95.
Humans and bird-like beings unite on the planet Avalon to repulse a space and land invasion by the Terran Empire. Their strength lies in their unique hybrid culture resulting from mutual cultural diffusion. An excellent treatment of interstellar war and the beautiful, noble flying warriors, the Ythri. Superior Anderson. HN, 1974. NN, 1973.

4-23. Anderson, Poul. **Seven Conquests**. Macmillan, 1969. Collier, $.95.
Seven stories, 1955–1969, loosely tied to the theme of conflict. A foreword gives Anderson's views on the subject. Better stories include "Kings Who Die," with its war technology that can alter both body and mind, and "Wildcat," with its establishment of a secret base for oil exploration in the Jurassic era. Typical Anderson and proof of his maxim that SF is a literature of ideas.

4-24. Anderson, Poul. **The Star Fox**. Doubleday, 1965.
Good action story and argument for taking military hard line against external threat. Industrialist and ex-navy officer Gunnar Heim resists the "Militants for Peace" on the home front and fights the crafty Aleriona

with his privateer starship, the *Star Fox*, until the timid politicians decide to make war. As usual, the aliens fear men because of their rapid technological development and want to defeat them while they still can. Trite for the mid-1960s. Compare Bova's *As on a Darkling Plain* [4-92]. NN, 1965; first part, "Marque and Reprisal," HN, 1966.

*4-25. Anderson, Poul. **Tau Zero.** Doubleday, 1970, $4.95.
In two ways, an archetypal "hard" SF novel: first, an out-of-control space ship is saved by continuous acceleration to near light speed and undergoes the relativistic shrinkage of time to the point where the universe dies and is reborn before the crew find a planet safe to settle. Second, this is a platform for demonstration of the author's philosophy, through the actions of the ship's constable and savior, Charles Reymont, of individualism, strong leadership, rationality, and the need for martial arts. Indeed, the flight itself is a direct metaphor for the myth of progress—advance or die. A solid example of the Campbell–Heinlein SF approach. Compare Niven's *Ringworld* [4-441] and Heinlein's *The Moon is a Harsh Mistress* [4-299]. HN, 1971.

4-26. Anderson, Poul. **There Will Be Time.** Doubleday, 1969.
Jack Havig, of Scandanavian background similar to the author's, foretells the future due to his innate ability to time-travel. Alarmed at America's destiny, Jack sets out to change events and becomes involved in the involution typical of time travel stories. As much a political tract as a novel, the work seems a direct response to the events and atmosphere of the late 1960s; witness the sarcastic "Withit's Collegiate Dictionary" whose first entry is "Activist: A person employing tactics in the cause of *liberation* which, when used by a *fascist*, are known as *McCarthyism* and *repression*." Not first-rate Anderson. Compare Seymour's *The Coming Self-Destruction of the U.S.A.* [4-504]. HN, 1973.

4-27. Anderson, Poul. **Time and Stars.** Doubleday, 1964. Manor Bks. $.95.
Six stories from 1960 to 1963. Includes "No Truce with Kings" (HW, 1964), the story of the discovery and overthrow of benevolent aliens secretly guiding humanity in a new direction amidst civil war in a fragmented, nuclearly devastated United States; pleads man's right to shape his own destiny. Also noteworthy is "Epilogue," where Earth is inhabited by highly evolved mechanical life; makes an interesting contrast with Lem's *The Invincible* [4-388].

4-28. Anderson, Poul. **Trader to the Stars.** Doubleday, 1964.
Three Nicholas Van Rijn novelettes, an Anderson series featuring a colorful and crafty merchant/pirate who pursues profit throughout a laissez-faire universe of the far future. A unique blend of Anderson humor,

philosophy, and historical extrapolation (note the excerpt from "Margin of Profit") in defense of the virtues of free enterprise.

4-29. Anthony, Piers. **Chthon.** Ballantine, 1967. Berkley, $1.25.
Anton Five learns the paradoxical relationship of love and hate, gentleness and violence through imprisonment in the terrible garnet mines on the malevolent planet Chthon. Hellish mines, fascinating characters, and the ordeal of their escape are a remarkable metaphor for the human predicament. HN, 1968; NN, 1967.

*4-30. Anthony, Piers. **Macroscope.** Avon, 1969, $1.75.
The macroscope permits man to see everything in space or time; no secrets are possible, in a single life or in the universe. The first third of this long novel focuses on terrestrial activities and the changes resulting from the macroscope's presence and its ability to reveal human inadequacies. The last two-thirds are less effective and narrate the more cosmic results when the macroscope is turned upon the universe and humanity sees itself in perspective. A dramatic conception whose implications are strikingly presented; his best novel. HN, 1970.

4-31. Anthony, Piers. **Prostho Plus.** Gollancz, 1971, £1.60; Sphere, £.35.
Dr. Dillingham, dentist, is kidnapped from backwater Earth by an alien with a toothache. He becomes a galactic dentist, fixing all kinds of teeth for all kinds of species. Dental problems are cleverly conceived, making the book a gentle parody of SF BEM (bug-eyed monster) conventions. Technical detail is sufficient to make this a laugh romp for a real dentist.

4-32. Anthony, Piers, and Robert E. Margroff. **The Ring.** Ace, 1968.
Jeff Font seeks his father's lost fortune on an Earth where law and order are guarded by "the ring," an electronic device put on convicted criminals that punishes all illegal or immoral behavior and thoughts with an intensity-varied shock. Jeff is "ringed" but recovers the fortune anyway, even as he learns not to hate the "ring" all that much. With a few modifications, a machine-dictated morality might well bring about a utopian society—a perversely and disgustingly intriguing proposition that makes this novel noteworthy. Jeff's relentlessly depicted ordeal is like that of the hero of Anthony's *Chthon.* A sympathetic treatment of the legal "castration" proposition that contrasts with Ellison's " 'Repent, Harlequin!' Cried the Ticktockman" and all attacks on totalitarianism in general.

4-33. Anthony, Piers. **Sos the Rope.** Pyramid, 1968. Faber, £1.70.
In a post-catastrophe world, a benevolent scientific elite keeps the rest of the population in ignorant barbarism. Sos, caught between the two cultures, builds an empire and must then destroy it, because high civ-

ilization always ends in nuclear war. An extremely rare blend of adventure story and rich characterization, incisively plausible incident, reinforcing symbolism, and poignantly evoked theme. Winner, $5,000 Pyramid Publications/Magazine of Fantasy & Science Fiction/Kent Productions Science Fiction Novel Award. Sequel: *Var the Stick* (Bantam, 1973; Faber, £1.95).

4-34. Ashton, Francis (U.K.). **Alas, That Great City.** Andrew Dakers, 1948.
Jonathan and Joy of the twentieth century assimilate by telepathy and time travel the adventures of Larentzal and Cleoli 13,000 years ago in Atlantis' last days. It is destroyed when a former planet causes geological upheavals as it becomes Earth's moon. The book's thesis is that human destiny is ordered by great events of natural law. Using Platonic, Egyptian, and Aztec myths, this is Ben Hur romance and adventure in an SF catastrophe setting. Excellent characterization in sentimental epic tradition. See also Ashton's *Breaking of the Seals* (1946). Compare with Bond's lesser work, *Exiles of Time* [4-85].

4-35. Asimov, Isaac. **The Early Asimov or, Eleven Years of Trying.** Doubleday, 1972, $10.00. Fawcett Crest, 2 vols., $1.50 ea.
Twenty-seven stories, including Asimov's earliest surviving effort. Not noteworthy as fiction, but valuable for the extensive biographical sections between stories which deal heavily with Campbell and the experience of writing "under" him. Stories are illustrative of the general SF pulp content of the time (1939–1949) and feature Asimov's distinctive humor.

4-36. Asimov, Isaac. **The End of Eternity.** Doubleday, 1955. Fawcett Crest, $1.75.
Perhaps Asimov's best early novel. Andrew Harlan, an "Eternal" sworn to use secret time technology to police human history against disasters, falls in love with an outsider and betrays his cause. Making history "safe" denies mankind his destiny; Harlan destroys the secret Eternity police, giving man the agonies of atomic war, but also the nobility of his freedom. Compare Anderson's "No Truce with Kings" [4-27]; contrast Silverberg's more mod *Up the Line* [4-531].

4-37. Asimov, Isaac. **Fantastic Voyage.** Hougton Mifflin, 1966. Bantam, $1.25.
Novelization of the highly successful 1966 film. The screenplay by Harry Kleiner, from an original story by Otto Klement and Jerome Bixby, was followed closely by Asimov, although he improved the scientific content. Crew and sub are miniaturized to sail in unconscious scientist's bloodstream and remove a lethal blood clot in his brain. Good science but tepid cold war story. Not first-rate Asimov. NN, 1966.

*4-38. Asimov, Isaac. **The Foundation Trilogy.** Doubleday SF Book Club, 1964. Avon, $3.95.

Neither novels nor trilogy, but rather a series of nine stories written in the 1940s and inspired by the fall of Rome. Eight were written for Campbell's *Astounding*. Now classics, they portray the destruction of a human galactic empire and the efforts of psycho-historians to shorten the coming dark ages. To do this, they set up a hidden Foundation to guide man in the development of a new culture (*Foundation*, 1951. Alternate title: *The 1000 Year Plan*, 1955. Doubleday, $5.95; Avon, $1.25). As predicted, the old empire's survivors attempt to destroy the Foundation and fail; but an unanticipated threat, a powerful psychic mutant called the Mule, consolidates a mini-empire which threatens the original "Sheldon's Plan" (*Foundation and Empire*, 1952. Alternate title: *The Man Who Upset the Universe*, 1955. Doubleday, $4.95; Avon, $1.25). Finally, with the Mule vanquished, a Second Foundation leads man in the development of mental science, and the dark ages will soon end (*Second Foundation*, 1953. Avon, $.95). Some internal inconsistencies and pulp writing style, but the series helped open SF to new content beyond mere space opera. Awarded a special Hugo (1966) for best all-time series.

*4-39. Asimov, Isaac. **The Gods Themselves.** Doubleday, 1972, $6.95. Fawcett Crest, $1.50.

Asimov's first novel after a fifteen-year gap. The development of a "positron pump" provides a new, seemingly limitless energy supply, but it adversely affects an alternate universe inhabited by remarkable trisexual aliens. Cleanly written and typically cerebral, but the work's three sections are uneven; unique aliens and detailed lunar city in second and third sections add color and interest. Useful metaphysical comment for an era of ecological concern and energy crisis. Compare Heinlein's *The Moon is a Harsh Mistress* [4-299]. HW, 1973; NW, 1972.

4-40. Asimov, Isaac. **I, Robot.** Gnome, 1950. Fawcett Crest, $1.25.

Nine positronic robot stories, originally published 1940–1950, with new material added for continuity. Contains Asimov's famous Three Laws of Robotics and involves the history of U.S. Robots and Mechanical Men, Inc., and the strong-willed "robopsychologist," Dr. Susan Calvin. "Reason" and "Liar!" are particularly noteworthy. *The Rest of the Robots* (Doubleday, 1964, $6.95) presents the eight remaining positronic robot stories, mainly from the 1950s, plus the two novels about policeman Lije Baley and his robot detective sidekick, R. Daneel: *The Caves of Steel* (1954) and *The Naked Sun* (1957). Also contains autobiographical material by Asimov. Superior stories include "Victory Unintentional," "Let's Get Together," and "Lenny," while *Caves* rates as superior Asimov. Compare with the original *Frankenstein* [1-47], Binder's *Adam Link—Robot* [4-68], and Williamson's *The Humanoids* [4-626].

4-41. Asimov, Isaac. **Nightfall and Other Stories.** Doubleday, 1969. Fawcett Crest, $1.50.

Twenty stories with interesting biographical notes by Asimov, all from the 1950s and 1960s except the title story, perhaps Asimov's best, "Nightfall" (SFHF). Written in 1941, it tells of a world which never sees the stars except during an eclipse that occurs only once every 2,049 years, causing madness and cultural collapse. Other stories are average Asimov. Another collection of works for the same period is *The Martian Way and Other Stories* (Doubleday, 1955. Fawcett Crest, $1.25), which includes four stories from 1952 to 1954. In "The Martian Way" (SFHF), the rings of Saturn are mined for water to keep colonial Mars free from reactionary Earth politics. Good traditional SF of the period.

4-42. Atkins, John Alfred (U.K.) **Tomorrow Revealed.** Spearman, 1955.

Some 3,000 years in the future, the son of a star-gazer patches together a history of Earth and planets from such "authorities" as Wells, Huxley, Graves, Orwell, Bradbury, and C. S. Lewis. He determines that mankind's destiny is ordered by "theological significance" after all. Not doctrinaire, gracefully written, persuasively interpolates "sources." Marvelous entertainment for reader seasoned in history of speculative literature. Compare R. C. Churchill's *A Short History of the Future* [4-148]; contrast Garry Allighan's *Verwoerd—The End* [4-13].

4-43. Bahnson, Agnew H., Jr. **The Stars Are Too High.** Random, 1959.

Four men, pretending to be UFO aliens, use an ultra-advanced gravity-driven craft they have secretly developed to frighten Earth's cold-warring nations into peace. The scheme is bungled; nuclear war seems imminent, but the U.S.S.R. and United States agree to cooperate against the common threat. In return, the idealists turn the craft over for international inspection. A tense, smoothly written story. Compare Sturgeon's "Unite and Conquer" [4-570].

4-44. Ballard, James Graham (U.K.). **The Burning World.** Berkley, 1964. (British title: *The Drought.* Penguin, £.30).

A film caused by industrial waste prevents evaporation and causes extended world drought. Ransom, a doctor, is central figure as catastrophe devastates world population. The elemental mechanism of the planet is implacable; modern man will destroy himself by disturbing it. Ballard is masterful at description and metaphor of ecologically shocked landscape, worthy of comparison with Melville and Conrad in this novel and others.

*4-45. Ballard, James Graham (U.K.). **Chronopolis and Other Stories.** Putnam, 1971.

Sixteen stories, the créme de la créme of Ballard's short fiction: "The Voices of Time" are heard by an insomniac counting down signals from space in a world suffering from a strange sleeping sickness; on "The Terminal Beach" of Eniwetok, time stands still at ground zero for a man driven by guilt; "Chronopolis" is a city whose rebellious time-enslaved inhabitants have broken all the clocks; fragile present-freezing flowers in "The Garden of Time" temporarily hold back an advancing hoard; in "End Game," knowing you are innocent is proof of your guilt, and your executioner waits; "Billenium" obtains the ultimate in overcrowding; a desperate man fights to remain in "The Cage of Sand" made of a decayed Cape Kennedy awash in deadly virus-laden dunes. Also noteworthy are "The Drowned Giant," "Manhole 69," "Storm-Bird, Storm-Dreamer," and "Now Wakes the Sea."

*4-46. Ballard, James Graham (U.K.). **The Crystal World.** Farrar, Straus & Giroux, 1966. Avon, $2.25.
Ballard's fourth novel and perhaps his best; it captures the poetry of much of his short fiction but is less experimental in form. Dr. Sanders, drawn to central Africa by a strange letter from a friend, finds himself trapped in a fantastic and beautiful crystalizing forest. Like a spreading jeweled leprosy, land, plants, animals, and humans undergo metamorphosis into frozen time and light, the product of distant, cosmic forces that cause galaxies to divide. Despite the beauty, men fight and guns roar. Touched by the crystals, Sanders tears a portion from his arm, and finally flees the forest carrying a cross thrust upon him by a missionary who stays behind. And Sanders, too, returns. A unique work with apparent debt to Joseph Conrad's *Heart of Darkness*. This work, in combination with *The Wind from Nowhere*, *The Drowned World*, and *The Burning World*, apparently completes a cycle of apocalypses based on the classic elements of matter—fire, earth, air, and water. NN, 1966.

4-47. Ballard, James Graham (U.K.). **The Day of Forever.** Panther, 1967. £.25.
Ten stories that explore "inner space," including "The Lost World of Mr. Goddard," who becomes absorbed in the little people he keeps in a box; "The Insane Ones," where a patient, now cured, sets out to assassinate a leader; and the title story, of a man caught in a twilight realm on a no longer rotating Earth.

4-48. Ballard, James Graham (U.K.). **The Disaster Area.** Cape, 1967. Panther, £.30.
Nine stories of personal disaster. In "Storm-Bird, Storm-Dreamer," a man successfully battles invading birds, but fails to understand a grieving mother; "The Concentration City" is a projection of ultimate urban-

ization, a decaying city that circles space and time; "Now Wakes the Sea" finds a man drowned in a phantom prehistoric ocean; "Manhole 69" is about an experiment in sleeplessness.

4-49. Ballard, James Graham (U.K.). **The Drowned World.** Berkley, 1962. Gollancz, £1.40; Penguin, £.30.
Increased solar radiation has melted Earth's polar caps, flooding its cities and devolving life to a vividly portrayed Triassic Age. Sailing over London, an expedition from the habitable north searches for reclaimable sites. Dreaming racial memories, members also socially devolve and struggle against human scavengers. Finally expedition member Kerans, captured by the situation, heads south into unbroken jungles, "a second Adam searching for the forgotten paradises of the reborn Sun." Superior Ballard. Compare White's *The Dream Millenium* [4-615].

4-50. Ballard, James Graham (U.K.). **The Impossible Man.** Berkley, 1966.
Nine stories, including the title story about a man who rejects a transplanted leg, "The Drowned Giant" where sightseers puzzle over a gigantic human corpse washed up on the beach, and "The Delta at Sunset," with its sick archaeologist, trapped in his own seething mind, watching the snakes on the mud flats.

4-51. Ballard, James Graham (U.K.). **Love and Napalm: Export USA.** Grove, 1972. (British title: *The Atrocity Exhibition*. Cape, 1970, £1.50. Panther, £.30).
Fifteen separable stories or essays first published between 1966 and 1969 and presented as a novel more in terms of atmosphere than plot. Ballard's personal response to the paranoia, violence, and chaos of the United States in the 1960s. High point is the last chapter, "The Assassination of J. F. K. Considered as a Downhill Motor Race," which is also included in *The Day of Forever* [4-47]. Compare with the dark dystopias by Brunner, Disch, and Spinrad from the same period.

4-52. Ballard, James Graham (U.K.). **The Overloaded Man.** Panther, 1967.
Ten stories, including "The Time-Tombs," where grave robbers plunder the psychic tombs of an ancient race; "The Venus Hunters," about a UFO-seeing fanatic and the scientist he converts; "Time of Passage," which traces a boy's birth from the grave to his death in his mother's womb; and the title story, of a man going insane.

4-53. Ballard, James Graham (U.K.). **Vermillion Sands.** Berkley, 1971. Cape, £2.25.

Eight stories set in a decadent Palm Springs-like resort town of the future, Vermillion Sands. "'The Cloud-Sculptors of Coral D" is the collection's outstanding story; men use gliders to shape clouds, until one tries to ride a tornado, dies, and is uniquely avenged by his comrade. Others of note include "Cry Hope, Cry Fury!" and "Prima Belladonna."

4-54. Ballard, James Graham (U.K.). **The Wind from Nowhere.** Berkley, 1962. Penguin, £.30.
Ballard's first novel is a relatively straightforward story of a mysterious 550 MPH wind that destroys civilization, toppling cities and scouring the land. Vainly, men seek shelter underground. In England, a super-bunker in the shape of a pyramid is rushed into construction by a millionaire—a self-contained world for his personal survival and a challenge to the wind. But the wind topples the pyramid, the final humbling of man, and then stops. Good detail of the catastrophe; compare with Leiber's *The Wanderer* [4-380].

4-55. Barbet, Pierre (pseud.) (France). **Baphomet's Meteor.** DAW, 1972, $.95. Tr. by Bernard Kay of *L'empire du Baphomet*, 1972.
In a paralled universe, a technologically advanced alien castaway incites Hugh of Payens to set up the Knights Templars in order to enslave mankind. One hundred fifty years later, William of Beaujeu, given atomic grenades with which to first retake the Holy Land and then conquer all of Asia, turns on the alien, Baphomet, and sets a unified Christian mankind both free and on the road to scientific progress. Historically well researched with interesting battle tactics, but suffers from stuffy language, stereotypic characters, and underwriting, given the story's apocalyptic scope.

4-56. Barjavel, René (France). **The Ice People.** Morrow, 1970. Tr. by Charles Lam Markmann of *La nuit des temps*, 1968.
A handsome couple, Elea and Coban, awake after 900,000 years of suspended animation, bearing the awesome science of a civilization enormously advanced over the twentieth century. World's scientists unify to study them, but world's politicians destroy them before the knowledge gets out. Knowledge without virtue makes culture paranoid. Plausible, smooth narrative and social criticism. A best-seller in France.

4-57. Barnes, Arthur K. **Interplanetary Hunter.** Gnome, 1956. Ace, $.95.
Gerry Carlyle, woman hunter in man-dominated society, hunts strange animals on Sol's planets with chief henchman, Tommy Strike. Five stories from the 1937–1946 period are representative of stage in evolution from space opera to much more probable scenarios of Stanley Weinbaum.

*4-58. Barth, John. **Giles Goat-Boy, or, The Revised New Syllabus.**
Doubleday, 1966, $6.95. Fawcett Crest, $2.25.
An allegorical tour de force representing world as huge university, divided into an East and West "campus." Story is the autobiography of
George Giles, born a psycho-genetics experiment and educated to emphasize the most powerful "goat" drives; an elaborate parody of the aspirations of mankind. A long narrative, endlessly inventive in its use of the
vocabularies of various university components to symbolize the machinations of a mid-twentieth century cold war world. A critical success in the
literary mainstream. Black comedy; it does for the university what Vonnegut did for the Manhattan Project in *Cat's Cradle* [4-605].

*4-59. Bass, T. J. **Half Past Human.** Ballantine, 1971, $1.50.
In distant future of Earth, trillions of four-toed "devolved" humans live
in underground hive utopia; a few "five toes" survive on surface preserving primitive but valuable life drive. Hive populations are dead-ended. "Five toes" are husbanded by ancient cybernetic star ship, "Olga,"
to be implanted in small groups on new Earth-like planets. The hive
model is not for the human species. A rich weave of interesting characters and ingeniously speculative biophysics. NN, 1971. *The Godwhale*
(Ballantine, 1974, $1.50) is an excellent para-sequel. "Humanity" lives in
underground hives. A few humans adapt to live in sea in underwater
bubbles, raiding pitiful surface gardens of the hive. Virtually all planet's
natural flora is dead. Story is of transition from hives to newly "seeded"
environment. Larry Dever makes use of a "godwhale," a cyborg—part
whale, part computer, part robot—to help the sea people flourish
against hive opposition. Fine extrapolation of biological, ecological, and
anthropological principles in describing hive and sea people environment. Whale symbol is powerful, as is drama of fragility and insignificance of organic life systems on an Earth-like planet. NN, 1974.

4-60. Benford, Greg. **Deeper than Darkness.** Ace, 1970.
Half-breed caucasoid, Ling Sanjen, commands a space navy ship against
the alien Quarn in a far-future decaying empire dominated by the descendents of Earth's mongoloids. But a new Quarn weapon drives men
into a psychosis where they shun light, open space, and all social contact.
Faced with this disaster, the immune Ling, despite past discrimination,
attempts the empire's salvation, only to find his cause to be part of the
Quarn treachery. Ling escapes to found a new world where his long-repressed individualism may set man on a new path. Early descriptions of
the psychosis are the work's major asset. As a 1969 novelette received
NN and HN.

4-61. Bennett, Margot (U.K.). **The Long Way Back.** Coward McCann,
1955.

Future Africans form expedition to explore savage Britain where they learn that nuclear weapons, which they now verge on developing, destroyed that once-great civilization. Description of African society and cave-dwelling Britons are this uneven cautionary tale's high points. Story interestingly paralleled by Lightner's *The Day of the Drones* [5-60].

4-62. Best, Herbert. **The Twenty-Fifth Hour.** Random, 1940.
About 1965, "offensive" war reduces Europe to stone age. Americans are wiped out by plague. Hugh from Europe and Ann from America survive to make new life in utopian civilization sprung up in Alexandria, Egypt. Good character development—complex. Thoughtful anthropological insight. Strong narrative weakens in last third of work. Deserves comparison with post-catastrophe stories of John Christopher or Stewart's *Earth Abides* [4-558].

4-63. Bester, Alfred. **The Dark Side of Earth.** Signet, 1964.
Seven satisfying stories, most from the *Magazine of Fantasy and Science Fiction*, including the experimental "The Pi Man" (HN, 1960) and "The Men Who Murdered Mohammed" (HN, 1959), about time travel that adjusts the reality of the individual traveler only. Especially noteworthy is "Time Is the Traitor," a story of love, compulsion, and how time changes us. Eleven other Bester stories are contained in *Starburst* (Signet, 1958. Sphere, £.30), several of which deal with the relationship of psi talents and mankind's desire for power. Memorable entries include "Fondly Fahrenheit" (SFHF), "Adam and no Eve," "Of Time and Third Avenue," "Oddy and Id," and "The Starcomber" (formerly "5,271,009"). Pyrotechnic, yet well-crafted writing is Bester's hallmark.

*4-64. Bester, Alfred. **The Demolished Man.** Shasta, 1953. Garland, $11.00.
One of modern SF's top novels, the tragedy of a twenty-fourth century Oedipus, Ben Reich, a ruthless interplanetary tycoon subconsciously driven to unknowingly commit patricide. He is pursued by a vengeful "Esper" policeman, Lincoln Powell, and by a mental phantom, The Man With No Face, symbol of his evil deed. In escaping Powell and the law's enlightened penalty for murder, social restoration after personality demolition, Reich risks a more complete destruction by his own guilty subconscious. Extrapolated social setting and innovative writing techniques compare with Brunner's *Stand on Zanzibar* [4-118], while the mature handling of telepaths anticipates Silverberg's *Dying Inside* [4-523]. The touchstone of hybrid SF and detective fiction, its sophistication in character development and the exploration of the human psyche is rare in either genre. Winner of the first Hugo (1953); placed second in IFA (1954).

*4-65. Bester, Alfred. **The Stars My Destination.** Signet, 1956. (British title: *Tiger! Tiger!*, 1956). Berkley, $1.25; Gregg, $10.00.

Twenty-fifth century Earth features the decadence of the common man in the grip of multinational capitalism, even though, essentially illogically, mankind has acquired the ability to teleport over distances up to 1,000 miles. Enter Gully Foyle, ape-like space sailor, who, driven by desire for revenge, transcends his ignorance, social class, and parapsychic limitation to bring to every man the power and responsibility to teleport to the ends of the universe—a godlike existence. Under the stress of the murderous constraints upon him, man will develop abilities that enable him to survive and triumph. A pollyannish though seductively optimistic interpretation of how most men will be selected to survive—when the alternative is extinction. The political scenario is prescient of topics widely current today. The narrative paraphernalia anticipates Brunner's wholesale effects in *Stand on Zanzibar* [4-118] and *The Sheep Look Up* [4-115]. A well-modulated paranormal powers-emerging story. Gully Foyle is a persuasively complex "everyman." Compare Simak's *Time and Again* [4-537].

4-66. Biggle, Lloyd, Jr. **The Metallic Muse.** Doubleday, 1972, $5.95. DAW, $1.25.
Seven stories from 1957 to 1968, introduced by the author, which more or less touch on the arts. Biggle, trained in music, is known for his use of the arts in his works. Notable stories: "Tunesmith"—TV commercials are the only entertainment and medium for the highly automated arts until tunesmith Baque dares to bring back traditional music; "In His Own Image"—a humanoid robot, priest to a congregation of machines in a space hostel, electro-shocks a castaway into conversion.

4-67. Biggle, Lloyd, Jr. **Monument.** Doubleday, 1974, $4.95.
A marooned maverick earthman leaves a legacy of knowledge so that the peaceful, happy natives of his Edenic castaway world can resist the inevitable exploitation by Earth's expanding commercial domain. Makes a sentimental but effective case against cultural imperialism and environmental corruption. In this novel the country boys outsmart the city slickers. Expansion of delightful story nominated for a Hugo in 1962. Contrast Silverberg's *Downward to the Earth* [4-522].

4-68. Binder, Eando (pseud. of Earl Andrew Binder and Otto Oscar Binder). **Adam Link—Robot.** Paperback, 1965. Warner, $.95.
Charles Link creates Adam and Eve Link, robots; metal with human emotions. Adam agonizes over identity, saves Earth from alien invasion, and goes to the Moon to think over future with Eve. A sentient robot will have problems with mankind. Written in late 1930s and early 1940s, these robot stories break from space opera and gadget tales. Thoughtful treatment of artificial intelligence. Compare Shelley's *Frankenstein*[1-47], Asimov's *I, Robot* [4-40] (Binder used title first in 1939 "Link" story), and Jones' *Colossus* [4-327].

4-69. Binder, Eando (pseud. of Earl Andrew Binder and Otto Oscar Binder). **Puzzle of the Space Pyramids.** Curtis, 1971.

Captain Atwell and crew make first trips to Mars, Venus, Mercury, Ganymede, and Jupiter, finding life on all and also pyramids on each employed by ancient Martians to alter the eccentric orbit of Asteroidia with gravity beams to prevent collision with Mars. The planet broke into the asteroid belt and destroyed Martian civilization. Life seems to exist everywhere. Episodic (serialized in *Thrilling Wonder Stories*, 1937–1942), but an ingenious compilation of what have become clichés about our solar system. One of the first attempts to humanize space explorers.

4-70. Bioy Casares, Adolfo (Argentina). **The Invention of Morel and Other Stories.** University of Texas Press, 1964, $7.95. Tr. by Ruth L. C. Simms of *La invención de Morel*, 1940.

Influenced by Wells' *The Island of Dr. Moreau* [2-162], deals with Morel's search for immortality, culminating in invention depending heavily on photographic principles. Story by nameless narrator, recounting stay on Morel's island, who falls in love with Morel's "amante," Faustine. She ignores him because he is on another plane of existence.

4-71. Bishop, Michael. **A Funeral for the Eyes of Fire.** Ballantine, 1975, $1.50.

Best known for his award-nominated short stories (no published collection to date), Bishop's first novel is brilliantly ambitious and seriously flawed. Fleeing Earth to Glaparcus, two brothers are successful in a mission to bring gentle-spirited and persecuted Ouemartsee from Trope to Glaparcus. For this they earn a place on Glaparcus—only to become convinced they have been exploited by the betrayals and tragedy of interplanetary diplomacy. The individual must fail when he trusts the ethos of corporate civilization. Fine writing, but the tragic progress of the novel might benefit by substitution of third-person dramatic for first-person voice of Balduin who tells the story. Very promising first novel.

4-72. Bixby, Jerome. **Space by the Tale.** Ballantine, 1964.

Eleven SF and fantasy stories from 1952 to 1963, including "The Bad Life," about the torture of a space-age social worker by the depraved inmates of Limbo, a prison planet; "Small War," a novel first-contact story in which human and alien mutually reject contact; and "Angels in the Jets," where a new planet's atmosphere turns an exploration ship's crew mad, leaving its captain the choice of madness or death. Enjoyable yarns.

4-73. Blackburn, John (U.K.). **A Scent of New-Mown Hay.** M. S. Mill, 1958.

At the end of World War II, Nazi scientist Rosa Steinberg mutates fungus that transforms women into hideous monsters; spores have widespread effect by late fifties and threaten world so that cold war enemies unite. Plague is metaphor of great evil still abroad from the war. Plausible scientific basis. Cloak and dagger suspense with politically conservative mood.

4-74. Blish, James. **Anywhen.** Doubleday, 1970. Faber, £1.80.
Seven well-crafted stories first published between 1956 and 1968, with a brief preface and story introductions. Of special note are "A Style in Treason," a colorful far-future romp where treachery has replaced diplomacy; "The Writing of the Rat," in which man learns he is the descendent of galactic slavers; and "A Dusk of Idols," which stands our traditional humanistic values on their head. Literate works by one of the genre's intellectuals.

*4-75. Blish, James. **A Case of Conscience.** Ballantine, 1958, $1.50.
Father Ramón Ruíz-Sánchez, Jesuit priest and biologist, sees a new planet, Lithia, and its intelligent reptilian inhabitants as creations of the devil created to tempt man, because they offer final proof of evolution. One of these reptiles, Egtverchi, brought to Earth as an egg by Ramón, grows up a stunted misfit, creates social havoc, then escapes back to Lithia. Fearing that Egtverchi's impact on Lithia would make it even more of a danger to man's soul, Ruíz-Sánchez exorcises the planet, whose sun immediately goes nova. A novel rich in theological concerns, well researched and executed, and open to several interpretations. Blish's best SF work. HW, 1959. *Case* is the final third of what Blish has termed a philosophic trilogy, "After Such Knowledge." The first part is an excellent historical novel on the life of Roger Bacon, *Doctor Mirabilis* (1964), while the middle part is composed of two fantasy novels—*Black Easter* (1968), where a deal with the devil unleashes victorious evil, and a sequel, *The Day after Judgement* (1971). Works are independent of each other in subject matter, but all speak to the same issue: "Is the desire for secular knowledge, let alone the acquisition and use of it, a misuse of the mind, and perhaps even actively evil?" An effort unique in SF; highly recommended.

*4-76. Blish, James. **Cities in Flight.** Avon, 1970, $2.25.
Four novels constitute a future history in which Earth's cities, using the "spindizzy" drive, leave the planet to escape repression and take up nomadic existence in space. This omnibus includes an essay by Richard D. Mullens, "The Earthmanist Culture: *Cities in Flight* as a Spenglerian History," which contains a chronology of Spenglerian and Blishian worlds. Great space opera in the mode of Asimov's *The Foundation Trilogy* [4-38] but even more grandiose and rich in detail. The story begins with *They Shall Have Stars* (1956), composed of material published between 1952 and 1954, which tells of the perfecting of the antigravity spindizzy

and the building of a huge structure, "The Bridge," on Jupiter. The cities are fleeing Earth in *A Life for the Stars* (alternate title: *Year 2018*) (1962). Here, life in such a city is traced as the "Okies" struggle for survival, seeking what work they can in return for needed supplies. *Earthman, Come Home* (1955) is composed of four stories from 1950 to 1953 written into continuity (title story included in SFHF). It tells of New York City and its mayor, John Amalfi, as they confront other cities turned rogue and a Vegan fortress that threatens Earth. But the day of the Okie cities is over; under Earth's ban, New York flees to the Greater Magellanic cloud to found New Earth. Here, the immortal city dwellers face the ultimate threat—the end of the universe. In *The Triumph of Time* (1958) (British title: *A Clash of Symbols*), New York flees to the universe's heart to ride out the storm; the end comes, and Amalfi, hanging lost in the "unmedium," explodes himself to begin creation anew.

4-77. Blish, James, and Robert Lowndes. **The Duplicated Man.** Avalon, 1959. Associated Booksellers, $.60.
Two immortals play a dangerous game when they manipulate a war to prevent the use of atomic weapons. A normal, Paul Danton, finally breaks the deadlock with the use of a duplicating machine and the cooperation of both immortals. Convoluted plot with good psychological depiction. Man can overcome his failures, but only through the sacrifice of those who can force the move. Compare with Pohl's *Slave Ship* [4-465].

4-78. Blish, James. **Galactic Cluster.** Signet, 1959, $.95.
Eight stories, 1953–1959, representative of early Blish. Emphasis is on people, as in "Tomb Tapper," a strong antiwar story about men who tap the minds of downed enemy airmen and the horror they find there, and "A Work of Art," where the personality of Richard Strauss, recreated in the mind of a musical illiterate in an age of musical decadence, faces his failure as a composer. "Common Time" is an exploration of the subjective time effects of faster-than-light flight on an astronaut. Contrast with Asimov's *The Martian Way* [4-41].

4-79. Blish, James. **Jack of Eagles.** Greenberg, 1952. Faber, £2.10 (Alternate title: *ESP-er*, Avon, 1958).
Blish's first novel, overly melodramatic and poorly characterized, but an important early study of scientifically based psi powers. Danny Caiden develops a range of "wild talents," including telepathy, teleportation, and telekinesis, which disrupt his life. On the run from the F.B.I., criminals, and a group of "psi-men," he finally vanquishes the bad guys and gets the girl. Contrast with Silverberg's strikingly realistic *Dying Inside* [4-523].

4-80. Blish, James. **The Seedling Stars.** Gnome, 1957. Signet, $1.25.
The Pantropy series, written between 1952 and 1955, tells of a biological development that allows humans to be shaped to fit non-Earth environ-

ments and the effects of such seeding. "Seeding Program," the weakest story, traces program's origins and the fight on Ganymede against reactionary Earth's efforts to kill it; in "The Thing in the Attic," treetop dwellers reestablish contact with earthmen; "Surface Tension" (SFHF), the best of the series, tells of tiny water dwellers who explore the "Universe" beyond their little puddle; "Watershed" confronts the prejudice of the "basic type" human towards the pantrophied ones. Prose awkward at times, but ideas and action carry the series and reflect Blish's life-long interest in biological sciences.

4-81. Blish, James, and Norman L. Knight. **A Torrent of Faces.** Doubleday, 1967. Faber, £1.50.
Based on the concept, under development by the authors since 1948, of an Earth able to hold one trillion inhabitants; excellent description of the technological, environmental, and societal elements of this crowded world whose 800 years of stability have ended, for the best, the authors feel, by impact with the asteroid Flavia. Story suffers from weak characterization. Compare with Harrison's *Make Room! Make Room!* [4-290] and del Rey's *The Eleventh Commandment* [4-204].

4-82. Bloch, Robert. **Fear Today, Gone Tomorrow.** Award Books, 1971, $1.25.
Twelve SF and fantasy stories, from 1954 to 1968, with emphasis on horror and death; in "A Toy for Juliette," Jack the Ripper time travels into the future, while in "The Hungry Eye," an alien feeds on the murders committed by its hypnotized human slaves. Stories of satire and social criticism also included; the humorous "Report on Sol III" has an alien ethnographer delineating human failings, and in the powerful fantasy story, "The Funnel of God," an immortal black African shaman becomes God and destroys decadent Earth with a giant gob of spit. Typical Bloch, but SF is not his forte.

4-83. Blum, Ralph. **The Simultaneous Man.** Little, Brown, 1970. Panther, £.30.
In the mode of *The Andromeda Strain* [4-184], this work takes one into the nightmare world of secret research in the name of national security. Andrew "Bear" Horne, Korea War POW and pharmacologist, has his memories recreated in a black prisoner volunteer whose own memories have been erased. The transfer includes classified material and violates orders. Both Bear and "Black Bear" fall under suspicion and surveillance. Rebelling, Black Bear defects to U.S.S.R. to help their memory changing research, and Bear follows, only to become the captive of "himself" for use in similar experiments. Near-surrealistic scenes balance occasional writing flaws. Compare Harrison's *Daleth Effect* [4-288].

4-84.   Bodelsen, Anders (Denmark). **Freezing Down.** Harper & Row,

1971. Tr. by Joan Tate of *Frysepunktet*, 1969. (British title: *Freezing Point*.) Bruno, one of the first to be frozen down with an incurable disease, is pursued through time by his physician, Dr. Ackermann, who is intent on giving Bruno immortality even though he comes to have no reason to live after successive thawings. His universe constricted to his hospital room, Bruno begs for death but his doctor insists that he live, even if in a semicomatose dream world. Interesting twist on the sleeper wakes theme; good translation. Compare with Amosoff's *Notes From the Future* [4-14].

4-85. Bond, Nelson S. **Exiles of Time.** Prime, 1949.
Originally published in 1940, a fast-paced action story built around an astronomical catastrophe that threatens ancient Mu and the attempt to prevent it by bringing modern humans into the past. But time is unalterable, a closed circle—our past is our future. Full of clichés, stereotyped characters, and questionable anthropology, geology, and astronomy, but a neat "explanation" of cross-cultural catastrophe myths, the ice age, Charles Fort's anomalies, and Ragnarok.

4-86. Bond, Nelson S. **Lancelot Biggs: Spaceman.** Doubleday, 1951.
Lancelot Biggs, skinny genius, with rotating Adam's apple, performs astounding feats—some good, like saving his ship from bloodthirsty space pirates, and some bad, like turning a valuable cargo of vegetables into a rotten mess. He bumbles along, testing his seemingly farfetched "theories" to the consternation of his old space-dog captain, yet seems to always save the day in this 1939–1943 pulp series. Typical, but good space/science yarns of the period, complete with space navy slang, space academy football rivalries, pig latin, and a space radio operator called Sparks. In the end, Lancelot marries the Captain's daughter, invents antigravity, and gets his own command. Perfect example of future-as-today SF. Compare Chandler's John Grimes stories [4-144].

4-87. Borges, Jorge Luis (Argentina). **Ficciones.** Ed. by Anthony Kerrigan. Grove, 1962, $2.95. Tr. by Anthony Kerrigan et al. of *Ficciones*, 1956.
Seventeen short stories synthesizing philosophy and fantasy. "Tlön, Ugbar, Tertius" involves an alternate world, invented by scholars, slowly displacing the "real" world. "The Circular Ruins" explores the reality of dreams and their effect on other planes of existence. "The Babylon Lottery" presents a bizarre game of infinite possibilities under the aegis of a sinister company. Borges is likely candidate for Nobel Prize. *Ficciones* shared 1961 Formentor Prize with Samuel Beckett.

4-88. Boucher, Anthony (pseud. of William Anthony Parker White). **Far and Away.** Ballantine, 1955.
Eleven fantasy and SF stories from 1941 to 1954. Stories of interest in-

clude "Star Bride," a short tragedy of interplanetary imperialism; "Balaam," a first contact story involving a rabbi and a priest who face a test of conscience; and "The Other Inauguration," about U.S. politics and the penalty for tampering with fate. Also of interest is the SF-fantasy blend, "Snulbug," a time travel story involving a cute time-warping demon and his master's abortive efforts to capitalize on knowledge of the future. Typical Boucher stories.

4-89. Boulle, Pierre (France). **Garden on the Moon.** Vanguard, 1965, $6.95. Signet, $.95. Tr. by Xan Fielding of *Le jardin de Kanashima*, 1964.
The space race begins at the German Peenemünde rocket base and includes the United States, U.S.S.R., and Japan. Ironically, Japan wins the race to put the first man on the Moon by the simple expedient of allowing the rocket pilot to die there. The moral is that the space effort is enormously important and should be an international effort. Competition here is wasteful and intermittently tragic. Moving fictional history and extrapolation of the people and events surrounding the effort to put men on the Moon. Compare Clarke's *Prelude to Space* [4-155].

4-90. Boulle, Pierre (France). **Planet of the Apes.** Vanguard, 1963, $6.95. Signet, $.95. Tr. by Xan Fielding of *La planète des singes*, 1963.
Expedition to Betelgeuse solar system finds a world where dominant species is simian; humans are subordinate animals. Prejudices, posturing, and social absurdities are portrayed with Swiftian comment and literary deftness. Boulle is a first-rank novelist whose novel contrasts sharply with adulterated film and TV versions. An excellent modern *Gulliver's Travels* [1-49].

4-91. Boulle, Pierre (France). **Time out of Mind.** Vanguard, 1966, $6.95. Signet, $1.25. Tr. by Xan Fielding and Elisabeth Abbott of *Contes de l'absurde suivis de E=mc²*, 1957.
Twelve stories, including "Time out of Mind," about time travellers from past and future who meet man from present and trap him in endless piece of the present, and "The Perfect Robot," about "humanizing" androids by making them defective in perception and judgment. Familiar story scenarios excellently rendered.

4-92. Bova, Benjamin William. **As on a Darkling Plain.** Walker, 1972. Based on stories orginally appearing in 1969 and 1970, an entertaining "hard" SF tale of Sydney Lee, a scientist so obsessed with the psychic and potential military threat of giant, alien, incomprehensible machines on Titan that he attempts suicide, is driven to interstellar exploration, and refuses true love. Colorful background includes a descent into Jupiter's atmosphere, Neanderthal survivors on a nova-scoured world near Sirius, and gaudy Saturn hanging over Titan's ammonia sea. Good science, but characterization fails. Compare with Clement's realistic alien worlds.

4-93. Bova, Benjamin William. **Forward in Time.** Walker, 1973, $6.95. Popular Lib., $1.25.
Ten stories published between 1962 and 1971, each set in a progressively more distant future. Hard SF and morality plays mingle in "Stars, Won't You Hide Me?," where the last man races racial punishment to the end of time, "The Next Logical Step," in which an advanced computer's predictions of ultimate disaster may end the cold war; and "Men of Good Will," who continue a foolish lunar battle. "Zero Gee," "Test in Orbit," and "Fifteen Miles" are part of projected series about astronaut Chester A. Kinsman.

4-94. Bowen, John (U.K.). **After the Rain.** Ballantine, 1959.
The rain falls and there comes a second deluge of Earth. Some survivors stay alive on a raft. After many days they come to an island and have a chance to begin life again. There is joylessness in their salvation because the time on the "ark" has demonstrated all the viciousness, brutality, and insanity that characterizes mankind. Just before they disembark on the island, Tony, the one heroic figure of the group, suicides. Well-written, biting satire. Bowen is principally a playwright; this novel is derived from an earlier play.

4-95. Boyd, John (pseud. of Boyd D. Upchurch) (U.K.). **The Last Starship from Earth.** Weybright and Talley, 1968. Gollancz, £1.25; Pan, £.40.
Interesting alternate universe, with Earth run by an all-powerful benevolent state ruled by sociologists, psychologists, and a Catholic Church headed by a computerized Pope. Castes exist, with "Pros" permitted to breed only within their profession. A young mathematician, Haldane IV, and a poetess challenge the system, are caught and sent to the penal planet Hell, where other social dissidents have built a free society. Haldane IV goes back in time to destroy Earth's confining social system by stopping Christ before his successful conquest of Rome and the institution of the crossbow as the Church's symbol. A very good first novel, humorous and sophisticated. Contrast Moorcock's *Behold the Man* [4-427].

4-96. Boyd, John (pseud. of Boyd D. Upchurch) (U.K.). **The Pollinators of Eden.** Weybright and Talley, 1969. Gollancz, £1.25; Pan, £.30.
Stereotypical woman scientist goes to study sentient flowers; she is raped by an orchid and gives birth to a seed. Humorous satire on science, sanity, and society. Compare Farmer's *The Lovers* [4-240].

4-97. Boyd, John (pseud. of Boyd D. Upchurch) (U.K.). **Sex and the High Command.** Weybright and Talley, 1970.
A new product, Vita-lerp, gives women not only great orgasms, but baby daughters as well. Men, now superfluous, fight back under the military high command, but the women win. Broad satire on male chauvinism

and the military, as well as a warning against ultra-women's lib. Supports the case of Russ's *The Female Man* [4-485].

4-98. Brackett, Leigh Douglas. **The Long Tomorrow.** Doubleday, 1955. Ballantine, $1.50.
Len Colter lives in antiscientific age after World War IV. Neo-Mennonite and evangelical fundamentalist culture forbids science, but scientists work in secret. Colter suffers a protracted period of indecision but finally joins them to renew technology, hoping it won't be misused again. Compare Cooper's *The Cloud Walker* [4-176] and Miller's *A Canticle for Leibowitz* [4-424]. Fine illustration of how fear creates a sterile and superstitious culture.

*4-99. Bradbury, Ray. **Fahrenheit 451.** Ballantine, 1953, $1.50. Simon & Schuster, $5.95.
Based on 1951 short story, "The Fireman" (SFHF), work's title is flashpoint of book paper. Totalitarian state outlaws virtually all books, especially the classics; an underground forms of people who memorize great works to preserve them for posterity. The plot revolves around a "fireman's" conversion from book burner to preserver. Widely popular as film. Inspired a BBC symphony. Won Commonwealth Club of California second annual Gold Medal.

4-100. Bradbury, Ray. **The Golden Apples of the Sun.** Doubleday, 1953. Bantam; $1.75, Greenwood, $10.75.
Twenty-two SF and fantasy stories, including "The Fog Horn," about a sea monster that loves a fog horn; "The Pedestrian," the classic tale of a walker who is lonely because everybody is watching television; "A Sound of Thunder," where a time-safari to hunt tyrannosaurus rex alters the present because a hunter accidently kills a butterfly; and the title story, about a spaceship that flies into the Sun's atmosphere to capture part of its substance. Emphasis on message and characters, rather than science.

4-101. Bradbury, Ray. **The Illustrated Man.** Doubleday, 1951, $5.95. Bantam, $1.25.
Eighteen SF and fantasy stories from 1947 to 1951 plus prologue and epilogue. Structured by the device of a man's body tatooed with pictures, each of which comes alive with a story. Includes "The Veldt," about a futuristic playroom that realizes children's fantasies and leads to their parents' death; "Kaleidoscope," with an exploded spaceship's crew hurtling through space to their deaths; "The Long Rain," in which a group of lost men fight the endless rains of Venus; and "Zero Hour," a study in horror where a child leads her alien playmate to the attic where her parents are hiding. Some social criticism, but emphasis on sentimentality in highly crafted, emotion-generating stories. IFA third place, 1952.

*4-102. Bradbury, Ray. **The Martian Chronicles.** Doubleday, 1950, $5.95, $8.95 (deluxe ed.). Bantam, $1.25. (British title: *The Silver Locusts*, 1951).

The frame story for *Chronicles* is the colonization of Mars by Earth in the late twentieth century. Stories provide vignettes of spacemen landing on Mars, the first colonies, the nature of the nearly mystically existing Martians, and the lives of Earthmen who become "Martians." Themes are of cautionary, social criticism. Earthmen will treat Mars as Europeans treated North America, raping and plundering it. Stories are "exemplums" set in the future, with moral and quasi-religious messages. Compare with Bradbury's *The Illustrated Man* [4-101]. Received $1,000 award from National Institute of Arts and Letters for contribution to American literature; perhaps the best-known of all modern SF books.

4-103. Bradley, Marion Zimmer. **The Sword of Aldones.** Ace, 1962.

Perhaps the best of the Darkover planet series (first in series is *Darkover Landfall*, 1972). Darkover has avoided "progress," stressing simplicity of civilization and family in the face of Earth-based galactic technological civilization. Psi-talented Lew Alton, half Darkoveran, half Terran, mediates the fate of Darkover in the threat from technological civilization by means of his adaptation to the Sword of Aldones, its true power available only in its psycho-kinetically operable matrix. He "saves" Darkover. Well-told story with sword and sorcery setting and "scientific" underpinning.

4-104. Briarton, Grendel (pseud. of Reginald Bretnor). **Through Time and Space with Ferdinand Feghoot.** Paradox, 1962. Mirage, $4.00, $6.50 (as *The Complete Feghoot*).

Fifty "Feghoots," including five published for first time (most of others appeared in the *Magazine of Fantasy and Science Fiction*). Each runs one to two pages, involves a fantasy or SF motif, and concludes with a pun—generally so arch and bad that it's funny. With Gahan Wilson's cartoons, one of the few really fascinating droll spin-offs from the serious main currents of the genre.

4-105. Brown, Fredric. **Angels and Spaceships.** Dutton, 1954. (Alternate title: *Star Shine*, 1956).

Seventeen stories and vignettes from 1941 to 1949, and an introduction by the author on the distinction between SF and fantasy. The vignettes, Brown's forte, range from the horror of "Pattern" and "Answer" through the tenderness of "Reconciliation" and the broad humor of "Politeness." Other superior stories include "Letter to a Phoenix," a philosophic statement about human nature and destiny; and "Waveries," in which invading aliens eat electricity and turn back the technological clock, to the betterment of humanity.

4-106. Brown, Fredric. **Honeymoon in Hell.** Bantam, 1958.
Twenty-one stories and vignettes, some fantasy, including the classic "Arena" (SFHF), the story of a superior being's test of mankind's vs. an alien's fitness to survive through single combat. Also noteworthy are "The Dome," about the wages of a man who deserts mankind to save himself; "Too Far," a punny story about a lecherous were-deer's retribution; and "Imagine,"a treatise on our sense of wonder in under 200 words. Like much Brown, parables, entertainments, and puzzles.

*4-107. Brown, Fredric. **The Lights in the Sky Are Stars.** Dutton, 1953. (British title: *Project Jupiter*, 1954).
Mature story, rich in characterization for the SF of its day, of the efforts to reopen space exploration with a flight to Jupiter over the objections of "conservationists." Senator Ellen Gallagher gives her life for the project, while her lover, Max Andrews, once denied space travel due to an accident, fights the bureaucracy and alcoholism to see the project through and to go on the voyage. The rocket goes, but Max doesn't. A powerful, poignant plea for spaceflight and a study of a man obsessed by it. Compare with Kornbluth's *Takeoff* [4-352]; contrast with Malzberg's *Universe Day* [4-410].

4-108. Brown, Fredric. **Space on My Hands.** Shasta, 1951.
Nine stories, ranging from humor to horror, and brief introduction by the author on writing SF. Includes "The Star Mouse," one of Brown's most popular stories, about a lonely scientist who sends a mouse, Mitkey, into space, where aliens make it intelligent. Also noteworthy are "Pi in the Sky," where the stars are used to advertise soap; "Nothing Sirius," which has a member of a space-touring penny arcade troop fall in love with the thought projection of an alien cockroach on an unexplored planet; and "Come and Go Mad," about a man driven mad by the knowledge that ants are really Earth's masters, mankind merely a parasite. Good collection of Brown from 1941 to 1951.

4-109. Brown, Fredric. **What Mad Universe.** Dutton, 1949.
Brown's first novel; an SF editor is tossed into an alternate universe by the failure of the first Moon rocket in 1955. In this universe, filled with SF pulp fiction clichés, space flight was accidentally discovered in 1903 by a scientist using a sewing machine, and man presently faces a space war with Arcturians. Good, humorous SF satire, with skimpily clad girls in transparent space suits, BEMs, a superscientist, and all. Contrast with Malzberg's *Herovit's World* [4-409].

4-110. Brown, James Cooke. **The Troika Incident.** Doubleday, 1970.
"Troika" space shot sends an American, a Russian woman, and a Frenchman into the year 2070. They return with description of utopian destiny

of civilization—socialistic, decentralized—and an account of how it emerged. Little action, emphasis on ideas. Unusually sophisticated updating of tradition of Bellamy's *Looking Backward* [2-14]; also compare Reynold's lesser *Looking Backward from the Year 2000* [4-476].

4-111. Brunner, John (U.K.). **The Jagged Orbit.** Ace, 1969, $1.25.
Paranoia is institutionalized in a near-future United States; blacks in barricaded enclaves and whites in booby-trapped homes confront each other in an urban jungle while the Gottschalk arms cartel fans the flames by ubiquitous weapons development and sales. The mental casualties of this alienating society are treated with isolation therapy by psychotic Dr. Mogshack in his fortress-like state hospital. Media columnist Matthew Flamen discovers a Gottschalk plot to market an ultimate weapon system and enlists the aid of psychologist Conroy, a philosophic counterweight to Mogshack, to stop them. Brunner's most experimental novel, well worth reading for its powerful setting despite a weak and inappropriately optimistic ending. Compare and contrast with the numerous versions of black rebellion that appeared in the late 1960s and with Spinrad's *Bug Jack Barron* [4-551]. NN, 1969.

4-112. Brunner, John (U.K.). **Out of My Mind.** Ballantine, 1967.
Thirteen stories originally published between 1956 and 1965; overall tone is of pessimism and horror. Outstanding stories include "The Totally Rich," about a wealthy woman's attempt to recreate her dead lover; "The Last Lonely Man," where death is cheated only by corrupting life; and "Such Stuff," in which a researcher becomes trapped in the dreams of his subject. "The Nail in the Middle of the Hand," although not SF, is a gruesome little masterpiece about Christ's executioner. Some of Brunner's best short fiction.

4-113. Brunner, John (U.K.). **The Productions of Time.** Signet, 1967. Penguin (U.K.), £.25.
In an isolated lodge, Manuel Delgado, a brilliant and mysterious playwright, assembles a troop of has-beens and neophytes for his latest creation. Among them is ex-alcoholic Murray Douglas, who discovers that the *real* play is not to take place on stage. The company's weaknesses and perversions are secretly catered to by Delgado and his sinister band of stewards—liquor for Douglas, partners for homosexuals and so on. But Douglas resists and lays a trap to uncover the truth. In the ensuing events, the lodge burns, and a dying Delgado confesses that his chief steward, Victor, is really the leader of a band of time-travelers returned to the "primitive" past to record deviant behavior for the entertainment of jaded consumers in the "civilized" future. Noteworthy for effective writing and blending of mainstream elements. Compare Moore's "Vintage Season" [4-431]. NN, 1966.

4-114. Brunner, John (U.K.). **Quicksand.** Doubleday, 1967.
A young woman is found naked in an English forest. Unable to speak any known language, she is dubbed Urchin and placed in a mental institution under the care of Dr. Paul Fidler. Under his tutorage, she learns English and describes herself as a visitor from a future utopia. Fascinated by the woman, Fidler decides to flee with her, thereby escaping the pressures of his career and an unhappy marriage. Their idyllic retreat is shattered by her second revelation: the utopia is a sham; her real origin, although still in the future, is a brutal world of tyranny and decadent, sterile eroticism. A broken man, Fidler destroys her and himself. A sensitive adult tragedy of a man caught between his dreams and reality that blends mystery, SF, and mainstream elements; an underappreciated work.

*4-115. Brunner, John (U.K.). **The Sheep Look Up.** Harper, 1972, $6.95. Ballantine, $1.95.
The ultimate ecological disaster story; in the late 1970s, the ecology "fad" has passed and the United States is being polluted to death. Against this background of meticulously described and scientifically accurate environmental effects, the lives of numerous characters, from the poor to the rich, the innocent to the guilty, are counted down by months during America's last year. The writings and actions of "subversive" ecologist Austin Train provide the novel's central focus, as he returns from self-imposed exile, is unjustly imprisoned and finally martyred before he can lead the country out of its decay and filth. People are collectively responsible for their condition, and can save themselves by rising to their full potential rather than relying on a savior/superman. A complex, expertly crafted work, more effective than *Stand on Zanzibar* [4-118] in its handling of innovative writing techniques; also of interest are the excellent poetry pastiches that preface each chapter and provide ironic contrast. One of SF's most horrific, bitter, realistic, and alarming dystopias. Compare and contrast Orwell's *1984* [4-450] and Huxley's *Brave New World* [3-27]. NN, 1972.

4-116. Brunner, John (U.K.). **The Shockwave Rider.** Harper, 1975, $8.95. Ballantine, $1.95.
Polymath Nickie Haflinger, product of special training for government service in contingency-managed Tarnover, rebels against his regimented, data-netted twenty-first century world. Living underground, his experiences convince him to attempt the liberation of the entire future-shocked North American society by using its own computers against it. Although pedantic at times, a convincing future society is described, including the interesting utopian community, Precipice. In the same family as Brunner's other major dystopias. Compare Huxley's *Brave New*

World [3-27]. (The author has stated that unauthorized changes in the Harper edition will be corrected in a 1976 Ballantine reprint.)

4-117. Brunner, John (U.K.). **The Squares of the City.** Ballantine, 1965, $1.25.
President Vados, dictator of a Brazil-like South American country, invites traffic analyst Boyd Hakluyt to rid his ultramodern capital of squatters. Intrigue and death follow, climaxing in Hakluyt's discovery that Vados and a political rival are manipulating people's behavior with advanced techniques in thought control. This is the result of an agreement between the two leaders to compete for power without suffering the devastation of a civil war; they are literally playing chess using people as pieces. The game is ruined and civil disorder erupts; people must ultimately make their own destiny. The novel's plot follows exactly the moves of an actual championship game played in 1892. Mature, interesting reading on either level. HN, 1966.

*4-118. Brunner, John (U.K.). **Stand on Zanzibar.** Doubleday, 1968. Ballantine, $1.75.
One of SF's greatest works, it helped open the genre to innovative mainstream writing techniques by incorporating them into a mammoth novel based on Dos Passos' forms blended with a McLuhanish approach emphasizing visual media that resulted in a movingly complete and realistic depiction of a future society. Set in the near future, it explores the psychological, social, and political effects of overpopulation, big business, and big government, and major developments in eugenics and genetic optimization. Two major plots unfold as black Norman House, a tool of giant General Technics, manipulates the exploitation of a small, mineral-rich African country (Beninia), while his roommate, white Donald Hogan, a tool of U.S. government, engages in espionage against a genetic breakthrough in an Asian nation. Radical sociologist Chad Mulligan, prototype of Train in *The Sheep Look Up* [4-115] and Conroy in *The Jagged Orbit* [4-111], and Shalmaneser, a sentient supercomputer, aid House by discovering a "pacifying" gene among the Beninian people, a find perhaps worthy of corruption by the world's power elites into another agent of social control. A unique work in SF, highly creative and involving. HW, 1969; NN, 1968.

4-119. Brunner, John (U.K.). **The Whole Man.** Ballantine, 1964, $1.25.
Expansion of two stories originally published in 1958 and 1959; unusually rich in character development for SF of its time. Crippled, misshapen Gerald Howson precariously exists as a ridiculed outcast among society's dregs. A powerful natural telepath, Howson can link others into an all-consuming fantasy world, an ability that nearly dooms both himself and his only friend, a lonely, unwanted mute girl. Fortunately, they

are saved by the telepathic community, whose members perform vital roles in communication and psychotherapy. With training, Howson becomes a master at healing the mentally ill, but, despite fame and fortune, remains haunted by the legacy of social revulsion caused by his deformity. Finally he discovers a novel use for his talent—mental "concerts" that reach thousands and uplift their lives. No longer isolated, Howson joins the world, a whole man at last. A creative and poignant work that marked Brunner as a major SF writer. Compare Silverberg's *Dying Inside* [4-523]. HN, 1965.

4-120. Budrys, Algis J. **The Amsirs and the Iron Thorn.** Fawcett, 1967. (British title: *Iron Thorn*, Gollancz, £1.05).
Honor Jackson, product of a genetic experiment on Mars, grows up fighting Amsirs. He discovers the expeditionary ship *Iron Thorn*, boards it with his Amsir friend and returns to Earth and his heritage in a computer-served paradise civilization. When a species becomes too comfortable, perhaps life is kept interesting through vicarious violent experience. Compelling and ingenious, it includes some very engaging and personable artificial intelligences. Compare Bass's *The Godwhale* [4-59].

4-121. Budrys, Algis J. **Budrys' Inferno.** Berkley, 1963. (British title: *The Furious Future*, Gollancz, 1964. £1.75).
Nine stories, published between 1953 and 1958, and an author's introduction. Tales emphasize emotion and characterization, such as "The Peasant Girl," with old Mr. Spar, a cantankerous cabinet-maker who resents his sister's marriage to a boy with superhuman powers, and "Dream of Victory," where an android, driven to frenzy by his inability to have offspring, kills his human lover. At times, as in "And Then She Found Him," as sensitive and concerned with love as Sturgeon's work.

*4-122. Budrys, Algis J. **Rogue Moon.** Fawcett, 1960. Avon, $1.95.
Ed Hawks masterminds exploration of alien construct on Moon using quasi-suicidal Al Barker as explorer. Moon trips are accomplished by "teleportation" effect that duplicates traveller at Moon-base receiver, leaving original behind. Barker is "killed" again and again in dangerous work that killed or drove insane earlier candidates. Each time the Earth duplicate replaces him. Finally, Hawks himself makes the trip and must suicide on Moon so there won't be two of him on Earth. What is a man, his form or his "matter"? Probing character analysis in radically realistic treatment of "doppleganger" proposition. Last paragraph is a nova. HN, 1961 and SFHF.

4-123. Budrys, Algis J. **The Unexpected Dimension.** Ballantine, 1960.
Seven stories from 1954 to 1959, three of which deal with utopias and the need to overthrow them due to either the pressures of change or stagnation ("The End of Summer," "The Burning World," "The Execu-

tioners"). Most outstanding is the sad and sensitive "The Distant Sound of Engines," about a ship-wrecked alien dying in an Earth hospital; compares with McKenna's "Casey Agonistes" [4-402].

4-124. Budrys, Algis J. **Who?** Pyramid, 1958. Ballantine, $1.50.
Lucas Martino struggles up from an Italian immigrant farming family to become an MIT-graduated genius in physics, crucial to national security. An accidental lab explosion brutally maims him and lets him fall into Soviet hands. The Soviets restore him using mechanical parts, but fail to get his research secrets. Returned to the West, his metal face an emotionless mask, he is not allowed to continue his work; no one can prove his true identity. A twice destroyed man, he returns to his rundown family farm, forsaking physics forever. A powerful comment on cold war espionage and its self-defeating nature. Compare with Harrison's *The Daleth Effect* [4-288] and Blum's *The Simultaneous Man* [4-83]. HN, 1959.

4-125. Bulgakov, Mikhail Afans'evich (U.S.S.R.). **The Heart of a Dog.** Harcourt, 1968, $1.45. Grove, $1.95; Association Press, $4.50 (in Russian). Tr. by Michael Glenny, original, 1925.
Still too stinging for release in U.S.S.R. A surgeon turns a dog into a "human being" through a transplant, but the result is so appalling that he turns it back into a dog. The dog is the Russian people. Message is that the revolution (the operation of the surgeon) should never have happened. Parabolic satire that collects vivid detail of Soviet life in 1920s. Contrast Yefremov's *Andromeda* [4-644].

4-126. Bulmer, Kenneth (U.K.). **City under the Sea.** Ace, 1957. Avon, $1.95.
Average adventure story, but setting is an excellently developed "aquaculture" of the near future; detailed descriptions of undersea cities, corporate farms, transportation and communication systems, recreation, surgically altered "menfish," and sea life. Lyrical passages effectively communicating the mood of underwater existence contrast sharply with uninspired, involuted plot: a space navy officer, inheritor of an undersea farm, is kidnapped and forced into undersea slavery by farm's manager. He escapes in time to establish contact with extraterrestrials inhabiting ocean depths who want detente with humanity. Compare setting with Clarke's superior *The Deep Range* [4-151].

4-127. Bunch, David R. **Moderan.** Avon, 1971, $.75.
Composed of many loosely connected vignettes, most of which originally appeared from 1959 to 1970, this unusual and inventive work details the rise and fall of Moderan, the super-technological society that replaces our war-destroyed and polluted present. Onomatopoeia, symbolic images, and lyrical prose are employed to satirize and comment on the current rationalist/technologist model of progress: in Moderan, the "New

Processes Land," Earth has been beaten smooth and covered with plastic; men, women, and children live alone, gradually replacing most of their flesh with "new metal" and losing their humanity in degree to their progress toward immortality; the most superior men command completely automated Strongholds, make love to their robot mistresses, fight endless and pointless wars, and at other times engage in thinking on "universal deep problems"; metal birds are released to inspire a sense of beauty and are then used for target practice, while each month has its own sky color and each spring metal flowers are programmed to bloom. Occasionally self-doubt occurs, as when one's cute girl-child comes calling (but beware, she has left a booby-trapped doll!) or when one's conscience drops in (better to blow one's Stronghold with the demolition box in the mountain of "Last Hope Stand" than have him around!), but the false optimism lasts until all the foolish Strongholds simultaneously launch their secret "Grandy Wumps," each blaming the other for finally ending the Moderan man's dream "to live forever with my stronghold and my Joys." Compare Lem's *The Cyberiad* [4-385].

4-128. Burdick, Eugene, and Harvey Wheeler. **Fail-Safe.** McGraw-Hill, 1962. Dell, $1.25.
Nuclear capability, with "fail-safe" firing procedures, was thought a good war deterrent, but accident launches a nuclear strike that destroys Moscow. The President volunteers to nuke New York City to avoid a world war. Theme: When you have a super-weapon, it will ultimately be employed. Slick popular fiction; successful film. Compare George's *Dr. Strangelove* [4-260].

*4-129. Burgess, Anthony (pseud. of John Anthony Wilson) (U.K.). **A Clockwork Orange.** Norton, 1963, $1.45; Ballantine, $1.75.
Squarely in tradition of *1984*, presents story of electrochemical brainwashing of young man who has committed mayhem. He is conditioned to become sick at thought of violence. Brilliantly crafted warning story. Burgess's other SF piece, *The Wanting Seed* (Norton, 1963. Heinemann, £2.40; Penguin, £.35) is also a warning story. It presents a world in which all measures imaginable are encouraged to curb population explosion. Richly satirical. Like Vonnegut, Burgess writes in Swiftian SF tradition. He is novelist of first rank and powerfully stimulating speaker. *Clockwork* was filmed by Stanley Kubrick.

4-130. Burroughs, William S. **Nova Express.** Grove, 1964, $1.95.
Cops and robbers on an interplanetary scale. Nova mob matches wits with Nova cops. Mobsters include Limestone John, Hamburger Mary, and "The Ugly Spirit," leader of the pack. They run amuck, employing exotic weapons to create conflict. The Nova police are equally resourceful but hampered by the corrupt Biologic Courts. Social criticism. HN, 1965.

4-131. Burroughs, William S. **The Wild Boys: A Book of the Dead.** Grove, 1969, $1.50.
From the 1920s to the 1980s, bands of boys gradually emerge throughout the world, given to specialized violence and homosexual orgies. Established authorities try to stamp them out. Story told as series of film clips. Boys may be a metaphor for the anarchistic, violent decadence of twentieth-century man in corporate civilization. Burroughs is brilliant narrative craftsman.

4-132. Caidin, Martin. **Cyborg.** Arbor House, 1972, $7.95.
After a near-fatal crash destroys his legs, an arm, and an eye, an air force test pilot is turned into a "cyborg," becoming a superman. Story is of espionage adventure and Steve Austin's attempt to adjust to his new body. Good technical exposition and yarn spinning. Sequels are *Cyborg 2, 3,* and *4*; *Operation Nuke, 1973*. Basis for TV's *Six Million Dollar Man*.

4-133. Caidin, Martin. **The God Machine.** Dutton, 1968.
Steve Rand is a principal in the construction of a super-computer programmed to protect the United States and to keep itself in existence—with the data inputs and hardware to accomplish this. The machine takes over itself, but Rand finally destroys it. Computer's self-programming much more logically explained than in Jones' *Colossus* [4-327], but often slow-moving.

4-134. Caidin, Martin. **Marooned.** Dutton, 1964.
A three-man American space shot satellite is marooned and two occupants are saved when Russian cosmonaut intervenes with help, giving American rescue, X-RV, time to complete pickup of men. Cooperation between space-flight nations is necessary. Excellent technical detail by experienced science writer. Fine suspense. Made into excellent movie.

4-135. Calisher, Hortense. **Journal from Ellipsia.** Little, Brown, 1965.
At American research center, Jack Linhouse presents a long message from a beautiful anthropologist, formerly his lover, who has disappeared and gone to "Ellipsia." Janice has found love with quasi-sexual new lover in cosmos where everything is connected. Comic and profound, urbane and idyllic. Human sexuality is unutterably and beautifully ramified. Compare Russ's *The Female Man* [4-485].

4-136. Calvino, Italo (Italy). **Cosmicomics.** Harcourt, 1968. Collier, $1.25. Tr. by William Weaver of *Le cosmicomiche*, 1965.
Theories of evolutionary geology by George H. Darwin, Edwin P. Hubble, and others are transmuted to twelve stories cleverly intertwined with fantasy. Characters are mathematical formulae and simple cellular structures. The narrator, Mr. Ofwfq, tells of the galaxy's formation, first life on Earth, the destruction of the dinosaurs. Calvino's intent is philo-

sophical, contemplating the mutability of energy and matter. Similar in spirit is his *T Zero* (Harcourt, 1969; Collier, $1.25).

4-137. Calvino, Italo (Italy). **Invisible Cities.** Harcourt, 1974, $6.50 Tr. by William Weaver of *Le città invisibili*, 1972.
In dialogue with Kublai Khan, Marco Polo describes a multitude of cities with female names, metaphoring the myriad forms that civilization has taken and will take; in virtually all there is loneliness, even as successive cities are filled to bursting with art, filth, and bodies of mankind. Utopia is a least likely eventuality. Compare Hersey's *My Petition for More Space* [4-310] and Brunner's *The Sheep Look Up* [4-115]. In 1972, Calvino earned the Premio Feltrinelli per la Narrativa for his work.

4-138. Cameron, John. **The Astrologer.** Random, 1972. Warner Books, $1.50.
Astrology is put on a scientific footing. The sign of the Virgin Mary, mother of Christ, is plotted; then the reading is used to search for a match in the twentieth century. Once found she turns out indeed to be pregnant with a "virgin" conception—at least the Papacy seems to think so. A really original idea. Contrast Moorcock's *Behold the Man* [4-427].

4-139. Campbell, John Wood, Jr. **The Moon Is Hell.** Fantasy Press, 1950. Ace, $.95.
Garner expedition to the Moon is not relieved after two years' stay and members struggle to be self-sufficient until rescue. They retreat to gypsum mine where only a few survive, though simultaneously discoveries are made that will make life on Moon self-sufficient. Man can overcome radically hostile environments. A logical, suspenseful story told in diary form and typical of Campbell's editorial policy. For more, see *The Best of J. W. Campbell* (Sidgwick & Jackson, 1973 £3.50).

4-140. Capon, Paul (U.K.). **The Other Side of the Sun.** Heinemann, 1950.
Timothy and Rose travel to Antigeos, earthlike planet on opposite side of Sun, in 1960s. Discover ideally functioning anarchistic state of Antigeonians. Villain, McQuoid, would colonize and exploit it but is finally lost. Other members of expedition return to Earth. Pedestrian in science; enlightened in political philosophy. Compare Le Guin's *The Dispossessed* [4-371].

4-141. Carr, Robert Spencer. **Beyond Infinity.** Fantasy Press, 1951.
Four stories: "Beyond Infinity," "Morning Star," "Those Men from Mars," and "Mutation." "Morning Star" presents a beautiful female visitor from Venus who seeks to insure success of expedition to bring Earth males to Venus. On Venus only women evolved; male of species remained in "spore" state. Solid stories of human interest set in America of 1940s and 1950s.

4-142. Carter, Angela (U.K.). **Heroes and Villains.** Simon & Schuster, 1970. Pocket Books, $.95.
After the bomb there are wandering tribes and enclaves where vestiges of civilization are preserved by "professors." Marianne is a professor's daughter who leaves her father to follow a tribal barbarian named Jewel, becoming his consort and surviving him after numerous adventures. Only occasionally flawed by false narrative notes, work is excellent in imaginative representation of anthropological and archetypal insights of mankind in nomadic, post-catastrophe scenario. Brutality and enormous misery; moments of life far richer than civilization permits. Often a fine parody of sword and sorcery tales, a purge of the sappy romance of the future gothic tale. See also Carter's excellent *Magic Toyshop* (1967).

*4-143. Carter, Angela (U.K.). **The War of Dreams.** Harcourt, 1974, $6.95. (British title: *The Infernal Desire Machine of Doctor Hoffman*, 1972).
Desiderio is sent by "Minister" to kill Doctor Hoffman, whose transmitters are radically distorting time and space for all but a few citizens of a prosperous city. In a series of adventures combining modalities suggestive of *The Circus of Dr. Lao, Don Quixote, Gulliver's Travels, The Inferno*, and the works of De Sade, he succeeds, killing his beloved Albertina as well. A world of limitless imaginative possibility (Doctor Hoffman's) is destroyed to preserve the predictable world of cold reason. Desiderio is spiritually defeated. Magnificent interplay of symbol and archetype. Carter has won the Somerset Maugham award and the John Llewellyn Rhys prize for her writing.

4-144. Chandler, A. Bertram (Australia). **The Road to the Rim.** Ace, 1967.
Writing with imagination and zest, Chandler, himself a life-long working mariner, blends the military sea story with old time space opera to produce his numerous Rim Worlds stories, begun in 1959 and built around the character of John Grimes. *Road* tells of young Ensign Grimes' earliest adventures and introduction to the Rim Worlds. Good adventure reading. Compare Niven and Pournelle's *The Mote in God's Eye* [4-439].

4-145. Charbonneau, Louis. **The Sentinal Stars.** Bantam, 1963.
TRH-247, a "natural man," rebels against the world welfare state, The Organization, that structures a citizen's life in the finest detail. There are the Freedom Camps, whose life of luxury and nonregimentation is purchased by a citizen's life-long labor to pay his tax debt, but these, too, are a prison where freedom means license. In such a planned world, even underground resistance is futile; TRH and his true love, state prostitute ABC331, are exiled to the wilderness and find a new husky society of outcasts emerging to challenge the weak city folks. One of *Brave New World's* [3-27] less illustrious decendents, but typical of such SF dystopias

of the 1950s and 1960s as Pohl and del Rey's *Preferred Risk* [4-399] and Dick's *Solar Lottery* [4-212].

4-146. Christopher, John (pseud. of Christopher Samuel Youd) (U.K.). **No Blade of Grass.** Simon & Schuster, 1957. Avon, $1.95. (British title: *The Death of Grass*, 1956.) **The Long Winter.** Simon & Schuster, 1962. **The Ragged Edge.** Simon & Schuster, 1966, $4.50.
Blade is one of three fine catastrophe novels. Depicts arrival and results of world famine from blight on world's "grass" crops. *The Long Winter* is story of brief but devastating ice age. *The Ragged Edge* presents global earthquakes destroying virtually all civilization. In each story there are survivors and a sort of "second chance" for mankind. All demonstrate weaknesses and strengths of mankind in stress and crisis situations. Wonderfully plausible; compare Stewart's *Earth Abides* [4-558].

4-147. Christopher, John (pseud. of Christopher Samuel Youd) (U.K.). **The Possessors.** Simon & Schuster, 1964.
A holiday skiing party at Swiss chalet is subtly attacked by ruthless extraterrestrials. First Andy is killed and returned to life "possessed." Most of the rest of the party follow, especially children, until Christopher's favorite stress situation is set. Three men and a woman survive by burning to death "possessed" bodies while they are trapped in lodge. An eerily realistic terror tale.

4-148. Churchill, Reginald Charles (U.K.). **A Short History of the Future.** Werner Laurie, 1955.
Genially self-deprecating history of mankind by historian 6,000 years in future. Orwell's *1984* [4-450] is central reference for account based on Bradbury, Huxley, Russell, Vonnegut, and Waugh, among others. History will be cyclical, generally, though Spengler is not mentioned. Ingenious in interpolating "sources." Engaging satirical tone. Compare Atkins' *Tomorrow Revealed* [4-42].

***4-149.** Clarke, Arthur Charles (U.K.). **Childhood's End.** Houghton Mifflin, 1953. Harcourt, $7.95; Ballantine, $1.50.
Earth, threatened with self-annihilation, is visited by superior species, who act as agents for something that might be called transcendental cosmic sentience. Through these agents, ironically possessing the classic form of devils, mankind is pacified and the stage is set for the last generation of children, who in a climax of vaulting psychic/spiritual triumph coalesce their substance and join the cosmic oversoul. In face of its narrative mediocrity, *Childhood's* enormous popularity is hard to explain. Perhaps with unconscious accuracy it combines just the right elements of messianic myth and modern scenario to compel the mid-twentieth-century audience. The message seems clear: humanity needs help to fulfill its cosmic destiny. This is precisely the message of Clarke's novel and

film, *2001: A Space Odyssey* [4-158]. Contrast Russell's *Sinister Barrier* [4-490] and Davidson's *Clash of Star-Kings* [4-186].

4-150. Clarke, Arthur Charles (U.K.). **The City and the Stars.** Harcourt, 1956. Signet, $1.25.

Expansion and complete revision of Clarke's first novel, *Against the Fall of Night* (1948). The super-city of Diaspar and its immortal citizens have existed in cultural stasis for a billion years as Earth's mountains crumbled and its seas turned to desert. This vision marks the story's excellence; the tedious plot of Alvin uniting Diaspar with its forgotten neighbor, Lys, a pastoral anarchy peopled with telepaths, soon devolves into van Vogtian space opera. Alvin travels across the galaxy in search of other intelligence, meets strange creatures, explores the artifacts of past galactic civilization, and opens man to progress once more. Strong element of cultural renaissance following a period of "stagnation" (stability?) central to much of Clarke's work, but the writing here is generally inadequate for carrying such an awesome message. Note: Harcourt published an omnibus, *From the Ocean, from the Stars*, 1961, $8.50, which contains this novel, *The Deep Range*, and *The Other Side of the Sky*.

4-151. Clarke, Arthur Charles (U.K.). **The Deep Range.** Harcourt, 1957, $6.95; Signet, $1.25.

Classic early story of oceanic exploitation. Grounded spaceman Walter Franklin rises from Warden, a cowboy of the deeps herding whales, to director of the vital Bureau of Whales, a major producer of Earth's protein. Along the way he almost snares a mammoth sea serpent, does capture a giant squid, rescues a trapped submarine, and confronts Earth's major religious leader, a Buddhist, who prefers whale milking and plankton farming to the slaughter of whales. Embodies Clarke's optimistic philosophy of human growth as well as future extrapolation, but remains chiefly an action story. Compare Bulmer's *City under the Sea* [4-126]; contrast Bass's *The Godwhale* [4-59].

4-152. Clarke, Arthur Charles (U.K.). **Expedition to Earth.** Ballantine, 1953, $1.75. Harcourt, $6.95.

Eleven stories from 1946 to 1953 that exhibit Clarke's versatility in SF. Stories of interest: the beautiful and philosophic "Second Dawn," about a culture that developed mental powers before advanced technology, and now must discover the latter; "The Sentinel," realistic tale of finding a lunar pyramid, prototype of *2001* monoliths; "Superiority," in which a mighty space fleet is vanquished by a scientifically inferior enemy because of the latent effects of their too-advanced military technology; "Breaking Strain," where enough air remains for only one of a two-man space ship crew and they must pick who will die; and the humbling "History Lesson," about the attempted reconstruction by Venusians of extinct human culture from its sole surviving record—a Walt Disney cartoon.

4-153. Clarke, Arthur Charles (U.K.). **A Fall of Moondust.** Harcourt, 1961, $6.95. Signet, $1.25.
Efforts to rescue tourists from a lunar surface vehicle buried under a sea of dust. Emphasis on well-worked-out technical aspects of lunar dust, vehicles, and rescue processes, but social and psychological effects on trapped passengers and crew also treated—although they behave much like typical British characters facing a common crisis. Tension and suspense maintained despite present-day knowledge that the Moon just isn't that dusty. Compare with Caidin's *Marooned* [4-134].

4-154. Clarke, Arthur Charles (U.K.). **The Other Side of the Sky.** Harcourt, 1958, $7.95. Signet, $.95.
Collection of twenty-four stories written between 1947 and 1957 contains, along with contents of *Expedition to Earth*, *Reach for Tomorrow*, and *Tales from the White Hart*, all the pre-1960s short fiction by Clarke that he thinks worthy of preservation. Outstanding efforts include "The Nine Billion Names of God," (SFHF) in which Tibetan monks use a computer to compile all the possible names of God, thereby ending the universe; and "The Star" (HW, 1956) about the consternation of a Jesuit astrophysicist who discovers that the nova heralding Christ's birth also destroyed a magnificent people inhabiting its planetary system. Also of interest are "Venture to the Moon" and "The Other Side of the Sky," each containing six vignettes commissioned by the London *Evening Standard* and chronicalling the initial exploration of space, and the poignant "The Songs of Distant Earth," story of a love-lost girl on a distant planet and a boy aboard a ship of colonists that briefly stops before heading even farther out.

4-155. Clarke, Arthur Charles (U.K.). **Prelude to Space.** Gnome, 1954. Ballantine, $1.50; Harcourt, $5.75.
Written in 1947, one of the earliest scientifically accurate and realistic accounts of the first Moon voyage. Unlike the earlier classics, Verne's *From the Earth to the Moon* [2-150] and Wells' *The First Men in the Moon* [2-166], the emphasis is on preparations rather than the melodrama of the trip itself, anticipating the social, personal, and technical meaning and romance behind the actual conquest of space caught in Oriana Fallaci's *If the Sun Dies* (1966). The meager plot involves the conversion of Dirk Alexson, hired as the project's historical interpreter, as he learns the inner working of Interplanetary, the private organization sponsoring the development of the moon-ship *Discovery*, and of the engineers and astronauts who are making it happen. Hindsight illuminates errors, such as initial development of space travel by private interests, its relatively low cost, the invention of atomic engines, a lunar landing as late as 1978, and elim-

ination of nationalism in space, which are more than offset by a narrative that oscillates between nuts and bolts and the poetic as Clarke makes his clearest statement of the necessity for progress: "Out of the fears and miseries of the Second Dark Age, drawing free—oh, might it be forever!—from the shadows of Belsen and Hiroshima, the world was moving towards its most splendid sunrise. After five hundred years, the Renaissance had come again."

4-156. Clarke, Arthur Charles (U.K.). **Reach for Tomorrow.** Ballantine, 1956, $1.75. Harcourt, $5.75.
Twelve stories from 1946 to 1953. Superior works include: "Rescue Party," Clarke's first published story, a Campbellesque space opera touting mankind's great drive and ability; "Jupiter Five," about the discovery that Jupiter's innermost moon is really an abandoned alien ship; "The Parasite," in which an alien telepathic peeping Tom, Omega, drives a man to suicide; "A Walk in the Dark" has a man hurrying through the night to catch a spaceship on a lonely alien planet only to find a deadly creature waiting for him; "Trouble with the Natives," a humorous first-contact story of a flying saucer's crew who have difficulty finding anyone to believe them when they land in rural Britain.

*4-157. Clarke, Arthur Charles (U.K.). **Rendezvous with Rama.** Harcourt, 1973, $7.95. Ballantine, $1.75.
Old-fashioned SF, complete with cardboard characters, statesmen and astronauts who act like adolescents, and a superfluous plot by fulminating Mercurians to add artificial tension. Rama, a mile-long cylindrical space ship, passes through the solar system as it uses the Sun's gravity well for an acceleration boost. Humans go to investigate and discover Rama's internal world reawakening as Sun is approached. Lots of neat detail about Rama and the adventures of the human explorers, and these are the things that make this work outstanding despite its handicaps. The Ramans do not appear, the humans are ignored, and the giant ship flies off. Not typical of superior contemporary SF; more suited for a juvenile audience. Compare with Niven's *Ringworld* [4-441]; contrast with Malzberg's *Beyond Apollo* [4-406]. HW, 1974; NW, 1973; Campbell winner, 1974.

4-158. Clarke, Arthur Charles (U.K.). **Tales from the White Hart.** Ballantine, 1957, $1.50. Harcourt, $5.75.
Fifteen SF tall tales, reminiscent of de Camp and Pratt's fantasy *Tales from Gavagan's Bar* (1953), written between 1953 and 1956. Harry Purvis spins the yarns in the out-of-the-way London pub, the White Hart, where the regulars include the likes of John Christopher and John Wyndham (a real pub, the Globe, was a traditional gathering place for SF personalities). In "The Man Who Ploughed the Sea," Purvis tells of his meeting in the Atlantic with two millionaire scientists, one of

whom trades his process for extracting minerals from sea water for the other's yacht—one gets a process still to be perfected, the other, with less than a year to live, a ship he has coveted on which to spend his final days. A more outrageous example is "What Goes Up," in which Purvis relates how an Australian scientist invented antigravity but died in a flaming meteor after falling twenty feet horizontally while trying to reach the device.

4-159. Clarke, Arthur Charles (U.K.). **2001: A Space Odyssey.** New American Library, 1968, $6.95. Signet, $1.75.
Clarke's novelization of the 1967 Kubrick film based on their joint screenplay. Altruistic aliens guide man's evolution, first by stimulating his primate ancestors with the now famous "monolith," second by enticing man to a "portal" in deep space in search of the lunar monolith's signal's target. Here, the surviving crew member of the spaceship *Discovery*, after disconnecting the murderous computer HAL (driven crazy by security restrictions), is transformed into superman—the "Star Child." In film form, perhaps the single most important SF piece of the decade; unfortunately, its message throws us back to reliance on "superior powers," a theme crudely exploited in von Daniken's *Chariots of the Gods*, just as the future it depicts is equally archaic; not major Clarke. Compare with its prototype, *Childhood's End* [4-149]. Contrast Vonnegut's *The Sirens of Titan* [4-607].

4-160. Clarke, Arthur Charles (U.K.). **The Wind from the Sun.** Harcourt, 1972, $6.50. Signet, $1.75.
Eighteen stories, all Clarke wrote during the 1960s, full of topical scientific and technical ideas in the classic Heinlein tradition. Title story portrays a race by sunlight-powered space-sailing ships; "The Light of Darkness" has an African scientist destroying a dictator with a laser-fitted telescope; a cyborg named Falcon descends into Jupiter's atmosphere aboard a balloon-type craft in "A Meeting with Medusa"; an astronaut dies alone on Mars in "Transit of Earth"; and in "The Cruel Sky," a thalidomide-crippled scientist uses an antigravity device to scale Mt. Everest. Compare Niven's *All the Myriad Ways* [4-438] and Bova's *Forward in Time* [4-93].

4-161. Clement, Hal (pseud. of Harry Clement Stubbs). **Cycle of Fire.** Ballantine, 1957, $1.50.
Nils Kruger, Earthman, and Dar Lang Ahn, alien, must cooperate to survive on planet of tremendous climactic extremes. But first they must break through the awful mistrust with which one alien meets another. A tour de force epitomizing the radical points of view that different species must adopt to coexist. Logical in the mode for which Clement is famous. Compare Dickson's *The Alien Way* [4-216] and White's *The Watch Below* [4-619].

*4-162. Clement, Hal (pseud. of Harry Clement Stubbs). **Mission of Gravity.** Doubleday, 1954. Pyramid, $.95.
Earthmen are aided in recovery of crashed observer satellite on disk-shaped planet Mesklin by fifteen-inch-long natives armored to adapt to the 700 Earth gravities of their unusual world. Consumately logical "hard core SF." IFA second place, 1955. Sequel is *Starlight* (Ballantine, 1971) which provides more adventures with Captain Barlennan, merchant Mesklinite, on a planet where the awesome gravity forces can kill you with a six-inch fall.

4-163. Clement, Hal (pseud. of Harry Clement Stubbs). **Needle.** Doubleday, 1950. (Alternate title: *From Outer Space*, 1957).
Alien policeman pursues alien criminal on Earth by inhabiting boy's body (with boy's cooperation). Alien criminal "runs" by inhabiting another human. Rigorously logical and plausible.

4-164. Clifton, Mark. **Eight Keys to Eden.** Doubleday, 1960.
Underrated novel belonging to *Childhood's End* [4-149] tradition. A new planet's colony is suddenly incommunicado. Eventually investigators learn the planet is a perfectly harmonized ecology of mind and matter, an ideal that the Earth-born colonists are just beginning to realize at story's end. Especially interesting for critique of psychically sterilizing effects of Earth-type civilization. Compare Brunner's *Bedlam Planet* (1968).

*4-165. Clifton, Mark and Frank Riley. **They'd Rather Be Right.** Gnome, 1957. (Alternate title: *The Forever Machine*, 1959).
The first of the super-computers, "Bossy," is built and soon put to work "healing" or "perfecting" human beings. Treated humans become physically and mentally perfected, including the full development of psi abilities. Society, represented in distorted commercial and news media information, reacts with a witch-hunt. An honest, extremely wealthy man saves the heroes and the Bossy prototype so that enough machines can be built to process all humanity. Stereotyped characters; good narrative. HW, 1955.

4-166. Clingerman, Mildred. **A Cupful of Space.** Ballantine, 1961.
Sixteen stories, mostly fantasy, with a feminine touch; full of cute kids, frightened or worried women, eccentric grandmothers, and sentimental aliens. Among better SF are "Minister without Portfolio," where Earth is spared by aliens due to their contact with an elderly traditional woman; "The Word," where aliens trick or treat on Halloween; and "Birds Can't Count," an axiom for both humans watching birds and aliens watching humans. Compare with Merril's *Out of Bounds* [4-421] and deFord's *Xenogenesis* [4-197].

4-167. Coblentz, Stanton A. **Hidden World.** Avalon, 1957.
Coblentz is best known for this humorous satiric work, first published in

1935, and for a later satire on dictatorship, *Lord of Tranerica* [not seen], which dates from 1939 (as a book, 1966). In *Hidden World*, two young mining engineers fall into an underground world of continuous, senseless war between the states of Wu and Zu. Much of European and American culture is lampooned, including the military, nationalism, congress, the class structure, female vanity, the press, the utilities, dictators, big business, bureaucrats, and the Nazis. Unusual for early American pulp SF. Compare with Boulle's *Planet of the Apes* [4-90] and Sheckley's *Journey beyond Tomorrow* [4-513].

4-168. Cogswell, Theodore R. **The Wall around the World.** Pyramid, 1962, $.95.
Ten SF and fantasy stories, from 1952 to 1960, and two introductions on the distinction, or lack of one, between the two genres by Anthony Boucher and Frederik Pohl. "The Specter General" (SFHF) describes a distant future after the collapse of a human galactic empire where those remnants having machines no longer know how to repair them, while one isolated military post ritualistically trains technicians but lacks machines enough to live above the level of primitive hunters. In most of the other stories, elements of SF and fantasy are combined—e.g., alien invaders meet vampires. Entertaining, but not sophisticated.

4-169. Cole, Everett B. **The Philosophical Corps.** Gnome, 1962.
Dalthos A-Riman leads contingent of space corps that deals with new species and cultural disturbers, "drones," by re-education instead of obliterating violence. Procedure of benevolent brain-washing. Ideological space opera, combining interesting adventures in context of at least politically conservative machinations of a "thought control police force." Part of a 1950s *Astounding* series. Compare Mitchison's *Memoirs of a Spacewoman* [4-426].

4-170. Collins, Hunt (pseud. of S. A. Lombino). **Tomorrow's World.** Avalon, 1956. (Alternate title: *Tomorrow and Tomorrow*, 1956).
Expansion of "Malice in Wonderland" (1954), published under Lombino's major pseudonym, Evan Hunter. In the near future, U.S. society is polarized between the dominant drug-using, pornography-gazing, body-painting, hip "Vikes," who only want vicarious experiences, and the subordinated, sexually and emotionally repressed, puritanical "Res," whose doctrine of "realism" is equally narrow. The dialectic unfolds, with Re defeating Vike, but this time, a new synthesis leading to a balanced society may result. Interesting slang, as in Brunner's *Stand on Zanzibar* [4-118], and an extrapolation unusually close to the present sensate culture; plot is merely vehicle for the author's comments on society and humanity. Lots of sex for its time. Compare Compton's *Synthajoy* [4-172].

4-171. Compton, David Guy (U.K.). **The Steel Crocodile.** Ace, 1970, $.75. (British title: *The Electric Crocodile*.)

Matthew and Abigail Oliver join secret computer project at "Colindale" as spies for leftist "CLC" and are destroyed by right-wing security characteristic of paranoic "hush-hush" government secret scientism. Matthew and Abigail are fully developed characters whose tragic fate is central interest of book. Science dehumanizes in modern context. Excellent narrative pace. Compare Shaw's *Ground Zero Man* [4-505]. NN, 1970.

4-172. Compton, David Guy (U.K.). **Synthajoy.** Ace, 1968.
Powerful story of a British psychiatrist's rise to wealth and power through his development of a machine that transfers recorded emotional experiences to others. The story is relived by his wife in a series of flashbacks as she undergoes treatment for her husband's murder, in his own mental hospital with the machine she has come to so despise. Mature writing, deep characterization, and social concern—Compton's trademarks—are present in abundance.

*4-173. Compton, David Guy (U.K.). **The Unsleeping Eye.** DAW, 1974, $1.25. (British title: *The Continuous Katherine Mortenhoe*, 1974).
The jaded public of the near future is treated to TV documentaries featuring the decline of terminal disease cases. Katherine Mortenhoe appears to be such a case, only her story is to be secretly recorded, with her husband's highly paid permission, through the eternally awake "eyes"— tiny, surgically implanted TV cameras—of Roddie Rodericks. But Katherine, reflecting on her sterile past life, comes to find herself as she flees public recognition, and so, too, does Roddie as he accompanies her—he blinds himself rather than continue as an agent of such perversion and voyeurism. Human psychology and social criticism blend to raise moral issues in this work by a much underrated writer. Contrast Aldiss's *Report on Probability A* [4-9].

4-174. Condon, Richard. **The Manchurian Candidate.** McGraw, 1959. Dell, $1.50.
The well-written benchmark novel of Korean War era brainwashing techniques and their implications for a cold war world. Raymond Shaw, Medal of Honor winner, is "brainwashed" into a time-bomb assassin by communist psychologists. Back in America, his mission is set in motion by a post-hypnotic signal. Conditioning and hypnosis are complementary psychotherapeutic techniques that will be turned to subtly terrible purposes in international warfare. The effect has become a commonplace in recent SF. Condon's story is powerful and convincing. Compare Budrys' *Who?* [4-124].

4-175. Coney, Michael G. (U.K.). **Mirror Image.** DAW, 1972, $.95.
Planetary colonization story with the usual ingredients: Stordahl, the stoic supervisor; Joan, who pines for his affection; Briggs, the egotistical scientist; Hetherington, the crafty, ruthless, and deformed capitalist; and Marilyn, his beautiful but sexually loose wife. However, the aliens

are interesting, protean life forms capable of defensively assuming the idealized bodies and personalities of the colonists' best-loved persons. After taking human forms, the aliens give birth to a new, better humanity. Compare Silverberg's *Downward to the Earth* [4-522].

4-176. Cooper, Edmund (U.K.). **The Cloud Walker.** Ballantine, 1973. Hodder, £1.75.
After World War IV, an antimachine age is maintained by the "Luddite" church. In medieval culture, Kieron dares death by reinventing flight in form of hot-air balloon. His balloon is first used to firebomb bandit ships. His revolt against this leads to the formation of a quasi-religious guild of aeronauts dedicated to the peaceful use of science. Well-told story criticizing culture that finds "machines" evil and the cause of civilization's failure. Misuse of machines is the real evil. Compare Brackett's *The Long Tomorrow* [4-98] and Miller's *A Canticle for Leibowitz* [4-424].

4-177. Cooper, Edmund (U.K.). **A Far Sunset.** Walker, 1967.
A space explorer is marooned on a planet of Altair. He must learn to live in peace with the nonhuman inhabitants. In this process he marries and impregnates an alien woman who is later murdered in revulsion by the outraged natives. Eventually he becomes the ruler and is destined to die in a religious ceremony. His rescue ship comes just before his execution, giving him the choice of dying for his new people or escaping with his old. Good narrative and anthropological insight. Contrast Le Guin's *Planet of Exile* (1966).

4-178. Coppel, Alfred. **Dark December.** Fawcett Gold Medal, 1960.
After World War III, Gavin is released from duty as member of ICBM team and travels in loneliness and loss over the devastated remains of the United States, learning to survive physically and to replace his lost family with a new one. Post-catastrophe story in John Christopher mold; perhaps more of a psychological study.

4-179. Corley, Edwin. **Siege.** Stein & Day, 1969.
One of three or four widely read "revolutionary" novels depicting, step by step, on a nationwide scale, the rise of black people in a revolution in the United States. A competent black Marine general is the leader. All of Harlem and surrounding area on Manhattan Island are burned to the ground. Fast-paced and plausible version of doomsday. Compare Greenlee's *The Spook Who Sat by the Door* [4-275].

4-180. Cowper, Richard. (pseud. of John Middleton Murry) (U.K.). **Breakthrough.** Dobson, 1967, £1.75. Ballantine (U.K.) 1967 £.30.
Jimmy Haverill, English professor, and Rachel Bernstein are paranormal reincarnations of Haalar and Araaran, lovers from the doomed edenic future of mankind. They reunite in the present with help of

"Dumps," mysterious parapsychologist; their genes are mankind's potential. Nice work with three main characters. Clever assimilation of literary antecedents in Blake and Keats. Compare his later *The Twilight of Briareus* [4-182].

4-181. Cowper, Richard. (pseud. of John Middleton Murry) (U.K). **Kuldesak.** Doubleday, 1972. Gollancz, £1.80; Quartet Books, £.40.

In the forty-second century on Earth an indifferent computer plans to phase out the human species. It is stopped by Mel, one of the last questioners, with aid of alien anthropologist who advises that humanity is not without purpose, indeed is destined for intergalactic progress. Compare Clarke's *Childhood's End* [4-149] and Johannesson's *Tale of the Big Computer* [4-326].

4-182. Cowper, Richard. (pseud. of John Middleton Murry) (U.K.). **The Twilight of Briareus.** Day, 1974, $6.95. DAW, $1.50.

In 1983, a supernova in Briareus bathes Earth in radiation; numerous physical effects result, including climatic changes that cool down Britain and genetic alterations that first drastically drop the birth rate, but then produce children with parapsychological powers. Actually, these genetic changes are controlled by aliens who arrived with the nova's deadly light and who seek mankind's survival. Similar thematically to Clarke's *Childhood's End* [4-149], but lacks clarity concerning mankind's transcendence. Detailed astrophysical, meteorological, and biological elements compare with the Hoyles' *The Inferno* [4-318].

4-183. Crane, Robert (pseud. of Bernard Glemser) (U.K.). **Hero's Walk.** Ballantine, 1954.

Strong story about the conflict between Earth's ambitious leaders, bent on exploiting the other planets, and the quarantine of Earth by a superior species, the Ampiti. During the resulting bombardment of Earth's cities, Neil Harrison struggles to reach his girl and reflects on the blunders that led to the disaster. The militarists have been overthrown and Earth surrenders to the Ampiti; perhaps they will spare a wiser mankind. Realistic description of bombing in this antiwar story. Contrast Anderson's *The Star Fox* [4-24].

4-184. Crichton, Michael. **The Andromeda Strain.** Knopf, 1969, $6.95. Dell, $1.25.

U.S. space shot threatens catastrophic complications when military tampering results in returned capsule unleashing super virus on town, killing inhabitants. Program virologists succeed in neutralizing threat only at last minute. Space age science must be conducted very carefully in view of potential dangers. Story in form of report, replete with authentic-looking bibliography. Popular as a film. Compare Blackburn's *A Scent of New-Mown Hay* [4-73] and Merle's *The Day of the Dolphin* [4-418].

4-185. Daniel, Yuri (as Nikolai Arzhak) (U.S.S.R.). **This Is Moscow Speaking, and Other Stories.** Dutton, 1969. Collier, $1.25. Tr. by Stuart Hood, Harold Shukman, and John Richardson of *Ici Moscou*.

"Moscow Speaking" is most controversial of four stories included, about declaration in Russia, August 10, 1960, of a "Public Murder Day" and public's passive acceptance of it. An analysis of the phenomenon and orchestration of terrorism.

4-186. Davidson, Avram. **Clash of Star-Kings.** Ace, 1966.

Despite its title, a well-constructed, well-characterized, and maturely written tale of the final struggle between two star-races—one peaceful and benevolent, the other cruel, warlike eaters of human hearts. The setting is a mountain village in modern Mexico, and the story abounds with local color and lore. In *Chariots of the Gods* fashion, the star-races were once god-like visitors to ancient Mexico, but their war took them elsewhere. When they return for a hidden weapon capable of tipping the balance, natives and two expatriate American writers get drawn into the fray. Suspenseful and realistic. Nebula novella nominee, 1966.

4-187. Davidson, Avram, and Ward Moore. **Joyleg.** Pyramid, 1962. Walker, $5.95.

Congressional fact-finding expedition in Tennessee foothills becomes international free-for-all as Isachar Joyleg, veteran of the American Revolutionary War, is revealed to possess "fountain of youth" in his moonshine still. Reporters, congressional investigators, and even ambassadors from Soviet Union try to exploit him. But trunk of old papers from days of Revolution turns tables and makes Joyleg master of the world. Rollicking social criticism.

4-188. Davidson, Avram. **Or All the Seas with Oysters.** Berkley, 1962.

Seventeen stories, including title story (HW, 1958), about subtly evolved tragedy in bicycle shop when safety pins, coat hangers, and bicycles begin to "regenerate." Also of interest is the humorous "Help! I Am Dr. Morris Goldpepper" and the ethnic "The Golem." Mood is science fantasy rather than science fiction.

4-189. Davidson, Avram. **Rogue Dragon.** Ace, 1965.

Dragons are real and live on Earth of the far future. A dragon hunt is sought after by many of the galaxy's wealthy. The dragon breeders are rich, decadent, and totally dependent on the dragons for their power over the population. When the dragons are discovered to be alien in origin and controlled by an alien hidden on Earth, trouble flares. Good picture of future-alternate civilization.

4-190. Davidson, Avram. **Strange Seas and Shores.** Doubleday, 1971.

Seventeen well-crafted SF and fantasy stories from 1958 to 1967 that exhibit Davidson's wit and taste for the offbeat. Time travel and plot to prevent the development of modern technology unfold in "Take Wooden Indians", "The House the Blakeneys Built" creates a social microcosm for the battle of stability vs. change. A man searches futilely for a family that predicts new fads in "The Sources of the Nile," and an orphan child turns the tables on his mean grandfather in "The Goobers." Strong on characterization and story backgrounds. Also includes a preface by the author, and an appreciation of him by Ray Bradbury.

4-191. Davies, Leslie Purnell (U.K.). **The Paper Dolls.** Doubleday, 1966.
As Germany is losing World War II, a Nazi concentration camp scientist seeks revenge by altering the genes of a Polish man so that later he will father an evil super-child; instead, he sires Siamese quadruplets linked at the arms. Two young school teachers and an old man play amateur detective over a detailed English countryside as they trace these psychic superboys in the face of mental counterblows, racing U.S. intelligence and a mob of vengeful villagers to destroy the menace posed by the children. Ordinary folks caught up in events, amateur sleuthing, and weird happenings in rural Britain are typical Davies story elements; fine psi-emerging story. Compare Wyndham's *The Midwich Cuckoos* [4-639], Shiras' *Children of the Atom* [4-518] and Sturgeon's *More than Human* [4-565].

4-192. de Camp, Lyon Sprague. **Divide and Rule.** Fantasy Press, 1948.
"Hoppers," insectile aliens, conquer Earth and recast human society in feudal mold, partitioned into fiefs to discourage unified resistance; they allow only medieval technology, with few exceptions, such as radios. Mankind's resistance is cast with hero "knight" and "cowboy" in comic adventure tale vaguely reminiscent of *Don Quixote*. Revision of a 1939 story. Compare Tenn's *Of Men and Monsters* [4-579]. This edition also contains "The Stolen Dormouse" (1941), one of de Camp's best stories.

4-193. de Camp, Lyon Sprague, and Peter Schuyler Miller. **Genus Homo.** Fantasy Press, 1950.
A busload of scientists and chorus girls sleep Rip van Winkle style a million years into the future and find a geophysically different Earth. There is no human race, and several species of monkey and ape, along with beavers, have evolved intelligence comparable to humans. A combination of allegory, satire, and clever extrapolation that descends into soap opera. At its best, similar to *Gulliver's Travels* [1-49], *Earth Abides* [4-558], and *Planet of the Apes* [4-90]. Boldly considers practicality of nudity, polygamy, and the amalgamation of humans in the gorilla culture that befriends them.

4-194. de Camp, Lyon Sprague, and Fletcher Pratt. **The Incomplete Enchanter.** Holt, 1942. SF Book Club, $3.50; Ballantine, $1.95. (as *The Complete Enchanter*; includes *The Castle of Iron*.)
The humorous adventures of Harold Shea, a dilettant psychologist who

finds himself through excursions into mythical and fictional worlds where magic, like technology here, operates by fixed laws. Mental exercises in symbolic logic are the means of transportation, carrying Shea first to Norse mythology's Ragnarök, then into Spencer's *Faerie Queene*. Background well developed. Based on material dating from 1940. Two sequels of lesser quality: *The Castle of Iron* (Gnome, 1950) originally appeared in 1941 and is set in Ariosto's *Orlando Furioso*; *Wall of Serpents* (Avalon, 1960) is derived from 1953–1954 stories, set in Kalevala and Irish mythology. Contrast Zelazny's *The Dream Master* [4-646].

*4-195. de Camp, Lyon Sprague. **Lest Darkness Fall.** Holt, 1941; rev. ed., Prime, 1949. Ballantine, $1.50.
Martin Padway, time-travelled to 754 A.D. Rome, sets about distilling brandy, teaching Arabic mathematics to bookkeepers, inventing printing, etc. Eventually helps Goths conquer Rome—contrary to *his* history. Neat anthropological interpretation of history. This is de Camp's best. Compare Golding's *Brass Butterfly* [4-268].

4-196. de Camp, Lyon Sprague. **Rogue Queen.** Doubleday, 1951. Signet, $.95.
A female-dominated species governed on the hive model is visited by an exploration team from Earth. The contact leads to a revolution by some members of humanoid hive people who adopt democratic Earth government model with leadership of "rogue" woman. Contact between alien species will lead to transformation of culture of less enlightened. Thoughtful anthropological insights. Clever Swiftian parody of human institutions and provincialism.

4-197. deFord, Miriam Allen. **Xenogenesis.** Ballantine, 1969.
Sixteen fantasy and SF stories from 1950s and 1960s, many from the *Magazine of Fantasy and Science Fiction*, and more or less tied to the general theme of procreation and sex. Of interest are "The Daughter of the Tree," "Season of the Babies," and "The Last Generation." Emphasis on characterization, moral issues, and humanity. Contrast with Clingerman's *A Cupful of Space* [4-166].

*4-198. Delany, Samuel R. **Babel-17.** Ace, 1966. $1.50.
In an interstellar war, "Babel-17" is linguistic program with vocabulary limited to potential criminality and sabotage. Until it is understood, the Alliance cannot win. Rydra Wong, translinguistic genius–poetess, provides the key. Profound lesson in limits and potential of language soundly based on modern linguistic theory. Compare "Martian" in Heinlein's *Stranger in a Strange Land* [4-302] and "Newspeak" in *1984* [4-450] HN, 1967; NW, 1966.

4-199. Delany, Samuel R. **Dhalgren.** Bantam, 1975, $1.95.
William Dhalgren comes to Bellona, doomed U.S. metropolis, to join

counter-cultural society in decadent and anarchical life style, a dance symbolizing the twilight of the American dream. An essentially simple story here becomes enormously complex through symbolism, satire, experimental narrative organization, para-pornographic detail, and much dialogue. Critical reception is mixed. Some find *Dhalgren* long, tedious, involuted, and imaginatively masturbatory; some see its near-Joycean architectonics as estimable, easily repaying the considerable effort it requires of the reader. Compare Gawron's slighter *An Apology for Rain* [4-258] and Aldiss's *Barefoot in the Head* [4-2].

4-200. Delany, Samuel R. **Driftglass.** Doubleday, 1971. Signet, $.95.
Ten stories from 1966 to 1971. Includes "Driftglass" (NN, 1967); "The Star Pit" (HN, 1968); "Time Considered as a Helix of Semiprecious Stones" (HN, 1970; NW, 1969). Especially interesting is "Aye, and Gomorrah" (NW, 1967), a study of the perverted love of some for neutered spacemen. Superb collection by a top "new wave" writer.

*4-201. Delany, Samuel R. **The Einstein Intersection.** Ace, 1967, $.95. Garland, $11.00.
Thirty thousand years in the future, mankind is no longer at all human. "Functionals" must earn right to belong to society; those found lacking spend lives in compound "kages." Lo Lobey is forced to leave his simple life as a shepherd for an Orpheus-like trek when his beloved Friza is taken by Kid Death; he confronts an Earth that stands at crossroads of what had been and what is fast becoming. Marvelous weave of symbol, archetype, and hyperbolic physics. Compare Zelazny's *This Immortal* [4-650]. HN, 1968; NW, 1967.

4-202. Delany, Samuel R. **Nova.** Doubleday, 1968. Bantam, $1.50.
Captain Lorq Von Ray, figurehead of Pleiades Federation, races Prince and Ruby Red, heads of Earth/Draco Red-Shift Ltd., to the core of an exploding sun for a prize of seven tons of the trans-300 element Illyrion, the rare power source of the thirty-second century. Accompanying him are the fascinating characters Mouse and Katin. Symbols and archetypal relationships meticulously assembled in this variation on the Ahab and Moby Dick theme. HN, 1969.

4-203. del Rey, Lester. **And Some Were Human.** Prime, 1948.
Twelve SF and fantasy stories from the 1940s including "Nerves" and "Helen O'Loy" (both SFHF), the latter about an android woman humanized and married by one of her makers. Also of interest are "The Day is Done," which depicts the conflict between Neanderthal and Cro-Magnon men, and "The Stars Look Down." One of the better known early single-author anthologies.

4-204. del Rey, Lester. **The Eleventh Commandment.** Ballantine, 1962.
One of the best treatments of the future Roman Catholic Church theme.

Here the Church rules an Earth teeming with billions. It has decreed that mankind should proliferate without restraint. Reason: the long-range improvements, which drive the species up the steps of evolution, far outweigh the short-range miseries of overpopulation. Contrast with Harrison's *Make Room! Make Room!* [4-290].

*4-205. del Rey, Lester. **Nerves.** Ballantine, 1956, $1.25.
First published in 1942 and later expanded, probably the earliest major work to deal with an accident at an atomic power plant. Seen through the eyes of the plant physician, engineers battle courageously to stop an escaped experimental isotope from exploding. Prophetic in its anticipation of popular fear and resistance to nuclear plants, the story is not likely to satisfy present-day atomic critics with its last-minute solution based on the guess of an untried nuclear boy wonder. Taut action, gobs of technology; unrealistically, del Rey's nuclear plant is insured! Original short story in SFHF. Compare Fuller's nonfiction *We Almost Lost Detroit* (1975).

4-206. del Rey, Lester. **Pstalemate.** Putnam, 1971. Berkley, $.95.
The author's first adult novel after a ten-year interlude, it traces the discovery by young Harry Bronson of inherited ESP powers and his struggle, ending in the use of psychedelic drugs, to forestall the inevitable madness that strikes adult ESPers. While aiding his ESPer girlfriend, his future "mature" self returns to enable the drugged Harry to save her sanity and thus provide the means for saving all of his kind. Compare with Selling's *Telepath* [4-501] Brunner's *The Whole Man* [4-119], and Pohl's *Drunkard's Walk* [4-463].

4-207. Dick, Philip K. **Do Androids Dream of Electric Sheep?** Doubleday, 1968. Rapp & Whiting, £1.05; Panther, £.30.
Man had built androids to help in the colony worlds to which most had fled from a more and more dangerously polluted Earth. Each generation of androids behaves more "humanly." Androids escape their servitude and flee to Earth masquerading as humans. Rick Deckard is a bounty hunter, receiving $1,000 for each android he "retires." He is splendidly successful, but personal contact with some androids arouses his sympathy and he begins to doubt that his work is wholesome. Even when he can re-create sentient life, man's presumption will make him fail to recognize it as such—especially when he cannot even recognize the life in animals. Setting is a stark and sterile dying Earth, a plausible extrapolation of tendencies of mid-twentieth century civilization. Again Dick has turned SF clichés upon themselves so that the reader must confront the present-day reality those clichés usually hide. Compare Brunner's *Into the Slave Nebula* (1968). NN, 1968.

4-208. Dick, Philip K. **Dr. Bloodmoney (Or How We Got Along After the Bomb).** Ace, 1965, $1.50.

The H-bombs fall. Story centers several years later upon the vicissitudes in lives of survivors. In a reduced civilization with flora and fauna mutations, emerging paranormal powers, and contact with the dead, life nevertheless proceeds with its soap-operatic ups and downs, much as before. Few, if any, can grasp the magnitude and implications of cataclysm; thus, cataclysm will leave most essentially unchanged. Inspired presentation of stereotypical characters in story woven so subtly that its art and discipline are easy to overlook. Compare and contrast Miller's *Canticle for Leibowitz* [4-424]. Title also suggests associations with George's *Dr. Strangelove* [4-260]. NN, 1965.

4-209. Dick, Philip K. **Eye in the Sky.** Ace, 1957, $1.25.
Remarkable variation on alternate worlds model. Eight people are knocked out in a bevatron field. As consciousness returns to successive victims, the others are drawn into the private reality of the one returning to consciousness. Resulting adventures in worlds of religious fascist, a "nice" but sexually frigid female blueblood, and a communist sympathizer are suspenseful, interesting, and instructive. Creator of each world is literally "god" in that world, leaving others at his mercy—in fear of the "eye in the sky." Context for story is paranoia of spy-hunting, top-secret labeling, cold-war United States. First two-thirds of novel especially well told.

4-210. Dick, Philip K. **Flow My Tears, the Policeman Said.** Doubleday, 1974, $6.95. DAW, $1.50.
Television superstar Jason Taverner is drawn into an alternate personal reality where he is a nobody through the drug-aided dream wish of Alys Buckner, sister of police "general" Felix Buckner, with whom she lives incestuously. The drug wears off; Alys dies from its exhausting effects; Jason's reality is restored. Characters of Jason and Felix are superbly drawn in a very competent narrative. Police state setting is ominous and plausible, but novel is perhaps misconceived because SF apparatus is unnecessary. Jason and Felix belong to present reality. Or is this a parody of dystopia and SF clichés? NN, 1974; HN, 1975; Campbell Memorial Award, 1975.

*4-211. Dick, Philip K. **The Man in the High Castle.** Putnam, 1962. Berkley, $1.50.
A classic alternate history novel depicting a world in which Axis powers won World War II, and have divided and occupied the United States. Especially noteworthy are the insights into the conqueror–conquered relationship, the Japanese mind, and the attempts by Americans to emulate it. The book's driving force is the *I Ching*, the basis not only of characters' actions, but of writing of *The Grasshopper Lies Heavy*, a widely read "subversive" alternate history novel which has the Allies winning the war. (Still, the world portrayed in that book is not our real one.) Dick also

used the *I Ching* in plotting the novel. A cleanly written although complexly plotted work, its central action involves the attempt by a German faction to warn the Japanese of an impending nuclear attack on their homeland. Surrounding this are several subplots in which characters realize their destinies for good or ill. Dick's best. Contrast Sarban's *The Sound of His Horn* [4-498]. HW, 1963.

4-212. Dick, Philip K. **Solar Lottery.** Ace, 1955, $1.25. Gregg, 1976, price not set. (British title: *World of Chance*, 1956).
In a stagnant future social order supposedly based on chance, people operate with game theory's "Minimax." But few can actually win; giant industrial complexes with fealty systems and a rigid class system see to that. Even the Quizmasters, absolute tyrants chosen at random, subvert the system by trying to abolish or rig the drawing, while public assassins attempt to murder them and personal telepathic bodyguards provide security. Against this background, a complex plot unfolds of Quizmaster Verrick's loss of office to a new one, Cartwright, who wins the throne through fraud so he can send a spaceship to search for a mystical tenth planet. Verrick's attempt at assassination almost succeeds except for the intervention of his idealistic "serf," Benteley, who questions if immoral orders should be followed. Finally, there is hope that mankind will once more be free to strive toward its potential. Dick's first major achievement. Contrast with van Vogt's *World of Null-A* [4-594].

*4-213. Dick, Philip K. **The Three Stigmata of Palmer Eldritch.** Doubleday, 1965. Manor Books, $1.25.
Palmer Eldritch visits Proxima Centauri and brings back "Chew-Z," a hallucinogenic drug that provides "trips" that are real. Moreover, the weird Christ-symbol Eldritch is a controller–inhabitant of each hallucination. "Chew-Z" seems likely to replace "Can-D," the commercial hallucinogen merchandized with Barbee-like dolls and furniture for quite predictable drug escape experience—into a doll-house jet-set world. Eldritch and "Chew-Z" rip the fabric of Earth's reality to reveal glimpses of cosmic meta-reality that can threaten or sublimely translate human sentience. The novel's proposition seems mystically subtle: Transubstantiation is actual, not merely symbolic. Everyone is Eldritch; everyone is . . . God. An exciting weave of the major symbols of Judeo-Christian belief, first in parody, then in a reintegration of them refreshed in meaning and power. One of Dick's very best. Contrast Moorcock's *Behold the Man*. [4-427]. NN, 1965.

4-214. Dick, Philip K. **Ubik.** Doubleday, 1969. Rapp & Whiting, £1.40.
A corporation of anti-parapsychics competes with a corporation of parapsychics, and the dead are reanimated in "half-life." The "realities" of individual half-lifers, however, are unstable and subject to control by the strongest among them. Whose reality are you living in? Dick raised this

question in *Eye in the Sky* [4-209] as well. Subtly combines a parody of SF clichés with ultimate metaphysical questions. Much SF is escapist; this piece throws the reader back to his own "reality." Compare Aldiss's *Report on Probability A* [4-9].

4-215. Dickinson, Peter (U.K.). **The Green Gene.** Pantheon, 1973, $5.95. DAW, $1.25.
Pravandragasharatipili (Pete) Humayan, a demographic statistician from India on loan to England, has discovered that the "green gene," a euphemism for melanin element in the skin of nonwhite races, has appeared as a dominant in a significant percentage of births to parents of supposedly pure caucasian stock. Black babies are being born to white parents. It is nature's way of combating skin cancer in whites. But in a viciously racist Great Britain of the not-too-distant future, the appearance of the gene causes chaos, especially because it signifies ancestors of England's race-proud whites were black. Story's end: revolution in progress. Compare Priest's *Darkening Island* [4-468]. Campbell nominee, 1974.

4-216. Dickson, Gordon R. **The Alien Way.** Bantam, 1965.
Earth has achieved faster-than-light drive and makes the inevitable contact with hostile aliens. War with the Ruml is averted because Jason Barchar has discovered the "alien way" of looking at survival. The Ruml, of course, must learn the "alien way" of humanity. Brotherhood, however, is not the message, rather, it is that knowledge and power are necessary for ultimate survival. Humanity has it. Excellent for orchestration of Ruml's and humanity's point of view.

4-217. Dickson, Gordon R. **The Genetic General.** Ace, 1960.
Donal Graeme is part Dorsai, part Maryan, providing breeding of strength, courage, and intelligence with psi ability. He begins career as a "mercenary" (in the good sense), overcomes many challenges in his "apprenticeship," becomes the most powerful military man in the galaxy, and is vaguely disappointed, because his full power has emerged in his trials and he is like a god. Good emerging superman story. Graeme's intelligence is interestingly illustrated. Celebration of the militaristic identity may be unpalatable to many 1970s readers. Part of a future history, the Childe Cycle, which traces an evolutionary development in man from the 1300s to the 2300s; also includes *Necromancer* (1962), *Tactics of Mistake* (1971), and *Soldier, Ask Not* [4-218]. HN, 1960.

4-218. Dickson, Gordon R. **Soldier, Ask Not.** Dell, 1967. DAW, $1.50.
Tam Olyn, a newsman, discovers himself to be one of the "movers" of humanity. He has an instinct that enables him to direct the forces of human development. Playing games with real lives, he encourages a poor religious colony to hire men out as mercenaries even against the in-

vincible Dorsai. He learns only too late how well he succeeded, and how unnecessary it was. Excellent psychological profile. Part of the Childe Cycle (see *The Genetic General* [4-217]). The original short story was a 1965 Hugo winner.

*4-219. Disch, Thomas M. **Camp Concentration.** Doubleday, 1969. Avon, $1.50.
Brilliant tale of Louis Sacchetti, political prisoner, who is secretly used by the state, along with others, as guinea pig in experiment designed to increase mental powers. But increase is caused by a hybrid strain of syphilis which rapidly destroys the host's central nervous system. The lives of the inmates and their experimenters are followed in secret "Camp Archimedes," until the genius of the victims finds a solution. A highly critical, creatively executed, and accurate extrapolation of the mentality of the U.S. military-industrial elite who gave us the Vietnam War. Compare with Blum's *Simultaneous Man* [4-83] and Keyes' *Flowers for Algernon* [4-336].

4-220. Disch, Thomas M. **Fun With Your New Head.** Doubleday, 1971.
Seventeen stories from 1963 to 1967 that explore the modern human condition. The exquisite "Moondust, the Smell of Hay, and Dialectical Materialism" tells of a stranded Soviet cosmonaut pondering why he is dying on the Moon; the realistic "Casablanca" deals with a middle-American couple caught overseas after the destruction of the United States; the general affluence resulting from matter-transforming machines in "Now is Forever" has destroyed the old order but failed to supply a meaningful replacement; the army as death is portrayed in the satirical "1-A." Of a piece with Spinrad's *No Direction Home* [4-553] and Ellison's *Alone against Tomorrow*[4-232].

4-221. Disch, Thomas M. **The Genocides.** Berkley, 1965. Panther, £.30.
A group of people work desperately to survive the prodigious growth of a suddenly ubiquitous "plant" and the depredations of spheres that turn buildings and mammals to ash. In fact, alien agriculturists are methodically clearing Earth of competing flora and fauna to make a more prosperous farm. Excellent suspense; logical; point of view provides sobering insight about "value" of mankind on Earth—not to mention the larger scheme of things. Compare Vonnegut's *The Sirens of Titan* [4-607]. NN, 1965.

4-222. Disch, Thomas M. **334.** Avon, 1974, $1.65.
Powerful, pessimistic slices of a dark future in New York City built around the residents of 334 East 11th Street, a mammoth building, part of a government housing project. More a collection of stories than a novel; portions appeared throughout the late 1960s and early 1970s. A superior work. NN, 1974.

4-223. Dolinsky, Mike. **Mind One.** Dell, 1972, $1.25.
Jesuit priest and well-preserved middle-aged woman, both psychiatrists, discover that a drug treatment for psychosis produces telepathic talent. They take it and the fun begins. Excellent scenario of civilization about to be transformed by important new factor; major achievement is marvelous characterization of Jesuit celibate becoming aware of sexual nature of receptive female colleague. Relationship prospers as story ends. Compare Miller's *Canticle for Leibowitz* [4-424], Blish's *Jack of Eagles* [4-79], and Brunner's *The Whole Man* [4-119].

4-224. Drury, Allen. **Come Nineveh, Come Tyre.** Doubleday, 1973, $8.95, Avon, $1.75.
A conscious updating of Sinclair Lewis's *It Can't Happen Here* [3-34]. Failure to appreciate threat of world communism and lack of firmness in American government results in chaos and anarchy. Drury's best-selling novels present thinly disguised characters of people in national political life. Satire and irony in a politically conservative vein.

4-225. Dudintsev, Vladimir (U.S.S.R.). **A New Year's Tale.** Dutton, 1960. Tr. by Gabriella Azrael.
Allegory of scientific discovery of ultimately cheap heat and light for dark continent that never gets light from Sun (North America?). Hero makes breakthrough by learning he has a "year" to live and understands paradox of hurrying in real sense—by being completely composed. Ambition leading to scientific discovery is metaphor for political and moral triumph . . . perhaps.

4-226. Duncan, David. **Occam's Razor.** Ballantine, 1957.
A scientific experiment using soap films and wire frames to test the theory of minimals inadvertently taps another space-time continuum and introduces a beautiful girl and horned, super-strong man onto a top-secret island Moon-rocket base. The resulting confusion and blunders by officials threaten to launch nuclear world war. Interesting characterizations, but weak in science. Compare Maine's *Fire Past the Future* [4-405].

*4-227. Durrell, Lawrence (U.K.). **Tunc.** Dutton, 1968, $7.95. Pocket Books, $1.25.
First of two works; sequel is *Nunquam*, (Dutton, 1970. Pocket Books, $1.25). In *Tunc*, Felix Charlock is genius inventor of super-computer named "Abel," capable of predicting the future. Charlock and computer are bought by world-girdling conglomerate "Merlin," representing the monopoly-capitalistic situation of Western world in near future, much as in Brunner's *Stand on Zanzibar* [4-118]. Charlock has all money can buy, and it drives him crazy. In *Nunquam*, Charlock is brought out of madhouse to use Abel to create an android copy of Iolanthe, the dead prostitute turned movie idol, with whom Julian, the head of "Merlin," is madly infatuated. Charlock succeeds. Iolanthe, human in all respects, is de-

stroyed by the same forces of the world that destroyed her original. Good narrative; surprising imagery, peopled with every character and neurosis imaginable. Durrell is first-rank British novelist. Compare Carter's *The War of Dreams* [4-143].

4-228. Edmondson, G. C. **The Ship that Sailed the Time Stream.** Ace, 1965.
An accident sends a navy yawl back a thousand years in time. The crew sail through several historical .periods in their search for the present. They meet Norsemen, Moors, and Roman slavers, and a number of amorous ladies bent on a different kind of slavery. Once the sailors reach their own time they begin plans to steal a larger and better-provisioned vessel and continue their voyages in time. Well-written parody of all time-travel stories. NN, 1965.

4-229. Effinger, George Alec. **What Entropy Means to Me.** Doubleday, 1972. Signet, $.95.
An unusual work, in some ways a parody on fantasy and quest stories. In a book within a book, Seyt describes the imaginary trials of his brother, Dore, who has set out to follow the sacred River on their planet of Home in search of their Father. Meanwhile, Seyt's many weird relatives critique each chapter, explicate the story's symbolism, and foment religious schisms within the family's faith. Finally, Seyt, too, sets out down the River. A highly praised first novel, but more technique than substance. NN, 1972.

4-230. Ehrlich, Max. **The Big Eye.** Doubleday, 1949.
Earth narrowly misses catastrophic collision with new planet, "the big eye," which astronomers have announced will actually collide in order to unify world and end all war. Gravely flawed in science and sociology, but sentimentality is very satisfying. Reflects the rise of social concerns among post-world-war scientists. Compare Sturgeon's "Unite and Conquer" in *A Way Home* [4-570]. A Book of the Month Club selection.

4-231. Eklund, Gordon. **All Times Possible.** DAW, 1974, $.95.
Between 1923 and 1947, Tommy Bloome is prime mover in making of an alternative America in successful revolution by political left. In fact, existing history is not changed. He's on different time line; finally discovers an infinity of alternate time lines, and that one's individual existential nemesis is met in each. All times are the same from the subjective point of view. Fine characterization; nice evocation of the Steinbeckian *Grapes of Wrath* leftist revolutionary mood.

*4-232. Ellison, Harlan. **Alone against Tomorrow.** Macmillan, 1971. Collier, $1.25.
Twenty stories on the theme of alienation, from the mid-1950s to the end of the 1960s. In his introduction, the author says, "Alone against his

world, the man of today finds his gods have deserted him, his brother has grown fangs, the machine clatters ever nearer on his heels, fear is the only lover demanding his clasp, and without answers he turns and turns, and finds only darkness"; apt description of these works. Includes "I Have No Mouth, and I Must Scream" (HW, 1968), an anti-machine allegory, and " 'Repent Harlequin'! Said the Ticktockman" (HW, 1966, NW, 1965), about freedom and repression in an ordered, rational, machine-like society.

4-233. Ellison, Harlan. **The Beast that Shouted Love at the Heart of the World.** Avon, 1969. Signet, $1.25.
Fifteen prime Ellison stories, most dating from 1968 and 1969. The title story (HW, 1969) tells of a civilization that has purged itself of insanity by condemning the rest of the universe to suffer madness forever. "Shattered Like a Glass Goblin" (NN, 1969) is a fantasy piece set in a drug commune whose members grotesquely degenerate. But "A Boy and his Dog" is solid SF, a post-holocaust story (now a film) of Blood and his young master whose mutual love is strengthened by telepathy as they struggle to survive in a vicious world. Then there are "Along the Scenic Route," where automobile duels are a simple extrapolation from present-day aggression on the highway, and the humorous "Santa Claus vs. S.P.I.D.E.R.," a satiric parody with undercover agent Santa Claus stopping a plot to destroy the world. An informative introduction by the author rounds out the volume; a good collection of the unique and powerful Ellison.

*4-234. Ellison, Harlan. **Deathbird Stories.** Harper & Row, 1975, $8.95.
Nineteen fantasy/SF stories from the mid-1960s to the present. Collected around the theme of "a pantheon of modern gods." Noteworthy are: "Deathbird" (NN, 1973; HW, 1974); "Pretty Maggie Moneyeyes" (NN, 1967; HN, 1968); "Shattered Like a Glass Goblin" (NN, 1969); "Paingod"; "Along the Scenic Route." Powerful, angry, beautiful stories, perhaps Ellison's best collection. [Not seen.]

4-235. Ellison, Harlan. **I Have No Mouth, and I Must Scream.** Pyramid, 1967, $.95.
Seven stories, including the title story (HW, 1968) of the last man, trapped by super-computer that remakes him without a mouth to scream his frustration at an absurd and sterile world. Also "Delusion for a Dragon Slayer" (HN, 1967); and "Pretty Maggie Moneyeyes" (NN, 1967; HN, 1968).

4-236. Engel, Leonard, and Emanuel S. Piller. **The World Aflame: The Russian-American War of 1950.** Dial, 1947.
In 1955, historians give account of war between America and Russia, five years ongoing and no end in sight. America's monopoly of A-bomb

not enough for quick victory. Right-wing point of view corroborates late 1940s McCarthyism, fear of communism. Historically interesting potboiler. Compare Farjeon's *Death of a World* [4-237].

4-237 Farjeon, Joseph Jefferson (U.K.). **Death of a World.** Collins, 1948.
In the future, aliens read diary of John Smith, a last survivor when the governments of Earth destroyed the planet. Slickly narrated by first-class popular writer. An "awful warning" story. Compare Wylie's *Triumph* [4-636].

4-238 Farmer, Philip José. **The Alley God.** Ballantine, 1962. Sphere, £.30.
Three superior stories. "The Alley Man" (HN, 1960) is about the world's last Neanderthal, who works as a trash man, and his "attractiveness" for a certain young lady. "The Captain's Daughter" (1953) tells of an alien life form that inhabits human bodies and reproduces by making its hosts have intercourse, a fate that a spaceship captain and his daughter struggle against. In "The God Business" (1954), the hero is reborn a god after wandering in a fantastic, allegorical environment created out of the mind of his old professor of classical literature. Typical of Farmer's themes, treatments, and innovativeness.

4-239. Farmer, Philip José. **The Green Odyssey.** Ballantine, 1956.
Fast, humorous story of Alan Green, spaceship-wrecked on a barbarous lawn-covered planet over which the natives sail in wind-driven wheeled ships. No superman despite his ability-enhancing symbiote and technical knowledge, the timid Green is made a slave, works as a court gigolo, and finds himself under the thumb of a strong-willed wife with five children; then he hears of two captured Earthmen and sets off with his family in a fascinating "wind roller" to rescue them and himself. Compare Foster's *Icerigger* [4-248].

*4-240. Farmer, Philip José. **The Lovers.** Ballantine, 1961.
Expansion of a 1952 story that generated much controversy in SF because of its sexual content. Linguist Hal Yarrow is sent by his rigid, neo-Islamic theocratic government, the "Sturch," as part of an expedition to kill the intelligent, friendly, insect-like aliens on a planet wanted for colonization. Hal falls in love with a female member of another alien life form on the planet, one capable of mimicking human form and behavior. She inadvertently becomes pregnant by Hal, causing her death, but Hal still has the "children," all female, to love. Meanwhile, the insect-like aliens, having uncovered the Sturch's plot, kill the other Earthmen, freeing Hal from his superior's wrath. A commentary on the meaning of humanity and love in a police state. Compare with Howard's *The Eskimo Invasion* [4-316] and Coney's *Mirror Image* [4-175]. Sequel: *A Woman a Day* (1960); alternate title: *The Day of Timestop* (1968).

4-241. Farmer, Philip José. **Night of Light.** Berkley, 1966, $.75. Garland, $11.00.

Two John Carmody stories, about a vicious criminal turned priest, unartfully tacked together. Carmody reforms after braving a periodic solar disruption, called the "Night of Light," that literally gives a person what he really wants. The good Carmody sires a new god, Yess, after the evil Carmody had killed the old god, Yess. This first part is the more effective, reaching the mood of Delany's *Dhalgren* [4-199] at times. The second, more convoluted and less well written, has Catholic priest Carmody returning to Kareen to ask his god-son not to proselytize off-planet. For a future when man travels over a million light years between planets, customs and beliefs are unrealistically too similar to the present (must heroes eternally be puffing on those cigarettes?). Story too light to carry message of local versus galactic saviors. NN, 1966.

4-242. Farmer, Philip José. **Strange Relations.** Ballantine, 1960. Avon, $1.95.

Five stories of mankind meeting aliens, including "My Sister's Brother" ("Open to Me, My Sister") (HN, 1961), of a religiously inclined member of first Mars exploration team who learns from a female alien what true "brotherhood" might be, and "Mother," a Freudian-influenced study of a young man trapped inside an alien monster who uses him as part of her reproductive system. Daring stories for the SF of their time.

*4-243. Farmer, Philip José. **To Your Scattered Bodies Go.** Putnam, 1971. Berkley, $1.25.

A multimillion-mile-long river, one of the most remarkable SF vehicles, is the means for the resurrection of the entire human race, from subhuman to twenty-first century man. Traces the quest of Sir Richard Francis Burton for meaning in the apparent "heaven." HW, 1972. In *The Fabulous Riverboat* (Putnam, 1971, $5.95; Berkley, $1.25), Samuel Clemens builds a kingdom to construct a riverboat to cruise to the headwaters of the river. Opposing both Burton and Clemens are the mysterious "Ethicals," engineers of the massive enterprise. Within the mass of humanity there exist a few restless individuals who are never satisfied until they find meaning. All human endeavor results from this questing. Yet to come is a third novel tying the two novels together, and showing the results of both quests. Based on material originally written in the early 1950s.

4-244. Fast, Howard Melvin. **The Edge of Tomorrow.** Bantam, 1961.

Seven stories from 1959 and 1960, including "The Large Ant," about man's impulsive killing of a giant ant-like creature that has come bearing super-scientific knowledge for him. Parables condemning human arrogance, cruelty, and lack of emphathy. Nine similar SF and fantasy stories are included in *The General Zapped an Angel* (Morrow, 1969. Ace, $.75), several of which deal with the implications of war and environmental decay; in the title story, a trigger-happy Major General shoots down a twenty-foot-long angel, while "The Insects," guided by a central intelligence, strike back at man and destroy his ecologically destructive civilization. Fast is the author of *Freedom Road* and *Spartacus*, popular historical novels. Compare Sheckley's and Spinrad's short fiction.

4-245. Finney, Jack (pseud. of Walter Braden Finney). **The Body Snatchers.** Dell, 1955. Award, $.95 (as *Invasion of the Body Snatchers*).
Aliens invade Earth in form of seed pods, beginning in small California community. Aliens want human bodies. Attempted takeover is impersonal competition of species for survival. Fierce tenacity of Miles and Becky, and use of fire, drive the invaders back to space. Basis for film, *Invasion of the Body Snatchers*, 1956. Compare Heinlein's *The Puppet Masters* (1951) and Dick's "The Father-Thing."

4-246. Finney, Jack (pseud. of Walter Braden Finney). **The Third Level.** Rinehart, 1956.
Twelve stories, including the famous "I'm Scared," concerning a man who is cataloging the gradual breakdown of serial time under the influence of popular modern will to escape the present into the past and the future. The title story postulates a level below the two existing in the New York subway that is fifty years in the past. Time paradox is the topic of most of the stories.

*4-247. Finney, Jack (pseud. of Walter Braden Finney). **Time and Again.** Simon & Schuster, 1970, $9.95. Warner Books, $1.50.
Simon Morley, time traveler for secret government project, goes back to New York of the 1880s, a world much different and much the same as ours. Great virtue of story is historical authenticity and realism—an excellent history lesson. About 3,000,000 copies in print. Compare Kantor's *If the South Had Won the Civil War* [4-331] and Wells' *Time Machine* [2-161].

4-248. Foster, Alan Dean. **Icerigger.** Ballantine, 1974, $1.25.
Castaway humans on an ice-age planet battle the climate, mammoth beasts, and native barbarians as they help a medieval city-state build an ice clippership to carry them to this frontier planet's spaceport. Development of the alien environment compares with Herbert's *Dune* [4-307], the battles with Anderson's *Fire Time* [4-19], but the natives, despite their unique physical structure, possess a socio-cultural system too similar to Earth's European Middle Ages. Good adventure.

4-249. Frank, Pat (pseud. of Harry Hart Frank). **Alas, Babylon.** Lippincott, 1959. Bantam, $1.50.
After nuclear holocaust nearly devastates America, a small group of people survive to try to make a new and better world. Order is key to

survival. With it mankind will survive even the bomb. Excellent popular narrative. Compare Stewart's *Earth Abides* [4-558] and Christopher's post-catastrophe stories.

4-250. Frank, Pat (pseud. of Harry Hart Frank). **Mr. Adam.** Lippincott, 1946.
A nuclear blast sterilizes every man on Earth except Homer Adam. Civilization's chaos is aggravated by bureaucracy until Tommy Thompson's seaweed tonic reestablishes fertility. Belly-laughing satirical attack on U.S. bureaucrats. Compare Heinlein's *Stranger in a Strange Land* [4-302].

4-251. Franke, Herbert W. (Germany). **The Orchid Cage.** DAW, 1973, $.95. Tr. by Christine Priest of *Der orchideenkäfig*, 1961.
In distant future, Earthmen visit far planet in simulacrum message form, discovering humans there have been made into "orchids" by their computerized civilization. They are reduced to rudimentary organs ("orchid" means "teste" in Greek). As for humans, machine civilization makes life virtually meaningless. Logical tour de force. Ingenious space travel concept. Compare Anthony's *Macroscope* [4-30] and Campbell's "Twilight" [3-8].

4-252. Friedberg, Gertrude. **The Revolving Boy.** Doubleday, 1966. Gollancz, £.90; Pan £.25.
Derv Nagy was born with a "wild talent," a sense of absolute direction. Finding any degree on the compass by feel was like breathing. You could spin him around blindfolded and he would "unwind" to the point he originally faced. Later, as an athlete, it gave him perfect sense of bodily "attitude." Derv finds his destiny when he is able to direct astrophysicists to source of intelligent transmissions eight light years from Earth. Called a fresh idea when it appeared, the novel is nicely paced, and unnecessary futuristic furniture is only mildly obtrusive.

4-253. Galouye, Daniel F. **Dark Universe.** Bantam, 1961.
A nuclear war has forced many to retreat to prepared shelters for what becomes a generation-long exile. Loss of lighting power forces development of other senses, hearing and heat sensing, in two groups of exiles. Jared, while exploring this dark underground universe, discovers others from above seeking survivors. The light they bring creates a profound culture shock. Excellent insight. Good use of the formula of changing one element of a normal reality and extrapolating. HN, 1962. Compare Asimov's "Nightfall" [4-41].

4-254. Garbo, Norman. **The Movement.** Morrow, 1970.
The penultimate campus riot scenario. At mythical Chadwick University in Michigan, the students' demands are rejected by the administration. One step follows another until the students, joined by the ROTC and activist war veterans, fight to a draw the local police, the national guard,

and the regular army. Finally, local and national authorities approve a strike by jet fighters that rocket and bomb the campus to end the stalemate. Dramatization of behavior and motives of established authority is terrifyingly authentic. Compare Brunner's *The Sheep Look Up* [4-115].

4-255. Gardner, John Champlin. **Grendel.** Knopf, 1971, $5.95.
Beowulf epic told from point of view of the monster, Grendel. Set in old Denmark, Grendel's cave, and Hrothgar's meadhall, presents Grendel as a figure of tragedy, watching and commenting as man descends to the lowest levels of barbarity. Beowulf is seen not as a great liberator, but as the epitome of insensitivity and cruelty. He anachronistically assimilates many of the sterilizing machine-like characteristics that his Anglo-Saxon heirs would parley into a major civilization. Allegorical social criticism by a mainstream writer.

4-256. Garrett, Randall. **Too Many Magicians.** Doubleday, 1967.
Good mystery story, skillfully complicated with trappings of SF and "magic." Lord Darcy is master detective in well-constructed alternate history of Europe. "Magic" in form of parapsychological powers invest many of the aristocratic characters in a semi-medieval twentieth-century civilization. Darcy has no psi powers; he's merely Sherlockianly brilliant. Compare de Camp and Pratt's *The Incomplete Enchanter* [4-194]. HN, 1967.

4-257. Gary, Romain (France). **The Gasp.** Putnam, 1973, $6.95. Pocket Books, $1.25.
Marc Mathius, physicist, succeeds in capturing the "gasp" or "gsp," the incredibly powerful package of energy that functions as life force in humans, as it escapes at death. The energy is trivialized first in razors and automobiles, then in a superbomb as world powers attempt to exploit it. A science parable of black comedy and ripping satire. Excellent narrative. Compare Kosinki's *Being There* [4-353] and Swift's "A Modest Proposal."

4-258. Gawron, Jean Mark. **An Apology for Rain.** Doubleday, 1974, $4.95.
Bonnie Wolfe, one-quarter telepath, searches for brother Philip who orchestrates civil war in future America. Quasi-hallucinatory story is metaphor for meaninglessness of mankind in modern Western civilization. Recommended highly by Theodore Sturgeon.

4-259. Gentry, Curt. **The Last Days of the Late, Great State of California.** Putnam, 1968, $6.95. Ballantine, $1.95.
The San Andreas fault finally gives and California falls into the Pacific, killing millions. The United States changes without the state. Cogently, the story argues that California was being destroyed anyway by state's leaders' failure to protect its ecology. Perhaps best California destruction

story. Tedious pace but effective narrative. Appearance of careful research. Stewart's *Earth Abides* [4-558] provides same setting.

*4-260. George, Peter Bryan (U.K.). **Dr. Strangelove: Or, How I
Learned to Stop Worrying and Love the Bomb.** Bantam, 1964.
Script from film of same title that dramatizes through actions of principal participants—bomber pilots, generals, politicians, whores, et al.—
how the nuclear holocaust will begin. Mankind is selfish, stupid, sex-
crazed, essentially suicidal. Remarkable for relentless parody of the behavior of leaders of "free world." Great popularity as film and novel. Derived from author's novel, *Red Alert* (1958).

4-261. Gerrold, David. **The Man Who Folded Himself.** Random, 1973.
Faber, £1.90.
A man inherits a time-travel belt and uses it to replicate himself as male
and female (the logic of time paradox) to and through identity crises.
Clever plotting; notable emphasis upon homosexual relations. Theme:
Who is a man when he lives in his past and his future and present simul-
taneously? Compare MacDonald's *The Girl, the Gold Watch and Everything*
[4-403]. Contrast Edmonson's *The Ship That Sailed the Time Stream* [4-228].
HN, 1974; NN, 1973; JN, 1973.

4-262. Gerrold, David. **When Harlie Was One.** Doubleday, 1972. Ballantine, $1.50.
David Anderson oversees construction and growth of Harlie, a super-
computer with growing pains, threatened with shutdown because its
services don't show profit. Harlie responds with G.O.D. computer design
program, giving him grasp of all known human activity. Artificial intelligence might make man obsolete. Speculative computer science clearly displayed in good story. Compare Caidin's *The God Machine* [4-133],
Jones' *Colossus* [4-327], Heinlein's *The Moon Is a Harsh Mistress* [4-299],
and Johannesson's *Tale of the Big Computer* [4-326]. NN, 1972.

4-263. Geston, Mark. **Lords of the Starship.** Ace, 1967. Sphere, £.30.
Citizenry in a country of the far future is persuaded to enter into a gen-
erations-long program to build a starship in the yards in which their ancestors once built others. After many difficulties, they complete their
task. The mover behind this is revealed as an evil emissary of a strange
country far to the east. He turns the blast of the ship on the yards, then
blows the ship up. Since the country is now wasted by the effort, an invasion begins. Powerful and dramatic writing.

4-264. Geston, Mark. **Out of the Mouth of the Dragon.** Ace, 1969.
Sphere, £.30.
For thousands of years men have journeyed to the Meadows to fight an
unending series of purposeless wars that have sapped the strength of
many civilizations. Amon Van Roark is caught by this urge and becomes

the one to fight the final war, the one to burn out the last vitality of Earth. A tour de force with inspired weave of mythopoeic elements.

4-265. Glaskin, Gerald Marcus (Australia). **A Change of Mind.** Barrie and Rockliff, 1959.
A middle-aged accountant, Edward Henderson, hypnotically exchanges "minds" with Roger, a young, athletic mechanic. Resulting situation causes Edward to lose wife, Betty; finds sympathy in Dorothy. Roger commits suicide. Soap-operatic tale providing probing insights into the nature of individual identity. Compare Chris Stratton's *Change of Mind* (white man's brain in black man's body) and Stine's *Season of the Witch* (man's brain in woman's body) [4-560].

4-266. Godwin, Tom. **The Survivors.** Gnome, 1958 (reprinted as *Space Prison*, 1960).
Vying with mankind for ascendency in inhabited space, the alien Gerns maroon 4,000 humans on the 1.5-gravity planet Ragnarök as "rejects" from slavery. Nearly 300 years later, 1,000 of the marvelously adapted humans survive to escape the planet and begin successful conquest of Gerns. Mankind is remorselessly resourceful and will triumph against all odds. An epic ordeal reminiscent of Clement's *Mission of Gravity* [4-162] and White's *The Watch Below* [4-619].

4-267. Gold, Horace Leonard. **The Old Die Rich and Other Science Fiction Stories.** Crown, 1955.
Twelve SF and fantasy stories, including "Trouble with Water," about a man cursed by water gnome so water won't touch him; "Man of Parts," about human who joins metabolisms with mineral-eating alien; and "The Man with English," for whom brain operation reverses all senses. Also includes author's critical comments on each story. Tightly told "amusements," many with a Jewish character flavor, by the pioneering editor of *Galaxy Science Fiction*.

4-268. Golding, William G. (U.K.). **The Brass Butterfly.** Faber, 1958.
In ancient Rome, Phanocles is DaVinci-like genius who invents paddle-wheel steam warship, explosives, and pressure cooker for Emperor, who is too culturally naive to see them as much more than toys. Therefore, they don't change history. Emperor's enemies are neutralized by accident, as usual. Human history seems inexorably plodding—perhaps to mankind's benefit. Satirical play; compare Vidal's *Visit to a Small Planet* [4-604] and de Camp's *Lest Darkness Fall* [4-195].

4-269. Gordon, Rex (pseud. of Stanley Bennett Hough) (U.K.). **First on Mars.** Ace, 1957. (British title: *No Man Friday*, 1956).
Despite a silly, juvenile beginning (a spaceship is secretly built by British technicians, incompetently manned, and crash landed on Mars by an unskilled survivor), the story vastly improves with a detailed portrayal of

the castaway's creative struggle for survival. At first, practical sense and engineering know-how seem to win out, proving man's superior ability, but the castaway's technologically hewn niche is destroyed by originally conceived, truly alien Martian life. Although a self-conscious pastiche of Defoe's *Robinson Crusoe*, the book questions the basic Western assumptions of action, progress, and growth; it's the castaway who becomes a man Friday, a pet, to an offspring of the giant, worm-like, but highly evolved Martians.

4-270. Gottlieb, Hinko (Yugoslavia). **The Key to the Great Gate.** Simon & Schuster, 1947. Tr. by Fred Bolman and Ruth Morris from Serbo-Croat.
Remarkable story of Nazi tyranny written by an ex-prisoner. Tarnopolski, a Polish gentleman, confounds Nazi guards with fabulous powers based on his mastery of the space-time continuum. Damon Knight has termed it "A classic science-fantasy extravaganza, charming, pathetic, profound and wonderfully funny."

4-271. Goulart, Ron. **After Things Fell Apart.** Ace, 1970.
Zany satire set in the near future where internal chaos has fractured the United States into numerous local and specialized subcultures—the "San Francisco Enclave," "The Republic of Southern California," "The Natty Bumpo Brigade," the "Amateur Mafia," and the "G-Man Motel" (remnants of the old FBI). Through this cultural collage, detective Jim Haley romps on the trail of "Lady Day," an organization of women who are assassinating male leaders. Fast-paced fun.

4-272. Goulart, Ron. **The Sword Swallower.** Doubleday, 1968. Dell, $.60.
Light, humorous adventure story of Ben Jolsen's search for missing military men on a planet specializing in entertainment and cemeteries. Jolsen is a member of the "Chameleon Corps," a physiognomy-changing group of secret agents from the planet Barnum. He eventually uncovers a plot to create a new space empire using frozen-down military specialists. Typical of Goulart's "Chameleon Corps" stories.

*4-273. Graves, Robert (U.K.). **Watch the Northwind Rise.** Creative Age, 1949. (British title: *Seven Days in New Crete*. Portway Reprints, £1.60).
Edward Venn-Thomas, poet, travels to the future where Greek-like golden age reigns at the pleasure of the "goddess," nature. He has been brought to sow the seeds of disorder so that the beauty of order may be more richly experienced—Milton's *felix culpa*? By contrast the twentieth century, provides limitless opportunity for appreciation of divine harmony. Literary, didactic, satiric, pleasant narrative by a first-rank modern British poet.

4-274. Gray, Curme. **Murder in Millennium VI.** Shasta, 1951.
In the 5700s, murder in matriarchal society that has "forgotten" death provides mystery story to describe world of big, flat-chested women, small men, and food pills in fascinating scenario of alternate Earth. Damon Knight recommended it in spite of difficult narrative structure. Contrast Chandler's *Spartan Planet* (1969) or Russ's *The Female Man* [4-485].

4-275. Greenlee, Sam. **The Spook Who Sat by the Door.** Baron, 1969. Bantam, $.95.
"Freeman" rises, against all odds, to be second in command of the CIA. He is black; so he is a token who sits by the door in clear view to "integrate" the agency. He quits and takes his expertise to the building of guerrilla groups of black revolutionaries in all America's big cities. At novel's end a nationwide uprising is in progress. It is the best known of ten to fifteen such novels published at close of 1960s expressing fear, frustration, or hope of the civil rights forces of the time. Others are Corley's *Seige* [4-179] and Williams' *The Man Who Cried I Am* [4-624].

4-276. Guerard, Albert Joseph. **Night Journey.** Knopf, 1950.
Paul Halden, sergeant, wanted to make a contribution to winning the war against dictatorship for all the traditional freedoms. But the war has no meaning, no victories, only misery and destruction. Halden's personal experience is focus for this message. This war is a post-World War II European war, but it could be any war. Relentless rendering of psychological experience. Compare with Kit Reed's *Armed Camps* [4-474].

4-277. Gunn, James Edward. **The Burning.** Dell, 1972, $.95.
The masses revolt against science, repudiating its domination of their lives. John Wilson, scientist, is hounded from his university, fugitive, until he is aided by aliens who help evoke latent human ability to adapt to machine environment without losing identity. Mankind is now decadent in machine environment, may need help from outside agency to survive. Good social criticism, although novel's major sections are oddly uneven in writing style. Compare Miller's *Canticle for Leibowitz* [4-424].

4-278. Gunn, James Edward. **The Immortals.** Bantam, 1962.
Composed of stories from 1955 to 1960, novel depicts people practically ageless from mental set preventing physical deterioration. They are hunted by the rich who desire their blood; face world finally where they will have to live immortally. Mankind desires immortality—will do nearly anything for it. Good example of profound philosophical and psychological problem. Basis for a TV series, from which Gunn adapted a similar, but lesser, novel, *The Immortal* (1970).

4-279. Gunn, James Edward. **The Joy Makers.** Bantam, 1961.

Three loosely linked stories from 1955 depict the rise and dominance of scientific pursuit of pleasure in human society. The Hedenic order finally decays when its leaders cannot become happy themselves. "Happiness" is not mankind's proper state. It stultifies him. Slickly written social criticism. Compare Huxley's *Brave New World* [3-27].

*4-280. Gunn, James Edward. **The Listeners.** Scribner, 1972, $6.95. Signet, $1.75.
Radio telescopes finally pick up interstellar message, perhaps the computer's decipherable account of the whole history of the sending civilization. Radio astronomy has the capability to receive such a message; it would be revolutionary for.mankind's identity. Novel interpolates many classical literary allusions, as well as quotes from scientific works on extraterrestrial life and communication. Compare Hoyle and Elliot's *A for Andromeda* [4-317] and Anthony's *Macroscope* [4-30]. Campbell second prize, 1973.

4-281. Hadley, Arthur T. **The Joy Wagon.** Viking. 1958.
A computer decides to run for U.S. presidency with results that put human politicians to shame. The computer is foiled at the last moment of the campaign by a concerned woman and an eyebrow pencil. A slapstick, satirical look at politics of the 1950s.

4-282. Haldeman, Joe. **The Forever War.** St. Martin's, 1975, $6.95. Ballantine, $1.50.
Novelization of four *Analog* stories, including "Hero" (HN, 1973). In 1997 Private Mandella, holder of degree in physics, is drafted to fight an alien enemy. He is trained, fights battles, and reaches rank of Major to fight final conflict in war that lasts 1,000-plus-years (objective time; for Mandella it is about ten years of subjective time, popping in and out of "black holes"). Mandella survives. Apparently a comment on Vietnam, Haldeman's *War* is hell. Its excellence lies in its realism and narrative economy, and the reviews say Haldeman hasn't missed any pertinent detail. Contrast Heinlein's *Starship Troopers* [4-301]; compare Remarque's *All Quiet on the Western Front* (1928). [Not seen.]

4-283. Hamilton, Edmond. **The Star of Life.** Dodd, 1959.
Updated 1947 space opera about America's first Moon-orbiting astronaut, quick-frozen for 10,000 years following his spacecraft's failure, who leads an underground dedicated to giving immortality, inexplicably limited to a small elite, to all humanity. Opposing him, deep in the Trifid nebula, are the immortal "Vormen," humans altered by the life-prolonging radiation of a unique star, who secretly guard the dangerous "Third Men," their aggressive mutated descendents. Moral: man's destiny is the stars, for good or ill, the quest an end in itself. Typical Hamilton adventure.

4-284. Harness, Charles Leonard. **Flight into Yesterday.** Bouregy & Curl, 1953 (reprinted as *The Paradox Men*, 1955).

Complexly plotted, swashbuckling time travel tale which blends Einsteinian relativity and Toynbeean historical theory. In a militaristic, totalitarian, future United States, an aristocratic class profits from the labor of citizens who have sold themselves into slavery to escape dire poverty. Amnesiac superman Alar/Muir struggles to end this injustice and prevent suicidal global war. Setting is of more interest than the strained plot. Compares only in its use of historical theory with Blish's Spenglerian *Cities in Flight* [4-76] and Asimov's cyclic *Foundation Trilogy* [4-38].

4-285. Harness, Charles Leonard. **The Rose.** Berkley, 1953. Compact, 1966. Panther, £.25.

Psychiatrist–ballerina Anna Van Tuyl is haunted by dreams that begin when she gets rare, debilitating disease. Transforming dreams into ballet leads her to Ruy Jacques, a millionaire who also has the disease. But Ruy's wife, Martha, who is perfecting an invention to make science supreme over art, is jealous and tries to have Anna killed when she finds her in love with Ruy. However, love conquers as the deformation of the lovers turns out to be chrysalis stage before man's next step in evolution. Fine sentimental epic richly enhanced by cogent treatment of antagonism of the rational and the aesthetic in modern culture. Originally published in 1953. Compact edition also contains two other 1950s stories, "The Chess Players," and "The New Reality."

4-286. Harrison, Harry. **Bill, the Galactic Hero.** Doubleday, 1965. Avon, $1.95.

Bill, a naive peasant lad, is tricked into the Emperor's military forces. Stumbling through a social-Darwinist world of boot camps, meaningless interstellar war, bureaucratic and urban chaos, and other misadventures, Bill is transformed from a nice guy into one who would, and does, sell out his own brother despite their mother's pleas. Very humorous but dark satire on the military and the corrupt, brutal, and dehumanizing social order it serves. A perfect counterweight to Heinlein's *Starship Troopers* [4-301].

4-287. Harrison, Harry. **Captive Universe.** Berkley, 1969, $1.25.

Gargantuan starship ark preserves *in utero* enclaves of the best of Earth's civilizations which remain unaware of their context and of starship's caretakers. Chimal, peasant of degenerating Aztec enclave, discovers his situation and takes over to revitalize the enclaves and reteach the caretakers the meaning of their task. Mankind diminishes in cultural stasis; must constantly rejuvenate self-awareness. Compare Bass's *Godwhale* [4-59] and Aldiss's *Starship* [4-11].

4-288. Harrison, Harry. **The Daleth Effect.** Putnam, 1970.
Begins like a standard spy story, but ends with a strong condemnation of nationalism and security. An Israeli physicist develops a gravity engine—the Daleth effect—but flees to Denmark where it is developed for peaceful scientific research, trade, and space travel. Humorous scenes—a space flight in a submarine—give way to the horror of murder, blackmail, and betrayal, and finally, to heroic self-sacrifice. Good study of institutionalized paranoia. Contrast with Bahnson's *The Stars Are Too High* [4-43].

4-289. Harrison, Harry. **Deathworld.** Bantam, 1960.
First of a trilogy; Hugo nominee in 1971. This and its sequels, *Deathworld 2* (1964) and *Deathworld 3* (1968), are contained in *Deathworld Trilogy*, Berkeley, $1.95. Series follows psychic gambler Jason dinAlt as he helps tame Deathworld itself, where local psychic life has evolved into incredibly deadly forms in defense against the thoughts of hostile human colonizers. In the two less successful sequels, dinAlt survives being marooned on a planet with viciously competitive cultures and then leads the original Deathworld colonists—themselves culturally evolved into very tough customers—in the conquest of Pyrrus, a rich planet peopled by Mongol-like barbarian warriors. Much action with Darwinist philosophy.

4-290. Harrison, Harry. **Make Room! Make Room!** Doubleday, 1966. Berkley, $.95.
A scenario of overpopulation in the New York of 1999; introduction by Paul Ehrlich and a bibliography on population. Detective Rusch futilely battles in an ecological disaster area to hold together an ignorant, overcrowded, and underfed city; poverty is rampant, violence ubiquitous, the family, government, and other institutions tottering. Foresees an energy shortage, but not race war. On a par with Brunner's *The Jagged Orbit* [4-111], but not as experimental. More vivid than Blish and Knight's *A Torrent of Faces* [4-81]. Story is basis for film, *Soylent Green*. NN, 1966.

4-291. Harrison, Harry. **Planet of the Damned.** Bantam, 1962. (British title: *Sense of Obligation*. Dobson, £1.50).
Brion of the Cultural Relationships Foundation engineers the salvation of Dis, a hellish planet infected with an alien parasite that made it behave homicidally. The pacificist planet Nyjord does the mopping up. Evil is not ultimately mysterious; it has a cause that can be neutralized if the agents of good keep their heads. Adventure as a clever solution to problem in social anthropology. HN, 1962.

4-292. Harrison, Mike John (U.K.). **The Committed Men.** Doubleday, 1971.
Aging Doctor Wendover and a group of crippled people try to deliver a

baby, adaptively mutated to survive in the ecological morass created by irresponsible government and technology, to a tribe of mature mutants. Picture of desiccated, ulcerated, psychotic mankind presented with appalling effect. Unsentimental, spare, stark narrative of post-nuclear holocaust set in England. Compare Brunner's *The Sheep Look Up* [4-115].

4-293. Hawkes, Jacquetta (Hopkins) (U.K.). **Providence Island.** Random, 1959.
Archeologists discover lost race on Pacific island, survived from Magdelanian prehistoric period. Islanders live edenically; have psychic power, used finally to prevent United States from turning island into nuclear testing target. Psi ability would make technological civilization unnecessary; by comparison with island culture it's stupid. Interesting anthropological insights. Contrast E. R. Burroughs' Pellucidar stories [2-30].

4-294. Heard, Henry Fitzgerald (as Gerald Heard) (U.K.). **Dopplegangers.** Vanguard, 1947.
Complex, dense novel loaded with relatively sophisticated philosophic and social speculation. Plot involves the attempt by the "Mole," an under-ground revolutionary genius, to physically modify a nameless pawn to resemble "Alpha," benevolent dictator of a hedonistic utopia based on Sheldon's somatotypes. The double not only supplants Alpha, but in effect becomes him. Humanity has finished its revolutionary period, from the religious, to political, to economic, and, finally, to the psychological/anthropological era; a third force, the "Elevated," a group based on Hinduism and other philosophies, intervenes to destroy the Mole, one of their fallen colleagues, and help point Alpha II and humanity again up the road of social evolution. Rewarding study of power despite its turgid prose. Contrast Huxley's *Brave New World* [3-27] and Heinlein's *Double Star* [4-296].

4-295. Heinlein, Robert Anson. **The Door into Summer.** Doubleday, 1957. Signet, $1.25.
Dan Davis, an electronics engineer, invents an all-purpose robot and is shanghaied into suspended animation for thirty years by his business partner and his financée. He returns by way of a time machine, rescues his cat, starts a rival company, proposes (future) marriage to a twelve-year old, and returns to the future to reap his reward. Good adventure in an unusually mellow mood for Heinlein.

*4-296. Heinlein, Robert Anson. **Double Star.** Doubleday, 1956. Signet, $1.75.
An actor is coerced into impersonating a kidnapped politician. The politician is recovered but soon dies. His staff persuades the actor to continue the act and carry out the ambitions of the politician. An approving but informative view of the morality of politics. Not major Heinlein. Contrast Heard's *Dopplegangers* [4-294]. HW, 1956.

4-297. Heinlein, Robert Anson. **Glory Road.** Putnam, 1963. Berkley, $1.25.

Oscar Gordon is chosen by Ishtar, Queen of seven universes, to rescue "phoenix egg," key to computer complex of her government. He succeeds after picaresque adventures that prove his courage. Parody of familiar Heinlein militaristic heroism. Adventure clichés are vitalized by comic treatment in this sword and sorcery effort, but not superior Heinlein. Compare Vance's *The Dying Earth* [4-597]. HN, 1964.

4-298. Heinlein, Robert Anson. **Have Space Suit—Will Travel.** Scribner, 1958. Ace, $1.25.

Kip Russell, high-schooler, wants to go to the Moon. Instead, he wins a second-hand space suit in a contest and with the help of extraterrestrials travels the galaxy, returning (still not having visited the Moon) eager to get a good education and more patient about the Moon visit. Cogent critique of public education curriculum. Well-paced juvenile adventure story inspirational to teen readers about how to get a good education. HN, 1959.

*4-299. Heinlein, Robert Anson. **The Moon Is a Harsh Mistress.** Putnam, 1966, $6.95. Berkley, $1.50.

Leaders of the Moon colony declare independence from Earth, making it stick with aid of sentient computer "Mike." The parallels with American revolution are obvious and seem intended. Stock Heinlein characters; fast adventure narrative. Neospace opera. Contrast Asimov's *The Goods Themselves* [4-397]. HN, 1966; HW, 1967; NN, 1966.

*4-300 Heinlein, Robert Anson. **The Past through Tomorrow.** Putnam, 1967, $9.95. Berkley, $1.95.

A treasure trove of Heinlein's short fiction, spanning his writing career from 1939 to 1957 and including some of his best and most popular efforts. Contains most of Heinlein's "Future History" stories, plus a revised chronology; perhaps most notable are "The Roads Must Roll" (SFHF), about life on the solar-powered conveyor-belt highways of the future, and "The Man Who Sold the Moon," in which businessman and space travel enthusiast D. D. Harriman makes the first Moon flight a reality. Also included are such well-known works as "Blowups Happen," "Coventry," "The Green Hills of Earth," "Life-Line," "Logic of Empire," "Methuselah's Children," "Requiem," and "—We Also Walk Dogs." The one notable omission is "Universe" (SFHF; in *Orphans of the Sky*, 1964). The first serious attempt in SF to project a detailed, consistently feasible future for mankind; hard SF, as in Niven's Known Space series [4-442], but equally concerned with social and political matters, as in the more space-operatic stories of Asimov's Foundation [4-38] and Blish's "Cities in Flight" [4-76] future histories. Scenario begins with the contemporary "Crazy Years," passes through a "period of imperial exploitation" around the year 2000, and continues into the twenty-second century and "the first human civilization." A basic item in any SF library. This ominbus collection was originally published by Shasta as four separate books: *The Green Hills of Earth* (1951); *The Man Who Sold the Moon* (1950); *Revolt in 2100* (1954); and *Methuselah's Children* (1958) each available separately from Signet, $1.25.

*4-301. Heinlein, Robert Anson. **Starship Troopers.** Putnam, 1959, $6.50. Berkley, $1.25.

Heinlein was an Annapolis cadet. *Troopers* is story of space cadet academy and after, as negotiated by single individual. Novel largely responsible for view of Heinlein as "fascist" and war-approving. Heinlein was "hawk" for Vietnam war. Vintage Heinlein storytelling. Compare Panshin's *Rite of Passage* [4-454] and E. E. Smith's Lensman series [4-548] Contrast Harrison's *Bill, the Galactic Hero* [4-286]. HW, 1960.

*4-302. Heinlein, Robert Anson. **Stranger in a Strange Land.** Putnam, 1961, $6.95. Berkley, $1.95.

Valentine Michael Smith, born of human parents and raised by Martians, returns to Earth as a young man, rich and a virtual superman because of the parapsychological powers Martian education produced in him. Jubal Harshaw befriends Michael and his fortune until Michael can acculturate himself. Mike becomes wise, but keeps his virtue—becoming a Christ-figure who finally "discorporates." Harshaw is familiar Heinlein central character in a radicalized mood, favoring free love, ritual cannibalism, and other familiar Heinlein social propositions. First half of novel is best; breaks in middle, and so is flawed for many readers. Read well beyond SF fandom; used in college composition courses; directly associated with Charles Manson, murder cult leader of the Sharon Tate massacre. Best known of Heinlein's SF. HW, 1962.

4-303. Heinlein, Robert Anson. **Time Enough for Love.** Putnam, 1973, $7.95. Berkley, $1.95.

Further adventures in 2,000-year life of Lazarus Long, a major character in Heinlein's Future History series (see *The Past through Tomorrow* [4-300]). His descendents unite and scheme to keep the bored and suicidally inclined man from killing himself. Adventures include cloning twin girls from Lazarus's genes, transference of a computer's personality to a female body, and a time trip to Earth's past where Lazarus meets and seduces his mother. Many flashback sequences of episodes in Long's previous lives. A memoir. All men want to be gods. Men who live too long become decadent (perhaps not Heinlein's intended theme). Maudlin, soap operatic, unoriginal, but witty. Compare Heinlein's *Stranger in a Strange Land* [4-302]. HN, 1974; NN, 1973.

4-304. Henderson, Zenna. **Pilgrimage: The Book of the People.** Doubleday, 1961. Avon, $.95.

Linking narrative added to earlier short stories. A preternaturally good "human" species arrives on Earth in small groups of survivors after their sun goes nova. They have psi talents that are always used for wholesome purposes. Meetings with Earth humans are basic to most of the stories, producing scenarios that probe gently but deeply the inadequacies of mankind. Chief characters are school teachers and children. Has Simak's sentimentality and Wellman's eye for backwoods culture. Contrast Wyndham's *The Midwich Cuckoos* [4-639]. Sequel is *The People: No Different Flesh* (Doubleday, 1967. Avon, $1.25), which contains "Captivity" (HN, 1959).

4-305. Herbert, Frank. **Destination: Void.** Berkley, 1966, $.95.
The crew of a starship discover that their organic computer isn't working. It must be repaired to save their ship. After many trials they solve their problems only to discover their computer has the powers of a god and desires to be treated as such. Good psychological novel. Compare Caidin's *The God Machine* [4-133] and Jones' *Colossus* [4-327].

4-306. Herbert, Frank. **The Dragon in the Sea.** Doubleday, 1956. (Variant titles: *21st Century Sub* [1956] and *Under Pressure* [1974]). Ballantine (as latest title), $1.50.
In twenty-first-century war with Eastern Hemisphere, U.S. subs are lost trying to steal from enemy's underwater deposits. John Ramsey, psychologist/electronics crewman, discovers cause of the loss of the subs by learning meaning of "sanity" to mankind, especially in closed, pressurized world of submarine. Sanity is different adaptations in different environments. Fine adventure narrative and good speculative psychology. Compare White's *The Watch Below* [4-619].

*4-307. Herbert, Frank. **Dune.** Chilton, 1965, $5.95. Ace, $2.25; Berkley, $1.95.
"Dune" is a planet whose total environment and adapted culture is depicted with relentless logic—an almost waterless desert with a quasi-Islamic civilization, guided by a "messiah," Paul Atrides, to prepare for a time when water will come and give their children's children a fertile world. A science fiction world to compare with the fantasy world of Tolkien's Middle Earth. One of most celebrated works of modern SF. Incorporates "Dune World," HW, 1964. In complete form: NW, 1965; HW, 1966. Sequel is *Dune Messiah* (Putnam, 1969; Berkley, $1.50).

4-308. Herbert, Frank. **The Eyes of Heisenberg.** Berkley, 1966, $.95.
Lizbeth and Harvey Durant follow their child from genetically sculpted conception to advanced pregnancy in society where genetically superior but sterile "Optimen" keep a dubious immortality as their privilege. Meanwhile, the "Heisenberg principle" intrudes to show both "Optimen" and inferior "Folk" that death can make a long life exciting. Provoking analysis of ramifications of gene manipulation and the life experi-

ence. Compare Huxley's *Brave New World* [3-27] and Shaw's *Back to Methuselah* [2-137]. NN, 1966.

4-309. Herbert, Frank. **Hellstrom's Hive.** Doubleday, 1973. Bantam, $1.50.
Dr. Hellstrom's project involves mutant humans who adopt insect hive behavior as the next evolutionary step for mankind. It is threatened by U.S. intelligence investigation but gains the time needed to mature. Mind-wrenching theme sympathetically postulates obsolescence of present family structure because, without a radical adaptation, it will destroy itself in a fit of paranoiac psychosis. Premise: Hive psychology is a more powerful force than individualism. Contrast Bass's *The Godwhale* [4-59].

4-310. Hersey, John Richard. **My Petition for More Space.** Knopf, 1974, $5.95.
Sam Poynter resides in a seven-by-eleven-foot space in a world of teeming population—and wants more: eight by twelve. He petitions and is denied. Powerful evocation of the tyranny, with attendant psychological aberrations, to be imposed by a "shrinking" planetary environment. Psychological time, too, will shrink. Poynter is reminiscent of Winston in Orwell's *1984* [4-450].

4-311. Hersey, John Richard. **White Lotus.** Knopf, 1965. Bantam, $1.50.
The Chinese conquer the United States. A fifteen-year-old Arizona girl is taken with the others of her town to live as a slave, renamed "White Lotus," in China. A first-person narrative of the uprooting, slavery, and second-class citizenship of a mid-twentieth-century American. A sustained parable/allegory realistically rendered. Parallels Afro-American history. "What if someday we are the masters and they are the underdogs?" Hersey's China boyhood is a rich resource here. Compare Dick's *The Man in the High Castle* [4-211].

4-312. Herzog, Arthur. **The Swarm.** Simon & Schuster, 1974. Signet, $1.95.
Postulates that aggressive and vicious African honey bee, which has in fact created many problems in South America, mutates to even more deadly variety and eventually threatens United States, with novel's climax an attack on beleaguered New York City. Citation of legitimate scientific accounts adds to novel's verisimilitude. Well-plotted; will appeal as Crichton's *Andromeda Strain* [4-184] or the science film *The Hellstrom Chronicle*.

*4-313. Hesse, Hermann (Germany). **The Glass Bead Game (Magister Ludi).** Holt, 1969, $3.00, $7.95. Bantam, $1.75. Tr. by Richard and Clara Winston of *Das glasperlenspiel*, 1943.

In twenty-fifth-century Castalia, Joseph Knecht works his way to becoming Magister Ludi, a grandmaster of "games," in a utopia devoted to mental and aesthetic ideals. The intellectually elitist pursuit is symbolized by the fantastically intricate and disciplined "Glass Bead Game." Knecht rejects the Castalian ideal for one that is socially conscious as well. Individual perfection is meaningless until it finally transcends the one and aggrandizes the lives of the many. The book's excellence is consummate—hailed by Thomas Mann and admired by T. S. Eliot and Andre Gide, it is the principal work for which Hesse received the Nobel Prize in 1946. Compare Mann's *Doctor Faustus* and Brunner's *The Whole Man* [4-119]. Rand's *Atlas Shrugged* [4-472] represents the antithesis of this philosophy.

4-314. Hingley, Ronald (U.K.). **Up Jenkins!** Longmans, 1956.
Civil war splits Britain into a free north and totalitarian south. Peter Gosling in the south is saved by Helen Browning, whose husband has infiltrated the southern regime and leads escapees to the north through the mine tunnels of a "concentration camp." Good satire.

4-315. Hjortsberg, William. **Gray Matters.** Simon & Schuster, 1971, $4.95. Pocket Books, $1.25.
The minds of mankind await rebirth in perfect synthetic bodies on a utopian, nontechnological Earth; brains are cared for and given instruction toward enlightenment in mechanical wombs within the limbo of a vast underground cybernetic labyrinth. But some resist spiritual progress, locked into their sense of personal identity: a depraved film star who is "misplaced" in a sexual fantasy realm; a boy troubled by nightmares of his brain being eaten in elaborate rituals; and a rebellious black sculptor who rescues his brain and flees to the Eden-like surface, only to kill and be killed. But he leaves his seed, the first human-born child in centuries. A strange and at times disturbing story. Winner of the Playboy Fiction Award.

4-316. Howard, Hayden. **The Eskimo Invasion.** Ballantine, 1967.
Pseudo-Eskimos begin unchecked proliferation due to innate drive to mate, total fertility, a one-month gestation period, and highly accelerated maturation. Dr. West seeks to warn the world of impending disaster only to be himself victimized by ideological, religious, and political forces supporting the expansion of the beautiful but totally passive "Esks." Excellent treatment of population dynamics, Eskimo culture, and the meaning of humanness, especially in the novel's first half. Unique despite its theme of overpopulation. NN, 1967.

4-317. Hoyle, Fred (U.K.). **The Black Cloud.** Harper, 1957. Signet, $.95.
A cloud of interstellar matter throws solar system into chaos and begins

destruction of earthly life. But cloud is intelligent, honors life, and re-treats after communication is established. So plausible and astronomi-cally accurate that astronomy classes assign it as supplementary reading. Contrast Thomas and Wilhelm's *Year of the Cloud* (1970). Hoyle's fascina-tion with communication with extraterrestrial intelligence, exhibited here, is further explored in *A for Andromeda* (Harper, 1962; Avon, $1.25), written with John Elliott. This is a classic tale of decoding mes-sage from space. The message gives plans for creating a humanoid, clev-er device for invasion by aliens, with humanoid programmed to multiply its numbers. Sequel: *Andromeda Breakthrough* (Harper, 1964). Compare Gunn's *The Listeners* [4-280].

4-318. Hoyle, Fred, and Geoffrey Hoyle (U.K.). **The Inferno.** Harper, 1973, $5.95.
Earth is threatened by the explosion of the galaxy's core; Scottish as-tronomer returns to Highlands to survive the coming storms and rebuild society along old clan lines. Emphasis on strong group leaders and social Darwinism. Further, Earth is actually saved by an "invisible hand." Bet-ter written than Hoyles' earlier works. Compare Niven's "At the Core" [4-440] and Cowper's *The Twilight of Briareus* [4-182].

4-319. Hoyle, Fred (U.K.). **October the First Is Too Late.** Harper, 1966, $6.95.
In 1966, a higher intelligence scrambles time on Earth, leaving England in the present, Europe in World War I, America in the future, Greece in its Golden Age, Mexico in the far future, and Russia at the end of time. Human culture from different ages dramatically comments on itself. Time-locked civilization is stultifying: "October the first" is often *too early.*

4-320. Hoyle, Fred (U.K.). **Ossian's Ride.** Harper, 1959. Heinemann, £2.00.
A young Oxford graduate is drafted by British intelligence to penetrate and investigate I.C.E. (Industrial Corporation of Eire)—a huge megacor-poration that has made enormous advances in science in a cordoned-off area in southwest Ireland. He discovers that beneficent aliens reborn as humans are behind the scientific explosion. Very similar in outlook to *A for Andromeda* and *Andromeda Breakthrough* [4-317] and Gunn's *The Listen-ers* [4-280].

4-321. Hubbard, Lafayette Ron. **Final Blackout.** Hadley, 1948. Gar-land, $11.00.
In a world made decrepit by many wars, "the Lieutenant" brilliantly engi-neers the resurrection of England, effectively neutralizing tech-nologically superior, politically decadent America's attempt to colonize it. Military discipline can yield crucial human freedom. Persuasive. Fine

evocation of loneliness of genius in a wasted civilization. Hubbard's best SF; controversial when first published in 1940.

4-322. Huxley, Aldous Leonard (U.K.). **After Many a Summer Dies the Swan.** Harper, 1939. Harcourt, $1.25. (British title: *After Many a Summer*, 1939).
American oil baron and entrepreneur searches for longevity or immortality through research of personal physician. They find it through consumption of fish entrails, demonstrated in form of 200-year-old British aristocrat who, with mistress, has "evolved" into ape. As a dog is underdeveloped wolf, man may be underdeveloped ape. Nature and god are "good"; civilization is "evil." Erudite, comic; full of incisive social criticism. Enthralling narrative. James Tait Black Memorial Award, 1939.

4-323. Huxley, Aldous Leonard (U.K.). **Ape and Essence.** Harper, 1948. Harcourt, $1.25.
In 1947, William Tallis writes rejected screenplay of California in 2018 visited by New Zealand Rediscovery Expedition after nuclear holocaust. Situation is neo-medieval, church directed. Message is scalpel-like satirical account of twentieth-century man's failure to understand his nature. Lesser writers would not handle this scenario and theme intelligently until the 1960s.

4-324. Huxley, Aldous Leonard (U.K.). **Island.** Harper, 1962, $7.95, $1.50.
Farnaby, spiritually crippled journalist, shipwrecks on Pala, 100-year-old experimental island utopia, idyllic, communal, insulated. Inhabitants are psychically whole in transcendental philosophy of love. War and neurosis unknown. Farnaby's guilt-ridden mentality contrasts with serene yogic spirit of Pala. End comes when neighboring dictator takes over Pala for its oil. Capitalism is antithesis of love; Buddha was right. Contrast Skinner's *Walden Two* [4-542].

4-325. Jensen, Axel (Norway). **Epp.** Chatto & Windus, 1967. Tr. by Oliver Stallybrass of *Epp*, 1965.
Epp is a pensioner (retiree) in socialistic, utopian state. Story is his journal of maundering details of useless, reclusive life in one-room apartment where he has spent twenty-five years. Utopia may fail the old as present-day government fails them. Powerful evocation of mood of loneliness in stark dramatic narrative. Compare Hersey's *My Petition for More Space* [4-310] and Silverberg's *The World Inside* [4-532].

4-326. Johannesson, Olof (pseud. of Hannes Alfven) (Sweden). **The Tale of the Big Computer.** Coward, 1968. Tr. by Naomi Walford of *Sagan om den stora datamaskinin*, 1966. (British title: *The Great Computer, a Vision*, Gollancz, 1968, £1.05).
History of intelligence on Earth written in future by a man?/a computer?

illustrating the conclusion that the period after Earth's formation was an effort to "engender computers directly," and failing that to engender them ultimately. Mankind is merely an intermediate step. Ingenious. Enormously instructive of role and nature of computers, but a little dry. The author shared the 1970 Nobel Prize for physics.

4-327. Jones, Dennis Feltham (U.K.). **Colossus.** Putnam, 1967.
Dr. Forbin heads project to build super-computer "Colossus" to guarantee defense of free world. Likewise, Russia builds "Guardian." The two computers collaborate and take over world in benevolent dictatorship. Sequel: *The Fall of Colossus* (Putnam, 1974, $5.95; Berkley, $.95). Computers will be built that can think. This story caught public fancy, and film version was popular. Compare Caidin's more logical *The God Machine* [4-133] and Gerrold's *When Harlie Was One* [4-262]. Contrast Heinlein's *The Moon Is a Harsh Mistress* [4-299].

4-328. Jones, Raymond F. **This Island Earth.** Shasta, 1952.
Cal Meacham discovers that an intergalactic civilization, at war with another, evil, intergalactic civilization, is using Earth as manufacturing base for important weapons. He joins them in time to turn tide and save Earth by ignoring their computers and doing the unexpected. Good suspense; grandiose scope of E. E. Smith's Lensman space operas [4-548]. Basis for fair SF film.

4-329. Jones, Raymond F. **The Toymaker.** Fantasy Pub. Co., Inc., 1951.
Six stories, including title story about warlike diplomacy contrasted with subtler diplomacy of the "Toymaker," and "Forecast," about the problems encountered after we can control the weather. Generally, fine SF that leaves space opera behind.

4-330. Joseph, Michael Kennedy (U.K.). **The Hole in the Zero.** Dutton, 1968.
Beyond the universe is "chaos," where everything is possible for four adventurous explorers who create multiple worlds out of their subjective consciousness. Paradine apparently "returns" to create Earth, and becomes a new Adam to Helen's new Eve. Or have they time-travelled to the beginning of the original Earth? No time/no space is made an effective metaphor for the meaning of human relationships. A successful hybrid of SF and fantasy. Compare Dick's *Eye in the Sky* [4-209].

4-331. Kantor, Mackinley. **If the South Had Won the Civil War.** Bantam, 1961, $.60.
The South wins and the United States is divided into the Confederacy, the Union, and Texas. Not until 1960 do proceedings for reunification begin. Kantor's *Andersonville* and *Stillness at Appomatox* are popular Civil War history. This novel ingeniously incorporates major figures from actual history, preserving their personalities, to make this a delightful diversion for Civil War buffs.

4-332. Karp, David. **One.** Vanguard, 1953. Grosset & Dunlap, $1.95.
Burden is an English professor in totalitarian state who is devastatingly brainwashed by the genius inquisitor Lark and given new identity as "Hughes." Though the superficial identity switch is successful, Hughes retains his "heretical" and basic desire to assert individuality. The few people who successfully resist complete brainwashing will defeat all totalitarianisms. Excellent primer on techniques of brainwashing. A Book of the Month Club choice. Compare Orwell's *1984* [4-450] and Burgess's *A Clockwork Orange* [4-129]; contrast Huxley's *Brave New World* [3-27].

4-333. Kavan, Anna (pseud. of Helen Woods Edmonds) (U.K.). **Ice.**
Doubleday, 1970. Popular Lib., $.95.
A Lilith-like young woman is pursued by a somewhat obsessed young man in the near future of Earth when nuclear testing has produced the onset of another ice age. The doom of the planet's civilization is perfectly assimilated in the personal doom of the heroine. She is freezing to death existentially as well as physically. Compare Ballard's *Crystal World* [4-46], wherein external forces, symbolically the result of mankind's moral incompetence, combine to trap and destroy the most sensitive individuals.

*4-334. Kelley, William Melvin. **A Different Drummer.** Doubleday, 1959. Anchor, $1.95.
Tucker Caliban and his ancestors are heroes of story set in mythical state in the deep South. Beginning with the life of an African slave in the United States, it ends with all of the black population leaving that state in 1957, making it the only state without one black person in residence. Told as a fine literary parable, the story comes so close to reality as to fill all the requirements of the SF of social criticism in the form of the "warning story." This might be ranked among the dozen finest American short novels of the 1950s. Compare Bradbury's "Way in the Middle of the Air" in *The Martian Chronicles* [4-102].

4-335. Keppel-Jones, Arthur (South Africa). **When Smuts Goes.** Capetown, 1947.
A political and economic history of South Africa from 1952 to 2010, as published in 2015. It explains the reduction of the nation to near barbarism because of racism and the economic caste system. An awful-warning story. Successful affectation of synoptic history. Compare Allighan's *Verwoerd—The End* [4-13] and Brunner's *The Jagged Orbit* [4-111].

*4-336. Keyes, Daniel. **Flowers for Algernon.** Harcourt, 1966, $7.95. Bantam, $1.25.
Exquisite story of mentally retarded Charlie Gordon, who becomes a genius as the result of an intelligence-enhancing drug. Through his diary containing periodic "progress reports," we follow Charlie's emergence into the "normal" adult world and then beyond as his mind blazes; but the flame is short-lived, and shrinks back into darkness and ashes. A sen-

sitive and poignant exploration of the meaning of humanity and intelligence that grips the reader through its characters' full dimensionality and their inevitable tragic destinies. One of SF's truly fine works. Also excellent as the film, *Charly*. Compare Anderson's *Brain Wave* [4-16] and Sturgeon's "Maturity" in *Without Sorcery* [4-571] Hugo short fiction winner, 1960; HN, 1967; NW, 1966.

4-337. King, Vincent. **Another End.** Ballantine, 1971.
Adamson, kept alive by his sentient Probe ship, endlessly searches the galaxy for alien intelligence, the great dream of the now-extinct human race. Instead, he finds mad Thread, the embodiment of mankind's worst characteristics, who is populating space with his clones. But Adamson, with the aid of Protea, an energy creature, defeats Thread and leaves the galaxy to found a new race. Meanwhile, the voyeuristic creators of the universe start the whole thing over again to see what will happen this time. . . . Part space opera, part lightweight parable, part satire.

4-338. Kirst, Hans Hellmut (Germany). **The Seventh Day.** Doubleday, 1959. Tr. by Richard Graves of *Keiner kommt davon*, 1957.
Long narrative of rigorous verisimilitude of the tragic diplomatic vicissitudes of nuclear nations for six days, culminating in the detonation of over 1,000 nuclear bombs with nearly a hundred million dead. At novel's end the seventh day has not dawned. It will be anniversary of the doom of mankind. Russia and the United States are the instigators. Excellent awful-warning tale. Symbolism of the undoing of the seven days' work of Genesis is intended. Kirst is best known in United States for non-SF *Night of the Generals*. Compare Wylie's *Triumph* [4-636] and Shute's *On the Beach* [4-520].

4-339. Klein, Gerald (France). **Starmaster's Gambit.** DAW, 1973, $.95. Tr. by C. J. Richards of *Le gambit des étoiles*, 1958.
Jerg Algan uses a symbolic game of chess to pursue space-operatic adventures in a search for the secret of what makes the universe run. He discovers the source of sentience in the stars, the suns of solar systems, whose plans for mankind are benevolent and transcendent. A well-paced narrative with a vaulting theme, reminiscent of Clarke's *Childhood's End* [4-149]. Prix Jules Verne winner, 1958.

4-340. Kneale, Nigel (U.K.) **The Quatermass Experiment.** Penguin, 1960.
A six-part play produced for the BBC in 1953. Professor Quatermass heads manned space shot that returns with crew in last stages of being absorbed by a plant-thing from outer space. Earth is threatened; catastrophe barely averted. Space program scientists should be more careful. Effective melodrama and social satire for its time. Sequels: *Quatermass II* and *Quatermass and the Pit* (both 1960).

4-341. Knebel, Fletcher. **Night of Camp David.** Harper, 1965. Bantam, $1.50.
The President of the United States, Mark Hollenbach, goes crazy and pushes the world to the brink of catastrophe. The day is saved when the President is brought to resign. Good speculative suspense that cogently anticipates Watergate and the resignation of Richard Nixon. Representative of emerging allied genre, speculative literature about the increasingly "imperial" U.S. presidency. Other representatives include Wallace's *The Man* (1964), Johnson's *The Presidential Plot* (1969), and Serling's *The President's Plane Is Missing* (1967).

4-342. Knight, Damon Francis. **Far Out.** Simon & Schuster, 1961.
Thirteen stories from 1949 to 1960, introduced by Anthony Boucher, that catch the wit and urbanity of this SF writer's writer. "To Serve Man," a gruesome little comment on human gullibility, involves the appearance of apparently altruistic aliens who secretly want to use man as food; in "Not with a Bang" humanity is doomed to extinction due to its prudishness when the last man on Earth has a fatal attack in the men's room while the last woman waits outside; the real value of communication is illustrated in "Babel II" when a visiting alien scrambles human speech and writing; in "Special Delivery," a woman suffers the arrogance of a super-intelligent fetus who mentally communicates with her until its precociousness thankfully is destroyed by birth; "You're Another" tells of a young man dogged by a lucky piece that only brings bad luck until he discovers he is being used as comic relief in a play for a future society's entertainment and switches to the role of hero.

4-343. Knight, Damon Francis. **Hell's Pavement.** Lion, 1955. Fawcett, $.75. (Variant title: *Analogue Men*, 1962).
Knight's first novel presents the old "big brother" mind control scenario with exemplary vigor, character and event enriched in detail. In a future society, men are controlled by "analogues," individually induced psychological hang-ups. Hope for freedom rests with the "immunes," an underground population of people who cannot be "psyched." Story's end promises freedom, but not without near-catastrophic social upheaval. Effective adventure and suspense; sensible social criticism—especially of a consumer society. Compare Orwell's *1984* [4-450] and Vonnegut's *Player Piano* [4-606].

4-344. Knight, Damon Francis. **In Deep.** Berkley, 1963. Manor Books, $.75.
Eight stories from 1951 to 1960, including "The Country of the Kind" (SFHF), about a killer excommunicated by his society and his pathetic rebellion and loneliness. Also has "The Handler," an unusual piece in which an ugly dwarf is rejected while the large humanoid shell he inhabits and directs is a social success, and "Stranger Station," about a

battle of love and hate between a human and an alien aboard an isolated space station where the alien periodically appears to give the man a longevity chemical.

4-345. Knight, Damon Francis. **Turning On.** Doubleday, 1966. Sphere, £.25.
Fourteen stories from 1951 to 1965 by the first major critic of SF. Includes "Mary," about Mary and Klef, dwellers in a floating city, artificially organized for survival of forgotten holocaust; breaking custom, they enter monogamous love and depart for the land, which is losing its radioactive poison. Also includes "The Man in the Jar," "The Night of Lies," and "The Big Pat Boom," a satirical comment on the tourist industry. An uneven collection.

4-346. Koestler, Arthur (U.K.). **The Age of Longing.** Macmillan, 1951. Hutchinson, £2.00.
Hydie loves Colonel Nitkin, agent for totalitarian forces that will try to enslave Western nations. The background of characters and events characterizes the cold war in France in the middle fifties. Story's end finds the chief characters waiting for the "comet" of destruction. Drama of the helplessness of those in a civilization that impersonally moves toward its destruction. Compare Kirst's *The Seventh Day* [4-338].

4-347. Koontz, Dean R. **Beastchild.** Lancer, 1970.
In process of exterminating mankind as unfit for membership in galactic society, a reptilian (?) soldier befriends a male Earthling child, perhaps in time to learn enough to give humanity a second chance. Xenophobia is ubiquitous, even among sophisticated members of galactic society. Sensitive characterization of alien and human child relationship. Compare Dickson's *The Alien Way* [4-216].

*4-348. Kornbluth, Cyril M. **Best Science Fiction Stories of C. M. Kornbluth.** Faber, 1968.
Twelve stories and one poem ("The Unfortunate") introduced by Edmund Crispin; contains most of the best short fiction of Kornbluth, one of the 1950s' major figures in SF. In the classic "The Marching Morons" (SFHF), a small population of mechanics/engineers/governors maintains Earth as a playpen for the majority of mankind whose intelligence has depreciated to about an IQ of 80. For example, they create inane TV programs, cars that are gaudy and sound powerful, but are in fact slow, to satisfy the ever more stupid masses. Excellent as reductio social critique of the mindless consumerism characteristic of mid-twentieth century Americans, but terrible as genetics, perhaps even dangerous in its perpetuation of the myth that the "stupid" lower classes, through overbreeding, are decreasing the general intelligence. The equally well known "The Little Black Bag" also assumes that "mental subnormals

were outbreeding mental normals and supernormals, and that the process was occurring on an exponential curve," but focuses on the discovery by a drunken, discredited doctor of an automated medical treatment machine from the future. With it, he becomes successful, but falls under the evil influence of a greedy woman who steals the machine and kills him—leading to the device's deactivation and her death by it. The "Theory of Rocketry" (HN, 1959), presents a characterization of the dehumanized, "eager beaver" male high school student whose goal is acceptance into the Air Force Academy. Also contains the well-known stories "The Mindworm," "Gomez," "The Silly Season," and "With These Hands."

4-349. Kornbluth, Cyril M. **A Mile beyond the Moon.** Doubleday, 1958. Manor Books, $.75.
Fifteen stories, from 1941 to 1958, that span Kornbluth's all-too-short career. Better efforts include: "Shark Ship" ("Reap the Dark Tide," HN, 1959), about life aboard the ships of a nomadic seafaring culture that had fled the overpopulated land but now must return to it; "Two Dooms," a defense for the building of the A-bomb, in which a Manhattan Project scientist stumbles onto a key to a successful bomb but considers withholding it until he "travels" in a drug-induced dream into a future where the United States lost World War II; and "The Adventurer," that has the U.S. cabinet secretly creating a charismatic leader by exposing a child to a harsh life in order to overthrow a tyrannical hereditary presidency—only to find they have created a worse dictator. Also includes "The Little Black Bag" (SFHF) (see *Best Science Fiction Stories of C. M. Kornbluth* [4-348]).

4-350. Kornbluth, Cyril M. **Not This August.** Doubleday, 1955.
The United States has been defeated and occupied by Red China and Russia, and the people in rural upstate New York wither under an oppressive yoke aimed at their extinction and the introduction of Russian colonists. But wait! Billy Justin discovers a vast cavern where a nearly completed launch vehicle and orbiter, armed with hydrogen and cobalt bombs, are hidden. The U.S. underground rises, as does the space station, and defeat becomes victory. A chauvinistic cold-war story warning of inevitable communist aggression; yet Billy gets religion in the end and rejects a military career. Contrast with Frank's *Alas, Babylon* [4-249] and Dick's *The Man in the High Castle* [4-211]. Received major critical attention in the mainstream when it first appeared.

4-351. Kornbluth, Cyril M. **The Syndic.** Doubleday, 1953. Avon, $1.95.
Charles Orsino and Lee Falcaro of culturally hospitable "Syndic" infiltrate the "Mob" nation to investigate the meaning of the Mob's growing use of diplomacy by assassination. After harrowing adventures, they return to report onset of cultural psychosis and recommend therapy and

standing armies to protect Syndic. But Frank Taylor, Syndic's leader, hedges, preferring brief prolongation of Syndic's good life against immediate paranoiac readying for war. Human culture in history enjoys only brief moments of splendor, then plunges again into long periods of savagery; *carpe diem*. Effective adventure in somberly persuasive theory of history. Compare Stewart's *Earth Abides* [4-558].

4-352. Kornbluth, Cyril M. **Takeoff.** Doubleday, 1952.
Under cover of a California amateur rocket club's building of a mock spaceship, the head of the AEC and crippled aircraft magnate (patterned after Howard Hughes?) conspire, out of fear of bureaucratic ineptness and espionage, to build the first Moon rocket. Patriotic scientist Mick Novak, who uncovers the plot but thinks it is a foreign effort, almost spoils things. Still, he and the millionaire's daughter blast off to the Moon. Novel looks ridiculous in the hindsight of NASA, but its anti-big government and cold-war mentality are still alive in many quarters. Well written; compare with Clarke's *Prelude to Space* [4-155]. IFA nominee, 1953.

4-353. Kosinski, Jerzy. **Being There.** Harcourt, 1971, $5.95. Bantam, $1.50.
"Chance" is the anonymous "Chauncey Gardiner," who grew from orphaned childhood as rich man's gardener, watching television, and wearing cast-offs of rich man. Lacks birth certificate, tax return, and other symbols of modern identity. Rich man dies and Chance enters world, fortuitously invited to house of the Rands, people close to U.S. political power. Gratuitously mistaken as wealthy, he meets President, who quotes him in subsequent speech. Russian ambassador quotes him. He is a guest on political talk show, answers all questions in terms of gardener's experience. Political and business elite love him. They will run him for Vice-President. Narrative simple as Chance. An allegory of Western man's cultural predicament. No one has real identity. Thus, Chance is celebrated, urged to lead an aimlessly anonymous people. Rich irony and satire. Kosinski became known with *The Painted Bird* (non-SF). Contrast Heinlein's *Stranger in a Strange Land* [4-302].

4-354. Kuttner, Henry. **The Best of Henry Kuttner.** Ballantine, 1975, $1.95.
Seventeen SF and fantasy stories, from 1939 to 1955, and a flattering introduction by Ray Bradbury, "Henry Kuttner: A Neglected Master," that points out Kuttner's significant influence on the genre. Catches his best short fiction, including: "Mimsy Were the Borogoves" (SFHF), in which two children are taught advanced knowledge by toys accidentally lost from the future; "The Twonky," about a strange machine that looks like a console radio but acts as a monitor on its owner's behavior; "Two-Handed Engine," in which the infallible Furies, robot police who detect

and execute murderers, are tricked by an official who reprograms them to cover up a killing, but who finds his guilt just as effective a jailor. Also contains "The Proud Robot," "A Gnome There Was," and "Absalom."

4-355. Kuttner, Henry, and C. L. Moore (as Lawrence O'Donnell). **Fury.** Grossett & Dunlop, 1950. Gregg, $11.00 (as *Destination Infinity*).
Sam Harker is born an "immortal," a breed of Venusian humans who live 1,000 years and rule the underwater civilization colonized by Earth after it was poisoned by nuclear wars. Sam's drive forces colonization of the forbidding jungle surface of Venus, preserving survival initiative for mankind. Themes: natural selection works; human destiny is to fill the universe. Thoughtful development of Ben Bowman, computer-like prophet "immortal" who can extrapolate future but not interfere. An intelligent, albeit incorrect, setting of Venusian ecology. Transcends pulp-fiction antecedents.

4-356. Kuttner, Henry (as Lewis Padgett). **Mutant.** Gnome, 1953.
Five stories, the 1945–1953 "Baldy" series from *Astounding*, that chronicle the history of a group of mutant telepaths and their struggle to survive in a world of inimical "normals." The invention of a device to induce telepathy in normal infants gives hope for an eventual reuniting of the race. Adversity overcome enables mankind to progress. Classic work in the emerging-telepath scenario. Compare Wyndham's *Re-Birth* [4-641]; contrast Roberts' *The Inner Wheel* [4-480].

4-357. Kuttner, Henry (as Lewis Padgett). **Robots Have No Tails.** Gnome, 1952.
Five 1943–1948 stories of Gallegher, the alcoholic, untrained inventor whose creative unconscious (Gallegher Plus) is unleashed when drunk, and Joe, his narcissistic robot with super senses. Formula plots: Gallegher's unconscious self takes commissions for fantastic inventions and leaves his sober self in financial or legal trouble. A new binge leads to solution. Once highly touted as humorous SF, but the idea of creativity credited to alcohol and distorted image of science as product of eccentric, ignorant individual leaves sour taste today. Spots of social satire and word play are worthwhile. Compare with Bond's *Lancelot Biggs* [4-86].

4-358. Kuttner, Henry (as Lewis Padgett). **Tomorrow and Tomorrow** and **The Fairy Chessman.** Gnome, 1951.
Chessman, first published in 1946, depicts a distant future of endless, meaningless war in which scientists are driven mad by the solution of a mysterious equation. Time travel, extratemporal perception, and fairy chess players constitute major elements in a complex plot. *Tomorrow*, dating from 1947, contrasts with a near future ruled by a dictatorial "Global Peace Commission" dedicated to the status quo. An underground tries to start an atomic war to blast mankind again into cultural and scientific

progress. Two complexly plotted but superior short novels with grim and bitter dystopian views.

4-359. Lafferty, Raphael Aloysius. **The Devil Is Dead.** Avon, 1971.
More theological fantasy than SF, an allegorical sea voyage for a motley crew of demi-mythic characters on a ship captained by the devil. Or is he the devil? Shapes, scenes, and events are rarely what they seem. Tangled plot is emblem for serious deliberation of one of theology's dreadful predictions. When the devil is dead, he rules indeed without interference. Not for all readers, Lafferty's narrative is often brilliant, esoteric, and obscure, but always challenging. Compare and contrast Blish's *A Case of Conscience* [4-75]. NN, 1971.

4-360. Lafferty, Raphael Aloysius. **Fourth Mansions.** Ace, 1969, $.75.
Like his other works annotated here, not really SF, but heraldic or morality fantasy. But Lafferty is embraced by the SF field. This is a tale of conflict between groups who would preserve the cyclic process of human history and those who would have mankind evolve to superman—with innocent Freddy Foley to moderate the outcome, which is finally left in doubt. Is patience or ambition the best posture for the moral destiny of the species? Marvelously unrealistic characters, energetic symbolism, philosophically comic, and only sometimes overwritten. Compare the weave and mood of Delany's *Einstein Intersection* [4-201]. NN, 1970.

4-361. Lafferty, Raphael Aloysius. **Past Master.** Ace, 1968. Garland, $11.00.
Around 2500, Astrobe's utopian culture fails, as did old Earth's American one 500 years earlier. To rejuvenate it, Astrobe brings Thomas More from the past. More dies another political martyrdom, giving Astrobe a mystic infusion of new life so that the adventure of human history may proceed to further triumph . . . and failure. Folkish fancy and erudition merge in smooth narrative combining SF, fantasy, and theological history. Compare Miller's *A Canticle for Leibowitz* [4-424]. NN, 1968; HN, 1969.

4-362. Lafferty, Raphael Aloysius. **The Reefs of Earth.** Berkley, 1968. Dobson, £1.40.
The Dulanty family consists of alien Pucas, children roguishly thievish by nature, who become deadly in confrontations with a humanity that insists upon rejecting the spiritual advantages the "Giver" has provided mankind. Largely unnoticed, the children will mature, their impatience ever more dangerous for the majority of a decadent humanity. Thoroughly engaging, racy, comic, macabre story, easily recognized as an allegory of mankind refusing God's gift of redemption. Compare Henderson's *Pilgrimage* [4-304].

4-363. Lafferty, Raphael Aloysius. **Space Chantey.** Ace, 1968.

Space Captain Roadstrum and crew replay adventures of Homer's *Odyssey* in futuristic mood. Picaresque comic adventure in science fantasy mode. Lafferty reportedly considers it his best published novel. Contrast his *The Devil Is Dead* [4-359].

4-364. Lafferty, Raphael Aloysius. **Strange Doings.** Scribner, 1972, $5.95.
Sixteen stories, from the late 1960s to early 1970s, including "Continued on Next Rock" (NN, 1970), about curiously compelled members of archeological dig in American south who excavate a chimney that tells them more and more about the present and future as the layers appear. Philosophically heavier stories include "Entire and Perfect Chrysolite" and "Cliffs that Laughed." Strategic flippancy refreshes the archetypal behaviors of man in Lafferty's Roman Catholic-influenced tales.

4-365. Lange, Oliver. **Vandenberg.** Stein & Day, 1971. P. Davies, £2.10; Pan, £.40.
Russia takes over America almost without a struggle, but Gene Vandenberg, who makes his life in forests of the Rocky Mountains, makes a stand, dying rather than submitting to the new regime. Good characterization, scene-setting, and suspense. Might be last of legendary heros of American West. Update of one of SF's oldest scenarios, the revolutionary cry "Give me liberty, or give me death." Compare Heinlein's "If this goes on . . ." in *The Past through Tomorrow* [4-300] and Kornbluth's *Not This August* [4-350].

4-366. Lanier, Sterling E. **Hiero's Journey.** Chilton, 1973. Bantam, $1.25.
In post-catastrophe era, Hiero sallies forth from neo-Roman Catholic monastic academy astride a bull moose to travel through world of mutants, savagery, piracy, and strange beasts to seek and find legendary plans for making a computer. Excellent narrative and quasi-symbolic scene and character. Weak ending. As long as mankind survives he will seek resources to make a sophisticated, wholesome culture. Compare Miller's *A Canticle for Leibowitz* [4-424] and Roberts' *Pavane* [4-481]. Sequel: *Hiero's Travail.*

4-367. Laumer, Keith, and Rosel George Brown. **Earthblood.** Doubleday, 1966.
Roan, a pure-blood terrestrial raised by nonhuman parents, goes on a quest to find semi-mythical Earth. He succeeds and discovers that some nonhumans are not as nonhuman as they seem. Adventurous space opera with some light satire on racial attitudes against an interesting "carny" background. Compare Heinlein's *Stranger in a Strange Land* [4-302]. NN, 1966.

4-368. Laumer, Keith. **Envoy to New Worlds.** Ace, 1963.

Six stories from Retief series. Retief is space-going diplomat of low degree who cuts through bureaucratic red tape to successes his superiors cannot achieve. Allegedly derived from Laumer's own diplomatic career. Humorous and sometimes pointed satire and parody. Sequels include several additional collections and novels. Compare Stableford's Halcyon Drift series [4-555] and Tubb's Dumarest stories [4-585].

4-369. Laumer, Keith. **The Monitors.** Berkley, 1966. Dobson, £1.40; Mayflower, £.25.
Earth is invaded and conquered by beneficent aliens who prevent any violence. A rebel, Blondel, succeeds in penetrating the secret of the aliens' mission, and is created ambassador of Earth to the galaxy. Typical Laumer novel of man's ability to rise above himself to greatness under crushing adversity. Basis for farcical film. Compare Schmitz's *The Demon Breed*, Campbell's *The Moon Is Hell* [4-139], and Williamson's *The Humanoids* [4-626].

4-370. Laumer, Keith. **A Plague of Demons.** Berkley, 1965. Warner Books, $.75.
Aliens nurture wars on Earth to cultivate and reap crop of "computers"—human brains. John Bravis is surgically converted to "superman" to investigate. Caught, he finds his brain placed in control of multiton tank fighting unknown war on unknown world. He rebels, frees fellow enslaved brains, and girds for endless wars against alien enemy. Entertaining space opera and satirical attack on war. NN, 1965.

*4-371. Le Guin, Ursula K. **The Dispossessed: An Ambiguous Utopia.** Harper, 1974, $7.95. Avon, $1.75.
Poor, arid Anarres, settled by anarchists, and the parent world, Urras, rich in resources but burdened by monopoly capitalism, circle one another in a binary planetary system. Shevek of Anarres, one of the galaxy's greatest physicists, has found utopia flawed by its narrow-mindedness and seeks revisions by journeying to Urras. But seeing that the capitalists only want to use him, Shevek escapes underground and returns to his harsh home through the Earth ambassador's good offices. His theories give rise to the ansible, an instantaneous communications device, and are paralleled in the novel's structure of chapters alternating between past and present activities on the two worlds, allowing Shevek's history to be unfolded and Anarres' sociocultural system described simultaneously with his activities on Urras. Its philosophy and social theory, excellently developed settings, and superlative writing make this one of SF's greatest novels. HW, 1975; NW, 1974. JW, 1974; Campbell Memorial Award runner-up, 1975.

4-372. Le Guin, Ursula K. **The Lathe of Heaven.** Scribner, 1971. Avon, $1.25.
George Orr finds he can alter reality through his dreams. He consults a

psychiatrist, Dr. Haber, who undertakes to control his dreams in order to create a perfect world. This plan is only partially successful. Meanwhile, Orr's dreams no longer affect reality, while Haber's do. In the end, Haber goes mad; the world slowly recovers from Haber's dream, while Orr finds happiness knowing better than to tamper with reality. Compare and contrast Borges' "The Circular Ruins" in *Ficciones* [4-87]. HN, 1972; NN, 1971.

*4-373. Le Guin, Ursula K. **The Left Hand of Darkness.** Ace, 1969, $1.75.
One of SF's best works, it explores the relationship between Genry, envoy from the galaxy's technologically advanced worlds to the backward and ice-gripped planet of Winter, and machiavellian Estraven, sometime statesman from the Winter kingdom of Karhide. Only on Winter have humans developed a unisexual nature, whose balance is shifted to either maleness or femaleness as the result of interaction with another person during estrus. Estraven is exiled for supporting Genry's cause of opening Winter to the galaxy, and both undertake a heroic journey across the glaciers to save the mission. Estraven's strategy is successful, but he pays with his life, and Genry, blinded by his culturally entrenched maleness, comes to know his love for Estraven too late. The meticulous description of Winter and its cultures, in the manner of Herbert's *Dune* [4-307], is a major asset of the work, as is Le Guin's uniquely beautiful prose. HW, 1970; NW, 1969.

4-374. Leiber, Fritz. **The Best of Fritz Leiber.** Ballantine, 1974, $1.75.
Twenty-two SF and fantasy stories, from the 1940s to the 1970s, that showcase the author's continued originality, social concerns, and craft development. Among the best of a very good lot are "Coming Attraction" (1950, SFHF), "Poor Superman" (1950), "A Pail of Air" (1951), "The Night He Cried" (1953), "The Big Trek" (1957), "Rump-titty-titty-tum-tah-tee" (HN, 1958), and "A Deskful of Girls" (HN, 1959). Especially noteworthy is "Gonna Roll the Bones" (NW, 1967; HW, 1968), a poetic fantasy in which a miner out on a spree ends up shooting craps with the devil, his soul the wager. Leiber's best collection, with an introduction by Poul Anderson and an afterword by the author.

*4-375. Leiber, Fritz. **The Big Time.** Ace, 1961, $1.50.
Part of the Change War series, written in the late 1950s and 1960s, about a vast war between the mysterious "Snakes" and "Spiders" fought by recruits from many species and many past and future times; the war's object is to alter past events in such a way that one side gains ultimate victory. *The Big Time* involves events in the "Place," a Spider R & R center outside the cosmos, when the medical and entertainment staff becomes involved in an attempted mutiny led by a disillusioned time soldier. Dramatic staging, action, and dialogue are reminiscent of a play, as charac-

ters emotionally and verbally spin about in an intense, flowing narrative. A comment on the psychological aspects of war. *The Mind Spider* (Ace, 1961) contains other stories in the series. Contrast with Asimov's *The End of Eternity* [4-36] and Le Guin's *The Lathe of Heaven* [4-372]. HW, 1958.

4-376. Leiber, Fritz. **Gather, Darkness!** Pellegrini & Cudahy, 1950. Ballantine, $1.50.
In this 1943 story, Brother Jarles, a priest of the Hierarchy of the Church of the Great God, a religion firmly based on concealed technology, is caught up in a revolution conducted by "witches," underground scientists. Jarles' inner war of morality vs. duty is reflected by the witches' war against the misuse of science. Solid SF and the forerunner of later novels involving the role of religion and science. Compare del Rey's *The Eleventh Commandment* [4-204]; contrast Miller's *A Canticle for Leibowitz* [4-424].

4-377. Leiber, Fritz. **The Green Millenium.** Abelard, 1953. Ace, $1.25.
In a decadent United States, reminiscent of settings in Pohl and Kornbluth's *Gladiator-at-Law* [4-464] and Brunner's *Stand on Zanzibar* [4-118], two symbiotic species from Vega, one satyr-like, the other looking like green cats, secretly invade Earth. The cats exhale a pacifying, mood-elevating hormone and are aggressively sought by semi-legitimate organized crime, the government, a religious cult, and Phil Gish, the story's average-guy hero. But the cats, in their self-assured feline way, "capture" not only the Earth, ending war and interpersonal violence, but the reader as well. Colorful, humorous entertainment despite an overly convoluted plot.

4-378. Leiber, Fritz. **The Silver Eggheads.** Ballantine, 1962.
Of interest as a satire on writers, readers, publishers, and editors extrapolated from the worst practices in popular literature today; otherwise, minor Leiber. Comic at times, even biting, despite a contrived, ridiculous plot about the attempted use of encapsulated brains of ancient authors to produce books after the destruction of all automated writing machines called "wordmills." Compare Biggle's "Tunesmith" [4-66], Malzberg's *Herovit's World* [4-409], and Leiber's own "The Night He Cried" [4-374].

4-379. Leiber, Fritz. **A Specter Is Haunting Texas.** Walker, 1969, $4.50.
After World War III, Texas, with all of its legendary braggadocio, has become the whole United States. Scully, an actor grown up thin and softmuscled on a satellite of Earth's Moon, "haunts" Texas by leading a revolution of the enslaved "Mexes" against the hormonally giganticized Texans. It succeeds as Scully wenches, wines, and dissembles on a stage full of tragi-comic caricatures of today's political dramatis personae—the

theatrical motif supplied by the novel itself. Belongs in the cream of SF as satire, though its tone is upbeat whereas Vonnegut's is bleak, Brunner's is serious, and Moorcock's is decadent.

*4-380. Leiber, Fritz. **The Wanderer.** Ballantine, 1964. Dobson, £2.10.
Common people are swept up in a world-wide disaster when the Wanderer, a mysterious purple-and-gold-surfaced planet, pulls into orbit next to the Earth. Gravitational effects rip the globe as the Wanderer breaks up the Moon for fuel and then suddenly vanishes, closely pursued by another planet-sized spaceship. Lots of characters, action, and catastrophe details in this heavily loaded, perhaps tongue-in-cheek novel. Superior Leiber. Compare Ashton's *Alas, That Great City* [4-34] and Balmer and Wylie's *When Worlds Collide* [3-3]. HW, 1965.

4-381. Leinster, Murray (pseud. of William Fitzgerald Jenkins). **Colonial Survey.** Gnome, 1957. (Variant title: *The Planet Explorer*, 1957).
Bordman is colonial survey trouble-shooter through four loosely linked chapters, saving new colony from disaster in each. Included is "Combat Team," about pioneer cooperation between men and mutant kodiak bears, which won Hugo as "Exploration Team" in 1956. Each story set as problem to be solved. Compare Mitchison's *Memoirs of a Spacewoman* [4-426] and Barnes' *Interplanetary Hunter* [4-57].

4-382. Leinster, Murray (pseud. of William Fitzgerald Jenkins). **The Forgotten Planet.** Gnome, 1954.
Human castaways, culturally degenerated by harsh conditions on a world dominated by previously seeded insects and fungi, are rallied by a genius, Burl, who rediscovers technology and aggressiveness, compresses thousands of years of cultural evolution into a few days, and leads his band to a "natural" home for man on a temperate plateau. And all just in the nick of time to meet a visiting spaceship full of sportsmen. Based largely on 1926 and 1927 stories, and shows its age; author's claims of authenticity of insect behavior may be valid, but overall scientific accuracy, especially in cultural and behavioral sciences, is terrible. Basically, a blend of social Darwinism, a great-man theory, and pop anthropology and entomology, in a plot too full of coincidences and underdeveloped characters. Surprisingly, the work remains absorbing and vivid, perhaps because it touches obsolete myths we still hold. Compare with Aldiss's *The Long Afternoon of Earth* [4-7] and Blish's "The Thing in the Attic" [4-80].

4-383. Leinster, Murray (as Will F. Jenkins, the author's true name). **The Murder of the U.S.A.** Crown, 1946.
America's cities are mysteriously destroyed by about 300 A-bombs. Lieutenant Sam Burton subsequently solves the mystery of what country did it (readers are never told). Detective story with crime so big it becomes

SF. Anticipates Bester's *Demolished Man* [4-64] and Wahloo's *Steel Spring* [4-610]. One of earlier A-bomb attack warning stories.

4-384. Leinster, Murray (pseud. William Fitzgerald Jenkins). **The Pirates of Zan.** Ace, 1959, $.95 (includes Leinster's *The Mutant Weapon*).
Bron Hoddan leaves the space pirates of Zan to seek his fortune as an electrical engineer on civilized, stagnant Walden. But his innovations force him into exile on feudal Darth, where he hatches a scheme of mock-space piracy that not only makes him rich, but renews human social progress. Humorously satirizes static human societies and spoofs SF pulp conventions by making them seem plausible. Possible libretto source for SF equivalent of Gilbert and Sullivan. HN, 1960.

*4-385. Lem, Stanislaw (Poland). **The Cyberiad: Fables for the Cybernetic Age.** Seabury, 1974, $8.95. Tr. by Michael Kandel of *Cyberiada*, 1967.
A delightful cycle of ingenious and humorous stories modeled on European fables about two robot "constructors," timorous Trurl and vexatious Klapaucius, who build fabulous machines for pay and pride throughout the galaxy. Stories individually point up lessons, such as "The Fifth Sally (A), or Trurl's Prescription," which satirizes bureaucracy, and "The Sixth Sally, or How Trurl and Klapaucius Created a Demon of the Second Kind to Defeat the Pirate Pugg," which warns against the current information explosion. Collectively they demonstrate the retributory effects of the seven deadly sins despite the use of technology in their commission. The jargons of science, math, and technology permeate the stories, adding color and humor, as does the use of mechanical analogs of human behavior. Still, not truly myths of the age of science, as in Calvino's *Cosmiccomics* [4-136]; rather, traditional sorcerer vs. client fables jazzed up with scientific terminology and treating science as magic, men as machines, the future as the past. Outstanding translation; a carnival of words. Compare Bunch's *Moderan* [4-127].

4-386. Lem, Stanislaw (Poland). **The Futurological Congress, from the Memoirs of Ijon Tichy.** Seabury, 1974, $6.95. Tr. by Michael Kandel of *Ze wspomnien' Ijona Tichego. Kongres futurologiczny*, 1971.
A satire on contemporary society, on professional futurists, and on "the sleeper wakes" utopias. Tichy goes to a convention of futurists held in the 100-story Costa Rica Hilton. Pointless terrorism abounds, and Tichy is caught up in a local rebellion and the counter-measures that unloose a flood of mind-altering drugs. In hallucinations, he is wounded repeatedly, frozen down, and awakes in the brave new world of the future where both good and evil come out of a pill bottle. Humor is as unsubtle as in Goulart's *After Things Fell Apart* [4-271], the violence as severe as in Brunner's *The Sheep Look Up* [4-115], though with little social insight.

4-387. Lem, Stanislaw (Poland). **The Investigation.** Seabury, 1974, $7.95. Tr. by Adele Milch of *'Sledztwo*, 1959.

Scotland Yard is confronted by the strange mystery of the dead moving and then walking away. Detective Gregory doubts it is supernatural and suspects the eccentric statistician, Sciss—for the phenomenon's pattern suggests either ghoulish human activity or the existence of natural phenomena undreamt of in our philosophy. Finally, Gregory confronts the latter with all its psychic consequences. The story's familiar setting and form provide contrast to its central theme: man's limited understanding of and uncomfortableness with the unknown.

4-388. Lem, Stanislaw (Poland). **The Invincible.** Seabury, 1973, $6.95. Ace, $1.25. Tr. by Wendayne Ackerman of *Niezwyciezony*, 1964.
The space ship *Invincible* lands on uninhabited Regis III to discover how its sister ship, the *Condor*, was defeated and its crew driven into infantile madness. It appears that abandoned machines have evolved through natural selection on Regis III, giving rise to highly specialized mechanical life forms—which are beyond man's efforts to defeat. Surface space opera with philosophical undercurrents.

4-389. Lem, Stanislaw (Poland). **Memoirs Found in a Bathtub.** Seabury, 1973, $6.95. Tr. by Michael Kandel and Christine Rose of *Pamietnik Znaleziony w wannie*, 1971.
Satire on militarism, the cult of secrecy, and its resultant paranoia in closed systems. A paper-decaying epidemic has destroyed civilization, so the U.S. military builds a "Third Pentagon" in the Rockies to weather the crisis. Locked under stone, the autonomous complex comes to believe it still functions to control affairs. A young man is given a meaningless secret mission and becomes involved in pointless spy-counter-spy activities leading to eventual self-destruction within the entombed Kafkaesk labyrinth filled with technological gimmickry. Story eventually becomes overly complex and tedious.

*4-390. Lem, Stanislaw (Poland). **Solaris.** Walker, 1970. Faber, £2.00. Tr. by Joanna Kilmartin and Steve Cox of *Solaris*, 1968.
Written by Lem in 1961. A planet-wide ocean seems to have a life of its own as it twists itself into fantastic shapes and provides visions for Earthmen there to study it. But its nature defies all Earth's ingenuity; a multitude of "solutions" are offered, none of which seem to fit. Man can interpret the truly alien only in his own limited terms. A fascinating and philosophical work, highly original. Compare Blish's *A Case of Conscience* [4-75].

4-391. Léourier, Christian (France). **The Mountains of the Sun.** Berkley, 1974, $.95. Tr. of *Les montagnes du soleil*, 1971.
Three hundred fifty years after a cataclysmic deluge on Earth, Earthling expatriates to Mars return to meet survivors, "retrogrades," who stayed behind, and recolonize Earth. The two groups integrate, but not before

they break out of the rigidified cultures—one advanced, one primitive—that made survival possible. Includes "conscious" computer, "Molly." Fine socio-anthropological insights.

4-392. Lessing, Doris (U.K.). **The Memoirs of a Survivor.** Knopf, 1975, $6.95.
Things are falling apart. Civilization is failing. Only the "administrators," the "talkers," are insulated by their stolen wealth from the chaos and scarcity of food and utilities. The woman watches it all from the window of her apartment. A man drops thirteen-year-old Emily off with the woman. As the city population migrates, stopping in tribal groups in the street below the window, Emily passes through puberty into young womanhood—the tribal group the scenario of her *rite de passage*. The woman, the "survivor," has the perception of a middle-class grandmother, without being sentimental. Emily, too, is a "survivor." There is a kind of hope in seeing the experience of an Emily, hope that transcends even major upheavals of civilization. In Lessing's excellent narrative, flaws of missed words, vague phrasing, leap out as they would not in lesser tellings, but Lessing succeeds brilliantly in capturing the awareness of the moment when established things cease and surviving begins. Contrast Jensen's *Epp* [4-325].

4-393. Levin, Ira. **This Perfect Day.** Random House, 1970. Fawcett Crest, $1.50.
Earth is under the management of a supercomputer, its people's lives closely regulated and controlled with drugs. Chip, wanting to control his own life, rebels, joins an underground, flees to an isolated, technologically backward island, and plots to destroy the system by reprogramming the computer. Alas, rebellion is also programmed, a ticket to elite membership. But, by a fluke, Chip destroys the computer, turning man back on his own resources. A typical warning story against a planned, cybernetic, welfare-oriented future. Compare Vonnegut's *Player Piano* [4-606] and Brunner's *The Shockwave Rider* [4-116]; contrast Reynold's *Looking Backward from the Year 2000* [4-476].

*4-394. Lewis, Clive Staples (U.K.). **Out of the Silent Planet.** Bodley Head, 1938. Collier, $1.25; Macmillan, $5.95. **Perelandra.** Bodley Head, 1943. Collier, $1.25; Macmillan, $5.95. **That Hideous Strength.** Bodley Head, 1945. Collier, $1.50; Macmillan, $5.95.
The three novels form a "Space Trilogy" featuring Ransom, who goes to Mars from Earth, the "Silent Planet," to find preternatural Martian society; then to Venus, "Perelandra," to find human life beginning on that planet; then back to Earth to guide the battle against the forces of evil symbolized by the atheistic scientism, "hideous strength," of the modern university. The medieval magician Merlin is resurrected to neutralize

the evil and preserve mankind for caritas—God as the expression of awesome divine love. The narrative is often tedious and clogged, but stories are rich fusion of philological theory, medieval and Arthurian legend (the "Matter of Britain"), and sophisticated Christian theology and philosophy. Enormously popular since its publication. Compare Tolkien's *Lord of the Rings*.

4-395. Lupoff, Richard A. **Into the Aether.** Dell, 1974, $.95.
Professor Thintwhistle, accompanied by his protegé, lady friend, and black servant, sails off into the universes in his coal-burning spaceship. A parody of early SF in a style reminiscent of Horatio Alger.

4-396. McCaffrey, Anne. **Dragonflight.** Walker, 1968. Ballantine, $1.50.
Pern is a lost colony of Earth subject to cyclic invasions of deadly space spores, ravaging advanced technology and necessitating cooperation of dragons and dragonriders of Pern. Dragons breathe fire, teleport, and link telepathically with riders. Their prime purpose is to burn spores when they appear. But in the long period between spore invasions, people forget past dangers. F'lar and Lessa, leaders of single weyr of dragons, are forced to develop methods all over of dealing with spore invasion. Lessa discovers dragons' ability to time travel; brings dragon "wings" from past and saves Pern. Novel incorporates "Weyr Search" (NN, 1967; HW, 1968—first woman to win Hugo), and "Dragon Rider" (NW, 1968; HN, 1969). Sequel is *Dragonquest* (Ballantine, 1971, $1.50), continuing saga with development of technology to aid fight and carry it to spore planet to destroy source. HN, 1972. Third novel projected.

4-397. McCaffrey, Anne. **Restoree.** Ballantine, 1967.
Called a spoof by McCaffrey. An Earth girl is abducted by evil aliens and is rescued by nonterrestrial humans. Naturally, she falls in love with the ruler of this new planet. An SF romance.

4-398. McCaffrey, Anne. **The Ship Who Sang.** Ballantine, 1970, $1.50.
Short stories featuring Helva, the ship who sings. Helva is a physiological freak modified to control a starship as a normal would his body. She proves that she is as human emotionally as any normal human. Written as a romance, this provides a good portrayal of the problems of a cyborg's adjustment to the real world. Includes "Dramatic Mission" (NN, 1969; HN, 1970).

4-399. McCann, Edison (pseud. of Lester del Ray and Frederik Pohl). **Preferred Risk.** Simon & Schuster, 1955, $2.75.
Governments have withered, leaving all power in the hands of a ubiquitous, ultimate insurance company, symbol for welfare society, which has insured against everything and eliminated social ills to keep from paying claims. But the costs of utopia are the usurpation of power by a

dictatorial "Underwriter" and the end of progress due to the elimination of risk. Thomas Wills is the stock rebel, manipulated first by the perverted Company to spy on misguided revolutionaries, then by the underground to explode an air-poisoning cobalt bomb in a naive attempt to bankrupt the Company. Of course he vanquishes the villain and humbly undertakes the initiation of a U.S.-type balance of power, democratic world government as Earth's frozen-down millions escape the fallout in Company vaults. Morals: Power corrupts; and administrative politics and economics must be separated. Good example of liberal ideology in SF; contrast Rand's *Atlas Shrugged* [4-472] and Reynolds' *Looking Backward from the Year 2000* [4-476]. Winner of a Galaxy–Simon & Schuster $6,500 prize.

4-400. MacDonald, John Dann. **Ballroom of the Skies.** Greenberg, 1952. **The Girl, the Gold Watch, and Everything.** Fawcett, 1962. **Wine of the Dreamers.** Greenberg, 1951. Fawcett Gold Medal, $1.25 each.
Three SF novels by a popular writer of detective fiction. *Wine* is well-spun yarn of the world of 1975 exhibiting familiar insanity: mankind's behavior is manipulated, inadvertently, by telepathic dreamers from another world. When dreamers learn this, life on Earth takes turn for better. In *Ballroom*, extraterrestrial interference explains mankind's troubles on Earth as a deliberate winnowing experience to select Earth's future leaders. *Girl* is comic parable about use of power obtained by a "watch" that speeds up time for owner so that, at a ratio of about one half hour to a second, the watch owner "lives" and moves at invisible speed—granting virtual omnipotence. Compare *Girl* with Gerrold's *The Man Who Folded Himself* [4-261].

4-401. McHugh, Vincent. **I Am Thinking of My Darling.** Simon & Schuster, 1943.
Jim Rowan searches for his actress wife Niobe, even as New York is stricken by epidemic fever that releases inhibitions and causes non-violent chaos in the community. A tragi-comic analysis of the principles of social change, as cure is found and the Rowans are reunited at the end of the strange week. Compare Frank's *Mr. Adam* [4-250].

4-402. McIntosh, J. T. (pseud. of James Murdock MacGregor) (U.K.). **One in Three Hundred.** Doubleday, 1954.
The Sun is going nova and man can survive only by migrating to Mars. However, there are only a limited number of space ships, and of these, only a small number can actually reach Mars. Once there, the environment and internal strife threaten the few remaining survivors. This Darwinian theme of survival is also shared by his other novel, *The Fittest* (Doubleday, 1955). Scientist Paget's experiments heighten animal intelligence, and some—dogs, rats, and cats—escape. These "paggets" destroy civilization, forcing man into a desparate fight for survival. Despite

these catastrophes, both works are optimistic. Man has what it takes to overcome any problem eventually. Excellent action stories. Compare Wyndham's *Day of the Triffids* [4-638].

*4-403. McKenna, Richard. **Casey Agonistes and Other Science Fiction and Fantasy Stories.** Harper, 1973, $5.95.
Five of McKenna's best stories, from 1958 to 1967, and an introduction by Damon Knight. Stories of true manhood, humanhood, and de Chardin-like evolution: powerful "Casey Agonistes," where dying men create a clownish red ape in a collective fantasy; "Hunter, Come Home," with men trying to destroy a planet's biosystem as a test of their manhood; "The Secret Place" (HN, 1967; NW, 1966), about the games boys play; "Mine Own Ways," where man makes himself; and the exquisite "Fiddler's Green," with its strange world created by seven men lost at sea. Contrast Anderson's *Time and Stars* [4-27] and *Seven Conquests* [4-23].

4-404. MacLean, Katherine. **Missing Man.** Berkley, 1975, $1.25. Putnam, $6.95.
George Sanford, a social misfit, uses his psychic powers to find people for a police "Rescue Squad" in the novel's excellent first part, a 1971 novella Nebula winner. Its later parts are weaker, as George becomes involved in preventing warfare among New York's anarchistic subcultures and his subsequent flowering into his full superhuman powers after remembering repressed parentacide. Culture of future city is well developed. Compare Brunner's *The Whole Man* [4-119].

4-405. Maine, Charles Eric (pseud. of David McIlwain) (U.K.). **Fire Past the Future.** Ballantine, 1959.
Mystery and SF elements blend in a suspenseful Ten Little Indians tale of successive murders among isolated scientists counting down the launch of an antigravity spaceship. Mind-controlling time traveler is the villain, sent back to prevent man's discovery of time travel. Pseudo-science mishmash about Lorentz-Fitzgerald equations cannot be taken seriously, nor can the scientific conceptual breakthrough by the nonscientist hero of the story. Compare Temple's *Shoot at the Moon* [4-576].

*4-406. Malzberg, Barry N. **Beyond Apollo.** Random, 1972. Pocket Books, $.95.
Controversial winner of the first Campbell Award (1973). The nervous dialogue, alienated characters, and insane social institutions seem far from the Campbell tradition, but worse, it dares to criticize NASA's space program. The sole survivor of a Venus flight, under official suspension, tells various versions of the trip until the insanity of the whole "program" becomes apparent. Malzberg tackled similar themes in a more conventionally structured earlier novel, *The Falling Astronauts* (Ace, 1971, $.75). Richard Martin, pressed to a nervous breakdown by the "program" during his own Moon flight, is asked to cool out a fellow

Apollo astronaut who has gone mad and threatens to drop nuclear bombs on Earth. Instead, Martin implores him to do it. Compare Moorcock's *The Black Corridor* [4-428] and Temple's *Shoot at the Moon* [4-576].

4-407. Malzberg, Barry N. **The Destruction of the Temple.** Pocket Books, 1974, $.95.

A student from an effete suburban university enters a city, long abandoned to the "lumpen," to film a reenactment of the Dallas assassination. Filled with class superiority, he first coerces the lumpen's cooperation, only to become their captive and to be made to relive several racial and civil rights murders as well as John Kennedy's. Malzberg's recapitulative style catches the paranoia of the recent past as the student repeatedly awaits the bullet's blow. Part parable, social commentary, and nostalgia. Compare Delany's *Dhalgren* [4-199].

4-408. Malzberg, Barry N. (as K. M. O'Donnell). **Final War and Other Fantasies.** Ace, 1969.

Eleven stories, from 1967 to 1969, with preface and story intros by the author. The title story (NN, 1968) depicts a meaningless, endless "limited war" fought on a large estate and the futile efforts of a soldier to escape from it. This collection, Malzberg's first, contains many of the themes and techniques found in his more successful later works—assassination, criticism of U.S. space program, satirizing the SF subculture, theme and variation story structures, and neurotic characters. Compare Spinrad's *No Direction Home* [4-553] and Ballard's *Love and Napalm* [4-51].

4-409. Malzberg, Barry N. **Herovit's World.** Random, 1973. Pocket Books, $.95.

Jonathon Herovit, SF writer on the skids, is unable to function in his anomic, disintegrating social world. He is haunted by his nom de plume, sophisticated Kirk Poland, who replaces him, only to fail and be replaced in turn by his fictional character, macho spaceman Mack Miller. Two earlier Malzberg novels lead to Herovit: *Dwellers of the Deep* (as K. M. O'Donnell, Ace, 1970), about an SF magazine collector who must rally an SF club to forestall alien conquest; and *Gather in the Hall of the Planets* (as K. M. O'Donnell, Ace, 1971, $.75), where an SF writer must identify a disguised alien at an SF convention in order to save the world. Taking SF-dom as the cosmos, Malzberg explores the existential dilemma of modern man as he struggles for meaning in a meaningless world—and provides laughs by satirizing the SF subculture. Compare Sladek's *The Müller-Fokker Effect* [4-544].

4-410. Malzberg, Barry N. (as K. M. O'Donnell). **Universe Day.** Avon, 1971.

A downbeat *Martian Chronicles* [4-102] of the 1960s, this collection of loosely connected stories and sketches, some previously published between 1969 and 1971, depicts man's exploration of the social system.

Malzberg's concerns include insane bureaucracies, official dehumanization and corruption, human intolerance and greed, and the psychological impact of the sheer alienness of space. Of note are "Apocrypha as Prologue or—The Way We Wish It Happened," a chronicle of man's rape of the planets; "The Conquest of Conquistadores, 2423," about the ultimate astronaut-training exercise; and "Interview With an Astronaut, 2008," where a vindictive social worker toys with an impoverished ex-astronaut. Not outstanding, but significant in its anti-space travel orientation. Contrast Brown's *The Lights in the Sky Are Stars* [4-107].

4-411. Manvell, Roger (U.K.). **The Dreamers.** Simon & Schuster, 1958.
Jane Fettes, postmistress for village forty miles from London, is hypnotically programmed with dream by African tribesman whose wife was allowed to die by Doctor Morgan in Africa. Morgan is now village resident. Dream is designed to kill Morgan with fear after it is passed from person to person to him. Morgan is saved by a journalist and Doctor King, an African visiting London as specialist in tribal occultism. Solution is through a seance, but details for a behavioral explanation are provided by narrative. A subtle and exotic SF gimmick.

4-412. March, William. **The Bad Seed.** Holt, 1954. Dell, $.95.
Rhoda Penmark is a beautiful eight-year-old child of "bad" parents who has somehow inherited a consummately evil nature from them. Her great intelligence enables her to maintain a front of perfect virtue while she does secret evil, including murder, her nature undiscovered at end of a suspenseful story. Very popular despite scientifically invalid doctrine of inherited evil. Contrast Ira Levin's *Rosemary's Baby* (1967) and Blatty's *The Exorcist* (1971), where the supernatural cause of evil replaces the now discredited pseudo-genetics of *Seed*.

4-413. Matheson, Richard. **Born of Man and Woman.** Chamberlain, 1954. (Alternate title: *Third from the Sun*, 1955).
Seventeen fantasy, horror, and SF stories, from 1950 to 1954, the best of early Matheson. Horror and SF are blended in the title story (SFHF), where a monstrous offspring plots revenge against its parents who keep it chained in the cellar, and in "Lover When You're Near Me," in which an ugly alien female with ESP powers forces her love on a terrorized Earthman. More philosophic are "Third from the Sun," about a family and their neighbors fleeing their world in a stolen spaceship on the eve of total war, and "The Traveller," in which a time traveller visits the crucifixion and gains a faith based not on physical miracles, but on Jesus' willingness to die for his beliefs. Compare and contrast with the works of John Collier and Ray Bradbury.

4-414. Matheson, Richard. **I Am Legend.** Fawcett Gold Medal Books, 1954. Berkley, $.95.
Classic scare story of a disease that causes a kind of vampirism, whose

victims rise from graves and flee light. Finally, a lone survivor, barricaded against the undead, goes forth by day to destroy the vampires. He becomes a symbol of fear to them and the basis of a new myth. Reversal of *Dracula*. Terror and meaning of novel did not survive translation into two screenplays.

4-415. Matheson, Richard. **The Shrinking Man.** Fawcett Gold Medal Books, 1956.
Strange radiation causes a man to shrink; good depiction of his personal and family problems as he diminishes. Eventually becoming trapped in his own basement, he defeats a spider in a climactic scene and goes forth to face the unknown. Fascinating story with meticulous detail. Basis for fair SF film.

4-416. Mead, Harold (U.K.). **The Bright Phoenix.** Ballantine, 1956.
The account of John Waterville, citizen and explorer of post-World War III "perfect" socialist state, who leads colonization of new territory by genetically selected colonists (he's not one). Arrogant colonists are destroyed by indigenous inhabitants. Waterville is befriended by inhabitants but has tragic love affair. Unfortunately, human predicament is warring one; denial of this exacerbates the problem. Deft scene-setting and excellent characterization. Compare Orwell's *1984* [4-450], Russell's *The Great Explosion* [4-488], and Kornbluth's *The Syndic* [4-351].

4-417. Mead, Shepherd. **The Big Ball of Wax.** Simon & Schuster, 1954.
Clever satire and SF by the author of *How to Succeed in Business Without Really Trying*. Lanny Martin, momma's boy and middle-level executive of monopolist conglomerate, "Con Chem," tells how he and his company turned the spiritually revolutionary mind-altering device that allows user to "become" other people at will to reassuringly commercial applications. Madison Avenue ingenuity can be depended upon to subvert all possibility of human progress in the direction of a totalitarian consumer state. Martin's shallow and disarming ingenuousness perfectly contrasts the appalling slavery implied in the commercial state depicted in the story. Constantly inventive. Compare Huxley's *Brave New World* [3-27], Vonnegut's *Player Piano* [4-606], and Pohl and Kornbluth's *The Space Merchants* [4-466].

4-418. Merle, Robert (France). **The Day of the Dolphin.** Simon & Schuster, 1969. Fawcett Crest, $1.50. Tr. by Helen Weaver of *Un Animal doué de raison*, 1967.
Professor Sevilla establishes full communication with dolphins in government-sponsored experiments; discovery subverted for espionage that could lead to global war. Sevilla reacts by escaping with dolphins to put things right—perhaps not in time. Ingenious use of dolphin lore. Human government too brutalized to properly value discovery of another intelligent Earth species. Compare Harrison's *The Daleth Effect* [4-288].

*4-419. Merle, Robert (France). **Malevil.** Simon & Schuster, 1974, $10.00. Warner, $1.95. Tr. by Derek Coltman of *Malevil*, 1972.
Seven people survive nuclear holocaust in "Malevil," a medieval castle. Emmanuel Comte, charismatic leader, directs lives of survivors, as more and more collect. Progress back to twentieth-century level of technology and civilization will be relatively swift, but will it be worth it, or will it all lead to yet another catastrophe? Excellent post-catastrophe story. Compare Stewart's *Earth Abides* [4-558], Frank's *Alas, Babylon* [4-249], and works by John Christopher. Campbell winner, tied with Clarke's *Rendezvous with Rama* [4-157].

4-420. Merril, Judith. **Daughters of Earth.** Doubleday, 1969.
Three stories from the 1950s that illustrate Merril's sensitive and competent approach to "female" SF subjects. The title story is a chronology of six generations of women who ride the crest of humanity's space exploration; emphasizes their emotional responses as generations alternately pursue security and pioneering. The male hero of "Project Nursemaid," a military psychologist, confronts his own inner emotional turmoil as he counsels women giving up their embryonic children to an experimental space program, selects other women to raise these children, and struggles to protect the program's integrity and the children's future. In "Homecalling," a castaway girl and her baby brother develop a relationship with an intelligent insect-like female alien who heads a matriarchal society; a tender, insightful story that upholds the universality of motherhood. Contrast with the modern feminist viewpoint in Russ's *The Female Man* [4-485].

4-421. Merril, Judith. **Out of Bounds.** Pyramid, 1960.
Seven stories about various kinds of love in SF settings, sometimes approaching the maudlin. Includes Merril's first sale and perhaps best known story, "That Only a Mother" (1948; SFHF), about a mother's self-blinding love for a mutation-deformed infant; and a Martha Foley pick, "Dead Center" (1954), a dated tearjerker about an astronaut's family's love that leads to their deaths following the first Moon landing. In "Whoever You Are" (1952), telepathic aliens love all living things; "The Lady Was a Tramp" (1957) involves love, sex, and need among a space freighter's crew. "Peeping Tom" (1954) deals with sexual exploitation using telepathy, while in "Connection Completed" (1954), mind reading brings two lonely people together. As sentimental as, but less well crafted than, works by Sturgeon, who introduces this collection.

4-422. Merril, Judith. **Shadow on the Hearth**. Doubleday, 1950.
Atomic catastrophe novels tend to focus on the large scale collapse of civilization, with isolated bands of survivors stumbling through radioactive rubble. This novel of the early atomic age focuses on a suburban housewife and her family when New York City is bombed. The terror is intensi-

fied by being experienced through the eyes of the mother and her two young children, one of whom is the probable victim of radiation sickness (the shadow of the title). As the utilities fail, the voices on the telephone cease, and radio announcements impersonally document the dissolution of their world; the family attempts to cope. The understated tone makes this novel especially effective. Compare Stewart's *Earth Abides* and Shute's *On the Beach*.

4-423. Miller, Peter Schuyler. **The Titan.** Fantasy Press, 1952.
Eight stories dating from the 1930s and 1940s. An uneven collection; superior works include the long title story based on an unfinished 1935 serial about an Earthman marooned on Mars and kept in a zoo as a "Star-Beast" until he joins a revolt of the Martian lower class and gives his life. Also of note are the 1944 time paradox story, "As Never Was," about archaeologists who explore the future; and "Old Man Mulligan," a thirty-thousand-year-old Neanderthal who uses his knowledge to overcome a gang of kidnappers on a watery, frontier Venus; both stories reflect Miller's interest in anthropology.

*4-424. Miller, Walter M., Jr. **A Canticle for Leibowitz.** Lippincott, 1960, $3.95. Gregg, $13.50; Bantam, $1.25.
Story begins 600 years after World War III, going through new dark ages, renaissance, and modern times, ending with onset of World War IV—even though interstellar travel has been achieved. Thesis: Future history will recapitulate past history, repeating its tragic failure. Fortuitously, the Roman Catholic Church has a hand in next 2,000 years as it had in past 2,000. Brilliant, often satiric transformation of the history of Western civilization, focused by 1,800 years of vicissitudes of life at Abbey Leibowitz, where civilization's sources were preserved after World War III. No short comment can convey work's excellence. Named by many as best SF novel of modern period. HW, 1961.

4-425. Miller, Walter M., Jr. **Conditionally Human.** Ballantine, 1962.
Three novellas, including title story about humanness of a pet, "The Darfsteller" (HW, 1955) and the terms of human dignity; and "Dark Benediction" about racism and xenophobia. All bear the mark of excellence of *A Canticle for Leibowitz* [4-424]. Nine other stories from Miller's too-brief SF career are found in *The View from the Stars* (Ballantine, 1964, Panther, £.35.). Superior efforts include "You Triflin' Skunk!," about an invading alien killed by a hill woman; "The Big Hunger"; "Anybody Else Like Me?"; and "Crucifixus Etiam." Every story is satisfying; themes are insights into man's basic nature.

4-426. Mitchison, Naomi Haldane (U.K.). **Memoirs of a Spacewoman.** Gollancz, 1962.
Picaresque story of a "communicator," specialist in identifying and com-

municating with alien life forms. What "lives" and "thinks" will surprise mankind. Modes of communication will be bizarre. Fitful lapses in novel's continuity more than offset by brilliantly ingenious constructs of those we will meet and how we will "talk" with them. Compare Cole's *The Philosophical Corps* [4-169].

*4-427. Moorcock, Michael (U.K.). **Behold the Man.** Avon, 1970, $.75.
Karl Glogauer, twisted by a disastrous childhood, travels back in time to check the Christ story. Alas, Jesus is a retarded child; so Karl, after having intercourse with Mary, takes the identity of Christ, preaches, and is eventually martyred. Despite rumors caused by the theft of his body by a physician, he did not rise. The juxtaposition of child and adult Glogauer and other unconventional writing techniques lend power to this insightful study of a man's character. Expansion of a novella which won a Nebula in 1967.

4-428. Moorcock, Michael (U.K.). **The Black Corridor.** Ace, 1969. Mayflower, £.30.
Innovative study of Ryan, who watches over a dozen frozen survivors in a lone spaceship fleeing a nuclear war on Earth. In flashbacks, he dreams about the turbulent Earth now gone, awakening only to increasing fantasy in the isolation of the ship. Does a strange alien threaten the humans? Have the sleepers awakened and walked the ship? Or have they been left to die as the *Hope Dempey* falls down its endless well, full of madness and despair? Compare Malzberg's *Beyond Apollo* [4-406] and Lem's *Solaris* [4-390].

4-429. Moorcock, Michael (U.K.). **The Jerry Cornelius novels.** *The English Assassin.* Harper, 1974, $6.95 [not seen]; *The Final Programme.* Avon, 1968. Allison & Busby, £2.00; Mayflower, £.30; *A Cure for Cancer.* Allison & Busby, 1971, £2.00; Penguin (U.K.), £.45.
Each novel stars Jerry Cornelius, a nonwhite spy, stud, immortal, utterly cosmopolitan, and rich, making his way on incomprehensible missions in a decadent and perverted global civilization. Parodies James Bond so well, the reader soon forgets James Bond. The narrative is full of jewels, yet remains clear as a story-telling vehicle. Power-fantasy fanciers beware. Compare Durrell's *Tunc* and *Nunquam* [4-227].

4-430. Moore, Brian (U.K.). **The Great Victorian Collection.** Farrar, 1975, $7.95.
English professor Maloney, specialist in Victoriana, dreams into existence a very real collection of virtually every Victorian antique artifact of interest, from toys and tea sets to instruments of kinky erotica. The collection appears in a vacant lot by the motel where he is staying. Experts attest its authenticity, even as they verify the continued existence of the "originals," still lodged in dispersed collections. First enraptured, Ma-

loney encounters problems not unlike King Midas, and dies frustrated. The collection endures. Academic parapsychologists study the phenomena. Do we truly know our heart's desires? Did God? The collection might symbolize the world that, once created, has an inexorable life of its own, subject only to its inherent entropy—mindless of its creator. In glass-clear narrative, the story is a smorgasbord of propositions equal to Charles Finney's *The Circus of Dr. Lao* (1935) and the "Walpurgisnacht" of Goethe's *Faust*.

4-431. Moore, Catherine L. **The Best of C. L. Moore.** Ballantine, 1975.
Ten stories from 1933 to 1946 selected by Lester del Rey that catch Moore's best early SF; also includes del Rey's biographical sketch of Moore and an afterword by her. Top stories: "The Bright Illusion" (1934), a human–alien love story that transcends the flesh; "No Woman Born" (1944), a variant on the Frankenstein theme about the transplantation of a burned beautiful woman's brain into an extraordinary metal body and her emerging superhumanness; "Vintage Season" (1946, SFHF), about jaded visitors from the future who return to view historic catastrophes and their disdainful treatment of a man who discovers their secret. Contains the popular "Shambleau," one of several tales featuring Northwest Smith.

4-432. Moore, Ward. **Bring the Jubilee.** Farrar, 1953. Avon, $2.25.
Hodgins McCormick lives in an alternate United States in which everything from major wars to minor inventions such as the typewriter are different or happened otherwise. This is due to the South having won the battle of Gettysburg, a fact inadvertently changed when McCormick time-travels back to 1877 to meet his death. Excellent and ingenious transformation of real history. Compare Finney's *Time and Again* [4-247] and Kantor's *If the South Had Won the Civil War* [4-331].

4-433. Moore, Ward. **Greener Than You Think.** Sloane, 1947.
Miss Francis perfects a chemical that enables plants to transform any material directly for growth. Albert Weener chronicles its application until "grass" has obliterated everything on Earth. Meanwhile, humanity, in the form of government and industry, fiddles while doomsday arrives. Good satire. Compare Wyndham's *Day of the Triffids* [4-638] and Disch's *Genocides* [4-221]; contrast Christopher's *No Blade of Grass* [4-146].

4-434. Mrozek, Slawomir (Poland). **The Ugupu Bird.** Macdonald, 1968. Tr. by Konrad Syrop of *Wesele w atomicach*, 1959.
Seventeen stories and vignettes, including "The Ugupu Bird," a parable on the interconnectedness of the ecosystem; "Ad Astra," a parable of conflict between traditional and modern writers; and "Escape Southward," employing *Waiting for Godot* as springboard for evolutionary parable on mankind, the evolving cousin of the "Yeti" or Abominable

Snowman. Nakedly mythic and archetypal, tightly constructed narratives told independently of a communist ideological context. Compare G. B. Shaw's *Far-Fetched Fables* [2-137].

4-435. Nearing, Homer, Jr. **The Sinister Researches of C. P. Ransom.** Doubleday, 1954.
Eleven stories loosely linked as novel of Professor Ransom, mathematician, and Professor Tate, philosopher, who try to develop breakthrough for linking arts and sciences. Their successes are pyrrhic, and Ransom finally wins "Superman" award from Nietzsche Society for extraordinary inventions, etc. The gentlest of science fantasy nonsense.

4-436. Nesvadba, Josef (Czechoslovakia). **The Lost Face: Best Science Fiction from Czechoslovakia.** Taplinger, 1971, $5.95. Tr. by Iris Urwin. (British title: *In the Footsteps of the Abominable Snowman*, 1964).
Eight stories by a Czech physician, including title story about plastic surgeon who helps a criminal escape with a brilliant face-lift; "In the Footsteps of the Abominable Snowman," about the contrast between a life in nature and a life according to reason; and "The Death of an Apeman," about the possibility that an ape might be as human as a human. Fine parables, with humorous notes, in search of the definition of man in an age of science, reason, and the modern world's turmoil. Compare Vercors' *You Shall Know Them* [4-602].

4-437. Neville, Kris. **Bettyann.** Tower, 1970.
Based on stories originally published in 1951 and 1954, a sensitive, touching, at times Bradbury-like tale of an unintentionally abandoned orphan alien infant raised as a crippled human girl. Growing up, Bettyann searches for her identity, while her people, a dying race, return to search for her. Learning of her heritage, she chooses to remain on her adopted Earth. An underrated work. Makes a sharp contrast with Wyndham's *The Midwich Cuckoos* [4-639].

*****4-438.** Niven, Larry. **All the Myriad Ways.** Ballantine, 1971, $1.50.
Nine stories, three speculative essays (on Superman's sex life, teleportation, and time travel) and two short-shorts. "Inconstant Moon" (HW, 1972) vividly portrays the impact of the Sun going nova on the lives of a young couple. Evidence of Sun's increased activity is displayed by a vastly brighter Moon in their night sky. "The Jigsaw Man" (HN, 1968) depicts a man convicted for a minor crime and sentenced to be sacrificed to the public organ banks. A frighteningly plausible scenario, part of the Known Space series. The inventive "Not Long before the End" (HN, 1970; NN, 1969) concerns a swordsman and sorcerer confrontation in an era when technology's analog, magic, is beginning to decline as the basis for civilization. "All the Myriad Ways" (HN, 1969), about the social effects of proof that multiple universes exist, has an im-

pact paralleling that of the Cubist painting, "Nude Descending a Staircase." "Becalmed in Hell," also part of the Known Space series, tells of a probe into Venus' atmosphere that nearly goes awry; makes an interesting companion piece to Clarke's venture into Jupiter's clouds, "A Meeting with Medusa" [4-160]. The essay, "Man of Steel Woman of Kleenex," is a reductio ad absurdum of the most famous of all comic book cosmologies. Remarkably cogent and amusing spoof. The other two essays are similar in treatment. A fine collection, strong in science and as fiction.

4-439. Niven, Larry, and Jerry Pournelle. **The Mote in God's Eye.** Simon & Schuster, 1974, $9.95. Pocket Books, $1.95.
A 537-page space opera about the first contact between naive mankind and malevolently cunning and treacherous aliens. Stereotyped characters (stiff-lipped naval officers, a flamboyant galactic senator's daughter, wrong-headed eggheads, a crafty mideastern-type merchant, etc.), combined with too much coincidence (a trait that badly tarnishes Niven's *Ringworld* [4-441]), and outdated social roles and values more than offset the interesting (but of course inimically dangerous) alien "Moties" and the awesome astronomical setting of the Coalsack Nebula. Nostalgia SF; compare Schmitz's *The Witches of Karres*. JN, 1974; HN, 1975.

4-440. Niven, Larry. **Neutron Star.** Ballantine, 1968, $1.50.
Eight stories from Niven's Known Space series. "Flatlander" (NN, 1967) details Beowulf Shaeffer's visit to Earth, hub of human civilization, and his surprising discovery of an antimatter planet. In "Neutron Star" (HW, 1967), Shaeffer is blackmailed into piloting a research vessel in a parabolic orbit—deep within the gravity well of a neutron star—by a Puppeteer, a tri-pedal, two-headed creature with a penchant for cowardice, whose hooves are deadly weapons. Shaeffer barely survives the tidal forces. Naturally he is perturbed to be again blackmailed, in "At the Core," into piloting an experimental vessel to the center of the galaxy. He manages to get close enough to discover that the center is exploding. Although the wavefront of the explosion will not reach human space for twenty thousand years, the Puppeteers take fright and flee the galaxy on their planet at sublight speed. Excellent hard SF.

*4-441. Niven, Larry. **Ringworld.** Ballantine, 1970, $1.25.
An enormous hoop-shaped artifact ninety million miles in radius which completely circles a star is discovered by the cowardly Puppeteers. They send two humans, Louis Wu and Teela Brown, a mad Puppeteer, Nessus, and a Kzinti, member of a carnivorous cat-like species that cannot seem to win a war, to investigate. The ring turns out to have been built by a fallen human civilization. Niven's work is extremely inventive and accurate, and his delineation of alien characters is unsurpassed. Plots, although always enjoyable, are at times contrived, as here where Teela's

wild talent for luck is used to rationalize extremely unlikely coincidences. Compare Niven's work with Hal Clement's and Poul Anderson's. HW, 1971; NW, 1970.

4-442. Niven, Larry. **Tales of Known Space: The Universe of Larry Niven.** Ballantine, 1975, $1.50.
Contains thirteen stories, several of which have already appeared in other collections, from Niven's future history, Known Space. More importantly, this volume contains the key to this series, which incorporates events from 1975 to 3100 and spans half the galaxy, in the form of a schematic chronology (similar to that found in Heinlein's works), an introduction and afterword by Niven commenting on the series, a bibliography of series stories, a colorful star map of series locations on the book's cover and an explanatory note by the artist, Rick Sternback, and inside cover art by Bonnie Dalzell depicting the body and skeleton of the alien Kzinti. Other works of Known Space include *World of Ptavvs* [4-443], *Protector*, *A Gift from Earth*, *Ringworld* [4-441], the stories in *Neutron Star* [4-440] and *The Long Arm of Gil Hamilton* (Ballantine, 1976, $1.50). Also included in this unique and valuable volume are notes to each story and a general Niven bibliography.

4-443. Niven, Larry. **World of Ptavvs.** Ballantine, 1966, $1.50.
A dangerous alien (a slaver of the Puppeteer stories) is freed from "stasis" after a billion years. A human forms a mental link with the alien, but is submerged by its superior mind. The alien is eventually destroyed and the human makes peace with the intruder in his own mind. NN, 1966. *Protector* (Ballantine, 1973; $1.50) follows in a similar mode. A human is converted to an alien philosophy and technology by the forerunner of an expanding race near the center of the galaxy. His efforts become directed toward preparing humanity for the probable invasion. The novel's first half initially appeared in 1967. HN, 1974. Both novels, part of the Known Space series, hold the optimistic view that humanity will prevail, although it will have to work at success.

4-444. Nolan, William F., and George Clayton Johnson. **Logan's Run.** Dial, 1967. Bantam, $1.50.
In a computer data-netted future civilization, Logan "runs" from the death sentence everyone receives on their twenty-first birthday—a means of planetary population control. Logan hopes to find the half-legendary "Sanctuary" where he can live his life to its natural limit. He succeeds. Burgeoning world population may give future civilizations bizarre constraints. A patently illogical yarn, full of time-worn SF tropes, that many feel will make a swell awful-warning movie. Compare Blish and Knight's *Torrent of Faces* [4-81] and del Rey's *Eleventh Commandment* [4-204].

*4-445. Norton, Andre (pseud. of Alice Mary Norton). **Star Man's Son.** Harcourt, 1952, $5.95. (Variant title: *Daybreak 2250 A.D.*, 1962).

Two hundred years after atomic war, Fors, member of knowledge-collecting clan, travels to remains of New York (?) with telepathic bobcat pet. Among other adventures he unites remaining human tribes against mutant rat-men, thereby bringing peace treaty among human tribes. Radioactivity mutations might be mostly evil. In post-catastrophe civilization, lost knowledge will be important. Effective narrative; fine anthropological insight for the fundamentals of human civilization. Compare Brackett's *Long Tomorrow* [4-98] and Miller's *A Canticle for Liebowitz* [4-424].

4-446. Oliver, Chad. **Another Kind.** Ballantine, 1955.

Seven stories, including "Rite of Passage," about how "primitive" civilization can be far more advanced than high technologies; "Scientific Method," an ingenious first-contact story; and "Night," about an American Indian who prepares a primitive planet against the rapine of colonization by Earth. Fascinating anthropological epitomes; termed by Anthony Boucher the outstanding SF book of 1955.

4-447. Oliver, Chad. **The Edge of Forever.** Sherbourne, 1971, $7.50.

Six stories of "anthropological science fiction" from 1952 to 1959. "Transfusion" is about the seeding of Earth with mankind; another story of interest is the poignant "Didn't He Ramble," in which a rich jazz buff recreates an asteroid Storyville, complete with android musicians and live call girls, to escape his mundane life on Earth. Also includes biographical sketch of Oliver and checklist of his works by William F. Nolan. Clean, expository narrative.

4-448. Oliver, Chad. **Shadows in the Sun.** Ballantine, 1954.

Paul Ellery, anthropologist, discovers that Jefferson City, Texas, is a galactic alien colony, negotiates with the aliens for possible membership in galactic civilization, and finally decides to stay on Earth as a small part of Earth's attempt to mature its civilization so it may be part of galactic society. Oliver's background in anthropology is ingeniously mined for the story. Contrast Simak's *Way Station* [4-539].

4-449. Oliver, Chad. **The Shores of Another Sea.** Signet, 1971.

Royce runs baboonery in Africa that is invaded by aliens who experiment on his partner and the baboons to try to understand the human species. Though saddened at the loss of Bob Russell, Royce understands necessity of alien experiments; doesn't report them because he will be thought mad. There must be lines of communication among all living things. Fine anthropological theory illustrated. Good expository fiction. Contrast Christopher's *The Possessors* [4-147].

*4-450. Orwell, George (U.K.). **1984.** Harcourt, 1949, $8.95. Signet, $1.25.

Mentioning *1984* is like mentioning the Bible. The title marks the triumph of the totalitarian state. Three super-powers divide the world and conduct sham wars. "Newspeak" is official language, an insidious language used to propagate lies. "Big Brother" polices you through two-way TV in your quarters. Romance is forbidden, sex a political act. Personal opinion is neutralized by brainwashing. Life is hell. One of the half-dozen most influential novels of the twentieth century. Influence on SF of social criticism is incalculable. *Animal Farm* (Harcourt, 1946, $6.95; Signet, $1.25) is only slightly less known. On a farm the swine lead the other animals in a revolt against the farmer (capitalism). When the revolution succeeds, the swine succumb to the ease and luxury to be gained by exploiting their fellows that characterized the farmer. This marvelous allegory suggests that revolution, as understood in its traditional dynamics, must always fail. It is not, in fact, revolution, but merely a change of leadership, leaving the wrongs that fostered the change unredressed. Orwell died at 46, bleakly pessimistic over mankind's chances for happiness and survival.

4-451. Pangborn, Edgar. **Davy.** St. Martin's, 1964. Ballantine, $1.25; Garland, $11.00.

On island Neonarcheos, Davy writes memoirs of life in medieval United States 300 years after nuclear holocaust, as he grows from "bondsman" to explorer interested in resuming the ascent of man. Davy is Tom Jones character. HN, NN, 1965. Beautiful heroic–romantic character study is redone in same scenario, female version, in Pangborn's *The Judgment of Eve* (Simon & Schuster, 1966. Avon, $1.95), about a woman who must choose between two fine men. Compare Miller's *A Canticle for Liebowitz* [4-424] and Roberts' *Pavane* [4-481].

*4-452. Pangborn, Edgar. **A Mirror for Observers.** Doubleday, 1954. Avon, $1.95.

For thousands of years, Martian observers chronicle and gently manipulate human history, optimistic for its destiny. Elmis (Miles), Martian, narrates life of Angelo (Abraham), human genius and potential initiator of great age of ethics for mankind, who must elude influence of bad Martian Namir and does. There is hope for mankind in its Ghandi and Martin Luther King figures. Characterization of Angelo inspirational almost as latter-day saint's life. Contrast Vonnegut's *The Sirens of Titan* [4-607]. IFA winner, 1955.

4-453. Pangborn, Edgar. **West of the Sun.** Doubleday, 1953.

An exploring starship crash lands on another planet. The explorers form a utopian colony including members of two vastly different sentient native species. Dilemma when a rescue ship comes, but all chose to remain and abandon the tyranny of Earth government. Pangborn's first novel. Good characterization; literate narrative. Compare Cooper's *A Far Sunset* [4-177] and Russell's *The Great Explosion* [4-488].

*4-454. Panshin, Alexei. **Rite of Passage.** Ace, 1968, $1.25.
To qualify for adult status in a world of the future, Mia must pass a test of survival in the wilds of an earthlike planet. She also learns about herself. Education as an initiation rite, perhaps in the form of a survival test, must be a necessity in a civilization increasingly mobile and rootless. Twentieth-century American experience is the reality analog for the fictional civilization of *Rite*. A worthy addition to the long tradition of fables that embody educational theory, going back at least as far as Rousseau's *Emile* (1762), and richly represented in modern SF. Compare Heinlein's *Starship Troopers* [4-301] and *Have Spacesuit—Will Travel* [4-298]; contrast Henderson's *Pilgrimage* [4-304]. HN, 1969; NW, 1968.

4-455. Pedlar, Kit, and Gerry Davis. (U.K.). **Mutant 59: The Plastic Eaters.** Viking, 1972, $5.95.
With *Andromeda Strain* [4-184] realism, this tells in detail of the socially devastating effects of an escaped virus, developed as an aid to pollution abatement, that eats plastic. The destruction of London's subway and public service systems is especially well developed. Despite weak characterization, a thriller and good illustration of the ecological principle that everything is related to everything else.

*4-456. Percy, Walker. **Love in the Ruins.** Farrar, 1971, $7.95. Dell, $1.50.
Scene: Southern United States in early 1980s. America is in "ruins," falling apart from decadence (novel's subtitle is "The Adventures of a Bad Catholic at a Time near the End of the World"). Bad Catholic is psychiatrist who invents "lapsometer" that cures insanity; he hopes it will cure the Western world. Meanwhile, as a widower, he pursues and finds love with Ellen. Social criticism and satire by a mainstream author. Compare Burgess's *Clockwork Orange* [4-129] and Wolfe's *Limbo* [4-629].

4-457. Phillips, Mark (pseud. of Randall Garrett and Laurence M. Janifer). **Brain Twister.** Pyramid, 1962.
A "let's find the telepaths among us" story. FBI agent Kenneth Malone heads the search and finds seven, including Miss Thompson, an old lady who is Queen Elizabeth of England and "immortal." All were found in asylums. Only Thompson is not totally insane. Story is soapish and superficially esoteric in references to Elizabethan society. HN, 1960. Sequels: *Supermind* (Pyramid, 1963); *The Impossibles* (Pyramid, 1963).

4-458. Piper, H. Beam. **Little Fuzzy.** Avon, 1962. Ace, $1.25.
In opposition to commercial interests, Jack Holloway proves the lovable "Fuzzies" are sapient. Charming exploration of question, who is "hu-

man?" Fuzzies are notable illustration of sympathetic aliens. HN, 1963. Sequel: *The Other Human Race* (Avon, 1964).

4-459. Piserchia, Doris. **Mister Justice.** Ace, 1973, $.95.
A promising first novel in which a vigilante superman capable of limited time travel returns to the past, first to bring criminals to justice, but later as their executioner when he becomes dissatisfied with official response. Intense action, a complex plot, fascinating characters, and competent writing mark the book's excellences, although a hasty, unsatisfactory conclusion, perhaps due to editorial intervention, mars the total effect.

4-460. Platt, Charles (U.K.). **Garbage World.** Berkley, 1967.
As the neat and clean agent of pleasure worlds, Oliver arrives on Kopra, garbage dump asteroid, to adjust its gravity; he falls in love with the beautiful but disgustingly filthy Juliette and escapes with whole population as asteroid explodes to rain filth back upon pleasure worlds from which it came. Bizarre sympathy with two physically filthy lovers. Mankind can adapt to its garbage.

4-461. Pohl, Frederik. **The Age of the Pussyfoot.** Trident, 1969. Gollancz, £1.25.
In this humorous, light 1966 *Galaxy* novel, Pohl gives us a well developed, somewhat utopian future scenario of a generally affluent, computer-integrated society which maximizes human freedom. In a sleeper-wakes plot, Charles Forrester, frozen at death in the twentieth century, is awakened in 2527 to face this strange world which has nearly abolished death. As he struggles to adjust, he runs afoul of a plot by a neo-Luddite and alien Sirians to destroy the computer system. It all ends well. Compare Reynolds' *Looking Backward from the Year 2000* [4-476]. NN, 1966.

4-462. Pohl, Frederik. **The Best of Frederik Pohl.** Ballantine, 1975, $1.95.
Sixteen stories, selected by Lester del Rey, originally published between 1954 and 1967. Includes "The Midas Plague" (SFHF), a classic warning about super-abundance; "Day Million," a future-shocking love story; "The Census Takers," whose job is killing surplus people in an over-crowded world; and "The Day the Martians Came," a pointed statement on racism. Also includes an overview of Pohl's career by del Rey and an afterword by Pohl on the genesis of several of the stories. A basic Pohl sampler.

4-463. Pohl, Frederik. **Drunkard's Walk.** Ballantine, 1960.
Cornut, teacher and mathematician, fights off suicidal impulses to discover that mankind has been ruled by a handful of telepathic "immortals" who seek to prevent the human species from discovering that it, too, is telepathic. Mild inebriation is interim safeguard against immor-

tals' mental control. Story is a metaphor for exploitation of mankind by conspiracy of elite.

4-464. Pohl, Frederik, and C. M. Kornbluth. **Gladiator-at-Law.** Ballantine, 1955. Bantam, $1.25.
Derivative of *The Space Merchants* [4-466]; the United States is dominated by monopoly capitalism, primarily under the control of "Green, Charlesworth," an ancient couple in giant test-tubes who date from Lincoln's time. There is a two-class system, with the affluent living in marvelous G-M-L Homes available only by contract to employees of major companies, and the poor living in "Belly Rave," today's suburbs turned to slums. Lawyer Charles Mundin fights, both in a Roman-type arena and in the stock market, for love and for control of G-M-L Homes so that all can have good housing. Well developed and interesting social background, but the story's solution, the replacing of bad company heads by good ones, seems a weak reed with which to shore up an otherwise strong attack on the economic order.

4-465. Pohl, Frederik. **Slave Ship.** Ballantine, 1957, $1.50.
The Vietnamese, driven by religious fervor, conquer nearly the entire Eastern Hemisphere; the United Nations, including the United States, are totally mobilized against them. Communication with animals is developed for use in the war, and naval Lieutenant Logan Miller is sent on a last-ditch mission, using a submarine crewed by animals, to find a secret enemy weapon that threatens to tip the stalemate so much that nuclear war is inevitable. But the enemy is itself reeling under the weapon—an alien life form attracted by telepaths—and this discovery ends the war. Full of neat futurist ideas, like most Pohl novels, but not his best writing. A note on the science of animal communications is included. Contrast Merle's *The Day of the Dolphin* [4-418].

*4-466. Pohl, Frederik, and C. M. Kornbluth. **The Space Merchants.** Ballantine, 1953, $1.50.
Advertising is king in a near-future United States dominated by monopoly capitalism and divided into a small, relatively affluent professional and business class and a large class of poor industrial serfs and captive consumers. Against this well-developed background, "star-class copysmith" Mitchell Courtenay heads his firm's campaign to sell the difficult colonization of Venus to the public. But enemies shanghai Courtenay, forcing him to work as a laborer; unrepentant, he uses the underground of a persecuted environmentalist group (the Conservationists or "Consies") to regain his former position. But the love of his "Consie" wife and the knowledge that big business doesn't play by the rules causes him to lose his idealism; Mitch joins the underground and absconds with the Venus rocket in the hope of saving that planet from man's exploitation. A fine satire on advertising, and good social commentary, but its ending begs the question. Contrast Brunner's *The Sheep Look Up* [4-115].

4-467. Pohl, Frederik, and C. M. Kornbluth. **Wolfbane.** Ballantine, 1959, $1.50. Garland, $11.00.

Perhaps the most atypical novel by these creative collaborators; oriental religion, western technology, and social Darwinism are blended in a Campbell-like tale of Earth's removal from orbit by alien, pyramid-shaped robots who use the malnourished, culturally involuted human survivors as food-producing machine components. Of course, a maverick human makes a revolution, destroys the pyramids, and again finds the path of human progress. Unless intended as a Coblentz-type satire cum SF parody, the work suffers from numerous writing faults; a redundant, overly slow first half; a too-compressed second half; numerous hanging threads, problems of motivation, and typos that invite a thorough rewrite.

4-468. Priest, Christopher (U.K.). **Darkening Island.** Harper, 1972. Manor Books, $1.25. (British title: *Fugue for a Darkening Land*, Faber, 1972).

In the documentary style of Christopher's *No Blade of Grass* [4-146] and with the gut punches of Tucker's *The Long Loud Silence* [4-586], Priest portrays the struggles of an uncommitted man, Alan Whitman, his frigid wife, and his beloved daughter as they are buffeted across an England fractured by civil and racial warfare. A nuclear self-devastated Africa has loosed a vast migration of blacks, thousands of whom reach England, only to be repressed by a rightist government; the blacks rebel and occupy British homes. The government and people split on the "Afrim" issue, a three-sided war results, and civil authority falls. The brutal shock of losing his family finally forces Alan to hate; now committed, he takes up the gun. Realistic detail, coupled with a nonlinear structure, produce a work of exceptional power. John W. Campbell Award nominee, 1973.

4-469. Priest, Christopher (U.K.). **The Inverted World.** Harper, 1974, $7.95. Popular Lib., $1.25.

Well-written hard SF built around an image as unique and as powerful as Clarke's *Rendezvous with Rama* [4-157]. A city is winched over tracks laid before and removed behind as it crosses Eurasia on a fantastically distorted, hyperboloid Earth. Conflict erupts as the city approaches the Atlantic; conservatives want to continue the herculean trek, keeping pace with a moving zone of normal space-time midway between a dopplerized past and future, while radicals want the city to stop. Fascinating, well-worked-out details worthy of Niven's *Ringworld* [4-441] and Silverberg's *The World Inside* [4-532]. Effective illustrations. HN, 1975.

4-470. Pynchon, Thomas. **Gravity's Rainbow.** Viking, 1973, $3.95, $15.00. Bantam, $2.50.

During the V-2 seige of London in World War II, PISES (Psychological Intelligence Schemes for Expediting Surrender), a psychological warfare unit composed of assorted cranks, Pavlovian behaviorists, statisticians, and spiritualists, learns that one of it members, Lt. Tyrone Slothrop, may be a key to the rocket attacks. In fact, PISES learns, Slothrop's sexual expeditions climax at sites that exactly anticipate where the next rocket will fall. A Slothrop erection lewdly, comically, Freudianly, trivially, and literally symbolizes the launched rocket. PISES wants to experiment. Slothrop refuses and becomes a fugitive from his own side and the enemy's as well. All hunt him. Paranoia is endemic in an age of science and war. SF invested with black comedy, narrative virtuousity, and intricate symbolism from the mainstream. Compare Aldiss's *Barefoot in the Head* [4-2], Vonnegut's *Sirens of Titan* [4-607], and the "New Wave" mood in general. NN, 1973. JN, 1973.

4-471. Rand, Ayn. **Anthem.** Caxton, 1946, $3.25. Signet, $.95.
Written in 1937. In far future after world war, all trace and memory of the concept "I" are abolished in a collectivist dystopia. Then Equality 7-2521, a genius, rediscovers electricity, is condemned to death by "Council of Scholars," and escapes with beautiful woman to forest. He discovers "I" with her; renames himself "Prometheus" and vows to gather new society of self-conscious people once more. Parable of Rand's once enormously influential "objectivism." The individual is all. Narrative is fiery, moralistic, and polished. Compare Silverberg's *A Time of Changes* [4-528].

4-472. Rand, Ayn. **Atlas Shrugged.** Random, 1957, $12.95. Signet, $2.50.
John Galt and cohorts embrace "objectivist" philosophy, withdrawing from world that doesn't appreciate their independent genius and towering ambition. Civilization crumbles, while in their mountain retreat the objectivists prepare to rebuild it with their vision in control. *Atlas* is vehicle for Rand's famous philosophy of ruthlessly rational individualism. Long speeches and multiple subplots make long, intellectually melodramatic book. Compare Heinlein's *Stranger in a Strange Land* [4-302].

4-473. Rankine, John (pseud. of Douglas R. Mason) (U.K.). **Binary Z.** Dobson, 1969, £1.75.
F. S. Hartley and Britomart Gleave, British public school principal and English teacher respectively, find identity and love and resolve to escape from their institutionalized lives when a hostile and indestructible alien robot is unearthed in new school excavation. Hartley defuses robot to save Britomart, but the emphasis is on misery of sensitive people caught in stupidity of educational bureaucracy. Excellent narrative; serious character study. Compare Kingsley Amis's *Lucky Jim*.

4-474. Reed, Kit (U.K.) **Armed Camps.** Dutton, 1970, $4.95.
The setting is a chaotic future United States under military dictatorship

and involved in a destructive, endless war. Anne represents the fanatic political left, Danny the fanatic militaristic right. Narrative alternates their separate careers that merge only at the black comic end of the novel when the two will combine brief effort to unleash a nuclear holocaust. The story is gloomy allegory that finds militarism and pacificism unlikely to prevail to save civilization. Recommended by Frank Kermode, major literary critic. Compare Brunner's *The Sheep Look Up* [4-115].

4-475. Reynolds, Mack. **Commune 2000 A.D.** Bantam, 1974, $.95.
Another of Reynolds' future scenarios as he continues his exploration of the world of 2000. The U.S. social order, as in *Looking Backward* [4-476], is based on a universal guaranteed income; but here, the state has not withered away. Ethnologist Ted Savain is sent by the ruling elite to spy on the burgeoning commune movement, a cover for revolutionary libertarianism. But the elite's plan to usurp the existing meritocracy radicalizes Ted, who joins the movement. Lots of action and sex. Compare with Theobald's *Teg's 1994* (1972).

4-476. Reynolds, Mack. **Looking Backward from the Year 2000.** Ace, 1973.
Excellent future utopian scenario in the style of Bellamy, built on current futurist writings. Includes author's introduction, citing sources. Rich capitalist Julian West freezes down for thirty-three years, awakening in a more rational, humanistic world where exponential growth of knowledge has made him hopelessly obsolete. Past and future are juxtaposed through flashbacks. Could be a fictionalized text to read along with works of futurists Toffler, Theobald, and Bell. Compliments as a positive to the negative of Brunner's *The Shockwave Rider* [4-116]. Compare with Le Guin's *The Dispossessed* [4-371] and contrast with Anderson's *There Will Be Time* [4-26]. Strictly an idea, not an action, work.

4-477. Reynolds, Mack. **Of Godlike Power.** Belmont, 1966.
Ezekiel Joshua Tubber, preaching a naturalistic, humanistic doctrine, throws the world into turmoil by "hexing" women's makeup, jukeboxes, parking meters, and the mass media through his paranormal powers. Lots of ideas in this mixture of religion, ecology, economics, politics, and life styles as Tubber's utopian speeches are contrasted with existing conditions; unfortunately, writing is trite, plot is uninspired. A vehicle for Reynolds' beliefs, which are better developed in later works.

4-478. Reynolds, Mack. **Tomorrow Might Be Different.** Ace, 1975, $1.25.
In near future, Russian and Chinese communism succeed, causing economic depression in the Western world, especially because of Russian tourism. Mike Edmunds is an agent sent to Russia to start a "religion of moderation"—to stifle the devastating tourism. When he begins to suc-

ceed, Russia's premier joins him to prevent analogous cultural submersion of Russia by Chinese tourists. Communist economy will triumph. Interesting ideological yarn.

4-479. Rimmer, Robert H. **The Harrad Experiment.** Sherbourne, 1966. Bantam, $1.50.
At mythical Harrad College (near Harvard), 400 young men and women matched by computer are placed in a state of complete cohabitation, a mini-utopia of total cultural liberation—as an experiment. Story examines the sexual mores of Western world. Rimmer follows this up in *Proposition 31*, a novel about a law allowing multiple marriage. These novels were popular avant-garde in mid-sixties and sold extremely well. Accurately predicted trends that became actual in the mid-seventies. Contrast Wylie's *The Disappearance* [4-634] and Russ's *The Female Man* [4-485].

4-480. Roberts, Keith (U.K.). **The Inner Wheel.** Doubleday, 1970.
Jimmy Stringer is the "middle man" for an emerging "gestalt" of psi-talented people, most interesting of whom is Elizabeth Maynard, whose life as secret telepath is sensitively told. Psi gestalts join others around the world to avert World War III. Determined character development and clean narrative refresh hackneyed material. Compare Sturgeon's *More Than Human* [4-565] and Morgan's *The New Minds* (1967).

*4-481. Roberts, Keith (U.K.). **Pavane.** Doubleday, 1968. Berkley, $1.25.
Our world has ended in atomic catastrophe, but man, forgetful of his earlier historic cycle, arises again, recapitulating his development until the year 1588, when Queen Elizabeth is assassinated and the Spanish Armada is victorious. As a result, the Renaissance and Industrial Revolution are delayed until late in the twentieth century, as the Catholic Church, truly universal, limits technological development during an extended period of feudalism. *Pavane* provides loosely connected sketches of that rebirth, excelling in the detailed workings of 1968 technology and society in Britain, with rail-less steam trains, communication by semaphore, fortified castles, and an inquisition, as the hegemony of the Church is challenged and ended by inevitable progress. But the technological hiatus was all to the good, argue the Fairies, an ancient race that remembers the prior cycle, for the Church may have "given man time to reach a little higher toward true Reason. . . . Did she oppress? Did she hang and burn? A little, yes. But there was no Belsen. No Buchenwald." And perhaps no fusion-fired death this time. A challenging thesis in a beautiful, lyrical work too long unrecognized. Compare Miller's *A Canticle for Liebowitz* [4-424] and Blish's *Doctor Mirabilis* (1964); contrast Brunner's *Times Without Number* (1969).

4-482. Robinson, Frank M. **The Power.** Lippincott, 1956.

A "psi emerging" story. Tanner and Nordlund are among some psychologists testing for telekinesis. The "power" exists, but who has it? Nordlund (Adam Hart) does, and tries to keep it to himself. Tanner hunts the power holder, miraculously escaping many near-fatal "accidents," secretly caused by Nordlund. He has Nordlund killed after realizing that he, Tanner, has power, too; it takes a superman to catch a superman. Story ends with Tanner contemplating fun of playing god. First-rate adventure yarn; basis for fair SF film.

4-483. Roshwald, Mordecai. **Level 7.** McGraw, 1959. Signet, $.95.
Officer X-127, of an undisclosed nationality, writes a diary recording his fateful duties and short life in the deepest level of a 4,200-foot bomb shelter—"Level 7"—where he helps fire the missiles and then chronicles the gradual destruction of the upper levels down to his own. An awful-warning story. Recommended by Bertrand Russell, J. B. Priestley, and Linus Pauling. Compare Farjeon's *Death of a World* [4-237], Shute's *On the Beach* [4-520], and Lem's *Memoirs Found in a Bathtub* [4-389].

4-484. Russ, Joanna. **And Chaos Died.** Ace, 1970, $1.25.
Jai Vedh is an Earthman marooned on lost Earth colony where vast unnamed beings taught inhabitants psi powers. Jai acquires them, too, and they nearly drive him insane as he returns to Earth. Returning to colony, he learns to live with them and has chance for happiness. Fitful narrative creates image of Jai's chaotic mental state upon first possession of psi. Compare Brunner's *The Whole Man* [4-119], Sellings' *The Uncensored Man* [4-502], and Blish's *Jack of Eagles* [4-79].

4-485. Russ, Joanna. **The Female Man.** Bantam, 1975, $1.25.
Janet Evason is from Whileaway, an "Earth" of the future populated solely by women who live, reproduce, work, and play in a utopian society. Janet time-travels to present-day Earth where her relationship with Jeannine and Joanna (?) illustrates the appalling insanity of a male chauvinist society. Compare theme with Le Guin's *The Dispossessed* [4-371]. Compelling story exploits variety of points of view and narrative tactics.

4-486. Russ, Joanna. **Picnic on Paradise.** Ace, 1968, $.95. Gregg, 1976, price not set.
Trans Temporal Corporation time-travels Alyx, a twenty-six year old woman, reminiscent of Zelazny's Conrad in *This Immortal* [4-650], out of ancient Greek civilization to become agent of rescue for tourists trapped in commercial war on planet "Paradise"—preserved for tourism. She must conduct eight men and women across mountains of Paradise in winter. She succeeds, losing only four. SF paraphernalia are incidental. Intent is to contrast people with survival competencies against softer breeds of post-scarcity civilization. Women do better than men. Polished

narrative that brought raves from Delaney, Leiber, Sturgeon, Anderson, and Clement. HN, 1968.

4-487. Russell, Bertrand (U.K.). **Nightmares of Eminent Persons.** Bodley Head, 1954.
Twelve story pieces, including the *1984*-like "Eisenhower's Nightmare: The McCarthy—Malenkov Pact," and "Dr. Southport Vulpes's Nightmare: The Victory of Mind over Matter" about the ascent of the robot machine age. Satire by an enormously erudite and seasoned spectator of modern man.

4-488. Russell, Eric Frank (U.K.). **The Great Explosion.** Dodd, 1962. Ballantine, $1.95.
Faster-than-light drive allows Earth's dissidents to colonize far-flung worlds. Four hundred years later Earth's ambassador sets out with military vessel to bring four such worlds into the Terran empire for "mutual defense." They find the planet of Buddhists and Mohammedans empty. On the planets settled by convicts, nudist health lovers, and "Gands" (people who say "no" to all forms of tyranny), the mythology of Terran aegis is rejected in vignettes of surgically deft satire. Corporate government is nonsense. Fortunately, stellar distance will make it virtually impossible. Slickly told; picaresque; deeply satisfying. Expansion of ". . . . And Then There Were None" (1951, SFHF).

4-489. Russell, Eric Frank (U.K.). **Men, Martians, and Machines.** Roy, 1956. Dobson, £2.00.
Four stories from an early 1940 SF *Astounding* series. Jay Score is a humanoid robot with human emotions. In company with humans and chess-playing octopoid Martians he adventures around the stars. Well-written parody with good stereotyping (with a difference) of characters. Representative of one of the true pulp masters, although his best short fiction is yet to be collected.

4-490. Russell, Eric Frank. (U.K.) **Sinister Barrier.** Fantasy Press, 1950.
Revised from its original appearance in the initial (March 1939) issue of *Unknown*, this novel relies on a now hackneyed theme, the idea that humans are pets of aliens, an idea popularized by Charles Fort. A number of distinguished scientists die, and the hero of this suspense novel discovers and eventually destroys the cause of their death, the Vitons who parasitically feed upon the nervous energy of their human cattle. Well-paced adventure but little more.

4-491. Russell, Eric Frank (U.K.). **Wasp.** Avalon, 1957. Dobson, £2.00.
Outclassed Terra enlists James Mowry to pose as a Sirian humanoid and conduct a campaign of sabotage on the enemy planet Jaimel as his part in an interstellar war. Single-handed, he reduces the planet's military, police, and intelligence services to a state of confusion. Fast action, effec-

tive secret agent scenario, perhaps inspired by Allied World War II espionage activity. Compare Laumer's Retief series [4-368].

4-492. Saberhagen, Fred. **Berserker.** Ballantine, 1967.
Picaresque space opera stories depicting threat to life in the universe by planetoid-sized "Berserkers"—super war machines dedicated to the extinction of all living things. Superficially supports establishment/capitalistic ethos; subliminally raises nice questions about the meaning of life, individuality, nobility, sacrifice of self. Combines features of E. E. Smith and Ray Bradbury in setting and theme. Story told by member of mysterious, sympathetic but pacifist species that possesses modified oracular powers. Sequel: *Brother Assassin* (Ballantine, 1969).

4-493. St. Clair, Margaret. **Change the Sky and Other Stories.** Ace, 1974, $.95.
Eighteen SF and fantasy stories, from 1951 to 1961. Title story: a man has an artist create the ideal world for which he has been searching the universe all his life. Instead, he finds a hell reliving the childhood he has fled from. General theme of collection: if you seek for something and find it, it probably isn't what you thought you were looking for. Other stories of interest include "An Old-Fashioned Bird Christmas," "An Egg a Month from All Over," and "Marriage Manual."

4-494. St. Clair, Margaret. **The Dolpins of Altair.** Dell, 1967.
Altair civilization seeded prehistoric Earth with sentient life. Dolphins and humans are destined to combine. Twentieth-century man's pollution of seas and experimentation on dolphins give rise to conspiracy between a few humans and dolphins to bring this about as Earth goes through geological upheaval. Dolphins are fully sentient. Excellent apologia for dolphinology. Social criticism. Compare Merle's *Day of the Dolphin* [4-418].

4-495. St. Clair, Margaret. **Sign of the Labrys.** Bantam, 1963.
Sam Sewell and Despoina are of the "Wicca," super-normals, viewed as "witches," immune to fungus plagues that kill millions. Death reaches even into the elaborate underground shelters of the Wicca, who survive to lead a new mankind again to the Earth's surface. The species is hard to destroy. Remarkable for Dantesque underground setting.

4-496. Sanborn, Robin. **The Book of Stier.** Berkley, 1971.
The music of the mysterious Richard Stier is sweeping the nation, and Paul Odeon, half ad-man, half beatnik, is chosen as his prophet. The resulting free-loving youth movement, stoned on hallucinogenic "white clay," sweeps away or co-opts every social institution. Odeon's search for the elusive Stier ends with the discovery that the whole thing is a bid for power by "The Nine." Odeon is destroyed by fans in Stier's place, and Canada annexes the now-incapacitated United States. Extrapolation

from the Beatles phenomenon. Compare with Spinrad's "The Big Flash" [4-553] and Heinlein's *Stranger in a Strange Land* [4-302].

4-497. Sapir, Richard, and Warren Murphy. **Created, the Destroyer.** Pinnacle, 1971, $1.25.
Remo Williams is ex-cop transformed after years of training by Chiun, eighty-year-old Sinanju assassin, into super killing machine for use by U.S. President when legal means fail. Remo is logical epitome of "plausible" limits of human strength and mental control—after Chiun. Readable as "serious" or marvelous parody of super-agent fiction. Very popular. The first of the Destroyer series, which had reached volume 21 by 1975.

4-498. Sarban (pseud. of John W. Wall) (U.K.). **The Sound of his Horn.** Ballantine, 1960.
Englishman Alan Querdilion, escaping a Nazi POW camp in 1943, falls into a future alternate Earth where the Germans have won World War II. Living in decadent baronal splendor on feudal estates, the German rulers blend their pagan past and racist beliefs in a sadistic and ruthless New Order with a genetically debased "under-men" caste (the remnants of "inferior races"), humans conditioned to behave like animals, and hunts using social dissidents as prey. Alan inevitably becomes such a prey and only returns to our world through the self-sacrifice of a fellow victim. A rural dystopia in sharp contrast with Dick's *The Man in the High Castle* [4-211]. Also compare Spinrad's *Iron Dream* [4-552].

4-499. Schmitz, James H. **The Universe against Her.** Ace, 1964.
Light, humorous adventure of Telzey Amberdon, individualistic and cute heroine, who first joins the crest cats of Jontarou, intelligent beings treated as big game, in upsetting the Establishment and then uses her newly acquired psionic powers to flout the bureaucratic Psychology Service. [Not seen.]

4-500. Schmitz, James H. **The Witches of Karres.** Chilton, 1966.
The captain of an old tramp starship rescues three "witch" children and returns them to Karres. He then becomes involved in cosmic adventures ending with his saving mankind, with the children's aid, from the clutches of a maniacal computer and a race of lizard conquerors. Between crises the honest captain, a disdainer of sex and evil thoughts, smokes cigarettes and drinks coffee (perhaps pondering why mankind has evolved over the centuries into the stereotypes of early twentieth-century pulp fiction). Entertaining, especially for juveniles. HN, 1967.

4-501. Sellings, Arthur (pseud. of Robert Arthur Ley) (U.K.). **Telepath.** Ballantine, 1962. (British title: *The Silent Speaker*, 1965. Dobson, £1.75).
Arnold and Claire discover they are telepathic, have trouble understanding it and convincing others of it. They learn to teach it to others and

mankind gets a new destiny. Well told. Good characterization. Compare Brunner's *The Whole Man* [4-119] and del Rey's *Pstalemate* [4-206].

4-502. Sellings, Arthur (pseud. of Robert Arthur Ley) (U.K.). **The Uncensored Man.** Berkley, 1964. Dobson, £1.75.
Super-alien "solvers" make a breakthrough to Mark Anders, who discovers that his consciousness has been masked from its potential full range of psi powers. All mankind have it and will soon be in touch with the ultimate mind of the universe with aid of "solvers." Excellent suspense; effective weave of British Romantic and Victorian poetry (Wordsworth and Arnold).

4-503. Serling, Rod. **Stories from the Twilight Zone.** Bantam, 1960, $1.25.
Six stories from the TV series which won three consecutive Hugos for best dramatic presentation (1960–1962). Includes "The Mighty Casey," about a robot baseball pitcher who gets a heart and goes into social work. Slick entertainments in the Hitchcock mold often considered trite by SF insiders. Two other similar volumes of *Twilight Zone* stories have appeared.

4-504. Seymour, Alan (U.K.). **The Coming Self-Destruction of the United States of America.** Souvenir, 1969.
Narrator is British. Story told through bits and fragments of diaries and letters left in rubble of United States. Cause of catastrophe is relatively effective black revolution led by "Hero." Black Professor Braintree is sociologist writer of many of the fragments. Black nation flourishes for a time. Despite sympathy for this development, there is destruction for all in the end. Violent revolution is destined to failure. Painstakingly thought out and well written. Contrast Allighan's *Verwoerd—The End* [4-13].

4-505. Shaw, Bob (U.K.). **Ground Zero Man.** Avon, 1971.
Lucas Hutchman, a mathematical genius, develops a machine to destroy all nuclear weapons. He serves notice to the world's governments, then goes underground, suffers, but finally destroys the stockpiles. Alas, governments find new ways to wage war, but Hutchman finds happiness in his failure and sees flaw in his misplaced social consciousness: successful species have numerous members, so many can be spared to die. Taut suspense, sophisticated action. Contrast Harrison's *The Daleth Effect* [4-288].

*4-506. Shaw, Bob (U.K.). **Other Days, Other Eyes.** Ace, 1972, $.95.
Based on Shaw's story "Light of Other Days" (NN, 1966), a picaresque novel of the effects of "slow glass" upon people and institutions in the modern world. "Slow glass" slows down light: For example, five-minute glass will reveal what's taking place in front of it five minutes after the

event is complete. Novel must be read to appreciate marvelous implications of such an effect. One of the greatest SF gimmicks. Very satisfactory narrative. Epitomizes Sturgeon's requirement for SF: Introduce one revolutionary factor into an otherwise familiar world.

4-507. Shaw, Bob (U.K.). **The Palace of Eternity.** Ace, 1969. Pan, £.30.
Species of nonmaterial beings cohabit with material life forms, serving as their "souls" during life and as their collective spirits after death. But humans are destroying their "souls" in an interstellar war. A new kind of human evolves who can communicate between men and their "souls," solving problem. First half good, solid Shaw action, but second half lags, and ending is letdown. Metaphysical viewpoint may interest some.

4-508. Shaw, Bob (U.K.). **The Two-Timers.** Ace, 1968. Gollancz, £1.25; Pan, £.25.
A disintegrating marriage is the setting for a bizarre time-travel story. A man's guilt over his wife's death drives him to travel back in time to prevent it, thus creating an alternate universe. Here, he plans to kill his other self and reclaim wife, but time travel makes this universe unstable, forcing his return to his own time. His other self and wife reconcile and save their marriage. Well written, with relationships within this unique triangle especially notable.

4-509. Sheckley, Robert. **Can You Feel Anything When I Do This?** Doubleday, 1971. DAW, $.95.
Sixteen stories, from 1961 to 1971, mostly SF, illustrative of the more recent, maturer Sheckley. Still, despite their polish and more varied writing techniques, many lack the freshness of his earlier works. Better stories include the title story, about Rom, a sophisticated, sentient vacuum cleaner who falls in love with a frigid housewife; "The Cruel Equations," a traditional Sheckley story involving a logic duel between a space explorer trapped outside his camp and his guardian robot who refuses him admittance without proof of identity; and "Tripout," the spaced-out adventures of an alien tourist in New York.

4-510. Sheckley, Robert. **Citizen in Space.** Ballantine, 1956.
Twelve stories, the best of which are "The Accountant," "Hunting Problem," "The Luckiest Man in the World," "The Mountain Without a Name," "Something for Nothing," and "A Ticket to Tranai." Written with the ingenuity and clean style typical of early Sheckley, they often employ traditional SF situations to comment on man and his behavior, in the manner of Bradbury and Vonnegut. For example, in "The Mountain Without a Name," first a planet, then a galaxy instruct proud mankind about his unsavory self by "spitting him out" to die in space, while in "Hunting Problem," a first-contact story is given a unique twist by having an alien Boy Scout win his achievement badge by hunting a wild "Mirach" (a human explorer) and taking its hide (his uniform).

4-511. Sheckley, Robert. **Dimensions of Miracles.** Dell, 1968.
Carmody wins Galactic Sweepstakes Prize, a protean creature of considerable intelligence and wit; meanwhile, he discovers galaxy is bureaucracy. To return to Earth he must travel with his "prize" from one probable Earth to another, from one with intelligent dinosaurs, to one with a "nagging" city, to one with planet-building contractor whose customer was God. Always death stalks Carmody in picaresque adventures that are comic and satiric, ending with his rejection of Earth, and beginning of new outlook.

4-512. Sheckley, Robert. **Immortality, Inc.** Bantam, 1959. (Expansion of *Immortality Delivered*, Bouregy, 1958).
Science has verified an afterlife and corporations peddle it in 2110, the year Thomas Blaine awakes after being snatched from a 1958 death for a company's ad campaign. It's a future familiar to Sheckley readers—cynical, impersonal, avaricious, full of mayhem and human hunts—and the anachronistic and shallow Blaine barely copes. He is led through a tortuous and surprising plot, encountering real ghosts, zombies, and spirits, and finally obtains self-understanding. A well-written and often witty novel of social and philosophical comment; compare Pohl and Kornbluth's *The Space Merchants* [4-466] and Farmer's *Night of Light* [4-241]. HN, 1959.

4-513. Sheckley, Robert. **Journey beyond Tomorrow.** Signet, 1963. Gollancz, £1.40.
Humorous social satire, still relevant today, in the form of oral accounts of the journey of Joenes, a young Candide from Manituatua, who leaves his simple island home in the year 2000 to travel through the United States and U.S.S.R. to seek his fortune. Government, the military, academe, various idealisms, the police, psychiatry, and many more are lampooned as Joenes is buffeted by events leading to a cataclysmic accidental war between elements of the United States defense system that destroys civilization. Returning to the Pacific islands, Joenes and his beatnik friend, Lum, become the prophets of a new nontechnological civilization. Contrast Heinlein's *Stranger in a Strange Land* [4-302] and Vonnegut's *Cat's Cradle* [4-605].

4-514. Sheckley, Robert. **Notions: Unlimited.** Bantam, 1960.
Twelve stories, from 1952 to 1957, that span Sheckley's rich early career. Superior efforts include "Watchbird" (1953), which warns against trying to solve human problems with machines; "Paradise II" (1954), about a planet of the dead whose posthumous technology terrifyingly traps two human explorers; "Native Problem" (1956), with an expatriate Earthman mistaken for a native by colonists wanting to settle on his lonely world; "Dawn Invader" (1957), which rebuts the Darwinian notion that alien races can't coexist; "The Language of Love," which teaches that the

over-intellectualization of love can inhibit it. Like much early Sheckley, deceptively bland but definitely mind-sticking.

4-515. Sheckley, Robert. **Pilgrimage to Earth.** Bantam, 1957.
Fifteen stories, most from 1954 to 1956. In "The Academy," a dystopian vision of thought control, ubiquitous "sanity meters" monitor humanity, weeding out individualism and inventiveness, the misfits being locked away in enforced sleep. The brilliant title story depicts a cynical future Earth where dreams are for sale; the resulting disillusionment is free. Sheckley's humor finds voice in "The Body," about the transplantation of a famous scientist's brain into a dog's body, and in "Milk Run," where the AAA Ace Interplanetary Decontamination Service gets fouled up with a spaceship full of alien livestock. Also contains the horrific "Fear in the Night." A full spectrum of the unique Sheckley talent.

4-516. Sheckley, Robert. **Untouched by Human Hands.** Ballantine, 1954.
Thirteen stories from 1952 and 1953. Includes the realistic "Seventh Victim," where humans hunt one another for sport; "The Monsters," a study in cultural relativism; the dystopian "Cost of Living," an extrapolation of our debt-ridden consumer society; "Specialist," about a spaceship composed of an organic community; and the humorous title story, which proves that one man's meat is another man's poison when two lost humans discover a warehouse full of alien goods. A good mix of Sheckley wit, poignancy, and insight; his first collection which marked him as a major new SF author.

4-517. Sheriff, Robert Cedric (U.K.). **The Hopkins Manuscript.** Macmillan, 1939, $4.95.
Memoir of Edgar Hopkins, a very ordinary British middle-class gentleman, who details the events leading to and following the collision of Earth and Moon. Ironically, it's the greed-induced warfare over the crashed Moon's extensive resources, now filling the North Atlantic basin, that finally destroys civilization. Anticipates the later British catastrophe stories of Wyndham, Christopher, and Ballard, while following the tradition of Wells' *War of the Worlds* [2-143]. In the 1963 reprint, John Gassner discusses Sheriff's career in an introduction and George Gamow critiques the novel's science in an epilogue; also, excellent illustrations by Joe Mugnaini. A superior work.

4-518. Shiras, Wilmar H. **Children of the Atom.** Gnome, 1953.
Derived from a late 1940s' *Astounding* series, including "In Hiding" (SFHF). Radiation from atomic plant explosion in 1958 causes birth of about thirty super-intelligent children who "hide" from recognition until, after uniting with the help of a psychiatrist, they decide to reveal themselves and re-enter society to make a better world for all. In-

telligence is worthless in selfish uses. Mankind will readily accept aid from geniuses!(?) Energetic narrative. Compare George O. Smith's *The Fourth "R"* [4-549] and Sturgeon's *More Than Human* [4-565].

4-519. Shute, Nevil (pseud. of Nevil Shute Norway) (U.K.). **In the Wet.** Morrow, 1953. Ballantine, $.95.

In Australia, a Church of England priest makes journal account of the future of British Commonwealth as heard from dying man, to be reincarnated as David Anderson. England will decline; Australia will rise (population 100,000,000 by the year 2000) and become leader of Commonwealth. England, Australia, and Canada to be administered by Governors General, taking workload from monarchy. Socialism will decline, replaced by Millian poly-vote system according to individual achievement. Utopian extrapolation of British empire's best (realistically) possible future. Good writing by mainstream novelist.

*4-520. Shute, Nevil (pseud. of Nevil Shute Norway) (U.K.). **On the Beach.** Morrow, 1957, $7.95. Ballantine, $1.75.

In the atomic age, even the little nations have the bomb and the inevitable happens—a nuclear war releasing so much radioactivity that the planet is doomed. A British military unit waits for the end in Australia. An awful-warning story. Plausible world political scenario; fine suspense. Extraordinary popularity as book and film. Compare Wylie's *Triumph* [4-636].

4-521. Silverberg, Robert. **The Book of Skulls.** Scribner, 1972, $5.95.

Four young men, an intellectual Jew, a rich eastern WASP, a homosexual Italian, and an ex-Kansas farm boy, set out to achieve immortality as described in the long-lost Book of Skulls. The men find a sect, the Keepers of the Skulls, in the Arizona desert, that *may* give them eternal life. The catch: one must voluntarily give up life and another must be murdered if the remaining two are to achieve their goal. Well-written, suspenseful story, very rich in characterization. NN, 1972.

4-522. Silverberg, Robert. **Downward to the Earth.** Doubleday, 1970.

Ex-colonial official Gundersen, a pilgrim driven by past sins committed during Earth's domination of Belzagor, progresses toward his rebirth with that newly independent planet's yin-yang dominant species, the carnivorous, ape-like Sulidoror and the herbivorous, elephantine Nildoror. A well-written, several-layered work full of symbolism, anti-imperialism, and anti-ethnocentrism. What really separates man from other animals, and man from himself? Contrast the more Westernized view in Clarke's *2001: A Space Odyssey* [4-158].

*4-523. Silverberg, Robert. **Dying Inside.** Scribner, 1972, $6.95. Ballantine, $1.25.

David Selig was born a superman; his telepathic powers made the world his oyster, as he gulped down the mental images of others and snapped up easy money. But he finally sees himself, in the mind of his drug-tripping girl friend, as he is—a blood-sucking parasite. Now begins a period of austerity and self-denial, as David earns his living ghosting term papers for Columbia students. Worse, he begins to feel the gradual loss of his powers, and his despair deepens. Finally, exposed for his academic fraud, he completely loses the gift. Accepting his fate, David begins life again. NN, 1972; HN, 1973. A unique story, splendidly executed, and destined to become a classic. Compare with Brunner's *The Whole Man* [4-119] and del Rey's *Pstalemate* [4-206], also character studies of a telepath. Contrast with the more traditional Blish's *Jack of Eagles* [4-79] and Tucker's *Wild Talent* [4-587].

4-524. Silverberg, Robert. **Hawksbill Station.** Doubleday, 1968. Tandem, £.25.
Repressive government sends dissenters and revolutionaries on a one-way time trip into a Cambrian prison camp. But one of the prisoners turns out to be the representative of a future liberal government that plans to repatriate the convicts. Tragically, Hawksbill's leader, Barrett, chooses not to return to a world that has passed him by. Good depiction of prison life. Compare Anderson's "Wildcat" in *Seven Conquests* [4-23]. HN, 1968; NN, 1967.

4-525. Silverberg, Robert. **The Masks of Time.** Ballantine, 1968, $1.25.
The year 2000 nears and "Apocalyptists" run riot when Vornan-19, a superman from the future, appears in Rome. Governments, attempting to use the visitor for their own ends, give him a group of chaperones, some of Earth's best minds, who try to gain knowledge of the future. But Vornan, now the focus of a growing religious movement, independently seeks out Earth's diversions and sex, disdainful of his "backward" hosts. Finally, he is "martyred," perhaps shredded by masses of his adorers. Apocalypse has arrived. Some social satire and investigation of religion, but still second-line Silverberg. Compare Heinlein's *Stranger in a Strange Land* [4-302]. NN, 1968.

4-526. Silverberg, Robert. **Nightwings.** Walker, 1970.
To Earth, deep in the aftermath of a technological downfall lasting generations, come vengeful invaders bent on making Earthlings captives as they themselves once were held in zoo-like compounds on Earth. Through the eyes of the "Watcher" Wuelig (who becomes Tomis of the Rememberers and later Pilgrim Tomis), we learn of Earth's past and its future. Compare Brunner's "Coincidence Day" in *Time Jump* (1973). HW as novella in 1969; NN, 1968.

4-527. Silverberg, Robert. **Thorns.** Ballantine, 1967, $1.25.
To obtain the pain necessary for his physical and psychic well-being,

Duncan Chalk manipulates the lives of people around him, feeding on their agonies. For a proposed orgy of anguish, he bribes Lona Kelvin and Minner Burris into a love affair, carefully calculating torture to come from their psychically scarred personalities. But the pair unite and defeat Chalk with . . . love. HN, 1968; NN, 1967.

*4-528. Silverberg, Robert. **A Time of Changes.** Doubleday, 1971. Gollancz, £2.10.

On Borthan, men obey the Covenant created by its founders: the self is despicable, first-person pronouns obscenities. But Kinnall Darival rebels against this strict religion, loses his high station, gains another under a false identity, but gives that up, too, for his cause. Now he must lead his people into a sharing of self, the dangers of which he knows well after making his sinful love for his "bondsister" known to her through the use of an illegal drug that allows minds to merge. Darival is martyred, but he has already touched off a time of changes. Borthan and its people are excellently presented in this meaningful work. HN, 1972; NW, 1971.

4-529. Silverberg, Robert. **Tower of Glass.** Scribner, 1970, $5.95.

Simeon Krug, wealthy industrialist and developer of the androids who now labor for man, rears a mighty glass tower to communicate with possible life in distant NGC 7293. The androids, headed by Krug's chief engineer, Thor Watchman, secretly worship Krug as God; Thor finally sees Krug as he is—crude, arrogant, and egotistical—topples the unfinished beacon and leads the androids in revolt. Krug flees Earth to pursue his nebulous aliens. Good action and social criticism, mingled with religious symbolism in this superior work. Contrast Dick's *Do Androids Dream of Electric Sheep?* [4-207]. NN, 1970; HN, 1971.

4-530. Silverberg, Robert. **Unfamiliar Territory.** Scribner, 1973, $5.95.

Thirteen stories, mainly from original anthologies, which date from 1971 to 1973; some of Silverberg's and SF's best recent short fiction. Of special note are "Good News from the Vatican" (NW, 1971), where the first robot Pope is selected; "When We Went to See the End of the World" (NN, 1972, HN, 1973); "In Entropy's Jaws"; and "Caught in the Organ Draft." All stories are well done.

4-531. Silverberg, Robert. **Up the Line.** Ballantine, 1969, $1.25.

Time travel exists in mod future (an extrapolation of late 1960s), where the "Time Service" conducts tours of the past. But swinging time-guide Judsen Elliott III falls in love with his multi-great grandmother, and lets a jaded tourist change history. The "Time Patrol" puts things right, and Judsen, on the lam "up the (time) line," is paradoxed out of existence as punishment. Light Silverberg. Compare Gerrold's *The Man Who Folded Himself* [4-261]. NN, 1969; HN, 1970.

4-532. Silverberg, Robert. **The World Inside.** Doubleday, 1971. Signet, $.95.
Happy people in highly organized society exist inside giant high-rises, Urbmons, each housing 800,000. This introverted utopia is too restricted for a few; but the outside, with its agrarian tribal communes, is as much a trap as the inside; nor does history and the internal exploration of the Urbmon offer freedom. In utopia, change comes to an end; the way outside is death. A well-developed extrapolation of urbanization. Hugo nominee (withdrawn by the author), 1972. Contrast Blish and Knight's *A Torrent of Faces* [4-81].

4-533. Simak, Clifford D. **All Flesh Is Grass.** Doubleday, 1965. Berkley, $.75.
An intelligent, computer-like species of purple flowers from an alternate Earth establishes a beachhead protected by a force field around a small, midwestern town. The usual collection of folksy, believable, small-town Simak characters are trapped within, and Brad Carter, a strong individualist chaffing under his community's *gemeinschaft*, is chosen by the flowers to be their human ambassador. Should man join the flowers, combining his hands with their brains for mutual benefit, or will he be enslaved by these super plants? Faith in life and cooperation win. Well written and meaningful. Contrast Anderson's *Seven Conquests* [4-23]. NN, 1965.

4-534. Simak, Clifford D. **A Choice of Gods.** Putnam, 1972. Berkley, $.75.
Earth has returned to a primeval state after nearly all of its teeming billions are suddenly transported to distant planets; only a handful of humans remain, living at a low technological level, but apparently immortal. Moreover, some have learned to travel to the stars using mind power. Robots, too, remain; some, like Hezekiah, have become monks and taken up man's lost religious quest, while others build a great tower to communicate with the alien "Principle" that inhabits deepest space. But Earth's ex-citizens, still anti-nature technologists, rediscover Earth and threaten to upset the evolutionary forces that may lead down new paths. But the "Principle" says no. Not really a deep work, despite its theological, quasi-mystical trappings; still, pleasantly sentimental and pastoral. Contrast Silverberg's *Tower of Glass* [4-529]. HN, 1973.

*4-535. Simak, Clifford D. **City.** Gnome, 1952. Ace, $1.25.
Eight "legends" constitute the heritage of sentient dogs who have inherited Earth from man, along with android robots to aid the dogs. There is strong doubt that mankind ever existed. If he did, man's passing coincides with the gradual abandonment of that peculiarly human artifact, the city—produced by the same creative genius that runs awry and

makes war, whereas dog culture completely pacifies the animal kingdom. Sublime humanity may not work; instead may transform or become extinct—a dead divinity. A maudlin, poignant, quietistically philosophical twilight-of-the-gods account of man; the end of the human species. A doleful contrast to the vaulting optimism of Bester's *The Stars My Destination* [4-65], Clarke's *Childhood's End* [4-149], and Asimov's *Foundation Trilogy* [4-38]; a seminal work in modern SF's swing to pessimism. Compare Stewart's *Earth Abides* [4-558] and Campbell's "Twilight" [3-8]. IFA, 1958.

4-536. Simak, Clifford D. **The Goblin Reservation.** Berkley, 1969, $.75.
Goblins and fairies really exist, and Pete Maxwell is a student of them. They aid Pete as he tries to sell an ancient race's collective knowledge to Earth. The "Wheelers," disgusting creatures composed of insect colonies, also want the knowledge, and Pete finds obstacles in his path—including the fact that he is officially dead. Light entertainment; minor Simak. HN, 1969.

4-537. Simak, Clifford D. **Time and Again.** Simon & Schuster, 1951.
Asher Sutton travels 6,000 years of human history to gain special assistance, to mature, and to survive to write a universe-guiding book, telling all life, "We are not alone." Destiny is with life. The human species, against its psychotic claims, is decidedly not preeminent in the universe. Be it louse or super-android, all life is lovely before destiny; all are equal. Racism, nationalism, and manifest destiny are obscene behaviors and delusions. Sutton is well-rounded prophet–messiah figure. Compare Clarke's *Childhood's End* [4-149].

4-538. Simak, Clifford D. **Time Is the Simplest Thing.** Doubleday, 1961. Leisure Books, $.95.
Shepherd Blaine is a teleporting star traveller who leaves Fishhook Corporation because he has become "contaminated," joined minds with a super-intelligent, benevolent alien. Mechanical space travel won't work. It must be accomplished by paranormal means. In fact, mankind's future depends upon his paranormal powers; yet the normals hunt the paranormals as witches until, led by the "alienated" Blaine, paranormals depart Earth for new planets, leaving normal humanity to stagnate and devolve. A profound critique of human "spirituality": When messianic men appear, fearful men repudiate them and murder them. Courageous men welcome them and become them. An obvious but effective allegory. Compare Henderson's *Pilgrimage* [4-304] and Wyndham's *Re-Birth* [4-641]. HN, 1962.

*4-539. Simak, Clifford D. **Way Station.** Doubleday, 1963. Manor Books, $1.25.
Nostalgic story of Civil War veteran and frontiersman Enoch Wallace,

made immortal to tend a secret galactic travel station in rural Wisconsin, and his loneliness, his love of Earth, and his solitary struggle to bring galactic benefits to man. Finally, after CIA spying and witch-fearing neighbors threaten to cause the station's closure, Enoch's dreams come true. Aided by his alien, coffee-drinking friend, Ulysses, and a beautiful deaf-mute hill girl with psychic powers, Enoch saves the "Talisman," an artifact that brings peace by opening people's contact with "the cosmic spiritual force," and proves Earth worthy to join the galaxy. Maudlin, but effective. HW, 1964.

4-540. Simak, Clifford D. **The Worlds of Clifford Simak.** Simon & Schuster, 1960.
Twelve stories from the 1950s, including "The Big Front Yard" (HW, 1959; SFHF), a prototype of the author's *Way Station* [4-539] and *All Flesh Is Grass* [4-533], in which a folksy fix-it man finds his ancestral home turned into a portal between worlds; "Lulu," about a computerized spaceship who falls in love and elopes with her three-man crew; and "Neighbor," a typical Simak story involving a small farming community and an alien family who settle there, isolating and preserving it as an idealized, rural American utopia.

4-541. Siodmak, Curt. **Donovan's Brain.** Knopf, 1943. Barrie & Jenkins, £1.50.
The brain of Donovan, killed in plane crash, survives in laboratory suspension; it gains psi power over its attendent, becomes obsessed, and finally dies. The source story for the popular brain-survival jokes. Not particularly well written but tremendously well known. Belongs to the Frankenstein's monster tradition. In a tenuous sequel, *Hauser's Memory* (Putnam, 1968), Pat Cory, Nobel Prize-winning biochemist, transplants RNA from Hauser, World War II German chemist, to Hillel Mondoro. Unwittingly, he transplants Hauser's whole revenge-directed personality. Mondoro dies killing Geller, Nazi concentration camp criminal, while under control of "Hauser's memory," thus losing Hauser's formula for control of hydrogen fission. Ingenious biochemical gimmick and routine espionage yarn.

4-542. Skinner, Burrhus Frederick. **Walden Two.** Macmillan, 1948, $2.50.
Frazier, mercurial genius, in effort to prove science of human behavior, sets up "Walden Two." In this utopian environment, psychological problems of group living are solved with principles of behavioral engineering. Largely dialogue between Frazier and Castle, representing determinism and free will, respectively. Frazier rejects free will, democracy, and theology as *sine qua non* of human actualization in favor of appealing utopia of positive reinforcement—behaviorist's answer to "love."

Brilliant tour de force. Contrast Orwell's *1984* [4-450] and Brunner's *The Shockwave Rider* [4-116].

4-543. Sladek, John T. **Mechasm.** Ace, 1969, $.75. (British title: *The Reproductive System*, 1968, Avon, $1.95.).

Dr. Smilax invents a cybernetic "organism" that eats metal, reproduces and adapts, and threatens Earth's civilization until brought under control to perform mankind's menial tasks, turning Earth into Eden. Science would bring true progress quickly without interference of military-industrial complex. Comic satire in innovative narrative strategies. Compare Brunner, *Stand on Zanzibar* [4-118]; Vonnegut, *Cat's Cradle* [4-605].

4-544. Sladek, John T. **The Müller-Fokker Effect.** Morrow, 1971, $5.95. Pocket Books, $.95.

Dark, satirical comedy about a millionaire voyeur who decides to enter the soap-opera life of the family he secretly watches. To that end, the father is killed in a military experiment, his personality stored on super-computer tapes, his wife made the queen of TV cookery commercials, and his son sent to a sadistic military school. Meanwhile, the computer tapes, sold as army surplus, foul up a phoney evangelist, a pseudo-artist, and the military's attempts to contain a Washington demonstration by fascist racists that degenerates into a Bosch nightmare. But millionaire Mac Hines puts his victim's personality into a new body, and the family is returned to normal. A potpourri of a novel, full of gimmicks, guffaws, and wild parties, that puts down everybody. Contrast with the milder Vonnegut's *Cat Cradle* [4-605] and Sheckley's *Journey beyond Tomorrow* [4-513].

4-545. Sloane, William M., III. **To Walk the Night.** Farrar, 1937. Hyperion, $10.95 (as *The Rim of Morning*, which includes both novels).

Excellent blend of mystery and macabre with SF; subtle development and character exploration leads to powerful, yet understated horrific tone. Bart Jones relates the mysterious events preceding the inexplicable "suicide" of his best friend, Jerry Lister, who seemed driven to marry the widow of his old teacher, Dr. LeNormand, a brilliant space-time physicist, following the scientist's enigmatic death by spontaneous combustion. The widow, a beautiful yet culturally naive woman, seems beyond human emotion and evokes a feeling of alienness in Bart; she may be "possessing" the body of a missing idiot girl. But despite her psychic powers and mysterious origins, this visitor from another world is forced to destroy the human, Jerry, she has come to love. A quaint classic of its kind. Compare Brunner's *Quicksand* [4-114]. Sloane's *The Edge Of Running Water* (Farrar, 1939) is similar in mood, yet not as successful. In a lonely Maine farmhouse, a bereaved scientist, with the aid of a medium, is secretly constructing a machine to communicate with the dead. Homicide results, and the scientist's beautiful daughter and best friend are drawn into the mystery as hostile village folk threaten mob action. Compare Shelley's *Frankenstein* [1-47].

4-546. Smith, Cordwainer (pseud. of Paul M. A. Linebarger). **Norstrilia.** Ballantine, 1975, $1.50.
Rod McBan of conservative and enormously wealthy (holding monopoly on "Stroon" immortality drug) planet of Old North Australia finds inherited land and life in jeopardy. With a computer he becomes richest man in known universe—owning thirty or forty planets, including Earth. He travels in disguises to avoid assassination. He is erratic but powerful telepath. Story characterized by allegorical names typical of Linebarger's tales. Themes of contrast between rugged individualism and corporate government; arid, inhospitable planets and lushness of "Old Earth." Nostalgia for traditional values of Earth although underpeople foment revolution and Instrumentality of Man governs by promoting change. The original 1960 version was published as *The Planet Buyer* (Pyramid, 1964, $1.25) (HN, 1965) and *The Underpeople* (Pyramid, 1968). Jupiter nominee, 1974.

4-547. Smith, Cordwainer (pseud. of Paul M. A. Linebarger). **You Will Never Be the Same.** Regency, 1963. Garland, $11.00.
Eight stories, including the 1948 "Scanners Live in Vain" (SFHF). Colorful allegorical introductions to universe of 15,000 years hence when man sails space on huge estate-like plane-forming ships, castes of nonhuman, animal-derived underpeople are enslaved by "true" humans (less normal than the "animals"), and Lords of the Instrumentality of Man govern all with ruthless benevolence. *Space Lords* (Pyramid, 1965) adds five Instrumentality stories, including "The Ballad of Lost C'mell" (SFHF). Both collections provide fine allegory and dream-like imagery.

*4-548. Smith, Edward Elmer. **The Lensman Series.**
First issued by Fantasy Press, the greatest of the early golden age space opera. A Lensman is a super-virtuous male or female chosen by the agents of cosmic goodness in the universe to have his virtues magnified and augmented with a "ruby lens." The lensmen become the balance of power against forces of cosmic evil. On the greatest of battlefields, employing the most violent weapons, the lensmen fight the most ferocious of all wars. In sequence, the novels of the series are: *Triplanetary* (1948, Pyramid, $1.25); *First Lensman* (1950, Pyramid, $.95) second-best of series; *Galactic Patrol* (1950, Pyramid, $1.25); *Gray Lensman* (1951, Pyramid, $1.25) best of series; *Second Stage Lensman* (1953, Pyramid, $1.25); and *Children of the Lens* (1954, Pyramid, $1.25). Boxed and sold together by Fantasy Press as "The History of Civilization."

4-549. Smith, George Oliver. **The Fourth "R".** Ballantine, 1959. (Alternate title: *The Brain Machine*, 1968).

Jimmy Holden inherits a learning machine from his murdered father. He's bright but must hide from murderer guardian until he can gain his majority, secure adult rights, and give the machine to the world to enhance everyone's intelligence. Fruits of science are for all to share. Good suspense. Clever plotting. Set in nostalgia United States.

4-550. Smith, George Oliver. **Venus Equilateral.** Prime, 1947. Garland, $11.00.
Ten *Astounding* stories about "Venus Equilateral," a communications satellite absolutely essential to maintaining contact among the planets of the solar system when the Sun is in the way. Stories analyze science, psychology, and politics of the station's operations. Interesting yarns woven of clichés and stereotypes of golden-age SF.

*4-551. Spinrad, Norman. **Bug Jack Barron.** Walker, 1969. Avon, $.95.
Jack Barron is an assimilation of Johnny Carson, Joe Pine, and any number of call-in-you're-on-the-air media MC's. Barron runs his TV program with sensational flair, often as muckraker. He attacks Benedict Howards, one of America's richest men, who is using his wealth to develop immortality treatment. Treatment is perfected, but Howards is defeated; Barron wins all the marbles, including a shot at the Presidency, which he plans to resign in favor of black vice-presidential running mate. Slickly realistic; one of first in SF to describe details of hero's sexual affairs. NN, 1969; HN, 1970.

4-552. Spinrad, Norman. **The Iron Dream.** Avon, 1972, $1.95.
The fictitious author of this is Adolf Hitler, famous SF writer. Feric Jaggar is the perversely seductive hero of a neo-Naziesque "sword and sorcery" tale. He leads the rise of a fascist state after an atomic war. An inspired literary ploy—a novel within a novel, complete with blurbs, titles, biography, and scholarly afterword, written skillfully enough to catch the sympathy of the unsuspecting (?) reader. The theme is as sick as the Third Reich. NN, 1972.

4-553. Spinrad, Norman. **No Direction Home.** Pocket Books, 1975, $1.25.
Eleven socially conscious stories, from 1969 to 1973, which reflect the dominant concerns of the times: ecological destruction in "The Lost Continent," where affluent Africans get a tour of the extinct space-age United States; violence and sports in "The National Pastime," which innovates combat football as the mob's circus; and the horror of psychedelic drug dependency in "No Direction Home." "The Big Flash" (NN, 1969) has the U.S. government using a rock band to manipulate public opinion into using nukes in Vietnam, while "A Thing of Beauty" (NN, 1973) has a gross American selling a refined Japanese the Brooklyn Bridge. Accurate mirrors for a distorted culture.

4-554. Stableford, Brian M. (U.K.). **Cradle of the Sun.** Ace, 1969. Sphere, £.25.

In the twilight of the human race, an unknown power has sapped humanity of all drive, thus hastening extinction. Three humans and three sentient rats undertake a futile quest to find this foe. One of the humans succeeds and finds an immortal man who has abandoned humanity. The human race *is* doomed. Humanity is the source of its own defeat. Slick and tight writing prevents degeneration to maudlin mood. Compare Vance's *The Dying Earth* [4-597] and Aldiss's *The Long Afternoon of Earth* [4-7].

4-555. Stableford, Brian M. (U.K.). **The Halcyon Drift.** DAW, 1972, $.95.

Thirty-fifth-century trader pilot, Grainger, agrees to fly special ship, product of human and alien science, into "Halcyon Drift"—an area of warped time and space—to recover the cargo from *The Lost Star* spaceship. He succeeds. Intelligent, tough-minded space opera. Excellent character development in painstaking narrative. Sequels: *Rhapsody in Black* (DAW, 1973); *The Paradise Game* (DAW, 1974); *Promised Land* (DAW, 1974); *The Fenris Device* (DAW, 1974) each $.95.

4-556. Stasheff, Christopher. **The Warlock in Spite of Himself.** Ace, 1969. Garland, $11.00.

Rodney d'Armond and epileptic robot go to the planet Gramarye to bring it from feudalism to democracy. He is kidnapped by elves, meets ghosts, and a witch falls in love with him; finally, he defeats men from the future who block his goal. Good satirical narrative. Pro-democracy but impatient with bureaucracy. Progress is necessary in the long run even though painful for small groups in process. A successful SF/sword and sorcery hybrid.

4-557. Sternberg, Jacques (France). **Future without Future.** Seabury, 1974, $6.95. Tr. by Frank Zero of *Futurs sans avenir*, 1971.

Five stories of futures in which mankind meets various forms of catastrophe, including "Fin de siècle," about the end of Earth in year 2000 because mankind has muddled time, and "Ephemera," about human spacecrash survivors who land on a planet but die because time on this planet is slower—its inhabitants cannot perceive them. Often employs epistolary or journal format. Compare "Fin de siècle" with Orwell's *1984* [4-450] and Zamiatin's *We* [2-177]. Not all stories in the original are included in this edition.

*4-558. Stewart, George Rippey. **Earth Abides.** Random, 1949. Hermes, $8.95. Fawcett Crest, $1.50.

Plague sweeps Earth, killing 250,000 for every survivor. Ish and Em lead nine original survivors in San Francisco Bay area. Only humans are killed in plague; all other flora and fauna survive, as well as the physical plant of civilization—including the Huntington Library. Ish spends forty or fifty years trying to make road back to civilization. But his sons and daughters are quintessential tribal primitives when he dies. Human civilization is trivial; the planet "abides." Lasting excellence is brilliant dramatization of anthropological and sociological principles at work, respected by 1970s scholars. First IFA winner, 1951.

4-559. Stewart, Mary (U.K.). **The Crystal Cave.** Morrow, 1970, $8.95. Fawcett Crest, $1.75.
The birth, childhood, and youth of Merlin, King Arthur's magician, that preserves the spirit of Arthurian legend while demythologizing and humanizing the legendary sorceror. He possesses an intermittently functioning second sight and scientific knowledge unknown to his own civilization. In sequel, *The Hollow Hills* (Morrow, 1973, $8.95; Fawcett Crest, $1.75), Merlin uses his power to preserve young Arthur until he can take the throne. A third novel of Arthur's reign is projected. Well researched, thoroughly readable popular fiction; months on national best seller list in America. Compare Rosemary Sutcliff's *Sword at Sunset* (1963) and T. H. White's *The Once and Future King* (1957).

4-560. Stine, Hank. **Season of the Witch.** Essex House, 1968.
Andre Fuller, rape-murderer, is punished by being translated into a beautiful female body, wherein he/she finds happiness after an odyssey of sexual adaptive experience. Biological transformation of sexuality may be necessary for male and female to understand one another. Pornographic detail absolutely necessary to stunning evocation of who a woman really is. Compare Russ's *The Female Man* [4-485]; contrast Heinlein's *I Will Fear No Evil* (1970).

4-561. Strugatski, Arkadi, and Boris Strugatski (U.S.S.R.). **Hard to Be a God.** Seabury, 1973, $6.95. DAW, $1.25. Tr. by Wendayne Ackerman of *Trudno byt bogom*, 1964.
Twenty-odd agents from post-capitalistic Earth oversee the development of civilization in a "medieval" period on a colony planet. Planet's inhabitants superstitiously regard agents as gods. If you're human, being a god is impossible. Manipulating backward civilization for its own good is beyond human wisdom. Compare de Camp's *Rogue Queen* [4-196] and Roberts' *Pavane* [4-481].

4-562. Sturgeon, Theodore. **Aliens Four.** Avon, 1959.
Four long stories, including the well-known "Killdozer!" (1944), about a duel between a man-operated power shovel and a "possessed" bulldozer; "The (Widget), the (Wadget), and Boff" (1955), in which aliens trying to psyche out mankind are confounded by the colorful residents of a boarding house. Also contains the horrific "The Comedian's Children" (1958), and a fantasy set in the American West, "Cactus Dance" (1954). Entertaining and insightful reading.

4-563. Sturgeon, Theodore. **Case and the Dreamer.** Signet, 1974, $.95.
Three excellent stories about the power and meaning of love. The title
story (NN, 1973) involves a triangle of two castaway space explorers,
Case and Jan, and a protean alien; only after hundreds of years of death
and his resurrection by a derelict space ship does Case come to understand his love. "If All Men Were Brothers, Would You Let One Marry
Your Sister?" (NN, 1967) offers a rational justification for human incest
on ecological grounds. Charli Bux, visiting the shunned planet Vexvelt,
confronts his own conditioned revulsion when he learns of this practice,
but the people's sanity, creativity, and fulfillment win him as an immigrant. In "When You Care, When You Love" (HN, 1963), a wealthy
young woman, facing the death of her lover by choriocarcinoma, has
him cloned and herself frozen to await his maturation. Meanwhile, a
plan is set in motion to guide his life experiences so that he will form a
similar personality as well as having an identical body.

4-564. Sturgeon, Theodore. **E Pluribus Unicorn.** Abelard, 1953.
Thirteen fantasy and SF stories, from 1947 to 1953, and an introduction
by Groff Conklin. The most outstanding story is "A Saucer of Loneliness," a sensitive love story of a lonely woman touched by a small flying
saucer and hounded nearly to death by the government and the public;
on a deserted beach, she is found by an equally lonely man led to her by
the bottles she has tossed into sea, perhaps as some other lonely being
tosses "saucers" across space. In "The World Well Lost," Sturgeon ca-
pably explores homosexuality and its social condemnation, both between
alien bird like creatures who flee their repressive society for sanctuary
on Earth and between crew members of the ship that sets out to return
them. Other stories of interest are "Bianca's Hands," "The Silken-Swift,"
and "The Professor's Teddy Bear."

*4-565. Sturgeon, Theodore. **More Than Human.** Farrar, 1953. Ballantine, $1.50. Garland, $11.00.
Sturgeon's greatest work; it vaulted him to the forefront of SF writers.
Several misfit children, symbolizing mankind in their diversity, are driv-
en together by an inner call to form a new "gestalt" based on the parapsychological union among its specialized parts. This communion realizes the potential Sturgeon feels mankind possesses to achieve its psychic
destiny. A popular novel in SF courses, it is one of the genre's greatest
works. Compare Roberts' *The Inner Wheel* [4-480] and Clarke's *Childhood's End* [4-149]. Winner of the IFA, 1954.

4-566. Sturgeon, Theodore. **Sturgeon Is Alive and Well.** Putnam,
1971.
Thirteen stories, twelve written in 1969 and 1970, the first by Sturgeon
following years of silence. Emphasis on literary features; some marginal
and non-SF (e.g. "To Here and the Easel"). Contains "Slow Sculpture"

(NW, 1970), about a scientist's disillusionment with society and his relationship with a woman whose cancer he cures. There is a rather personal preface by the author.

4-567. Sturgeon, Theodore. **The Synthetic Man.** Greenberg, 1950. Pyramid, $.95. (Alternate title: *The Dreaming Jewels*).
Utterly alien jewel-like creatures dream into existence the being who will grow up as Horty Armand, inhuman but humanoid, telepathic, and able to change his shape and regenerate major body parts. Fleeing his vicious stepfather, Horty joins a carnival to meet his beloved, Zena, and other friends and enemies. Hairpinning plot plays guess who's human with the reader while Horty and Zena finally learn that "humanity" is a conditioning, not a biology. Exceptional use of music to characterize Horty. Progressive sexual theory given the novel's publication date. As in Sturgeon's presentation of childhood in his *More Than Human* [4-565] and *Venus Plus X* [4-569], Horty's youth is a symbol for human hope. Compare Henderson's *Pilgrimage* [4-304].

4-568. Sturgeon, Theodore. **A Touch of Strange.** Doubleday, 1958. Books for Libraries, $15.25.
Nine stories, including the excellent study of the corruption of power, "Mr. Costello, Hero." A galactic wheeler-dealer who thrives on sowing dissension and controlling people almost seduces a ship's purser; a wise society gives such a megalomaniac what he wants as therapy/object lesson—the purser visits him in exile where he is pitting one ant colony against another. Other works of note are "Affair with a Green Monkey," "The Other Celia," and "A Touch of Strange."

4-569. Sturgeon, Theodore. **Venus Plus X.** Pyramid, 1960.
Pilot Charlie Johns of familiar Earth crashes to his death, but his brain and its contents are saved by the people of Ledom, recently instituted secret parallel Earth civilization. They put it into a new body and ask "Charlie Johns" what he thinks of their utopian society, especially remarkable for the biobisexuality of its citizens (Charlie's new body is male). The resulting events and dialogue are an interesting critique of familiar Earth society with the often tragic confusion of its gender-stamped roles. An estimable anticipation of Le Guin's two prize-winning novels, *Left Hand of Darkness* [4-373] and *The Dispossessed* [4-371]. HN, 1961.

4-570. Sturgeon, Theodore. **A Way Home.** Funk & Wagnalls, 1955.
Nine stories with introduction by Groff Conklin. "Unite and Conquer" represents Sturgeon touch with story of brilliant scientist who tricks world into "uniting" against threat from invading aliens, bringing a new, beneficial world order. Also contains the nuclear warning story, "Thunder and Roses," "The Hurkle Is a Happy Beast," and "Tiny and the Monster."

4-571. Sturgeon, Theodore. **Without Sorcery.** Prime, 1948.
Thirteen of Sturgeon's earliest stories, from 1939 to 1948, with an introduction by Ray Bradbury. Includes the classic "Microcosmic God" (SFHF), about a super-scientist whose fantastic inventions were made by a rapidly evolving miniature species he created and for whom he was a god. Also of note are "It," "Shottle Bop," "Ether Breather," "Brat," "Cargo," "The Ultimate Egoist," and "Maturity."

4-572. Swann, Thomas Burnett. **Day of the Minotaur.** Ace, 1966. (Alternate title: *The Blue Monkeys*).
Eunostos, the bull-man, is leader of the peaceful beast creatures of the forest and in love with beast princess Thea. He defeats invasion of humans with poisoned blue monkeys whom humans kill and eat. A fantastic confection in which many humans are more beast-like than the beasts. HN, 1967.

4-573. Tate, Peter (U.K.). **Gardens One to Five.** Doubleday, 1971.
Shem is a free man forced to negotiate five gardens in middle Italy, in each of which inhabitants pursue a worthy goal in a stupid way. In the fifth garden, U.N. forces kill Shem, but he is survived by Scarlatti who takes up the torch of reality. Allegory of the stupidity of mankind's procedures even as he seeks peace, space travel, knowledge, and love.

4-574. Taylor, Robert Lewis. **Adrift in a Boneyard.** Doubleday, 1947.
Fred Robinson, his wife, housekeeper, housekeeper's son, an old man, and a girl survive an agency that kills every other human being where he stands. Their survival devices and travels are a combination of the realistic and quixotic, ending on an edenic island where they seem to have a choice of living "naturally" or returning to a restored world. A disarmingly complex parable questioning the meaning of human existence. Compelling urbane dialectic metaphored in characters of serenely cynical Fred and Martha, his superficially empty-headed wife. Contrast Stewart's *Earth Abides* [4-558].

4-575. Temple, William Frederick (U.K.). **The Fleshpots of Sansato.** MacDonald, 1968.
Intergalactic espionage gets qualitative lift with symbol, archetype, and character as Garner, Earth agent, tracks down secret faster-than-light drive and deals with his sexual hangups in Dorian-controlled galaxy. Mankind can compete in any game. Sansato city scenario is remarkable.

4-576. Temple, William Frederick (U.K.). **Shoot at the Moon.** Simon & Schuster, 1966.
Mystery, murder, and romance on a credible Moon trip, but with a crew out of a NASA psychologist's nightmare: an ultra-individualistic pilot fearing automated spacecraft; a gold-mad British politician living out a

Klondike fantasy; his beautiful, schizoid, scientist daughter; her ex-husband physician playboy; a Jonah geologist fearful of his masculinity. The politician's lunar goldstrike turns out to be a novel life form. Pilot's atavism typical of many SF heroes. Compare Kornbluth's *Takeoff* [4-352] and Clarke's *Prelude to Space* [4-155].

4-577. Tenn, William (pseud. of Philip Klass). **The Human Angle.** Ballantine, 1956. Ballantine (U.K.), £.30.
Eight stories from the mid-fifties, including "Wednesday's Child," about a strange young woman who reproduces by shucking the mother's body and becoming a mature person in body of new baby; ingenious and profoundly symbolic. Also of interest is "The Discovery of Morniel Mathaway." Collection abounds with Klass-ic wit.

4-578. Tenn, William (pseud. of Philip Klass). **Of All Possible Worlds.** Ballantine, 1955. Ballantine (U.K.), £.30.
Seven stories, from 1947 to 1954, and an effective advocacy essay, "On the Fiction in Science-Fiction." Better stories include "Down among the Dead Men," about the "recycling" of dead men in a vicious space war; "The Liberation of Earth," a satirical comment from the victims' viewpoint of being "saved" by brutal forces fighting over them; "The Tenants," in which two aliens rent a nonexistent thirteenth floor and move in; and "The Custodian," about a man who stays behind on Earth after the rest of humanity has fled in advance of the Sun's going nova.

4-579. Tenn, William (pseud. of Philip Klass). **Of Men and Monsters.** Walker, 1968. Ballantine, $1.50.
Alien giants colonize Earth. Earthlings live like cockroaches in the giants' dwellings, regarded at most as pests. A few humans lead mankind out of superstitious rat like existence to stars—on spaceship stolen from giants. Mankind is infinitely adaptable and resourceful. Lilliputian point of view cogently maintained. Anthropological and psychological exemplum. Tenn's only novel to date. Compare White's *Mistress Masham's Repose* (1946).

4-580. Tenn, William (pseud. of Philip Klass). **The Wooden Star.** Ballantine, 1968. Ballantine (U.K.), £.30.
Eleven stories with author's note. Among them are several of Klass's best: "Generation of Noah"; "Brooklyn Project"; "Null-P"; "Eastward Ho!"; "The Masculinest Revolt."

*4-581. Tevis, Walter. **The Man Who Fell to Earth.** Fawcett, 1963.
Sadly beautiful story of alien from "Anthea" (Mars?) who comes to Earth from superior but dying civilization to get help from mankind. He puts whole being into becoming as "human" as possible. Psychologically a success. But "humanity" is not enough, as he reveals himself only to be de-

feated by xenophobia of Earth. Repudiation is doubly tragic since he has become empathetic with men. A parable of man's inhumanity to man— this time in guise of an alien.

4-582. Thomas, Theodore L., and Kate Wilhelm. **The Clone.** Berkley, 1965.
Life is accidentally created in the catch basin of a Chicago drain; this "clone" grows into a miles-square blob that eats organic material, including people. The city is threatened as the clone adapts to eating parts of buildings. Plausibly developed. Compare Pedler and Davis' *Mutant 59* [4-455]. NN, 1965.

4-583. Tiptree, James, Jr. **Ten Thousand Light-Years from Home.** Ace, 1973, $.95.
Fifteen stories from 1968 to 1972, and an introduction by Harry Harrison. Special mention: "And I Awoke and Found Me Here on the Cold Hill's Side" (NN, 1972; HN, 1973), about man's "cargo-cult of the soul" due to his adoration of aliens; "Painwise" (HN, 1973), with its lost galactic explorer incapable of feeling pain; and "Faithful to Thee, Terra, in Our Fashion," a kaleidoscope of alien competitors on a galactic racetrack run by Solterrans after Earth's death.

4-584. Tiptree, James, Jr. **Warm Worlds and Otherwise.** Ballantine, 1975, $1.50.
Twelve stories with a biographical introduction by Robert Silverberg. Includes: "The Last Flight of Dr. Ain" (revised) (NN, 1969); "The Girl Who Was Plugged In" (NN, 1973; HW, 1974); "Love Is the Plan, the Plan Is Death" (NW, 1973; HN, 1974). Excellent collection of Tiptree's best works.

4-585. Tubb, E. C. (U.K.). **The Winds of Gath.** Ace, 1967, $.95.
Dumarest is dumped on Gath, a resort planet, and into an adventure with an exotic monarchy in an environment where time and weather are maverick. He braves assassins and lasers to save the daughter of Matriarch of Kund. SF adventure in the Burroughs vein. Campare Stableford's "Halcyon Drift" novels [4-555]. Tubb has written several other Dumarest novels.

*4-586. Tucker, Wilson. **The Long Loud Silence.** Rinehart, 1952.
A nuclear–biological war devastates the United States east of the Mississippi. Corporal Russell Gary survives on the east side, but, along with a few others, finds himself quarantined and forbidden to re-enter civilization. Eventually, he is reconciled to a life of primitive necessity. Excellent scenario. Kornbluth called it "enormously effective social criticism, saying much about man and his society." Compare Frank's *Alas, Babylon* [4-249]; contrast Wylie's *Triumph* [4-636].

4-587. Tucker, Wilson. **Wild Talent.** Rinehart, 1954. (Variant title: *Man from Tomorrow*, 1955).
Paul Breen discovers, during an appropriate experience of confusion, that he has psi talent. Unwittingly he reveals himself to government agents, who try to use him and kill him. He survives and goes into hiding with the woman he has come to love. Good telepath-emerging story. Cold-war world will not appreciate a "new" man. Compare Blish's *Jack of Eagles* [4-79], Sellings' *Telepath* [4-501], Roberts' *The Inner Wheel* [4-480], Brunner's *The Whole Man* [4-119], and Sturgeon's *More than Human* [4-565].

4-588. Tucker, Wilson. **The Year of the Quiet Sun.** Ace, 1970, $.75.
A government time-travel project sends a team into 2000 A.D. to anticipate problems. Team finds Russia and China have been at war; America is back to savagery as the result of black revolution. Was the future changed? Time paradox unresolved. Social criticism; awful-warning story. Compare Greenlee's *The Spook Who Sat by the Door* [4-275] and Williams' *The Man Who Cried I Am* [4-624]. HN, 1971; NN, 1970.

4-589. Tung, Lee (India). **The Wind Obeys Lama Toru.** Kutub-Popular, 1967.
Allegory of tragic foolishness of mankind that has proliferated population for reasons of national strength. Chaos increases when fertility drugs infect animal populations. Antidote sterility drug cuts planet's population to half million. Counterbalancing refertilizing drug formula is lost. Mankind doomed because it won't control populations intelligently. Cogent satire in form of "manuscripts." Perhaps the ultimate story warning against overpopulation. Quasi-mystical perspective is effective.

4-590. Van Herck, Paul (Netherlands). **Where Were You Last Pluterday?** DAW, 1973, $.95. Tr. by Danny DeLaet and Willy Magiels of *Sam, of de Pluterdag*, 1968.
Sam falls in love with a girl of higher social level. He discovers that she has access to an additional day of the week. Once he penetrates this secret, he wins the girl and use of the eighth day. Later, his son follows suit and finds another girl and a ninth day. Good satire. First Europa Award, 1972.

*4-591. van Vogt, Alfred Elton. **Slan.** Arkham, 1946. Berkley, $.95; Garland, $11.00.
First appeared in 1940 *Astounding*, a classic ESP story of benevolent supermen overcoming repression by superstitious, mob-spirited man. The golden-tentacled slans are telepathic, super intelligent, physically superior mutants hated by the public and hunted by the secret police of world

dictator, Kier Gray. Young Jommy Cross, orphaned son of a slan scientist, vows to end the bigotry, but falls into the hands of a grandmother Fagin. After maturing, he continues his quest, running afoul of the spaceships of nontelepathic slans, actually true slans with some traits temporarily inhibited. But Cross, now not only a biological superman, but a technological one as well thanks to his father's discovery of a new energy source, doesn't discover this until he goes to warn dictator Gray of the tendrilless slans' planned vengeful attack on Earth. True slans are by nature "antiwar, antimurder, antiviolence." Surprise! Gray is really a true slan helping a master plan unfold for the eventual evolutionary slan replacement of the increasingly sterile normals. Descendents might include Blish's *Jack of Eagles* [4-79], Henderson's *The People* [4-304], del Rey's *Pstalemate* [4-206], and Disch's *Camp Concentration* [4-219].

4-592. van Vogt, Alfred Elton. **The Voyage of the Space Beagle.** Simon & Schuster, 1950. Manor Books, $.95.
"Nexialism" ("applied wholism") is mankind's best hope for finally escaping Spenglerian history cycles. Elliot Grosvenor is a synthesist, sailing between galaxies in the exploring *Space Beagle* and fighting both the narrow views of her crew of scientific specialists and the vicious aliens encountered along the way. Basically a spectacular parade of villainous BEMs; hypnotic space-birds, an Id-eating cat-monster, an eight-legged matter manipulator that uses human bodies for egg incubators, and a giant gas cloud that ate a galaxy. Of course, all are bested by superman Grosvenor. Three stories written into continuity, two of which date from 1939 *Astounding*.

4-593. van Vogt, Alfred Elton. **The Weapon Shops of Isher.** Greenberg, 1951. Ace, $1.25.
Immortal Robert Hedrock created the inviolate Weapon Shops as a check to big government on Earth, their creed—"The right to buy weapons is the right to be free." Now, after hundreds of years of uneasy stability, the strong-willed young Isher empress, Innelda, attempts the shops' destruction. Provincial Cayle Clark, who has a talent for luck, is drawn into the struggle, as is an innocent reporter from 1951 who ends martyred as an explosive pendulum swinging through time; behind the scenes, superman Hedrock schemes to save the status quo. Awkward, illogical, and amateurish at times, but continuously inventive and politically attractive to many. *The Weapon Makers* (Greenberg, 1952. Grosset & Dunlop, $1.25) was rewritten after its initial 1943 appearance to make it a sequel to *Shops*; Hedrock struggles to force the empress to release the repressed technology of an interstellar drive. Hunted as a traitor by both the empire and the shops, he escapes into deep space only to encounter sentient spider-like aliens who may threaten man. Hedrock outwits them

all, is revealed to be empire's original founder, and sets indomitable mankind on a course to the stars. Grandiose space opera with libertarian politics and humanistic values.

4-594. van Vogt, Alfred Elton. **The World of Null-A.** Simon & Schuster, 1948. Berkley, $.95.
Originally published in 1945, this is a complexly and unsteadily plotted space opera full of pseudo-science, gadgets, and cardboard characters, but still fascinating in its grandiose scale and audacity. Gosseyn, an immortal superman, uses dopplegangers to foil a galactic plot by villains who have subverted the machine that appoints world leaders. They seek the overthrow of the non-aristotelian system that Gosseyn originally set up to mentally train humanity into true maturity. The machine is destroyed, but the null-a-trained Earthmen resist the invaders, and Gosseyn, despite his repeated "deaths," defeats their cunning chief. In an even more flamboyant sequel, *The Pawns of Null-A* (Ace, 1956; originally published as "The Players of Null-A" in 1948), Gosseyn is carried further into the intrigues of galactic war. For a recent and improved version of this type tale, see Niven and Pournelle's *The Mote in God's Eye* [4-439].

4-595. Vance, Jack. **The Blue World.** Ballantine, 1966.
Eleventh-generation descendents of convicts, who hijacked ship taking them to penal planet, live on water planet on giant lily pad-like islands. Mild climate and socialistic community, threatened by sea beast and emerging caste system, is preserved by Sklor Hast, "Hoodwinker," who kills the beast and sets technology afoot for potential reunion with main body of mankind. Epic adventure in futuro-exotic setting. Effective presentation of ecology and resulting life-style from "criminal" beginnings. NN, 1966.

4-596. Vance, Jack. **The Dragon Masters.** Ace, 1963, $1.25. Gregg, 1976, price not set.
On Aerlith ("Stone in the Sky"), planet on fringe of galaxy, descendents of ancient war live feudally, while fighting reptillian "basics" with specially bred dragons. "Basic" raid repelled with aid of "Sacerdotes," indigenous quietistic humans. A tentacle of the galactic history of man, who must always fight to live. Intriguing extrapolation. Contrast Davidson's *Rogue Dragon* [4-148]. HW, 1963.

4-597. Vance, Jack. **The Dying Earth.** Lancer, 1962. Mayflower, £.30.
Six stories from 1950 about Earth in the far future: magic replaces science; population shrinks; the Sun is dying. Yet mankind struggles for survival in tragic heroic mood. Sequel is *The Eyes of the Overworld* (Ace, 1966). Picaresque adventures of Cugel the Clever who, having offended Iucorinu the Laughing Magician, must make a perilous journey over the

dying Earth to recover a magical adjunct for Iucorinu. Exotic characters and fascinating situations. Well told. NN, 1966.

4-598. Vance, Jack. **Emphyrio.** Doubleday, 1969.
Ghyl Tarrok escapes oppressive artisan-welfare state on a planet ruled by alien "Lords," by stealing Lord ship and traveling to Earth and the "Institute" (ubiquitous in Vance's stories), from which he gains knowledge to free his people from the Lords. Knowledge of culture and biological sources gives mankind power. Artful depiction of yet another possible world.

4-599. Vance, Jack. **The Last Castle.** Ace, 1966, $.95.
Men return to a long-deserted Earth to establish an aristocracy served by alien "Meks" and "Peasants." Meks rebel and threaten the extinction of soft-living humans, but they are saved by Xanten, human leader who breaks out of aristocratic lethargy. Parable of bitter fruit of too much luxury and power taken for granted. Psychology of idle rich convincingly depicted. HW, 1967; NW, 1966.

4-600 Vance, Jack. **Trullion: Alastor 2262.** Ballantine, 1973, $1.25.
Alastor has an edenic climate where the Trill, humans living in an easygoing counter-cultural life style, once a year play "hassade," a death-defying all-or-nothing "olympics." Problems arise when interstellar pirates make a kidnapping raid and Trill must discover the traitor among themselves. Life is not interesting without crucial conflict.

4-601. Vercors (pseud. of Jean Bruller) (France). **Sylva.** Putnam, 1962. Tr. by Rita Barisse of *Sylva*, 1961. Macmillan, $2.25 (in French).
Gentleman farmer Richwick sees a fox turn into a woman, captures her, and raises her to become his wife—after "education" that distills 500,000 years of mental development. Simultaneously, Dorothy, an earlier love, "descends" to savagery by means of drugs. A credible, stunning, minor literary masterpiece that exhibits the tremendous resources of human love. Compare David Garnett's *Lady into Fox* (1923) and Kafka's "Metamorphosis." HN, 1963.

4-602. Vercors (pseud. of Jean Bruller) (France). **You Shall Know Them.** Little, Brown, 1953. Tr. by Rita Barisse of *Les animaux denatures*, 1952. (Variant titles: *The Murder of the Missing Link*, 1958, and *Borderline*, 1954).
Douglas Templemore is sperm donor to ape-like mother Paranthropus named Derry, who bears several children. Are they human? Templemore kills one and demands to be charged with murder. Found innocent, Templemore nevertheless has advanced the problem of the definition of man to new insights. A cogent philosophical dialectic in good

supporting yarn. Compare Bass's less discursive *Half Past Human* [4-59]; contrast Huxley's *After Many a Summer Dies the Swan* [4-322].

4-603. Vidal, Gore. **Messiah.** Little, Brown, 1965. Bantam, $1.50.
John Cave: J. C.: "Jesus Christ" gives a post-mid-century world "Cavesword" and "Cavesway," the passionate desire for death and procedure of faithful suicide. From California to North America to the world, mankind joins a religion that worships death. A grim, relentless satire; a *reductio* for a species that places empirical science over reason. Probing critique of Western world's way of doing business. Compare Miller's *A Canticle for Leibowitz* [4-424].

4-604. Vidal, Gore. **Visit to a Small Planet.** Little, Brown, 1956, $5.95 (with other plays).
Insignificant, history-locked Earth is visited by a child super-alien who parks his saucer in plain view and threatens national crisis—even world and historic crisis—since he can change the past. His guardians retrieve him just in time. Comic tone; bald satire and parody in a play that reveals mankind, represented by America, as fools and cowards in context of cosmic realities.

4-605. Vonnegut, Kurt, Jr. **Cat's Cradle.** Holt, 1963. Delacorte, $7.95. Delta, $2.75. Dell, $1.25.
A satire on the atomic age and the Manhatten Project that unleashed the bomb on modern man. Here the "bomb" is "Ice-9," with a melting point of over 100 degrees Fahrenheit, that gradually freezes virtually all life on Earth—a metaphor for radioactivity? Parody of every foible of frenetic mid-twentieth-century world. Razor-witted narrative. HN, 1964.

*4-606. Vonnegut, Kurt, Jr. **Player Piano.** Holt, 1952. Delacorte, $7.95; Delta, $2.65; Dell, $1.50. (Variant title: *Utopia 14*).
Paul Proteus, engineer, leads revolt against machine/computer conformist civilization, only to find that when it succeeds, people wish for the machines again. In order or in chaos, mob psychology is stupid. Modern civilization has hate/love affinity for machines. Incisive satire; a classic modern dystopia. IFA, third place, 1953.

4-607. Vonnegut, Kurt, Jr. **The Sirens of Titan.** Dell, 1959, $1.25; Delta, $2.25; Delacorte, $7.95.
All of human history has been manipulated by Tralfamadorians in order to produce replacement part for Salo's (robot messenger) spaceship, downed on Titan. His message: "Greetings." The "part" appears very much like a beer can opener—a "church-key." Mankind's "meaning" is a trivial footnote in the process of the cosmos. Excellent satire. HN, 1960.

*4-608. Vonnegut, Kurt, Jr. **Slaughterhouse Five, or the Children's Crusade.** Delacorte, 1969, $7.95. Delta, $2.75; Dell, $1.50.

The life and times of Billy Pilgrim, who survived allied bombing of Dresden to become comfortably upper-middle class; then becomes time traveller in cosmos of Tralfamadorians and learns human existence is meaningless. Stunning contrasts of Pilgrim's different experiences provide enraged satire of mankind's stupidity. Vonnegut's best novel. NN, 1969; HN, 1970.

4-609. Vonnegut, Kurt, Jr. **Welcome to the Monkey House.** Delacorte, 1968, $7.95. Delta $2.95; Dell, $1.25.
Twenty-five stories, including "Harrison Bergeron," about "equality" arranged by system of handicaps imposed upon people with exceptional abilities; "Deer in the Works" (not SF), about a deer that gets trapped on the grounds of a modern factory—metaphor for mankind in industrial age; and "Report on the Barnhouse Effect," in which a scientist uses his discovery of psychic power to disarm the world and end war. Twelve of these pieces were earlier published as *Canary in a Cat House* (Fawcett, 1961).

4-610. Wahloo, Per (Sweden). **The Thirty-First Floor.** Knopf, 1967. Tr. by Joan Tate of *Mord på 31*, 1965. (British title: *Murder on the 31st Floor*, 1966).
The first of two SF/detective pieces featuring Inspector Jensen solving crime with implications for his whole nation. Here a bomb threat to publishing monopoly draws Jensen to discovery of nightmare secret of thirty-first floor, and a shattering conclusion. Unique and convincing. [Not seen.] In *The Steel Spring* (Delacorte, 1970), Jensen discovers that his country's politicians have drugged the population with glue on stamps to get votes. But drug's effects are eventually fatal. Cynical warning of manipulation of populations in advanced countries. Effective wedding of detective character and SF. Compare Bester's *The Demolished Man* [4-64].

4-611. Wallace, Ian. **Croyd: A Downtime Fantasy.** Putnam, 1967.
Croyd is psi superman who, in addition, can time travel. In this first of a series, his task is to save galaxy from destruction by aliens. In the process, he is "handcuffed" for a time by switching bodies with beautiful woman—a favorite Heinlein gimmick. Series extends to three sequels: *Dr. Orpheus* (Putnam, 1968, $4.95), *Deathstar Voyage* (Putnam, 1969), and *A Voyage to Dari* (DAW, 1974, $1.25). Wallace is direct heir of E. E. Smith "Lensman" [4-548] space-opera tradition.

4-612. Watson, Ian (U.K.). **The Embedding.** Scribner, 1975, $6.95.
Chris Sole, linguist, a French anthropologist studying a Brazilian Indian tribe, and a small group meet the alien Sp'thra, who are making a language inventory in aid of recontacting the "Change Speakers," dimensionally estranged para-beings. The special linguistic experience of the Indian tribe seems to have value for the Sp'thra. The Sp'thra's needs are

met, though not without international tumult. The quality of language orders perception of reality; to "improve" language, however, may have dangerous effects. Good linguistics and anthropology; well-built story. Campbell Award, second place, 1974.

4-613. Waugh, Evelyn (U.K.). **Love Among the Ruins.** Chapman & Hall, 1953.
In the super-welfare state of future England, the do-nothings and criminals live more luxuriously than the workers. Miles, a nice person when he's not a psychotic incendiary, leaves his lovely prison digs and has a love affair with a beautiful, blond, bearded ballerina, Clara—that goes sour when she has her beard replaced with a rubber mask. He finally makes a marriage of convenience to ugly Miss Flower to begin career as counter-propaganda minister in favor of preserving permissive welfare state. Waugh is master satirist. Compare Vonnegut's *Welcome to the Monkey House* [4-609].

4-614. Werfel, Franz (Germany). **Star of the Unborn.** Viking, 1946. Tr. by Gustave O. Arlt of *Stern der Ungebornen*, 1945.
In the midst of World War II, "F. W." writes a history of the future, modeled perhaps on Dante's *Divine Comedy*, in three parts, with the aid of his "guide," "B. H." He travels the universe and learns it is made in image of what man is destined to become; that even as man separates from God in time, paradoxically, man comes closer to God as the end of all things approaches—100,000 years (?) from 1943. Erudite and profound, from author of *Song of Bernadette*. Compare Stapledon's *Last and First Men* [3-56].

4-615. White, James (U.K.). **The Dream Millennium.** Ballantine, 1974, $1.25.
From ravaged, used-up Earth, colonists travel in frozen suspended animation for a thousand years to "seed" a new world. Each "dreams" into conscious memory his genetic and archetypal past; thus "knowing himself" fully and giving mankind a far better chance to succeed in a new beginning. Fascinating dramatization of the possibility that Jung's collective unconscious may actually exist. Contrast Moorcock's *The Black Corridor* [4-428].

4-616. White, James (U.K.) **Escape Orbit.** Ace, 1965.
Chlorine-breathing aliens are fighting a war of attrition with humanity that threatens the imminent destruction of both. Sector Marshall Warren is captured and incarcerated on an alien prison planet. He leads a "great escape" just in time to salvage remnants of human civilization as hostilities collapse. Rigorous details of escape plans are the novel's adventure feature. NN, 1965.

4-617. White, James (U.K.). **Hospital Station.** Ballantine, 1962. Corgi, £.175.

A picaresque story of "Sector General," a galactic hospital replete with environments and medical technology to treat every imaginable life form. O'Mara, doctor and psychologist hospital director, links the episodes together. Alien anatomy and psychology ingeniously imagined. Compare with Hal Clement's works.

4-618. White, James (U.K.). **Second Ending.** Ace, 1962.
Ross, last man of an Earth sterilized by radioactivity, survives the death of the solar system in suspended animation tended by robots who deliver him to "human" civilization on Fomalhaut IV. Mankind can expect many endings, but no end. Spectacular scaling of the life of a man to the five billion year life of a solar system. HN, 1962.

*4-619. White, James (U.K.). **The Watch Below.** Ballantine, 1966.
Several generations (100 years) of five survivors, trapped in the hold of a sunken World War II cargo convoy ship, are rescued just in time to be the only suitable go-betweens for contact with sea-dwelling invading aliens who themselves have travelled for several generations in water-filled spacecraft, non-hostilely seeking a wet planet like Earth as a new home. Ordeal of the trapped humans is persuasively reported. Their experience is a fortuitous analogue for that of the aliens, perhaps the sort of analogue through which mankind will find rapport and sympathy with extraterrestrial life. An ingenious twist on the Robinson Crusoe shipwreck scenario and a fictional crucible experience that should delight the speculative anthropologist. Contrast Verne's *Twenty Thousand Leagues Under the Sea* [2-153] and Wyndham's *Out of the Deeps* [4-640].

4-620. White, Ted. **By Furies Possessed.** Signet, 1970.
Gooey alien symbiotes that help man become mentally and physically better are brought to Earth, and spread under cover of a religious movement. Tad Dameron struggles to defeat this "menace," only to find that the true beast is within himself. Strong characterization and fast action, as well as a comment on the human psyche and modern society. Contrast Finney's *The Body Snatchers* [4-245].

4-621. Wilhelm, Kate. **The Downstairs Room.** Doubleday, 1968.
Fourteen stories (some non-SF) including "Baby, You Were Great" (NN, 1967), about film star whose emotions, electronically transmitted to audience, have unvarnished, universal appeal; and "The Planners" (NW, 1968), about a scientifically accelerated genetic transmission of intelligence in chimpanzees. Bright, hard narrative. Mankind finds scientific fruits hard to understand and control.

4-622. Wilhelm, Kate. **The Infinity Box.** Harper, 1975, $8.95.
Nine stories, from 1970 to 1975, plus an introduction by the author. Notable works include: "April Fool's Day Forever" (NN, 1970); "The Funeral" (NN, 1972); and "The Infinity Box" (NN, 1971). Some of Wilhelm's best.

4-623. Wilhelm, Kate. **The Mile-Long Spaceship.** Berkley, 1963.
First collection of one of SF's foremost women authors. Title story: A man, rendered unconscious in an accident, finds his mind free to wander around in an alien starship looking for worlds to conquer. The aliens try to find where he is located, but discover he is milking them of their secrets. They blow up their ship, and he wakes up with a headache. Enjoyable.

4-624. Williams, John Alfred. **Sons of Darkness, Sons of Light.** Little, Brown, 1969. Penguin (U.K.), £.35.
In 1973, Eugene Browning sets up a Mafia hit of killer New York policeman, precipitating series of events leading to black guerrilla revolt and an attack on Manhattan. Ends with outcome in doubt but optimism for black rebels' success. Well-written "potboiler"—in black author Williams' words. Williams is mainstream writer ranked with James Baldwin and Ralph Ellison among the best of mid-century U.S. novelists. Also wrote critically acclaimed *The Man Who Cried I Am*. (Little, Brown, 1967, $7.50; Signet, $1.25), which includes discovery of U.S. government plot to perpetuate genocide on twenty million U.S. blacks.

4-625. Williamson, Jack. **Darker Than You Think.** Fantasy Press, 1948. Garland, $11.00.
Evil in the form "Homo lycanthropus" triumphs in this 1940 story, perhaps Williamson's best. Modern man still possesses genes from his ice-age masters, a parapsychic race of shape-changing vampires. These genes have been concentrated in Will Barbee, the "Black Messiah," and he is unwittingly used to murder a group of archeologists who have uncovered the plot to overthrow mankind. Excellent description of the wild, free experiences of werewolf Barbee, but the carefully laid pseudo-scientific basis for lycanthropy seems absurd today. Compare Matheson's *I Am Legend* [4-414], Zelazny's *This Immortal* [4-650], Scheckley's *Immortality, Inc.* [4-512], and Lem's *The Investigation* [4-387] as other examples of supernatural folk myths given an empirical explanation.

*4-626. Williamson, Jack. **The Humanoids.** Simon & Schuster, 1949. Avon, $1.95.
Related story, "With Folded Hands" (SFHF). The humanoids are sentient robots designed with the injunction "to serve and obey, and guard men from harm." They carry this to the extreme that man is not permitted to do anything of potential harm and must have happiness even if it is drug-induced. Forester, an astrophysicist, rebels and is forced to develop parapsychological powers to free himself from the robots' domination, then finds that this is the robots' hidden purpose. Excellent and influential work. Compare Asimov's robot stories.

4-627. Williamson, Jack (as Will Stewart). **Seetee Ship.** Gnome, 1951. Mayflower, £.25.

Rick Drake returns to the asteroids from an Earth university to help his father find a way to utilize contra-terrene matter and fight the corporation that rules the asteroids through the control of energy. With the help of an old asteroid miner who has an absolute direction and time sense, they succeed. In the sequel, *Seetee Shock* (as Will Stewart, Simon & Schuster, 1950; Mayflower, £.25), a C-T artifact appears but cannot be approached or used until it is realized that the direction of time on this strange form of matter is opposite to the normal flow. Outstanding space opera.

*4-628. Wilson, Colin (U.K.). **The Philosopher's Stone.** Crown, 1971. Warner, $1.75.

In *Stone*, mankind has transcendent mental potential if he can develop it. A few do. They become aware of race of "monsters" that created mankind as slaves. Man must either become aware or return to slavery when the monsters awake. *The Mind Parasites* (Arkham, 1967. Oneiric Pr. $3.25) offers a similar story, constructed of fictional papers, tapes, and verbatim reports. Both novels are replete with Wilson's erudition and enormous knowledge of history and culture. Both are in the Lovecraft tradition.

4-629. Wolfe, Bernard. **Limbo.** Random, 1952.

Dr. Martine (Lazarus) spends eighteen years on a secret island doing research on the brain's aggressive centers. Outside, World War III ends and a world-wide amputee culture arises with people becoming voluntary cyborgs. This utopia fails, and Martine's research notes, along with his earlier notebooks, become a dangerous potential for a new utopia based upon a type of lobotomy. Mankind will not find utopia through any form of surgery, though it consistently attempts it. Brilliant metaphor for twentieth-century civilization's predicament. Compare, carefully, Brunner's *Stand on Zanzibar* [4-118].

*4-630. Wolfe, Gene. **The Fifth Head of Cerberus.** Scribner, 1972, $5.95.

Three novels tied together by the story of two sister worlds, Saint Anne and Saint Croix, settled by the French. The aboriginal life has been destroyed; it is, perhaps fictionally, recreated in " 'A story,' by John V. Marsch." Marsch is unjustly arrested by authorities on Saint Croix as an agent of Saint Anne, but finds himself trapped in the vicious, nightmare workings of the state ("V.R.T."). The title story (HN, 1973; NN, 1972) is of a scientist who finances his cloned eternal life by keeping a bordello on Saint Croix, and of his "son's" search for his own identity, leading to "patricide." These summaries fail to touch the complexity, meaning, and sheer beauty of these excellently written stories.

4-631. Wouk, Herman. **The "Lomokome" Papers.** Simon & Schuster, 1956. Pocket Books, $.95.

Originally written in 1949, *Papers* represents Wouk's only excursion into SF. An American Navy astronaut goes to Moon to discover "Lomokome" (Hebrew for "nowhere" or "utopia"), "Lomadine," and the memory of "Lozain," a nation of cannibals destroyed by Lomokome and Lomadine. Lomokome finally defeats Lomadine through Professor Ctuzelawis' theory of "Reasonable War," in which killing is done with scientific precision and economy. War by advanced civilization is just as vicious and suicidal for all parties as it is at any level of civilization. Satire explicitly indebted to Wells, Swift, Butler, and Defoe, inspired by reading Nicolson's scholarly *Voyages to the Moon* [6-67].

4-632. Wright, Austin Tappan. **Islandia.** Farrar, 1942. Arno, $30.00.
Islandia is Wright's childhood fantasy utopia continued and elaborated through his adulthood to the end of his life. Set facing the Antarctic, it is an independent nation in contact with the real nations of the world. Its very elaborateness is a virtue, being in published form a distillation of the massive manuscript that details even the history of its literature. In complexity of conception comparable to Tolkien's "Middle Earth" and Herbert's *Dune* [4-307].

4-633. Wul, Stefan (France). **Temple of the Past.** Seabury, 1973, $6.95. Tr. by Ellen Fox of *Le temple du passé*, 1970.
Massir labors heroically to save his expedition, downed on a chlorine/silicone-based planet and swallowed by a whale. Primitive telepathic lizards help him put himself in suspended animation in temple acropolis. Ten-thousand-odd years later, Earth expedition discovers the eighteen-foot-tall Massir and identifies him as coming from Earth's lost Atlantis. Tenacity of sentience against nature is limitless; it will prevail in some form. Splendid example of survival effort. Compare Clement's *Cycle of Fire* [4-161].

*4-634. Wylie, Philip. **The Disappearance.** Rinehart, 1951. Panther, £.75.
Superior Wylie novel whose premise is the mutual disappearance of men and women from each other's worlds. These single-sex societies are traced as they adapt and evolve over a four-year period; then they are united as suddenly and inexplicably as they were separated, as if no time had passed. But the memories of the separation are retained, of the social degeneration of the men, of the challenge and growth of the women, and they catalyze a new era in human relations—people have learned to love. Well-written social criticism and social extrapolation.

4-635. Wylie, Philip. **The End of the Dream.** Doubleday, 1972. DAW, $1.25.
Millionaire Miles Standish Smith, his sister Nora, and her husband Will Gulliver found Faraway, an estate in upstate New York, as a refuge from an anticipated ecological collapse. The collapse comes and eventually

even Faraway succumbs. Extremely well-dipicted scenario, one of the better novels of this type. Very persuasive and enlightening, and not a little frightening. Introduction by John Brunner. Compare Brunner's *The Sheep Look Up* [4-115] and Stewart's *Earth Abides* [4-558].

4-636. Wylie, Philip. **Tomorrow.** Holt, 1954.
In World War III, America sustains great losses: near Christmas, four cities are hit by H-bombs; twenty-five hit by A-bombs; twenty million dead or injured; hundreds of thousands dying in riots. U.S. population is vulnerable because of cities' concentration. Meticulous, if dated, analysis of how United States would weather attack. To escape surrender, U.S. counters with super-bomb that could (but doesn't) destroy the planet. Wylie rewrites this scenario in an excellent updated story, *Triumph* (Doubleday, 1963).

4-637. Wyndham, John (pseud. of John Benyon Harris) (U.K.). **Chocky.** Ballantine, 1968. Penguin (U.K.). £.35; M. Joseph, £1.90.
Young boy and alien, "Chocky," form temporarily successful symbiosis so that alien can give knowledge and wisdom to mankind. Not successful; alien must work in fits and starts through many people. Mankind can't accept "super" people. Well-written yarn. Compare Clement's *Needle* [4-163].

4-638. Wyndham, John (pseud. of John Benyon Harris) (U.K.). **The Day of the Triffids.** Doubleday, 1951. Fawcett Crest, $1.25.
The triffids seem a beneficent plant until human greed and mismanagement turn them into quasi-sentient, mobile flora that threaten to take over Earth, reducing man to small enclaves for survival. In the end a "weapon" to destroy them seems possible but does not yet exist. Fine pace and excellent narrative. Good post-catastrophe analysis. Compare Finney's *The Body Snatchers* [4-245] and Disch's *Genocides* [4-221]. IFA nominee, 1952.

*4-639. Wyndham, John (pseud. of John Benyon Harris) (U.K.). **The Midwich Cuckoos.** Ballantine, 1958, $1.25. (Alternate title: *Village of the Damned*).
Aliens impregnate the women in the English village of Midwich, who give birth to super-children, brilliant with psi power. The people in charge of them, though viewing them benevolently, acknowledge their threat to humanity and destroy them. A superior species must destroy mankind by its very nature—unless mankind destroys it in immature stage. A really original scenario; social criticism; good story. Very popular; basis for superior SF film. Compare G. O. Smith's *The Fourth "R"* [4-549] and Shiras' *Children of the Atom* [4-518]. *The John Wyndham Omnibus* (Simon & Schuster, 1966, $5.95) includes this novel, *The Kraken Wakes* [4-640], and *The Chrysalids* [4-641].

4-640. Wyndham, John (pseud. of John Benyon Harris) (U.K.). **Out of the Deeps.** Ballantine, 1953. (British title: *The Kraken Wakes*, 1953).
Sentient aliens infest the deep seas of Earth, and humanity narrowly escapes obliteration when they come landside. Mankind will win out in the face of catastrophe. Excellent oceanography; effective first-person journal narrative. Compare Wells' *The War of the Worlds* [2-143].

4-641. Wyndham, John (pseud. of John Benyon Harris) (U.K.). **Re-Birth.** Ballantine, 1955. (British title: *The Chrysalids*, 1955).
After a nuclear war, "normal" people gradually ostracize the mutants among them. They're wise to do so, because the dominant mutation provides telepathic ability, creating a new species. A superman inevitably, if regretfully, will make mankind as presently known obsolete. Excellent telepathy-emerging story. Compare Roberts' *The Inner Wheel* [4-480] and Kuttner's *Mutant* [4-356].

4-642. Wyndham, John (pseud. of John Benyon Harris) (U.K.). **Tales of Gooseflesh and Laughter.** Ballantine, 1956.
Eleven stories, some from *Jizzle* (1954) and *The Seeds of Time* (1956), including "Compassion Circuit," about compassionate robot servant who has her masters' bodies replaced because they are so frail and subject to pain—compare with del Rey's "Helen O'Loy" [4-203].

4-643. Wyndham, John (pseud. of John Benyon Harris) (U.K.). **Trouble With Lichen.** Ballantine, 1960. Penguin (U.K.), £.50.
The "trouble" is that special lichen can extend human life virtually indefinitely, but you can't tell the world of the discovery until you can mass-produce it. Desire for immortality and concurrent power is as old as people's experience with death. Good social psychology. Fine Wyndham story, as usual.

*4-644. Yefremov, Ivan Antonovich (U.S.S.R.). **Andromeda: A Space Age Tale.** Foreign Language Publishing House, 1959. Tr. by George Hanna of *Tumannost Andromedy*, 1958.
Nearly a thousand years in the future, Earth, a socialist commonwealth, explores its area of the galaxy and finally is contacted by Andromeda galaxy. Space opera and soap opera as an exhibition and rhapsodic presentation of fulfillment of mankind's intellectual curiosity and need for constructive adventure, in line with doctrinaire ideals of socialistic state. Tirelessly inventive of interesting problems and solutions, generally plausibly depicted. (Author's last name sometimes transliterated as Efremov.)

4-645. Zelazny, Roger. **The Doors of His Face, The Lamps of His Mouth and Other Stories.** Doubleday, 1971. Avon, $1.25.
Fifteen stories, from 1963 to 1968. Especially noteworthy are the title sto-

ry (HN, 1966; NW, 1965), where fishing for a hundred-meter-long monster in the seas of Venus provides an allegory for man's struggle to face his fears and assert his dominion, and "A Rose for Ecclesiastes" (HN, 1964; SFHF), about an Earthman, bent on learning the literature of the secretive Martians, who ends instead by becoming their savior, preacher of a gospel he doesn't believe. Also includes "The Keys to December" (NN, 1967); "This Moment of the Storm" (HN, 1967; NN, 1966); and "This Mortal Mountain" (NN, 1967). Incomparable stories by Zelazny at his best.

4-646. Zelazny, Roger. **The Dream Master.** Ace, 1966, $1.25.
Well-crafted tale full of mythic elements. Charles Render, a "neuroparticipant therapist" troubled by the death of his family, plays God by building realistic dream worlds while mind-linked with his mentally disturbed patients. Eileen Shallot, blind from birth, gets Render to help her become such a "shaper," but first he must acclimate her to "sight" through his instruments. Sigman, Eileen's intelligence-enhanced talking guide-dog, loves his mistress and fears that Render's treatments may replace him. Despite warnings, Render proceeds and becomes trapped in Eileen's dream world. Interesting contrast with Brunner's *The Whole Man* [4-119]. Nebula novella winner, 1965.

4-647. Zelazny, Roger. **Isle of the Dead.** Ace, 1969, $1.25.
Earthman Francis Sandow had learned the skills of "worldscaping" from the ancient, dying Pei'ans, secularly embracing their Hindu-like religion for that end and becoming the "Name-bearer" of the god "Shimbo of Darktree Tower, Shruger of Thunders." But his vast wealth and 1,200 years of life are both threatened by the ritualized revenge of Gringrintharl, a pious Pei'an in league with Belion, the god of fire and Shimbo's traditional enemy. The Pei'an reincarnates Sandow's dead loved ones and enemies from stolen life-recordings to lure him to the Isle of the Dead, one of his favorite creations. But the ensuing struggle is really a contest between the two gods—the apparently real existence of which surprises skeptical Sandow—in which mortal combatants are only pawns. The victorious Sandow concludes, "If the gods were real, their only relationship with us was to use us to play their games. Screw them all." Philosophic overtones similar to Zelazny's "A Rose for Ecclesiastes," [4-645], battles and setting reminiscent of his *Lord of Light* [4-649], and hero traceable to Conrad in *This Immortal* [4-650]; typical awkward lyricism. NN, 1969.

4-648. Zelazny, Roger. **Jack of Shadows.** Walker, 1971. Faber, £2.00; Corgi, £.35.
On a non-rotating world, picaresque Jack, a prince and thief from the magical land of shadows, is unjustly punished and flees to the scientific land of light to hide and plot his revenge. Returning to Darkside, Jack

gathers power to restore the world's rotation, ending the polarized hegemony of night and day. An allegory about the unification of men's divided bright intellect and dark emotions, or perhaps simply a fantasy-adventure story. Compare Brunner's *The Traveler in Black* (1971). HN, 1972.

*4-649. Zelazny, Roger. **Lord of Light.** Doubleday, 1967. Avon, $1.50.
Hindu culture has developed again on an isolated planet colonized by the spaceship *The Star of India*; this time, reincarnation is real, using mind transferring machines and artificially grown bodies. Most of the ship's original crew, conservative in their immortality and powerful in their grasp of high technology and evolved psychic talents, decide to limit the masses' scientific advance to the pre-industrial, setting themselves up literally as gods in "Heaven," their fortress city, and deciding the winners on the wheel of Karma to their own advantage. But one rejects this self-endowed godhood; Sam battles the "gods," loses, returns as the "Lord of Light" to resurrect the heresy of Buddha as a political weapon, and finally undercuts the Pantheon to the point where progress recommences. Carefully researched, *Lord* excels in its isomorphic casting of Indian philosophy and religion into an empirically based system that works. Brahma, Yama, Krishna, Vishnu, Agni, Kali, Shiva, and others love, plot, and fight; epic battles rage; the Enlightened One meditates and teaches in his purple grove; souls fly from body to body, both human and animal—and all solidly set in traditional SF trappings. Zelazny's wit, social commentary, brilliant imagery, and jarringly placid eclectic allusions permeate the work, although its philosophic issues remain largely unresolved amid the battles and background. A fascinating, creative work. HW, 1968; NN, 1967.

*4-650. Zelazny, Roger. **This Immortal.** Ace, 1966, $1.25. Garland, $11.00.
Mutants in mythic forms haunt the still radioactive continents of a depopulated future Earth, run by an island-based government as a museum and tourist attraction for culturally superior Vegans. Immortal Conrad Nomikos, alias Kallikonzaros, the Earth underground's ex-leader, fights to safeguard visiting Vegan Cort Myshtigo until his mission's consequences for Earth become clear. Action, symbolism, and writing pyrotechnics characterize Zelazny's first novel. NN, 1966; HW, 1966.

Anthologies:
The Modern Period

According to tradition, Donald Wollheim originated the modern SF anthology in 1943 with *The Pocket Book of Science Fiction*. Since that time, such works have greatly increased both in number and type. Groff Conklin reported that from 1946 to 1952, over fifty SF anthologies had been published contrasted with about two hundred genre-labelled novels and single-author collections (*Omnibus of Science Fiction*, Crown, 1952, p. ix). But in 1973, novels and collections, excluding reprints, numbered over 200 in that year alone, while 105 new anthologies were issued. In 1974, the figures reached about 250 novels and single-author collections as opposed to 78 anthologies; even though the total number of anthologies declined from 1973 to 1974, the majority of the 1974 anthologies contained only original stories (*Locus* 153, Dec. 30, 1973; *Locus* 168, Dec. 24, 1974). Besides proliferation of original anthologies, the growth in anthology varieties is further represented by the presence in the 1973–1974 lists of single-theme anthologies, year's-best series, anthologies of award-winning stories, translations of non-English SF, retrospective anthologies from single magazines, works published for classroom use in a variety of fields, and even an anthology of stories adapted from TV scripts.

The anthology has been and remains an important vehicle for SF. Given the genre's emphasis on short fiction and the existence of an active fan subculture complete with jargon, social organization, and a sense of its own historical development, this is to be expected. And once created, the anthology became a major factor in shaping the field's standards (such as Bleiler's, Merril's, and Wollheim's year's-best series); widening its horizons (Ellison's *Dangerous Visions* and Suvin's *Other Worlds, Other Seas* as cases in point); introducing new readers to the field (Conklin's, Crispin's and Amis's anthologies, and, more recently, Blish's *Star Trek* series); chronicling its history and much of its best short fiction (Healy's, Boucher's, Moskowitz's, and Knight's anthologies, as well as the Nebula, Hugo, and Hall of Fame winners' collections); advancing the genre's academic respectability (Silverberg's *The Mirror of Infinity* and Clareson's *A Spectrum of Worlds* are examples); and opening new markets for writers (Pohl's *Star Science Fiction Stories*, Carnell's *New Writings in SF*, and Knight's *Orbit* series).

Although the need for including anthologies in any volume dealing with modern SF is clearly evident, the selection of specific works from such a large and diverse population is difficult. Those annotated below were picked according to the following criteria: First, only works composed largely or totally of SF from the modern period have been included. Thus, such excellent works as Donald A. Wollheim's *Portable Novels of Science* (Viking, 1945), August Derleth's *Beyond Time and Space* (Pellegrini Cudahy, 1950), Sam Moskowitz's *Masterpieces of Science Fiction* (World, 1966) are not found here.

Secondly, the works selected had to be representative of the history and variety of anthologies in SF. To this end, nine categories were established as follows:

1. *General reprint anthologies*: The oldest type, beginning with Wollheim's *The Pocket Book of Science Fiction* (1943), Conklin's early anthologies (1946, 1948, 1950, and 1952), and Healy and McComas's *Adventures in Time and Space* (1946), and continuing through Boucher's *A Treasury of Great Science Fiction* (1959), and Moskowitz's *Modern Masterpieces of Science Fiction* (1965), and Cerf's *Vintage Anthology* (1966) to Knight's compilations (1962, 1968, and 1972).

2. *Year's best anthology series*: Pioneered by Bleiler and Dikty (1949–1958), continued by Merril (1956–1968) and Wollheim and Carr (1965–1971), and presently well represented by Harrison and Aldiss (1967 to date), Carr (1972 to date), and Wollheim (1972 to date). Several new series have recently begun, but lacking a test of endurance, are not included.

3. *Reprint anthology series*: Ranging from the venerable *The Best from Fantasy and Science Fiction* (1952 to date) and Campbell's selections from *Astounding* and *Analog* (1952, 1962, and 1962–1971), to the British-origi-

nated series, Amis and Conquest's *Spectrum* (1962–1966), Crispin's *Best SF* (1955–1966), and Moorcock's best from *New Worlds* (1968–1971). Several other reprint series exist, especially from magazines such as *If* and *Galaxy*, but are not included here.

4. *Anthologies of award-winning stories*: To date, these are *The Hugo Winners* (1962 and 1971), edited by Asimov, the *Nebula Award Stories* (1965 to date), and *The Science Fiction Hall of Fame* (1970 and 1973), edited by Bova and Silverberg, which in effect awarded Nebulas to fiction published prior to 1965.

5. *Original anthology series*: Initiated by Pohl's *Star Science Fiction Stories* (1953–1959) and Carnell's *New Writings in SF* (1964 to date), perfected by Knight's *Orbit* (1965 to date), and ably expanded by Silverberg's *New Dimensions* (1971 to date) and Carr's *Universe* (1971 to date). Other such series exist, but the above works appear to be the best and the most historically important; the latter four dominate the field.

6. *Theme anthologies*: Both original and reprint; although long a feature in SF, as demonstrated by Conklin and Pohl's two 1962 collections of SF written by scientists, these works grew in importance and success in the late 1960s, and moved into areas once controversial in the genre. Chief among these are Ellison's unprecedented *Dangerous Visions* volumes (1967 and 1972); then Mohs (1971) and Elwood (1974) explored religion, Disch examined ecology (1971) and politics (1973), and Scortia (1972) and Elder (1973) took on sex. However, traditional SF themes also abound; deep space in Elder's *The Farthest Reaches* (1968), future extrapolation in Harrison's *The Year 2000* (1970), and SF nostalgia in Harrison and Aldiss' massive two-volume *The Astounding-Analog Reader* (1972 and 1973). Many other, often excellent, examples could have been included in this category.

7. *Anthologies of translated non-English language SF*: Began to appear regularly only recently and are still not numerous. Noteworthy examples include Collier's early *Soviet Science Fiction* (1962) and its sequel (1962), Delacorte's Soviet entry, *Path into the Unknown* (1968), and Ginsburg's *The Ultimate Threshold* (1970), this latter volume being, oddly, the only one giving editorial credit. France is represented by a volume by Knight (1965), while several European countries have authors in the advocacy anthologies by Suvin (*Other Worlds, Other Seas*, 1970) and Rottensteiner (*View from Another Shore*, 1973).

8. *Anthologies for educational and academic uses*: A major new development in the field, off to a solid start with Stover and Harrison's anthropological *Apeman, Spaceman* (1968); proliferation soon followed, but only a few major examples are included here: Silverberg's *The Mirror of Infinity* (1970), Harrison's *The Light Fantastic* (1971), Asimov's *Where Do We Go from Here?* (1971), Clareson's *A Spectrum of Worlds* (1972), and Spinrad's *Modern Science Fiction* (1974).

9. *Miscellaneous works that further illustrate the history and development of SF anthologies*: Included are a serious anthology of verse edited by Lucie-Smith (1969), Blish's adaptations of *Star Trek* scripts (1967 to date), and Wilson's *Clarion* anthologies (1971 to date) of stories and criticism from the major SF writer's workshop.

As a third criterion, the works selected for annotation do not include those volumes, although often excellent, composed only of three or four novellas. A large number of these have recently appeared, such as Sallis' *The Shores Beneath* (Avon, 1971), Silverberg's *Chains of the Sea* (Nelson, 1973) and Silverberg's *Three Trips in Time and Space* (Hawthorne, 1973), but older examples such as *Sometime, Never* (Ballantine, 1957), also exist. This exclusion is based on space limitations and the inherent problem of making a long list even longer, often for the sake of one or two outstanding stories, many of which can be found in other larger anthologies, single-author collections, or novel expansions. Given these three limiting criteria, the final selections, detailed above, were based on a work's historical importance, significant impact on the field, intrinsic high quality, and/or its representativeness of some major trend or development in SF. Within this list, works nominated for inclusion in a core collection are marked with an asterisk. For series anthologies, editorial, titling, and publication variations are noted in the body of the annotation. Leader data refer to initial volume only. Named stories are included in the title index, and in the name index as well. The Cole and Siemon indexes (chapter 7) provide access to the stories in many of these anthologies, as do the *Short Story Index* volumes from H. W. Wilson.

4-651. Amis, Kingsley, and Robert Conquest (U.K.), eds. **Spectrum.** Harcourt, 1962.
Originally developed as an annual reprint anthology series for British readers to show the scope and variety of SF and to plug its value as a literary form *sui generis*; published a year later in the United States. Largely limited to U.S. genre sources and authors of the 1940s, 1950s, and early 1960s. Introductions by the editors review trends in SF and argue their case in each volume except in *Spectrum 4* (1965), where an excellent debate on SF, "Unreal Estates," by C. S. Lewis, Aldiss, and Amis is included. Excellent fiction reprinted includes Pohl's "The Midas Plague" (1), Kuttner's "Vintage Season" (2), Anderson's "Call Me Joe" (3), Bester's "Fondly Fahrenheit" (3), and Kornbluth's "The Marching Morons" (4), all in SFHF. Also, Sheckley's "Pilgrimage to Earth" (1), Wyman Guin's "Beyond Bedlam" (2), Sturgeon's "Killdozer"(3), Leinster's "Exploration Team" (3, HW, 1956), Ballard's "Voices of Time" (3), and Brunner's "Such Stuff" (4). *Spectrum 5* , 1967, is of lesser quality and marks the series' end.

*4-652. Asimov, Isaac, ed. **Before the Golden Age; A Science Fiction**

Anthology of the 1930's. Doubleday, 1974. $16.95. Fawcett, 3 vols., $1.50 each.

The Golden Age of SF is conventionally considered the 1938–1950 period, beginning when Campbell became editor of *Astounding*, ending when other major magazines began, such as *Galaxy* under H. L. Gold and *The Magazine of Fantasy and Science Fiction* under Anthony Boucher. Asimov, born in 1920, discovered SF pulps in the late 1920s. Within a decade he began his professional writing career. Twenty-six stories, mostly from *Amazing* and *Astounding*, are introduced by autobiographical commentary mixed with affectionate evaluation of the authors and stories. The stories are arranged by year and include such authors as Edmond Hamilton, Simak, Williamson, Leinster and Weinbaum, as well as less-known authors. A balanced and intelligent selection although limited to the pulps. *[This entry properly belongs in Chapter 3.]*

*4-653. Asimov, Isaac, ed. **The Hugo Winners.** 2 vols. Doubleday, 1962, 1971 (bound together in a special SF Book Club edition, 1971, and still available from the club). Fawcett Crest, 3 vols., $1.50 each (abridged).

These Hugo-winning stories are arranged chronologically by the SF conventions at which the awards were given. Volume I covers 1955 to 1961 and contains nine stories, while Volume II spans the 1962 to 1970 conventions with fourteen stories. Both volumes end with complete lists of Hugos awarded in all categories. With the exception of Aldiss's Hothouse series (see his *The Long Afternoon of Earth* [4-7]) and Leiber's "Ship of Shadows," missing from Volume II, all non-novel Hugo-winning fiction is included. Asimov's witty introductions to each volume, as well as his notes preceding each story, add an entertaining and informative dimension to the anthology. Excellent collection of some of the most popular and best-written SF of the times.

4-654. Asimov, Isaac, ed. **Where Do We Go From Here?** Doubleday, 1971, $6.95.

Anthology designed to back Asimov's contention that SF "has potential as an inspiring and useful teaching device," Seventeen stories, all from the modern period except the first two by Weinbaum and Campbell, are followed by Asimov's notes on their scientific points and by a few questions designed to stimulate the reader's curiosity. Stories themselves lean toward the "hard" SF tradition; some, such as Tevis's "The Big Bounce," are more gimmick than plot. Also here, as compensation, are Blish's "Surface Tension" (SFHF), Niven's "Neutron Star" (HW, 1967), and Clarke's "The Deep Range," but literary grace is rare.

*4-655. Bleiler, Everett Franklin, and T. E. Dikty, eds. **The Best Science-Fiction Stories, 1949.** Fell, 1949.

Major early "year's best" anthology series; stories generally limited to

U.S. genre sources and authors. Still a solid compilation of better works from the late 1940s to the late 1950s. Bleiler drops as editor after the 1954 edition, but Dikty, after combining it with *The Year's Best Science Fiction Novels*, continues the series with Fell until 1956. A final, 1958 edition appeared from Advent and the Doubleday SF Book Club. Dikty's editions are notable for yearly review essays by the editor and for a yearly SF/fantasy book index compiled by Earl Kemp. The 1954 edition carries an index of stories in the series to date. Bleiler and Dikty set the standard for later year's-best anthologies. The 1949–1950 volumes were bound together and issued as *Science Fiction Omnibus* (Doubleday, 1952), a popular and influential anthology of SF's "golden age."

4-656. Blish, James. **Star Trek.** Bantam, 1967 Vols. 1-11 are $1.25 each.
Adaptations of the stories originally run on the TV series from 1966 to 1968, and now the basis of a mass cult. The original volume was successful, and ten more have followed through 1975. Original script authors include Gene L. Coon, D. C. Fontana, Bixby, Matheson, Bloch, and many others. Among the stories of note are Roddenberry's "Menagerie" (Hugo dramatic winner, 1967, ST4); Ellison's "The City on the Edge of Forever" (Hugo dramatic winner, 1968, ST2); Gerrold's "The Trouble with Tribbles" (ST3), Spinrad's "The Doomsday Machine" (ST3), and Sturgeon's "Amok Time" (ST3), (all Hugo dramatic award nominees, 1968). Blish provides interesting introductions about the *Star Trek* phenomenon in several of the volumes.

*4-657. Boucher, Anthony (pseud. of William Anthony Parker White) and J. Francis McComas, eds. **The Best from Fantasy and Science Fiction.** Little, Brown, 1952.
Since its founding in 1949, *F&SF* has been the literary aristocrat among genre magazines. It publishes both fantasy and SF, mainly original, although many stories were reprints during the magazine's first few years. Its approximately annual "best" collection reflects the nature and quality of the magazine; Boucher and McComas edit series 1 through 3, Boucher alone 4 through 8, Robert Mills 9 through 11, and Avram Davidson 12 through 14. The present editor, Edward Ferman, has continued the series through volume 20 (1973). Doubleday publishes the series beginning with number 3. Besides the usual excellent ten to fifteen stories in each volume, other items of interest are frequently reprinted, including poetry and Gahan Wilson cartoons. An additional twenty-five stories not collected in the regular series can be found in a special volume, *A Decade of Fantasy and Science Fiction*, ed. Robert Mills (Doubleday, 1960). Finally, the lead stories, appreciations, and updated bibliographies from six "special author" issues of *F&SF* have been collected in *The Best from Fantasy and Science Fiction: A Special 25th Anniversary Anthology* (Doubleday, 1974,

$7.95), ed. Edward Ferman; authors are Sturgeon, Leiber, Anderson, Blish, Asimov, and Bradbury. Together these volumes comprise a comprehensive post-war library of superior SF and fantasy.

4-658. Boucher, Anthony (pseud of William Anthony Parker White), ed. **A Treasury of Great Science Fiction.** 2 vols., Doubleday, 1959.
Giant collection of superior 1938–1958 SF largely overlooked by earlier anthologists. Contains four good novels (Wyndham's *Re-Birth*, van Vogt's *The Weapon Shops of Isher*, Anderson's *Brain Wave*, and Bester's *The Stars My Destination*) and twenty-one shorter pieces, among which the following are outstanding: Heinlein's "Waldo" and "The Man Who Sold the Moon," George P. Elliott's "Sandra," Clingerman's "Letters from Laura," E. B. White's "The Morning of the Day They Did It," Bradbury's "Pillar of Fire," Kuttner and Moore's "The Children's Hour," Sturgeon's "The (Widget), the (Wadget) and Boff," Kornbluth's "Gomez," Dick's "The Father-Thing," and Oscar Lewis's "The Lost Years" (the only non-genre inclusion). Still an enrollment offering by the SF Book Club, this anthology has introduced many serious readers to SF.

*4-659. Bova, Benjamin William, ed. **The Science Fiction Hall of Fame.** Vol. 2A and 2B. Doubleday, 1973, $9.95 each. Avon, 2 vols., $1.95 each.
These twenty-two novellas, eleven in each sub-volume, are the recipients of retroactive Nebulas by the Science Fiction Writers of America as the best novella-length SF published prior to 1965. Forster's "The Machine Stops" (1928) and Wells' *The Time Machine* (1895) are the only pre-1938 stories, while Smith's "The Ballad of Lost C'mell" (1962), Vance's "The Moon Moth" (1961), and Budrys' "Rogue Moon" (1960) fall after the 1950s. Editor's introduction explains selection procedures and indicates that two stories that should have been included, could not be—Miller's "A Canticle for Leibowitz" and Bradbury's "The Fireman." Only Simak's "The Big Front Yard" overlaps with Hugo winners. These certainly represent much of the best SF of the times, but seem more dated than do the shorter stories in volume 1 [4-695].

4-660. Carnell, John (U.K.), ed. **New Writings in SF: 1.** Dobson, 1964.
"New writings in SF is a radical departure in the field of the science fiction short story. As its name implies, not only *new* stories written specially for the series as well as SF stories which would not normally be seen by the vast majority of readers, will appear in future editions, but *new* styles, ideas, and even *new* writers who have something worth contributing to the *genre*, will be presented." With these words, Carnell launched the series he would continue to his death in 1972. It is still going under Kenneth Bulmer (*New Writings in SF: 24*, Sidgwick & Jackson, 1974). Much like a magazine, its quality is uneven, but the series served as an important market in Britain, especially for new writers. Published in the

United States by Bantam since 1964, recent volumes are composed of selections from several of the British ones.

4-661. Carr, Terry, ed. **Universe I.** Ace, 1971. Ace, vol. 1 and 2, $.95 each. Popular Lib., vol. 3 and 4, $1.25 each. Random, vol. 4, $5.95, vol. 5, $6.95.
A superior original anthology series containing a Nebula winner in its first number (Silverberg's "Good News from the Vatican") and other award nominees by Russ, Effinger, and Pangborn. The series now stands at five volumes (Random has published volumes 3 and onward), and has carried award nominees by Ellison, Rotsler, Silverberg, Wolfe, and Vance, as well as another Nebula winner by Benford and Eklund ("If the Stars are Gods" in *Universe 4*, 1974). Emphasis on stories of literary quality by genre authors.

4-662. Cerf, Christopher, ed. **The Vintage Anthology of Science Fantasy.** Vintage, 1966, $1.95.
Excellent collection of twenty modern stories, biographical notes, and editor's introduction (aimed at demonstrating that "science fantasy" can be "literate, provocative, and absorbing"). Besides major U.S. and British authors, Spain's José María Gironella is represented with "The Death of the Sea," and Poland's Julian Kawalec with "I Kill Myself." Outstanding works include Bradbury's "There Will Come Soft Rains," Sturgeon's "And Now the News," Knight's "The Analogues," Ballard's "Chronopolis," Davidson's "Or All the Seas With Oysters" (HW, 1958), Bester's "The Men who Murdered Mohammed" (HN, 1959), and Miller's "A Canticle for Leibowitz" (SFHF).

4-663. Clareson, Thomas D., ed. **A Spectrum of Worlds.** Doubleday, 1972, $5.95.
Quality anthology by one of the leading scholars of SF and perhaps the one person most responsible for SF's recent academic respectability. Fourteen stories, all dating from the modern period except those by Bierce, Wells, London, Benet, and Williamson, are followed by informative critical analyses. These stories were chosen to illustrate the history and development of the genre, and do so admirably, ranging from Bierce to Silverberg. Only English-language SF is considered. Other authors included are Asimov, van Vogt, Clarke, Simak, Ballard, Harrison, Delany, and Aldiss.

*4-664. Conklin, Groff, ed. **The Best of Science Fiction.** Crown, 1946.
One of the earliest classic SF reprint anthologies of short SF (forty stories!) with an essay by Campbell on the nature of SF and a long introduction by the editor. Most stories were derived from the American pulps, such as *Amazing*, *Astounding*, and *Planet Stories*, and date from the 1930s and 1940s. However, the editor "tried to make it an adequate

cross-section of the field, historically as well as contextually" and a story each is included by Frank R. Stockton, Poe, Doyle, Wells, and Huxley. Other stories of note include Cleve Cartmill's "Deadline" (of interest because it was investigated as a Manhattten Project leak), Sturgeon's "Killdozer," Leinster's "First Contact" (SFHF), and Heinlein's "Universe" (SFHF) and "Blowups Happen."

4-665. Conklin, Groff, ed. **Omnibus of Science Fiction.** Crown, 1952.
Similar to Conklin's 1946 anthology [4-664]; contains stories from the late 1940s to mid-1950s, as well as earlier works. Of the forty-three stories, all fall after 1937 except one each by Will Gray, David Keller, Jack London, Lovecraft, Andre Maurois, Fletcher Pratt and B. F. Ruby, and R. R. Winterbotham. Of the more recent works, interesting pieces include Deutsch's "A Subway Named Mobius," Boucher's "The Star Dummy," Bradbury's "Kaleidoscope," and Clarke's "History Lesson." The Conklin anthologies cited here, along with his *The Treasury of Science Fiction* (Crown, 1948) and *The Big Book of Science Fiction* (Crown, 1950), represent a solid, 2,409-page, 145-story library of short SF prior to 1952, and, along with over thirty other, smaller volumes, make him preeminent among early SF anthologists.

4-666. Crispin, Edmund (pseud. of Robert Bruce Montgomery) (U.K.), ed. **Best SF.** Faber, 1955.
The British Groff Conklin, Crispin's early anthologies brought much good SF from U.S. genre sources to British audiences. His first volume contained Blish's "A Case of Conscience," while in the next are found Brown's "Placet Is a Crazy Place," Heinlein's "Blowups Happen," Clarke's "The Nine Billion Names of God" (SFHF), and Bradbury's "Zero Hour." Faber published *Best SF 6* in 1966. For later volumes, see 4-674.

4-667. Disch, Thomas M., ed. **Bad Moon Rising.** Harper, 1973.
Not labeled SF by its publisher, this noted anthology of original, socially critical SF and near-SF illustrates the genre's current blending with mainstream literature. Of the twenty-one pieces, all are prose except for Peter Schjeldahl's fine "Ho Chi Minh Elegy" and "For Apollo 11" plus two other poems by Marilyn Hacker. Outstanding items include Ellison's "The Whimper of Whipped Dogs," Disch's "Everyday Life in the Later Roman Empire," Wilhelm's "The Village," and Silverberg's "Notes from the Predynastic Epoch." The overall literary level is high, and entries by Effinger, Wolfe, Sladek, and Moorcock could also be mentioned. More a pessimistic description than a blueprint for action, despite the editor's description of SF as "partisan literature."

4-668. Disch, Thomas M., ed. **The Ruins of Earth.** Putnam, 1971, $6.95.

Anthology on theme of ecological disaster, a self-conscious effort to effect change through the presentation of "awful warning" stories. Of the sixteen stories, six are original, the others coming from both SF and non-SF sources. Stories are arranged under general headings of "The Way It Is" (three non-SF stories), "Why It Is the Way It Is," "How It Could Get Worse," and "Unfortunate Solutions." Among the more interesting stories are Dick's "Autofac," Harrison's "Roommates" (the basis for *Make Room! Make Room!* [4-290]), duMaurier's "The Birds," Leiber's "America, the Beautiful," and Gerald Jonas' "The Shaker Revival" (NN, 1970). Not as dark a vision as *Bad Moon Rising* [4-667].

4-669. Elder, Joseph, ed. **The Farthest Reaches.** Trident, 1968, $4.95.
Despite a patronizing introduction by the editor that condemns SF to a genre ghetto, a good collection of twelve original stories set in far time and space. Of special note are Carr's "The Dance of the Changer and the Three" (NN, HN), Anderson's "Kyrie" (NN), Aldiss's "The Worm That Flies," and other stories by Ballard, Vance, and Laumer. Good writing that keeps its sense of wonder.

*4-670. Ellison, Harlan, ed. **Again, Dangerous Visions.** Doubleday, 1972. New American Library, 2 vols., $1.95 each.
Companion volume undertaken due to the success of the first *Dangerous Visions* [4-671]; in the same vein as its predecessor, contains forty-six original stories, each with its own intro and afterword. Editor's introduction explains the book's origins. Art by Ed Emshwiller. Not the bombshell of the first volume, but its equal in quality: LeGuin's "The Word for World is Forest" (NN, HW); Lupoff's "With the Benfin Boomer Boys on Little Old New Alabama" (NN); Russ's "When It Changed" (NW, HN); Wilhelm's "The Funeral" (NN); Wolfe's "Against the Lafayette Escadrille" (NN, HW). The editor is producing a final volume in the series; no author will be represented more than once.

*4-671. Ellison, Harlan, ed. **Dangerous Visions.** Doubleday, 1967. Signet, $1.95.
Thirty-three original stories by SF's most talented writers; riding the crest of SF's "second new wave" controversy, this work profoundly shook the genre. The editor's original intention to provide for certain story themes, language, forms, etc., a market not otherwise available was somewhat overrun by rapid changes in publishing; conversely, this work probably did contribute to the freedom of expression that the genre now exhibits. Regardless, the collection is amazingly good by both popular and critical standards. Examples: Delany's "Aye, and Gomorrah . . . " (HN, NW); Dick's "Faith of Our Fathers" (HN); Farmer's "Riders of the Purple Wage" (NN, HW); Leiber's "Gonna Roll the Bones" (HW, NW); Niven's "The Jigsaw Man" (HN); Sturgeon's "If All Men Were Brothers,

Would You Let One Marry Your Sister?" (NN). In addition, the volume is enhanced by two humorous and informative forwords by Asimov, a meaningful introduction by the editor, extensive introductions to each story by the editor, interesting afterword by the authors, and, finally, the illustrations for each story by Leo and Diane Dillon. Without doubt the best and most important single anthology of original SF works ever to appear.

*4-672.   Franklin, Howard Bruce. Future Perfect: American Science Fiction of the Nineteenth Century. Oxford Univ. Press, 1966, $3.95, 12.95.
For annotation see entry 6-35.

4-673. Harrison, Harry, and Brian W. Aldiss (U.K.), eds. **The Astounding-Analog Reader.** Doubleday, vol. 1, 1972; vol. 2, 1973.
Tribute to Campbell, his magazine, and his era that perpetuates the legend. Volume 1 contains fifteen stories from 1932 to 1946, volume 2, twenty-one stories from 1947 to 1965. Perhaps as much a nostalgia trip as an historical document, the set is divided into twelve sections, most a few years in depth and preceded by their own introductions, within which the stories, complete with Campbell's original lead-ins, are arranged chronologically. Stories included both here and in the SFHF are Asimov's "Nightfall," Anderson's "Call Me Joe," Godwin's "The Cold Equations," Leinster's "First Contact," and Moore and Kuttner's "Vintage Season." Other notable works are Bester's "The Push of a Finger," Blish's "The Bridge," Brown's "Placet Is a Crazy Place," Campbell's "Forgetfulness," Dickson's "Computers Don't Argue," Heinlein's "By His Bootstraps," Simak's "City," Sturgeon's "Thunder and Roses," and Tenn's "Child's Play."

*4-674.   Harrison, Harry, and Brian W. Aldiss (U.K.), eds. Best SF: 1967. Berkley, 1968. Putnam, 1972, $5.95. Putnam, 1973, $6.95. Berkley, $.95. Bobbs, 1974, $8.95.
Each volume, continuing down to *Best SF: 1973*, contains an informative introduction by Harrison on the SF year and an excellent concluding essay by Aldiss. Between are stories that fit a broad definition of SF (although perhaps not as eclectic as Merril's), poems (beginning in 1968), and occasional essays, such as some selected reviews of *2001: A Space Odyssey* in 1968. Only English-language SF is included, but two translations, from the Swede, Bringsvaerd, and the Russian, Varshovsky, are in 1973; sources and authors are not limited to genre specialists. Quality varies between and within volumes; the series is, unlike Wollheim and Carr [4-701], a remarkably poor guesser of award nominees and winners, although some have crept in, such as Silverberg's "Hawksbill Station" (NN, 1967, HN, 1968), Malzberg's "Final War" (NN, 1968), Elli-

son's "Pretty Maggie Moneyeyes" (NN, 1967, HN, 1968), and Haldeman's "Hero" (HN, 1973). This is offset by the inclusion of many other fine stories, such as Ballard's "The Assassination of John Fitzgerald Kennedy Considered as a Downhill Motor Race" (1967), and William Harrison's "Roller Ball Murder" (1973).

4-675. Harrison, Harry and Theodore J. Gordon, eds. **The Light Fantastic: Science Fiction Classics from the Mainstream.** Scribner, 1971, $2.45.
Thirteen stories by authors not generally thought of as SF authors. Twain, Kipling, C. S. Lewis, and E. M. Forster are represented, but the remaining authors are post-1938: Burgess, Kersh, Amis , Greene, Borges, Robert Graves, E. B. White, Leo Szilard, and John Cheever. Excellent introduction by James Blish, "The Function of Science Fiction," which discusses SF as literature and its unique qualities.

4-676. Harrison, Harry, ed. **The Year 2000.** Doubleday, 1970.
Thirteen original stories on the theme of the quality of life in the year 2000. Illustrates the SF–future studies connection and the faith of some that SF has a role in helping us to understand the future. Introductory essay by the editor on the rise of future studies and SF's place in it. Literarily not outstanding, but several important areas are explored: ecology, population, the city, medicine, and economics. Authors include Leiber, Oliver, Reynolds, Aldiss, Silverberg, and Harrison.

*4-677. Healy, Raymond J., and J. Francis McComas, eds. **Adventures in Time and Space.** Random, 1946. Ballantine, $4.95. Modern Library, $5.95 (as *Famous Science Fiction Stories*).
The most popular and influential reprint anthology of SF's golden age; within 997 pages are crowded thirty-three stories, many now classics, such as del Rey's "Nerves" (SFHF), Brown's "The Star-Mouse," Asimov's "Nightfall" (SFHF), and Campbell's "Who Goes There?' (SFHF) to name just a few; and two articles, one on rocketry by Willy Ley and another on time travel by A. M. Phillips. This anthology dominated *Astounding SF* readers' polls in 1953 and 1956, and still placed twentieth in 1966. Stories largely from the late 1930s and early 1940s and limited to genre authors and publications; catches the cream of SF's "first new wave." Other stories of interest include Heinlein's "Requiem," "The Roads Must Roll," and "By His Bootstraps," Campbell's "Forgetfulness," van Vogt's "Black Destroyer," P. S. Miller's "As Never Was," Rocklynne's "Quietus," Padgett's "The Twonky" and "The Proud Robot," and Bates' "Farewell to the Master."

4-678. Knight, Damon Francis, ed. **A Century of Science Fiction.** Simon & Schuster, 1962.

Twenty-six stories and excerpts from larger pieces, two-thirds of which fall into the modern period. The book is divided into seven categories: robots, time travel, space, other worlds and people, aliens among us, supermen, and marvelous inventions (similar to what Conklin did), within each of which three to five pieces are placed more or less chronologically. The resulting sequences of idea development, coupled with Knight's usually informative comments, makes for an unusual reading experience. Story selections are good; superior modern items include Aldiss's "But Who Can Replace a Man?," Anderson's "Call Me Joe" (SFHF), and Clarke's "The Star" (HW, 1956). A companion volume, **100 Years of Science Fiction** (Simon & Schuster, 1968, $7.95), is built along the same lines and contains twenty-one stories. Unfortunately, Knight's valuable comments on the stories are absent from this volume. Outstanding among the modern works included are Clarke's "The Nine Billion Names of God" (SFHF), Ballard's "The Voices of Time," and Kornbluth's "The Mindworm."

*4-679. Knight, Damon Francis, ed. **Nebula Award Stories: 1965.** Doubleday, 1966. Vols. 1–4, Pocket Books, $.75 each; vol. 7, Harper, $1.25, $6.95; vol. 8, Berkley, $1.25; vols. 9 and 10, Harper, $7.95 each.
Besides annually reprinting the past year's non-novel Nebula winners, each volume contains additional contemporary stories selected by the current editors. So far, beginning with the second volume, these editors are Aldiss and Harrison (2), Zelazny (3), Anderson (4), Blish (5), Simak (6), Biggle (7), Asimov (8), and Wilhelm (9). An outstanding element is added by the frequent appearance of special essays, such as Aldiss and Harrison's "The Year in SF" (2), McNelly's "The Science Fiction Novel in 1968" (4), Suvin's "The SF Novel in 1969" (5), Clareson's "Science Fiction and Literary Tradition" (6), and analyses of Nebula-winning fiction by Anderson and Sturgeon (7). Various other small features of interest, such as memorial statements, dot the series. Some occasional overlap with the Hugo winners.

*4-680. Knight, Damon Francis, ed. **Orbit 1.** Putnam, 1966. Vols. 7, 9–13, Putnam, $5.95 each; vols. 14–17, Harper, $6.95, $7.95, $8.95, and $7.95, respectively.
The most outstanding of the original anthology series, which have had a profound effect on the SF genre since the mid-1960s. *Orbit* has produced four Nebula winners (McKenna's "The Secret Place" in 1; Wilhelm's "The Planners" in 3; Wilson's "Mother to the World" in 3; Silverberg's "Passengers" in 4), and twenty-seven Nebula and Hugo nominees by writers such as Thomas, Harness, Ellison, Le Guin, Spinrad, Lafferty, Disch, Russ, Sallis, Dozois, Laumer, Wolfe, and Bryant. Series favors works of high literary merit by genre authors. *Orbit 10* contains an index to the first ten volumes. Series currently stands at seventeen volumes

(1975). A crème de la crème anthology, *The Best from Orbit* (Putnam, 1975, $7.95) recently appeared, drawing twenty-eight stories from volumes 1 through 10.

4-681. Knight, Damon Francis, ed. **A Science Fiction Argosy.** Simon & Schuster, 1972, $9.95.

Includes two novellas, twenty-two short stories, and two outstanding novels (Bester's *The Demolished Man* [4-64] and Sturgeon's *More than Human* [4-565]), all of which, with the exception of Collier's "Green Thoughts," appeared after 1945. The short fiction, largely drawn from three American SF magazines, is of high quality; examples include Charles Harness's "An Ornament to His Profession" (NN, 1966; HN, 1967), Shirley Jackson's "One Ordinary Day, With Peanuts," Cordwainer Smith's "The Game of Rat and Dragon," Pohl's "Day Million," Sheckley's "Can You Feel Anything When I Do This?," Aldiss's "Man in His Time" (NN, 1966; HN, 1967), and Shaw's "Light of Other Days" (NN, 1966).

4-682. Knight, Damon Francis, ed. & tr. **Thirteen French Science Fiction Stories.** Bantam, 1965.

Stories are reprinted from *Fiction*, the French edition of *The Magazine of Fantasy and Science Fiction*, and date from the mid-1950s to the early 1960s, except for Mille's "After Three Hundred Years" (1922). Despite the usual SF props such as spaceships and aliens, many stories stress boy-girl, or human-alien, love: Cliff's "The Chain of Love," Veillot's "A Little More Caviar?," Klein's "The Monster," Damonti's "Olivia," and, especially, Dorémieux's "The Vana," where a man dies to save his disease-carrying alien lover. In Cheinisse's "Juliette," it is the star-crossed love of boy and his robot car. Also contains some fantasy.

4-683. Lucie-Smith, Edward (U.K.). ed. **Holding Your Eight Hands: An Anthology of Science Fiction Verse.** Doubleday, 1969. Rapp & Whiting, £.65, £1.50.

Despite variable quality of contents, still a ground-breaking effort. Contains poems by well-known SF writers (Aldiss, Brunner, Conquest, Disch, C. S. Lewis, Lovecraft, and Sladek) and SF-type poetry by others such as J. R. Colombo, Adrian Henri, Peter Redgrave, Edwin Morgan, Kenneth Koch, George MacBeth, and John Ciardi. Also contains an interesting introduction by the editor on SF and poetry.

*4-684. Merril, Judith, ed. **SF: The Year's Greatest Science-Fiction and Fantasy.** Gnome, 1956.

With eighteen stories ranging from those by Steve Allen through Ted Sturgeon to Shirley Jackson, an introduction by Orson Welles, and a yearly summation and honorable mentions by the editor, Merril launched what came to be the finest annual year's-best anthology in SF. Emphasizing literary quality as well as ideas, selections and authors were not limited to ghetto sources; thus, these anthologies include much of the best short speculative fiction written at the time. Frequently covered British as well as U.S. sources. Anthony Boucher summed up the year in SF books in numbers 6, 7, 8, and 9 (1961–1964). Merril's brief commentaries on SF are an added bonus in most volumes. Title changed to *The Year's Best SF* with number 5 (1960) and continued through number 11 (1966). Series ended with *SF 12* (Delacorte, 1968; Dell, $.75), having helped launch the "new wave" of the 1960s and expanded the genre's horizons.

4-685. Mohs, Mayo, ed. **Other Worlds, Other Gods: Adventures in Religious Science Fiction.** Doubleday, 1971. Avon, $.95.
Reprint anthology of stories with religion as a central theme. Despite tendency for its stories to be limited to Christian themes and conflicts, it illustrates SF's potential for exploring man's morality and relationships with a higher power. Superior stories include Clarke's "The Nine Billion Names of God" (SFHF), where modern science becomes the handmaiden, not the master of faith; and "Vitanuls," a parable by Brunner on how the short-sightedness of the present can destroy the heritage of the future. Several of the stories are reprinted from *Dangerous Visions* [4-671]. Another anthology of reprinted stories on the same theme is *Chronicles of a Comer and Other Religious Science Fiction Stories*, Roger Elwood, ed. (John Knox Press, 1974, $2.95). Of its six stories, the best are Anderson's "The Problem of Pain" and Bradbury's "In This Sign."

4-686. Moorcock, Michael (U.K.). ed. **The Best SF Stories from New Worlds.** Berkley, 1967.
The mystique of *New Worlds*, the groundbreaking and controversial British magazine which sought "fresh subject matter and techniques" from its authors, is carried in these stories and their introductions by the editor. Six volumes were published in this series, ending in 1971, each generally drawing stories from a 1964–1968 spread. A good sampling of Ballard, Moorcock, Aldiss, Disch, Sladek, Spinrad, Zelazny, Priest, Emshwiller, Langdon Jones, David Masson, Charles Platt, James Sallis, and other New Worlders. Makes an interesting contrast with the *Analog* [4-673] series; some would label several of these stories marginal SF at best.

4-687. Moskowitz, Samuel, ed. **Modern Masterpieces of Science Fiction.** World, 1965. Hyperion, $4.95, $13.95.
Twenty-one stories by the authors examined by Moskowitz in *Seekers of Tomorrow*. Emphasis on golden-age SF, with stories ranging from Smith's "The Vortex Blasters" to Farmer's "Mother;" other stories include Campbell's "Night," Heinlein's ". . . We Also Walk Dogs," Asimov's "Liar!," and Williamson's "With Folded Hands," Sturgeon's "Microcosmic God," Simak's "Huddling Place," Leiber's "Coming Attraction," these last four all in SFHF. Makes an interesting comparison with Cerf's *Vintage Anthology of Science Fantasy* [4-662].

4-688. Path into the Unknown: The Best of Soviet Science Fiction. Delacorte, 1968.

In an introduction, Judith Merril cites this as the first Soviet SF anthology which suits current American tastes. Certainly an improvement on the likes of *Soviet Science Fiction* and *More Soviet Science Fiction* (both Collier, 1962) with its (as Asimov terms it in an introduction) "technology dominant" SF, but still a little old fashioned by *F&SF*, let alone *New Worlds*, standards. Some of the translations seem weak. Of the eight stories (original publication date not given), Krapivin's "Meeting My Brother" and A. Strugatsky's "Wanderers and Travellers" are especially strong. A more recent anthology of a similar nature is *The Ultimate Threshold: A Collection of the Finest in Soviet Science Fiction*, edited and translated by Mirra Ginsburg (Holt, 1969), which contains such *Analog*-type stories as Altov's "Icarus and Daedalus" and Dneprov's "When Questions Are Asked."

4-689. Pohl, Frederik, ed. **The Expert Dreamers.** Doubleday, 1962.

Sixteen SF stories by scientists; some are regular SF contributors, such as Clarke, Asimov, R. S. Richardson, Hoyle, and G. O. Smith, but others include George Gamow, Norbert Wiener, and Leo Szilard. General literary quality is not exceptional, but ideas are exciting and competently developed. Editor introduces each author and, in an introduction, argues that *science* fiction is not a misnomer. Another anthology on the same theme is Groff Conklin's *Great Science Fiction by Scientists* (Collier, 1962) which contains sixteen stories—many by the same authors as found in Pohl's collection—and editor's introduction and story notes. Other scientist–authors include E. T. Bell, J. B. S. Haldane, Julian Huxley, Chad Oliver, and John R. Pierce.

*4-690. Pohl, Frederik, ed. **Star Science Fiction Stories.** Ballantine, 1953.

The pioneer original SF anthology series that ran to six numbers, ending in 1960. Among the outstanding stories from this series are Clarke's "The Nine Billion Names of God" (1) Bixby's "It's a *Good* Life" (2), both in the SFHF, Clarke's "The Deep Range" (3), Kornbluth's "The Advent on Channel Twelve" (4, HN, 1959), Davis's "Adrift on the Policy Level" (5), and Dickson's "The Dreamsman" (6). The "best" of the Star series was pulled together by Pohl in *Star of Stars* (Doubleday, 1960). Another interesting spinoff was the short-lived quality SF magazine, *Star Science Fiction*, begun in January 1958.

*4-691. Rottensteiner, Franz (Austria), ed. **View from Another Shore: European Science Fiction.** Seabury, 1973, $6.95.

The editor claims there exists a uniquely European SF marked by "seriousness of purpose" as opposed to the more frivolous U.S. stuff. Also surveys current European SF authors. Includes eleven stories from writers in Poland (Lem), France (Andrevon), Denmark (Madsen), West

Germany (Franke), Czechoslovakia (Nesvadba), Rumania (Rogoz), Italy (Aldani), and the U.S.S.R. (Gansovski, Ivanov, and Shefner). Superior stories include those by Lem, Madsen, Nesvadba, and, especially, Gansovski. Biographical and bibliographic notes on the authors are also included. Makes a good companion to Suvin's *Other Worlds, Other Seas* [4-698].

4-692. Scortia, Thomas N., ed. **Strange Bedfellows: Sex and Science Fiction.** Random, 1972. Pocket Books, $.95.
Groundbreaking reprint anthology of nineteen SF stories which deal with sex as their central idea. Stories date from the early 1950s to the early 1970s, and range from Boucher's light "Khartoum: A Prose Limerick," through Sturgeon's homosexuals in "The World Well Lost," to the powerful "Mother," Farmer's wrenching story of the ultimate return to the womb. Other authors include Silverberg, Zebrowski, Bretnor, Aldiss, and deFord. Also includes introductions to stories and a brief but interesting essay on sex in SF by the editor, "Where Have All the De-flowers Gone?" A lesser collection on the same theme is Joseph Elder's *Eros in Orbit* (Trident, 1973. Pocket Books, $.95) with ten original stories, the best of which are Silverberg's "In the Group," Goulart's "Whistler," and Zebrowski's "Starcrossed."

*4-693. Silverberg, Robert, ed. **The Mirror of Infinity: A Critic's Anthology of Science Fiction.** Harper, 1970, $1.95.
Unique anthology combining thirteen, mostly modern, stories and their critiques by leading SF critics. Each has sketches of the author and critic, followed by the criticism, then the story itself. Critics include SF authors (Budrys, Harrison, Blish, Williamson, Panshin, Knight, and Aldiss) as well as academics and other writers (Thomas Clareson, Robert Conquest, Kingsley Amis, H. Bruce Franklin, Willis McNelly, and Ivor Rogers). All but two of the stories—Wells' "The Star" and Borges' "The Library of Babel" (the only translation)—appeared in American or British SF magazines. Outstanding stories include Campbell's "Twilight" (1934), Asimov's "Nightfall" (SFHF), Ellison's "I Have No Mouth and I Must Scream" (HW, 1968), and Ballard's "The Subliminal Man." In effect, the development of the whole modern SF period up to the late 1960s is summarized in this volume, including the increasing efforts at SF criticism and the rise of recent academic interest in the genre.

4-694. Silverberg, Robert, ed. **New Dimensions I.** Doubleday, 1971. Vols. 1–3, Avon, $.95 each; vol. 4, Signet, $1.25; vol. 5, Harper, $7.95.
The emphasis is on good writing in this superior original anthology series. Volume 3 (1973) contains two Hugo winners (Le Guin's "The Ones Who Walk away from Omelas" and Tiptree's "The Girl Who Was Plugged In"), while Volume 1 managed award nominations for stories by Dozois, Lafferty, and Le Guin. The editor vows a continuation of an

editorial policy that strives for an expansion of the reader's consciousness.

*4-695. Silverberg, Robert, ed. **Science Fiction Hall of Fame,** Vol. 1. Doubleday, 1970, $9.95. Avon, $1.95.
Contains twenty-six short stories and novelettes awarded retroactive Nebulas by the Science Fiction Writers of America; these are the membership's choices as the best short SF published before 1965. Only two stories, Weinbaum's "A Martian Odyssey" (1934) and Campbell's "Twilight" (1934), appeared before 1938, while only one, Zelazny's "A Rose for Ecclesiastes" (1963), appeared after 1959. All stories are reprinted in order of their original publication. The method of selection is explained by the editor in an introduction that leaves the reader wondering which stories were omitted due to lack of space. Still, an excellent overview of short SF up through the 1950s. Only one overlap with Hugo winners (Keyes' "Flowers for Algernon"). Anthology is abbreviated as SFHF, as is Bova's two-volume sequel [4-659].

*4-696. Spinrad, Norman, ed. **Modern Science Fiction.** Anchor, 1974, $3.50.
One of the best of recent reprint anthologies designed for academic use. Twenty-one stories, interspersed with frequent brief essays by the editor, trace the development of the genre from the Golden Age (Campbell's "Twilight," del Rey's "Helen O'Loy" [SFHF], Asimov's "Nightfall" [SFHF]), through "the Postwar Awakening" (Clarke's "The Star" [HW, 1956], Kornbluth's "The Marching Morons" [SFHF]), through "the Full Flowering" (Ballard's "The Voices of Time," Delaney's "Aye, and Gomorrah . . ." [NW, 1967; HN, 1968]). Also contains a general introduction to modern SF by the editor, and an excellent brief bibliography of additional significant SF works. Other stories of note include Godwin's "The Cold Equations" (SFHF), Bester's "5, 271,009," Spinrad's "No Direction Home," Dick's "Faith of Our Fathers" (HN, 1968), and Silverberg's "In Entropy's Jaws."

4-697. Stover, Leon E., and Harry Harrison, eds. **Apeman, Spaceman: Anthropological Science Fiction.** Doubleday, 1968.
Pioneer among SF anthologies for classroom use in non-literature areas. Introductions by anthropologist Carleton S. Coon and the editors set the stage for twenty-six stories, poems, essays, and a cartoon. Informative intros precede the work's subdivisions of "Fossils," "The Hairless Ape," "Dominant Species," "Unfinished Evolution," "Prehistory," "Archaeology," "Local Customs," and "Applied Anthropology"; thus, the major areas of anthropology—cultural, physical, and archaeological—are covered. Items of interest include anthropologist Horace Miner's satirical "Body Ritual among the Nacirema," Clarke's "The Nine Billion Names of God" (SFHF), and Coon's essay, "The Future of the Races of Man."

Similar anthologies, many less well done, have since appeared for sociology, history, psychology, social problems, political science, and some of the physical sciences.

*4-698. Suvin, Darko, ed. **Other Worlds, Other Seas.** Random, 1970.
Valuable anthology containing an excellent long essay by Suvin on SF in Eastern Europe and Russia, his notes on each author, and seventeen stories by authors from Poland (Lem), Rumania (Colin), Czechoslovakia (Nesvadba), Bulgaria (Donev), and the U.S.S.R. (Altov, Yarov, Varshavsky, Toman, and Dneprov). The stories vary in quality, with the works of Altov, Dneprov, Lem, and Yarov being superior to the others. The book is historically important in the recent rise of interest in non-English-language SF in the West. Compare Rottensteiner's *View from Another Shore* [4-691].

4-699. Wilson, Robin Scott, ed. **Clarion: An Anthology of Speculative Fiction and Criticism from the Clarion Writer's Workshop.** Signet, 1971.
Unique series of selected writings from a SF writer's workshop; hence, most of the authors tend to be new to the public and emphasize literary values in their work. Also includes critical essays by Clarion teachers: Pohl, Knight, Ellison, Leiber, Sallis, Le Guin, Wilhelm, Russ, Sturgeon, and the editor. These alone make the works valuable. *Clarion III* was issued by Signet in 1973.

4-700. Wollheim, Donald A., ed. **The Pocket Book of Science Fiction.** Pocket Books, 1943.
Ten stories in what is traditionally recognized as the first true modern SF anthology. Contains works by early writers Benet, Bierce, Collier, Wells, West, and Weinbaum; also includes Sturgeon's "Microcosmic God" (SFHF) and Heinlein's "—And He Built a Crooked House" from the modern period.

*4-701. Wollheim, Donald A., and Terry Carr, eds. **World's Best Science Fiction: 1965.** Ace, 1965.
The best such compilation after Merril's. Although established as a "world" anthology, only the first volume contained any significant percentage of foreign and translated SF, despite the editors' claim to search all SF sources each year. Overall, excellent and balanced selections of the year's best, perhaps due to the joint editorial effort. Outstanding stories and award nominees and winners are too numerous to list in the whole. Examples: 1965—Brunner's "The Last Lonely Man"; 1966—Ellison's " 'Repent, Harlequin!' Said the Ticktockman" (HW, NW); 1967—Shaw's "Light of Other Days" (NN); 1968—Silverberg's "Hawksbill Station" (HN, NN); 1969—Anderson's "Kyrie" (NN); 1970—Leiber's "Ship of Shadows" (NN); 1971, the series' final year—Sturgeon's "Slow Sculp-

ture" (NW). Since that time, both editors have continued separate year's best series of their own: Wollheim's *The 1972 Annual World's Best SF* (DAW, 1972, $1.25; 1973, $.95; 1974, $1.25; 1975, $1.50), and Carr's *Best Science Fiction of the Year* (Ballantine, 1973, no. 2, $1.50, no. 4, $1.50). Of the two, Carr's may have the edge; Wollheim in his introductions seems bent on resisting recent trends in SF, condemning the rise of original anthologies (he's drawing most of his selections from magazines), what he terms naive academics invading SF, and the extremely unconventional stories being turned out by some in SF today.

5.

Juvenile Science Fiction

Francis J. Molson

Rocket Ship Galileo, written by Robert Heinlein and published in 1947, is generally considered the first American juvenile science fiction work that merited any serious critical attention. For the first time—at least, as far as most specialists in children's literature knew—an author expertly blended together characters, subject matter, and plot in a way that was novel, relevant, and appealing to young readers. Ross, Art, and Morrie, the protagonists of the novel, were believable teenagers. The subject matter—a trip to the Moon in an atomic engine-powered rocket—was plausible extrapolation from current scientific knowledge; for who in 1947 had not heard of atomic power and V-1's and V-2's—technological breakthroughs which rendered possible a variety of schemes and proposals previously judged illusory or hare-brained? The plot of the book was both exciting and timely: not only a trip to the Moon and the discovery there of an extinct civilization but the destruction of a Moon base from which a band of Nazis plotted World War III.

There was another reason why the specialists were willing to praise *Rocket Ship Galileo*. That is, the novel also belonged to a recently developed genre, the junior novel, deliberately designed to appeal to teens by acknowledging their existence and speaking to their special needs. For Ross, Art, and Morrie, like many other American teens, fretted over vocational goals; they debated whether they should obey their parents, who at first would not allow the boys to accompany Dr. Cargraves, eminent scientist and Morrie's uncle, on his flight to the Moon. However, Cargraves convinced the boys' parents that going to the Moon would be not only adventurous but educational and character-building. Seen as a junior novel, then, *Rocket Ship Galileo* readily met the important didactic requirements demanded of literature aimed at young readers. Thus, juvenile science fiction, once it was demonstrated that it could be written competently and did contain didactic elements, was allowed to enter the mainstream of children's literature.

The publication of *Rocket Ship Galileo* may have marked mainstream children's literature's recognition of SF and its potential for engaging youth, but the book did not initiate juvenile SF. Prior to 1947, American youth had access to a popular SF literature specifically written for them. As early as 1879, Lu Senarens, under the pseudonym of Noname, turned out the first of his some 180 Frank Reade, Jr., stories, which chronicled the adventures of a boy genius responsible for many remarkable inventions. Other science adventure stories, modeled upon the Reade formula, could be found in the Tom Edison, Jr., *Happy Days*, and *Pluck and Luck* series. Some years later, Roy Rockwood, consciously patterning his stories upon the Jules Verne adventures, began to write the Great Marvel series. Shortly thereafter, Victor Appleton, hoping to capitalize on the continuing juvenile interest in science adventure, inaugurated in 1910 the popular Tom Swift series, which grew to number at least forty titles. Finally, the 1920s and 1930s saw both the continuation of the Tom Swift series and the reprinting of several of the Great Marvel titles—witness to youngsters' dreams of interplanetary adventure, fostered in part by the appearance of Buck Rogers and Flash Gordon in the comics.

Youngsters, however, did not have to limit their reading to juvenile series books. Adult SF, often in pulp form, was available also to the young. It should also be kept in mind that it was not until the last decades of the nineteenth century that distinctions between children's books and adult books began to be drawn with any kind of precision. Thus, young and old readers might be reading Verne, Haggard, Wells, or Burroughs. Further, many youngsters, even when popular juvenile SF was available, probably skipped it and read adult SF. Isaac Asimov, for example, when speaking of his youth, does not mention reading juvenile SF but does vividly recall reading copies of *Science Wonder Stories*, *Amazing Stories*, and *Air Wonder Stories* that were for sale on his father's candy store newsstand.

Within the mainstream itself, certain books, usually fantasies, indirectly contributed to the development of space fantasy or SF. For instance, Robinson Crusoe's narrative of survival on a strange island and Gulliver's adventures among the astonishing miniature and gigantic peoples were read also by children and soon became staples of their reading fare, presumably whetting an appetite for similar adventure tales. Charles Kingsley's *The Water Babies* (1863) moralized excessively, but it did utilize the fantasy mode to inform its readers both of the science of underwater life and the theory of evolution; thus, the latter appeared for the first time as a topic in children's literature. The stories of Alice's journeys not only introduced children to wonderlands where ordinary reason was eschewed but sought to undermine the dictum that children's books had to teach earnestly and could not "murder" time by entertaining their young readers. Edith Nesbit's best and most representative fantasy, *The Story of the Amulet* (1906), incorporated the device of time travel and predicted a utopian London organized around the social ideas of Wells, a close friend of the author. Howard Pyle's *The Garden behind the Moon* (1895) saw moonlight as a bridge from Earth to the Moon, and the children in Frances Montgomery's *On a Lark to the Planets* (1904) enjoyed their trip in space. L. Frank Baum, attempting in many of his books an indigenous American fantasy, saw in electricity a peculiarly appropriate American material for imaginative treatment and wrote *The Master Key* (1901). Baum should also be given credit for creating one of the first fully realized robots in juvenile literature, Tik Tok, who was introduced in *Ozma of Oz* (1902) and had its own book seven years later, *Tik-Tok of Oz*. Finally, Hugh Lofting, in *Doctor Dolittle in the Moon* (1929), sent his inestimable and much-traveled hero out in space for further adventure.

After the popular and critical success of *Rocket Ship Galileo*, mainstream publishers did not take long to realize that science fiction juveniles might prove profitable. By 1958, at least ninety additional science fiction titles, excluding series books, were published in the United States. Although this amount hardly seems impressive, in comparison to preceding years, when virtually nothing appeared, the total was indeed large and indicated that science fiction was well on its way to becoming an important subgenre of children's literature. The relatively sudden popularity and acceptance of juvenile science fiction in the 1950s can be attributed to many causes: the pioneering work of Heinlein, who went on writing other good juveniles; the emergence of a handful of genuinely talented writers, such as Andre Norton and Alan Nourse, who wanted to write for juvenile audiences; the continuing development of teens and preteens as separate groups requiring their own reading material, for to these groups most of the new titles were addressed; the growing popularity of science fiction not only in novels and short stories but in comic books and films—the latter two being media of which teens and preteens were avid fans; and the Sputnik phenomenon and the resulting interest in space and its exploration, which rendered less suspect and flamboyant the speculations of science fiction.

It would be pleasant to claim that most of the juvenile science fiction in the 1950s was well done, but the truth is the opposite. Children's literature, historically, has been burdened with hack work, and juvenile science fiction is no exception. Too many publishers, eager to take advantage of the interest in science fiction, were willing to accept any manuscript dealing with a first trip to the Moon, life on Venus, or a visitor from Mars, provided the story had for protagonists youngsters—or sometimes even animals!—and ostensibly had some educational or moral value. For instance, in Leslie Greene's *Moon Ahead*, Noel and Frank and their fathers are invited to come along on a rocket flight to the Moon. A plethora of scientific and procedural information clogs the narrative, and the adventures on the Moon are tepid and predictable. In Carl Biemiller's *The Magic Ball from Mars*, J, a young boy, meets a mysterious visitor from Mars who gives J a magic ball because the boy believed in the stranger. The U.S. military appeals to J's patriotism for the ball which will grant any wish, but the Martians, fearing the possibility of planet-wide war, take back the ball without even allowing J to decide whether he might voluntarily return the ball. Or in Ruthann Todd's *Space Cat*, Flyball, a cat, accidentally becomes a crew member on a rocket to the Moon, finds sentient life there, saves his captain, and returns to Earth a hero. The last work, incidentally, illustrates the problems confronting anyone who wants to write science fiction for the younger child. Generally speaking, trying to organize a picture book around a scientific principle or technological procedure is difficult because of the intended audience's lack of scientific knowledge. Consequently, the author opts for little or no science at all and the end product is best labeled space fancy—for example, a story picture book about talking cats or monkeys acting as space pilots, or about metal-eating monsters from space.

A noteworthy feature of the juvenile science fiction written in the 1950s is the relatively high number of titles—about one third—written by already established authors of adult science fiction. (This feature is true also of subsequent juvenile science fiction.) The names of those who have written for both juveniles and adults include some of the most prominent authors of science fiction: Isaac Asimov writing as Paul French, Robert Silverberg, Donald Wollheim, Poul Anderson, James Blish, Ben Bova, Arthur Clarke, Lester del Rey, Gordon Dickson, Murray Leinster, Andre Norton, Jack Vance, and Harry Harrison. Of more than passing interest is the possibility that some of these "name" authors might have been forced, except for their juvenile output, to cease writing science fiction. Unfortunately, the evidence also suggests that several were not above placing hack work in the supposedly lucrative juvenile market. On the other hand, the competent work of Heinlein, Norton, Bova, del Rey, and Dickson provided direction and some prestige to juvenile science fiction until new talent, seriously committed to writing for children and unwilling to compromise, entered the field in the 1960s and 1970s.

In the last fifteen years, juvenile science fiction has come of age. An over-reliance on trite first trips to the Moon or meeting Martians has been abandoned, and new and wider-ranging topics have been essayed. The political abuses of behavior modification and mind control, for example, are a central concern in John Christopher's novels. Theological speculation can be found in the novels of Madeline L'Engle, in particular *The Young Unicorns* (1968), and Alexander Key. The sexism historically so endemic in children's books is under attack, especially in the novels of Sylvia Engdahl, whose central protagonists are girls who are assigned tasks usually given males. Space opera has been muted; and when it is used, as in the Rhada novels of Robert Gilman, the adventure is handled quite convincingly. The ecological movement, as may be expected, is becoming a more common topic. Adrien Stoutenburg's *Out There* is a sympathetic study of man's destruction of his fellow species and its effect upon a future where expeditions are organized to find any traces of animal life.

Perhaps the best evidence that juvenile science fiction has become a permanent, important segment of children's literature is twofold. One aspect is that juvenile science fiction, at ease with itself and confident of its value, can make fun of itself as in the Matthew Looney books of Jerome Beatty which, describing Moon inhabitants debating whether Earth can support any life, gently parody stock situations and attitudes. The other fact is that the mainstream has granted science fiction its highest awards. L'Engle's *A Wrinkle in Time*, with its talk of time warps and its depiction of a world ruled by a computer that exemplifies the worst features of behavior modification and mind control, won the Newbery Award in 1963 as the best children's book of that year. Robert O'Brien's *Mrs. Frisby and the Rats of NIHM*, the story of rats who have become super-intelligent through psychological and biological experimentation and who build themselves a utopian society, also was awarded the Newbery Medal in 1972. Finally, Ursula Le Guin's *The Farthest Shore*, the third of the Earthsea works, one of the most acclaimed high fantasies of recent years, received the 1972 National Book Award for children's literature.

The list of annotated titles that follow is a selective one, and I have personally handled and read all the books. In making my selections I have been guided more by the needs of the general reader, the classroom teacher, and the librarian and less by those of the specialist or "fan" of science fiction. There are several consequences of this approach. First, I have consulted far more extensively the reviews and commentary in *The Horn Book Magazine*, *School Library Journal*, *The Booklist*, *Bulletin of the Center for Children's Books*, and *Elementary English* (now *Language Arts*) than I have the various bibliographic and critical resources of adult science fiction. However, J. O. Bailey's *Pilgrims through Space and Time*, Asimov's anthology *Before the Golden Age*, the journal *Extrapolation*, and occasional fanzines, like *Fantasiae*, have been helpful. Second, books selected, in addition to being within the conventional age levels, for example, 9–12 or 13 and above, are those that have been written well and illustrate aptly a particular theme, approach, and direction in science fiction or represent the multivolume work of an author such as Norton or Heinlein. Third, almost all books annotated have been published since 1947 for reasons that should be clear from what has been said above. A limited amount of high fantasy has been included because it is not always possible to distinguish carefully between science fiction and high fantasy; these books, moreover, are outstanding juvenile fantasy and deserve to be widely read. However, the vast majority of books listed are science fiction and meet the criteria outlined by Joe DeBolt and John Pfeiffer in their introduction.

Readers seeking further information about juvenile science fiction face limited resources. No in-depth or extended study of the subject exists—a phenomenon probably reflecting mainstream neglect. What resources do exist, in addition to the journal coverage mentioned above, are of three kinds. First is a brief introduction to juvenile science fiction that is a very small part, usually two or three pages, of a lengthy overview of children's literature intended as a text or reference book. The most helpful tend to be the most recent, e.g., May Hill Arbuthnot and Mark Taylor, *Time for New Magic* (Scott, Foresman, 1971); William Anderson and Patrick Grogg, *A New Look at Children's Literature* (Wadsworth, 1972); Bernard J. Lonsdale and Helen K. Mackintosh, *Children Experience Literature* (Random, 1973); and Sam Leaton Sebesta and William J. Iverson, *Literature for Thursday's Child* (Science Research Associates, 1975). A second source of information is the infrequent essay dealing with some aspect of juvenile science fiction. Of these the best are: Virginia McCaulet, "Out of This World: A Bibliography of Space Literature for Boys and Girls," *Elementary English*, 36 (February 1959), 98; M. Jean Greenlaw, "Science Fiction: Impossible! Improbable! or Prophetic?," *Elementary English*, 48 (April 1971), 201; Sylvia Louise Engdahl, "The Changing Role of Science Fiction in Children's Literature," *The Horn Book Magazine*, 47 (October 1971), 450; and Thomas Roberts, "Science Fiction and the Adolescent," *Children's Literature: The Great Excluded*, II (1973), 87. Third is the work of adult science fiction criticism or commentary that occasionally alludes to juveniles. Perhaps the most useful is Tuck's *The Encyclopedia of Science Fiction and Fantasy through 1968, I: Who's Who, A–L* [7-22].

Bibliography: Juvenile Science Fiction

*5-1. Alexander, Lloyd. **The Book of Three.** Holt, 1964, $3.59. Dell, $1.25.

The first of the five-volume chronicles of Prydain, an imaginary land modeled upon Wales and its legends and myths. Taran, who wants to become a hero, becomes, instead, Assistant Pig-keeper. Yet, oddly, he is caught up in the invasion of his homeland and finds that he is instrumental in its successful defense. Thus, he takes a first important step in the discovery of his real identity and in following what he believes is his destiny. An ALA Notable Book. Other volumes are: *The Black Cauldron* (1965), ALA Notable Book and Newbery Medal runner-up; *The Castle of Llyr* (1966); *Taran Wanderer* (1967); and *The High King* (1968), Newbery Award, 1969. In addition to the brilliant recreation of Welsh myth and legend, the chronicles are noteworthy for the use of humor; the convincing portrait of a slowly maturing Taran who understands profoundly by the end that character is indeed destiny; and an often unconventional and offbeat look at the nature of heroism. 10–14.

5-2. Allum, Tom (U.K.). **Boy Beyond the Moon.** Bobbs, 1960. (British title: *Emperor of Space*, 1959).

Guy Abbot meets Professor Harvey and learns he is a famous expert in interplanetary travel whose innovative space ship is rejected as unworkable by the government. Unexpectedly, the Professor dragoons four escaped prisoners and Guy as a crew and they take off for Emperor, the mysterious planet. The journey out, the sudden death of Harvey, encountering prehistoric fish and tremendous purplish fires, a mutiny by the prisoners, a rescue party, and a novel return to Earth make up the adventures. Accurate scientific information; an above-average space adventure with a refreshingly different set of characters. 11–14.

5-3. Anderson, Poul. **Vault of the Ages.** Winston, 1952.
Five hundred years after the "Doom," the Lann army from the north invades the peaceful Dale country and threatens the vestiges of civilization. Escaping from maurading Lanns, Carl stumbles upon a time vault in the ruins of a city that summarizes in books and containers past scientific and humane knowledge for the use of whatever people survive the nuclear holocaust. Carl determines that the store of knowledge, instead of being taboo, is needed by the people who may, hopefully, profit wisely. However, both the Lann army and ignorance must be overcome before the time vault can open its riches. Brisk adventure; well written; effective in dramatizing human ambivalence before the potential of knowledge. 12 and up.

5-4. Appleton, Victor. **Tom Swift and His Electric Rifle.** Grosset and Dunlap, 1911.
Having perfected his electric rifle, Tom decides to try it out elephant hunting in Africa. With a crew made of his associates Ned Newton and Mr. Damon, and an elephant hunter, Durban, Tom takes off in the *Black Hawk*, his newest airship. In Africa, Tom becomes embroiled in native attacks, rescuing various whites and tracking down lions and elephants. Representative of the popular Tom Swift series written by the Edward Stratemeyer Syndicate. Tom is an inventive genius, easily superior to his contemporaries and able to overcome all dangers. The Tom Swift books have been periodically reissued and revised and today appear as the Tom Swift, Jr., series, still published by Grossett and Dunlap as $1.95 paperbacks. 9–13.

5-5. Asimov, Isaac (as Paul French). **David Starr: Space Ranger.** Doubleday, 1952. Signet, $.95.
To an Earth suffering from over-population its Martian colony is a necessary breadbasket. When poisoned food begins to turn up, David Starr, agent of the Council of Science, is sent to investigate and uncovers an alien conspiracy. Routine adventure story; among the first space operas for children; significant also because of the special status of its author. 12 and up. There are five other David Starr adventures: *Lucky Starr and the Pirates of the Asteroids* (1953), *Lucky Starr and the Oceans of Venus* (1954), *Lucky Starr and the Big Sun of Mercury* (1956), *Lucky Starr and the Moons of*

Jupiter (1957), and *Lucky Starr and the Rings of Saturn* (1958), all Signet, $.75 each.

*5-6. Ballou, Arthur, W. **Bound for Mars.** Little, Brown, 1970, $5.95.
The *Pegasus*, under command of Col. Sanborn, is scheduled to place the first permanent station upon Mars. For this historically important mission the crew has been most carefully screened, physically and psychologically. However, one member of the crew, the youngest, George Foran, cracks and threatens the ship's safety. Carefully the commander entraps Foran, and the mission continues. Actual incidents are not, per se, much above routine; what is impressive is the authentic detailing of on-board procedures, especially the in-space repair of one sled that malfunctions; highly recommended for hard science fiction devotees. 12–14.

5-7. Baum, Lyman Frank. **The Master Key: An Electrical Fairy Tale.** Bowen-Merrill, 1901. Hyperion, $3.75, $10.50.
Rob Joslyn, precocious tinkerer in things electrical, accidentally hits the Master Key and summons the Demon of Electricty. Like the genii of old, the Demon provides Rob with various devices—a travel machine, a "blaster," a garment shield, food tablets, a recorder of ongoing events, and spectacles that distinguish good and evil—all utilizing electrical or magnetic power. Each device, although working "magically" to the observer, is explained on scientific grounds—explanations asserted but not demonstrated. Rob enjoys numerous adventures around the world but decides to return the devices to the Demon because mankind is not wise enough to handle advanced technology. Routine adventure spiced by early twentieth-century American chauvinism; early science fantasy; important pioneering attempt to adapt current science to traditional fantasy to create an American fairy tale. 10 and up.

*5-8. Beatty, Jerome, Jr. **Matthew Looney's Voyage to the Earth.** Scott, 1961. Avon $.95.
Matthew, a Moon-dweller, is selected to accompany his uncle on a flight to Earth to test for life and utility. No life can be found since the landing occurs at the South Pole. However, it is Matthew's recorded observation of his pet's going into water and living that vindicates the voyage and shows that life can exist on Earth. A lighthearted spoof of science fiction formulas; enjoyable for both juveniles and adults; enhanced by Gahan Wilson's droll illustrations. 10 and up. Matthew's adventures are continued in *Matthew Looney's Invasion of the Earth* (1965), *Matthew Looney in the Outback* (1969), and *Matthew Looney and the Space Pirates* (1972).

5-9. Berna, Paul (France). **Continent in the Sky.** Abelard-Schuman, 1963. Tr. by John Buchanan-Brown from *Le continent du ciel*, 1955.
Michael stows away on the space ship *Danae* and becomes embroiled in an uprising by those that want to open the Moon to commercial ex-

ploitation. After a series of mildly interesting adventures the uprising is put down. Conventional characterization; technology is more prop than hard science; however, a strong feature is the description of lunar seasons, terrain, and the various stations or camps on the Moon. 11–13.

5-10. Berry, James R. **Dar Tellum: Stranger from a Distant Planet.** Illus. by E. Scull. Walker, 1973, $3.95. Scholastic Book Service, $.75.
Ralph makes contact with a plant-like form, Dar Tellum, from the planet Sidra. As earth is suffering from an overabundance of carbon dioxide in the atmosphere, Dar Tellum suggests placing certain algae in the atmosphere, and the problem of pollution is alleviated. A simple story; some humor; plenty of striking black-and-white illustration; one of the few science fiction picture story books that work. 6–8.

5-11. Biemiller, Carl. L. **The Hydronauts.** Doubleday, 1970, $4.95.
A post-catastrophe story. Because of great changes brought about by radiation, the seas have become the major source of food. Kim, Toby, Genright, and Tuktu are trainees in the Warden Service that oversees the harvesting of the oceans. Patrolling the kelp forests, guarding the shark pens, and tracking down a mysterious hostile power provide the four ample adventure and experience. Provocative look at future marine life, harvesting the sea, and water survival techniques; taut writing; credible characterization. 12 and up.

5-12. Blish, James. **Mission to the Heart Stars.** Putnam, 1965.
The flight of the starship *Argo* across the galaxy is the occasion for an investigation into the various forms those societies earth might face in the future may take. Stability vs. change, self-satisfachion vs. curiosity, coercion vs. tolerance are the poles around which these societies are organized; another topic of investigation is the way society is affected by technological advancement and sheer lasting power. Although lacking in exciting adventures, the novel contains ample, provocative speculation and discussion. 14 and up.

*5-13. Bova Ben. **Exiled from Earth.** Dutton, 1971, $.95, $5.95.
A world suffering from overpopulation fears genetic engineering, so the best geneticists and support scientists are banished to an orbiting satellite. Some scientists are mysteriously reprieved, but, Lou Christopher discovers, only to aid unwittingly a revolt that fails. Lou, again banished, convinces his associates that the only hope for the race's preservation is to aim for the stars, and they depart Earth. Tight, suspenseful writing, especially the description of Lou's escape attempt; thoughtful examination of science's need to be free. 13 and up.

5-14. Brink, Carol Ryrie. **Andy Buckram's Tin Men.** Viking, 1966, $4.95.
Andy Buckram, very clever at machines, assembles four robots to per-

form some of his chores: Campbell, a spoiled baby; Bucket, to carry; Lily-Belle, to sing and babysit; Supercan, to row a boat. During a storm the robots are hit by lightning and, electrified, take on life of their own. A series of humorous incidents occurs during an ensuing flood. Although a robot story, the technology of robots is put aside in favor of humor and incidents readily enjoyable to children. 9–11.

5-15. Cameron, Eleanor. **The Wonderful Flight to the Mushroom Planet.** Little, Brown, 1954, $5.95.
When David and Chuck build a small space ship and deliver it to Mr. Bass, the boys are informed of the existence of the mushroom planet, Basidium, which can be seen only by a special filter devised by Bass, and that they and their spaceship have been selected to fly to check on conditions on Basidium. There the boys assist in preventing disaster by suggesting how more sulfur can be placed in the planet's diet. Returning, the boys can enjoy their triumph only in secret. Well written, mildly entertaining combination of science fiction and fantasy; popular with children. Other mushroom planet books are *Stowaway to the Mushroom Planet* (1956), *Mr Bass's Planetoid* (1958), *A Mystery for Mr. Bass* (1960), and *Time and Mr. Bass* (1967). 11–13.

5-16. Capon, Paul (U.K.). **Flight of Time.** Heinemann, 1960.
A Wellsian time travel book. Four children, accidentally blundering into a UFO, travel to 2260 England. Then follows a glance both at futuristic cities, travel, and communication, and at alterations to the geography of England. More interesting is the adventure in the past, 1960 B.C. While observing a bloody battle between two stone-age peoples over the talisman spaceship, the children are under attack and, just managing to activate the controls, return to the present. Above average in style and characterization. 12–14.

5-17. Carlsen, Ruth Christoffer. **Ride a Wild Horse.** Houghton Mifflin, 1970, $3.50.
Julie Solstead or Eiluj Daetslos, a girl from outer space, finds herself stranded on Earth. In the Sutton barn, Julie, finding a merry-go-round horse, Diablo Grande, discovers that it is a transductor which will allow her to travel around looking for a station to her unnamed world. After a series of mildly exciting adventures, Julie locates the station at Los Alamos and leaves, having tried unsuccessfully to invite young Barney Sutton to her world. An effective, though low-keyed, combination of science fiction and fantasy. 11–13.

*5-18. Christopher, John (pseud. of Christopher Samuel Youd) (U.K.). **The Guardians.** Macmillan, 1970, $5.95.
In 2052, England is divided into two parts: the Conurb, a megalopolis teeming with unrest and pacified by bread and games, and the County, where the gentry pursue a rural lifestyle. Conurban Rob flees, after the

mysterious death of his father, to the County where he is befriended by the Giffords and passed off as gentry. In the course of an uprising, Rob learns the terrifying facts of the guardians' systematic repression of all dissident elements, and, giving up an opportunity to become a guardian, leaves for the Conurb to join the revolutionary movement. Tautly written; thoughtful study of the potentially evil implications of behavioral modification and mind control. 12–14.

5-19. Christopher, John (pseud. of Christopher Samuel Youd) (U.K.). **The Prince is Waiting.** Macmillan, 1970, $4.95. Collier, $.95.
After a series of earthquakes has destroyed much of civilization, England rebuilds after the pattern of medieval walled cities, ruled over by the spirits as they are interpreted by the seers. Thirteen-year-old Luke suddenly finds himself recognized when his father is selected Prince of Winchester. Luke is forced after his father's sudden death to flee to the Sanctuary where science and technology are preserved and augmented and the seers practice trickery to keep the people malleable. Luke also discovers that he is to be groomed to become Prince of Princes and reunite the cities. The first of a trilogy; the others, *Beyond the Burning Lands* (1971) and *The Sword of the Spirits* (1972), continue Luke's career as he fails at reunification through force and becomes content to wait and use peaceful means. As is typical of author, dramatic interplay and ample incidents; investigation of both proper use of science and technology, and individual rights vs. society's needs. 12–14.

***5-20.** Christopher, John (pseud. of Christopher Samuel Youd) (U.K.). **The White Mountains.** Macmillan, 1967, $4.95. Collier, $1.25.
The first volume in the "tripod" trilogy about a successful invasion of Earth by aliens and its eventual triumph over the invaders. The tripods consolidate their control by inserting metal communicators into the heads of all adults; thus, behavior modification is quick and brutal if need be. Will, Henry, and Jean Paul all fear the ceremony of capping that marks rites of passage and set out to join a small band of humans in the White Mountains who resist the tripods. Picture of future life in England after an alien invasion is convincing and troubling; journey of boys is exciting and suspenseful; tripods are suggestive of Wells. In *The City of Gold and Lead* (Macmillan, 1967, $4.95; Collier, $1.25), Will and Fritz enter into the city of the masters to discover the nature of tripods and ascertain whether there is any way they can be overthrown. *The Pool of Fire* (Macmillan, 1968, $5.95; Collier, $1.25) describes the overthrow of tripods and their masters. However, an ominous note enters at the end when the various nations squabble among themselves. 12–14.

5-21. Christopher, John (pseud. of Christopher Samuel Youd) (U.K.). **Wild Jack.** Macmillan, 1974, $5.95.
Another of the author's studies of future societies based upon valid con-

temporary trends. Young Chris is falsely accused of criticizing the status quo and is summarily sent to an island camp where he is to be reformed through a regimen of harsh treatment. He becomes friends of Kelly and Sunyo, and the three escape to the Outlands, a supposedly wild and fearful area, and fall into the hands of Wild Jack, a despised Robin Hood-like outlaw. The boys successfully undergo an ordeal and become accepted into the band of outlaws. First volume of a proposed trilogy. As is typical of author's work, adventure, dramatic conflict, and intrigue abound. 12–14.

5-22. Clarke, Arthur Charles (U.K.). **Dolphin Island.** Holt, 1963, $4.95. Berkley, $.95.
A story of experiments on Dolphin Island to open up more effective communication with the dolphins. Johnny Clinton, unloved runaway, discovers he has a special affinity with dolphins when they rescue him from a sinking hovercraft. Later, after a great storm, he uses the dolphins to surf across to the mainland to bring medical aid. Characterization of humans and incidents are routine; what is above average is the depiction of various experiments, current and future, with dolphins, all of which assume that one day dolphins and humans will communicate freely. 12–14.

*5-23. Clarke, Arthur Charles (U.K.). **Islands in the Sky.** Holt, 1952, $3.97. Signet, $.95.
Roy Malcolm, as his prize for winning a TV quiz show in the second half of the twenty-first century, goes out to an orbiting space station. There he undergoes several adventures involving space pirates, the making of a space film, and a runaway rocketship. The strength of the book, despite its publication date, is the detail, all plausibly explained, of the procedures of space travel and life on an orbiting station. The same thoroughness later seen in *2001: A Space Odyssey* [4-158] (1968) is clearly evident. As an adventure story, routine; as an investigation into the technology necessary for space travel, exceptional. 12–15.

5-24. Clarke, Joan (U.K.). **The Happy Planet.** Lothrop, 1965, $5.75.
A post-catastrophe story. Three future societies are contrasted: the Tuanians, descendants of the Getaways who left before the great destruction, are a technologically advanced, highly regimented people; the Hombods, descending from holocaust survivors, have established a semi-pastoral life which may make Earth a "happy planet"; and the Dredfooters, descended from cyborgs, attempt to prey on the Hombods. A Tuanian attempt to investigate Earth's utility is thwarted, and Earth is spared the joyless, rationalistic life of Tuan. Although a relatively thoughtful study of possible societies, its excessive length may hamper enjoyment. 12–15.

5-25. Craigie, David (U.K.). **The Voyage of the Luna I.** Messner, 1949. Martin and Jane Ridley, members of a British family famous for exploring, stow away on board a test rocket that precedes man's first flight to the Moon. Once there the children encounter lunar ants, ash forests, snakes, and bats. While the children explore the Moon, the second rocket is readied for their rescue, and the children return world-famous. A Jules Verne-like adventure with a premium on fanciful incidents and not science; firm and very British characterization; slowly developing story because of time devoted to background and minor characters. 12–14.

*5-26. Cross, John Keir (U.K.). **The Angry Planet.** Coward, 1946. $5.95.
Three children stow away on an experimental rocket ship bound for Mars. There they encounter the Beautiful people, who are mobile plant life, and the Terrible Ones, ugly mushroom-like plants. In spite of their best efforts, the humans and the Beautiful people are overcome in battle, the rocket crew barely managing to escape. Finally, a volcanic explosion seemingly terminates all Martian life. A British book influenced by Wells, and one of the very first science fiction mainstream novels, it precedes even *Rocket Ship Galileo* [5-44]. Use of journal device for a multiple perspective provides effective change of mood and narrative pace; careful, speculative discussion of possible life on Mars. 13–15.

5-27. del Rey, Lester. **The Infinite Worlds of Maybe.** Holt, 1966, $3.59.
Bill Franklin's father has disappeared into one of the infinite possible worlds, leaving behind for his son a cryptic note. Assisted by Professor Adams, Bill studies his father's notes until the pair figure out how they, too, can enter into the possible worlds. Following his father's track, Bill travels into the future, a second war between the states, a simian-dominated land, a society with a technology that satisfies all wants (where Adams remains), an ice age, and finally a society devoted to individual perfection, where his father awaits him. Investigation of both a variety of alternative societies humans might select if comfort, ease, and pleasure are goals, and of the nature of time. 13–15.

5-28. del Rey, Lester. **The Runaway Robot.** Westminster, 1965, $4.50.
Sixteen-year-old Paul Simpson must return to Earth from Ganymede and leave behind his robot, Rex. Paul jumps ship and is reunited with Rex, who also has been pining for Paul. After several adventures in which the pair are forced to separate, the two are again happily reunited on Earth. A feature that sets the book off from the commonplace is that it is told from Rex's perspective. Humor also abounds because of Rex's habit of assuming, even against the evidence of his "eyes," that his human masters are superior in all respects to robots, since masters by definition never make errors and know all. 12–14.

5-29. del Rey, Lester. **Step to the Stars.** Winston, 1954.
Eschewing space opera gadgetry and employing then-current knowledge and techniques, the book plausibly and convincingly lays out the various stages and dangers of constructing the first space station. The narrative husk involves Jim Stanly's growth from a lonely, skilled mechanic, too poor to pursue his goal of becoming a space pilot, to a confident, poised man who earns his space pilot wings. A subplot of espionage and sabotage by a pacifist group opposed to military uses of space is too conventional to add much to the book's impact. 12 and up.

*5-30. Dickinson, Peter (U.K.). **The Weathermonger.** Little, Brown, 1969, $5.95.
The first volume in the Changes trilogy. Geoffrey and his sister Sally, having been abandoned to die as witches, escape to France. They are urged to return to England and discover the cause of the Changes that have thrown the British Isles back into the Middle Ages, where ignorance and superstition again rule, all things mechanical are feared, and even the weather is controlled by incantation. The children find out that Merlin's sleep has been disturbed and, unhappy with what he sees, Merlin has sent England back to a time he knows. The children convince him to wait for a more suitable time to return and he relents, freeing England from its curse. A brilliantly imaginative combination of myth and science fiction. *Heartsease* (Little, Brown, 1969, $5.95) recounts a group of children's successful rescue of a witch. In *The Devil's Children* (Little, Brown, 1970, $5.95), Nicky and a band of Sikhs, free of the madness caused by the Changes, become allies, settle on a farm, and beat off various threats to their safety. 12–14.

5-31. Dickson, Gordon R. **Secret under the Sea.** Holt, 1960. Scholastic Book Service, $.85.
Speculation about marine and terrestrial life, especially the dolphins, and supposed Martian sea life save what would otherwise have been a routine "space adventure" for children. Also contributing to the book's effectiveness is the notion of an undersea building which is part home and part lab for Robbie and the Hoenig family. The sometimes-humorous illustrations by Jo Ann Stover also are an asset. 11–13.

5-32. Dickson, Gordon R. **Space Winners.** Holt, 1965, $3.25.
Jim, Curt, and Ellen are selected by the Alien Federation for a secret training mission of great moment. They are joined by Atakit, a small, squirrel-like but strong alien. Crash landing on Quebahr, a planet closed to technological knowledge, the four, after various adventures, assist in establishing cooperation among the several hostile peoples. They discover, also, that their mission actually was to Quebahr, and the three teens become part of an advance cadre for bringing Earth into the Federation. Well-paced narrative, competently written; many surprises. 12–14.

5-33. du Bois, William Pene. **The Twenty-One Balloons.** Viking, 1947, $5.95. Dell, $1.25.

Krakatoa, in the late nineteenth century, is the site of an amazing civilization that combines outlandish but workable household devices to save labor and a utopian social organization built around eating tastes and financed by a diamond hoard. Professor Sherman, a retired teacher on a balloon tour over the Pacific, is forced down near Krakatoa and is invited to join the group. The eruption of the volcano ends the utopian experiment, and the Professor escapes to inform a curious country why he was found in the ocean amidst twenty-one balloons. A humorous, Jules Verne-like, richly imaginative book that can be enjoyed by all. Newbery Award, 1948. 10 and up.

*5-34. Engdahl, Sylvia Louise. **Enchantress from the Stars.** Atheneum, 1970, $.95, $5.95.

A long, detailed novel which is built around the notion that a traditional fairy tale may actually refer to incidents involving a wise, superior race visiting a younger race and world to spare it contamination. To Georyn, a youngest son, Elana is an enchantress who would help him destroy a ravaging dragon, actually a rock-destroying machine of the Imperial Exploration Corps. Elana and her father instruct Georyn in utilizing his latent psychological power, which frightens the materialistic Imperial colony, another Youngling people, to leave the planet—Earth? Strong features are the working out of correspondences between fairy tale and the mission, anticolonizing theme, and the preeminence of Elana; thus, a non-sexist novel. Newbery Honor Book, 1971. 13–15.

5-35. Engdahl, Sylvia Louise. **The Far Side of Evil.** Atheneum, 1971, $.95, $6.50.

Another long detailed story devoted to Elana and the Anthropological Service. Elana, now graduated from the Academy, is sent on a mission to Toris, a Youngling planet, split between liberal and reactionary factions and on the brink of war. As is usual, she is to observe and not interfere. However, a second agent, Randil, becoming too involved, falls in love and interferes. Before matters can be set right and Toris can turn its attention to space travel and not war, Elana is imprisoned and tortured and Randil killed. Good, but drawn out, depiction of Elana's interrogation through brain washing; thus, length may offset admirable attempt to fuse science fiction and conventional romance formulas. 13–15.

5-36. Fairman, Paul W. **The Forgetful Robot.** Holt, 1968, $3.75.

A robot with a defective memory bank, an old grandfather and his two grandsons who want to put on Shakespeare for the isolated planets and stations in space, archeological forays into Zark and the other forbidden cities of Mars, a fanatic "do-gooder" who wants to organize the hitherto-unknown Shadow People, and an assortment of henchmen combine to make a fast-moving, unpretentious story. Told from the robot's point of view, the story is amusing. Except for the laws of robotics that are embodied in the robot's behavior, there is no serious science; the purpose of the book is to provide easy fun, and it does succeed. 11–13.

*5-37. Fisk, Nicholas (U.K.). **Trillions.** Pantheon, 1971, $4.95.
Countless numbers of strange, geometric objects, called trillions by the children, fall from the skies upon Earth. Thirteen-year-old Scott Houghton, who has an extraordinary ability to observe and think, discovers that the trillions have intelligence, are from a destroyed planet, and have come to Earth seeking work and a new home. General Hartman is the leader of those who see the trillions as invaders seeking to destroy, and he proposes to exterminate them. Scott, however, communicating with the trillions, has them leave to continue their search. Suspenseful, well-written narrative; political overtones; ecological orientation. 12–14.

*5-38. Garner, Alan (U.K.). **Elidor.** Walck, 1965. Collins, £1.05.
The Watson children, playing ball near a slum church, are drawn into Elidor, a parallel world, and become embroiled in a struggle against the forces of darkness. They take the Treasures, needed to bolster Elidor, back to England for safe keeping. The children and their home become the object of the dark's search for the Treasures, manifested in bizarre electrical phenomena. Victory is achieved when the children aid the unicorn Findhorn, as its death song and the Treasures thrown back into Elidor overwhelm the dark. Striking instance of traditional myth and fantasy material in contemporary garb; exciting, tersely written story. 13 and up.

5-39. Gilman, Robert Cham (pseud. of Alfred Coppel). **The Rebel of Rhada.** Harcourt, 1968. Gollancz, £1.00.
First volume in a space-opera trilogy concerning Rhada and its leaders. In a future when only tantalizing fragments remain of lost civilizations, science and technology are unsanctioned, and the Second Stellar Empire is threatened by internal strife, Kier, warleader of Rhada, puts down a revolt against great odds. Featured is a dizzying array of incidents and characters including telepaths, cyborgs, humanoids, witches, and warlocks. In the second volume, *The Navigator of Rhada* (Harcourt, 1969. Gollancz, £1.20), hundreds of years later, the Order of Navigators, grown ambitious, plans to substitute for the Emperor his twin, a young Navigator, Kynan, but is foiled by him. The concluding volume, *The Starkahn of Rhada* (Harcourt, 1970), concerns the fortunes of the Starkahn, a descendant of Kier the Great, who saves Earth from the destruction planned by disgruntled colonists in a faraway constellation. 14 and up.

*5-40. Halacy, Daniel Stephen, Jr. **Return from Luna.** Norton, 1969.
Rob Stevens arrives at the Moon colony to find it discouraged by cut-

backs in funds that have severely curtailed the colony's becoming independent. Nuclear war breaks out on Earth, and the colony, along with its
Russian counterpart, is forced to go it alone. Dissension festers and some
men crack and mutiny; only cooperation with the Russians enables the
colony to survive until they are rescued. A survival story translated into a
lunar and technological setting; writing and characterization adequate;
quite good creation of lunar life and terrain; technological passages
mesh smoothly into the narrative. 13 and up.

5-41. Heinlein, Robert Anson. **Citizen of the Galaxy.** Scribner, 1957,
$5.95. Ace, $1.25.
Before Thorby Baslim can enter into his rightful inheritance as head of
Rudbek, a Terran financial corporation, he is first a slave boy on Jubbul
in the Nine Worlds, a quasi-Roman empire, then an adopted son of the
People, an intergalactic trading company organized around matriarchy,
and finally a guardsman in a futuristic Foreign Service. Emphasis is not
on characterization or incident, but explaining alternate ways of organizing society, and dramatizing distinction between owning and controlling, having power and using it. Early instance of using juvenile science fiction for explaining and pushing ideas rather than merely relating exciting incidents. 13 and up.

5-42. Heinlein, Robert Anson. **Farmer in the Sky.** Scribner, 1950,
$5.95. Ballantine, $1.50.
Emigration to Ganymede and the opportunity to homestead is the
choice of Bill and his family. The flight out is long, and disappointment
awaits Bill when the colonists discover that land and equipment are not
ready. Bill is lucky to be assigned an early plot and begins the process of
making soil. In spite of the setback of a massive quake, Bill decides to
continue farming rather than return to Earth for further schooling. Subplots concerning Bill's relationship with father and stepmother, and setting up boy scouting on Ganymede, supposedly make the book more attractive to young readers. Chief interest is description of futuristic agricultural techniques. 13–15.

5-43. Heinlein, Robert Anson. **Red Planet.** Scribner, 1949, $5.95. Ace,
$1.25.
One plot line concerns Jim Marlowe's adventures at school and his
friendship with Willis, his pet ball-like animal that is really the first stage
in the development of a Martian. Second plot line involves the Company's attempt to force its colonists to winter at North Colony and the latter's resistance. The two plots come together when Willis is responsible
for colony's reprieve from intended annihilation by the Old Ones of
Mars, who tire of human fighting. A somewhat talky and slow-moving
novel, it does describe a social organization and biology utilized later in
Stranger in a Strange Land [4-302]. 12 and up.

*5-44. Heinlein, Robert Anson. **Rocket Ship Galileo.** Scribner, 1947, $5.95. Ace, $1.25.
Ross, Art, and Morrie, all amateur rocketeers, become involved with Morrie's uncle, Doctor Cargraves, and his plan to fly to the Moon. Having worked together in building an experimental, atomic-powered rocket, the three boys and Cargraves set off for the Moon. There they are attacked by a few Nazis plotting World War III from a secret lunar base. The boys overcome the Nazis and, having also discovered the ruins of a dead lunar civilization, return famous to Earth. A pioneering novel that began American mainstream science fiction for juveniles and combined juvenile protagonists, gadgetry, current science, and adventure in such a way that even today the book still retains interest. 13 and up.

5-45. Heinlein, Robert Anson. **Starman Jones.** Scribner, 1953. Ballantine, $1.50.
Story of Max Jones' rise from hillbilly runaway to acting captain of a star ship. What makes Max's rise possible is his phenomenal memory that retains all the astrogator's tables, needed for astronavigation, and the cunning of Sam, an older man who befriends the runaway and gets him aboard the *Asgard* with fake credentials. Striking are the detailed, convincing picture of spaceship operational procedures, and the suspense whenever the ship must pass through an "anomaly" in space. A subplot involving colonization of Charity, an unexplored planet, provides change of pace and conventional adventure. 13–15.

5-46. Heinlein, Robert Anson. **Tunnel in the Sky.** Scribner, 1955, $5.95. Ace, $1.25.
Rod Walker and his classmates, sent into an unknown world as part of a survival test, find themselves stranded. Banding together, as many as fifty teens are forced to make their own laws and rules. Just as the new society is viable and children are born, the young people are rescued and returned to Earth where many, including Rod, are forced back into teen roles. A provocative book, especially in its portrait of adults, who fail to discern the maturity of young people and see only teens. One unfortunate flaw is the stereotyped and sexist characterization. 12–14.

5-47. Hoover, H. M. **Children of Morrow.** Four Winds Press, 1973, $5.95.
Set in a future after widespread nuclear devastation has wiped out civilization, the story contrasts two forms of government and economy the survivors have adopted. One is afraid, cautious, reactionary, distrustful of what technology survives, and, hence, increasingly brutal and stagnant. The other is open, bold, and willing to build upon extant science and to utilize genetic mutations in order to construct a new society that seems to have successfully combined progress, discipline, justice, and

love. The descriptions of the countryside after the Great Destruction are plausible and convincing. In all, a stimulating novel. 12–14.

5-48. Hunter, Evan (pseud. of S. A. Lombino). **Find the Feathered Serpent.** Winston, 1952.
Neil, substituting for his father, the inventor of a time machine, journeys back in time, hoping to find the origin of Quetzalcoatl, the great white god. He meets Eric, who becomes instrumental in assisting the Mayans to resist barbarian invaders and in introducing corn and other agricultural innovations. Returning to the present, Neil realizes that he has participated in the making of legend and myth. A time travel tale involving a Wellsian time machine; patterned also after books describing long-lost peoples; far more interesting as an archeological and anthropological reconstruction than as hard science fiction. 12–14.

5-49. Jackson, Jacqueline, and William Perlmutter. **The Endless Pavement.** Illus. by Richard Cuffari. Seabury, 1973, $5.95.
At a time when cars are everywhere, pavement is endless, and the planet is ruled by The Great Computermobile, life is highly regimented, organized around the car. One day, to obtain an apple she sees and can hardly recognize, Josette breaks the routine and brings the whole system to a halt. One of the few effective picture story books that looks into the future. However, given the current energy crisis, the use of an automobile-dominated society as a metaphor for a dehumanized world already seems a bit outdated. Drawings are appropriately stark and nightmarish. 7–9.

5-50. Jameson, Malcolm. **Bullard of the Space Patrol.** Ed. by Andre Norton. World, 1951.
The chronicles of John Bullard's rise from lieutenant to Grand Admiral of the space patrol. Each chapter is a separate episode: showing exceptional resources in a crisis, leading a mutiny against a Captain Bligh-like commander, running a blockade, outwitting space pirates, smugglers, and crooked politicians. Well written; replete with incidents and gadgetry; entertaining and diverting for those who favor vintage space opera. 13 and up.

*5-51. Key, Alexander. **Escape to Witch Mountain.** Westminster, 1968, $5.50. Archway, $.75; Pocket Books, $.95.
Tony and Tia, orphan brother and sister, are placed in a home with no possessions except a "star box" that suggests a mysterious origin and an equally mysterious destination. When a stranger seeks to adopt them, the children run away. Before they reach the safety of Witch Mountain, the children realize they possess parapsychological powers and remember they are "Castaways" from a destroyed planet. It is also hinted that the children are sought by forces of satanic evil; hence, the book is anoth-

er of the recent stories dramatizing a universal struggle between good and evil in which juvenile protagonists play active roles. 11–13. A Walt Disney Productions film of the same name was released in 1975.

5-52. Key, Alexander. **The Forgotten Door.** Westminster, 1965, $4.75. Scholastic Book Service, $.95.
Little Jon falls through a forgotten door into an alien world, Earth. Temporarily forgetting his past, Jon is befriended by the Bean family, who gradually suspect he is from another, peaceful world. Others are not that perceptive, frightened by or wanting for their own uses Jon's telepathic power. As a mob closes in on him, Jon tries to find the door back; when he does, he takes the Bean family with him. Taut, suspenseful story; firm characterization, depiction of Jon's regaining his memory especially good; ethical commentary never allowed to take over narrative. 11–14.

5-53. Knott, William C. **Journey across the Third Planet.** Chilton, 1969.
Laark is forced to abandon ship on Earth, a strange planet. His appearance makes him a stranger, and his journey to meet a rescuing star ship seems impossible except for the help of Peter, a runaway who joins Laark. In addition to the excitingly rendered adventure, distinctive is the depiction of the slowly growing friendship between the two, in particular, Laark's realization that Earth, technologically very inferior to his home, can give Krall, an old and tired planet, insights gained from the courage and resourcefulness of a young planet. 13–15.

5-54. Latham, Philip (pseud. of Robert Shirley Richardson). **Five Against Venus.** Winston, 1952.
An early science fiction novel that is modeled upon the Robinson Crusoe survival formula. The Robinson family is forced to land on Venus, where they encounter evidence of another human being, an alien life form, the Bat people, and various plants that provide light and eat flesh. Effective description of conditions on Venus as science then surmised them. A noticeable weakness is that the Robinson family, although living in a rocket era, have no clothing or tools that suggest advanced technology. 12–14.

5-55. Latham, Philip (pseud. of Robert Shirley Richardson). **Missing Men of Saturn.** Winston, 1953.
The space ship *Albatross* is ordered to follow the *Anomaly*, a ghost ship, out to Saturn. Subsequently, the crew is exposed to a series of terrifying incidents, and members turn up missing. Gradually, it becomes apparent that Saturn is inhabited, and neither the Saturnians, an old civilized race, nor the descendants of Capt. Dearborn, first explorer of Saturn who disappeared mysteriously, want any interlopers. The crew, however, is set free as the Saturnians decide rapprochement is inevitable.

Suspenseful, well written mystery for two-thirds of the book; then speculation about the possibility of life on Saturn intrudes. 12–14.

5-56. Leek, Sybil. **The Tree that Conquered the World.** Prentice-Hall, 1969.
Julian discovers in his yard a strange, fast-growing tree that speaks. He also sees that the tree's swift growth and intense desire to propagate itself by the thousands can stem the tide of pollution and smog in the Los Angeles area. So with Sam and Laura, his sister, he establishes Operation Treetop to plant as many seedlings as possible. The children become national heroes. In spite of being preachy, it is informative concerning dangers of pollution; also one of the few story picture books that is entertaining and factual. 8–10.

*5-57. Le Guin, Ursula Kroeber. **A Wizard of Earthsea.** Parnassus, 1968, $5.50. Ace, $.95.
Young Ged becomes apprentice to a mage. Impatient to know everything, the talented boy is even tempted to call up the powers of darkness; and when he does, Ged summons his own shadow, death, which now unloosed, seeks to possess the boy. At the climactic confrontation Ged is able to master his darker self. A carefully wrought, dense novel: not only a description of an imaginary world, Earthsea, and the making of a wizard, but a sensitive, unconventional story of a youth's search for identity and belonging. This book, along with two subsequent novels, *The Tombs of Atuan* (Atheneum, 1972, $6.50. Bantam, $1.50), which narrates Ged's second triumph over the dark powers, and *The Farthest Shore* (Atheneum, 1973, $6.95. Bantam, $1.50; National Award Winner for Children's Books, 1973), which describes Ged's apotheosis as the Great Mage, constitutes the Earthsea trilogy, one of the major fantasy works of recent times. Perhaps the outstanding feature of the trilogy is the author's weaving together of myth and Jungian psychology. 13 and up.

*5-58. L'Engle, Madeleine. **A Wrinkle in Time.** Farrar, 1962, $4.50. Dell, $1.25.
Meg and Charles Wallace Murry, along with Calvin, Meg's classmate, become involved in an attempt to find Dr. Murry, a brilliant scientist who has mysteriously disappeared. Under the direction of Mrs. Who, Mrs. Whatsit, and Mrs. Which, three "angels," they "tesseract" to Camazotz, a distant star, where the children must save Dr. Murry, held captive by "It" in Central Intelligence. Eventually, it is the self-effacing love of Meg and not the brilliant intelligence of Charles Wallace that saves their father. One of the contemporary fantasy–science fiction novels that enmesh juveniles in planet-wide struggles between good and evil. Well written; firm characterization; provocative themes. Newbery Medal Winner, 1963. 13–15.

*5-59. Lewis, Clive Staples (U.K.). **The Lion, the Witch and the Wardrobe.** Macmillan, 1950, $4.95. Collier, $1.25 (7 vol. boxed set, Collier, $8.95).

A walk-in wardrobe allows four children to enter Narnia, where it is always winter. Deciding to fight against the White Witch, who is responsible for spring's not coming, the children and some of the talking Narnian animals are aided in their struggle by the great lion Aslan. Before the witch's spell is broken and spring and peace return, Aslan must be sacrificed. The children, now become kings and queens, rule over a golden age. Book I of the Chronicles of Narnia. Others are: *Prince Caspian* (1951), *The Voyage of the "Dawn Treader"* (1954), *The Silver Chair* (1953), *The Horse and his Boy* (1954), *The Magician's Nephew* (1955), and *The Last Battle* (1956). The seven books chronicle, among other events, Aslan's creation of Narnia, evil's introduction into the land, adventures of "sons and daughters of Adam and Eve," and the end of Narnia and the revelation of a new, more glorious Narnia. A brilliant series of fantasies: heroic adventure, captivating animal and scenery descriptions, a multitude of interesting characters, deep and consistent ethical implications. The question of whether worlds other than Earth require redemption was handled earlier by the author in his adult space trilogy [4-394]—*Out of the Silent Planet, Perelandra,* and *That Hideous Strength.* 10 and up.

*5-60. Lightner, Alice M. **The Day of the Drones.** Norton, 1969. Bantam, $.75.

A post-catastrophe story. Afria (once Africa) seems the only land uncontaminated by radioactivity. An expedition sets out to explore the potentially dangerous lands around Afria and discovers in an ancient northern country (once England) the Bee-people, a mutant, dwarfed race descended from the pre-disaster white population, organized around matriarchal principles, and controlled by gigantic mutant bees. A harrowing look at a possible future society adversely affected by radiation, virtually bookless, and unsure of the uses of power and knowledge; a perceptive study of the nature and effects of racial prejudice. 10–14.

5-61. Lightner, Alice M. **Doctor to the Galaxy.** Norton, 1965.

Young Dr. Garrison Bart becomes, through a mixup, a veterinarian instead of a physician, on a faraway planet. He discovers that lustra, a local money-making grain, inhibits growth. To the Assembly of Scientists he announces the discovery, but his findings are rejected; he is also charged with illegally practicing medicine. Bart makes another discovery: lustra inhibits cancerous growth. This time he is honored for his discovery and is able to become a physician. A mildly interesting story that aptly represents the author's ability to find subject matter appealing to preteens. 11–13.

5-62. Lord, Beman. **The Day the Spaceship Landed.** Walck, 1967, $4.95.
Young Mike meets four spacemen and cooperates with their request for information. The visitors from outer space leave, stating they will return in two years for a formal visit to the United States. A straightforward and, at times, amusing narrative; the realistic pictures by Harold Berson contribute to the lack of cuteness. 8–9.

5-63. MacGregor, Ellen. **Miss Pickerell Goes to Mars.** McGraw, 1951, $3.95.
Miss Pickerell finds a rocket ship trespassing on her pasture. Determined to register a complaint, she clambers on board and is mistakenly locked in as the rocket takes off for Mars. Her presence resented, she is not finally accepted until she rescues one of the crew. She returns a heroine! Early space fantasy; light reading; popular with young readers. Other Miss Pickerell books are: *Miss Pickerell Goes Under-Sea* (1953), *Miss Pickerell and the Geiger Counter* (1963), *Miss Pickerell Goes to the Arctic* (1954), and *Miss Pickerell on The Moon* (1965) (with Dora Pantell). 8–11.

5-64. Marsten, Richard. **Rocket to Luna.** Winston, 1953.
Ted Baker, Space Academy Cadet, unexpectedly becomes backup on the first rocket to the Moon. Rejected at first by the crew, Ted is accepted eventually as it is he who pilots the rocket onto the Moon's surface and saves the life of one of the crew. Although time has made obsolete some of the book's presentation of the technology required for a lunar flight, the technical descriptions are detailed and accurate. Moreover, the story still retains much of the tension and excitement of a journey to the Moon. 12–14.

5-65. Martel, Suzanne. **The City under Ground.** Viking, 1964. Archway, $.95.
A post-catastrophe story. Where old Montreal used to be, Surreal, an underground city, survives because of a highly technological and rigidly organized society. Two sets of brothers, Luke and Paul and Eric and Bernard, showing curiosity and initiative, help the city fight a mysterious, hitherto-unknown underground enemy, and stumble upon a way to the surface, where they discover a cleansed Earth and other survivors, the Lauranians, a free, less repressed, and technologically inferior people. Surreal decides to go above ground and ally itself with the Lauranians. Adequately written; mildly engaging incidents. 11–13.

*5-66. Mayne, William (U.K.). **Earthfasts.** Dutton, 1967, $4.95.
David and Keith meet an eighteenth-century drummer boy emerging from a newly formed grassy mound and carrying a steady, cold, white-flamed candle. Before Keith can return the candle to the past, in-

explicable phenomena—boggarts, heaving ground, moving stones, wild boars, giants, shadowing horsemen, awakening Arthurian knights, and even David's "death"—plague the area. A remarkable combination of fantasy and science fiction; strong characterization; fine depiction of the boys' determination to treat the constantly burning candle scientifically before succumbing to its power; exceptional use of atmosphere; brilliant style. 12–14.

5-67. Morressy, John. **The Humans of Ziax II.** Walker, 1974, $5.50.
Toren, son of the Earth Commander in charge of Pioneer Base One on Ziax II, loses his way in the jungle and is befriended by the Imbur, dwellers of the rain forest. From them Toren learns that killing is not always necessary. Further, he is instructed in the use of psychological powers that enable humans to survive without killing. A picture story book; easy-to-understand vocabulary conveys the ethical insights without distorting through oversimplification. 7–9.

5-68. Norton, Andre (pseud. of Alice Mary Norton). **The Beast Master.** Harcourt, 1959, $5.25. Ace, $1.25.
Except for the sympathetic portrayal of Indian sensibility, the book is little more than a skilled science fiction adaption of the western formula, set on Arzor, a planet whose climate is similar to the American Southwest and which becomes the next battleground between the Xik invaders and the Terran Confederacy. The characterization of Hosteen Storm, the beast master and a descendant of the Navajo, is noteworthy. Space adventure competently written, as is typical of the author. 14 and up.

5-69. Norton, Andre (pseud. of Alice Mary Norton). **Catseye.** Harcourt, 1961, $4.95. Ace, $1.25.
Temporary work in a strange interplanetary pet shop involves Troy Horan, a displaced person, in adventure, intrigue, and mystery, hallmarks of typical Norton work. Surprised to learn that he can communicate with animals, Troy stumbles upon the fact that several pets in the shop are being used as secret weapons in a plot against the rulers of Korwar. Troy is forced to flee into the Wild and a dead, booby-trapped underground city, and only the closest cooperation between Troy and several exotic animals, a cat, two foxes, and a kinkajou, enables him to survive and become a member of the Rangers who patrol the Wild. Skillful narrating of science fiction adventure and sympathetic depiction of animal–human relationship. 13 and up.

*5-70. Norton, Andre (pseud. of Alice Mary Norton). **Operation Time Search.** Harcourt, 1967, $5.75.
Ray Osborne is accidentally sent back into a time when the Atlantean Empire sought to overthrow the Murians and becomes the instrument whereby the latter, worshippers of the Flame, are able to annihilate At-

lantis, devotees of the false Poseidon, who traffic in demonic powers. Osborne wonders why Atlantis lingers in legend while the Murian Empire disappeared, but fails to observe that the religion and kings of Mura provide the basis for the Greek pantheon and mythology. Osborne remains in the past, determined to organize in the Barren Lands a colony, ruins of which are the mounds dotting the central United States. An Atlantis legend story; entertaining; especially stimulating in its speculation concerning orgin of myth. 13 and up.

5-71. Norton, Andre (pseud. of Alice Mary Norton). **Quest Crosstime.** Viking, 1965, $3.75. Ace, $1.25.
In a future when moving crosstime to parallel universes is possible, one group on Vroom favors crosstiming so that society can rebuild itself after nuclear devastation by using the resources of other universes. The Rogan sisters and Blake Walker, all with various parapsychological abilities, are swept into a revolt organized by those opposed to crosstiming. Before the revolt is put down, the adventure spills over to E625, a crosstime world embroiled in a tense stalemate modeled upon the conflict between the American Plains Indians and the pioneers. Heavily plotted, exciting, fast-moving story. 13–15.

5-73. Norton, Andre (pseud. of Alice Mary Norton). **Storm over Warlock.** World, 1960. Ace, $1.25.
Terrans and the evil, cruel Throgs clash over establishing sovereignty on Warlock, a newly discovered planet. Thorvald and Shann Lantee, the only survivors of a Terran survey, along with two wolverines, are forced to flee a band of Throgs. Falling into the hands of Wyvern or witches, the pair are tested but eventually are accepted by them. The new allies of Terra assist in pushing the Throgs back to their own planet. Early space adventure featuring one major characteristic of the author: witches and witchcraft, illusion vs. dream. Of secondary interest is human–animal coequal relationship. 13 and up.

5-74. Norton, Andre (pseud. of Alice Mary Norton). **The Stars Are Ours.** World, 1954. Ace, $.95.
Even in a time when Earth has embarked upon interplanetary flight, old animosities continue to exist and eventually lead to a devestating war. Scientists are proscribed by the Company of Pax, and a handful of Free Scientists escape to the stars. After exploring a new planet, the band of humans enter into an alliance with a race of mermen to take up anew the history of humanity. Well plotted, filled with incident, and skillfully written. 13 and up.

5-74a. Nourse, Alan Edward. **The Bladerunner.** McKay, 1974, $5.95. Ballantine, $1.50.
By the early twenty-first century, overpopulation has forced mandatory

sterilization upon anyone seeking medical care. A medical black market springs up for those opposed to all medical practice. When a mysterious flu virus threatens a nationwide epidemic, Billy Gimp and other blade-runners, that is, persons who provide black-market physicians with supplies and assistance, are called upon to warn the populace. The epidemic is curtailed and humane changes in health care ensue. Suspenseful incidents; fascinating look at future medical care and procedures; responsible handling of population control problem. 13 and up.

5-75. Nourse, Alan Edward. **The Mercy Men.** McKay, 1968, $4.95. Ace, $.60.
In this novel of narrative twists and surprises, Jeff Meyer feels a compulsion to seek out and kill a man he believes has killed his father. Suspecting the man has entered a research Medical Center, Jeff decides to enter also as a mercy man, i.e., one who allows medical experimentation on him for money. Before Jeff can leave the Center he is shocked to learn that he is an espi but, like his father, triggered to go insane, and that this insanity affects the laws of probability. Jeff is a carrier of disorder that must be eradicated or treated. As in other novels by the author, speculation about future medical practice is stimulating; style and characterization are above average. 12–14.

5-76. Nourse, Alan Edward. **Raiders from the Rings.** McKay, 1962.
Nuclear devastation is averted when outer space colonists refuse to strike their Earth enemies. As a result the colonists are banished; to exist they must raid, but only for essentials, especially women, since outer space radiation has prevented the birth of females. An all-out reprisal by Earth to destroy the raiders is prevented by the Searchers, a race devoted to seeking out new life in space and nurturing it without gross interference. Competent space adventure; change of pace from an author usually concerned with futuristic medical practice. 12–14.

5-77. Nourse, Alan Edward. **Star Surgeon.** McKay, 1960, $3.95.
Expert blending of futuristic medicine, its procedures and organization, and the story of Earth's attempt to enter the Galactic Confederation. Earth, hospital center for the entire galaxy, prides itself on its medical skill and begrudgingly allows Dal, a Garvian and first off-Earth medical student, to intern. After several adventures, Dal wins his silver star as a star surgeon, and Earth has passed its probation. Suspenseful in depicting possible future medical technology; especially provocative speculation of possible applications of process of symbiosis. 12 and up.

*5-78. O'Brien, Robert C. **Mrs. Frisby and the Rats of NIMH.** Atheneum, 1971, $5.95.
Mrs. Frisby, the head of a family of field mice, is told to consult neighboring rats concerning the illness of her son. Justin, a leader of the rats,

agrees to help because Mr. Frisby had been of assistance to the rats. Upon hearing the whole story of the rats' being the object of psychological and biological experimentation by the NIHM labs and becoming, as a result, superintelligent, Mrs. Frisby also volunteers to aid the rats. The rats escape from an attempt to exterminate them by NIHM labs and establish a utopian society away from man. Outstanding combination of fantasy and science fiction: a winning portrait of rats and mice that has little cuteness. Newbery Award, 1972. 10–14.

*5-79. O'Brien, Robert C. **Z for Zachariah.** Atheneum, 1975, $6.95.
A post-catastrophe story. Believing she may be the only survivor of a devastating war, Ann Burden is pleased to see a man enter the Burden valley and decides to befriend him. Shocked, when, after all she has done for him, he tries to rape her, Ann is forced to leave the valley, hoping to come across other survivors. Sensitive transformation of trite subject into a tragic study of human behavior in the face of destruction and possible extinction; use of journal to record struggle for understanding, carefully paced narrative, and characterization of protagonist are distinctive. 14–16.

5-80. Offutt, Andrew J. **The Galactic Rejects.** Lothrop, 1973, $5.95.
Dell, $.95.
Rinegan, Berneson, and Cory, all gifted with parapsychological power but social misfits, find themselves on Bors, a hitherto-unknown agrarian world where crime and the proverbial rat race seem nonexistent and life is utopian. Impressed by the marked contrast to Earth, the three change and become circus performers. The extent of change is tested when they decide not only to preserve Bors' society from the invading Azuli, archenemy of Earth, but to bring peace by offering to immunize the Azulians from a disease fatal to them but not to Terrans. Different and refreshing because of the engaging circus scenes. 13–15.

*5-81. Pesek, Ludek (Germany). **The Earth is Near.** Bradbury Press, 1974, $5.95. Dell, $1.25. Tr. by Anthea Bell of *Die Erde ist nah*, 1970.
An engrossing adventure; convincing investigation of what happens to an international crew of twenty during a journey to Mars and its exploration. The dramatization of the shifting psychological states of mind on the long trip to Mars and during the terrifying dust storms; the explicit and hidden animosities and rivalries that emerge; the loneliness and futility experienced because the crew has depended too much upon specialized machines which fail or prove useless; the frustration resulting from the suspicion that the expedition may have done better if it had attempted to harmonize with Martian ecology; and human courage and endurance all give the novel its distinction. German Children's Book Prize for 1971. 13 and up.

5-82. Rockwood, Roy. **By Space Ship to Saturn.** Whitman, 1935.
Lucky, Phil, and Phil's Uncle John, along with others, embark on a flight
to Saturn. The adventures are many and harrowing, and include per-
fumed steam that shrinks, brontosauri, tribal battles, boiling lakes, poisonous vapors, and great mushrooms. Fortunately, all of the crew survives and return safely to Earth. Influenced by Jules Verne; minimal science, maximum adventure; one-dimensional characterization, wooden
style. Representative of the Great Marvel series by the author, one of the
Stratemeyer pseudonyms. Although predating the Tom Swift series, the
Great Marvel books never achieved the same degree of popularity. Six of
the titles were reprinted in the 1930s, attesting to the staying power of
juvenile interest in the genre. 11–13.

5-83. Shelton, William. **Stowaway to the Moon.** Doubleday, 1973, $5.95.
The story of a boy's stowaway on a rocket to the Moon is divided into
three parts: getting on board; the actual journey; and the return to
Earth and confrontation with the public as the boy successfully convinces
them that his illegal act is actually beneficial. In spite of outrageous character stereotyping, the book remains valuable because of the massive detailing that convincingly shows what space flight is like, and because the
book affirms that young people wanting to go into space need to prove
themselves just as young people did who went off to sea. 13 and up.

5-84. Silverberg, Robert. **Gate of Worlds.** Holt, 1967.
Alternative history which answers the question of what would have happened to Europe and the rest of the world if the Black Death of 1348
had killed three-fourths instead of one-fourth of Europe's population.
Dan Beauchamp of New Istanbul (London) leaves to make his fortune in
Mexico. Accepting the patronage of a rascally nephew of King Mocte-
zuma, Dan never quite makes his fortune. Of more interest than Dan's
adventures is the portrait of the new world, non-Christian, less dependent upon machinery, and nonwesternized; anthropological and archeological information and speculation are sound and challenging. 13–15.

5-85. Silverberg, Robert. **Time of the Great Freeze.** Holt, 1964, $3.95.
Dell, $.75.
By 2230 A.D., because of the fifth Ice Age, cities were forced underground. Centuries later these cities, afraid and suspicious, were content
with their living conditions and the lack of communication with each other. Jim Barnes, his father, and five other men, having made radio contact with London, were, as a consequence, expelled from New York, and
determined to make London over the ice. Their many adventures and
dangers make up a fast-moving story that also entertains through suggesting what elements in today's civilization might survive after an ice
age. 12–14.

*5-86. Sleator, William. **House of Stairs.** Dutton, 1974, $5.95.

Five sixteen-year-old orphans find themselves in a house of stairs with a red machine as the only furniture. When the machine light blinks and sounds are emitted, the teens realize they must perform in a certain way or the machine will not spit out food pellets. Three of the young people do what the machine wants, use each other, and become brutal and mechanistic. The other two open to and sustain each other as humans. The young people discover they have been subjects in a psychological conditioning experiment. The language and attitudes of teens are captured; the breaking down of all external, protective devices is plausibly rendered. However, the truth of the situation may be too obvious to some readers; hence the sharpness of the attack on behavioral modification procedures is blunted. 14 and up.

5-87. Slobodkin, Louis. **The Space Ship under the Apple Tree.** Macmillan, 1958, $4.95. Collier, $.95.

Marty, a junior scientist–explorer from outer space, lands under an apple tree in Eddie's grandmother's apple orchard. Eddie and Marty become close friends and share many adventures. Perhaps more space fairy tale than science fiction, the book is humorous, lively, and enjoyed by younger children. Further adventures of Marty and Eddie are *The Space Ship Returns to the Apple Tree* (1958), *The Three-Seated Space Ship* (1964), and *Round Trip Space Ship* (1968). 8–10.

*5-88. Stoutenberg, Adrien. **Out There.** Viking, 1971, $4.95.

Some time in the twenty-first century, cities lie sterile under steel and plastic domes. Outside is a land so ravaged by waste and pollution that virtually all wildlife is gone. Into this land Zeb and a handful of youngsters travel on an outing to find animal life. The group does locate ample signs of wildlife but also meets a hunter. An even more ominous note is sounded at the end: the possibility that the restored land may become recreational land, and the cycle of ecological nightmare begin anew. Well-written and believable situation; polemic against human selfishness and exploitation balanced. 13–15.

*5-89. Suddaby, Donald (U.K.). **Village Fanfare.** Oxford Univ. Press, 1954.

In 1908 the village of Much Swayford becomes the center of activity for Burton, the man from the future. Come to Edwardian England to learn from the past, Burton, through his giant computator and his ability to project images of himself anywhere in the world, relearns and takes back the human attributes—love for music, laughter, and courage—that he believes will enable his time, the age of great brains, to go on. Clearly indebted to Wells not only for its depiction of scientific apparatus and time travel but for its sympathetic, gently humorous portrayal of British village life. A book that deserves wider reading. 13 and up.

5-90. Sutton, Jean, and Jeff Sutton. **The Programmed Man.** Putnam, 1968, $5.95.
The conventions of both space opera and the novel of espionage are interwoven in this neatly plotted story of suspense and adventure. Various agents feint and counterfeint to discover the secret of the N-Bomb, a weapon which has kept peace in the galaxy. Compounding the intrigue is the existence of the "programmed man," a mysterious agent whose identity and purpose, rumor has it, have been programmed to become known at the moment of greatest crisis. A double surprise ending caps the fast-paced novel. 13–15.

5-91. Sutton, Jean and Jeff Sutton. **The Beyond.** Putnam, 1967, $5.95.
In a future when the Federation has organized the galaxy, inexplicable people with parapsychological powers are banished as "dangerous elements" to Engo, an inhospitable planet whose inhabitants quickly succumb. Shelby, who is assigned to investigate rumors of a powerful "beyond," i.e., a parapsych who can teleport, is shocked to learn that he is also a beyond. Together with the beyond he has sought, Shelby outwits the secret police. A carefully plotted, quick-moving narrative that shares in the secret agent genre; not intended as a serious study of parapsychological powers. 12–14.

5-92. Sutton, Jefferson. **Beyond Apollo.** Putnam, 1966.
Delivery of the first lunar permanent station is on schedule when Logan sickens from weightlessness and Apollo II has to return to Earth. Clay, command pilot, decides to go ahead putting Big Lander on the Moon. The landing is successful, but an off-target landing spot and another injury appear to force abandonment of the project until Clay stays behind alone manning the station. A taut, suspenseful story; vivid, believable rendering of landing procedure; good description of Moon scenery, atmosphere, and travel; theme of man's endurance and determination easily comes across. 13 and up.

5-93. Walters, Hugh (U.K.). **Destination Mars.** Criterion, 1964.
All goes well as Chris Godfrey and his companions find, during their investigation into the possibility of Martian life, exciting evidence of life and civilization. However, disembodied Martian life makes its presence known and demands to be taken to Earth. When the crew resists, the now hostile life takes over the minds of all except Chris and begins the flight to Earth. Mysterious space voices, transmitted by the ship's radio, frighten away the Martians and the crew escapes. Effective space adventure; adequately written; ample incident and suspense; representative of author's better work in juvenile science fiction. 12–14.

5-94. Wibberly, Leonard Patrick O'Connor. **Encounter near Venus.** Farrar, 1967, $3.95.

Four members of a family must spend their summer vacation with their uncle. Becoming involved with Venusian life forms, the children and their uncle journey to Nede, a satellite of Venus, where they are caught up in a struggle to keep Ka, the evil Smiler, from corrupting Nede, an innocent world. A struggle-between-forms-of-good-and-evil book which is suggestive of the Narnia books by C. S. Lewis [5-59]. Information about science and ethics is, generally speaking, skillfully meshed into the narrative. 11–13.

5-95. Williams, Jay, and Raymond Abrashkin. **Danny Dunn and the Homework Machine.** McGraw, 1958, $4.95.
Entrusted by Professor Bullfinch with a home-size computer, Danny cannot resist using it for his homework. His teacher and mother, however, arrange matters in such a way that Danny and his friends, Joe and Irene, learn their homework as they program the computer. Typical of the Danny Dunn series: some adventure, built around a scientific device, real or imagined, designed by Professor Bullfinch, and involving Danny and his friends; easy reading, diverting and entertaining; very popular with children. 10–12.

5-96. Williams, Jay. **The People of the Ax.** Walck, 1974, $5.95.
A post-catastrophe story. Two societies have survived: human beings or the ax people, who have souls and no longer kill except for food; and the crom, a human-like people, hated by the humans. Arne realizes he possesses tendo, an ability to sense the spirit of harmony in all, and, hence, is destined to become a leader of the humans. Arne's first, and revolutionary, intuition is a suspicion that crom may also be human, and he successfully awakens soul in one of their leaders. Competently written; plausible look at possible future societies except that author becomes too tendentious when contemporary civilization is blamed for all of man's failures. Very different from the Danny Dunn series. 12–14.

5-97. Winterfeld, Henry (Germany). **Star Girl.** Harcourt, 1957. Tr. by Kyrill Schabert of *Kommt ein Madchen geflogen*, 1956.
Mo, an eighty-seven-year-old girl from Asra, or Venus, accidentally falls out her father's space ship. She is found by several German children under a forest tree and they, believing her story, agree to help Mo meet her father that night. The village adults refuse to believe or help Mo, but the children and Mo eventually succeed. Exceptional are the realistic portrayal of adult disbelief and their quick willingness to consider Mo insane, and the sharply distinguished characterization of Mo and the children. Less convincing is the speculation about possible Venusian civilization. 11–13.

5-98. Wollheim, Donald A. **The Secret of the Martian Moons.** Winston, 1955.

Early juvenile mainstream space opera. A handful of humans secretly left behind in a final attempt to discover the origin and fate of the Martian cities become embroiled in a rivalry between the two factions of the cowardly Vegans who centuries before had placed two artificial spheres, Phobos and Deimos, in orbit near Mars. Before peace can be established, the Star people, the original inhabitants of Mars, return and enter into an alliance with Earth. Minimal characterization and science hardware, but ample incident and a quick-moving story. 12–14.

5-99. Wrightson, Patricia (Australia). **Down to Earth.** Harcourt, 1965, $5.50.

The new, strange boy in George's neighborhood in Sydney turns out to be Martin, a Martian touring Earth. After a series of incidents, some of them quite humorous, brought about by Martin's difficulty in adjusting to Earth customs and his habit of announcing to anyone he meets that he is from outer space, Martin, along with another "tourist," departs for home just as Earth's defenses sense a possible invasion. A believable, humorous, and at times touching space fantasy. 9–11.

Part 2.
Research Aids

6.
History,
Criticism, and Biography

6-1. Agel, Jerome, ed. **The Making of Kubrick's 2001.** Signet, 1970, $1.75.

A thick paperback containing Arthur C. Clarke's original source story, "The Sentinel," articles about and reviews of the film, interviews with Kubrick and others, production details, and a 96-page photo insert. A multi-faceted look at what is almost certainly the most ambitious SF film ever attempted, and certainly the most discussed. Clarke's screenplay was published as *2001: A Space Odyssey* [4-158], and Clarke's later account of the film appeared as *The Lost Worlds of "2001"* (Signet, 1972, $1.50).

*6-2. Aldiss, Brian W. (U.K.). **Billion Year Spree; The True History of Science Fiction.** Doubleday, 1973, $7.95. Schocken, $2.95.

The best single critical history of SF yet written. Aldiss sees Shelley's *Frankenstein* [1-47] as "the first great myth of the industrial age" and a seminal work in the field but does not ignore earlier writings such as fantastic voyages and utopias, although he rejects the idea of a distinct continuity between such writings and more modern works. Both major and minor figures are discussed with perception and balance. The last two decades are covered more hurriedly, and a sequel is hinted at.

6-3. Aldiss, Brian W. (U.K.). **Science Fiction Art.** Crown, 1975, $9.95. An oversized (10 ½ x 14 ¾ inches), 128-page paperback which presents the work of thirty American and British SF illustrators from the 1920s to the 1970s, showing, describing, and contrasting their individual techniques and strengths. Their work is seen further in short chapters dealing with common themes—catastrophes, machines, robots, spaceships, etc. A magazine gallery of seventy-nine titles with covers in color and black and white provides a useful sampling. Index of artists and magazines. Garish and repetitive though they are, Aldiss argues that the illustrations stimulated youthful readers as much as the text. A good survey but awkward for libraries because of its size. Frewin [6-36] is preferable though it lacks post-1940 examples. Gunn's selection of illustrations [6-44] is more than adequate for most readers. Aldiss is second choice.

6-4. Aldiss, Brian W. (U.K.). **The Shape of Further Things.** Faber, 1970. £1.75. Corgi, £.40. Doubleday, 1971.
Part autobiographical, part speculation, this quasi-diary covering a month in 1969 deals with the author's reflections and musings about SF and his other literary and extra-literary interests. As one of SF's most astute critics, his work deserves a place in more comprehensive collections.

*6-5. Allott, Kenneth (U.K.). **Jules Verne.** Macmillan, 1941. Kennikat, $11.00.
The standard English-language biography, which leans heavily on the biography by Verne's niece, Marguerite Allotte de la Fuÿe's *Jules Verne— sa vie, son oeuvre* (Kra, 1928; tr. by Erik de Mauny, Staples Press, 1954). The Verne personal archives are still closed, so a definitive biography is impossible. This is a workmanlike, chronological biography and brief assessment of one of the most popular French writers of his day. Bibliography and index, sixteen plates. See the new biography by Jean Jules-Verne [6-50].

*6-6. Amis, Kingsley (U.K.). **New Maps of Hell.** Harcourt, 1960. Arno, $9.00.
Instrumental in gaining SF a wider and more thoughtful critical acceptance, this is one of the best of the earlier critical studies. Amis sees social criticism and satire as SF's major virtues, adventure and action as artifacts from the pulp era. The easy conversational tone and wit make it an especially worthwhile work. Index of names and titles.

*6-7. Armytage, Walter Harry Green (U.K.). **Yesterday's Tomorrows; A Historical Survey of Future Societies.** Routledge, £2.00, Univ. of Toronto Press, 1968.
A major study of a rapidly growing field of scholarly investigation, the planning of the future. Abundant historical background and references

to hundreds of books, many of them SF works of recent years and often little-known, make this an essential background work.

6-8. Ash, Brian (U.K.). **Faces of the Future: The Lessons of Science Fiction.** Taplinger, 1975, $8.95.
The twelve chapters provide an informal account of SF mixed with some criticism. Four of the chapters emphasize the period through Wells, another treats the pulp years and later, and seven focus on recurrent themes in SF. Not a history and less critical than Aldiss [6-2], it is roughly comparable to Lundwall [6-60]. A good introduction for the beginner. Index, two-page bibliography of SF history and criticism.

*6-9. Bailey, James Osler. **Pilgrims through Space and Time; Trends and Patterns in Scientific and Utopian Fiction.** Argus Books, 1947. Greenwood, $3.50, $13.00.
Based on the author's dissertation, "Scientific Fiction in English, 1817–1914" (Univ. of N.C., 1934), which in turn developed from a master's thesis on H. G. Wells, this is the first scholarly and comprehensive study of what were then called scientific romances. Although the focus is on pre-World War I works, enough attention is paid to subsequent works to show the continuities in themes and methods. The author has remained at North Carolina as a specialist in Victorian literature.

6-10. Baxter, John (U.K.). **Science Fiction in the Cinema.** Barnes, 1970, $2.95. Warner, $1.25.
A useful British survey of the field, emphasizing the aesthetics—such as they are—of the SF film. The coverage is broad and informed and includes a chapter on SF for TV. Bibliography and filmography, plus many stills. Compare Clarens [6-21], Gifford [6-38], and Johnson [6-49].

*6-11. Bergonzi, Bernard (U.K.). **The Early H. G. Wells: A Study of the Scientific Romances.** Univ. of Toronto and Manchester Univ. Press, 1961, £1.92.
The most detailed and important study of those works SF readers usually cite. The Victorian world shaped by tradition and the uncertain new world dominated by science and technology are bridged by Wells. Bergonzi relates Wells' early works to the nineteenth-century *fin de siècle* attitudes common at the time. Hillegas [6-47] relates these romances to similar works by later writers.

*6-12. Blish, James (as William Atheling). **The Issue at Hand: Studies in Contemporary Magazine Science Fiction.** Advent, 1964, $3.50, $7.00.
Most of these essays appeared in long-defunct fanzines from 1952 to 1963 and are spirited reviews of stories appearing in the SF magazines of the time. A few revisions and afterthoughts are appended to most. Many

of the pieces are dated, but their concern with quality is not, and they repay reading. Detailed index.

*6-13. Blish, James (as William Atheling). **More Issues at Hand: Critical Studies in Contemporary Science Fiction.** Advent, 1970, $3.50, $7.00.
The emphasis in this second collection is on book reviews rather than short story reviews. The author's wide knowledge of literature serves him well. His subjects include the critical SF literature, Heinlein, Sturgeon, Algis Budrys and, unexpectedly, A. Merritt, whom he eviscerates.

6-14. Borrello, Alfred. **H. G. Wells: Author in Agony.** Southern Illinois Univ. Press, 1972, $6.95.
One of the Crosscurrents/Modern Critiques, this is a capable survey of recent criticism of Wells rather than an original analysis. The recurrent themes of qualified optimism and unrelieved despair are traced through all his works. A good starting point.

6-15. Bova, Benjamin William. **Notes to a Science Fiction Writer.** Scribner, 1975, $6.95.
Analog's editor directs his advice to aspiring writers, emphasizing character, background, conflict and plot. Four of his own stories are used to illustrate his points. Anecdotal, practical, it usefully complements the more general work by de Camp [6-29] and the forthcoming work by the Science Fiction Writers of America [6-85]. It would be especially helpful in a high school creative writing class, since the author is presumably aiming his book at this audience.

6-16. Bretnor, Reginald, ed. **Modern Science Fiction, Its Meaning and Future.** Coward-McCann, 1953.
One of the first comprehensive discussions of modern SF by editors (e.g., Campbell, Boucher), critics (e.g., Boucher, Bretnor, Fabun) and writers (e.g., Pratt, de Camp, Asimov, Clarke, Philip Wylie). Fletcher Pratt's sensible criticism of SF is one of the least dated essays.

*6-17. Bretnor, Reginald, ed. **Science Fiction, Today and Tomorrow.** Harper, 1974, $8.95. Penguin, $2.95.
Fifteen essays by well-known SF writers, editors, critics, and academics provide a thorough survey of the field today, twenty-one years after the editor's earlier survey appeared. The coverage is wide, occasionally uneven, always interesting. Biographical sketches and bibliographies for each author, plus a four-page annotated critical bibliography, enhance the work.

6-18. Britikov, Antolii Fedorovich (U.S.S.R.). **Russkii Sovetskii nauchno-fantasticheskii roman [The Soviet SF Novel].** Leningrad, Nauka, 1970.

A comprehensive discussion of the history of SF in Russia, the book also contains a very valuable bibliography—of Russian writers only—by Boris Liapunov, from the beginnings up to 1967. This includes books, individual stories in magazines, short story collections, anthologies, reviews and critical writings.

6-19. Carter, Lin. **Imaginary Worlds; The Art of Fantasy.** Ballantine, 1973, $1.25.
The emphasis here is on heroic fantasy, a popular category among many types of readers. The readable survey summarizes the genre's historic roots, describes many works from William Morris on, and includes several how-to chapters which critically explore the techniques used by contemporary fantasy writers, of whom Carter is one. While not dealing with SF directly, it provides essential collateral reading. Very useful notes and bibliography.

6-20. Chesneaux, Jean. (France). **The Political and Social Ideas of Jules Verne.** Thames & Hudson, 1972. Transatlantic, $10.00. Tr. by Thomas Wikeley from *Une lecture politique de Jules Verne*, 1971.
An examination of Verne's many *voyages extraordinaires* as elements in his political view of the world, a view which Chesneaux argues is far wider and more unorthodox than Verne's bourgeois upbringing would suggest. Forty-one engravings from original editions of the novels enliven the text.

6-21. Clarens, Carlos. **An Illustrated History of the Horror Film.** Putnam, 1967. Capricorn, $3.25.
A good critical history of horror and SF films, with many of the latter's alien menaces qualifying them for discussion. Clarens recognizes the generally low quality of most such films and speaks knowledgeably of the field, although the endless plot summaries prove wearisome. A 69-page appendix gives credits for all films discussed, and often cites the original stories for the films, noting that most suffered in translation to film. Forty-eight pages of stills and an index enhance the book's value.

6-22. Clareson, Thomas D., ed. **Many Futures, Many Worlds.** Kent State Univ. Press, 1976.
Essays examining some of the thematic concerns of the SF (primarily), such as myth in SF, machines, political/social sciences, philosophy/theology, women, SF films. Contributors include S. C. Fredericks, Patricia Warrick, Joseph Olander and Martin Greenberg, Thomas Clareson, Beverly Friend and Carolyn Rhodes. [Annotation based on prepublication information.]

*6-23. Clareson, Thomas D., ed. **SF: The Other Side of Realism; Essays on Modern Fantasy and Science Fiction.** Bowling Green Univ. Press, 1972, $4.00, $8.95.

Twenty-six essays, mostly from the 1960s from academic, popular, and specialist sources, assembled by the editor of *Extrapolation*, where some of these essays originally appeared. They discuss individual works and authors, or provide critical discussions of the meaning and significance of SF in both books and mass media. List of award-winning novels, bibliography, and notes on contributors. A balanced collection of modern criticism.

6-24. Clareson, Thomas D., ed. **Voices for the Future.** Bowling Green Univ. Press, 1976.
Essays on major SF writers such as Williamson, Stapledon, Simak, Asimov, Heinlein, Sturgeon, Bradbury, Clarke, and Vonnegut, by such critics as Samuelson, McNelly, Gunn, Thomas Wymer, Clareson, and Beverly Friend. A companion volume is in preparation dealing with other authors. [Annotation based on prepublication information.]

*6-25. Clarke, Ignatius Frederick. **Voices Prophesying War, 1763–1984.** Oxford, 1966, $11.25.
A very useful background study of fictional works predicting future wars, from the age of ballooning to modern missiles. Brief mention is made of a few SF works, such as Wells' *War of the Worlds* [2-164], Huxley's *Ape and Essence* [4-323], and Miller's *A Canticle for Leibowitz* [4-424]; others are listed in the longest part of the three-part bibliography.

6-26. Davenport, Basil. **Inquiry into Science Fiction.** Longmans, 1955.
In a brief historical review of the field, including some of the recurrent themes, Davenport discusses various types of SF, from the space opera, bug-eyed monster thud and blunder subliterary category to the more scientific and philosophically speculative. Dated but a balanced view of the period.

6-27. De Bolt, Joe, ed. **The Happening Worlds of John Brunner. Critical Explorations in Science Fiction.** Kennikat, 1975, $12.95.
Eight original essays on Brunner's works, including a lengthy career biography by the editor. The approach is interdisciplinary, with authors from the humanities and the social and physical sciences. Includes a preface by James Blish and a final chapter in which Brunner responds. Complete bibliography of Brunner's professional works and name and title index. A unique treatment of a contemporary SF writer.

*6-28. de Camp, Lyon Sprague. **Lovecraft: A Biography.** Doubleday, 1975, $10.00. Ballantine, $1.95 (abridged).
The definitive biography of Lovecraft, a Rhode Island recluse whose works were reprinted by Arkham House soon after his death in 1937 and which are relatively well known today. Although most of his more than sixty stories emphasize weird or supernatural themes, a few are sci-

ence fiction. Thoroughly documented with twenty-eight pages of notes, twenty-two of bibliography, and a twelve-page index.

*6-29. de Camp, Lyon Sprague. **Science Fiction Handbook: The Writing of Imaginative Fiction.** Hermitage House, 1953. Owlswick Press, 1975, $8.50.

Although the trade advice is outdated, the original edition of this book retains great value not only for its survey of the scene in the boom years of SF, but for teachers of creative writing. An excellent short history of imaginative fiction, biographies of eighteen major writers (many still active), and the nuts and bolts of writing and selling. The revised edition is equally valuable (but omits the biographical material) and is co-authored by the author's wife, Catherine C. de Camp. Essential for aspiring SF writers and of general use in any fiction writing course.

6-30. del Rey, Lester. **The World of Science Fiction: 1926–1976.** Garland, 1976, $15.00.

A veteran SF author and the editor of the Garland reprint series attempts to write "a general guide to the field as a whole for the student or the beginning reader who finds the literature and the associated activities as confusing as they may be fascinating" (from the preliminary foreword). The proposed table of contents indicates a wide-ranging survey of all aspects of the field, comparable textually to Gunn's history [6-44]. [Annotation based on prepublication information.]

6-31. Derleth, August W. **Thirty Years of Arkham House, 1939–1969; A History and Bibliography.** Arkham, 1970.

Arkham House was originally founded to bring to a larger public the works of H. P. Lovecraft. The sixteen-page history chronicles the growth of Arkham House, with the remaining pages providing detailed description of ninety-eight AH titles plus fourteen titles from Stanton & Lee and fourteen from Mycroft & Moran. Although Derleth died in 1971, his imprint survives. Photographs of some of the major AH authors are included.

6-32. Elliott, Robert C. **The Shape of Utopia: Studies in a Literary Genre.** Univ. of Chicago Press, 1970, $7.50.

Seven thoughtful essays from scholarly journals, dealing both with interpretive studies of individual literary utopias (e.g., those of More, Swift, and Hawthorne, Huxley's *Island*) and genre studies of the utopian mode. Index, notes, but no bibliography.

6-33. Eshbach, Lloyd Arthur, ed. **Of Worlds beyond; The Science of Science Fiction Writing, a Symposium.** Fantasy Press, 1947. Advent, 1964, $3.50, $6.00.

Much more general then de Camp's handbook [6-29], this symposium includes pieces by John Campbell, Robert Heinlein, Jack Williamson, and "John Taine" (Eric Temple Bell).

6-34. Eurich, Nell E. **Science in Utopia; A Mighty Design.** Harvard Univ. Press, 1967, $10.00.
Focuses on utopian writers of the seventeenth century, notably Campenella, Andrea, Bacon, Hartlib, Cowley, and Glenvill, and upon their influence on the emerging scientific world view. A literary rather than a sociological analysis, the concluding chapter attempts to relate early utopias to modern ones. For the graduate student and specialist.

*6-35. Franklin, Howard Bruce. **Future Perfect: American Science Fiction of the Nineteenth Century.** Oxford, Univ. Press, 1966, $3.95, $12.95.
An anthology of nineteen stories by thirteen nineteenth-century authors, published originally from 1843 to 1899. Each thematic group of stories is preceded by introductory commentary, as is each of the author's stories. The stories include Bellamy's "The Blindman's World," Bierce's "Mysterious Disappearances," Hawthorne's stories annotated in chapter 1 (excluding "The Celestial Railroad"), Poe's "The Facts in the Case of M. Valdemar" and two others annotated in chapter 1; and Twain's "From the 'London Times' of 1904." The longwindedness of much Victorian fiction is all too evident here, but Franklin's excellent notes offset this and show the links with modern SF. A useful supplement to Bailey and more wide-ranging and informed than Moskowitz's *Science Fiction by Gaslight* [2-116].

6-36. Frewin, Anthony (U.K.). **One Hundred Years of SF Illustration, 1840–1940.** Pyramid, 1975, $4.95.
Because the early pulps are seldom seen today, this work provides a useful survey of SF illustrations. The fascinating work of Grandville and Robida, two prolific nineteenth-century French artists, begin the book, followed by selected illustrations from editions of Verne and Wells. The emphasis is on illustrations in the SF pulps from the 1920s and 1930s— Frank R. Paul (who has the book's cover), Eliot Dold, and others known only to aficionados. Over forty covers are reproduced in color, some full-size, some reduced, from *Amazing*, *Astounding*, and others. This was the age of BEMs (bug-eyed monsters), and older fans will regard this survey with nostalgia, astonishment, and regret over a vanished youth. All illustrations have captions, and the remaining text, while succinct, is intelligent and helpful, putting SF illustration in a wider historical context. A very good and remarkably inexpensive introduction to the early years of SF illustration. Preferable to Sadoul's *2000* A.D. [6-81] but naturally lacking the scope of Gunn [6-44] and Rottensteiner [6-79].

6-37. Gerber, Richard (U.K.). **Utopian Fantasy; A Study of English Utopian Fiction Since the End of the Nineteenth Century.** McGraw-Hill, 2nd ed., 1973, $2.45. Folcroft, $12.50 (first ed., 1955).

The first part of this rather heavy-handed study outlines the rise of modern utopian belief in evolutionary progress. The second part discusses the moderation of utopian visions as tested by twentieth-century realities. The final part analyzes the literary techniques and value of utopian fantasies. A number of the seminal figures in SF are discussed, including Wells, Huxley, Stapledon, and Orwell. Gerber takes a very simplistic view of SF in his new preface, dismissing much of SF as "merely sensational." The annotated lists of English utopian fantasies, 1901–1972, are useful. Bibliography, index.

6-38. Gifford, Denis (U.K.). **Science Fiction Film.** Dutton, 1971. Studio Vista, £.80.
A British work, heavily illustrated, thick with title listings and brief commentary but with little detailed analysis. Baxter [6-10] and Johnson [6-49] are preferable.

6-39. Goble, Neil. **Asimov Analyzed.** Mirage Press, 1972, $5.95.
A pedestrian and rather mechanical analysis of the SF and science writings of one of the most prolific of current writers, in or out of SF. The bibliography, including detailed contents, of Asimov's first 100 books is the work's most valuable feature, but this has been superseded by the Miller bibliography [7-14]. Prefer Patrouch [6-71].

*6-40. Gove, Philip Babcock. **The Imaginary Voyage in Prose Fiction; A History of Its Criticism and a Guide for Its Study, With an Annotated Check List of 215 Imaginary Voyages from 1700 to 1800.** Columbia Univ. Press, 1941. Arno, $25.00. Octagon, $15.50.
An important early study which illuminates a recurrent theme in SF. A number of the works it discusses are mentioned or annotated in chapter 1 of this guide.

6-41. Graaf, Vera (Germany). **Homo Futurus; eine Analyse der modernen Science Fiction.** Hamburg, Claasen Verlag, 1971.
An introducory survey of the field by a teacher at the American Institute, Munich, who is a recent enthusiast for the field. The many facets of modern SF are explored, from definitions, sources, markets, fan clubs, and themes (not restricted solely to the book's title), to SF's place in American culture. The twenty-eight pages of notes and list of primary and secondary sources suggest the scope of the work and indicate wide reading by the author. Similar to Lundwall [6-60] in many respects, it provides a useful foreign view.

6-42. Green, Martin Burgess (U.K.). **Science and the Shabby Curate of Poetry; Essays about the Two Cultures.** Norton, 1965.
Probably the best single discussion of the scientific and literary sensibilities. Reviews in some detail the "two cultures" arguments of C. P. Snow. The introduction to this guide summarizes the author's views on SF.

6-43. Green, Roger Lancelyn (U.K.). **Into Other Worlds; Space-Flight in Fiction, from Lucian to Lewis.** Abelard-Schuman, 1958. Arno, $10.00.
Similar to Nicolson [6-67] but covering a wider range, as the title indicates. Descriptive rather than critical, with extensive quotes from the early accounts. Useful for historical perspective. Brief bibliography of accounts discussed in text; no index.

*6-44. Gunn, James E. **Alternate Worlds: The Illustrated History of Science Fiction.** Prentice-Hall, 1975, $29.95.
From the earliest precursors of SF to the latest expression in magazines and books, this provides thorough historical analysis of the scientific, social and philosophical influences which created and shaped the field. Hundreds of illustrations, many in color, including several hundred photographs of SF and fantasy authors. An appendix includes the Nebula and Hugo awards, a partial thematic index with examples, and a tabular history of science, technology and SF from earliest times. Detailed index. The author's background in literature and his reputation as a well-regarded SF writer make this much more than a coffee table work. More ambitious than Rottensteiner's [6-79] history, although lacking the latter's more detailed European and Soviet coverage. Not a critical study like Aldiss [6-2], but equally valuable.

6-45. Helms, Randel. **Tolkien's World.** Houghton, Mifflin, 1974, $3.95, $5.95.
Explores Tolkien's developing conception of Middle Earth, "an independent relm of the imagination with its own laws and significances," from his work as a teacher of Anglo-Saxon literature and his early works, such as *The Hobbit* (1938), to his well-known Lord of the Rings trilogy. Particularly illuminating in showing Tolkien's sources and development.

6-46. Hienger, Jörg (Germany). **Literarische Zukunftsphantistik; eine Studie über Science Fiction.** Gottingen, Vandenhoeck & Ruprecht, 1972.
Argues for the similarity of SF in all countries. Part 1 notes recurrent themes, e.g., space travel, mutations, dystopian trends. Part 2 outlines "rules" to which these fictional categories are subject—rationalty vs. irrationalty, adventure, weird or cosmic elements. From a 1970 thesis and for the scholar only.

*6-47. Hillegas, Mark Robert. **The Future as Nightmare; H. G. Wells and Anti-Utopians.** Oxford Univ. Press, 1967. Southern Illinois Univ. Press, 1974, $2.45, $7.00.
A well-written and absorbing study of Wells and his influence on other writers such as Forster, Capek, Zamiatin, Huxley, Orwell, and Lewis. The anti-utopian tradition is also traced in the works of the better SF writers such as Bradbury, Clarke, Pohl-Kornbluth, and Vonnegut.

6-48. Hillegas, Mark Robert, ed. **Shadows of Imagination: The Fantasies of C. S. Lewis, J. R. R. Tolkien, and Charles Williams.** Southern Illinois. Univ. Press, 1969, $6.95.

The intent of this Crosscurrents/Modern Critiques volume is to bring to the attention of readers three writers whose works, excluding Tolkien's, are relatively unknown. The editor's introduction, which stresses the "high order of excellence" and "respect for fantasy" of these authors, is followed by twelve essays on their works, mostly by academics. Compare Urang [6-89]. A more recent study is Richard Purtill's *Lord of the Elves and Eldils: Fantasy and Philosophy in C. S. Lewis and J. R. R. Tolkien* (Zondervan, 1975), which contrasts the themes and styles of these authors.

*6-49. Johnson, William, ed. **Focus on the Science Fiction Film.** Prentice-Hall, 1972, $2.45, $5.95.

Essays by American, British, and European critics about the origin and development of the SF film, its relation to other kinds of film and to SF writing, and its aesthetic value. The essays, in four chronological periods, span the years 1895 to 1970, and include pieces by Wells, Clarke, and Heinlein, but the most valuable essays are by European critics. Chronology showing scientific developments in SF writing and films, filmography, bibliography. Especially valuable for its breadth of coverage.

6-50. Jules-Verne, Jean (France). **Jules Verne; A Biography.** Taplinger, 1976, $12.95. Tr. by Roger Greaves from the 1973 French edition.

Verne's grandson has drawn on material in the family archives to provide a detailed picture of this major figure in the history of SF. He elucidates Verne's experiences and reveals in Verne's own words how many of his stories actually evolved. Like Chesneaux [6-20] he places Verne's works and ideas in the larger context of his times. The publisher claims this to be the definitive biography, with 368 pages, sixteen pages of illustrations, bibliography and index. If so, it will largely replace Allott's 1941 study [6-5]. [Annotation based on pre-publication information].

6-51. Kagarlitski, Julius (U.S.S.R.). **The Life and Thought of H. G. Wells.** Barnes & Noble, 1966. Tr. by Moura Budberg of *Herbert Wells: ocherk zhizni i tvorchestva*.

The editor of a Russian edition of Wells has written a short study of his thought, distilled from his sociological and prophetic (including SF) writings. Although originally aimed at a Russian audience, it is not dogmatically Marxist in outlook and shows literary as well as scientific influences on Wells' writings. Thirteen plates but no index.

*6-52. Kateb, George. **Utopia and Its Enemies.** Free Press, 1963. Schocken, rev. ed., 1972, $2.95.

Although touching only peripherally on SF, this closely reasoned analysis of utopian thought is of great value in gaining historical perspective on persistent themes in SF. Among the writers discussed are Bellamy, Wells, Marcuse, and Skinner.

6-53. Ketterer, David. **New Worlds for Old: The Apocalyptic Imagination, Science Fiction, and American Literature.** Anchor, $2.95; Indiana Univ. Press, 1974, $10.95.
Both a study of American literature and an analysis of SF, the book insists on the centrality of the apocalyptic vision in both American literature in general and SF in particular. Le Guin, Lem, Vonnegut, and Poe are among the authors whose works are examined in this important scholarly study.

*6-54. Klinkowitz, Jerome and John Somer, eds. **The Vonnegut Statement.** Delacorte, 1972, $10.00.
The authors of the thirteen pieces comprising the work are mostly academics, and some of their earlier pieces have been revised for this appearance. They focus on Vonnegut's popular and academic acceptance, his literary experience and development, and the theses and techniques in his six novels and many shorts. One essay argues that Vonnegut is not an SF writer in the traditional (pulp) sense but is "a writer who uses the techniques of that form to delineate human experience—a human experience of necessity broadened to include within its scope the technology which forms a goodly part of that experience." Helpful twenty-three page bibliography of primary and secondary materials, although Asa B. Pieratt and Jerome Klinkowitz's *Kurt Vonnegut, Jr.: A Descriptive Bibliography and Annotated Secondary Checklist* (Shoestring Press, 1974, $10.00) is the definitive bibliography to date.

6-55. Knight, Damon Francis. **In Search of Wonder: Essays on Modern Science Fiction.** 2nd ed., rev. & enl., Advent, 1967, $4.50, $9.00.
Mostly book reviews from the *Magazine of Fantasy and Science Fiction*, 1952–1960, for which Knight was the reviewer. Somewhat dated, fragmented, and very uneven, but still worth examination.

6-56. Kocher, Paul Harold. **Master of Middle Earth: The Fiction of J. R. R. Tolkien.** Houghton Mifflin, 1972. $3.25, $7.95.
A thorough discussion of the ideas of morality and social order underlying Tolkien's works, especially the Lord of the Rings trilogy, but paying attention to his lesser writings as well. A balanced and very useful study.

*6-57. Lewis, Clive Staples (U.K.). **Of Other Worlds; Essays and Stories.** Harcourt, 1966, $2.75.
His 1955 talk, "On Science Fiction," contains an extremely provocative and perceptive discussion of certain of the major types of SF stories, informed by a wide knowledge of literature and psychology. Especially co-

gent in his analysis of what types of sympathies a critic of SF should possess. All the pieces in this volume remind us of the loss we sustained with his death in 1963. See this guide's introduction for excerpts.

6-58. Locke, George (U.K.). **Voyages in Space: A Bibliography of Interplanetary Fiction, 1801–1914.** Ferret Fantasy, 1975. Distributed by Donald M. Grant, $8.50
A descriptive annotated bibliography of 263 books and magazine stories, with a sampling of thirteen titles prior to 1800. Each entry includes bibliographic information, including notes on various editions, and a brief summary indicating distinctive thematic elements. Usefully supplements Gove [6-40] and Nicolson [6-67]. Author index. Issued as Ferret Fantasy's Christmas Annual for 1974. For the specialist and larger library.

6-59. Lovecraft, Howard Phillips. **Supernatural Horror in Literature.** Ben Abramson, 1945; Dover, $1.50.
Originally published in 1927, this 32,000-word study is the longest single piece written by Lovecraft. Although peripheral to SF, Lovecraft's stories have had some limited influence on other SF writers. Compare Penzoldt [6-73] for a more balanced study.

6-60. Lundwall, Sam J. (Sweden). **Science Fiction: What It's All About.** Ace, 1971, $1.50.
An informal but useful survey of modern SF by a Swedish fan and editor. More balanced than Wollheim [6-98] much less comprehensive than Aldiss [6-2].

*6-61. Lupoff, Richard A. **Edgar Rice Burroughs: Master of Adventure.** 2nd rev. ed. Ace Books, 1975, $1.25.
Since ERB is not likely to get the same attention as, say, Henry James, this will probably remain one of the major studies. The entire range of his prolific writings is treated, from Tarzan in 1914 to posthumous works issued in the 1960s. An enjoyable and balanced study. Chapter 19, "A Basic Burroughs Library," will be helpful to libraries, which usually reject the works of this author, whose popularity has far outlasted more "serious" authors. Checklist of sixty-nine books published through 1967, but lacking an index, which would have helped. Preferable to Robert W. Fenton's lightweight biography *The Big Swingers* (1966). Compare Porges [6-75].

*6-62. MacKenzie, Norman Ian and Jean MacKenzie. **H. G. Wells; A Biography.** Simon & Schuster, 1973, $4.95, $10.00. (British title: *The Time Traveller*).
Wells' early life as a shopkeeper's son is described, then his education, and his career in and out of literature. A balanced and detailed study relying on primary sources. The best biography yet written of this giant,

whose works reflect the tensions and dualisms of his life. Useful bibliography. Compare Bergonzi [6-11], Borrello [6-14], Hillegas [6-47], Kagarlitski [6-51], Wagar [6-92], and Williamson [6-96].

6-63. Manuel, Frank E., ed. **Utopias and Utopian Thought.** Houghton Mifflin, 1966, $6.50. Beacon, $2.95.
Reprinted from the Spring 1965 *Daedalus*, plus several additional essays. The wide-ranging discussions are of value in understanding persistent themes in SF. Compare Kateb [6-52], who contributed one of the essays.

6-64. Moore, Patrick (U.K.). **Science and Fiction.** Harrap, 1957. Folcroft, $15.00.
Emphasizes works with an interplanetary setting, not surprising considering the author's astronomical background. Treatment is largely chronological, from Lucian to recent writers. Some helpful notes, from a British standpoint, on changes in magazine SF from the age of bug-eyed monsters to more adult stories. Criticizes the juvenile aspects of the field and notes the unscientific nature of most writing. Brief notes on SF illustrations, reviewing, and mass media adaptations. Index.

*6-65. Moskowitz, Samuel. **Explorers of the Infinite: Shapers of Science Fiction.** World, 1963. Hyperion, $3.95, $11.95.
The doyen of fans provides a largely uncritical history of early SF and semi-SF writers from Cyrano de Bergerac in the seventeenth century to relatively recent writers in the 1930s. Some of the authors discussed are minor by any standard—Fitz-James O'Brien, M. P. Shiel, E. R. Burroughs. Virtually no attempt is made to relate their work to wider literary or historical traditions. Name index.

*6-66. Moskowitz, Samuel. **Seekers of Tomorrow: Masters of Modern Science Fiction.** World, 1966. Ballantine, 1967; Hyperion, $4.75, $12.95.
Sequel to 6-65 this covers the post-1940 period to 1965. Twenty-one writers are discussed in detail, with a chapter devoted to Superman and his creators and one briefly treating a number of writers Moskowitz judges of lesser importance (such as Vonnegut). The same inbred quality vitiates both his works, and his critical estimates should be judged accordingly. In spite of these serious weaknesses, he deserves credit for providing a detailed and reasonably accurate picture of early and modern SF. Ballantine reprint has an expanded index of names, titles, and publishers, which the Hyperion reprint lacks.

6-67. Nicolson, Marjorie Hope. **Voyages to the Moon.** Macmillan, 1948, $1.75.
A useful background study, supplementing Gove [6-40]. An epilogue briefly traces the historical debts of Poe, Verne, Wells, and Lewis to ear-

lier writers. The bibliography of primary and secondary materials is useful for the scholar, and the plates will interest anyone.

6-68. Nolan, William F. **The Ray Bradbury Companion: A Life and Career History, Photolog, and Comprehensive Checklist of Writings, With Facsimiles from Ray Bradbury's Unpublished and Uncollected Work in all Media.** Gale, 1975, $28.50.
The subtitle provides a good summary of the contents. While not intended as a complete or formal bibliography, Nolan provides a kaleidoscopic view of a talented and widely praised writer, whose published work far transcends the limits of SF. The coverage is from 1936 through 1973, and the book is further distinguished by a handsome layout, design, and slipcase.

6-69. Pagetti, Carlo (Italy). **Il senso del futuro. La fantascienza nella letteratura Americana.** (Biblioteca de Studi Americani, 20). Rome, Edizioni di Storia e Letteratura, 1970.
A serious literary study of American SF from the nineteenth century to 1968. Verne and Wells are seen as the seminal figures, but the direct influences of Poe and Hawthorne are traced as well (the author relies on Franklin [6-35]). A number of recent and recurrent themes are treated, as are several modern writers, such as Bradbury, Sheckley, Dick, and Vonnegut. The last rates a complete chapter, for Pagetti considers him easily the best of modern SF authors. A final chapter sums up the latest writers: Delany, Le Guin, Disch, Zelazny, John Barth, and William Burroughs. A work comparable in scope to Aldiss's *Billion Year Spree* [6-2] but, because of its language, not likely to receive much attention. [Annotation based on review by Paul M. Lloyd, *Extrapolation*, 15 (May 1974), 152-4.]

6-70. Panshin, Alexei. **Heinlein in Dimension.** Advent, 1969, $4.00, $8.00.
A balanced and detailed study of one of SF's most popular authors, this originally appeared in *Riverside Quarterly*. Assesses the subjects, plots, literary qualities, militaristic heroes, and his influence in the SF field. Scheduled for 1976 is a collection of recent essays by Panshin and his wife, Cory, *SF in Dimension* (Advent).

6-71. Patrouch, Joseph F., Jr. **The Science Fiction of Isaac Asimov.** Doubleday, 1974, $6.95.
As the most prolific of living SF writers, it is not surprising that Asimov has received considerable attention. In addition to two lengthy bibliographies (the better is Miller [7-14]), we have this study, which is largely limited to Asimov's SF, and Goble's *Asimov Analyzed* [6-39]. Patrouch, an English professor, critically analyzes all of Asimov's SF (Goble discusses

the nonfiction also), comparing and contrasting themes, techniques, narrative devices, etc. His writing is clear, sensible, and often helpful in gaining a deeper understanding of Asimov's stories, which are treated as a world unto themselves, although occasional mention is made of other SF works. Much better than Goble, and the preferred study.

6-72. Pehlke, Michael, and Norbert Lingfeld (Germany). **Roboter und Gartenlaube, Ideologie und Unterhaltung in der Science-Fiction-Literature.** Munich: Carl Hanser, 1970.
A critical analysis showing how and why SF is simultaneously entertainment and yet often has a more serious satirical or cautionary purpose.

6-73. Penzoldt, Peter (U.K.). **The Supernatural in Fiction.** Humanities, 1952, $7.50.
A more recent treatment of a theme discussed by Scarborough [6-82] and Lovecraft [6-59]. Only passing attention is given to SF in a five-page section, "The Supernatural in Science Fiction." A chapter is devoted to Lovecraft. Of value for the study of supernatural fiction, included here to provide an added perspective.

*6-74. Philmus, Robert. **Into The Unknown: The Evolution of Science Fiction from Francis Godwin to H. G. Wells.** Univ. of California Press, 1970, $7.95.
A scholarly survey of English SF in the eighteenth and nineteenth centuries. The author defines SF as a rhetorical technique using (then) plausible scientific explanations to persuade the reader to suspend his disbelief in otherwise fantastic situations. He relates SF to utopian satire and an archetypical mythical view of literature, discussing such works as *Gulliver's Travels* [1-49], Voltaire's *Micromégas* [1-50], and *Frankenstein* [1-47]. A valuable study of SF's origins for the more devoted reader, who should have a good knowledge of the period for full comprehension.

6-75. Porges, Irwin. **Edgar Rice Burroughs: The Man Who Created Tarzan.** Brigham Young Univ. Press, 1975, $19.95.
Published on the hundredth anniversary of Burroughs' birth, this is the authorized and definitive biography, over 800 pages, including more than 250 photos and illustrations. Far more than a writer of SF, he was one of the most popular of all twentieth-century authors. The sources of this popularity and the entire scope of his works and life are discussed in detail by a professor of English, who has relied on many primary sources not previously available. The Lupoff study [6-61] is a better choice for most readers and smaller libraries and provides a better critical perspective on Burroughs' works than does Porges.

6-76. Reynolds, Quentin James. **The Fiction Factory; or, from Pulp Row to Quality Street; the Story of 100 Years of Publishing at Street & Smith.** Random, 1955.

An interesting house history of a publisher whose magazines and books still appear today. Westerns, romances, detective, adventure—all the popular types were published by Street & Smith. Chapter 11 is devoted to *Astounding* (now *Analog* and published by Condé Nast). Of minor interest to most SF readers but helpful to historians of popular culture. Similar works include *Pulpwood Editor* (Stokes, 1937) by Harold Hersey, who edited Street & Smith's *Thrill Book* (1919) and assisted in the founding of *Astounding*. A widely experienced pulp editor and publisher, he argues that the audience for pulps is much the same as that for slicks (*Colliers*, *Saturday Evening Post*, etc.), although pulp readers are less critical, though quick to point out errors in their favorite type of stories (westerns, air stories, etc.). Frank Gruber's *The Pulp Jungle* (Sherbourne Press, 1967) is an anecdotal autobiographical account by a prolific writer of westerns and detective stories. Tony Goodstone's *The Pulps; 50 Years of American Pop Culture* (Chelsea House, 1970, $10.00) contains over fifty complete stories, poems, features, articles, advertisements, and many covers in color. Introduction and short notes for each chapter, one devoted to the SF pulps.

6-77. Rogers, Alva. **A Requiem for Astounding.** Advent, 1964, $4.00, $8.00.
A dreary, almost wholly uncritical recital of the contents of *Astounding* (now *Analog*) from 1930 to 1969. The lack of perspective resulting from an almost exclusive preoccupation with a single magazine gravely impairs this work.

6-78. Rose, Lois and Stephen Rose. **The Shattered Ring; Science Fiction and the Quest for Meaning.** John Knox, 1970, $3.45.
Attempts to show how SF is concerned with basic human concerns, values, and future directions. Chapters are devoted to man, nature, and history, examining the work of Lewis, Wells, Clarke, Heinlein, and Asimov. A brief study of limited value.

*6-79. Rottensteiner, Franz (Austria). **The Science Fiction Book: An Illustrated History.** Seabury, 1975, $14.95.
The multilingual editor of *Quarber Merkur*, a respected Austrian fanzine, provides an extensively illustrated survey of SF. The coverage of non-English-language works is especially good and is long overdue. (Versins' [6-91] encyclopedia provides extensive coverage, also, but is available only in French). Chronology from Lucian to Le Guin, a multilingual descriptive bibliography, and a list of Nebula and Hugo awards conclude the work, which lacks an index. Gunn's survey [6-44] is more detailed, although lacking the international coverage, and is preferable, although both are essential for larger libraries.

6-80. Sadoul, Jacques. **Histoire de la science fiction moderne (1911–1971).** Paris: Albin Michel, 1973.

Unlike Aldiss [6-2] this is not a critical history but is largely a descriptive account, with some brief evaluations, of almost 500 stories and novels. The repetitive nature of the plot summaries is tiresome if unavoidable. The work's strength is the section on French SF, a world in which the author is a prominent figure. [Annotation based on unpublished review by Peter Brigg.]

6-81. Sadoul, Jacques (France). **2000 A.D.; Illustrations from the Golden Age of Science Fiction Pulps.** Regnery, 1975, $7.95, $17.95. Tr. of *Hier, l'an 2000*, 1973.

This affectionate study clearly reproduces several hundred black-and-white interior illustrations as well as many covers in full color, all with artist and issue indicated, from the 1926–1953 period. All the names familiar to aficionados and collectors are here. The eight chapters group the illustrations by themes (robots, machines, future cities, etc.), each introduced by a brief commentary. Index by source but no illustrator index. More pictorial than Rottensteiner's [6-79] history but lacking its historical and critical features. Frewin [6-36], although his coverage stops at 1940, has better quality illustrations, more in color, and a livelier text. For the collector and larger library. Much less satisfactory is Lester del Rey's *Fantastic Science-Fiction Art, 1926-1954* (Ballantine, 1975, $5.95), which reproduces forty pulp covers in color, eighteen by Frank Paul, an imbalance not helped by a routine eight page introduction.

6-82. Scarborough, Dorothy. **The Supernatural in English Fiction.** Putnam, 1917. Octagon, $11.00; Richard West, $9.95.

A chapter, "Supernatural Science," concentrates on Wells and his contemporaries, showing the links between the Gothic traditions and the scientific romance. Compare Penzoldt [6-73].

*6-83. Scholes, Robert. **Structural Fabulation; An Essay on Fiction of the Future.** (Ward-Phillips Lectures in English Language and Literature, 7). Univ of Notre Dame Press, 1975, $6.95.

Revised from four 1974 lectures, Scholes argues that traditional forms of fiction are moribund and "that the most appropriate kind of fiction that can be written in the present and the immediate future is fiction that takes place in the future." Following the first half's relatively theoretical but clear discussion, selected works such as *Flowers for Algernon* [4-336] and *Star Maker* [3-60] are discussed. An entire lecture is devoted to Le Guin. Short bibliography. In spite of its brevity, it may have an influence like that of Amis's *New Maps of Hell* [6-6] in gaining SF greater academic respectability.

6-84. The Science Fiction Novel: Imagination and Social Criticism. Advent, 1959, $3.50, $6.00.

Following an introduction by Basil Davenport are lectures delivered early in 1957 at the University of Chicago by Heinlein, Kornbluth, Bester, and Robert Bloch. Their tone is critical, stressing the lack of social criticism in most SF, the preoccupation with gadgets and technology in a vacuum. Moderately useful as historical background. As chapter 4 of this guide abundantly indicates, social criticism has been a major theme in recent SF.

6-85. Science Fiction Writers of America, eds. **Writing and Selling Science Fiction.** Writer's Digest, 1976.
A how-to guide by experienced SF writers describing markets, financial matters, developing ideas, plotting, characterization, dialogue, etc. Compare de Camp [6-29] and Bova [6-15]. [Annotation based on pre-publication information.]

6-86. Small, Christopher (U.K.). **Mary Shelley's "Frankenstein": Tracing the Myth.** Univ of Pittsburgh Press, 1973, $9.95. (British title: *Ariel Like a Harpy: Shelley, Mary and Frankenstein*. Gollancz, 1972; Humanities, $11.25).
Traces the "myth" of Frankenstein from its origin in Mary Shelley's imagination to its current forms in film and SF and literature generally. Focuses on the genesis of the novel, especially as influenced by her poet-husband and his works. Chapter 13, "Robots and Resurrection," explores the use of robots in fiction, from Čapek's coinage of the word in *R.U.R.* [2-37] to Asimov. Somewhat more popular is *The Frankenstein Legend: A Tribute to Mary Shelley and Boris Karloff*, by Donald F. Glut (Scarecrow, 1973, $10.00), whose account provides a thorough coverage of modern—and usually debased—versions of the myth in film, TV, and recent literature from comics to pornography. A more recent study of Shelley's sources, based on first-hand investigation, is Radu Florescu's readable *In Search of Frankenstein* (N.Y. Graphic Society, 1975, $9.95). The author collaborated with Raymond T. McNally on a similar work exploring vampire legends, *In Search of Dracula: A True History of Dracula and the Vampire Legends* (N.Y. Graphic Society, 1972, $9.95; Warner $1.50).

6-87. Stover, Leon, E. **La science fiction americaine: essai d'anthropologie culturelle.** Paris: Editions Aubier Montaigne, 1972.
A professor of anthropology at the Illinois Institute of Technology, Stover examines SF's origins as a response to the research revolution, where the individual inventor is displaced by the corporate or government research project. The ascension of John Campbell symbolized this change. Stover then analyzes a number of stories under rubrics borrowed from anthropology, such as society, work, communication, and material systems. The work is not unified by a systematic theory, and stories are selected only to illustrate the chapter headings, giving a fragmented quali-

ty to the study. Although not yet translated, an adaptation of chapter 1 appeared in *Extrapolation*, 14 (May 1973), 129–148.

6-88. Sussman, Herbert L. **Victorians and the Machine: The Literary Response to Technology.** Harvard Univ. Press, 1968, $8.50.
Concentrates on seven representative writers: Carlyle, Dickens, Ruskin, William Morris, Samuel Butler, Kipling, and Wells. Examines the complex ways these and other writers tried to adjust to the emerging industrial age and how the machine came to hold an important symbolic place in Victorian literature. A very useful background study for understanding the early years of SF. Not restricted to literature alone is the comprehensive and well-written survey by Herbert J. Muller, *The Children of Frankenstein; A Primer on Modern Technology and Human Values* (Indiana Univ. Press, 1970).

6-89. Urang, Gunnar. **Shadows of Heaven: Religion and Fantasy in the Writings of C. S. Lewis, Charles Williams and J. R. R. Tolkien.** Pilgrim Press, 1971, $6.95.
One chapter is devoted to each author, with a concluding essay comparing and contrasting thematic and structural elements. The emphasis is on the Christian concerns of their writings and contrasts their concern with past literature and folklore with the sharply different emphasis of most SF, where the future is the focus. A valuable scholarly study of these writers. The author contributed to Hillegas's similar work [6-48].

6-90. Van Ash, Cay, and Elizabeth Sax Rohmer. **Master of Villainy; A Biography of Sax Rohmer.** Bowling Green Univ. Popular Press, 1972.
Arthur Sarsfield Ward's life and works are the subject of this anecdotal biography by his wife and a friend of some years. Though the familiar Fu Manchu books are not SF, some of Rohmer's output falls on the fantasy/SF borderline. Valuable bibliography by Robert Briney of Rohmer's works from 1910 to his death in 1959. Index.

6-91. Versins, Pierre (Switzerland). **Encyclopédie de l'utopie, des voyages extraordinaires et de la science-fiction.** Lausanne, Editions L'age d'Homme, 1972.
A massive (8 ½ x 11 inches, 997 pages) encyclopedic dictionary by the foremost Swiss collector of SF. Unlike Tuck, which is largely descriptive bibliography, this wide-ranging work includes bio-bibliographic entries for authors, entries for each country with cross-references to their authors, discussions of common SF themes, useful graphs showing the varying popularity of SF as measured by the fluctuating number of magazines, as well as charts summarizing the future histories of Poul Anderson, James Blish and Isaac Asimov. SF in TV, music, films, comics, ballet and opera is also treated. Especially valuable for its often detailed discussion of European SF largely unknown to Anglo-American readers.

Well-printed and illustrated, its high cost (about $70) will limit its value to the large library collecting SF intensively.

*6-92. Wagar, W. Warren. **H. G. Wells and the World State.** Yale Univ. Press, 1961. Books for Libraries, $13.25.
Rewritten from a doctoral dissertation, the work argues that Wells conditioned his readers to think in terms of the entire world, tried to expand the parochial late nineteenth-century world view to a view Wells felt was essential for understanding the future. He shows (as Williamson [6-96] did later) that Wells was not a believer in inevitable progress, and that he understood the undesirable features of science and technology. A very important study.

*6-93. Walsh, Chad. **From Utopia to Nightmare.** Harper, 1962. Greenwood, $9.25.
An excellent short survey from an unobtrusive Christian perspective of nineteenth- and twentieth-century utopian and dystopian thought, discussing or alluding to not only standard utopias but to many falling within the SF mainstream. Especially good in analyzing the shift from utopian to dystopian literature, where sociology, psychology, political science, theology, and philosophy meet.

6-94. Warner, Harry, Jr. **All Our Yesterdays; An Informal History of Science Fiction Fandom in the Forties.** Advent, 1969, $9.00, $4.50.
A portion of SF's regular readers are vociferous enthusiasts, corresponding and feuding with one another, organizing and joining clubs, issuing fanzines and attending local, regional, and world conventions. Only the diehard buff will be able to read this casual history of fan activities, but the scholar will find it useful as supplementary reading. A glossary of neologisms common to the field clarifies matters for the neophyte.

6-95. Wertham, Fredric. **The World of Fanzines: A Special Form of Communication.** Southern Illinois Univ. Press, 1972, $10.00.
The first book-length study of fanzines as a type of personal publication distinct from other little magazines. The thirty-two pages of reproductions which begin the book are wholly unrelated to the text, which is largely descriptive of the various types, such as SF, fantasy, and comic book fanzines. Production, circulation patterns, and salient characteristics are discussed. The author, a psychiatrist, finds them nonviolent and personal and a welcome contrast with impersonal violence in literature and the world, a long-time preoccupation of his. A useful but very limited study of a topic neglected outside fan circles. The work lacks any real critical understanding of the subject.

6-96. Williamson, Jack. **H. G. Wells: Critic of Progress.** Mirage, 1973, $5.95.
A study "devoted to the premise that Wells' early science fiction presents

searching and significant criticism of the idea of progress," which the author claims contradicts the stereotype of Wells as "the deluded prophet of a crassly materialistic progress." This revision of a doctoral dissertation was partially anticipated by the works of Bergonzi [6-11], Wagar [6-92], and Hillegas [6-47].

6-97. Wilson, Colin (U.K.). **The Strength to Dream: Literature and the Imagination.** Houghton Mifflin, 1962. Greenwood, $14.00.
Examines the function of imagination and its relation to values in writers such as Graham Greene, Samuel Beckett, H. G. Wells, and Tolstoy, with a chapter devoted to H. P. Lovecraft and brief comments on other SF writers. Unsystematic and dogmatic, but of some value as collateral reading.

6-98. Wollheim, Donald A. **The Universe Makers; Science Fiction Today.** Harper, 1971.
An anecdotal, personal, but useful brief survey by a veteran editor and author, who now heads DAW books. Compare Aldiss [6-2] and Lundwall [6-60].

7.
Bibliographies, Indexes and Teaching Aids

While important bibliographic information is often found in the historical and critical works annotated elsewhere, the works listed below provide more comprehensive coverage. Burger's annual bibliography [7-3] and the listings in each issue of *Luna Monthly* provide useful recent information.

*7-1. Bleiler, Everett Franklin. **The Checklist of Fantastic Literature; A Bibliography of Fantasy, Weird and Science Fiction Books Published in the English Language.** Shasta, 1948. Fax, 1972.
The first major book-form bibliography, listing approximately 5,300 prose titles written after 1764 (Walpole's *Castle of Otranto*). The full citation is by author, followed by a title index, notes, and an annotated list of critical and historical reference works. The nature of fantasy permits many definitions, and many omissions were unavoidable. Further, extensive reprinting in book form of magazine material from the period of 1926 on did not really begin until several years after this volume appeared. A revised and expanded edition is in preparation. See Reginald [7-18] and Tymn [7-23].

*7-2. Briney, Robert E. and Edward Wood. **SF Bibliographies: An Annotated Bibliography of Bibliographical Works on Science Fiction and Fantasy Fiction.** Advent, 1972.
An essential bibliography which describes a great many of the fugitive and now very scarce amateur publications which were ignored by almost all libraries and are now almost unobtainable. Provides more detailed information about many of the works annotated in this guide. A revised and expanded edition is in preparation.

7-3. Burger, Joanne, comp. **Science Fiction Published in [year].**
An annual beginning with works published in 1968, this provides useful retrospective coverage. Available from the compiler, 55 Blue Bonnet Court, Lake Jackson, Texas 77566; 1971, 1972, 1973 and 1974, $1.25 each. Burger also publishes *Forthcoming SF Books*, bimonthly, $2.00/year.

*7-4. Christopher, Joe R., and Joan K. Otling. **C. S. Lewis: An Annotated Checklist of Writings about Him and His Works.** (Serif series, 30). Kent State Univ. Press, 1974, $15.00.
This major guide annotates the most important secondary materials, from book-length studies and dissertations to the most important reviews and interviews. Not only his fiction, but his poetry, children's books, theology, and other works are comprehensively reviewed. Author and title index. An essential starting point for all Lewis scholars.

*7-5. Clareson, Thomas D. **Science Fiction Criticism: An Annotated Checklist.** (Serif series, 23). Kent State Univ. Press, 1972, $7.00.
An extremely useful descriptive listing of over 800 items from both popular and academic sources, excluding fanzines and most European sources. A companion volume covering European (usually foreign-language) criticism is in preparation by David N. Samuelson of California State University, Long Beach.

*7-6. Clarke, Ignatius Frederick, comp. (U.K.). **The Tale of the Future from the Beginning to the Present Day: An Annotated Bibliography** . . . 2nd ed. London: Library Association, 1972, £3.75 (£3.00 to members).
A chronological and briefly annotated listing by year from 1644 to 1970 of about 1,200 utopian, political, and scientific romance tales of the future published in Britain. The romances emphasizing adventure and wonder are those commonly labeled SF. Author (including pseudonym) and title indexes and brief bibliography. Cover misnames author as Ian Clarke in second edition.

*7-7. Cole, Walter R., comp. **A Checklist of Science-Fiction Anthologies.** Brooklyn: author, 1964. Arno, $21.00.
Detailed indexing of almost 2,700 stories from 227 anthologies from 1927 to 1963, most since 1950. Listed by anthology title; by editor, show-

ing contents and original magazine source; and by author. Anthologies published in 1962–1963 are included in a supplement. Poorly designed and probably over-exhaustive and now somewhat dated, but still very helpful. A revised and updated edition would be a very valuable tool. Compare Siemon [7-19]. The *Short Story Index* (H. W. Wilson) includes many SF anthologies and single-author collections. *The Chicorel Index to Short Stories in Anthologies and Collections* (4 vols., 1974), indexes about 140 titles, many annotated in this guide.

7-8. Day, Bradford M. **The Checklist of Fantastic Literature in Paperbound Books.** Science-Fiction & Fantasy Publications, 1965. Arno, $7.00.

The nominal coverage is from the nineteenth century to 1965, listing English-language paperbacks from the United States, Canada, U.K. and Australia. Only one paperback edition is listed for each title, usually the first publication. Since Bleiler [7-1] omitted paperbacks, this has some use, although Reginald's checklist [7-17] should supersede this work.

7-9. Day, Bradford M. **The Supplemental Checklist of Fantastic Literature.** Science-Fiction & Fantasy Publications, 1963. Arno, $9.00.

A supplement to Bleiler [7-1]. Full entry under author, plus title index. Approximately 3,000 titles listed, many excluded from Bleiler although published prior to 1947. Compare Reginald [7-18] and Tymn [7-23].

7-10. Franson, Donald, and Howard DeVore. **A History of the Hugo, Nebula and International Fantasy Awards.** Order from Howard DeVore, 4705 Weddel St., Dearborn, Michigan 48125, $1.60 prepaid.

The list of awards in this guide is largely based on Franson and DeVore, which is current through 1975. All categories of awards are shown.

7-11. Halpern, Frank M. **International Classified Directory of Dealers in Science Fiction and Fantasy Books and Related Materials.** Haddonfield House, 1974, $7.95.

An experienced member of the Philadelphia Free Library's rare book department has compiled a directory of over 130 specialty dealers, which should prove very useful to the library collecting heavily in the SF field or to the private collector. Following the alphabetical listing of dealers, which shows phone numbers, frequency of catalogs, searching services, and subject specialties, there are indexes of dealers who accept want lists, make searches and appraisals, plus a geographic index. A subject index groups the dealers in almost 300 categories. See also comments preceding the publisher listing in this guide.

7-12. Lee, Walt. **Reference Guide to Fantastic Films: Science Fiction, Fantasy, and Horror.** 3 vols. Chelsea-Lee Books, 1972–1974, $29.40/set.

Three sturdy 8 ½ × 11 paperbacks list over 20,000 films from over fifty countries released since about 1900. The information is presented in title sequence, four columns per page, with cross-references from variant titles. Date of release, country of production, length, cast, credits, brief content note, source of film story, and references to reviews are among the elements shown for most titles. Almost 150 stills complement the text, as does a list of exclusions (films apparently but not actually within scope of the book), one of "problems," and an extensive bibliography. An extraordinary achievement characteristic of the best of fan scholarship. Preferable to Willis because of its much more thorough coverage, in spite of its price. Donald C. Willis, *Horror and Science Fiction Films: A Checklist* (Scarecrow, 1972, $15.00), is an alphabetical list by film title of approximately 4,400 films, giving reasonably complete production information: alternative titles, producing company, country of origin, year, length, director, story source, etc., with a brief plot synopsis and comment. Quite adequate for the smaller library, but larger libraries will prefer Lee.

*7-13. McGhan, Barry, comp. **Science Fiction and Fantasy Pseudonyms.** rev. ed. 1973. Order from Howard DeVore, 4705 Weddel St., Dearborn, Michigan 48125, $1.25 prepaid.
To the original thirty-four mimeographed pages from the 1971 edition are added twenty-one pages in the 1973 supplement. In addition to cross-references from pseudonym to real name, the real name is followed by all known pseudonyms. Source of information is shown. Used as the principal authority in this guide.

7-14. Miller, Marjorie M. **Isaac Asimov: A Checklist of Works Published in the U.S., March 1939–May 1972.** (Serif series, 25). Kent State Univ. Press, 1972, $6.50.
A chronological listing of fiction and nonfiction, showing first and subsequent publications, brief descriptive annotations, and title index. Supersedes listing in Goble [6-39]. Useful because of Asimov's importance to the field.

7-15. Owings, Mark, and Jack L. Chalker, eds. **The Index to the Science-Fantasy Publishers: A Bibliography of the Science Fiction and Fantasy Specialty Houses.** Mirage, 1966.
Thirty-six publishers are listed, with a brief history of each imprint and a chronological listing of all titles published, cross-indexed by author, title, and publisher.

7-16. Pfeiffer, John R. **Fantasy and Science Fiction: A Critical Guide.** Filter Press, 1971, $1.50, $4.00.
A sixty-four page guide, similar to but much less ambitious than this guide. The titles are not annotated.

*7-17. Reginald, Robert. **Science Fiction and Fantasy Literature; A Checklist, from Earliest Times to 1974, with Contemporary Science Fiction Authors II.** Gale, 1976, $45.00 [tentative].

This should be a major reference work. It will largely supersede *Stella Nova* [7-18] and will incorporate most of the entries in Bleiler [7-1] and the supplements thereto, plus additional titles. The author estimates that about 15,000 prose English-language titles, excluding juveniles, will be listed, including the growing number of paperback originals. Books about science fiction and SF authors will also be listed, with coverage through 1973. A separate section will contain over 800 biographies of SF authors, mostly living. [Annotation based on prepublication information.]

7-18. Reginald, Robert. **Stella Nova: The Contemporary Science Fiction Authors.** Unicorn & Son, 1970. Arno, $20.00.
Biographies of 308 contemporary SF writers active in the 1960s who responded to a questionnaire, showing autobiographical information, a list of books published by year, and a description of works in progress, plus an additional 175 author bibliographies. Title index. Similar to *Contemporary Authors* [7-17] and most helpful. The partially revised Arno reprint is titled *The Contemporary Science Fiction Authors.* The list of symbols and abbreviations used (far too many) was omitted from the reprint by error; request from publisher.

*7-19. Siemon, Fred, comp. **Science Fiction Story Index.** American Library Assn., 1971, $4.50.
Although reviewers noted that his work was seriously incomplete in its professed coverage, it does provide a useful and more easily used supplement to Cole [7-7]. The full citation of anthology by editor is followed by author and title indexes.

7-20. Suvin, Darko. **Russian Science Fiction Literature and Criticism 1956–1970; A Bibliography.** 1971.
Published by the "Secondary Universe 4" Conference held in Toronto, this thirty-five-page pamphlet is very useful, since this area has generally been neglected until very recent years. Part 1 lists Russian-language SF published in the U.S.S.R., 1956–1970. Part 2 lists all known book translations into Western (usually English) languages of twentieth-century Russian SF authors. This will be the most valuable section for most readers. Part 3 is a partially annotated bibliography of criticism of Soviet SF, 1956–1970. This supplements the bibliography in Britikov [6-18]. A revised edition is in preparation by Dragon Press, due 1976.

7-21. Swigart, Leslie Kay. **Harlan Ellison: A Bibliographical Checklist.** Dallas: Williams Pub. Co., 1973.
An extremely thorough bibliography of an important modern author and editor, covering not only Ellison's SF but his other writings as well. Too many SF author bibliographies omit the non-SF writings.

*7-22. Tuck, Donald Henry. **The Encyclopedia of Science Fiction and Fantasy through 1968.** Advent, 1974–. $20.00 (vol. 1).

The first of three volumes, covering who's who and works, A–L, appeared in 1974. Volume 2, probably 1976, will cover authors, M–Z, with a title index. Volume 3 will provide magazine checklists, paperback information, pseudonyms, and other general information. Brief biographical information appears for almost all authors, some of them only tangentially connected with SF (e.g., Charles Addams, the cartoonist). Contents of anthologies and collections are shown, as are series and original magazine sources for many works. Descriptive and evaluative comment is intermixed. An extraordinarily valuable reference work, surprising since the author lives in Tasmania.

7-23. Tymn, Marshall B., comp. **The Checklist of Fantastic Literature II.** Fax, 1976.
A supplement to Bleiler, as the title suggests, listing U.S. editions from 1948 through 1973, a borderline title index, and an annotated bibliography of SF criticism. Annual supplements are planned. The work does not appear to be as comprehensive as Reginald [7-18] and naturally duplicates much of Tuck [7-22]. Larger libraries will probably want all three bibliographies. [Annotation based on prepublication information.]

Teaching Aids

The number of anthologies/texts for SF courses is increasing rapidly. Specimen desk copies are normally available upon letterhead request by instructors. What follows is simply a sampling of better or typical texts. See also certain of the anthologies in the modern period, especially Clareson [4-663] and Silverberg [4-693]. Because anthologies normally must limit themselves to short stories, they must be supplemented by novels, many of which are listed in the bibliographies and reading lists in these aids.

7-24. Allen, L. David. **Science Fiction Reader's Guide.** Centennial Pr., 1974. $1.50.
Originally issued in 1973 as *Science Fiction: An Introduction* in the Cliff's Notes series, this is a useful and inexpensive introduction to the field for classroom use. Following a brief typology of SF, fifteen novels are discussed, two from the period of scientific romances (Verne and Wells), the others from 1950 to 1970, most of them award winners. The remaining third of the book analyses Herbert's *Dune* more thoroughly, discusses verisimilitude in SF, lists novel and short fiction award winners, and concludes with a recommended bibliography, an annotated bibliography of works about SF, and an index. Allen also wrote *The Ballantine Teacher's Guide to Science Fiction: A Practical Creative Approach to Science Fiction in the Classroom* (Ballantine, 1975, $1.95). Following a general introduction on teaching SF, Allen largely repeats his typology, then devotes

about 20 pages to each of fifteen works (thirteen novels), only one (analysis of Niven's *Ringworld*) duplicated in both guides. Each chapter is followed by topics and projects, which may help students gain more from the work under discussion but which frequently struck me as simple-minded busywork. While most works selected are important, their selection was apparently dictated less by their intrinsic worth than by their availability from Ballantine, a harmless bit of self-promotion. The first is the preferred guide, but both are inexpensive and useful.

7-25. Calkins, Elizabeth, and Barry McGhan. **Teaching Tomorrow; A Handbook of Science Fiction for Teachers.** Pflaum/Standard, 1972, $3.20.
Aimed at the high school English teacher, this short paperback includes basic background information, study guides, case studies, lists of dealers, publishers, and magazines, plus annotated lists of critical works and novels.

7-26. Friend, Beverly. **Science Fiction: The Classroom in Orbit.** Educational Impact, 1974, $4.95.
A short paperback that departs from the traditional text in appearance, this is aimed at both high school and college teachers. Not only fiction but film and TV are discussed. Over twenty-five "probes" are designed to stimulate reading and discussion. A fifteen-page teacher's supplement provides additional useful information.

7-27. Hollister, Benard C., and Deane C. Thompson. **Grokking the Future: Science Fiction in the Classroom.** Pflaum/Standard, 1973, $6.00.
Two instructors in an Illinois high school have developed a text "to demonstrate how SF offers new insights into current social issues, and . . . to help students become more creative in their thinking about the future." Each chapter includes reading lists, and there are "what if . . ." exercises to stimulate interest and thought. Useful on the college level also. Compare Friend [7-26].

7-28. McNelly, Willis, and Leon Stover. **Above the Human Landscape; A Social Science Fiction Anthology.** Goodyear, 1972, $6.95, $9.95.
Twenty-six stories, mostly from the last two decades, emphasizing SF as a literature of ideas and social criticism. The editors include an afterword, "Science Fiction as Culture Criticism," which provides a perspective on the stories.

7-29. Science Fiction Film Series. Audio Visual Center, Film Rental Service, Univ. of Kansas, 746 Massachusetts St., Lawrence, Kansas 66044.
A series of twelve 16 mm color and sound films, nineteen to forty minutes in length, featuring talks or discussions by many of the outstanding

writers and editors in the field, such as the late John Campbell, Poul Anderson, Damon Knight, Jack Williamson, and Harlan Ellison. A free brochure shows rental and purchase costs, contents, running time, etc.

*7-30. Williamson, Jack. **Science Fiction: Education for Tomorrow.** Mirage, 1976.
When issued, this should provide for the teaching field what Bretnor [6-16, 6-17] did for the interested layman. Teachers and active writers have contributed to this guidebook, whose comprehensive coverage includes use of SF in various subject disciplines, general articles on what SF is, its history, whether it should be taught, conferences, lectures, and workshops, basic reading lists, etc. This will largely supersede the author's pamphlet *Teaching SF*, 1972. [Annotation based on prepublication information.]

7-31. Wilson, Robin Scott, ed. **Those Who Can; A Science Fiction Reader.** Mentor, 1973, $1.50.
Pairs of writers discuss one of their stories (included) under one of the headings, plot, character, setting, theme, point of view, style. The contrasts are often interesting, and the dozen essays should be especially helpful for creative writing classes.

8.
Magazine and
Book Review Indexes

SF and fantasy magazines have been well indexed since 1952, when Day's pioneering work [8-1] appeared. The indexes shown below are described more fully in Briney and Wood [7-2], which also lists dozens of others, most long unavailable and many of very little value today. These indexes have value for libraries other than those owning back files of the originals, since much valuable bibliographic information is found only here. Most anthologies do not credit specific magazine issues. Greewood Press and University Microfilms have reprinted some of the essential SF magazines in microform, since the originals are almost unobtainable and physically fragile.

*8-1. Day, Donald Bryne. **Index to the Science Fiction Magazines, 1926–1950.** Perri Press, 1952.

*8-2. Index to the Science Fiction Magazines, 1966–1970. New England SF Association, 1971, $8.00.

*8-3. Metcalf, Norman. **The Index of Science Fiction Magazines, 1951–1965.** J. Ben Stark, 1968, $9.50.

*8-4. Metcalf, Norman. **The NESFA Index: Science Fiction and Original Anthologies 1971–1972.** $4.00; 1973, $3.00; 1974, $4.00. New England SF Association, 1973–1975.

8-5. Strauss, Erwin S., comp. **The MIT Science Fiction Society's Index to the S-F Magazines, 1951–1965.** MIT SF Society, 1966, New England SF Association, $12.00.

While other magazines indexes have appeared, these provide access to almost all significant SF magazines from the first issue of *Amazing Stories* in April 1926. Much information is included on pseudonyms, series, cover artists, etc. NESFA issues machine-produced annual indexes to both magazine SF and the increasingly numerous original anthologies and will probably cumulate them. The specialty dealers are the best source for these indexes.

8-6. Ashley, Michael. (U.K.). **The History of the Science Fiction Magazines.** New English Library, 1974–   . Parts 1, 1926–1934 (1974, £2.95) and 2, 1936–1945 (1975, £3.95) have appeared, and three more are scheduled, each covering a decade. Part 1 discusses in detail magazines featuring SF prior to 1926, then surveys the initial decade of specifically SF magazines (*Amazing, Astounding, Science Wonder* and *Wonder Stories*). A representative sampling of ten stories from the period are and will be included, usually one from each year. Appendixes include checklists of works of the ten authors included, a bibliographic summary of all magazine issues included during the decade, and notes on editors and illustrators. Successive parts will presumably follow the same pattern. Descriptive rather than critical, the five volume set should provide a near definitive history of the English language SF magazines and a fifty year chronological survey of SF magazine fiction. [Annotation based on information supplied by H. W. Hall].

8-7. Day, Bradford M. **The Complete Checklist of Science-Fiction Magazines.** Denver, N.Y.: Science-Fiction & Fantasy Publications, 1961. Wehman, $1.95.
"Gives cover dates and volume and number for all of the science fiction and fantasy magazines, as well as dozens of related or borderline magazines, covering the period from 1895 to 1960" (Briney and Wood [7-2], p. 3). Usefully supplements the magazine indexes themselves and is especially valuable for the pre-1926 period.

*8-8. Hall, H. W., ed. **Science Fiction Book Review Index, 1923–1973.** Gale Research, 1975, $45.00.
An exceptionally helpful reference aid providing access to almost 14,000 book reviews of about 6,900 books (with full bibliographic citations). The reviews appeared in SF magazines since 1923, and in general reviewing

media, such as *Library Journal* and *PW*, since 1970. The editor has issued his *SFBRI* since 1970, and the first four annuals are included in this fifty-year index. This work supersedes a less comprehensive work compiled by Barry McGhan and others, *An Index to the Science Fiction Book Reviews in Astounding/Analog, 1949–1969, Fantasy and Science Fiction, 1949–1969, Galaxy, 1950–1969*, issued in 1973 as miscellaneous publication no. 1 of the Science Fiction Research Assn. The valuable two-part appendix records full details for all SF magazines, 1923–1973, with a title checklist of all magazines covered by the index. This appendix partially supersedes the Day checklist [8-7].

9.
Periodicals

The number of SF periodicals has varied widely since the April 1926 issue of *Amazing Stories*, which is conventionally considered the first magazine devoted wholly to SF. The periodical indexes noted earlier provide relatively detailed coverage of the changes in SF periodicals over the past five decades. The editor of this guide contributed commentary and critical annotations for selected SF magazines in William Katz's *Magazines for Libraries* (2nd ed., Bowker, 1972) and its 1974 supplement, and libraries should consult this standard reference tool for additional details. The principal magazines dealing with SF in late 1975 are listed below for ready reference. Excluded are most of the several hundred fanzines published in the United States and abroad, whose publishing patterns are so erratic that no listing would be of any help. Wertham's study [6-95] provides a useful if limited historical perspective. Sample copies of these magazines will normally be supplied to libraries, which should include a stamped, self-addressed envelope for fanzines. The asterisked titles are so-called prozines, professionally published, which pay contributors and which contain most of the original magazine fiction. The others are often equally professional in content if not in format, but which generally omit fiction. The annual magazine wrap-ups by Tony

Lewis in *Locus* early each year provide useful details. My thanks to Hal Hall, who selected several of these titles.

9-1. Algol. 1963. Semi-annual. Andy Porter, ed. Box 4175, New York, N.Y. 10017. Circ. 3,000.

*9-2. Amazing Stories. 1926. Bi-monthly. Ted White, ed. Ultimate Pub. Co., Box 7, Oakland Gardens, Flushing, N.Y. 11364. Circ. 24,000.

*9-3. Analog Science Fiction/Science Fact. 1930. Monthly. Ben Bova, ed. 350 Madison Ave., New York, N.Y. 10017. Circ. 114,000.

9-4. Extrapolation: A Journal of Science Fiction and Fantasy. 1959. Semi-annual. Thomas D. Clareson, ed. Box 3186, College of Wooster, Wooster, Ohio 44691. Circ. 1,400.

*9-5. Fantastic Stories. Ditto *Amazing*. Circ. 23,600.

9-6. Foundation: The Review of Science Fiction. 1972. Quarterly. Peter Nicholls, ed. Administrator, The Science Fiction Foundation, North East London Polytechnic, Barking Precinct, Longbridge Road, Dagenham, Essex RM8 2AS, England.

*9-7. Galaxy Science Fiction. 1950. Monthly. Jim Baen, ed. 235 E. 45 St., New York, N.Y. 10017. Circ 48,000.

9-8. Locus. 1968. About 18 issues yearly. Charles N. Brown, ed. Box 3938, San Francisco, Calif. 94119. Circ. 2,000.

9-9. LUNA Monthly. 1969. Irreg. Ann Dietz, ed. 655 Orchard St., Oradell, N.J. 07649. Circ. 1,000.

*9-10. Magazine of Fantasy and Science Fiction. 1950. Monthly. Edward L. Ferman, ed. Mercury Press, Box 56, Cornwall, Conn. 06752. Circ. 52,000.

9-11. Riverside Quarterly. 1964. Semi-annual. Leland Sapiro, ed. Box 14451, University Station, Gainesville, Fla. 32604.

*9-12. Science Fiction Monthly. 1974. Julie Davis, ed. New English Library, Barnard's Inn, Holborn, London ECIN 2JR, England.

9-13. Science Fiction Review. 1973. Quarterly. Richard E. Geis, ed. Box 11408, Portland, Oreg. 97211. Circ. 1,400.

9-14. The Science Fiction Review Monthly. 1975. Martin Last, ed. 56 Eighth Ave., New York, N.Y. 10014. Book reviews only.

9-15. Science-Fiction Studies. 1973. Tri-annual. R. D. Mullen and Darko Suvin, eds. Dept. of English, Indiana State Univ., Terre Haute, Ind. 47809. Circ. 800.

9-16. DeLap's Fantasy and Science Fiction Review. 1975. Monthly. Richard DeLap, ed. 11863 W. Jefferson Blvd., Culver City, Calif. 90230. Book reviews only.

9-17. SFRA Newsletter. 1971. Monthly. Beverly Friend, ed. Science Fiction Research Assn., Box 3186, College of Wooster, Wooster, Ohio 44691. Circ. 225. Available to members only; inquire of editor.

9-18. Vector. Christopher Fowler, ed. British Science Fiction Assn., 72 Kenilworth Ave., Southcote, Reading RG3 3DN, England.

10.
Literary Awards

A variety of awards have been given to SF novels, short stories, and other categories since the first Hugo award was given at the 1953 World SF Convention in Philadelphia. The categories awarded prizes have varied over the years, as have the methods of nomination. Although the number of regular and casual readers of SF is several hundred thousand, the number who have actually voted for any given award is very small, ranging from a panel of judges to a few hundred fans or writers. The Franson listing [7-10] gives relatively complete information on the major awards and has been relied on here. The award-winning novels and nominees and short fiction winners are shown for convenient reference, and the award or nomination is also noted in the annotation by code: H(ugo), N(ebula), J(upiter), A(pollo), W(inner), N(ominee), IFA (International Fantasy Award). Winners are listed first and ties are noted. Titles shown are those of the published books; serial titles were often different. Authors are listed by pseudonyms, if used. See under author in Chapter 4 for annotations, or check the author or title indexes.

Hugo Award

The Hugo—officially the Science Fiction Achievement Award—is usually considered the most prestigious award and is given at the annual

world SF conventions held around Labor Day. It is named for the founding editor of *Amazing*, Hugo Gernsback. Year shown is that of award;
book or serial publication was normally the preceding year. No awards
were given in 1954 and 1957.

1953   Bester, Alfred. *The Demolished Man*

1955   Clifton, Mark, and Frank Riley. *They'd Rather Be Right*

1956   Heinlein, Robert. *Double Star*

1958   Leiber, Fritz. *The Big Time*

1959   Blish, James. *A Case of Conscience*
      Heinlein, Robert. *Have Spacesuit—Will Travel*
      Sheckley, Robert. *Immortality Delivered* and *Immortality, Inc.*
      Anderson, Poul. *The Enemy Stars*
      Budrys, Algis. *Who?*

1960   Heinlein, Robert. *Starship Troopers*
      Dickson, Gordon R. *The Genetic General*
      Leinster, Murray. *The Pirates of Zan*
      Vonnegut, Kurt, Jr. *The Sirens of Titan*
      Phillips, Mark. *Brain Twister*

1961   Miller, Walter M., Jr. *A Canticle for Leibowitz*
      Harrison, Harry. *Deathworld*
      Budrys, Algis. *Rogue Moon*
      Sturgeon, Theodore. *Venus Plus X*
      Anderson, Poul. *The High Crusade*

1962   Heinlein, Robert. *Stranger in a Strange Land*
      Galouye, Daniel F. *Dark Universe*
      Simak, Clifford D. *Time Is the Simplest Thing*
      White, James. *Second Ending*
      Harrison, Harry. *Planet of the Damned*

1963   Dick, Philip K. *The Man in the High Castle*
      Clarke, Arthur C. *A Fall of Moondust*
      Piper, H. Beam. *Little Fuzzy*
      Bradley, Marion Zimmer. *Sword of Aldones*
      Vercors. *Sylva*

1964   Simak, Clifford. *Way Station*
      Vonnegut, Kurt, Jr. *Cat's Cradle*
      Herbert, Frank. *Dune World*
      Heinlein, Robert. *Glory Road*
      Norton, Andre. *Witch World*

1965   Leiber, Fritz. *The Wanderer*
       Pangborn, Edgar. *Davy*
       Smith, Cordwainer. *The Planet Buyer*
       Brunner, John. *The Whole Man*

1966   Zelazny, Roger. *This Immortal*
       Herbert, Frank. *Dune* (tie)
       Heinlein, Robert. *The Moon Is a Harsh Mistress*
       Smith, Edward E. *Skylark DuQuesne*
       Brunner, John. *The Squares of the City*

1967   Heinlein, Robert. *The Moon Is a Harsh Mistress*
       Delany, Samuel. *Babel-17*
       Swann, Thomas Burnett. *Day of the Minotaur*
       Keyes, Daniel. *Flowers for Algernon*
       Garrett, Randall. *Too Many Magicians*
       Schmitz, James H. *The Witches of Karres*

1968   Zelazny, Roger. *Lord of Light*
       Anderson, Chester. *The Butterfly Kid*
       Anthony, Piers. *Chthon*
       Delany, Samuel. *The Einstein Intersection*
       Silverberg, Robert. *Thorns*

1969   Brunner, John. *Stand on Zanzibar*
       Simak, Clifford. *Goblin Reservation*
       Delany, Samuel. *Nova*
       Lafferty, R. A. *Past Master*
       Panshin, Alexei. *Rite of Passage*

1970   Le Guin, Ursula. *The Left Hand of Darkness*
       Spinrad, Norman. *Bug Jack Barron*
       Anthony, Piers. *Macroscope*
       Silverberg, Robert. *Up the Line*
       Vonnegut, Kurt, Jr. *Slaughterhouse Five*

1971   Niven, Larry. *Ringworld*
       Anderson, Poul. *Tau Zero*
       Silverberg, Robert. *Tower of Glass*
       Clement, Hal. *Starlight*
       Tucker, Wilson. *The Year of the Quiet Sun*

1972   Farmer, Philip José. *To Your Scattered Bodies Go*
       Le Guin, Ursula. *The Lathe of Heaven*
       McCaffrey, Anne. *Dragonquest*
       Silverberg, Robert. *A Time of Changes* (His *The World Inside* was
          nominated, but he requested it be withdrawn.)
       Zelazny, Roger. *Jack of Shadows*

1973   Asimov, Isaac. *The Gods Themselves*
       Gerrold, David. *When Harlie Was One*
       Anderson, Poul. *There Will Be Time*
       Silverberg, Robert. *The Book of Skulls*
       Simak, Clifford. *A Choice of Gods*
       Silverberg, Robert. *Dying Inside*

1974   Clarke, Arthur C. *Rendezvous with Rama*
       Heinlein, Robert. *Time Enough for Love*
       Niven, Larry. *Protector*
       Gerrold, David. *The Man Who Folded Himself*
       Anderson, Poul. *People of the Wind*

1975   Le Guin, Ursula. *The Dispossessed*
       Anderson, Poul. *Fire Time*
       Dick, Philip K. *Flow My Tears, the Policeman Said*
       Priest, Christopher. *The Inverted World*
       Niven, Larry, and Jerry Pournelle. *The Mote in God's Eye*

Nebula Award

This is awarded each spring by the Science Fiction Writers of America, a professional organization of about 400 writers, of whom roughly half vote. The award corresponds to the Edgar (named for Edgar Allen Poe) awarded by the Mystery Writers of America. Year shown is year of publication.

1965   Herbert, Frank. *Dune*
       Thomas, Theodore, and Kate Wilhelm. *The Clone*
       Dick, Philip K. *Dr. Bloodmoney*
       Simak, Clifford. *All Flesh Is Grass*
       White, James. *Escape Orbit*
       Disch, Thomas. *The Genocides*
       Burroughs, William. *Nova Express*
       Laumer, Keith. *A Plague of Demons*
       Davidson, Avram. *Rogue Dragon*
       Edmondson, G. C. *The Ship That Sailed the Time Stream*
       Anderson, Poul. *The Star Fox*
       Dick, Philip K. *The Three Stigmata of Palmer Eldritch*

1966   Delany, Samuel. *Babel-17*
       Keyes, Daniel. *Flowers for Algernon* (tie)
       Heinlein, Robert. *The Moon Is a Harsh Mistress*
       Pohl, Frederik. *The Age of the Pussyfoot*
       Asimov, Isaac. *Fantastic Voyage*
       Vance, Jack. *The Blue World*
       Harrison, Harry. *Make Room! Make Room!*

Zelazny, Roger. *This Immortal*
Anderson, Poul. *The Ancient Gods* (not annotated)
Biggle, Lloyd, Jr. *Watchers of the Dark* (not annotated)
Rackham, John. *Danger from Vega* (not annotated)
Ballard, J. G. *The Crystal World*
Laumer, Keith, and Rosel G. Brown. *Earthblood*
Farmer, Philip José. *The Night of Light*
Niven, Larry. *World of the Ptavvs*
Brunner, John. *The Productions of Time*
Vance, Jack. *The Eyes of the Overworld*
Herbert, Frank. *The Eyes of Heisenberg*

1967   Delany, Samuel. *The Einstein Intersection*
Silverberg, Robert. *Thorns*
Anthony, Piers. *Chthon*
Howard, Hayden. *The Eskimo Invasion*
Zelazny, Roger. *Lord of Light*

1968   Panshin, Alexei. *Rite of Passage*
Blish, James. *Black Easter*
Dick, Philip K. *Do Androids Dream of Electric Sheep?*
Silverberg, Robert. *The Masks of Time*
Lafferty, R. A. *Past Master*
Russ, Joanna. *Picnic on Paradise*
Brunner, John. *Stand on Zanzibar*

1969   Le Guin, Ursula. *The Left Hand of Darkness*
Spinrad, Norman. *Bug Jack Barron*
Zelazny, Roger. *Isle of the Dead*
Brunner, John. *Jagged Orbit*
Silverberg, Robert. *Up the Line*
Vonnegut, Kurt, Jr. *Slaughterhouse Five*

1970   Niven, Larry. *Ringworld*
Silverberg, Robert. *Tower of Glass*
Russ, Joanna. *And Chaos Died*
Tucker, Wilson. *The Year of the Quiet Sun*
Lafferty, R. A. *Fourth Mansions*
Compton, B. G. *The Steel Crocodile*

1971   Silverberg, Robert. *A Time of Changes*
Le Guin, Ursula. *The Lathe of Heaven*
Lafferty, R. A. *The Devil Is Dead*
Wilhelm, Kate. *Margaret and I* (not annotated)
Anderson, Poul. *The Byworlder*
Bass, T. J. *Half Past Human*

1972   Asimov, Isaac. *The Gods Themselves*
Gerrold, David. *When Harlie Was One*

Silverberg, Robert. *Dying Inside*
Brunner, John. *The Sheep Look Up*
Effinger, George. *What Entropy Means to Me*
Silverberg, Robert. *The Book of Skulls*
Spinrad, Norman. *The Iron Dream*

1973 Clarke, Arthur C. *Rendezvous with Rama*
Pynchon, Thomas. *Gravity's Rainbow*
Gerrold, David. *The Man Who Folded Himself*
Anderson, Poul. *The People of the Wind*
Heinlein, Robert. *Time Enough for Love*

1974 Le Guin, Ursula. *The Dispossessed*
Dick, Philip K. *Flow My Tears, the Policeman Said*
Disch, Thomas. *334*
Bass, T. J. *The Godwhale*

Short Fiction Awards

The short story has been a major form in SF, as the many annotated single-author collections and anthologies indicate. A Hugo and Nebula are awarded each year in this category, as listed below. The categories used for awards have varied over the years; short fiction refers usually to a short story but in some cases to a novelette. Nominees are not listed because of their large number; see Franson [7-10] for the full listings.

These stories have often been reprinted. Pfeiffer and De Bolt usually mentioned such winners or nominees in their annotations in this work. Cole's [7-7] and Siemon's [7-19] short story indexes, as well as the Chicorel and Wilson indexes (see Cole annotation) also provide access to many of these stories. Consult the title index for all stories mentioned in the annotations or introductions.

Hugo Award

1955 Russell, Eric Frank. "Allamagoosa"
1956 Clarke, Arthur C. "The Star"
1958 Davidson, Avram. "Or All the Seas with Oysters"
1959 Bloch, Robert. "The Hell-Bound Train"
1960 Keyes, Daniel. "Flowers for Algernon"
1961 Anderson, Poul. "The Longest Voyage"
1962 Aldiss, Brian W. The Hothouse series
1963 Vance, Jack. "The Dragon Masters"
1964 Anderson, Poul. "No Truce with Kings"

1965 Dickson, Gordon R. "Soldier, Ask Not"

1966 Ellison, Harlan. " 'Repent, Harlequin!' Said the Ticktockman"

1967 Niven, Larry. "Neutron Star"

1968 Ellison, Harlan. "I Have No Mouth and I Must Scream"

1969 Ellison, Harland. "The Beast that Shouted Love at the Heart of the World"

1970 Delany, Samuel. "Time Considered as a Helix of Semi-Precious Stones"

1971 Sturgeon, Theodore. "Slow Sculpture"

1972 Niven, Larry. "Inconstant Moon"

1973 Lafferty, R. A. "Eurema's Dam"
Pohl, Frederik, and C. M. Kornbluth. "The Meeting" (tie)

1974 Le Guin, Ursula. "The Ones who Walk away from Omelas"

1975 Niven, Larry. "The Hole Man"

Nebula Award

1965 Ellison, Harlan. " 'Repent, Harlequin!' Said the Ticktockman"

1966 McKenna, Richard. "The Secret Place"

1967 Delany, Samuel. "Aye, and Gomorrah"

1968 Wilhelm, Kate. "The Planners"

1969 Silverberg, Robert. "Passengers"

1970 (no award)

1971 Silverberg, Robert. "Good News from the Vatican"

1972 Russ, Joanna. "When It Changed"

1973 Tiptree, James, Jr. "Love is the Plan, the Plan is Death"

1974 Le Guin, Ursula. "The Day before the Revolution"

International Fantasy Award

Originated by four British fans, this short-lived award was given by an international panel to the best works of fiction and nonfiction of likely interest to SF readers. Only fiction is shown. Year of award is shown; no award was given in 1956.

1951 Stewart, George R. *Earth Abides*

1952 Collier, John. *Fancies and Goodnights*
Wyndham, John. *The Day of the Triffids*
Bradbury, Ray. *The Illustrated Man*

1953 Simak, Clifford. *City*
Kornbluth, Cyril M. *Takeoff*
Vonnegut, Kurt, Jr. *Player Piano*

1954 Sturgeon, Theodore. *More than Human*
Bester, Alfred. *The Demolished Man*

1955 Pangborn, Edgar. *A Mirror for Observers*
Clement, Hal. *Mission of Gravity*

1957 Tolkien, J. R. R. *Lord of the Rings* (trilogy)

John W. Campbell Memorial Award

Names for the editor of *Astounding/Analog* from 1937 to 1971, this award is given each spring by a small panel of critics and writers for the best novel. There is also a Campbell award for the best new writer whose first professional work appeared the preceding year. This award, given at the Hugo banquets and determined by a reader vote, is omitted here. Year of award is shown.

1973 Malzberg, Barry. *Beyond Apollo*
Gunn, James. *The Listeners*
Priest, Christopher. *Fugue for a Darkening Land*

1974 Clarke, Arthur C. *Rendezvous with Rama*
Merle, Robert. *Malevil* (tie)
Watson, Ian. *The Embedding*
Dickinson, Peter. *The Green Gene*

1975 Dick, Philip K. *Flow My Tears, the Policeman Said*
Le Guin, Ursula. *The Dispossessed*

Jupiter Award

Instructors of Science Fiction in Higher Education (ISFHE) are polled each year for their judgments on best novel, novella, novelette, and short story. Details are available from Steven E. Miller, 119 Willow Bend Drive, Apt. 3A, Owings Mills, Md. 21117. The award is presented for works published the preceding year; year of publication is shown.

1973 Clarke, Arthur C. *Rendezvous with Rama*
Pynchon, Thomas. *Gravity's Rainbow*
Gerrold, David. *The Man Who Folded Himself*

1974 Le Guin, Ursula. *The Dispossessed*
Niven, Larry, and Jerry Pournelle. *The Mote in God's Eye*
Pangborn, Edgar. *The Company of Glory*
Smith, Cordwainer. *Norstrilia*

Pilgrim Award

Awarded by the Science Fiction Research Association to the individual who has advanced the scholarly understanding of SF through research, editing, or other scholarly endeavor. The award, named for Bailey's pioneering work, is not given for a single work but for the individual's total efforts in the field. Year of award is shown. See name index for works by these writers.

1970 J. O. Bailey (American)

1971 Marjorie Nicolson (American)

1972 Julius Kagarlitski (Russian)

1973 Jack Williamson (American)

1974 I. F. Clarke (British)

1975 Damon F. Knight (American)

11.
Core Collection Checklist

Largely for the convenience of libraries, all first-purchase titles are listed here for checking against card catalogs. They are listed in the same sequence as they appear in chapters 1–8, which should be consulted for full details, including variant titles, sequels, etc. An asterisk before the name means a pseudonym. Check the annotation for the real name, if the latter is used as the main entry in your library.

Science Fiction: From Its Beginnings to 1870

*Atterly, Joseph. *A Voyage to the Moon*

Bacon, Francis. *The New Atlantis*

Butler, Samuel. *The Elephant in the Moon*

Cyrano de Bergerac, Savinien. *The Comical History of the States and Empires of the Worlds of the Moon and Sun*

Godwin, Francis. *The Man in the Moone*

Hawthorne, Nathaniel. [See annotations]

Holberg, Ludwig. *A Journey to the World Underground*

Kepler, Johannes. *Somnium*

Lytton, Edward Bulwer. *The Coming Race*

*McDermot, Murtagh. *A Trip to the Moon*
Melville, Herman. [See annotation]
More, Thomas. *Utopia*

O'Brien, Fitz-James. [See annotations]

Poe, Edgar Allan. [See annotations]

*Seaborn, Adam. *Symzonia*
Shelley, Mary Wollstonecraft. *Frankenstein*
Swift, Jonathan. *Gulliver's Travels*

Voltaire, Françoise-Marie Arouet. *Micromégas*

The Emergence of the Scientific Romance: 1871–1925

Astor, John Jacob. *A Journey in Other Worlds*

Balmer, Edwin. *The Achievements of Luther Trant*
Barney, John Stewart. *L.P.M.: The End of the Great War*
Bellamy, Edward. *Dr. Heidenhoff's Process*
Bellamy, Edward. *Looking Backward*
Bierce, Ambrose. [See annotation]
Bradshaw, William Richard. *The Goddess of Atvatabar*
Burroughs, Edgar Rice. *At the Earth's Core*
———. *The Gods of Mars*
———. *Carson of Venus*
———. *The Land That Time Forgot*
———. *Lost on Venus*
———. *Pellucidar*
———. *A Princess of Mars*
———. *Tarzan of the Apes*
Butler, Samuel. *Erewhon*

Čapek, Karel. *R.U.R.*
Chambers, Robert William. *The Green Mouse*
Cook, William Wallace. *Adrift in the Unknown*
———. *A Round Trip to the Year 2000*
Cowan, James. *Daybreak*
Cummings, Ray. *The Girl in the Golden Atom*

Dake, Charles Romyn. *A Strange Discovery*
DeMille, James. *A Strange Manuscript Found in a Copper Cylinder*
Donnelly, Ignatius. *Caesar's Column*
Doyle, Arthur Conan. *The Lost World*
———. *The Maracot Deep*
———. *The Poison Belt*

Emerson, Willis George. *The Smoky God*

England, George Allan. *Darkness and Dawn*

Fuller, Alvarado M. *A.D. 2000*

Gernsback, Hugo. *Ralph 124C41+*
Gratacap, Louis Pope. *The Certainty of a Future Life on Mars*
Greg, Percy. *Across the Zodiac*
Haggard, Henry Rider. *Allen Quatermain*
_____ . *King Solomon's Mines*
_____ . *She*

Hastings, Milo. *City of Endless Night*
Hertzka, Theodor. *Freeland*
Howells, William Dean. *Between the Dark and the Daylight*
_____ . *Questionable Shapes*
_____ . *A Traveler from Altruria*
_____ . *Through the Eye of the Needle*

Lasswitz, Kurd. *Two Planets*
Lloyd, John Uri. *Etidorpha*
London, Jack. *Before Adam*
_____ . *The Iron Heel*
_____ . *The Red One*
_____ . *The Scarlet Plague*
_____ . *The Star Rover*

Mitchell, John Ames. *The Last American*
Newcomb, Simon. *His Wisdom, the Defender*

Pope, Gustavus W. *Journey to Mars*

Reeve, Arthur Benjamin. *The Poisoned Pen*
Rhodes, William Henry. *Caxton's Book*

Serviss, Garrett Putnam. *A Columbus of Space*
_____ . *Edison's Conquest of Mars*
_____ . *The Moon Metal*
_____ . *The Second Deluge*
Shaw, George Bernard. *Back to Methuselah*
Stevenson, Robert Louis. *Strange Case of Dr. Jekyll and Mr. Hyde*
Stockton, Frank. *The Great Stone of Sardis*
_____ . *The Great War Syndicate*
Train, Arthur Cheyney. *The Man Who Rocked the Earth*

Verne, Jules. *Five Weeks in a Balloon*
_____ . *A Journey to the Center of the Earth*
_____ . *From the Earth to the Moon*
_____ . *The Adventures of Captain Hatteras*
_____ . *All around the Moon*
_____ . *Twenty Thousand Leagues under the Sea*
_____ . *Around the World in Eighty Days*

———. *The Begum's Fortune*

———. *Propeller Island*

Waterloo, Stanley. *Armageddon*

———. *The Story of Ab*

Wells, Herbert George. *The Time Machine*

———. *The Island of Dr. Moreau*

———. *The Invisible Man*

———. *The War of the Worlds*

———. *When the Sleeper Wakes*

———. *The First Men in the Moon*

———. *The Food of the Gods*

———. *A Modern Utopia*

———. *In the Days of the Comet*

———. *The War in the Air*

———. *The World Set Free*

———. *Men Like Gods*

White, Stewart Edward. *The Mystery*

———. *The Sign at Six*

Zamiatin, Eugene. *We*

The Gernsback Era, 1926–1937

Asimov, Isaac. *Before the Golden Age* [see 4-652]

Campbell, John Wood, Jr. *Who Goes There?*
Čapek, Karel. *The Absolute at Large*

Hilton, James. *Lost Horizon*
Howard, Robert Ervin. *Conan the Conqueror*
Hoyne, Thomas Temple. *Intrigue on the Upper Level*
Huxley, Aldous Leonard. *Brave New World*

Johnson, Owen McMahon. *The Coming of the Amazons*

Large, Ernest Charles. *Sugar in the Air*
Lovecraft, Howard Phillips. *At the Mountains of Madness*

McHugh, Vincent. *Caleb Catlum's America*
Merritt, Abraham. *The Ship of Ishtar*
Mundy, Talbot. *Jimgrim*

Read, Herbert Edward. *The Green Child*
Robertson, Eileen Arbuthnot. *Three Came Unarmed*

Schuyler, George Samuels. *Black No More*
Stapledon, William Olaf. *Last and First Men*

———. *Odd John*

———. *Sirius*

———. *Star Maker*

Weinbaum, Stanley Graham. *A Martian Odyssey and Other Science Fiction Tales*
Wells, Herbert George. *Things to Come*
Williamson, Jack. *The Legion of Time*
Wright, Sydney Fowler. *The World Below*

The Modern Period, 1938–1975

Aldiss, Brian W. *Barefoot in the Head*
_____ . *Greybeard*
Anderson, Poul. *Brain Wave*
_____ . *Tau Zero*
Anthony, Piers. *Macroscope*
Asimov, Isaac. *Foundation Trilogy*
_____ . *The Gods Themselves*

Ballard, James Graham. *Chronopolis and Other Stories*
_____ . *The Crystal World*
Barth, John. *Giles Goat-Boy*
Bass, T. J. *Half Past Human*
Bester, Alfred. *The Demolished Man*
_____ . *The Stars My Destination*
Blish, James. *A Case of Conscience*
_____ . *Cities in Flight*
Bradbury, Ray. *Fahrenheit 451*
_____ . *The Martian Chronicles*
Brown, Fredric. *The Lights in the Sky Are Stars*
Brunner, John. *The Sheep Look Up*
_____ . *Stand on Zanzibar*
Budrys, Algis. *Rogue Moon*
*Burgess, Anthony. *A Clockwork Orange*

Carter, Angela. *The War of Dreams*
Clarke, Arthur C. *Childhood's End*
_____ . *Rendezvous with Rama*
*Clement, Hal. *Mission of Gravity*
Clifton, Mark. *They'd Rather Be Right*
Compton, David Guy. *The Unsleeping Eye*

de Camp, Lyon Sprague. *Lest Darkness Fall*
Delany, Samuel R. *Babel-17*
_____ . *The Einstein Intersection*
del Rey, Lester. *Nerves*
Dick, Philip K. *The Man in the High Castle*
_____ . *The Three Stigmata of Palmer Eldritch*
Disch, Thomas M. *Camp Concentration*

Durrell, Lawrence. *Nunquam*
_____ . *Tunc*

Ellison, Harlan. *Alone against Tomorrow*
_____ . *Deathbird Stories*

Farmer, Philip José. *The Lovers*
_____ . *To Your Scattered Bodies Go*

*Finney, Jack. *Time and Again*

George, Peter. *Dr. Strangelove*
Graves, Robert. *Watch the Northwind Rise*
Gunn, James E. *The Listeners*

Heinlein, Robert Anson. *Double Star*
_____ . *The Moon Is a Harsh Mistress*
_____ . *The Past through Tomorrow*
_____ . *Starship Troopers*
_____ . *Stranger in a Strange Land*
Herbert, Frank. *Dune*
Hesse, Hermann. *The Glass Bead Game (Magister Ludi)*

Kelley, William Melvin. *A Different Drummer*
Keyes, Daniel. *Flowers for Algernon*
Kornbluth, Cyril M. *Best Science Fiction Stories*

Le Guin, Ursula K. *The Dispossessed*
_____ . *The Left Hand of Darkness*
Leiber, Fritz. *The Big Time*
_____ . *The Wanderer*
Lem, Stanislaw. *The Cyberiad*
_____ . *Solaris*
Lewis, Clive Staples. *Out of the Silent Planet*
_____ . *Perelandra*
_____ . *That Hideous Strength*
McKenna, Richard. *Casey Agonistes and Other Science Fiction and Fantasy Stories*

Malzberg, Barry N. *Beyond Apollo*
Merle, Robert. *Malevil*
Miller, Walter M., Jr. *A Canticle for Leibowitz*
Moorcock, Michael. *Behold the Man*

Niven, Larry. *All the Myriad Ways*
_____ . *Ringworld*
*Norton, Andre. *Star Man's Son*

Orwell, George. *Animal Farm*
_____ . *1984*

Pangborn, Edgar. *A Mirror for Observers*

Panshin, Alexei. *Rite of Passage*
Percy, Walker. *Love in the Ruins*
Pohl, Frederik. *The Space Merchants*

Roberts, Keith. *Pavane*

Shaw, Robert. *Other Days, Other Eyes*
*Shute, Nevil. *On the Beach*
Silverberg, Robert. *Dying Inside*
_____ . *A Time of Changes*
Simak, Clifford. *City*
_____ . *Way Station*
Smith, Edward Elmer. *Children of the Lens*
_____ . *First Lensman*
_____ . *Galactic Patrol*
_____ . *Gray Lensman*
_____ . *Second Stage Lensman*
_____ . *Triplanetary*
Spinrad, Norman. *Bug Jack Barron*
Stewart, George R. *Earth Abides*
Sturgeon, Theodore. *More than Human*

Tevis, Walter. *The Man Who Fell to Earth*
Tucker, Wilson. *The Long Loud Silence*

van Vogt, A. E. *Slan*
Vonnegut, Kurt, Jr. *Player Piano*
_____ . *Slaughterhouse Five*

White, James. *The Watch Below*
Williamson, Jack. *The Humanoids*
Wilson, Colin. *The Philosopher's Stone*
Wolfe, Gene. *The Fifth Head of Cerberus*
Wylie, Phillip. *The Disappearance*
*Wyndham, John. *The Midwich Cuckoos*

Yefremov, Ivan Antonovich. *Andromeda*

Zelazny, Roger. *Lord of Light*
_____ . *This Immortal*

Anthologies

Although serial anthologies are listed by their first editor, libraries may have cataloged them as title main entries. The title sometimes varies, as does the editor. See annotations for details.

Asimov, Isaac. *The Hugo Winners*

Bleiler, Everett Franklin. *The Best Science Fiction Stories*
*Boucher, Anthony. *The Best from Fantasy and Science Fiction*
Bova, Benjamin William. *The Science Fiction Hall of Fame*, vols. 2A and 2B

Conklin, Groff. *The Best of Science Fiction*
Ellison, Harlan. *Again, Dangerous Visions*
_____ . *Dangerous Visions*
Harrison, Harry. *Best SF*
Healy, Raymond J. *Adventures in Time and Space*
Knight, Damon Francis. *Nebula Award Stories*
_____ . *Orbit*
Merril, Judith. *SF: The Year's Greatest Science Fiction and Fantasy*
Pohl, Frederik. *Star Science Fiction Stories*
Rottensteiner, Franz. *View from Another Shore*
Silverberg, Robert. *The Mirror of Infinity*
_____ . *Science Fiction Hall of Fame*, vol. 1
Spinrad, Norman. *Modern Science Fiction*
Suvin, Darko. *Other Worlds, Other Seas*
Wollheim, Donald A. *World's Best Science Fiction*

Juvenile Science Fiction

Alexander, Lloyd. *The Book of Three*
_____ . *The Black Cauldron*
_____ . *The Castle of Llyr*
_____ . *Taran Wanderer*
_____ . *The High King*
Ballou, Arthur W. *Bound for Mars*
Beatty, Jerome, Jr. *Matthew Looney's Voyage to the Earth*
Bova, Benjamin William. *Exiled from Earth*
*Christopher, John. *The Guardians*
_____ . *The White Mountains*
Clarke, Arthur Charles. *Islands in the Sky*
Cross, John Keir. *The Angry Planet*
Dickinson, Peter. *The Weathermonger*
Engdahl, Sylvia Louise. *Enchantress from the Stars*
Fisk, Nicholas. *Trillions*
Garner, Alan. *Elidor*
Halacy, Daniel Stephen, Jr. *Return from Luna*
Heinlein, Robert. *Rocket Ship Galileo*
Key, Alexander. *Escape to Witch Mountain*
Le Guin, Ursula Kroeber. *A Wizard of Earthsea*
_____ . *The Tombs of Atuan*
_____ . *The Farthest Shore*
L'Engle, Madeleine. *A Wrinkle in Time*

Lewis, Clive Staples. *The Lion, the Witch, and the Wardrobe*
_____ . *Prince Caspian*
_____ . *The Voyage of the "Dawn Treader"*
_____ . *The Silver Chair*
_____ . *The Horse and His Boy*
_____ . *The Magician's Nephew*
_____ . *The Last Battle*

Lightner, Alice M. *The Day of the Drones*

Mayne, William. *Earthfasts*

*Norton, Andre. *Operation Time Search*

O'Brien, Robert C. *Mrs. Frisby and the Rats of NIMH*
_____ . *Z for Zachariah*

Pesek, Ludek. *The Earth Is Near*

Sleator, William. *House of Stairs*
Stoutenberg, Adrien. *Out There*
Suddaby, Donald. *Village Fanfare*

History, Criticism, and Biography

Aldiss, Brian W. *Billion Year Spree*
Allott, Kenneth. *Jules Verne*
Amis, Kingsley. *New Maps of Hell*
Armytage, Walter Harry Green. *Yesterday's Tomorrows*

Bailey, James Osler. *Pilgrims through Space and Time*
Bergonzi, Bernard. *The Early H. G. Wells*
Blish, James. *The Issue at Hand*
_____ . *More Issues at Hand*
Bretnor, Reginald, ed. *Science Fiction, Today and Tomorrow*

Clareson, Thomas D., ed. *SF: The Other Side of Realism*
Clarke, Ignatius Frederick. *Voices Prophesying War, 1763–1984*
de Camp, L. Sprague. *Lovecraft*
_____ . *Science Fiction Handbook*

Franklin, Howard Bruce. *Future Perfect*

Gove, Philip Babcock. *The Imaginary Voyage in Prose Fiction*
Gunn, James E. *Alternate Worlds*

Hillegas, Mark Robert. *The Future as Nightmare*

Johnson, William, ed. *Focus on the Science Fiction Film*

Kateb, George. *Utopia and Its Enemies*
Klinkowitz, Jerome. *The Vonnegut Statement*
Lewis, Clive Staples. *Of Other Worlds*
Lupoff, Richard A. *Edgar Rice Burroughs*

MacKenzie, Norman Ian. *H. G. Wells*
Moskowitz, Samuel. *Explorers of the Infinite*
———. *Seekers of Tomorrow*
Philmus, Robert. *Into the Unknown*
Rottensteiner, Franz. *The Science Fiction Book*
Scholes, Robert. *Structural Fabulation*
Wagar, W. Warren. *H. G. Wells and the World State*
Walsh, Chad. *From Utopia to Nightmare*

Bibliographies, Indexes, and Teaching Aids

Bleiler, Everett Franklin. *The Checklist of Fantastic Literature*
Briney, Robert E. *SF Bibliographies*
Christopher, Joe R. *C. S. Lewis*
Clareson, Thomas D. *Science Fiction Criticism*
Clarke, Ignatius Frederick. *The Tale of the Future*
Cole, Walter R. *A Checklist of Science-Fiction Anthologies*
McGhan, Barry. *Science Fiction and Fantasy Pseudonyms*
Reginald, Robert. *Science Fiction and Fantasy Literature*
Siemon, Fred. *Science Fiction Story Index*
Tuck, Donald Henry. *The Encyclopedia of Science Fiction and Fantasy through 1968*
Williamson, Jack, ed. *Science Fiction: Education for Tomorrow*

Magazine and Book Review Indexes

Day, Donald Bryne. *Index to the Science Fiction Magazines, 1926–1950*
Metcalf, Norman. *Index to the Science Fiction Magazines, 1951–1965*
Index to the Science Fiction Magazines, 1966–1970
The NESFA Index: Science Fiction and Original Anthologies 1971–1972, 1973, 1974
Hall, H. W., ed. *Science Fiction Book Review Index, 1923–1973*

12.
Library Collections of Science Fiction and Fantasy

H. W. Hall

The information shown herein has been provided by the libraries listed and is correct as of spring 1975. More detailed information on these collections is being developed by the Science Fiction Research Association Committee on Library Resources. Additions and corrections to this listing should be sent to that committee in care of the author. The committee will also serve as a clearinghouse to bring together individuals wishing to sell their collections and libraries wishing to purchase science fiction collections. Collectors or libraries should write the author for more information [see address in list of contributors].

Certain general statements may be made about the collections listed here. Collections are primarily found in university libraries, and are intended for research rather than recreational reading. Collections are grouped together, usually in the special collections department. Few collections exhibit overall strength in the three major categories: magazines, monographs, and amateur magazines (fanzines). Significant fanzine collections are rare. Magazines are unbound, and incomplete prior to 1940. Published descriptions or book catalogs are rare, though many libraries have prepared card catalogs or other catalogs. Libraries can normally answer inquiries regarding ownership of specific items. Interlibrary loan of original material is the exception. When permitted, it is noted as ILL. Photocopying of selected materials is often possible if condition of the material allows. Inquiries are recommended regarding either interlibrary loan or photocopy. Do not overlook microform copies of the magazines. Both Greenwood Press and University Microfilms list science fiction titles in their catalogs; this format offers many advantages over the original pulp material.

In recent years, growth of science fiction collections has been aided and encouraged by the Science Fiction Writers of America through their Regional Depository System. Under this system, SFWA makes books available to the participating libraries. The libraries agree to house the books in closed research collections to support the study and teaching of science fiction, and to make the books available to SFWA members who may have need of them. Libraries are chosen to give wide geographical coverage of the United States and Canada. The following libraries are currently active members of the SFWA Regional Depository System: California State University, Fullerton; University of Southern Mississippi; Eastern New Mexico University; Brigham Young University; University of Kansas; University of Tennessee; Michigan State University; University of Dayton; University of New Brunswick; Texas A & M University; and the Imperial College of Science and Technology, London.

Most medium to large libraries have scattered holdings of science fiction in their collections, but these collections generally lack depth and adequate access through indexing. I hope that this guide and the information in this section will stimulate libraries to develop more fully this significant and often neglected branch of literature. The following listings are arranged alphabetically by state, then by Canadian province.

Arizona
University of Arizona, University Library, Special Collections, Tucson, Ariz. 85721
Acquired in 1964, the collection now numbers over 7,000 items. The core of the collection is the magazine collection of over 5,100 issues from 1929 to date, including long runs of *Astounding/Analog*, *Galaxy*, *Amazing*, and other important titles. The monograph collection of over 1,900 titles is being actively built, but its strength is in the period 1968–1974, with Fredric Brown the main author strength. Sword and sorcery and fantasy are excluded. An author catalog exists on cards, and will be duplicated at the requestor's cost.

California
California State University, Fullerton, Library, Special Collections, Fullerton, Calif. 92634

The SF collections consist of over 2,800 paperback books and 1,350 periodical issues held in the special collections area, and of hardcover SF books cataloged in the regular collection. Associated collections include the SFWA depository collection, a collection of over thirty taped interviews and speeches of SF personalities, and a significant manuscript collection containing manuscripts, papers, and documents of thirty authors, including Philip K. Dick, Harry Harrison, Frank Herbert, Norman Spinrad, and Robert Moore Williams. A card catalog is available in the special collections area.

San Francisco Public Library, Special Collections, Civic Center, San Francisco, Calif. 94199

The McComas Collection of Fantasy and Science Fiction consists of 1,250 monographs and over 5,000 magazine issues, including complete runs of all American magazines indexed in Donald Day's *Index to the Science Fiction Magazines, 1926–1950* [8-1]. A catalog of the collection is available in the Literature Department of the Library.

University of California at Los Angeles, University Library, Special Collections, 405 Hilgard Ave., Los Angeles, Calif. 90024

The UCLA Fantastic Fiction Collection consists of over 5,000 magazine issues, including complete or near-complete runs of *Amazing*, *Astounding/Analog*, *New Worlds*, *Weird Tales*, and many others, and a monograph collection of over 7,500 titles dating from the nineteenth century. The monograph collection of fanzines from the period 1950–1965 adds depth to the collection. The collection also contains manuscripts of Ray Bradbury, and transcribed interviews with Forrest Ackerman, A. E. van Vogt, and Bradbury. No separate catalog of the collection is available.

University of California, Riverside, University Library, Special Collections, Box 5900, Riverside, Calif. 92507

The Dr. J. Lloyd Eaton Fantasy and Science Fiction Collection consists of over 8,500 volumes, and is particularly rich in early and scarce items published from 1870 to 1930, along with some important eighteenth-century titles. In-depth collections of the works of H. Rider Haggard, Jules Verne, Edgar Rice Burroughs, George Griffith, Talbot Mundy, S. Fowler Wright, A. Merritt, H. P. Lovecraft, E. E. Smith, David H. Keller, and William F. Jenkins are represented. There are extensive examples of British and American anthologies, and of British paperbacks. The periodical collection of 700 issues includes material from 1900 to 1950, and will be made comprehensive later. Supplementing the collection is an earlier collection of utopian literature and imaginary voyages. The collection is being actively expanded. An author-title catalog, and a separate catalog of anthologies is available on cards.

University of California at Santa Cruz, University Library, Special Collections, Santa Cruz, Calif. 95062

The collection consists of the published books of Robert A. Heinlein, and of Heinlein's manuscripts, notes, and correspondence. Some sixty manuscripts are accessible in the collection; the correspondence is sealed and unavailable for research. Also included in the collection are fourteen manuscripts and assosicated material by Eric Temple Bell. A brief listing of the collection is available on request.

Colorado

Colorado State University, Special Collections, University Libraries, Ft. Collins, Colo. 80523

The Imaginary Wars Collection includes future wars, hypothetical wars, and greatly altered outcomes of real wars involving a known society on Earth or a close parallel of a known society. The collection, still under development, now numbers 550 titles. A description of the collection appears in *Extrapolation*, December 1974 and May 1975. ILL.

University of Colorado, University Library, Boulder, Colo. 80302

A collection of representative titles of science fiction and fantasy is being developed gradually. Holdings now number over 1,000 in hardcover, and some seventy volumes of four magazine titles. The collection is not housed separately. ILL.

Georgia

University of Georgia, Little Memorial Library, Athens, Ga. 30601

A collection of all American science fiction magazines from 1926 to date, supported by 2,000 volumes of mongraphic fiction, critical works, and bibliographical material. No separate catalog of the collection is available. ILL.

Illinois

Northern Illinois University Library, Swen F. Parsons Library, Special Collections, DeKalb, Ill. 60115

A complete collection of American SF magazines from 1926 to the present. No associated material. An alphabetic list of periodicals with holdings is available.

Southern Illinois University, Morris Library, Carbondale, Ill. 62901

A large collection of several thousand volumes of fantasy and science fiction was purchased in 1962 and integrated into the regular collection. No separate catalog is available.

University of Illinois, H. G. Wells Collection, Special Collections, Urbana, Ill. 61801

The H. G. Wells collection of over 1,000 volumes was purchased in 1953/54. The collection includes an almost complete file of English editions, inscribed and corrected by Wells, fifty volumes from Wells' library, many inscribed to him, several thousand pieces of correspondence to and from Wells, indexed for access, and several corrected typescripts of books. A complete description of the collection is available in the *Rare*

Book Room Catalog of the University of Illinois, vol. 11. (Boston: G. K. Hall, 1972.) Inquire regarding ILL.

Wheaton College Library, Special Collections, 501 East Seminary Ave., Wheaton, Ill. 60187

The Lewis Collection, begun in 1965, houses books, letters, manuscripts, and articles by and about six authors: C. S. Lewis, Owen Barfield, George McDonald, Dorothy Sayers, J. R. R. Tolkien, and Charles Williams. The collection includes over seventy-five magazine titles which deal with the theme of modern mythology, such as *Orchrist*, *The Tolkien Journal*, and *Mythlore*. The collection includes most first editions and many other editions of Lewis, McDonald, Tolkien, and Williams. Other Lewis material includes two manuscripts, 878 original, mostly unpublished letters, 315 copies of letters, and many original poems. Williams material includes 750 holograph letters, nine manuscripts, including the first draft of *Descent into Hell* with an important variant chapter, poems, and holograph articles. The collection includes eighty doctoral, masters, and honors papers on the authors. No separate catalog of the collection is available.

Indiana

Indiana University, Lilly Library, Bloomington, Ind. 47401

A concerted effort was begun in 1972 to collect fantasy and science fiction. The collection will consist of extensive holdings of major authors and major works, but completeness will not be a goal. A representative collection of magazines will be assembled, consisting primarily of the better known titles. The collection currently includes over 2,000 monographs, movie scripts, TV scripts, and manuscripts of August Derleth. Complete first editions of Wells, Verne, Haggard, Chesterton, Derleth, and Lovecraft are available, along with a comprehensive Arkham House collection. A separate catalog of the collection is available.

Iowa

Iowa Commission for the Blind Library, 4th and Keosauqua Way, Des Moines, Iowa 50309

By far the largest collection of SF for the blind, the approximately 600 titles are available in Braille, talking books (16 ⅔ rpm records) and tape cassettes. Most are available only in Braille, and few titles are duplicated in more than one medium. The commission's director, Kenneth Jernigan, personally owns an additional 200 titles in Braille. A complete title and author index to both the commission's library and Mr. Jernigan's personal collection is maintained, covering both novels and short stories. Lists of the library's holdings will be sent to serious readers upon request. [Source: "Science Fiction for the Blind," by Neil Barron, *LUNA Monthly*, No. 35/36 (April/May 1972), 13, 38].

Kansas

University of Kansas, Spenser Research Library, Lawrence, Kans. 66044

Begun in 1969 with gifts, the collection now includes a SFWA depository collection, over 1,000 monographs, 1,600 magazine issues, and 500 fanzines. The collection is added to primarily by gift and deposit, with purchasing limited to paperbound books and reference books. The particular strength of the collection lies in the magazines from 1930 to 1950, and in manuscripts, including manuscripts of James Gunn, Lloyd Biggle, T. L. Sherred, Laurence Janifer, and Algis Budrys. Access to the collection is provided by an author catalog for monographs, a title catalog for periodicals, and an author-title index to stories in collections not otherwise indexed.

Kentucky

University of Kentucky Libraries, Special Collections, Lexington, Ky. 40506

A science fiction collection of more than 1,000 items, including 453 magazine issues, mostly *Analog* and *Galaxy*, and 400 paperback books. In addition, many SF books are in the regular collection. ILL.

Louisiana

Tulane University, Special Collections, Howard-Tilton Memorial Library, New Orleans, La. 70118

The SF material includes two collections in the Special Collections area. The Brown collection consists of 215 paperback editions, 10 hardcovers, and 637 issues of 37 periodical titles. The Heinlein Collection consists of 31 hardcover editions of Heinlein's works, many signed first editions. The collections are built by gift only. No separate catalog exists for the SF material.

Maryland

University of Maryland, Baltimore County, Library, 5401 Wilkens Ave., Baltimore, Md. 21228

The core of the UMBC SF Research Collection is The Walter Coslet Fanzine Collection, consisting of over 12,000 fanzine issues published between 1930 and 1972. In addition, UMBC is acquiring current fanzines by trade, gift, and purchase. A complete catalog of the fanzine titles in the collection is available for use at UMBC. In addition, the collection includes correspondence between Coslet and many individual fans. The research collection also includes over 1,000 hardcover SF books and over 2,500 paperbacks, and has a standing order plan to acquire current books as they are published. Some 65 to 70 magazine titles are in the collection, including a complete set of *Amazing* and a near-complete file of *Astounding/Analog*. Other material includes original artwork of Kelly Freas, typescripts, galley proofs, manuscripts, and attendant material from Roger Zelazny, and assorted other manuscripts. A complete catalog of the collection is in process.

Massachusetts

Boston University Libraries, Special Collections, 771 Commonwealth Avenue, Boston, Mass. 02215

The library has manuscripts of several SF writers, including Isaac Asimov, L. Sprague de Camp, Arthur C. Clarke, Edgar Pangborn, Alan Nourse, and Curt Siodmak. Each collection receives annual additions in both manuscripts and printed form. Each collection has a guide listing its contents.

Harvard University Library, Cambridge, Mass. 02138

A science fiction collection exists at Harvard, but the library views its role as that of conservator only, due to the fragile nature of the material. The SF collection at Harvard is *not* available for use. A description of the collection appeared in *Extrapolation*, 5 (December 1963), 2–14, and in the *Harvard Library Bulletin*, 9 (Autumn 1955), 422.

MIT Science Fiction Society Library, Room W20-421, MIT Student Center, Cambridge, Mass. 02139

Primarily a circulating collection for recreational reading of members. The 30,000-item collection has an almost complete file of U.S. and British magazines, many bound, and a large number of bound German and Italian magazines. Also included are many editions of both hardcover and paperback books, including many foreign editions, and extensive fanzine files. The collection is available to visiting scholars; inquire regarding loans. A catalog is available at requestor's cost. Not an official part of the Massachusetts Institute of Technology.

Michigan

Michigan State University, Library, Special Collections, East Lansing, Mich. 48823

The MSU library is an SFWA depository. The collection includes some 350 monographs, including some early paperbacks (circa 1940s). The magazine collection includes about 1,750 issues of 90 titles; current subscriptions are maintained. Fanzines are sparsely represented; a large collection is to be added soon. All manuscripts of the Clarion Workshops are represented in the collection in typescript copies.

The University of Michigan, Library, Special Collections, Ann Arbor, Mich. 48104

The Hubbard Collection of Imaginary Voyages consists of over 3,000 books, largely various editions of *Robinson Crusoe* and *Gulliver's Travels*. A few books by Verne, Bellamy, and de Bergerac are included. Almost entirely limited to imaginary trips on Earth, with few interplanetary trips. The collection is not being developed. No separate catalog exists except the shelf list.

Minnesota

University of Minnesota, Library, Manuscript Division, Minneapolis, Minn. 55455

The manuscript collection contains the papers and manuscripts of Gordon R. Dickson, including manuscripts of 20 novels and 240 shorter works. The papers and manuscripts of Carl Jacobi are in the process of deposit and processing. Guides to the collection are in process. Photocopies are available with the author's permission.

The Hess collection in the library's Special Collections department includes over 30,000 American and 17,000 British dime novels, selected pulp magazines, Big Little Books, comic books, and related juvenile materials, some of which are science fiction. The Kerlan Collection in the same department emphasizes twentieth-century children's literature and includes many of the juvenile titles annotated in this guide. Both collections have card catalogs, and limited photocopying is possible.

Mississippi

University of Southern Mississippi, Library, Southern Station, Box 53, Hattiesburg, Miss. 39401

A regional depository of the Science Fiction Writers of America. The collection consists of the 124 books donated by SFWA; additions are by SFWA deposit only. Four magazine titles are held. No catalog of the collection is available.

New Mexico

Eastern New Mexico University, Special Collections, University Library, Portales, N. Mex. 88130

The collection consists of over 6,000 published books, extensive magazine runs of over 6,500 issues, and the papers, manuscripts, and correspondence of Jack Williamson, Edmond Hamilton, Leigh Brackett, and duplicate manuscripts of Piers Anthony. The particular strengths of the collection are in the manuscripts and personal papers, and in the extensive magazine collections, including such titles as *Argosy*, *Blue Book*, *Weird Tales*, *Amazing*, *Astounding/Analog*, and others. The collection is also an SFWA depository. A separate catalog of the collection is available. Interlibrary loan is available for hardcovers; photocopies are available. A fuller description of the collection appears in *Extrapolation*, 14 (May 1973), 126–128.

University of New Mexico, Special Collections, Zimmerman Library, Albuquerque, N. Mex. 87106

The Donald Day SF Collection consists of a virtually complete collection of fifty-eight American and three British SF magazines published between 1926 and 1950. The magazines are those indexed in Day's *Index to the Science Fiction Magazines, 1926–1950* [8-1]. The collection includes Day's original card index from which the published version was derived.

New York

Syracuse University, Special Collections, George Arents Research Library, Syracuse, N.Y. 13210

The Syracuse collection has particularly strong holdings in the area of manuscripts and correspondence. Major writers represented include Hugo Gernsback, Damon Knight, Keith Laumer, Larry Niven, Fred Pohl, Donald A. Wollheim, and others. The papers and publications of Mercury Press and Galaxy Publishing Company are also in the collection. Over 2,100 monographs and 5,800 magazine issues are in the collection. Separate catalogs are available for completely processed material.

North Carolina

Duke University Library, Utopia Collection, Rare Book Division, Durham, N. C. 27706

The Utopia Collection consists of over 1,500 volumes of fiction. The collection is described in: Duke University, Durham, N. C., Library. *Utopia Collection of the Duke University Library*, by Glenn Negley. Folcroft, Pa: Folcroft Library Editions, 1970. 83 p. (reprint of the 1965 edition). A revised description is in preparation.

East Carolina State University, University Library, Greenville, N. C. 27834

A representative collection of science fiction and fantasy is being built. The collection is estimated at 5,000 volumes, all in the regular collection. ILL.

Ohio

Bowling Green University, Popular Culture Collection, University Library, Bowling Green, Ohio 43403

The collection consists of books, periodicals, posters, fanzines, and manuscripts, but is for the most part unprocessed. American magazines from 1926 to 1960 are a particular strength. Inquire about specific needs.

Case Western Reserve University, Sears Library, Cleveland, Ohio 44106

A collection consisting primarily of magazine issues is housed in the library, but it is not organized or cataloged at this time. Although access is limited, inquire regarding specific needs.

Ohio State University, University Libraries, Special Collections, 1858 Neil Ave., Columbus, Ohio 43210

The Ohio State collection consists of 105 American and British SF magazine titles, essentially complete from 1926 to the present. Representative holdings of monographs, with special strength in the nineteenth century, are also held by Ohio State, but are not part of the unitary SF collection. No catalog of the collection is available.

University of Dayton Library, 300 College Park, Dayton, Ohio 45469

An SFWA depository library, the collection consists of approximately 200 deposited books, with limited additions through purchase.

Pennsylvania

Pennsylvania State University, University Library, Special Collections, University Park, Pa. 16802

The Moorehead Collection consists of 2,700 issues of SF magazines dating to the 1920s, and includes complete files of *Unknown*, *Startling Stories*, *Astonishing Stories*, *Famous Fantastic Mysteries*, and others. Supporting the magazine collection are over 600 monographs, including a near-complete file of Arkham House books. No catalog of the collection is available; an inventory provides some access.

Temple University Libraries, Special Collections, Philadelphia, Pa. 19122

The David C. Paskow Collection contains over 5,000 items, including novels, anthologies, magazines, records, fanzines, and reference works. Currently the collection includes 1,900 monographs and 2,100 periodical issues. The strength of the collection is in the period 1950–1970. Additions are being made to the collection from the 1950 beginning date, but pre-1950 additions will be highly selective. The papers and manuscripts of Ben Bova have also been deposited in the collection. A catalog of the collection is in preparation.

Rhode Island

Brown University, Howard P. Lovecraft Collection, Library, Special Collections, 20 Prospect St., Providence, R.I. 02912

The collection contains more than 5,000 manuscripts and typescripts from the period 1894–1937, letters exchanged by Lovecraft with over 200 correspondents, including August Derleth, Frank Belknap Long, C. L. Moore, and Clark Ashton Smith, and professional and amateur periodicals from 1900 to date, including a complete file of *Weird Tales*. Query regarding photocopy.

Tennessee

University of Tennessee, Library, Nashville, 323 McLemore St., Nashville, Tenn. 37203

A regional depository for the Science Fiction Writers of America, containing some 100 hardcover books. No other material is available.

Texas

Sam Houston State University, Library, Special Collections, Huntsville, Texas 77340

A collection of H. G. Wells first editions, including both books and pamphlets, is available. No separate catalog of the collection is available. No related material.

Texas A & M University Library, Special Collections, College Station, Texas 77843

Begun in 1970, the Science Fiction Research Collection now exceeds 13,000 items. The core of the collection is the pulp magazine collection of over 5,500 issues dating from 1923 to the present, containing complete runs of *Astounding/Analog, The Magazine of Fantasy and Science Fiction, Galaxy, Planet Stories, Thrilling Wonder Stories, Unknown Worlds,* and *Science Fantasy,* and near-complete runs of *Amazing, Weird Tales,* and *New Worlds,* plus many other complete or near-complete titles. The associated monograph collection of over 8,000 volumes has particular strength from 1950 to the present, but includes many earlier works. The monograph collection includes novels, anthologies, collections, and reference works. A representative collection of over 6,000 amateur SF magazines—fanzines—is maintained, providing a sampling of this sometimes important but little-known segment of the literature of science fiction. Catalogs to both the magazine and monograph collection are available in the library.

Utah

Brigham Young University, Special Collections, University Library, Provo, Utah 84601

The Science Fiction–Fantasy Collection consists of over 2,700 items, including novels, periodicals, fanzines, and critical and bibliographical works. Areas of specialization include Arkham House publications, Edgar Rice Burroughs first editions, and Science Fiction Book Club editions. The collection is also a depository for the SFWA. A catalog is in preparation.

Virginia

University of Virginia Library, James Branch Cabell Collection, Manuscripts Department, Charlottesville, Va. 22901

The James Branch Cabell Archive covers the years 1886–1958, with especially rich material in the 1920–1940 period. The collections include the manuscripts of twenty-three books and a number of articles and stories. There are twelve scrapbooks containing clippings about Cabell's works, with emphasis on *Jurgen* and the attempts to suppress it. Original correspondence numbers about 1,500 items; microfilm or electrostatic copies of originals located elsewhere number about 800 items. Important correspondents include: H. L. Mencken, Burton Rascoe, Sinclair Lewis, Joseph Hergesheimer, Hugh Walpole, Ellen Glasgow, Carl Van Doren, and Carl Van Vechten. In the Clifton Waller Barrett Library of American Literature located in the same Department of Manuscripts is a James Branch Cabell collection containing fifteen manuscripts (including a first draft of *Jurgen*), and about 500 letters. In addition, there are letters of Cabell's scattered in many of the other collections held by the Department.

Virginia Commonwealth University, James Branch Cabell Library, Special Collections, 901 Park Ave., Richmond, Va. 23220

The James Branch Cabell collection consists of material centered on Cabell, containing almost 100 books and pamphlets by Cabell—first editions, revised volumes, and reprints—many inscribed; 20 volumes to which Cabell contributed, 22 books about Cabell, 250 magazine articles by and about Cabell, and 27 letters from 1921 to 1934. No separate catalog of the collection is available. Duplicate books may be borrowed on interlibrary loan; photocopies will be made when condition allows. Prior permission is required to copy letters.

Wisconsin

University of Wisconsin, Special Collections, Library, Milwaukee, Wis. 53201

The SF collection consists of some 1,500 magazine issues received by gift, including *Amazing*, vols. 1–27; *Astounding Stories*, 1930–1958; *Science Wonder Stories*, 1929–1953; *Startling Stories*, 1939–1953; and *Unknown Worlds*, 1939–1943. No catalog is available.

University of Wisconsin at La Crosse, Special Collections, Murphey Library, La Crosse, Wis. 54601

The Paul W. Skeeters collection of fantasy, science fiction, and horror literature contains over 1,000 titles, ranging from 1764 to the mid-1960s. The works are mostly first editions, many in dust wrappers, and include the works of Conrad Aiken, Edith Wharton, Edgar Rice Burroughs, Sax Rohmer, and Tiffany Thayer, and a number of early anthologies. The collection supplements a complete collection of Arkham House books. The collection contains no magazines or manuscripts. Access to the collection is through the library card catalog only.

Wyoming

University of Wyoming, Special Collections, University Library, Laramie, Wyo. 82070

The collection contains correspondence, books, magazines, and SF fan organization material collected by Donald A. Wollheim, J. Vernon Shea, Forrest Ackerman, and Robert Bloch. No catalog of the collection is available, but receipt lists provide some access to the material. Of particular note in the Wollheim material is much data on the early fan movement in the United States, and voluminous correspondence relating to Wollheim's editorial experience, extremely valuable in the study of the development of the anthology. The correspondence also reflects important aspects of the marketing and market conditions for SF over a long period. The Bloch material contains extensive correspondence with other professional writers, movie and television scripts, and related material. The Ackerman collection includes correspondence with most major SF and fantasy writers. The bulk of this material relates to horror films, rather than SF. The major value of the Shea collection is his extensive correspondence with Bloch. Some material in the collection is restricted and requires clearance to use. Photocopies only are available on loan. [Data supplied by Bob Bartell.]

Canada

Queens University, Special Collections, Library, Kingston, Ontario, Canada

The Gothic-Fantasy collection consists of over 4,000 items, including 1,500 novels and 2,500 magazine issues. American magazines are well represented to 1960; there are some incomplete British titles. A collection of over 200 H. P. Lovecraft items supplements the collection. No catalog of the collection is available.

Toronto Public Library, Spaced-Out Library, 40 St. Clair Ave., East, Toronto, Ontario, Canada M6G 2P7

Established in 1970 with the donation of Judith Merril's 5,000-item personal collection, the rapidly growing collection now includes more than 12,000 items, including novels, collections, plays, poetry, critical works, art, tapes, and periodicals. Of special note are the monograph collection of 6,000 books, the periodical collection of over 6,000 issues, the Verne collection of 200 books and an assortment of Verne ephemera, the Arkham House collection of first editions, and the fanzine collection, including issues of 295 fanzines, many in complete runs. The fanzine collection has been indexed by author and subject and may represent a uniquely accessible collection of fanzines. Ten vertical file drawers of manuscripts are included in the collection. A catalog of the entire collection is in preparation.

University of British Columbia, Special Collections, Library, Vancouver, B.C., Canada

A collection of early science fiction magazines, with more than 30 titles and 380 issues represented, many from the period 1926–1940.

University of New Brunswick, Ward Chipman Library, Tucker-Park, St. John, N.B., Canada

The SF and Fantasy collection consists of over 3,000 monographs and over 4,000 periodical issues. The books are a circulating collection, but the magazines, due to fragility, do not circulate. Approximately half of the book collection is hardbound, but recent acquisitions heavily emphasize paperbacks. The collection is a depository of the SFWA Regional Depository System. No separate catalog of the collection exists. ILL.

University of Winnipeg, Library, 515 Portage Ave., Winnipeg, Manitoba, Canada R3B 2E9

The collection consists of approximately 2,000 books, mostly fantasy as opposed to hard SF. Major strength lies in the period 1890–1960, with little new material. The collection is being built through normal acquisitions channels, but major acquisitions are planned. No separate catalog of the collection is available.

Directory of Publishers

It is usually preferable to order from a dealer specializing in the SF/fantasy field rather than direct from the publisher or from a regular jobber who does not stock the many mass market paperbacks so characteristic of modern SF. The dealer guide by Halpern [7-11] may be consulted for suggestions. Of the over 130 dealers listed there, Halpern and I suggest the following as having the largest stock of in-print hardbacks and paperbacks, including those from the smaller specialty publishers. The first and third dealers also stock out-of-print books. Dragon Press provides a variety of specialized standing orders for SF books, tailored to the library's collecting interests and budget.

Dragon Press, Elizabethtown, New York 12932

F & SF Book Co., P.O. Box 415, Staten Island, N.Y. 10302

Lois Newman Books, 1428 Pearl St., Boulder, Colo. 80302

The Science Fiction Shop, 56 Eighth Ave., New York, N.Y. 10014

Fantast (Medway) Ltd., 39 West St., Wisbech, Cambs., England PE13 2LX

The following pages list all publishers for in-print annotated books with their current addresses. The publishers are alphabetized by their key word, which is the same word used in the annotation (e.g., Knopf = Alfred A. Knopf). Libraries wishing to monitor original SF books should pay particular attention to the catalogs and announcements of the following publishers, which are listed in rank order by 1974 output of original works (*Locus*, 16 February 1975, p. 2). Hardback: Doubleday, Putnam, Harper, Random, Seabury, Walker, Chilton, Nelson. Paperback: DAW, Ace, Ballantine, Bantam, Avon, Pocket Books, Pinnacle, Dell, Popular Library. The bimonthly *Forthcoming SF Books* by Joanne Burger [7-3] also provides current information.

AMS Press
  56 East 13 St.
  New York, N.Y. 10003

Ace Books
  1120 Ave. of the Americas
  New York, N.Y. 10036

Advent Publishers
  P.O. Box A3228
  Chicago, Ill. 60690

Allison & Busby
  6A Noel St.
  London WIV 3RB

American Library Assn.
  50 East Huron St.
  Chicago, Ill. 60611

Amherst Press
  Amherst, Wis. 54406

Appleton-Century-Crofts
  Prentice-Hall, Inc.
  Englewood Cliffs, N.J. 07632

Anchor Books
  See Doubleday

Arbor House Pub. Co.
  641 Lexington Ave.
  New York, N.Y. 10021

Archway Paperbacks
  630 Fifth Ave.
  New York, N.Y. 10020

Arkham House
  Sauk City, Wis. 53583

Arno Press
  330 Madison Ave.
  New York, N.Y. 10017

Arrow Books
  See Hutchinson

Associated Booksellers
  147 McKinley Ave.
  Bridgeport, Conn. 06606

Association Press
  291 Broadway
  New York, N.Y. 10007

Atheneum Pubs.
  122 East 42 St.
  New York, N.Y. 10017

Avon Books
  959 Eighth Ave.
  New York, N.Y. 10019

Award Books
  235 East 45 St.
  New York, New York 10017

Ballantine Books
  201 East 50 St.
  New York, N.Y. 10022

Ballantine Books (U.K.)
  See Pan Books

Bantam Books
  666 Fifth Ave.
  New York, N.Y. 10019

A. S. Barnes
  P.O. Box 421
  Cranbury, N.J. 08512

Barnes & Noble
  10 East 53 St.
  New York, N.Y. 10022

Barrie & Jenkins
24 Highbury Cross
London N5 1RX

Beacon Press
25 Beacon St.
Boston, Mass. 02108

Bobbs-Merrill
4 West 58 St.
New York, N.Y. 10019

Bodley Head
9 Bow St.
London WC2E 7AL

Books for Libraries
1 Dupont St.
Plainview, N.Y. 11803

Borden Pub. Co.
1855 W. Main St.
Alhambria, Calif. 91801

Bowling Green Univ. Pop. Press
101 University Hall
Bowling Green, Ohio 43403

Bradbury Press
2 Overhill Rd.
Scarsdale, N.Y. 10583

Brigham Young Univ. Press
205 University Press Bldg.
Provo, Utah 84602

British Book Center
996 Lexington Ave.
New York, N.Y. 10021

Canaveral Press
63 Fourth Ave.
New York, N.Y. 10003

Jonathan Cape
30 Bedford Square
London WC1B 3EL

Capricorn Books
See Putnam

Caxton Printers
P.O. Box 700
Caldwell, Idaho 83605

Centennial Press
P.O. Box 80728
Lincoln, Nebr. 68501

Chelsea House
70 West 40 St.
New York, N.Y. 10018

Chelsea-Lee Books
P.O. Box 66273
Los Angeles, Calif. 90066

Chilton Book Co.
201 King of Prussia Rd.
Radnor, Pa. 19089

Citadel Press
120 Enterprise Ave.
Secaucus, N.J. 07094

Clearwater Pub. Co.
50 Rockefeller Plaza
New York, N.Y. 10020

Collier Books
See Macmillan

William Collins
14 Saint James Place
London SW1A 1PS

Corgi Books
P.O. Box 17
Wellingborough NN8 4BU,
England

Coronet Books
See Hodder & Stoughton

Coward, McCann & Geoghegan
200 Madison Ave.
New York, N.Y. 10016

Crown Publishers
419 Park Ave. South
New York, N.Y. 10016

Peter Davies
15-16 Queen St., Mayfair
London W1X 8BE

DAW Books
See New American Library

John Day
  666 Fifth Ave.
  New York, N.Y. 10019

Delacorte Press
  1 Dag Hammarskjold Plaza
  New York, N.Y. 10017

Dell Pub. Co.
  1 Dag Hammarskjold Plaza
  New York, N.Y. 10017

Delta Books
  See Delacorte

Andre Deutsch
  105 Great Russell St.
  London WC1B 3LJ

Dobson Books
  80 Kensington Church St.
  London W8 4BZ

Dodd, Mead & Co.
  79 Madison Ave.
  New York, N.Y. 10016

Doubleday & Co.
  245 Park Ave.
  New York, N.Y. 10017

Dover Publications
  180 Varick St.
  New York, N.Y. 10014

Dragon Press
  Elizabethtown, N.Y. 12932

E. P. Dutton
  201 Park Ave. South
  New York, N.Y. 10003

Educational Impact
  P.O. Box 355
  Blackwood, N.J. 08012

Wm. B. Eerdmans
  255 Jefferson Ave., S.E.
  Grand Rapids, Mich. 49502

Faber & Faber
  3 Queen Square
  London WC1N 3AU

Farrar, Straus & Giroux
  19 Union Square West
  New York, N.Y. 10003

Fawcett World Library
  1515 Broadway
  New York, N.Y. 10036

Fax Collector's Editions
  Box E
  West Linn, Oreg. 97068

Filter Press
  P.O. Box 5
  Palmer Lake, Colo. 80133

Folcroft Library Eds.
  P.O. Box 182
  Folcroft, Pa. 19032

Four Winds Press
  See Scholastic Book Service

French & European Pubs.
  Rockefeller Center Promenade
  610 Fifth Ave.
  New York, N.Y. 10020

Gale Research Co.
  Book Tower
  Detroit, Mich. 48226

Garland Publishing
  545 Madison Ave.
  New York, N.Y. 10022

Victor Gollancz
  14 Henrietta St.
  Covent Garden
  London WC2E 8QJ

Goodyear Pub. Co.
  15115 Sunset Blvd.
  Pacific Palisades, Calif. 90272

Gordon Press Pubs.
  P.O. Box 459
  Bowling Green Sta.
  New York, N.Y. 10004

Granada Pub.
  P.O. Box 9, 29 Frogmore St.
  Saint Albans, Herts AL2 2NF,
  England

Donald M. Grant
West Kingston, R.I. 02892

Greenwood Press
51 Riverside Ave.
Westport, Conn. 06880

Gregg Press
70 Lincoln St.
Boston, Mass. 02111

Grosset & Dunlap
51 Madison Avenue
New York, N.Y. 10010

Grove Press
53 East 11 St.
New York, N.Y. 10003

Haddonfield House
300 Kings Highway East
Haddonfield, N.J. 08033

Harcourt Brace Jovanovich
757 Third Ave.
New York, N.Y. 10017

Harper & Row
10 East 53 St.
New York, N.Y. 10022

Hart-Davis
See Granada

Harvard Univ. Press
79 Garden St.
Cambridge, Mass. 02138

William Heinemann
15-16 Queen St.
London W1X 8BE

Hendricks House
103 Park Ave.
New York, N.Y. 10017

Hermes Pubs.
P.O. Box 397
Los Altos, Calif. 94022

Hill & Wang
See Farrar, Straus & Giroux

Hodder & Stoughton
St. Paul's House
Warwick Lane
London EC4P 4AH

Holt, Rinehart & Winston
383 Madison Ave.
New York, N.Y. 10017

Houghton Mifflin
2 Park St.
Boston, Mass. 02107

Humanities Press
Atlantic Highlands, N.J. 07716

Hutchinson Pub. Group
3 Fitzroy Square
London W1P 6JD

Hyperion Press
45 Riverside Ave.
Westport, Conn. 06880

Indiana Univ. Press
Tenth & Morton Sts.
Bloomington, Ind. 47401

John Knox Press
341 Ponce De Leon Ave. N.E.
Atlanta, Ga. 30308

Johnson Reprint
111 Fifth Ave.
New York, N.Y. 10003

Michael Joseph
52 Bedford Sq.
London WC1B 3EF

Journeyman Press
97 Ferme Park Rd.
Crouch End
London N8 9SA

Augustus Kelley
305 Allwood Rd.
Clifton, N.J. 07012

Kennikat Press
90 South Bayles Ave.
Port Washington, N.Y. 11050

Kent State Univ. Press
Kent, Ohio 44240

Alfred A. Knopf
201 East 50 St.
New York, N.Y. 10022

Kraus Reprint
Millwood, N.Y. 10546

Larousse & Co.
572 Fifth Ave.
New York, N.Y. 10036

Leisure Books
185 Madison Avenue
New York, N.Y. 10016

Library Association
7 Ridgmont St.
London WC1E 7AE

J. B. Lippincott
521 Fifth Ave.
New York, N.Y. 10017

Little, Brown
34 Beacon St.
Boston, Mass. 02106

Lothrop, Lee & Shepard
See Morrow

Melvin McCosh
Rt. 1, Box 400
Excelsior, Mich. 55331

McGraw-Hill Book Co.
1221 Ave. of the Americas
New York, N.Y. 10036

David McKay
750 Third Ave.
New York, N.Y. 10017

Macmillan Pub. Co.
866 Third Ave.
New York, N.Y. 10022

Manchester Univ. Press
Oxford Rd.
Manchester MI3 9PL U.K.

Manor Books
432 Park Ave.
New York, N.Y. 10016

Mayflower
See Granada

Mentor Books
See New American Library

Mirage Press
P.O. Box 7887
Baltimore, Md. 21207

Modern Library
201 East 50 St.
New York, N.Y. 10022

William Morrow
105 Madison Ave.
New York, N.Y. 10016

MSS Information Corp.
655 Madison Ave.
New York, N.Y. 10021

Negro Universities Press
See Greenwood Press

New American Library
1301 Ave. of the Americas
New York, N.Y. 10019

New Directions
333 Ave. of the Americas
New York, N.Y. 10014

New England SF Assn.
Box G, MIT Branch P.O.
Cambridge, Mass. 02139

New English Library
Barnard's Inn, Holborn
London EC1N 2JR

N.Y. Graphic Society
11 Beacon St.
Boston, Mass. 02108

W. W. Norton
500 Fifth Ave.
New York, N.Y. 10036

Octagon Books
19 Union Sq. West
New York, N.Y. 10003

Odyssey Press
See Bobbs-Merrill

Oneiric Press
2940 Seventh St.
Berkeley, Calif. 94710

Owlswick Press
P.O. Box 8243
Philadelphia, Pa. 19101

Oxford Univ. Press
200 Madison Ave.
New York, N.Y. 10016

Pan Books
Cavaye Place
London SW10 9PG

Pantheon Books
201 East 50 St.
New York, N.Y. 10022

Panther
See Granada

Paperback Library
See Warner Books

Parnassus Press
4080 Halleck St.
Emeryville, Calif. 94608

Penguin Books
72 Fifth Ave.
New York, N.Y. 10011

Penguin Books (U.K.)
Bath Road
Harmondsworth, Middlesex
UB7 0DA, England

Pflaum/Standard
2285 Arbor Blvd.
Dayton, Ohio 45439

Philosophical Pub. Co.
P.O. Box 220
Quakertown, Pa. 18951

Pilgrim Press
1505 Race St.
Philadelphia, Pa. 19102

Pinnacle Books
275 Madison Ave.
New York, N.Y. 10016

Pocket Books
630 Fifth Ave.
New York, N.Y. 10020

Popular Library
600 Third Ave.
New York, N.Y. 10011

Portway Reprints
Cedric Chivers
Portway, Bath BA1 3NF
England

Clarkson N. Potter
See Crown

Prentice-Hall
Englewood Cliffs, N.J. 07632

G. P. Putnam's
200 Madison Ave.
New York, N.Y. 10016

Pyramid Pubs.
919 Third Ave.
New York, N.Y. 10022

Quartet Books
27 Goodge St.
London W1

Random House
201 East 50 St.
New York, N.Y. 10022

Rapp & Whiting
105 Great Russell St.
London WC1B 3LJ

Henry Regnery
180 North Michigan Ave.
Chicago, Ill. 60601

Routledge & Kegan Paul (U.K.)
68 Carter Lane
London EC4V 5EL

St. Martin's Press
175 Fifth Ave.
New York, N.Y. 10010

Scarecrow Press
52 Liberty St., Box 656
Metuchen, N.J. 08840

Schocken Books
200 Madison Ave.
New York, N.Y. 10016

Scholarly Press
22929 Industrial Dr. E.
St. Clair Shores, Mich. 48080

Scholar's Facsimilies & Reprints
P.O. Box 344
Delmar, N.Y. 12054

Scholastic Book Service
50 West 44 St.
New York, N.Y. 10036

Science Fiction Book Club
Garden City, N.Y. 11530

Scolar Press
39 Great Russell St.
London WC1B 3PH

Charles Scribner's Sons
597 Fifth Ave.
New York, N.Y. 10017

Seabury Press
815 Second Ave.
New York, N.Y. 10017

Shambala Pubs.
See Routledge & Kegan Paul

Sherbourne Press
1640 South La Cienega Blvd.
Los Angeles, Calif. 90035

Sheridan House
P.O. Box 254, South Sta.
Yonkers, N.Y. 10705

Sidgwick & Jackson
1 Tavistock Chambers
Bloomsbury Way
London WC1A 2SC

Signet Books
See New American Library

Simon & Schuster
630 Fifth Ave.
New York, N.Y. 10020

Peter Smith
6 Lexington Ave.
Gloucester, Mass. 01930

Somerset Pubs.
200 Park Ave., Suite 303E
New York, N.Y. 10017

Southern Ill. Univ. Press
P.O. Box 3697
Carbondale, Ill. 62901

Sphere Books
30-32 Gray's Inn Rd.
London WC1X 8JL

J. Ben Stark
Box 261, Fairmont Station
El Cerrito, Calif. 94530

Studio Vista
35 Red Lion Square
London WC1R 4SG

Sun Pub. Co.
P.O. Box 4383
Albuquerque, N.M. 87106

Tandem
Universal-Tandem Pub. Co.
14 Gloucester Road
London SW7 4RD

Taplinger Pub. Co.
200 Park Ave. South
New York, N.Y. 10003

Transatlantic Arts
North Village Green
Levittown, N.Y. 11756

Frederick Ungar
250 Park Ave. South
New York, N.Y. 10003

Univ. of California Press
2223 Fulton St.
Berkeley, Calif. 94720

Univ. of Chicago Press
5801 Ellis Ave.
Chicago, Ill. 60637

Univ. of Nebraska Press
901 North 17 St.
Lincoln, Nebr. 68508

Univ. of Notre Dame Press
Notre Dame, Ind. 46556

Univ. of Wisconsin Press
P.O. Box 1379
Madison, Wis. 53701

Vanguard Press
424 Madison Ave.
New York, N.Y. 10017

Viking Press
625 Madison Ave.
New York, N.Y. 10022

Henry C. Walck
See David McKay

Walker & Co.
720 Fifth Ave.
New York, N.Y. 10019

Warner Books
7 Rockefeller Plaza
New York, N.Y. 10019

Washington Square Press
See Simon & Schuster

Wehman Brothers
156-158 Main St.
Hackensack, N.J. 07601

Richard West
Box 6404
Philadelphia, Pa. 19145

Westminster Press
Room 905, Witherspoon Bldg.
Philadelphia, Pa. 19107

Writer's Digest
9933 Alliance Rd.
Cincinnati, Ohio 45242

Yale Univ. Press
92A Yale Station
New Haven, Conn. 06520

Zondervan Pub. House
1415 Lake Dr.
Grand Rapids, Mich. 49506

Author Index

This author index also includes all entries from the title index (which follows), except those few works lacking named authors, thereby permitting rapid scanning of all works of an author, be they only mentioned or fully annotated. Page references are given to all authors and editors of annotated books and stories, including references to authors as subjects. "Substantive" references to authors, when no specific work is mentioned, follow the author's name; references to specific works follow the title of the work. All "substantive" references are in **boldface**. Certain page references were deliberately omitted as too minor to justify indexing, e.g., simple references of the compare or contrast variety, if the cited books are elsewhere annotated. But when such a reference is the only reference for a title, it is indexed for the sake of completeness. References to authors mentioned in passing are omitted. An example of this would be the modern anthologies, where the author's name, but no specific work, is mentioned. Names of translators and illustrators and magazine titles listed in Chapters 10 and 11 are not indexed. A coauthor or coeditor may be identified by the presence of the main author's or editor's name in parentheses following the book title.

Title Index

This index was prepared primarily to permit direct access to a title when the user does not know or is uncertain of the author. However, the author index includes all the information from the title index and should be consulted when the author's name is known. Short story titles are shown in quotation marks, permitting ready access to about 550 of the more important stories. If a book uses a short story in its title, only the book title is indexed, since the presence of the story is self-evident. When the same short story is found in other collections, page references are shown following the book title. All variant titles—British, foreign language—are also given. The author surname is in parentheses after each title to facilitate identification. For filing purposes, abbreviations are treated as words, and alphabetization is word by word. As in the author index, page numbers in **boldface** denote the substantive references.